American Literary Scholarship

1976

American Literary Scholarship

An Annual / 1976

Edited by J. Albert Robbins

Essays by Wendell Glick, J. Donald Crowley, Donald B. Stauffer, Hershel Parker, Marvin Fisher and Willis J. Buckingham, Louis J. Budd, William T. Stafford, Stuart Y. McDougal, Panthea Reid Broughton, Jackson R. Bryer, Robert D. Arner, Warren French, David Stouck, Margaret Anne O'Connor, James H. Justus, Richard Crowder, Linda Welshimer Wagner, Winifred Frazer, Charles Nilon, Michael J. Hoffman, Jean Rivière, Hans Galinsky, Rolando Anzilotti, Keiko Beppu, Rolf Lundén

Duke University Press, Durham, North Carolina, 1978

PS
3
.A47
1976

Foreword

Beginning with this year's volume, James Woodress and I plan to alternate as editors of *American Literary Scholarship*. Anyone wishing to praise or deplore may correspond with either of us and we will share communications with each other.

As usual, we urge authors of books, monographs, and articles to send copies to the appropriate chapter author. If you are uncertain which chapter your work relates to, send to either editor and it will be forwarded.

Chapter authors for *ALS 1977* are the same as those for *ALS 1976*, with the following exceptions. Professor Willis Buckingham, who reviewed Dickinson for *ALS 1976*, will do both Dickinson and Whitman for *ALS 1977*. Professor Robert Gale (University of Pittsburgh) will write chapter 7 (Henry James); Professor George J. Bornstein (University of Michigan), chapter 8 (Pound and Eliot); Professor Thomas Wortham (UCLA), chapter 12 (19th Century Literature); and Professor James Breslin (California, Berkeley), chapter 17 (Poetry: The 1930s to the Present). Professor Michel Terrier will replace Jean Rivière as our French correspondent and in chapter 21 we will add coverage on scholarship in Eastern Europe by Professor F. Lyra of the University of Warsaw. We thank all who retire from work with ALS, with special acknowledgment of three veterans with long and distinguished service—Professors William T. Stafford, Warren French, and Linda Wagner.

A brief summary of these points of policy may be useful to some readers of these volumes. We do not attempt to cover dissertation literature. If you seek that type of scholarship, consult *DAI*, not *ALS*. Chapter authors are instructed to ignore (or give only brief notice of) inferior scholarship. In other words, do not assume that *ALS* equals the coverage of the annual *MLA International Bibliography*. It does not. And, of course, do not assume that *ALS* can accord even major books the close attention they may deserve. Our notices of necessity are briefly descriptive and evaluative. For extended commentary you should consult the detailed reviews in the appropriate general and specialized journals.

Finally, a brief note on a new but short-lived publishing enterprise, denoted in our list of abbreviations as *ESColl.* Series 1, number 1 of *English Studies Collections*, produced in East Meadow, New York, appeared in September 1976. The publisher issued scholarly articles as "separates" and sold them individually, each individually priced. One could purchase only essays in which one had an active interest and the publisher could promise prompt publication. Whatever the merits or disadvantages of this form of publication, it ceased operation late in 1977.

J. Albert Robbins
January 1978

Indiana University, Bloomington

Table of Contents

Key to Abbreviations

Festschrifts, Essay Collections, and Books Discussed in More than One Chapter

Aeolian Harps / Aeolian Harps: Essays in Literature in Honor of Maurice Browning Cramer, ed. Donna G. Fricke and Douglas C. Fricke (Bowling Green, Ohio: Bowling Green Univ. Press)

American Literary Naturalism / American Literary Naturalism: A Reassessment, ed. Yoshinobu Hakutani and Lewis Fried, Anglistische Forschungen, 109 (Heidelberg: Carl Winter, 1975)

Classical Traditions / Classical Traditions in Early America, ed. John W. Eadie (Ann Arbor: Center for Coordination of Ancient and Modern Studies, Univ. of Michigan)

Cunning Exiles / Cunning Exiles: Studies of Modern Prose Writers, ed. Don Anderson and Stephen Knight (Sydney: Angus and Robertson, 1974).

Discoveries & Considerations / Discoveries & Considerations: Essays on Early American Literature & Aesthetics Presented to Harold Jantz (Albany: State Univ. of N.Y. Press)

Educated Lives / Thomas W. Cooley. Educated Lives: The Rise of Modern Autobiography in America (Columbus: Ohio State Univ. Press).

Evolution of Consciousness / Evolution of Consciousness: Studies in Polarity, ed. Shirley Sugerman (Middletown, Conn.: Wesleyan Univ. Press)

Four Makers / Four Makers of the American Mind, Emerson, Thoreau, Whitman, and Melville: A Bicentennial Tribute, ed. Thomas E. Crawley (Durham, N.C.: Duke University Press)

Indian Studies / Indian Studies in American Fiction, ed. M. K. Naik, et al. (Delhi: Macmillan India, 1974)

Portraits / Portraits of a Nineteenth Century Family: A Symposium on the Beecher Family, ed. Earl A. French and Diana Royce (Hartford, Conn.: Stowe-Day Foundation)

Renaissance and Modern / Renaissance and Modern: Essays in Honor of Edwin M. Moseley, ed. Murray J. Levith (Saratoga Springs, N.Y.: Skidmore College)

Repossessing and Renewing / Sherman Paul, Repossessing and Renewing: Essays in the Green American Tradition (Baton Rouge: La. State Univ. Press.)

William Elliott Shoots a Bear / Louis D. Rubin, Jr. William Elliott Shoots a Bear: Essays on the Southern Literary Imagination (Baton Rouge: La. State Univ. Press, 1975)

Periodicals, Annuals, Series

AAAPSS / Annals of the American Academy of Political and Social Science

A-AS / Afro-American Studies, An Interdisciplinary Journal

ABR / American Benedictine Review

AHumor / American Humor
AI / American Imago
AL / American Literature
ALR / American Literary Realism
ALS / American Literary Scholarship
AmerS / American Studies
AmerSI / American Studies International (George Washington Univ.)
AmS / Amerikastudien
AmSS / American Studies in Scandinavia
AN&Q / American Notes and Queries
AntigR / Antigonish Review
Apollo
Approda / L'Approda Letheraria (Rome)
APR / American Poetry Review
AQ / American Quarterly
AR / Antioch Review
Arcadia: Zeitschrift für vergleichende Literaturwissenschaft (Berlin)
Ariel: A Quarterly Review of the Arts and Sciences in Israel
ArielE / Ariel: A Review of International English Literature
ArQ / Arizona Quarterly
ATQ / American Transcendental Quarterly
AWR / Anglo-Welsh Review
BALF / Black American Literature Forum
BB / Bulletin of Bibliography
BBB / Black Books Bulletin (Chicago)
BlackS / Black Scholar
BlackW / Black World
BNYPL / Bulletin of the New York Public Library
Book Forum, An International Transdisciplinary Review of Books (Rhinecliff, N.Y.)
Boundary 2: A Journal of Postmodern Literature
BP / Banasthali Patrika
BSUF / Ball State Univ. Forum
CanL / Canadian Literature
CE / College English
CEA / CEA Critic (College English Assn.)
CEAA / Center for Editions of American Authors

CentR / The Centennial Review
CimR / Cimarron Review
CLAJ / College Language Association Journal
CLC / Columbia Library Columns
ClioW / Clio: An Interdisciplinary Journal of Literature, History, and the Philosophy of History (Madison, Wis.)
CLQ / Colby Library Quarterly
CLS / Comparative Literature Studies
CollL / College Literature (Westchester State College)
ColQ / Colorado Quarterly
Commentary
Confrontation, A Literary Journal of Long Island University
ConL / Contemporary Literature
Costerus: Essays in English and American Language and Literature
CP / Concerning Poetry
CRevAS / Canadian Review of American Studies
Crit / Critique: Studies in Modern Fiction
CritI / Critical Inquiry
Criticism (Wayne State)
Critique (Paris)
CS / Concord Saunterer
CSE / Center for Scholarly Editions (formerly CEAA)
DAI / Dissertation Abstracts International
Delta (Montpellier)
Diacritics, A Review of Contemporary Criticism
DQ / Denver Quarterly
DR / Dalhousie Review
EA / Etudes Anglaises
EAL / Early American Literature
EAS / Essays in Arts and Sciences
EDB / Emily Dickinson Bulletin
EG / Etudes Germaniques
EigoS / Eigo Seinen [The Rising Generation] (Tokyo)
Éire / Éire-Ireland: A Journal of Irish Studies
ELH: Journal of English Literary History
ELN / English Language Notes

ELUD / *Essays in Literature*
(Univ. of Denver)
ELWIU / *Essays in Literature*
(Western Ill. Univ.)
Erz / *Erzählforschuung* (Vol. 1 otherwise denominated *Zeitschrift für Literaturwissenschaft und Linguistik*, Beiheft 4)
ES / *English Studies*
ESColl / *English Studies Collections*
(East Meadow, N.Y.)
ESQ: *Emerson Society Quarterly*
ESRS / *Emporia State Research Studies*
ETJ / *Educational Theatre Journal*
Expl / *Explicator*
Explor (Evanston, Ill.)
Extracts (Newsletter, Melville Society)
FOB / *Flannery O'Connor Bulletin*
ForumH / *Forum* (Houston)
FR / *French Review*
GaR / *Georgia Review*
GL&L / *German Life and Letters*
GrLR / *Great Lakes Review*
GSlav / *Germano-Slavica*
Gulliver: *Deutsch-Englische Jahrbücher* (Karlsruhe)
GWU / *Geshichte in Wissenschaft und Untericht*
GyS / *Gypsy Scholar* (East Lansing, Mich.)
HC / *Hollins Critic*
Helios (Texas Tech Univ., Lubbock)
HJP / *Higginson Journal of Poetry*
HLB / *Harvard Library Bulletin*
HMPEC / *Historical Magazine of the Protestant Episcopal Church*
HSE / *Hungarian Studies in English*
HSL / *Hartford Studies in Literature*
HudR / *Hudson Review*
IFR / *International Fiction Review*
IllQ / *Illinois Quarterly*
IowaR / *Iowa Review*
ItalAm / *Italian Americana*
(Buffalo, N.Y.)
JAAC / *Journal of Aesthetics and Art Criticism*
JAmS / *Journal of American Studies*
JBS / *John Berryman Studies*
JEGP / *Journal of English and Germanic Philology*

JEthS / *Journal of Ethnic Studies*
(Western Washington State Univ.)
JFI / *Journal of the Folklore Institute*
JML / *Journal of Modern Literature*
JNT / *Journal of Narrative Technique*
JPC / *Journal of Popular Culture*
JR / *Journal of Religion*
Kalki: *Studies in James Branch Cabell*
KuL / *Kunst und Literatur*
L&P / *Literature and Psychology*
Lang&S / *Language and Style*
LanM / *Les Langues Modernes*
LaS / *Louisiana Studies*
LC / *Library Chronicle* (Univ. of Pa.)
LCP / *Literary Criticism and Psychology* (Yearbook of Comparative Criticism, 7; University Park, Pa.)
LFQ / *Literature/Film Quarterly*
LGJ / *Lost Generation Journal*
LingL / *Linguistics in Literature*
LitR / *Literary Review*
LMonog / *Literary Monographs*
(Univ. of Wis.)
LMonogT / *Literary Monographs*
(Trinity College, San Antonio, Tex.)
LNL / *Linguistics in Literature*
(San Antonio, Tex.)
LSJ / *Lake Superior Journal*
(Duluth, Minn.)
LWU / *Literatur in Wissenschaft und Unterricht* (Kiel)
MarkhamR / *Markham Review*
McNR / *McNeese Review* (McNeese State College, La.)
MBL / *Modern British Literature*
(Butler, Pa.)
MD / *Modern Drama*
MFS / *Modern Fiction Studies*
MHRA / *Modern Humanities Research Assn.*
MichA / *Michigan Academician*
MidAmerica (East Lansing, Mich.)
Midstream
MinnR / *Minnesota Review*
MissQ / *Mississippi Quarterly*
MLN / *Modern Language Notes*
MLQ / *Modern Language Quarterly*
MLR / *Modern Language Review*

Mosaic: A Journal for the Comparative
    Study of Literature and Ideas
MP / Modern Philology
MPS / Modern Poetry Studies
MQ / Midwest Quarterly
MR / Massachusetts Review
MTJ / Mark Twain Journal
NALF / Negro American Literature
    Forum
N&Q / Notes and Queries
NCF / Nineteenth-Century Fiction
NCFS / Nineteenth-Century French
    Studies
NCHR / North Carolina Historical
    Review
NConL / Notes on Contemporary
    Literature
NDQ / North Dakota Quarterly
Neohelicon: Acta Comparationis
    Litterarum Universarum
    (Budapest)
NEQ / New England Quarterly
NG / National Geographic
NewRep / New Republic
NMAL / Notes on Modern American
    Literature (Jamaica, N.Y.)
NMW / Notes on Mississippi Writers
NOR / New Orleans Review
Novel: A Forum on Fiction
NYH / New York History
NYRB / New York Review of Books
NYTBR / New York Times Book
    Review
Obsidian: Black Literature in Review
    (Fredonia, N.Y.)
OhR / Ohio Review
OL / Orbis Litterarum
Olson: The Journal of the Charles
    Olson Archives (Storrs, Conn.)
ON / Old Northwest (Oxford, Ohio)
PAAS / Papers of the American
    Antiquarian Society
PAPA / Publications of the Arkansas
    Philological Association (Fayette-
    ville)
Pages: The World of Books, Writers,
    and Writing (Detroit: Gale
    Research Co.)
PAPS / Proceedings of the American
    Philosophical Society
Paragon
Parnassus: Poetry in Review

PAus / Poetry Australia
PBSA / Papers of the Bibliographical
    Society of America
PCLS / Proceedings of the Com-
    parative Literature Symposium
PH / Pennsylvania History
PHR / Pacific Historical Review
Players
PLL / Papers on Language and
    Literature
PMHS / Proceedings of the Mas-
    sachusetts Historical Society
PMLA: Publications of the Modern
    Language Association
PoeS / Poe Studies
PPNCFL / Proceedings of the Pacific
    Northwest Conference on
    Foreign Languages
Poétique: Revue de Théorie et
    d'Analyse Littéraires
Poetry
PR / Partisan Review
Prospects: An Annual Journal of
    American Cultural Studies
PsyR / Psychoanalytic Review
PULC / Princeton University Library
    Chronicle
QJS / Quarterly Journal of Speech
QQ / Queens Quarterly
RALS / Resources for American
    Literary Study
RANAM / Recherches Anglaises et
    Américaines
Renascence
RFEA / Revue Française d'Etudes
    Américaines (Paris)
RJN / Robinson Jeffers Newsletter
RLC / Revue de Littérature
    Comparée
RLV / Revue des Langues Vivantes
RUS / Rice University Studies
RS / Research Studies (Wash. State
    Univ.)
SA / Studi Americani
SAB / South Atlantic Bulletin
SAF / Studies in American Fiction
SALit / Studies in American
    Literature (Kyoto)
SAmH / Studies in American Humor
SAQ / South Atlantic Quarterly
SatR / Saturday Review
SB / Studies in Bibliography

SBL / *Studies in Black Literature*
SCN / *Seventeenth-Century News*
SDR / *South Dakota Review*
SELit / *Studies in English Literature*
  (Japan)
Semiotext(e) (Columbia Univ.)
SFS / *Science Fiction Studies*
SHR / *Southern Humanities Review*
SIH / *Studies in the Humanities*
SIR / *Studies in Romanticism*
SJS / *San Jose Studies*
SLitI / *Studies in the Literary*
  Imagination
SLJ / *Southern Literary Journal*
SN / *Studia Neophilologica*
SNNTS / *Studies in the Novel*
  (North Tex. State Univ.)
SoR / *Southern Review*
Soundings: A Journal of Inter-
  disciplinary Studies
SpTZ / *Sprache im technischen*
  Zeitalter (Stuttgart)
SR / *Sewanee Review*
SRC / *Studies in Religion/Sciences*
  Religieuses
SSF / *Studies in Short Fiction*
SSL / *Studies in Scottish Literature*
  (Univ. of S.C.)
StQ / *Steinbeck Quarterly*
Style (Univ. of Arkansas)
SwAL / *Southwestern American*
  Literature
SWR / *Southwest Review*

TCL / *Twentieth-Century Literature*
Thoth
THQ / *Tennessee Historical Quarterly*
TLS / *Times Literary Supplement*
Topic (Washington and Jefferson
  College)
TQ / *Texas Quarterly*
Trimestre (Pescara)
TSB / *Thoreau Society Bulletin*
TSL / *Tennessee Studies in Literature*
TSLL / *Texas Studies in Literature*
  and Language
TUSAS / Twayne United States
  Authors Series (Boston: G. K. Hall)
VLang / *Visible Language*
Vort
VQR / *Virginia Quarterly Review*
WAL / *Western American Literature*
W&L / *Women and Literature*
WC / *Wordsworth Circle*
WCWN / *William Carlos Williams*
  Newsletter (Middletown, Pa.)
WHQ / *Western Humanities*
  Quarterly
WHR / *Western Humanities Review*
WLB / *Wilson Library Bulletin*
WMQ / *William and Mary Quarterly*
WWR / *Walt Whitman Review*
WWS / Western Writers Series
YFS / *Yale French Studies*
YR / *Yale Review*
YULG / *Yale Univ. Library Gazette*

Part I

Part I

1. Emerson, Thoreau, and Transcendentalism

Wendell Glick

i. General Studies, Textual Studies, Reprints

The year was unpropitious, both for general studies in Transcendentalism and for CEAA-CSE-sponsored editions of Emerson and Thoreau. No in-depth study emerged to supplement those of Buell (see *ALS 1973*, p. 4), Boller (*ALS 1974*, p. 3), and Koster (*ALS 1975*, p. 3). Volume XII of *The Journals and Miscellaneous Notebooks of Ralph Waldo Emerson* was the only new, authoritatively edited volume of the works of either Emerson or Thoreau to see print.

Several articles directly or peripherally dealing with Transcendentalism, however, deserve note. Peter C. Carafiol in "James Marsh's American *Aids to Reflection*: Influence Through Ambiguity" (*NEQ* 49:27–45) argues plausibly that Marsh's attempts to popularize Coleridge in his "Preliminary Essay" were motivated by Marsh's intention to support religious orthodoxy; and that Marsh's stimulation of Transcendentalism by his facile interpretation of Coleridgean thought was an unintended by-product. Carafiol contends that the Transcendentalists ignored the *Aids*' orthodox intention and its systematic metaphysics and seized on its assertion of "the ability of the mind to derive spiritual knowledge from its own depths." The article is a follow-up of "James Marsh: Transcendental Puritan" (see *ALS 1975*, p. 15). Phillip K. Tompkins's "On 'Paradoxes' in the Rhetoric of the New England Transcendentalists" (*QJS* 62:40–48) demolishes a straw man erected on shaky postulates and misinformation by several earlier rhetoricians who argued that the Transcendental movement collapsed because of the ineffectiveness of its discourse. An understanding of the movement, one would surmise, should precede an explanation of its dissolution. In an explication of Bryant's "Thanatopsis" E. Miller Budick argues ("'Visible' Images and the 'Still

Voice': Transcendental Vision in Bryant's 'Thanatopsis' " [*ESQ* 22: 71–77]) that no contradiction exists (for Bryant) between the truth of Nature's visible images and her transcendental "still voice": "they collaborate in the production of nature's perpetual pageant of sense and consciousness." This in spite of Bryant's distrust of "the facile exuberances of Idealist faith." David M. Van Leer (*ESQ* 22:211–20) explores Hawthorne's using Transcendentalism fictionally in "Alymer's Library: Transcendental Alchemy in Hawthorne's 'The Birthmark.'"

Volume XII of *The Journals and Miscellaneous Notebooks of Ralph Waldo Emerson* (Cambridge, Mass.: Harvard University Press), edited by Linda Allardt and bearing the CEAA seal, prints nine Emerson lecture notebooks from 1835 to 1862, prefaced by an informative historical and textual foreword. Spanning twenty-seven of Emerson's most productive years, the notebooks contain notes for more than a hundred of his major lectures and essays. "Taken together with the journals and lectures already in print," Allardt alleges justifiably, "the publication of these notebooks rounds out the necessary resources for a searching reappraisal of the origins, composition, and interrelationship of Emerson's lectures and essays" (p. xxxix). Though lists of various types of material make up the bulk of the volume, some autobiographical entries are included, one of the most interesting being Emerson's dispute with his neighbor Bartlett over the latter's cutting trees on Emerson's property and Thoreau's role as surveyor in the dispute (pp. 210–13).

The year was fallow for the Princeton Edition of Thoreau, although at the press or near completion are *A Week on the Concord and Merrimack Rivers*; *Correspondence*; and volume 1 of the *Journal*. *A Catalog of Thoreau's Surveys in the Concord Free Public Library*, ably edited by Marcia Moss, was issued as *Thoreau Society Booklet*, no. 28. The monograph contains a list and description of more than 150 surveys by Thoreau donated to the library by Sophia Thoreau between 1874 and 1877, as well as reproductions of selected Thoreau drawings including his Concord River survey of all river bridges from Wayland to Billerica. Madeline Stern edited a sequel to *Behind a Mask: The Unknown Thrillers of Louisa May Alcott* (New York: William Morrow), titled *Plots and Counterplots: More unknown Thrillers of Louisa May Alcott*, issued by the same publisher. Stern's ear is perhaps more acute than most in hearing "the twentieth century audience that still clamors for more stories by Louisa May Alcott" (p. 24).

Reprint houses continued to issue out-of-print items, adding to the volumes by J. Benton, G. W. Cooke, and Raymond Adams produced in 1975. The single Thoreau volume, *Letters to Various Persons*, initially published in 1865, was reissued by Norwood (Norwood, Pa.) despite the imminence of the *Correspondence* volume in the Princeton Edition, which will contain a good number of hitherto unprinted items unearthed by the diligence of Walter Harding and Thomas Blanding. Four old Emerson items were resuscitated. H. D. Gray's premier study of Emerson's philosophy, often undeservedly neglected by modern researchers, was reprinted by Folcroft Library (Folcroft, Pa.); and Norwood reissued E. E. Hale's *Ralph Waldo Emerson* (1899), which included Hale's study of Emerson along with Emerson's prize undergraduate essays, "The Character of Socrates" and "The Present State of Ethical Philosophy." *ATQ* (29:49–52) reprinted Henry Van Dyke's sketch of Emerson in the Eleventh Edition of the *Britannica*, as well as Harriet Rodgers Zink's "Emerson's Use of the Bible" (30[part 2]:1–21) that originally appeared in *University of Nebraska Studies in Language and Literature*, No. 14 (1935), most useful for its tabulation of Emerson's Biblical allusions in each volume of the Centenary Edition. And finally Leonard Neufeldt, in his *ATQ* symposium on Emerson (31sup.:22–24) discussed below, included J. M. E. Ross's essay, "Ralph Waldo Emerson," reprinted from the *Encyclopedia of Religion and Ethics* (1914).

ii. Emerson

a. **Life and Thought.** Since "the man is only half himself, the other half is his expression," thought and expression are considered inseparable in sectioning this essay. Emerson scholarship, parenthetically, has been less concerned about language and expression than was Emerson himself; and the assumption by some scholars that the language of the fourth quarter of the 20th century is unchanged from that of the second quarter of the 19th has on occasion led to questionable conclusions. Ralph La Rosa's "Necessary Truths: The Poetics of Emerson's Proverbs" is an ambitious study relating Emerson's works to the proverbs of the time. It is available because of the laudable willingness of the University of Wisconsin Press to issue its *Liter-*

ary Monographs series to accommodate midlength studies. La Rosa's monograph is the third of three published in volume 8 (pp. 131–92), edited by Eric Rothstein and Joseph Anthony Wittreich, Jr. It is valuable for calling attention to the role of proverbs in illuminating Emerson's craft, and contributes as well to our understanding of Emerson's thinking about and concern for language. La Rosa's revelation as to how and why antithetical ideas are often juxtaposed in Emerson is particularly useful. More imaginative than La Rosa if less judicious, Gustaaf Van Cromphout, in "Emerson and the Dialectics of History" (*PMLA* 91:54–65), takes a different approach to Emerson's juxtaposition of antithetical ideas, interpreting Emerson's evolving view of history and biography as refracted through Hegel via Cousin, and concluding that by the midforties "Emerson began to see history not as a conflict between hero and society but as a synthesis of hero and society." The Emerson of *The Conduct of Life* according to this thesis had become "a Representative Man himself, a synthesis of his age and the Soul." This ideological explanation of Emerson's presumed late resolution of his conflict with society will doubtless provoke skeptical rejoinders. Merton M. Sealts, Jr., in "The American Scholar and Public Issues: The Case of Emerson" (*Ariel* 7:109–21) discusses Emerson's well-known difficulties in determining how and when to speak publicly on the political and social conflicts of the time, especially slavery, and concludes that Emerson remained justifiably within his chosen role as scholar-teacher. Sealts's view that it was "not because of any lack of personal courage" that Emerson remained relatively aloof may not convince all Emerson skeptics. In "Emerson's Unmoored Self" (*YR* 65:232–40) James McIntosh essays to treat a subtle problem without a sufficiently broad knowledge of Emerson or his terminology. McIntosh concludes that Emerson "blurs the hierarchy implicit in any traditional psychology he could have known," without demonstrating how "heart," "will," and "mind" related to Emerson's concept of the "self." Robert E. Spiller, in "The Four Faces of Emerson" (*Four Makers*, pp. 3–23), originally a lecture delivered at a Hampden-Sydney College Bicentennial celebration, reasserts the usefulness of Emerson to those seeking to understand the American character. William M. Moss, in " 'So Many Promising Youths': Emerson's Disappointing Discoveries of New England Poet-Seers" (*NEQ* 49:46–64) demonstrates a behavioral pattern by Emerson of initial enthusiasm for and subsequent disillusionment with younger poets such as Very, Thoreau, Channing, Cranch, Newcomb, and Whitman because of their shared intractability to criticism and, more important, their failure in Emerson's eyes to develop poetic talent to poetic greatness. Joseph Lawrence Basile in "The Crisis of Consciousness in Montaigne and Emerson" (*CS* 11,i:10–17) views Emerson's interest in Montaigne as motivated by his own search for self-knowledge and a personal *weltanschauung*. Daniel Brian Murteza (*ATQ* 29:52–55) prints several local newspaper reports of "Emerson's Lectures in Norwich, Connecticut." Harold Bloom in *Poetry and Repression: Revisionism from Blake to Stevens* (New Haven, Conn.: Yale Univ. Press, pp. 235–66) includes a chapter titled "Emerson and Whitman: The American Sublime." Bloom's terminology is characteristically eccentric; his esoteric study will no doubt be read appreciatively by those Emerson scholars who have taken the time to master Bloom's private mythology. With ingenuity Bloom links Emerson with Augustine, Kierkegaard, and Vico, exploding such pyrotechnic insights as, "What Emerson represses is *Ananke*, the Fate he has learned already to call 'compensation.' His vision of repetition is a metonymic reduction, an undoing of all other selves, and his restituting *daemonization* renders him solipsistic and free" (p. 237). The Emerson of *Nature*, one wonders, or "Experience"?

b. **Criticism of Specific Works.** Focusing on a single Emerson work, *Nature*, in "The Growth of the Soul: Coleridge's Dialectical Method and the Strategy of Emerson's *Nature*" (*PMLA* 91:385–95), Barry Wood develops a thesis along the same general lines as Van Cromphout (above), suggesting that Emerson's use of the dialectic method of Coleridge points directly toward his major purpose in the work, and leads him to a final synthesis in the chapter, "Spirit." Wood's focus upon one work rather than several lends a cogency to his argument that Van Cromphout's more expansive study lacks. Earlene Margaret Regan's "A Literary Introduction to Emerson's *Nature*" (*ATQ* 30:3–20), grew out of a master's thesis submitted at Trinity College, Hartford, in 1975. The diversity of her chapter titles suggests the problem of the essay: she writes of "genre," "foreshadowings," "figures of speech," "use of description," "diction," "architectonics." (I abstract the key words from some of her chapter titles.) In short, she attempts too much, and largely fails to achieve her stated purpose of suggesting "possibilities for research" in *Nature*. In "The Reader in Emerson's 'Circles' " (*AL* 48:140–51) David M. Wyatt has a tendency perhaps to transmute a personal response into a universal one: "While reading 'Circles' we enjoy a sense of resolved being and unstayed becoming." Emerson's prose in "Circles," Wyatt alleges, "dissolves successive distinctions between spiraling and staying." Wyatt's claim that "as every circle devolves into a spiral, its very center permanently shifts" calls for a more comprehensive demonstration of the phenomenon than he provides. Howard Vincent's "Two New England Snowstorms: From Fact to Poem, an Essay on Inspiration and Meaning" (*RLV* U. S. bicentennial issue:293–303) swirls through Emerson's Journal entries on snowstorms to the conclusion that Emerson's "The Snow-Storm," like Shelley's "Ode to the West Wind," is a poem about poetry. David Porter's " 'Threnody' and Emerson's Poetics of Failure" (*ESQ* 22:1–13) provides some useful insights to explain Emerson's failure as poet, arguing a disjunction between Emerson's "inner meditation on art" and "the particulars of experience" with the result that his poetry (in this instance, "Threnody") unlike that of Whitman, was drained "of its immediacy and personal voice." Porter relies heavily upon analysis of the text. Notes on separate works appear in *AN&Q*, "Emerson's 'Scoriae' " by Mario D'Avanzo (13:141–43) and "The Identity of Emerson's 'Titmouse' " by John H. McKee (13:151–52). In *Expl* (34:item 69) is a brief comment on Emerson's "Days" by Tyrus Hillway.

c. Influence.   About the usual number of articles appeared during the year discerning Emerson's influence on his contemporaries and on later writers. Two have considerable scope. Gay Wilson Allen in "Emerson's Audiences, American and British" (*Ariel* 7:87–108) retraces much of the familiar ground of Emerson's lecturing in America and England, but shows how Emerson adapted his material to contemporary audiences. The reminder is still useful that Emerson's essays were lectures first. In "Emerson and Rilke: A Significant Influence?" (*MLN* 91:565–74) Jan Wojcik elicits enough evidence of Rilke's interest in Emerson to raise the possibility of influence, but by no means closes the case, as the interrogation in the essay title suggests. Three other articles cite broad parallels between Emerson and other poets: G. Thomas Couser's "An Emerson-Whitman Parallel:

'The American Scholar' and 'A Song for Occupations'" (*WWR* 22: 115–18); Lee J. Richmond's "Emersonian Echoes in Dickinson's 'These Are the Signs'" (*ATQ* 29:2–3); and Walter Sutton's "Denise Levertov and Emerson" (*NMAL* 1:item 1). William L. Phillips shows ingenuity in drawing the slimmest of threads between Sherwood Anderson and Emerson in "Emerson in Anderson" (*AN&Q* 15:4–5).

The continued contributions of Kenneth Cameron, above and beyond the *ATQ* items mentioned above, deserve separate mention. Cameron's "Current Bibliography on Ralph Waldo Emerson" (*ATQ* 32:21–31) is comprehensive, up to date, hence immensely useful. A wide miscellany of primary materials is made available in *Sixty Years of Concord, 1855–1915: Life, People, Institutions and Transcendental Philosophy in Massachusetts—With Memories of Emerson, Thoreau, Alcott, Channing and Others*, by Franklin Benjamin Sanborn; edited with notes and index by Kenneth Walter Cameron (Hartford, Conn.: Transcendental Books). During the year Cameron published still another Emerson symposium (*ATQ* 31, sup. 1), which includes articles by six scholars, along with the reprint from J. M. E. Ross mentioned above, the whole gathered by Leonard N. Neufeldt, his second symposium to be issued by *ATQ*. Neufeldt's essay is perhaps the most stimulating of the group; in "'The Fields of my Fathers' and Emerson's Literary Vocation" (pp. 5–9), Neufeldt develops a plausible case for Emerson's discovery of a usable past in Concord history, though the essay ends with a possible overstatement of the link between "Historical Discourse" and *Nature*. Jeffrey L. Duncan in "The Curse and Blessing of Emerson's Art" (pp. 9–13), from "Experience" and other essays, draws some interesting though debatable conclusions on Emerson's use of dialectic as strategy. Duncan's essay invites comparison with those of Van Cromphout and Wood, above. Evelyn Barish in "Emerson and 'The Magician': An Early Prose Fantasy" (pp. 13–18) extracts some serious conclusions about Emerson from this trivial piece that are extravagant, to say the least. In "Metaphoric Imagery in Emerson's Later Essays" Brien R. Harding patently fails to deal with so ambitious a topic in three pages (pp. 18–21). Luther S. Luedtke's "Emerson in Western Europe (1955–1975)" is largely bibliographical. Luedtke's "Adolph Holtermann: Translator of Emerson" (*ATQ* 29:46–52) is an apparent spin-off of the same investigation. The last essay of the symposium, John J. Fenstermaker's "Emer-

son's Lexicon in 'The Poet'" (*ATQ* 31 sup.:42–45) makes the useful
point that much of the current difficulty in the reading of Emerson
stems from a failure to attend closely to his language.

iii. Thoreau

a. **Life and Thought.** First, the disparagements of Thoreau's
thought. Each year, since Stevenson called Thoreau a "skulker" (a
charge he later retracted), has produced its quota. (Walter Harding,
as a matter of fact, printed during the year a newly discovered 1901
response to Stevenson by Samuel Arthur Jones, "Thoreau as a Skulker" [*TSB* 135:2–5]). Kenneth S. Lynn in "Adulthood in American
Literature" (*Daedalus* 105:52–54) accuses Thoreau of "playing house
at Walden Pond," tarring 19th-century American writers from Cooper
to Twain with a broad brush of "childishness." Since Lynn has published a subsequent article on *The Adventures of Huckleberry Finn*
admitting that Henry Nash Smith, the Twain scholar, was more right
than he, perhaps he will review his position on other American writers
as well. William Lee Miller in *Of Thee, Nevertheless, I Sing* (New
York: Harcourt Brace Jovanovich, 1975, pp. 265–71) raises again the
problem of the moral absolutism of the man claiming to be "more
right than his neighbors." But nearly all Thoreau critics are of course
more positive. With the aid of the rhetoric of Kenneth Burke and
Harold Bloom, Lauriat Lane, Jr., in "Mountain Gloom and Yankee
Poetry: Thoreau, Emerson, Frost" (*DR* 55:612–30) is able to show
in separate poems from each author "three different Yankee responses
to the gloom or glory of the mountains of New England." The Thoreau
poem, "With Frontier Strength," Lane asserts, "could evoke several
Burkean 'mountings.'" Elsa Nettles in "'A Frugal Splendour':
Thoreau and James and the Principles of Economy" (*CLQ* 12:5–13)
develops some unexpected and perhaps overingenious linkages between the sensibilities of the two authors. Defining "economy" as "the
employment of one's resources so that one receives the fullest value
from them," Nettles alleges that "in general terms, economy means
for James what it means for Thoreau." Rosemary F. Franklin, in "The
Cabin by the Lake: Pastoral Landscapes of Poe, Cooper, Hawthorne,
and Thoreau" (*ESQ* 22:59–69), essays a great deal in a short space,
linking the four authors to aspects of the pastoral tradition, and concluding that the writings of Thoreau "contain the most fully realized

expression of the American pastoral impulse." Reviewing Thoreau's well-known relationships with women, and Journal passages in which Thoreau alludes to sexuality, Mary Elkins Moller in "Thoreau, Womankind, and Sexuality" (*ESQ* 22:123–48) suggests that by 1854 Thoreau acknowledged his own sexuality and that of others to be "a valued part of his and their emotional nature." Wendell Glick, in "Thoreau as Failed Poet" (*LSJ* 2:40–44), argues that Thoreau's romantic ideal for poetry was by definition unattainable. Frederick P. Lenz, III, in "Henry David Thoreau: The Forgotten Poems" (*CS* 11,i:1–9), takes the lonely position that Thoreau was a "major American poet." Kenneth Cameron in *Transcendental Apprenticeship: Notes on Young Henry Thoreau's Reading: A Contexture with a Researcher's Index* (Hartford, Conn.: Transcendental Books) provides us in one useful reference volume with a comprehensive source book of Thoreau's reading.

b. **Criticism of Specific Works.** Richard Fleck's "Mythic Buds in Thoreau's Journal" (*Ariel* 7:77–86) develops the argument that Thoreau's Journal is a record of "myths in bud" that develop later "into myths and mythic structures of his major books." Some confusion develops over Fleck's distinction between "myth" and "symbol," which are not synonymous terms, and the conclusion perhaps outruns the evidence. Thoreau's Journal, however, deserves more scholarly attention than it has hitherto received, which the publication of the augmented text in the Princeton Edition should stimulate. In "Thoreau in His Time—The First Installment" (*RLV* bicentennial issue:157–69) Edwin Fussell hazards "a Marxist reading of *A Week on the Concord and Merrimack Rivers*" that leads him on a tortured course through chapters on "Ellen Emerson, Freud, and Marx" and "Thoreau and Mao: From River to Poetry to Revolution" to a conclusion in his final sentence with which this reviewer concurs: "*A Week* . . . is *not* easy reading, but it is not impossible either, except for those who have an interest in making it seem so."

The majority of critical studies on individual works by Thoreau predictably deal with *Walden*. Mutlu Blasing, in "The Economies of *Walden*" (*TSLL* 42:759–75), argues that *Walden* should be considered autobiographical, "because its author, narrator, and hero have the same name, because it is devoted to self-cultivation, and because its other characters do not serve to 'mirror' the hero or to qualify the subjectivity of his point of view." This thesis leads him to consider "Economy" and the Narcissus legend as central. Michael Gates's "*Walden*: Yantra Above Yantras" (*ESQ* 22:14–23) views the book as a record of and espousal of a "religious" life, and develops with considerable cogency a predictable case for the influence of Hinduism upon Thoreau's thought, but a less predictable case for its influence on his artistry. Adrienne Baylop's "Music is the Sound of Universal Laws Promulgated" (*CEA* 39,iii:11–15) examines Thoreau's "view of sounds as the matrix which generates a deeper understanding of *Walden* and as one concordant element in Thoreau's system of metaphysics," reaffirming some of Sherman Paul's insights from a somewhat different evidentiary base. The "Annual Report for 1975" of the American Literature Section of MLA contains an abstract of Thomas Woodson's "Thoreau's Attitudes Toward His Prospective Readers during the Evolution of *Walden*" (p. 16) that makes one wish to see the entire paper in print. Willard H. Bonner, in "The Harvest of Thought in Thoreau's 'Autumnal Tints'" (*ESQ* 22:78–84), supports and extends Sherman Paul's judgment in *The Shores of America* that "Autumnal Tints" is "more about ripeness and ideas of harvest, than decay," and is not Thoreau's commentary upon his own approaching death.

c. **Influence.** The perception of the applicability of Thoreau's thought to problems of the present is widespread and leads annually to a plethora of appreciative essays, only a few of which yield new information and require mention here. The Hampden-Sydney College symposium, edited by Thomas Crawley (see above), included J. Lyndon Shanley's "Thoreau: His 'Lover's Quarrel with the World'" (pp. 25–42), which develops the theme that Thoreau's faith in and hope for the nation never wavered despite his criticisms of fellow-citizens and the state, and that his insights are therefore useful in understanding the American character. Thoreau's prescience in anticipating the problems of modern man is the general theme of Joseph Lawrence Basile's "Narcissus in the World of Machines" (*SoR* 32:10–13); Reginald L. Cook's "Looking for America: A Binocular Vision" (*TJQ* 8,iii:10–17), is an unusually fine example of how enlightening this sort of study can be when informed by the perceptiveness of broad knowledge.

The small journals specializing in Thoreau print varying mixes of brief, scholarly essays and appreciative ones. Generally speaking, since Lewis Leary relinquished the editorship of *TJQ*, the articles in that journal have become less scholarly and broader in appeal, Reginald Cook's article being the notable exception of the year. *CS*, the organ of the Thoreau Lyceum in Concord, ably edited by Anne McGrath, is moving in the direction of an increasing percentage of short, scholarly essays, spearheaded by the findings of the indefatigable Thoreau archeologist, Thomas Blanding of the Princeton Edition, who has uncovered much new material in private collections and public libraries. Since it is very difficult to develop substantive interpretive studies in the short space available in such journals, *CS* performs a service to scholars in printing this newly discovered matter. *TSB*, edited by Walter Harding, continues to publish in each issue the most useful current bibliography of Thoreau scholarship available, and along with its usual complement of anecdotal matter, an occasional genuinely scholarly piece of research, a case in point being Thomas Blanding's "Passages from John Thoreau, Jr.'s Journal" (*TSB* 136:4–6).

iv. Minor Transcendentalists

Attention upon minor figures studied for their own sake focused during the year largely upon Margaret Fuller and Bronson Alcott. By all odds, the preeminent achievement of the year in this category is Bell Gale Chevigny's *The Woman and the Myth: Margaret Fuller's Life and Writings* (Westbury, N.Y.: Feminist Press). A double intention (as typified by the title) and an implausible format (six chapters, each introduced by a biographical-critical essay, followed by an anthology of pertinent documents) would seem to portend diffusion and lack of focus. Instead, while conveying the frustration incumbent upon being a gifted, 19th-century woman, Gale Chevigny traces the evolution in Fuller's thought from early idealism to the political and social radicalism of her years in Italy preceding her death. Fuller's relationship to Emerson, particularly, both as woman and as intellectual disciple, is developed with scholarly attention to the evidence available. Each of the six essays, considered individually, is characterized by the restraint typical of the best research. Paul John Eakin, in "Margaret Fuller, Hawthorne, James, and Sexual Politics" (*SAQ* 75:323–38), contends that Zenobia in *The Blithedale*

Romance reflects Hawthorne's belief that an understanding of Margaret Fuller's sexuality would be needed to understand her ideas fully (an understanding that Chevigny perceptively conveys); and that Henry James drew extensively on the life of Fuller in writing his novel about sexual politics, *The Bostonians*. Marie Urbanski summarizes in "Henry David Thoreau and Margaret Fuller" (*TJQ* 8,iv: 24–29) the known facts about the relation between the two. Three of the five Alcott essays of the year are bibliographical: Joel Myerson prints "Additions to Bronson Alcott's Bibliography: Letters and 'Orphic Sayings' in the *Plain Speaker*" (*NEQ* 49:283–92) consisting of two Alcott letters to the editor of that reform journal and two collections of "orphic sayings"; Walter Hesford (*RALS* 6:81–84), in "Alcott's Criticism of *A Week*," prints entire Alcott's 1849 comment in his journal which Odell Shepard abridged in *The Journals of Bronson Alcott* (1938), pp. 213–15. Fordyce Richard Bennett prints matter from the 1825 and 1826 *Churchman's Magazine* alleged to be Alcott's earliest publications (*ATQ* 31:25–27). In an apparent spinoff of his Illinois dissertation on Alcott, Bennett suggests the Essenes, Pythagoreans, and the Englishman Greaves as inspirers of Alcott's Fruitlands ("Sources for Alcott's Fruitlands," *ATQ* 32:19–20). "The Transcendentalist as Mystic: Amos Bronson Alcott" (*ConnR* 9:90–99) by J. Wade Caruthers, begins with a statement on Alcott's mysticism, fails in definition, and diffuses into a collection of largely biographical facts.

University of Minnesota, Duluth

2. Hawthorne

J. Donald Crowley

Hawthorne criticism in 1976 strikes me as in some sense a replication of so much of Hawthorne's own art, defined as it is by what is not there as much as by what is. Several lines from Mark Strand's superb poem "Keeping Things Whole" might serve as a fitting epigraph: "In a field / I am the absence / of field. . . . / Wherever I am / I am what is missing." The year saw no new volumes of the Centenary Edition and thus no new commentaries on Hawthorne's revisions or on the problems of editing him. The annual *Nathaniel Hawthorne Journal* appeared too late to be remarked upon here, and the usual bibliographical and biographical notes it contains are absent from the year's work. Although two full-length biographical studies are under way, it still remains for us to see whether they will resolve the conflicts and contradictions between Randall Stewart's standard study and Frederick Crews's Freudian rejoinder. Publication of the collected letters is an event still to be wished for. Nonetheless, the season's crop is considerable. The freshest rethinking of Hawthorne's fiction since Crews's 1966 study, Nina Baym's *The Shape of Hawthorne's Career* (Ithaca, N.Y.: Cornell Univ. Press) is a most substantial analysis of Hawthorne's art as a process of elastic and coherent development informed largely by his self-conscious attitude toward it and his relationship with his audience. Not the least of Baym's achievements here is that she requires Hawthorne students to readjust their notion of the various stages or phases of his "career." Richard H. Brodhead's *Hawthorne, Melville, and the Novel* (Chicago: Univ. of Chicago Press) is likewise a carefully conceived and lucidly sustained exploration of its subject. With a very different definition of Hawthorne's "career," Brodhead focuses on the years of Hawthorne's concentrated creativity, discussing his shifts in experimentation and showing deftly the ways in which Hawthorne and Melville created different strategies to confront the same discontents with the form of the novel. Since I have reviewed both these studies elsewhere, I will add only that both critics manage exciting, sensitive readings of individual novels while elucidating those interstitial spaces between the fictions. Another event of major importance is the discovery—in Boulder, Colorado—of Hawthorne's earliest existing American Notebook, 86 pages in the author's own handwriting. For someone who once smiled that his name might come to be known best by way of stencilled cigar-boxes, Hawthorne turns out to be a man of letters who has travelled much, even in Colorado. Finally, especially given the chorus of complaints journal editors have been making these days about poorly researched and execrably written submissions, a pleasing number of essays on Hawthorne tend to be of generally high quality. There are some weeds with the flowers, to be sure, but much of the work deserves high praise: much of it should enhance and complicate our teaching of Hawthorne on virtually every level.

i. Manuscripts, Life, Bibliography

In "A Hawthorne Discovery: The Lost Notebook, 1835–1841" (*NEQ* 49:618–26), Hyatt Waggoner describes generally the nature of this manuscript, which he calls "one of the most important of all the American Notebooks." Consisting of 329 entries, the earliest dated May 28, 1835, the latest June 29, 1841, the manuscript contains 72 entries completely omitted by Sophia Hawthorne in her "rigorous editing." This Notebook is "the most inward-centered and idea-focused," and Sophia's changes have obscured its difference from others. Her changes have also served to conceal certain evidence about their courtship—as well as references to drunkenness, prostitution, shapely girlish legs, and various "morbid" ideas for tales. One of Waggoner's lasting impressions about such passages is that Hawthorne does appear to have been "unusually preoccupied not only with suffering, decay, and death, but with cruelty, guilt, and punishment" and does seem to describe himself accurately as "a detached, uninvolved, cold observer." The old biographical riddle holds on tight for us as for Hawthorne's contemporaries.

A thorough, vigorous attempt to see through and solve some part of that enigma is Sidney Moss's "Hawthorne and Melville: An Inquiry into Their Art and the Mystery of Their Friendship," in *Literary*

Monographs (Univ. of Wis. Press) 7[1975]:47–84). The primary urge in this long essay is psychographic, and its method is to use the fiction—and letters, notebooks, and the comments of friends and critics—to comprehend the life. For Moss, the riddle is not Hawthorne but the fact that he and Melville enjoyed for a time such a transport of friendship when their minds and their humanity were so irreconcilably opposite. When Moss says "opposite," he means just that: Hawthorne is an "*I* in profound conflict with the *Me*," in a self-constructed "cage of narcissism," and Melville is an "undivided" man, "a man of imagination" who wrote about actuality rather than his own "psychic preoccupations"; Melville is an authentic moral " 'ambiguist' " with a truly tragic vision, and Hawthorne is incapable of being "morally ambiguous" because he is a "moral absolutist" believing in "perfect certitude in the traditional moral order and in 'divine Providence' "—and "damned . . . to his private psychological hell" by his inability to feel deep sympathy for his characters. There are more of these tidily polar differences, and what they lead to relentlessly is this unambiguous judgment: "the mystery of their friendship dissolves when we understand that the Hawthorne we know, and the Hawthorne that Bridge, Emerson, Thoreau, Alcott, Duyckinck, Holmes, Lowell, Fields, and the others knew, and that even his wife and children knew, was not the Hawthorne that Melville knew." Though Moss insists that we can never really know Melville's Hawthorne, he does not demonstrate how—given the destruction of Hawthorne's letters to Melville—we can be so intellectually (and morally?) certain that Hawthorne was for Melville so singularly transformed a personality. Moss's assessment of that personality darkens inexorably: Hawthorne's life finally announces itself the victim of Hawthorne's art, becoming a rigid allegory of a man having "ice in [his] blood," Hawthorne himself being capable, in *Our Old Home*, of "a Dachau-type sentiment" regarding a small child in the workhouse. Emerson "was right," Moss tells us, "in suggesting that Hawthorne had committed the ultimate crime against life." Quoting Emerson directly again, Moss agrees that Hawthorne's tragedy was his "painful solitude" and that it—rather than cancer—killed him. Two compensatory paragraphs of conclusion cannot turn the tide of such judgments: Moss, curiously, condemns Hawthorne in much the same way he sees Hawthorne condemning others, in life and in fiction. At the same time, he makes nothing of Melville's passionate moral conservatism in his later writings and very little indeed of his decades of spiritual torment and nearly Hawthornian alienation.

Another essay essentially biographical, Robert Roulston's "Hawthorne's Attitude Toward Jews" (*ATQ* 29:3–8), takes Hawthorne to task as anti-Semitic: Miriam in *The Marble Faun*, the figure of the Wandering Jew in "Ethan Brand" and "A Virtuoso's Collection," and a reference in *The English Notebooks*, we are told, provide evidence of his hostility to Jews' "clannishness and social climbing, . . . uncleanliness, cosmopolitanism, ugliness, excessive sexuality, and, of course, greed." Hawthorne associates Jews with an almost "metaphysical isolation" in "Ethan Brand," and, in fact, with the devil, too. Why, we wonder, is Wakefield Wakefield? And aren't Chillingworth and Judge Pyncheon heaven-sent chances missed? Was the Wandering Jew compelling to Hawthorne as sociocultural racism or as universal fable? I have little doubt that Hawthorne's personal views were not what we would have them—about Jews, or slavery, or even contemporary nude statues. But it's only the third one of these items in this odd series that he risked in his fiction. Ezra Pound he was not.

The sole bibliographical study of 1976 is Robert J. Stanton's "Secondary Studies on Hawthorne's 'Young Goodman Brown,' 1845–1975" (*BB* 83:32–44,52), a compilation of critical works which, while not quite comprehensive, is a useful, welcome tool for virtually anyone writing about this tale.

ii. General Studies

Two essays take up the familiar issue of Hawthorne's use of allegory, and both disagree, albeit on different grounds, with Moss's conclusions. In "Allegory Versus Allegory in Hawthorne" (*ATQ* 32: 14–19), Dennis Grunes, like numerous previous critics, sees Hawthorne as an antiallegorist who employs the trappings of the technique primarily to expose unbending patterns of thought that distort actual experience. Thus, "Young Goodman Brown" is Brown's own allegorizing while it is Hawthorne's severe critique of the shortcomings of Brown's views. Brown's attitudes—and Aylmer's and those of the Puritan community in *The Scarlet Letter* and "Lady Eleanore's Mantle"—violate life and victimize heroines by persistently denying the senses and altogether repressing sexuality. Grunes both follows

Crews and doesn't: it is Hawthorne's fictional people, not Hawthorne, who are id-driven and self-concealing. Too little evidence is presented, however, to make the argument conclusive. On the other hand, Raymond Himelick, in "Hawthorne, Spenser, and Christian Humanism" (*ESQ* 21[1975]:21–28), is persuasive in suggesting that Hawthorne found in Spenserian allegory not "a ceremonious embalming of simplistic ethical values" but a profound vision of the complexity of the human situation. What Hawthorne responded to in Spenser—as well as in other writers—was an insistence upon an "ironic equipoise, or even synthesis, of opposites in the moral life," an awareness that the world, far from being a Manichean construct, is a place where good and evil fully interpenetrate, where blemish and ideal are inseparable, where faith engenders guilt and guilt becomes the simultaneous proof of faith. If Himelick does not clarify specific points of Hawthorne's fiction, he does provide a vital corrective to the charge that, insofar as Hawthorne is an allegorist, he is a rigid moral absolutist.

Several essays examine the metaphorical significance that habitations have, both aesthetically and psychologically, for Hawthorne. G. Thomas Couser's " 'The Old Manse,' *Walden*, and the Hawthorne-Thoreau Relationship" (*ESQ* 21[1975]:11–20), argues that there are many noteworthy similarities in subject, theme, imagery, form, and general intention in Hawthorne's sketch and Thoreau's book. Couser carefully reviews the friendship of the two men and explores, with sensible qualification, the possibility that their attitudes became mutually influential. Various readers, however, will find reason to quarrel with the notion that "The Old Manse" is as anomalous in Hawthorne's canon as Couser's thesis seems forced to make it, but the discussion of various parallels between the two pieces is penetrating and suggestive. Rosemary F. Franklin's "The Cabin by the Lake: Pastoral Landscapes of Poe, Cooper, Hawthorne, and Thoreau" (*ESQ* 22:59–70), examines the symbiotic relationship between the house and the pastoral ideal of a middle ground between nature and civilization. The function of the house as an emblem of the psyche promotes, ideally, a participation in the positive powers of both nature and society and a fortification against the negative threats and encroachments of both. Whereas the house connotes the conservation of forms, the lake or pond represents "the pure and revelatory face of nature, not the mysterious and chthonic forces of the dark wilderness." These balanced possibilities, Franklin says, are subverted in *The House of the Seven Gables* and *The Blithedale Romance* and sharply curtailed in *The Scarlet Letter*. The paradigm would seem to collapse when one considers that Hester's pond is nothing less than ocean. Whether Hawthorne can be said to have made "truly new contributions to the pastoral tradition" or radically inverted that tradition remains in question. In "Hawthorne's Houses of Fiction" (*AL* 48:271–91) Thomas H. Pauly advances the view that Hawthorne's portrayal in various sketches of rooms and homes associated with his everyday life transformed them into houses of fiction. Unlike James, however, Hawthorne was not comfortable in the process, being almost congenitally unable or unwilling to accommodate himself to "home." His earliest stories contain only an authorial sensibility while lacking any trace of the stories they would seem to want to tell. Even the Old Manse, his happiest home, leaves his imagination disaffected, as had the Province House of the four legends. His flight from fiction to the public life of the Custom-House he discovers to be a curse, since his fiction is once again out of sorts with both his condition of living and his audience. Defining himself as "invariably happiest elsewhere," Hawthorne, Pauly says, is at ease neither here nor there but questing always, and futilely, for a neutral territory capable of inducing, as Salem could not, a positive "home-feeling." The unfinished romances, the name Hawthorne gave to his last residence, his being on the road when he died—all point to his art's finally having nowhere to go. The theme of homelessness in Hawthorne's life and art is a matter deserving still further attention.

Hawthorne's shifting attitudes toward the meaning of the past continues to attract comment. In "Hawthorne, History, and the Human Heart" (*Clio* 5:175–80) Richard Harter Fogle finds Hawthorne expressing "conflicting theories about the source, the movement, and the structure of history," theories of a providential design on the one hand and, on the other, at least in some of the juvenile sketches, optimistically progressive and secular views. Hawthorne, however, is too consistent to be merely eclectic: he subjects all such theories, says Fogle, to the test of the human heart. The note, too general because too brief, is nonetheless provocative. Two other essays that elaborate much more fully similar attitudes toward the complexity of Hawthorne's pursuit of historical meaning are John P. McWilliams, Jr.'s "'Thorough-Going Democrat' and 'Modern Tory': Hawthorne and the Puritan Revolution of 1776" (*SIR* 15:549–71) and Lewis P. Simpson's "John Adams and Hawthorne: The Fiction of the Real American Revolution" (*SLitI* 9:1–18). Both are stimulating and substantial essays in historical criticism, and both are among the finest pieces reported on here. McWilliams's is the wider in range as it discusses *Grandfather's Chair*, the four Province-House tales, and "My Kinsman, Major Molineux" in the context of the complacent accounts of the Revolution most widely known among 19th-century readers—Weems's *Life of Washington* and Bancroft's *History of the United States*. These specious, uncomplicated reconstructions of the past—with their devotion to the nobility of character which inspired revolution and to the ideal of rationality and progress—could not address those issues that Hawthorne, with his disapproval of revolutionary motives and his distaste for violent events, found crucial: "such troubling facts as the conduct of popular crowds, the demagoguery of popular leaders and the plight of the American loyalist." The Revolution appeals to Hawthorne as subject, not because it is a revelation of timeless rights, but as a complex web of "generative conflicts" which enables him to trace the slow development of the New England mind, "from Province to Republic, from colonial to revolutionary." McWilliams's analysis of the fiction is astute and persuasive in showing how Hawthorne had to struggle to keep his "Tory" and "Democrat" sympathies in tandem. And he demonstrates how the "adult" historical sketches are a rather courageous affronting of the Jacksonian assumptions of his age. Taking issue with Q. D. Leavis and Frederick Crews, McWilliams sees Robin Molineux neither as symbol of America's coming of age nor as being involved in filial revolt. His Robin remains naive and uninitiated to the end; it is the violent mob and its leaders who register Hawthorne's assessment of pre-Revolutionary America. Simpson confines himself solely to this tale, which he calls "the archetypal story of the American imagination," and to its relationship with the definition of the real Revolution. That definition, as it resides in the Declaration of Independence, is one which makes "mind" the "very model of history," replacing the performances of heroes. While Jefferson the Enlightenment Deist drafted the document out of a fixed belief that perfectible rationality now molded history, John Adams, possesser of the Puritan heritage and of a vision of the fallen nature of man, lacked that faith in reason and thus becomes the clearest precursor of such fiction as Hawthorne's. Robin's story Simpson describes as "the fulfillment of Adams's search for the reality of our origins," the real Revolution having occurred long before the war itself. Simpson's interpretation of Robin's experience is at points dramatically different from McWilliams's. Robin, he contends, has out of his pastoral background already absorbed an intensely intellectual, rational spirit, Puritan rather than Deist; he is indeed initiated into that idea of history as the processes of consciousness. What Adams had intuited politically Hawthorne dramatizes fictionally: "While man had the opportunity as never before to be a rational creature, he was becoming as never before subject to his emotionality." For both McWilliams and Simpson Robin's "shrewdness" has in it the seeds of many another wild growth.

iii. Long Romances

Little new work on Hawthorne's romances appeared in 1976. Overlooked among 1975 essays are two studies of *The Scarlet Letter*. In "Self-Revelation in *The Scarlet Letter*" (*RUS* 61:141–50) J. A. Ward focuses on the ways in which prefatory sketch and romance alike grapple with the paradoxical strains on the individual as at once private and public self. The conditions of privacy are simultaneously a requirement of and a barrier to the revelation of self to community. This much has been said before, and in many ways, but Ward says it with fresh force. And his analysis of Hawthorne's arrangement of his materials and his chapters into three planes of being—introspective, conversational, and public occasions—provides insight into the book's structure. Elaine Tuttleton Hansen's "Ambiguity and the Narrator in *The Scarlet Letter*" (*JNT* 5:147–63) follows Charles Feidelson and other critics who see the narrator as the central character in a drama of consciousness about the function and meaning of the A. Seeing that narrator as Hawthorne's fiction, Hansen traces the modulations of the narrator's roles as editor and as romancer as his 19th-century-rational mind attempts to sort out the factual realities in the legendary-superstitious materials at hand. The attentive reader's business is to contemplate the meaning of the narrator himself, whose very "inconsistency" of consciousness guides the wary reader to that wider sympathy denied Hester by the Puritan community. The language of uncertainty, then, becomes "the language of moral flexibility." Hansen's Hawthorne would seem to lie about midway between Moss's and Himelick's. Is hers a Hawthorne who would accommodate himself, one wonders, to an age of "accountability"?

The extent to which Hawthorne's own attitudes can be, must be distinguished from those of his narrators and other characters has, of course, been a perennial question in post-Boothian analyses. Jeffrey Steinbrink, in "Hawthorne's Holgravian Temper: The Case Against the Past" (*ATQ* 31:21–23) argues that Hawthorne shares more fully in Holgrave's antipathy toward the past than critics have wanted to believe. He cites as evidence the author's adaptation of a notebook entry in one of Holgrave's indignant comments about the tyranny of the dead over the living; Holgrave's revolutionary zeal is, according to Steinbrink, Hawthorne's way of objectifying his own inhibitions and ambivalences. Ronald T. Curran's "'Yankee Gothic': Hawthorne's 'Castle of Pyncheon'" (*SNNTS* 8:69–79) looks at the romance as a skillful adaptation of European Gothic and its aristocratic intent to sustain feudal values of inheritance. Curran, however —unlike Steinbrink—has Holgrave's liberal enthusiasm flawed by his increasing conservatism and his skepticism about human progress: so much so that the radically democratic purposes of "Yankee Gothic" are defeated by the unavoidability of the past.

In "The Black Flower of Necessity: Structure in *The Blithedale Romance*" (*ELUD* 3:86–96) Vern B. Lentz and Allen F. Stein assert that whatever might be "providential" in the romance is nothing less than another mode of determinism, Coverdale being no freer than Dreiser's Clyde Griffiths. Hawthorne, they claim, completely refuses here to hold any of his characters "accountable" for their conduct. The illusory nature of freedom is embedded in the romance's structural rhythm of inevitability, which has Coverdale making four abortive attempts to commit himself wholesomely to others. Coverdale, however unsavory, is condemned to inhabit a personality that takes shape without choice. Far from assuming that this condition allows the characters to escape guilt, Lentz and Stein—like Hansen, unlike Moss—would see it as Hawthorne's expression of the need for compassion. What I sense as missing from the discussion is a workable definition of human freedom. Charles Swann's "A Note on *The Blithedale Romance*, or 'Call him Fauntleroy'" (*JAmS* 10:103–4), cites a few strands of evidence suggesting that forgery is the crime of old Moodie's fictional Fauntleroy, Hawthorne having seen the widely publicized history of a London banker by that name. The year's only essay on Hawthorne's last completed romance is Leland S. Person, Jr.'s "Aesthetic Headaches and European Women in *The Marble Faun* and *The American*" (*SAF* 4:65–77), which contends that for both Hawthorne and James the terrors that Europe held for the westering American crystallized in the European woman, who becomes the test of their heroes' capacity to relate to alien culture and symbolizes their problems in the creation of art. Person's discussion of Miriam as woman-artist is a sane, sensitive elaboration of various ideas cited in Crews and Baym, and his analysis of her artistic "supervision" of the romance's final chapters is illuminating.

iv. Short Works

In "The Function of the Lamp in Hawthorne's 'The Wives of the Dead'" (*SAB* 40,ii[1975]:62–64) Patricia Ann Carlson, claiming that most critics misread this early tale's events as occurring in wakeful reality, argues that the lamp's light is a symbolic projection of the two widows' susceptibility to illusion. The husbands are dead, the tale bleaker than usually supposed.

"My Kinsman, Major Molineux" continues to provoke all brands of comment. In "'My Kinsman, Major Molineux' as Mock-Heroic" (*ATQ* 31:20–21) Stanley J. Kozikowski compares the tale to Aeneas's descent into the underworld and concludes that Hawthorne inverts epic similitudes for essentially comic purposes. More substantial is P. L. Abernethy's "The Identity of Hawthorne's Major Molineux" (*ATQ* 31:5–8), which contends that the William Molineux of Hutchinson's *History of Massachusetts-Bay* is not the only historical source for Hawthorne's character, that Hawthorne's long familiarity with Swift would have made him aware of the William Molineux of the *Drapier's Letters*, champion of the Irish cause, and of his relative William Wood, who was hanged in effigy. Abernethy offers intriguing evidence—sufficient to make the argument plausible—that Hawthorne's tale amalgamates incidents from the Irish rebellion with those of his own New England ancestors. Abernethy appears curiously unaware of Roy Harvey Pearce's ground-breaking essay on the identity of the American Molineux, "Hawthorne and the Sense of the Past, or, The Immortality of Major Molineux" (1954); his essay would have done well to discuss the convergences of and the disparities between these materials. One of the year's finest essays is Peter

Shaw's "Fathers, Sons, and the Ambiguities of Revolution in 'My Kinsman, Major Molineux,'" (*NEQ* 49:559–76), an interpretation of the tale based on a rich cross-fertilization of Hawthorne's use of materials from history, literature, folklore, and an intuitive anticipation of both Frazer and Freud. Shaw does mention Pearce and builds on his insights, gracefully accounting as well for other critical assessments. Robin's story is Hawthorne's reconstruction of the colonial Molineux's ambiguous history, and it incorporates the Robin Goodfellow–Billy Bottom theatricals in *A Midsummer Night's Dream*, patterns of the Roman Saturnalia (learned from his reading of Strutt), English May Day disturbances and the ambivalent and contradictory roles therein of Robin Hood as at once mock-king and leader of the rebels. "It is no accident," Shaw says, "that rebel and revel are etymologically identical." For Shaw, Robin Molineux experiences a displaced aggression, having substituted Major for real father when joining the mob. Like that mob, he suffers both from excessive obedience and excessive rebelliousness in the same act: the boy who would become man joins a crowd of men maddened into boys. Shaw's Hawthorne, then, takes the measure of the moral and psychological significance of the Revolution by steeping it in profound ambivalence. He refuses to allow his readers to ascribe complacently to the idea that Robin enjoys moral growth even as he holds out hope that Robin's health, upbringing, and religious background will be sturdy equipment for living. Shaw's reading is richly, lucidly contextual. Joseph D. Adams's "The Societal Initiation and Hawthorne's 'My Kinsman, Major Molineux': The Night-Journey Motif" (*ESColl*, ser. 1, no. 1, 19 pp.), on the other hand, is single-mindedly mythic. Adams is almost totally optimistic about Robin's initiation, which consists of a stage of "Separation," moves on through seven encounters in the "Transition" of the night journey, and allows him to reach a reliable, kindly guide and undergo spiritual rebirth in the "Incorporation." At which point all problems cease: Adams ends by saying that "in a few days, Robin will have recovered from the severity of this ordeal. . . . He will learn that the townspeople with whom he has made identification are not infernal agents, but merely human beings, jealously guarding their right to self-dominion." Ah, Robin, would that it were so!

In "Image and Structure in Hawthorne's 'Roger Malvin's Burial'" (*SAB* 41,iv:3–9), Patricia Ann Carlson asserts that the recurring rock-grave image actually constitutes the organic evolution of the tale's dramatic action. Carlson explicates sensitively Hawthorne's multi-sided descriptions which endow the rock with physical, figurative, and allusive characteristics, but many readers will object to her mere word-play metamorphoses of it—from *stepping stone* to *touchstone* to *lodestone* to *altar stone*. No wonder, one begins to think, that Hawthorne gathered the tale in *Mosses*. In "The Geography and Frame-work of Hawthorne's 'Roger Malvin's Burial' " (*TSL* 21:11–20) John R. Byers, Jr., complains that Crews's interpretation makes the tale more complex than evidence warrants and offers a counterreading. Hawthorne turned to the Bible to draw on, not only the Reuben-Joseph story, but the Laban-Jacob-Rachel episode in *Genesis*. Byers's argument, however, seems less than solid: although he finds Hawthorne refusing to "create the least justification for Reuben's act," he calls Roger Malvin "the devil archetype, blood brother to Roger Chillingworth and Ethan Brand" because the older man "sought with generous art to wile [Reuben] to his own good." Child sacrifice, whether deliberate or not, is demanded as atonement for the abandonment of a devil figure?

James Duban's "The Sceptical Context of Hawthorne's 'Mr. Higginbotham's Catastrophe' " (*AL* 48:292–301) is a fresh and enlightening analysis of a folktale that critics have been hard pressed to account for except as a piece to be ignored. Duban proposes that it addresses, in farcically typological terms, "the question of the reality of Christ's resurrection in terms of David Hume's objections to human *testimony* as a reliable source of evidence in confirming Gospel miracles." Here as elsewhere in his fiction Hawthorne adapts for dramatic purposes the "Faith/Evidence apologetics" aroused by 18th- and 19th-century Deist and skeptical thought. In his sacrilegious tale, Dominicus Pike, a prodigal backslider run off from Parson Thumpcushion's orthodoxy, reenacts Hume's rejection of miracles established through human testimony. Duban's reading succeeds in demonstrating that the piece is not anomalous but an integral part of the Hawthorne canon. The reading puts the story in close touch with Hawthorne's concerns in one of his greatest allegories, at least as Leo B. Levy interprets matters in his masterful essay, "The Problem of Faith in 'Young Goodman Brown' " (*JEGP* 54[1975]:375–87). The title of the essay contains the problem of the tale: is Faith the belief or the character? Levy judiciously picks his way through previous

criticism and arrives at what strikes me as a brilliant clarification of
the tale's difficulties, which, he says, arise out of the fact that the
story is not only a dream vision and a conventional allegory but also
"an inquiry into the problem of faith that undermines the assumptions
upon which the allegory is based." The tale's meaning hinges on the
fact of Faith's pink ribbon, which links the dual roles of the character and, in the end, is the disruptive test of the entire allegory when
it reveals her physically at the same moment her allegorical presence
evaporates. The terror of the vision is that the story's "own simple
[allegorical] definitions do not work." If Brown had begun by abandoning Faith temporarily, his Faith finally leaves him forever. A
third essay, on another tale of the same vintage and elucidating Hawthorne's treatment of the effects of religious ideas, is Mario L.
D'Avanzo's "The Ambitious Guest in the Hands of an Angry God"
(*ELN* 14:38–42), which claims rather loosely that Edward's sermon
serves as a "frame of reference" which heightens this tale's theme and
tone.

Frederick Newberry's " 'The Gray Champion': Hawthorne's Ironic
Criticism of Puritan Rebellion" (*SSF* 13:363–70) and P. L. Reed's
"The Telling Frame of Hawthorne's 'Legends of the Province House' "
(*SAF* 4:105–11) are, like the studies of McWilliams and Simpson,
dedicated to complicating our awareness of Hawthorne's subtle ambivalence towards the Puritans, the Revolution, the past. Their approach, however, is by way of Hawthorne's rhetorical strategies. For
Newberry, Hawthorne appears to confirm his audience's jingoistic
attitudes on the tale's surface only to subvert them with his ironic
narrative tone. Only Bradstreet, a figure of true conciliation, escapes
Hawthorne's judgment; the spectral gray champion, evoked by the
dark antiprayer of the unruly mob, is himself demonic, satanic. Reed
extends earlier commentaries by Robert H. Fossum, Julian Smith,
and others in stressing the careful ordering of tales and frames into
a sequence which dramatizes the narrator's growing isolation in history and his final fearful escape back into the present.

David M. Van Leer's "Aylmer's Library: Transcendental Alchemy
in Hawthorne's 'The Birthmark' " (*ESQ* 22:211–20) raises questions
about the accepted view that Hawthorne's fiction of the 1840s turned
away from historical materials. The study is erudite, compact, penetrating. Van Leer, jumping off from Alfred Reid's study of Sir Ken-
helm Digby, the Neoplatonist scientist, as the prototype for Aylmer,

demonstrates that Hawthorne's allegory traces a tradition of "spiritualizing materialists" from the Royal Society through the French Enlightenment to Swedenborg. The story thus brings to bear on widespread contemporary attitudes the full weight of another, non–New England history. Van Leer's work and Duban's hint strongly that there are authentic continuities still to be uncovered even in Hawthorne's seemingly most disparate fictions. More conventional but a still worthwhile treatment of this tale is given in Elizabeth R. Napier's note, "Aylmer as 'Scheidekünstler': The Pattern of Union and Separation in Hawthorne's 'The Birthmark'" (*SAB* 41,iv:32–35). Images of union and separation, originally posited in Georgianna and Aylmer respectively, are gradually transferred to the other, establishing a complex polarity which deepens Hawthorne's psychological theme.

Shirley M. Detlaff's "The Concept of Beauty in 'The Artist of the Beautiful' and Hugh Blair's Rhetoric" (*SSF* 13:512–15) presents some evidence that Blair's aesthetic values, partly because they insist on social virtues, might be a more significant source for Hawthorne than those of Burke, even though Burke alone speaks of smallness as a criterion of the beautiful. The claim is modestly, plausibly put. Ted Billy, in "Time and Transformation in 'The Artist of the Beautiful'" (*ATQ* 29:33–35), thinks that Hawthorne imaginatively appropriated the Cupid and Psyche myth from Apuleius's *Metamorphoses* in order to construct a universalized parable in which Owen Warland himself, like Psyche and his butterfly, symbolically undergoes four distinctive stages of development. Artifact becomes the metaphor of the artistic process which creates it. The analysis, though stiffly schematic, is not without sense; but Billy errs, it seems, in not taking into account Hawthorne's ironic skepticism about Owen's fulfillment of his romantic-transcendental aesthetic. On the other hand, Lesley W. Brill, in "Conflict and Accommodation in Hawthorne's 'The Artist of the Beautiful'" (*SSF* 12[1975]:381–86), admits the problem but insists that Hawthorne enables his artist not to triumph but to enjoy conciliation. No longer needing external confirmation of his private vision, Owen can make his vision an actuality. But the study is to some degree vitiated by Brill's making the tale Hawthorne's literary celebration of his new marital happiness. How, on such grounds, is there room for Hawthorne's conceiving "The Birthmark" in the same year? Sheldon Liebman's "Hawthorne's Romanticism: 'The Artist of the Beautiful'" (*ESQ* 22:85–95) is the most persuasive argument for Hawthorne's vision of Owen as a heroically Romantic artist who, "caught between the antitheses of ideal and real, spirit and matter, imagination and understanding, and art and criticism," comes gradually to terms not only with his three antagonists but, more importantly, with himself. The discussion of Hawthorne's drawing upon the ideas of Coleridge and Carlyle is especially adept and illuminating.

Richard Brenzo's "Beatrice Rappaccini: A Victim of Male Love and Horror" (*AL* 48:152–64) asserts that the central symbol of "Rappaccini's Daughter" is the poison which infects Beatrice, the garden, and the exotic flower, and which signifies the destructive responses the three male antagonists make toward their victim. Beatrice herself is uncontaminated: it is the otherwise inadmissible fears, obsessions, and ambitions of these three hommes fatals who together create and destroy her. Just how this reading extends or qualifies Crews's is not made sufficiently clear. Mark Hennelly's "Hawthorne's *Opus Alchymicum*: 'Ethan Brand'" (*ESQ* 22:96–106), citing works of Eliade, Jung, and Erich Neumann, ventures an interpretation of the tale as an allegory of "the alchemical drama." Alchemy and metallurgy, in Hennelly's complex thesis, provide the metaphorical vehicle for Hawthorne's exploration of psychological processes and clarify what previous critics have scored as the tale's "confusion." The story pivots on the alchemical notion of transformation, and its five major image patterns—"construction, meteorology, landscape, hand, and . . . circle"—are pertinent, Hennelly shows, to the alchemical metaphor. His is a fascinating—and arcane—insight. Much less substantial, unfortunately, is Mark W. Estrin's "Narrative Ambivalence in Hawthorne's 'Feathertop'" (*JNT* 5[1975]:164–73), which strains to endow Hawthorne's last effort in short fiction with a "richness" of "narrative structure." To claim that Hawthorne, beginning with an ironic joke, ends with "a story that takes itself seriously," having put his readers in touch with "the secret ties . . . to the sources of evil," is too much like patterning criticism after Mother Rigby's art.

v. Hawthorne and Others

Lewis P. Simpson concludes his essay with an eloquent statement of the ways in which Hawthorne's insights in "My Kinsman, Major

Molineux" have influenced, if indirectly and implicitly, much of our later fiction. In "A Probable Source for Dorothea and Casaubon: Hester and Chillingworth" (*ES* 58:23–25) Robert K. Wallace presents succinctly and convincingly evidence that the Prynnes' unnatural marriage is very likely among the various ingredients involved in George Eliot's process of portraying the major characters of *Middlemarch*. More ambitious are two studies by Robert Emmet Long, "Henry James's Apprenticeship—the Hawthorne Aspect" (*AL* 48: 194–216) and "James's *Roderick Hudson*: The End of the Apprenticeship—Hawthorne and Turgenev" (*AL* 48:312–26). In the first of these Long attempts to substantiate specifically the general claims of several critics—among them F. R. Leavis and Peter Buitenheis— that Hawthorne was a very central influence in James's tales, 1865– 75, at least 12 of those 27 manifesting discernible Hawthornian elements and interests. The parallels and similarities Long points out seem by no means exaggerated: they show the young James maturing as a writer of fiction by way of sifting, whether consciously or not, Hawthorne's nuances throughout his canon. Nor was James simplistically imitative, as Long suggests; but Long's study reveals nonetheless some of the reasons why James, growing up, wanted to grow away from so large an influence and was compelled to condescend to his mentor's provinciality in his 1879 *Hawthorne*. Long's second essay is true to its title and elucidates persuasively the ways that Turgenev's influence operated both as an artistic qualification and as a cultural confirmation of the Hawthorne influence. Long's James is engaged in a process of "correcting" Hawthorne. *Roderick Hudson* is like *The Marble Faun* in its "mentalized cast" and in being "suffused with a lingering sense of Christian myth and allegory," but in its sharp delineation of manners and its unmelodramatic conception of the ensnarement of American innocence in corrupting civilization the book transcends its prototype. The only difficulty I find here is in the metaphor of "apprenticeship," which tends to overlook the later James's masterful fulfillment of his own manner as he reengages himself with the possibilities of Hawthorne's poetic romances.

That James never really let go of Hawthorne is implicit in Paul John Eakin's far-ranging essay on "Margaret Fuller, Hawthorne, James, and Sexual Politics" (*SAQ* 75:323–38). Eakin's interests do not involve the question of influence but of the profound (and depressing) stresses in our culture arising from the individual's need for a distinctly private life of feeling on the one hand and a compulsion to make a public profession of ideological faith on the other. The plight of Kate Millett—or, as Eakin puts it, the two Kate Milletts —is the plight of Margaret Fuller, and Eakin finds a comparison of *The Blithedale Romance* and *The Bostonians* a useful instrument in assessing the dynamics of the interplay of politics and personality. For both Hawthorne and James the lessons of Margaret Fuller's life are similar, the fates of Zenobia and of Olive Chancellor and Verena Tarrant symbolically parallel: the devotees of self-culture, by virtue of their very pursuit of freedom, suffer debilitating spiritual bondage. Just as very little "sexual history" had elapsed between 1852 and 1883, so, Eakin concludes, very little about it seems really to have changed since Margaret Fuller's day.

Another perceptively written study of Hawthorne's inroads into the development of American fiction is Samuel Coale's "Frederic and Hawthorne: The Romantic Roots of Naturalism" (*AL* 48:29–45), which advances the argument that Frederic's attachment to the values of literary naturalism is at best problematic. The reasons for this and for the confusion and compromised character of *The Damnation of Theron Ware* lie in Frederic's unsuccessful efforts to translate Hawthorne into his terms as fully as Howells and James were doing à la the demands of realism. Unsatisfied with deterministic explanations of Theron's fate, Frederic sought self-consciously in *The Scarlet Letter* and other Hawthorne works the resonances of an "emblematic, still-life approach" that could register causes deeper than merely sociological and historical ones. For Coale *The Damnation*'s "dreamlike sub-text" and the characters themselves have their roots in Frederic's reliance on Hawthorne's art. Yet the novel fails because Frederic was incapable of integrating its Hawthornian dimensions with his historical realism. Coale's remarks are perspicacious throughout; his essay comes close to being a model for "influence" studies. Of almost equal interest, if not equally convincing in its demonstration, is Kermit Vanderbilt's "From Passion to Impasse: The Structure of a Dark Romantic Theme in Hawthorne, Howells, and Barth" (*SNNTS* 8:419–29). Briefly, Vanderbilt's thesis is that Hester and Dimmesdale, in their thwarted sexual passion, their isolated existences and consciousnesses, and their separate deaths, symbolize Hawthorne's prefiguration of the perdurable darkness of American romance, a form whose pattern and sensibility are so essential in our culture that it has survived in an almost unbroken line into at least some of the fiction of Barth, Malamud, Bellow, and Updike—and even in Erica Jong's *Fear of Flying.* To be sure, Vanderbilt only alludes to the writers not mentioned in his title. Still, some of the implied connections here whiz by at frighteningly supersonic speed. There comes a point at which one has to ask, When is an influence no longer an influence? It's not for no reason at all, perhaps, that Hawthorne said he was not quite sure that he entirely comprehended his own meaning in some of these blasted allegories.

University of Missouri

3. Poe

Donald B. Stauffer

Looking back over what I have read this past year, I am struck by the fact that most people are still writing about Poe's short fiction rather than his poems or his criticism. But this year many are studying the texts themselves—although from two completely opposite directions. On the one hand there is a trend among American scholars and critics to look in earnest at the significance of Poe's revisions (which we have known of for seventy-five years) and at the evidence of his plans for future versions of his early tales, as in the Folio Club group. On the other hand, a pattern of French criticism that I dimly perceived last year is now more evident: the interest of Barthes, Derrida, and Ricardou in the text itself (*l'écriture*) as the repository of meaning has led them and others to seize, not surprisingly, on Poe's texts as a basis for some exercises in ingenuity and intellectual gamesmanship, with decidedly mixed results.

i. Sources, Influences, and Editions

Several new facts about sources and influences have come to light, some of which were unearthed by Burton R. Pollin. Southey's poetry had more of an influence on Poe than we might suspect, according to Pollin, who documents one example of his influence in "Southey's *Curse of Kehama* in Poe's 'City in the Sea'" (*WC* 7:101–6). In "Poe and Daniel Defoe: A Significant Relationship" (*Topic* 16:3–22), Pollin stresses the importance of Defoe's influence. Of particular interest are the parallels Pollin finds between Poe's review of the 1835 Harper edition of *Robinson Crusoe* and the biographical sketch of Defoe printed in that edition. Poe took the details of Defoe's life and works from the sketch, and some of the critical views that we attribute to Poe are actually those of the author of the sketch. In some cases his borrowing was hasty and inaccurate, but he also acquired from it some suggestions about the concept of verisimilitude that he later made his own. Pollin notes that we must be careful about citing Poe's critical views as his own without first reading the prefaces and texts of books he was reading and reviewing.

And in "Poe's 'Diddling': More on the Dating and the Aim" (*PoeS* 9:11–13) Pollin continues his controversy with Alexander Hammond (see *ALS 1972*, p. 224; *ALS 1975*, p. 38) and Claude Richard (see *ALS 1968*, p. 169). Pollin reasserts his conviction that the tale could not have been written before 1843 and rejects the idea that John Neal was the target of his satire.

Poe's borrowings from Benjamin Morrell's *Narrative of Four Voyages* are well known, but Pollin studies the question in detail, including the reputation of Morrell and his book among his contemporaries. He asserts that eighty paragraphs throughout the novel show traces of this source and provides an outline showing how Pym's voyages parallel those of Morrell. In light of the poor reputation of the book, it is surprising that Pollin does not suggest that Poe was satirizing it. However, he reminds us of another interesting point: the evidence that Morrell's narrative was probably ghost written by Samuel Woodworth, author of "The Old Oaken Bucket" ("The *Narrative* of Benjamin Morrell: Out of 'The Bucket' and into Poe's *Pym*," SAF 4: 157–73).

Erich W. Sippel, in "Another of Poe's 'Savans': Edward Tatham" (*PoeS* 9:16–21), cites Tatham's encyclopedic treatise, *The Chart and Scale of Truth* (1790–92), as another possible object of Poe's satire in the opening of *Eureka*, and as a possible source of passages in that work and in "The Poetic Principle" and "The Imp of the Perverse." Sippel is convincing in his argument that Poe is simultaneously borrowing from Tatham, parodying him, and, in "Imp," turning his thought back upon him.

Two notes by Kent Ljungquist cite Jacob Bryant's *Mythology* as a source. His note on "Poe's Nubian Geographer" (*AL* 48:73–75) was anticipated last year by Susan and Stuart Levine (see *ALS 1975*, pp. 39–40), but he also finds evidence that Bryant was a source of "The Raven" ("Poe's 'Raven' and Bryant's *Mythology*," ATQ 29:28–30). Ljungquist and Buford Jones, in "Monsieur Dupin: Further Details on the Reality Behind the Legend" (*SLJ* 9:70–77), provide additional evidence for believing that the notorious French jurist, André-Marie-Jean-Jacques Dupin (1783–1865) was Poe's model for his character, an idea first suggested by T. O. Mabbott. Judith D. Suther, in "Rousseau, Poe, and the Idea of Progress" (*PLL* 12:469–75), points out the similarities in tone and in their attitudes toward the idea of progress between Poe's "The Colloquy of Monos and Una" and Rousseau's *Discours sur les sciences et les arts* (1750), though she stops short of stating that Poe had actually read Rousseau.

Wayne R. Kime sees Poe's *Pym* as an important source of the Canadian writer James De Mille's posthumous novel, *A Strange Manuscript Found in a Copper Cylinder* ("The American Antecedents of James De Mille's *A Strange Manuscript Found in a Copper Cylinder*," *DR* 55[1975]:280–306).

Poe has been a fascinating subject for many writers, and John E. Reilly demonstrates the extent of this fascination with an informative survey of the almost three hundred poems written about Poe from 1830 to the present in *The Image of Poe in American Poetry*, a monograph published by the Enoch Pratt Free Library and the Edgar Allan Poe Society of Baltimore.

Those looking for a paperbound collection of all of Poe's tales will want to look at *The Short Fiction of Edgar Allan Poe*, ed. Stuart and Susan Levine (Indianapolis: Bobbs-Merrill). This is a simultaneously useful and annoying book which demonstrates some of the same tunnel vision that Stuart Levine displayed in his *Edgar Allan Poe: Seer and Craftsman* (see *ALS 1972*, pp. 215–16). The book is arranged by categories of tales—16 in all—which are sometimes helpful and sometimes not. Anyone, from George Woodberry on, who has tried to categorize the tales has discovered pitfalls, and the Levines are no exception. The most attractive feature of the book is its apparatus, including illustrations, headnotes, and extensive annotation, drawing on a vast amount of published scholarship, and in some cases (as in the notes indicating Poe's debts to Jacob Bryant) making new contributions. As useful as these annotations are, however, they concentrate almost exclusively on the tales; and there are few reminders that the tales do have relationships with the long fiction, with *Eureka*, with the poems, and with the criticism.

ii. Fiction

Although no books were published on Poe in 1976, the entire issue of three different periodicals has been devoted to his fiction, each with a different focus and approach. In the *Library Chronicle*, vol. 41, no. 1 (Univ. of Pa.) Benjamin Franklin Fisher, IV, has assembled a collection of essays concerned with textual history and Poe's revisions: "Poe the Craftsman: The Changing Fiction. Essays in Honor of Richard P. Benton and Maureen Cobb Mabbott." In a useful introductory essay, "Poe and the Art of the Well-Wrought Tale" (*LC* 41: 5–12), Fisher surveys the history of textual studies of Poe and lists the principal locations of existing Poe manuscripts and rare first printings of tales. James W. Gargano has edited *Topic 30* (vol. 16), devoted to a variety of critical essays on Poe. And Claude Richard is the editor of the first issue of a new French journal, *Delta*, containing a group of original and highly unorthodox articles under the heading, "Edgar Allan Poe et les textes sacrés." The approach is a disconcerting combination of structural linguistics and biblical criticism, in which the title of the collection takes on an ambiguous meaning and the emphasis is heavily upon *l'écriture*, in the vein of much French criticism. Instead of dealing with each of these collections as a whole, I shall discuss each article in connection with others on the same subject.

a. **Early Tales and Comic Tales.**   In "The Distorted Perception of Poe's Comic Narrators" (*Topic* 16:23–34), Gargano looks at Poe's treatment of defective intellectual and moral "sight" in five comic sketches: "The Spectacles," "The Angel of the Odd," "The System of Dr. Tarr and Professor Fether," "The Sphinx," and "The Devil in the Belfry." These tales, he says, are related thematically to the tales of terror in the way they dramatize "Poe's fascination with the unreliability and malfunctioning of human perception." This is an aspect of Poe's humorous tales largely overlooked, and those who have perceived similar lapses of perception in *Pym* and other "serious" tales would do well to look more closely at these and others, such as "The Man Who Was Used Up."

In "Edgar Allan Poe's *Tales of the Folio Club*: The Evolution of a Lost Book" (*LC* 41:13–43), Alexander Hammond chronicles the fortunes of the Folio Club Collection from 1831 to 1836, describes Poe's efforts to get the eleven-tale version published as a collection, and speculates on the probable makeup of the sixteen- and seventeen-tale collection Poe offered for publication in 1836. This is a reordering of material Hammond has published piecemeal before (see *ALS*

1972, p. 224; *ALS 1975*, p. 38), with additional textual and historical information. He speculates on the actual ordering of the tales, including the presumably lost section of burlesque criticism, and he offers "Von Jung, the Mystic" as a possible contender for the seventeenth tale.

In "*The Homo-Cameleopard* ou la mort de Dieu" (*Delta* 1 [1975]: 83–94), C. Lecompte argues for a new interpretation of "Four Beasts in One" which sees Poe attacking false religions rather than the Jackson administration, as most critics argue. In his view the excessive admiration of the populace for Antiochus Epiphanes is Poe's satirical or burlesque treatment of those who substitute the forms for the substance of religion; and the tale is not an attack on the Judeo-Christian God. However, the argument depends too heavily on the assumption that Poe was closely acquainted with Near-Eastern history in the 2nd century B.C. and the 2nd century A.D.

An example of the kind of insights that the study of revisions can reveal is James W. Christie's careful and modest "Poe's 'Diabolical' Humor: Revisions in 'Bon-Bon'" (*LC* 41:44–55), in which he looks closely at changes in the style and characterization of what was originally "The Bargain Lost" (1832) through its fourteen-year period of revisions in four subsequent versions. The direction of the revisions, Christie finds, was toward greater unity, toward a more convoluted style assuming a coterie of knowledgeable readers, and toward a different kind of devil: less like an eccentric rogue and more like an impoverished, if sinister, clergyman.

Benjamin Franklin Fisher's own contributions to his collection, "The Power of Words in Poe's 'Silence'" (*LC* 41:56–72), applies the same careful methods of textual and historical scholarship that he used in his study of "The Assignation" (see below). He prints a manuscript fragment of "Silence" and argues that, contrary to the views of Thompson and others, the tale, or "fable," is not a satire or parody of Bulwer or DeQuincey, but a serious visionary tale; and the revisions move toward increasing somberness of tone. He admits, though, that in the context of the Folio Club there may be certain comic elements including possible self-parody.

Fisher's masterful two-part study of the revisions of "The Visionary" is completed in "To 'The Assignation' from 'The Visionary' (Part Two): The Revisions and Related Matters" (*LC* 40:221–51). (Part 1, which reprinted the original *Godey's* version, is in *LC* 39[1973]:

89–105.) Fisher takes pains to support his conclusions, drawn from his study of the revisions, that the tale is essentially not a burlesque or satire but a serious visionary tale. Noting the changes which deepen the emotional range of its characters and tone down the humorous elements of the earlier versions, Fisher goes against prevailing opinion by emphasizing the serious Romanticism and viewing it as one of Poe's most poetic tales.

b. **Gothic Tales and Tales of Terror.** By examining some contemporary medical writers on the disease known as hypochondriasis, David W. Butler discovers some striking parallels between the symptoms they describe and the appearance and behavior of Roderick Usher, whom Poe describes as a "hypochondriac" ("Usher's Hypochondriasis: Mental Alienation and Romantic Idealism in Poe's Gothic Tales," *AL* 48:1–12). As the title of his essay suggests, Butler sees some important connections between the physicians' confusion as to whether the disease was physical or mental, and the romantics' concern with the bonds between the internal, subjective realm and the external world of physical objects. Butler concludes that "Usher" is "Poe's most thorough and sophisticated dramatization of the impossibility of developing unquestionably valid and complete medical, or unquestionably valid and complete mystical, explanations of some extraordinary private experiences." A rare introduction by Arthur Symons to a 1928 edition of "The Fall of the House of Usher" has been reprinted with commentary by J. Lasley Dameron in *PoeS* 9: 46–49. The original had illustrations by Alastair.

In an overwritten and repetitious essay, "The Aqua-Gothic Voyage of 'A Descent Into the Maelström'" (*ATQ* 29:85–93), Frederick S. Frank makes an important distinction between the narrator of "The Fall of the House of Usher" and the hero of "Maelström." This character, whom Frank calls "Aquarius" because his adventure and survival "belong to both sky and water," is heroic in his having achieved a vision of the divine that lies in the abyss. The "Usher" narrator, on the other hand, lacks the poetic intuition to perceive that beyond the Gothic horrors of the mansion lies a visionary experience; he therefore flees "aghast" and remains imprisoned in his rational self. While the pattern of descent and return represents a kind of rebirth for "Aquarius," then, a similar pattern has opposite results for the "Usher" narrator. Frank also methodically points out parallels to Gothic novels occurring in "Maelström."

A combination of Freud and Jung yields new insights when applied to "Maelström." Mark M. Hennelly, Jr., goes beyond Marie Bonaparte and draws upon Erich Neumann, Joseph Campbell, and others to develop a complex mythic reading containing Oedipal tension, return-to-the-womb desires, and a "culture dream" which "adumbrates the myth of the Orphic artist-questor who, though resolving his own Odeipal crisis by emerging from the underground womb, fails, in his art, to redeem others from the cultural wasteland." ("Oedipus and Orpheus in the Maelström: The Traumatic Rebirth of the Artist," *PoeS* 9:6–11).

The connection between the figure of the Red Death and time is developed in a complex and capable reading of the tale by Edward W. Pitcher in "Horological and Chronological Time in 'Masque of the Red Death' (*ATQ* 29:71–75). Pitcher sees a variety of symbols, private and conventional, operating to adumbrate the theme that time is cyclical and finally life-fulfilling rather than linear, mechanical, and futile. Grouping the seven varicolored rooms into three, representing Youth, Middle Age, and Old Age, he sees the arrogant Prospero's attempts to control Death mocked ironically by the arrival and ultimate triumph of the inevitable. By a careful explanation of the symbol he succeeds in showing that the plot "is both mechanically simple and hauntingly intricate on the level of causation and motivation."

E. Arthur Robinson, in "Cosmic Vision in Poe's 'Eleonora'" (*PoeS* 9:44–46), argues that certain paradoxes of plot and characterization in the tale "reflect that narrator's increasing awareness of a close relation between matter and spirit," and he places the tale in an intermediate position between "Usher" and *Eureka* in the development of Poe's thought. Charles A. Sweet, Jr., sees the narrator of "Ligeia" as an active rather than passive participant in a tale not of horror but of terror. He is actually, in Sweet's view, a warlock, with a knowledge of the occult which enables him to achieve through occult ritual the transmogrification of Ligeia ("'Ligeia' and the Warlock," *SSF* 13: 85–88). And in an explication written with annoying preciosity Walter Stepp sets out to show once again that Montresor is murdering his conscience ("The Ironic Double in Poe's 'The Cask of Amontillado,'" *SSF* 13:447–53).

"William Wilson" is the subject of four critical studies. Two essays reject reading the tale as a simple allegory of conscience, but they do so for different reasons. Eric Carlson, in "'William Wilson': The Double as Primal Self" (*Topic* 16:35–40), sees the tale as one of Poe's "psycho-epic visions of the primal, unified Self suffering internal split, conflict, and disintegration." Ruth Sullivan, on the other hand, uses straight Freudian psychology to argue that the surviving Wilson is not the one who committed the crime, but a tyrannical superego that is allowed to run rampant in his telling of the tale ("William Wilson's Double," *SIR* 15:253–63). Poe deliberately confuses the reader, Sullivan claims, in order to lead us to share in a limited view of evil as instinctual license. But the greater evil of the superego is an excessive and tyrannical morality, which operates as a vicious and destructive curb to instinct. She builds her case on some subtle internal contradictions in the tale.

Marc Leslie Rovner's study of the revisions of the tale compares the 1845 *Broadway Journal* version with the 1839 *Burton's* version. ("What William Wilson Knew: Poe's Disintegration of an Errant Mind," *LC* 41:73–82). He finds that Poe's general tendency was to reduce excesses of description and expression, to be more precise in details and to mute the Gothic or sensational qualities. An increased attention to details of clothing in the revisions, particularly in the closing paragraphs, suggests to Rovner that there is a relationship between clothes and "moral correspondences . . . for whenever he met another character, Wilson tended to evaluate the person in terms of his garments." And Sam B. Girgus uses R. D. Laing's theories of schizophrenia to explore the question of the divided self in several tales, including "William Wilson," "Usher," "The Imp of the Perverse," and "The Pit and the Pendulum" ("Poe and R. D. Laing: The Transcendent Self," *SSF* 13:299–309). Burton Pollin, on the other hand, adduces linguistic and historical evidence to support his claim that "The Imp of the Perverse" "can be considered a creative by-product of the Hamlet-theme" ("The Self-Destructive Fall: A Theme from Shakespeare used in *Pym* and 'The Imp of the Perverse,'" *EA* 29:199–202).

Three studies make some unusual observations on "The Tell-Tale Heart." In "Discours et Contre-Discours dans the Tell-Tale Heart" (*Delta* 1[1975]:43–65), Claude Fleurdorge undertakes what I can only describe as a linguistic scriptural exegesis of the tale. By studying the recurrence of certain letters in the tale, notably *T* and *H*, he develops reasons to suggest that some of the *T*'s should be dropped from the title, which then would become "The Hell Hale Heart." Reading the evil eye as the "evil I," Fleurdorge offers evidence to support his hypothesis that the "counter-discourse" of the tale concerns man's efforts to be free of guilt by "putting off the old man," or being born again, and he matches phrases from Poe with phrases from Scripture in support. Such an analysis leads me to conclude that Poe would have to have been a Fundamentalist cryptographer of truly extraordinary powers to have constructed such a code.

Claude Richard also finds two texts in the tale, but he finds the Biblical allusions much more submerged. For him, the "I" of the tale is split into the I/narrator and the I/protagonist, and his analysis leads from this to the conclusion that the tale is "about" the usurpation of the world of God for which the punishment is madness. But the tale may also be seen to deal with the humility of the writer before the act of writing (*l'écriture*) and the autonomous creativity of language itself ("La Double Voix dans *The Tell-Tale Heart*," *Delta* 1[1975]:17–41).

Like Fleurdorge, Pamela J. Shelden also calls attention to the possibility of the wordplay of Evil Eye/Evil "I" in "The Tell-Tale Heart" as well as in "The Black Cat." She is mainly concerned, however, with showing how the external Gothic props in the tales are reflections of the psychic confusions of the narrators, but she uses too much plot summary and does not add markedly to our understanding of the tales ("'True Originality': Poe's Manipulation of the Gothic Tradition," *ATQ* 29:75–80).

c. Tales of Ratiocination. The method of studying revisions is less successful for Joel Kenneth Asarch and Richard Fusco than for others in Fisher's collection. Asarch's "A Telling Tale: Poe's Revisions in 'The Murders in the Rue Morgue'" (*LC* 41:83–90), while showing how Poe's meticulous changing of small details, including punctuation and phrasing, made the tale more carefully crafted, does not go much beyond Ernest Boll's 1943 study, nor does he deal with some of the larger issues of interpretation raised by my own 1972 study (see *ALS 1972*, p. 222). When Fusco looks at the revisions of "The Mystery of Marie Rogêt" they suggest to him that between 1842 and 1845 Poe lost interest in showing how clever he was in his ratiocinative abilities and became more interested in constructing an effective tale ("Poe's Revisions of 'The Mystery of Marie Rogêt'—a Hoax?" *LC* 41:91–99).

Mireille Vincent, in "Le Grand Singe Fauve" (*Delta* 1[1975]: 67–82), applies a biblical reading to one of the ratiocinative tales equating the orangutan in "Murders in the Rue Morgue" with man's false vision of God, from which he has fallen into a confusion of tongues (Babel). Dupin as hero then assumes the role of "capturing" the ape, thereby restoring a primal unity and harmony of language that nullifies Babel. As in the other essays in Richard's collection, the bases for assigning such values to the characters and events appear to be whim and wordplay. It is not clear, for example, why we must see the murdered old women as representatives of England and America, a point which figures obscurely into the reading as a whole.

An essay that has obviously been influential upon such studies is that of the French psychoanalytic writer, Jacques Lacan, whose famous essay "Séminaire sur La Lettre Volée" was first published in France in 1966 (*Ecrits* [Paris: Editions du Seuil]) and translated into English in 1972 by Jeffrey Mehlman as "Seminar on 'The Purloined Letter'" in *French Freud: Structural Studies in Psycho-analysis* (*YFS* 48[1972]:38–72). Lacan's essay is a landmark in post-Freudian psychoanalytic structuralist criticism, to which others are reacting. One such is Jacques Derrida, in "Le Facteur de la Vérité" (*Poétique* 21[1975]:96–147). This essay was translated by Willis Domingo, James Hulbert, Moshe Ron, and Marie-Rose Logan in *YFS* 52[1975]:31–113. Lacan, says Derrida, is "a break from naïve semanticism and naïve psychobiographicism, an elaboration of a logic of the signifier . . . an appropriation of the problematic of *Beyond the Pleasure Principle*." Although Derrida objects to Lacan's approach, he is "not trying to save something like literature or literary form from the grips of psychoanalysis" but rather finds formal deficiencies in Lacan's analysis. The essay is impossible to summarize, as anyone familiar with Derrida will realize, and it is concerned more with critical theory and critical questions raised by the roles of Dupin, the narrator, and Poe than with the tale itself.

Lacan is also the starting point for Sergio L. P. Bellei, who says his reading implies a theory of perception which Bellei describes as "creative participation," in which Dupin becomes a part of his contextual reality in a way similar to that conceived of by Coleridge

("'The Purloined Letter': A Theory of Perception," *PoeS* 9:40–42).

Some other French criticism of recent years is being made more widely accessible to American readers through the new translation series in *Poe Studies*. Frank Towne has translated two of the influential essays of Jean Ricardou, "Le Caractère singulier de cette eau" ("The Singular Character of the Water") and "L'Or du scarabée" ("Gold in the Bug") in *PoeS* 9:1–6 and 33–39, respectively.

This is perhaps also the place to mention that three of Richard Wilbur's essays on Poe that have been difficult to obtain are collected in a paperbound volume of his essays: *Responses: Prose Pieces, 1953–1976* (New York: Harcourt). These include his critical essay printed in Perry Miller's 1962 anthology, *Major Writers in America*, his 1967 review essay for the *New York Review of Books*, and his important 1973 essay on *Pym*, first printed as the introduction to the David Godine edition of *Pym*.

d. The Narrative of Arthur Gordon Pym. Four essays on *Arthur Gordon Pym* attack the novel from various flanks. In "Metaphor and Meaning in Poe's *The Narrative of Arthur Gordon Pym* (*Topic* 16: 54–67), Joseph M. DeFalco works out a metaphysical correspondence between each vessel Pym sails on and the state of his mind while he is on it. In "'The Infernal Twoness' in *Arthur Gordon Pym*" (*Topic* 16: 41–53) J. Gerald Kennedy adds to the growing number of studies pointing out the elements of deception and hoax in the novel. Jeanne-Marie Santraud defends *Pym* against its detractors by calling the novel a drama of revolt and applying Gustav Freytag's old terms of "rising" and "falling" action to its structure. Her analysis of the allegorical content, turning on the pervasive theme of death, is not unconventional but defends well the need to read the story as allegory ("Edgar Allan Poe 'en sa maison de superbe structure': Étude du Récit d'Arthur Gordon Pym," *EA* 29:36–70).

In a long, discursive, and playfully disjointed essay, "L'Écriture d'Arthur Gordon Pym," Claude Richard brings structuralism to bear on the meaning of the novel in a number of different ways and attempts to reconcile the divergent views of the novel held by Asselineau, Ricardou, and others (*Delta* 1[1975]:95–124). Many of his discoveries depend too heavily upon wordplay; for example, in distinguishing between "verticality" and "horizontality" as opposing themes he notices that the dog is associated with the former because

Pym "perceived a slight *erection* of the hair." This is not an isolated example. Richard finds the unity of the novel in the word *blood*. The message Pym reads is written in blood, and from this point on, he—and the reader—learn to read. Reading becomes most crucial at the end, where the earth, and perhaps even the water (the "singular *character* of the water") must be read. Following Ricardou's idea that the novel's real struggle is between the text and the blank page, Richard writes, "The incompatibility of the ink . . . and the white paper will be progressively suspected, and, in the final chapter, ink and paper will reveal themselves as definitively strangers to each other."

iii. "The Raven"

In an important new reading of Poe's most famous poem, Barton Levi St. Armand argues for looking at "The Raven" from an alchemical, Jungian, and emblematic point of view ("Poe's Emblematic Raven: A Pictorial Approach," *ESQ* 22:191–210). In an argument difficult to summarize, he finds Poe working on both a popular and esoteric level, using traditional emblematic associations of the raven and modifying their meanings to suit complex purposes. St. Armand finds it fruitful to see "The Philosophy of Composition" as a commentary on the poem—as a "motto" to the "illustration," or pictorial quality of the poem itself, taking off from Poe's statement that the last line of the poem has the intention of making the bird "emblematic of *Mournful and Never-Ending Rememberance*." The student in the poem is seen as a Faustian or Promethean figure, tormented by the thirst for forbidden knowledge.

Claude Richard approaches the poem in quite a different way, discussing the progressive negative effect of the word "nevermore." In "Puissance de la Parole: 'The Raven' " (*EA* 29:353–59) he subjects the poem to close scrutiny in an *explication de texte* which reveals a movement from relative time to eternity, and a shift in meaning in its last word which comes to provide the narrator with a vision of his own self-annihilation through language.

iv. Philosophy and Aesthetics

In the Introduction to his edition of *The Science Fiction of Edgar Allan Poe* (New York: Penguin Books), Harold Beaver places Poe in the context not only of the scientific discoveries of his age but of philosophy and mathematics. He sees Poe, for example, as the heir of Condorcet in his interest in probability theory, which he discusses in "The Mystery of Marie Rogêt." But because Poe was basically hostile to mechanical reason and technical progress, he "used speculative theory from the start to frustrate technological progress" by merging mathematics with a mystical view of the universe, ending in *Eureka*: "He aspired to be nothing less than an American Keats with the mind of Newton, or rather a sublimer Newton with the soul of Keats." The case is well argued, but should be read in conjunction with David Ketterer (see *ALS 1975*, pp. 40–41), who argues that Poe was not a science-fiction writer. The book is well annotated, with selective bibliographies for each tale and a useful table of scientific developments from 1745 to 1876.

The concept of space and the role of the house in 19th-century American literature are receiving increased attention by scholars. Rosemary F. Franklin lays down some guidelines for future study in "The Cabin by the Lake: Pastoral Landscapes of Poe, Cooper, Hawthorne, and Thoreau" (*ESQ* 22:59–70). She locates both the cabin and the pond in the "pastoral middle-ground" between the city and the wilderness, and touches briefly upon "The Domain of Arnheim" and "Landor's Cottage" as examples of Poe's leaning toward art and artifice rather than nature.

Idealism and literary Gothicism are not so far apart in Poe's work as many believe, according to E. Miller Budick, who argues persuasively that Poe's blending of matter and spirit in *Eureka* reflects his view that a transcendental vision of the Ideal is coupled in his work with an awareness of the threat of physical annihilation inherent in it ("Poe's Gothic Idea: The Cosmic Geniture of Horror," *ELWIU* 3:73–85). Darlene Unrue, on the other hand, places emphasis on the subjective nature of man's perceptions—on the impressions of the physical world upon one's senses and the perceiver's reaction to them. Unrue sees Poe creating characters in his early tales for whom the only reality is what they believe to be real. She illustrates this with a close reading of "The Oval Portrait" ("Poe and the Subjective Reality," *ArielE* 7:68–76).

In "Poe's *Eureka* as a Prose Poem" (*ATQ* 29:61–71) Edward W. Pitcher detects an undercurrent of meaning in *Eureka* that challenges conventional modes of attaining knowledge and raises the intuitive mode to a position of equality with them. In a brilliant close analysis of the text Pitcher matches the upper current of statement with six major steps he finds in the undercurrent and concludes that Poe's theories of consciousness are intimately involved with his cosmological hypotheses.

Finally, in an article on Poe's aesthetics, Dwayne Thorpe challenges the idea that Poe views the poet as an escapist from the real world and the world of time; rather, he realizes that the poet is imprisoned in time, and his art represents attempts to transcend it ("The Limits of Flight: Poe and 'The Poetic Principle,'" *Topic* 16:68–80). Thorpe analyzes "The Poetic Principle" to show how thoroughly it is pervaded by Poe's sense of duality, leading to both delight in the fragmentary glimpses of the Supernal Loveliness which the poet achieves and frustration at being imprisoned in time, which leads to Poe's "petulant, impatient sorrow at our inability to grasp *now*" those "divine and rapturous joys." This is a stimulating reexamination of Poe's aesthetics, in spite of Thorpe's tendency to make sweeping statements about other critics in order to oppose his own view to theirs.

State University of New York at Albany

4. Melville

Hershel Parker

i. Biography, Bibliography, Reputation, and Miscellaneous

Two non-Melvilleans, Walter D. Kring, minister of the Unitarian Church of All Souls in New York City, and Jonathan S. Carey, then student assistant at All Souls, published at the end of 1976 the most important biographical article that has yet appeared on Melville: "Two Discoveries Concerning Herman Melville" (*PMHS* 87[1975]: 137–41). One revelation is that Melville was a member in good standing at All Souls. The main documents are a letter from Elizabeth Shaw Melville's half-brother Samuel S. Shaw to her minister at All Souls, Henry Whitney Bellows (May 6, 1867) and Mrs. Melville's own letter to Bellows (May 20, 1867). The first shows that Mrs. Melville's half-brothers had repeatedly—perhaps as early as the 1850s—urged her to separate from Herman Melville and had at last won some of the Melville family to their point of view. Indisputably now, there were times when Melville's wife believed he was crazy and thought of leaving him. Mrs. Melville's letter to Bellows is less significant except for what it shows of her character and intelligence. Revelations are not at an end, for other documents along with these two will be printed by the Melville Society in a booklet introduced by Dr. Kring. Meanwhile Melvilleans can be grateful that these discoveries were made by amateurs: none of us could have presented the basic documents so modestly and straightforwardly.

But score another one for the amateurs. Dorothy V. B. D. R. McNeilly offers an account of "The Melvilles and Mrs. Ferris" (*Extracts* 28:1–9), including correspondence of Mrs. McNeilly's grandmother, Mary Lanman Douw Ferris, with Mrs. Melville and her niece, Katherine G. Melville. Three letters are in facsimile, including Mrs. Melville's stalwart response to Mrs. Ferris's draft of an essay on Melville which was published in the September 1901 issue of *The American Author*. (What Mrs. Melville says about Melville's response to the reception of *Pierre* may be literal truth, but what she does *not* say is suggested in the letters printed by Kring and Carey.) Following the McNeilly article, Merton M. Sealts, Jr., offers a brief, formidable commentary on "Mary L. D. Ferris and the Melvilles" (*Extracts* 28:10–11), showing, among other things, just where Mrs. Ferris found the information she put into her essay. To the same issue Sealts also contributes "Additions to *The Early Lives of Melville*" (*Extracts* 28:11–13), the major item being the full text of Ferris Greenslet's letter to Willard Thorp about having heard the vigorous old Melville tell a barber a ribald tall tale of his adventures in the South Seas. In "Melville for Sale" (*Extracts* 26:18–19) Donald Yannella at the behest of Frederick James Kennedy calls attention to the recent sale of two Melville letters not in Davis and Gilman, one to John Murray (November 16, 1849), the other to George Palmer Putnam (May 16, 1854).

Now for a motley group. Some examples from Melville occur in G. Thomas Tanselle's "The Editorial Problem of Final Authorial Intention" (*SB* 29:167–211), the first attempt to reconcile "intention" as used by textual editors with the same term as used by aestheticians and speech-act theorists—a difficult, debatable, monumental article, a breakthrough for the New Scholarship. *A Melville Dictionary* by Shigeru Maeno (Tokyo: Kaibunsha) is a selective, alphabetical dictionary "of mythological, classical, Biblical, literary, religious, historical, and geographical references and allusions, and of capitalized hard words in the works of Herman Melville, designed to serve as a useful companion for the readers of Melville, especially for those readers whose mother tongues are not English and whose cultural traditions are quite different from Melville's." (The book is in English.) Alice P. Kenney's "Herman Melville and the Dutch Tradition" (*BNYPL* 79:386–99) is less documentary, more speculative than her earlier studies. Here she suggests that Maria Melville's having spoken Dutch in her family before and at times after her marriage is related to the absence of intimate expressions in her correspondence with her brother Peter Gansevoort, an absence that is "of the greatest importance in understanding Melville's apparent avoidance of some aspects of emotion and his reliance on literary conventions of sentimentality for expressing others." George Monteiro's "Herman Melville in the 1890s" (*PBSA* 70:530–36) offers eight new items, mainly reviews from the United States Book Company reprints of four of

Melville's books. A note for other contributors of *ALS* who may think they have no clout in the great world outside: following a suggestion in *ALS 1974* the Melville Society has reprinted and distributed to its members Wilson L. Heflin's "New Light on Herman Melville's Cruise in the *Charles and Henry*," the chief interest of which is the list of the ship's library—a major supplement to Sealts's *Melville's Reading*. Finally, one of the great treats of the year is Leon Howard's privately printed *Mysteries and Manuscripts*, which, among other articles old and new, contains "The Case of the Left-Out Letter" (pp. 17–26), an account of how he became a Melvillean despite himself as well as a wry, charming account of Jay Leyda on the way to the *Log*. We need a journal where old hands can tell wonderful tales about their lives as scholars and critics.

ii. Reviewing of Sealts and Miller

The reviews told something about Sealts's *Early Lives of Melville* (1974) and Edwin H. Miller's *Melville, A Biography* (1975) but told a great deal more about the state of reviewing. Sealts's work was found to be "impressive," "lucid," "richly detailed" (G. R. Thompson in *MFS* 22:298–302, a review of five books); and "impeccable" and "judicious" (Donald Yannella in *SNNTS* 8:214–22, a review of six books, of which only the Sealts book is also reviewed by Thompson, so prolific is the industry). In *Extracts* (27:5–7) Paul Metcalf, Melville's great-grandson, says that Sealts's book for the first time thrust modern Melville scholarship "into historical perspective" for him. And Robert Milder (*ESQ* 22:169–82) thoughtfully plays off the early biographers in Sealts's book against the biographers of the 1920s.

Yannella, Metcalf, and Milder also reviewed Miller. Characterizing Miller's approach as "adapted Freud, strongly laced with applied Adler," Yannella analyzes one of Miller's recurrent rhetorical strategies: "what is tentative or speculatively offered in one paragraph becomes the firm premise on which judgment is reached in a subsequent passage." Yannella treats the factual errors of the book in the context of Miller's failure to assimilate scholarship, much less employ "new hard information." Metcalf insists on a wider perspective than Miller's desire to believe and have the reader believe "that Melville propositioned Hawthorne": "Human relations are always more powerful where sex is involved—but its involvement may serve to stimulate, to provide an added incentive, rather than to override and obliterate all else." In about the most objective long review Miller is apt to receive, Milder challenges the "deft but often misleading presentation of evidence" and, more significantly, argues that the book oscillates between two extremes, "the thesis-ridden and the amorphous." Milder stresses that Miller's Freudian approach sometimes leads him into "an impoverishing reading, and an untenable one." More than any other reviewer, Milder elaborates the "methodological objections" to Miller's book. All in all, Milder shows a judicious, well-informed sense of trends in Melville biography even though he does not always know the facts of Melville's life well enough to be aware of when Miller does not know them. Except for Yannella, all the reviewers of Miller I have read either mentioned no errors or else dismissed them as unimportant. I think a moral needs to be pointed: Hard as it is to locate such scholars, editors of learned journals need to send biographies out to reviewers whose hands have been soiled in the manuscript collections, who know at least one period of an author's life as well as or better than anyone else.

iii. General

Last year I noted Charlotte Lindgren's cursory survey of some of Melville's opinions about England; now (*AntigR* 26:81–95) we have her similar "The Lion and the Stag: Herman Melville Views the Irish." Carolyn L. Karcher's "Melville and Racial Prejudice: A Reevaluation" (*SoR* 12:287–310) is an ambitious though not wholly responsible attempt to demonstrate that Melville was at least incipiently in accord with New-Leftist perspectives. Her reductive conclusion about *Moby-Dick* is that "the role which Ishmael's marriage with Queequeg performs in saving him from the *Pequod's* fate may well suggest that salvation for America lies in consecrating the marriage of her white and colored citizens." She holds that the title character of "Benito Cereno" perjures himself when he testifies against Babo, Melville being out to highlight "the one-sidedness of the original court records." Karcher's ideas are often bemusing enough, as when she suggests that Babo's torture of Captain Cereno was merely psychological, not physical (and therefore pretty nice torture, on the whole). Her style is often downright startling: "Mel-

ville came to grips with the thorny dilemma that lay at the root . . .";
Benito Cereno's allegation of cannibalism is "an innuendo which we
are left to flesh out. . . ."

iv. Early Books

Last year it looked as if we were in for another cycle of "Herman
Melville, author of *Typee, Omoo*, &c." but this year those books are
neglected except for a good little note by Rita K. Gollin, "The Quondam Sailor and Melville's *Omoo*" (*AL* 48:75–79). One of the "Yankee
lads" Melville mentions in chapter 51 of *Omoo* was William G. Lib-
bey, who recalled Melville and corroborated his account of Polynesian
farming in "Autobiography of a Quondam Sailor," which the *Shaker
Manifesto* published serially in 1878. In "The Influence of the Travel
Narrative on Melville's *Mardi*" (*Genre* 9:121–33) James Jubak un-
surprisingly concludes that travel literature did not determine the
shape of Melville's writing but "was an influence, providing themes,
problems and techniques." Jubak deduces a system of critical standards for the 1840's travel book from only three reviews in a single
magazine, but his article is a good sign of renewed interest in generic
conventions. Patricia Chaffee's "Paradox in *Mardi*" (*ATQ* 29:80–83)
briefly argues that Melville explores two paradoxes, "that of a free
agent in a mechanistic world and that of death that leads to life and
life that leads to death." Wayne R. Kime in "The American Antecedents of James De Mille's *A Strange Manuscript Found in a Copper
Cylinder*" (*DR* 55[1975]:280–306) establishes some affinity between
Melville and De Mille but does not make a case for *Mardi*'s being a
source for *Strange Manuscript*. Robert Sattelmeyer's "The Origin of
Harry Bolton in *Redburn*" (*ATQ* 31:23–25) suggests a direct debt to
a character in J. Ross Browne's *Etchings of a Whaling Cruise*, which
Melville reviewed for the *Literary World* in 1847. "Antidemocratic
Emphasis in *White-Jacket*" (*AL* 48:13–28) is Larry J. Reynolds's corrective to the usual democratic emphasis; the book is partly "an obviously democratic work that argues against social stratification" and
affirms "revolutionary ideals," partly "a subtly antidemocratic work"
that emphasizes "the depravity and vulgarity of the mass of men"
and "the legitimate superiority of a few gentlemanly individuals and
groups."

v. Moby-Dick

The most beautiful book of the year is in German, *Illustrationen zu Melvilles "Moby-Dick"* (Schleswig: Schleswig-Holsteinisches Landesmuseum), ed. Joachim Kruse. Illustrated editions are described in detail and dozens of illustrations of *Moby-Dick* are reproduced from movies, comic books, sculpture, paintings, and other sources, as well as from editions. See Leland R. Phelps's review (*Extracts* 29: 19–20) and try ordering a copy for five dollars from Schleswig-Holsteinisches Landesmuseum, Schloss Gottorf, D-2380 Schleswig, BRD (West Germany). After such foreign riches everything else pales, but illustrations (including some fine ones by Rockwell Kent, who is also well represented in Kruse's book) grace G. Thomas Tanselle's *A Checklist of Editions of "Moby-Dick"* (Evanston and Chicago: Northwestern Univ. Press and Newberry Library), a booklet issued on the occasion of an exhibition at the Newberry Library commemorating the 125th anniversary of the publication of *Moby-Dick*. Tanselle includes editions in English, "supplemented by a listing of abridgments, adaptations, and separately published extracts." The design of the booklet—happily an improvement over that of the Northwestern-Newberry Edition itself—visually enhances Tanselle's succinct, meticulous descriptions.

Leon Howard continues to reflect upon *Moby-Dick* and its author in "Melville and the American Tragic Hero," a graceful "bicentennial tribute" in *Four Makers* (pp. 65–82). Howard's revised opinion is that Melville's "plan for a Shakespearean tragedy in the form of a modern American novel" was of slower growth than he once thought. The famous events of the first week of August 1850, Howard now thinks, "lit a slow fuse which smoldered and sputtered through the fall and well into the winter before the charge was really set off." Together James Barbour and Leon Howard wrote "Carlyle and the Conclusion of *Moby-Dick*" (*NEQ* 49:214–24), which, as the title says, explores the influence of Carlyle in a part of the book where it has not regularly been noticed. Barbara Glenn's "Melville and the Sublime in *Moby-Dick*" (*AL* 48:165–82) is a very interesting essay, although before she finally makes her case for the influence of Edmund Burke's *Philosophical Enquiry* she will need to pay more attention to non-Burkean writing on the sublime and give fuller, more numerous parallels from Burke rather than relying so heavily on quotations from

Moby-Dick itself. A slight complementary note is Richard S. Moore's "Burke, Melville, and the 'Power of Blackness'" (*ATQ* 29:30–32), which treats the white whale as "the quintessence of the Burkean sublime." To G. B. Evans's *Shakespeare: Aspects of Influence* (Cambridge, Mass.: Harvard Univ. Press) David H. Hirsh contributed "Hamlet, *Moby-Dick*, and Passional Thinking" (pp. 135–62). Hirsh thinks that "the 'vocabulary for expressing passion' which Shakespeare released in Melville was in large part a biblical vocabulary that Melville had been accumulating and storing for years without being able to tap its most glittering peaks and most hidden recesses." In a related essay on Melville's language and syntax, "Blending Cadences: Rhythm and Structure in *Moby-Dick*" (*SNNTS* 8:158–71), Marden J. Clark points out "some of the rhythmic resonances as they build toward structural patterns" in the book. Neil R. Grobman goes at "The Tall Tale Telling Events in Melville's *Moby-Dick*" (*JFI* 12 [1975]:19–27) from the perspective of the newer (less item-centered) folklore studies; the categories are amusing in themselves (e.g., "The Lie With Provoked Interruption"). Joel Myerson's "Comstock's White Whale and *Moby-Dick*" (*ATQ* 29:8–27) consists mainly of a facsimile reprinting of William Comstock's *A Voyage to the Pacific* (Boston, 1838). Not the *Life of Samuel Comstock* mentioned in Melville's "Extracts," this pamphlet is nevertheless of great interest as an early account of a futile attempt to capture a white whale. In his chapter, "The Uncommon Long Cable: *Moby-Dick*" (pp. 134–62) in *Hawthorne, Melville, and the Novel* (Chicago: Univ. of Chicago Press), Richard H. Brodhead never quite gets a handle on the book; what he says is rambling and familiar.

vi. Pierre

It is hard to imagine why anyone accepted Richard H. Gamble's "Reflections of the Hawthorne-Melville Relationship in *Pierre*" (*AL* 47: 629–32), a flimsy equation of Melville with Pierre and Hawthorne with Glendenning Stanly. Carol Colclough Strickland's "Coherence and Ambivalence in Melville's *Pierre*" (*AL* 48:302–11) argues that the "imagistic patterns of *Pierre* provide a framework of coherence which shows the extent of Melville's effort in the book, but his ambivalence toward the hero undercuts this accomplishment." Far better is Richard H. Brodhead's chapter, "The Fate of Candor" (pp. 163–

93) in *Hawthorne, Melville, and the Novel*, especially its discussion
of "the relation between Pierre's conscious idealizings and his unconscious sexuality"—a topic also treated last year by R. Scott Kellner
(see *ALS 1975*, p. 76). The Strickland and Brodhead essays have in
common a New Critical blindness to possible biographical explanations of aesthetic problems. Strickland says that "Melville seems of
two minds about *Pierre*"—an observation long given in biographical
terms by Leon Howard. Having described Melville's effort to make
Pierre a great psychological novel, Brodhead says that "we must recognize at once that the second half of the book has little to do" with
that effort. Then he provides a fine description of how the second
half differs from the first, all the while defending the shift of purpose:
"Melville was wise not to let a foolish consistency keep him from
exploring the subjects and methods" of the Pamphlet chapter and
the books on "Young America in Literature" and "The Church of the
Apostles": "they are among the most interesting in *Pierre*." In "Why
Pierre Went Wrong" (*SNNTS* 8:7–23) Hershel Parker prints new
documentary evidence as to when Melville's intentions changed (the
first days of 1852, not February, as had been thought) and why (the
demeaning Harper contract drawn up by the first days of January,
which allowed Melville only 20 cents on the dollar after costs, not
the old 50 cents, and simultaneous appearance of hostile January reviews of *Moby-Dick*). Unlike Brodhead, Parker laments the shift in
purpose, holding that what Melville wrote "either in New York or
after his return to Pittsfield was often superb of its kind . . . but disastrous for the book he had first conceived and had brought far on
the way to completion in one sustained period of composition."
Moved by the painful biographical-critical evidence, Parker suggests
the possibility that "the greatest single tragedy in American literature
is that Melville broke off work on his manuscript when he did in
order to make a routine business trip to New York City."

vii. The Stories

I keep insisting that classic articles on Melville cry out to be written
despite the annual hoards of worthless essays. Well, the number of
unwritten classic essays is diminished by one, for "The Alternatives of
Melville's 'Bartleby'" by Allan Moore Emery (*NCF* 31:170–87) is
the best article ever published on "Bartleby" and may be the best

on any of the stories. Emery brilliantly does what Jay Leyda long ago suggested: he reads the story within the philosophical context implied by the narrator's reference to Jonathan Edwards and Joseph Priestley on the will. Emery's article has already received the Samuel Willis Medal for the best critical essay on Melville in 1976 and will surely be reprinted in future casebooks.

Christopher Bollas's "Melville's Lost Self: 'Bartleby' " (*AI* 31 [1974]:401–11) had escaped my notice, but it is now reprinted in a gathering of essays from *Criticism* and *American Imago*, *The Practice of Psychoanalytic Criticism*, ed. Leonard Tennenhouse (Detroit: Wayne State Univ. Press), pp. 226–36. Bollas's essay is a dull and jargon-ridden treatment of Bartleby as an "Ahab or Pierre come in out of the cold"; the "true self" is "finally existentially revealed in its condition of absolute need for the other." What's interesting is the editor's propagandistic introduction which (in the absence of better essays to celebrate) lays out some of the questions psychoanalytic critics should be asking: "how the text was made, how it was perceived by the author, how it may have been read by its original audience, and how it is read by a particular reader." Whatever the limiting bias, these questions are stimulating: Tennenhouse is moving toward the New Scholarship, that realm where textual scholarship, biography, literary history, and literary criticism are mutually enlightening and supportive.

Other articles are of little interest. David A. Roberts's "Structure and Meaning in Melville's 'The Encantadas' " (*ESQ* 22:234–44) argues "that Melville has made 'The Encantadas' an integrated whole by two means other than the common subject matter—by structural unity and by the coherence of the narrative point of view." (I contend, no one is going to write anything convincing about the unity of these sketches without a thorough consideration of the evidence as to the way they were composed and published. What of the possibility that Melville never wrote a last sketch as such but just stopped sending instalments to *Putnam's*?) David R. Eastwood in "O'Brien's Fiddler—or Melville's?" (*ATQ* 29:39–46) is an exercise in applying statistical tests to suggest that Melville probably wrote "The Fiddler," although Leon Howard (in a footnote too hastily added to a paperback reprinting of his biography) once accepted the *Harper's* index attribution to Fitz-James O'Brien. Eastwood is not aware that Mrs. Melville preserved the story and identified it as her husband's. Slight-

ing other critics, Kermit Vanderbilt in " 'Benito Cereno': Melville's
Fable of Black Complicity" (*SoR* 12:311–22) concludes that the story
"finally transcends historical oppression to become one of the bitterest
moments in Melville's quarrel with the first vengeful and deadly Master," God. Vanderbilt quotes briefly from some interesting letters
Charles Eliot Norton wrote from South Carolina in 1855. Arthur H.
Scouten, disclaiming any intention of pointing out a source or influence, glances at parallel situations in "The Derelict Slave Ship in
Melville's 'Benito Cereno' and Defoe's *Captain Singleton*" (*CLQ* 12:
122–25). "Babo's Name in 'Benito Cereno': An Unnecessary Controversy?" by Robert Cochran (*AL* 48:217–19) rather too tentatively
points out that arguments about the meaning of "Babo" are somewhat
beside the point since Melville got the name from Delano's *Voyages*.
Odds are that this sensible note won't stop the foolish speculation,
not nearly all of which is mentioned here. C. Sherman Avallone's
"Melville's 'Piazza' " (*ESQ* 22:221–33) forces the allusiveness of the
sketch into unlikely or ill-presented relationships, particularly with
Dante.

viii. *Israel Potter* and *The Confidence-Man*

Nothing much to report. Robert Zaller's "Melville and the Myth of
Revolution" (*SIR* 15:607–22) argues that in *Israel Potter* Melville
obsessively examined "the problem of authority and rebellion," in
the process turning the American Revolution into "a parable of the
human, and specifically the American condition." In "Melville's *The
Confidence-Man*: A 'Poisonous' Reading" (*PsyR* 63:571–85) C. Barry
Chabot moves from routine, derivative comments into a Freudian examination of oral and anal imagery; the immediate model is Erik
Erikson's notion of " 'basic trust vs. basic mistrust' " as "the central
issue to be resolved in the first, or oral, stage of the infant's development." Eugene Korkowski is reasonable in his titling of "Melville and
Des Périers: An Analogue for *The Confidence-Man* (*ATQ* 31:14–19),
since Bonaventure Des Périer's dialogues in *Cymbalum Mundi*
(1537) are indeed analogous to Melville's; but nothing here indicates
that the French work was an actual source for Melville. William Norris's "Abbott Lawrence in *The Confidence-Man*: American Success
or American Failure" (*AmerS* 17:25–38) suggests Lawrence (whom
Melville met in 1849) as a model for the man with gold sleeve-

buttons. What Norris says about Lawrence is interesting, but his arguments that Melville was satirizing Lawrence are never conclusive.

ix. Poetry

Douglas Robillard edited a not-very-special special issue, "Symposium: Melville the Poet," for *Essays in Arts and Sciences* (5,ii:83–206), with the following essays: Nathalia Wright, "The Poems in Melville's *Mardi*" (83–99); Bryan C. Short, " 'The Redness of the Rose': The *Mardi* Poems and Melville's Artistic Compromise" (100–112); Bertrand Mathieu, " 'Plain Mechanic Power': Melville's Earliest Poems, *Battle-Pieces and Aspects of the War*" (113–28); William H. Shurr, "Melville and Christianity" (129–48); William H. Wasilewski, "Melville's Poetic Strategy in *Clarel*: The Satellite Poems" (149–59); Agnes Dicken Cannon, "On Translating *Clarel*" (160–80); William Bysshe Stein, " 'The New Ancient of Days': The Poetics of Logocracy" (181–93); and Douglas Robillard, " 'I Laud the Inhuman Sea': Melville as Poet in the 1880's" (193–206). The collection is about on the level of those which have been appearing in *CLAJ* and *ArQ*. Some of the essays surely would have been published even in a refereed situation, but I like to think that others would not have. Of most durable interest is Agnes Dicken Cannon's essay, which reproduces some of Melville's markings in Matthew Arnold's "On Translating Homer." The titles of the other essays provide sufficient indication of their contents.

x. Billy Budd, Sailor

For all their unevenness and their mutually contradictory stances, three essays this year are better than anything that has been published in a long time: Joyce Sparer Adler's "*Billy Budd* and Melville's Philosophy of War" (*PMLA* 91:266–78); Edward M. Cifelli's "*Billy Budd*: Boggy Ground to Build On" (*SSF* 13:463–69); and Mary Everett Burton Fussell's "*Billy Budd*: Melville's Happy Ending" (*SIR* 15:43–57). Adler's article, overlong and sometimes badly written (see the recurrent verb "concretize"), somewhat reductively takes the book as Melville's final attempt to set forth "his view of the man-of-war world as a parody of the Christianity it feigns" and to awaken his audience "to 'holier' values than those civilized man had lived by";

the story contains a covertly hostile portrait of Vere as a man who sacrifices Billy "to Mars, an offering not demanded by law or ethics or even military necessity" but by his own obsessive dedication to the ritual of war. In an unusually responsible study Cifelli places Melville's problematical "late pencil revisions" (so named and discussed by Harrison Hayford and Merton M. Sealts, Jr., in their edition) in a broader context than the final characterization of Vere: "equivocation on large thematic issues is not to be wondered at from a writer who demonstrates, perhaps unconsciously, a parallel equivocation in elementary word choice"; from clearly categorized examples of equivocal language Cifelli argues that Melville "never intended to reveal himself in a straightforward manner" and that his late pencil revisions were meant "solely to veil, not negate, his sympathetic attitude toward Vere and thereby to recapture narrative consistency." Fussell treats Vere as a "rigorously self-disciplined man" who "suffers from a latent homosexuality which he can only control by projecting the self-hatred he feels toward his forbidden desires onto other men in whom the symptoms of homosexuality are more obvious." Billy's blow that kills Claggart is, she speculates, "a spontaneous gesture warding off the intolerable caress of the Captain," whose own sudden insight into his hidden motivations drives him "to his instant decision to hang the angel, and simultaneously to hysteria."

Cifelli knows the Hayford-Sealts Genetic Text exists; Adler makes nominal use of it; and Fussell actually works with it, a major breakthrough in criticism. With Fussell the results range between dubious and disastrous, for she misreads the passage she singles out as crucial, taking "Melville's astonishing 'Look at it. Look at it'" on leaf 238a as "obviously an exclamation of discovery addressed to himself," another "insight passage" like the one George R. Stewart thought he had found in *Moby-Dick*. Well, no such thing. Fussell has misread the Genetic Text. The symbols are not exactly self-evident, but they can be learned with a little effort. (Word to editors of learned journals: please reject any article that mentions Fussell's reading of leaf 238a as if it were fact.) Although Fussell's article is reckless, sometimes silly, and often outright wrong about facts, it is exhilarating to read because she does the main thing right—she uses the Genetic Text in order to gain a sense of the process of composition. She wonders, for instance, about "what significant synapses took place in Melville's mind as he flipped the pages of old poem holographs whose reverse sides he

used in composing *Billy Budd.*" Adler more often is nonprocessual, as
when she fails to focus on the anachronism of using *Bellipotent* and
Billy Budd, Sailor as if they had been ship's name and story title
throughout the composition, but she does argue that "in the development of the work an organic interaction between the poem and the
prose came into being, and as the narrative's implications grew,
changes took place in the ballad as well and in its role in the book."
Cifelli's categories would have been even better if he had mined
examples from the Genetic Text instead of restricting himself to words
remaining in the Reading Text. In varying ways Adler and Fussell
cheapen Melville's work (where is that lofty magnanimity Berthoff
wrote about?), and Cifelli's reassertion of the old testament of acceptance theory is imperfectly bolstered, but all three deserve close,
wary reading, and Fussell's approach, if rarely her conclusions, deserves wide imitation. More than one classic essay is going to come
out of responsible study of the interpretive implications of the evidence in the Genetic Text.

Two studies are less controversial and less stimulating. Kay S.
House in "Francesco Caracciolo, Fenimore Cooper and 'Billy Budd' "
(*SA* 19–20:83–100) interestingly uses Cooper's *Wing-and-Wing*,
Southey's *Life of Nelson*, and Cooper and Melville scholarship (es-
pecially Hayford's *The Somers Mutiny Affair*) to argue that in *Billy
Budd* Melville was indebted to Nelson's hanging of Caracciolo and to
later commentary on it. In her view, Vere is undoubtedly "based on
the character of Horatio Nelson." Superficial is Joseph C. Friel's
"Ustinov's Film *Billy Budd*, A Study in the Process of Adaptation:
Novel, to Play, to Film" (*LFQ* 4:271–85); film students may find more
in it than Melville readers do.

University of Southern California

5. Whitman and Dickinson

Marvin Fisher and Willis J. Buckingham[1]

On the whole, the published scholarship on Whitman in 1976 seems more conservative in tone, temper, and quantity than in 1975, and the number of dissertations is only one-third as many as in 1975. There are fewer bibliographical and critical studies but considerably more discussions of relationships and reputations.

A similar cautiousness prevails in Dickinson studies. Feminist criticism notably aside, work this year tends to evaluate and occasionally to reclaim already familiar approaches to the poetry rather than to strike out in new directions.

i. Whitman

a. **Bibliography and Editing.** The two letters reprinted by William White comprise a slight addition to Whitman documents. The more significant of the two, written to an unknown correspondent and dated 3/31/85, asserts that 800 copies of the first edition of *Leaves of Grass* were printed, that Whitman set some of the type, and that the 1876 *Leaves* was the sixth edition (rather than a new printing from the 1871 plates). Needless to say, Whitman's assertion does not constitute verification ("An Unknown Whitman Ms on the 1855 *Leaves*," *WWR* 22:172; "A New Whitman Letter to Mary Whitall Costelloe," *WWR* 22:42–43).

b. **Biography.** According to Jerome M. Loving, Whitman was not singled out for dismissal by Interior Secretary James Harlan because of Harlan's objection to *Leaves of Grass*. Loving cites a directive from Harlan to his bureau chiefs giving guidelines for pruning the Department—among them: disloyalty, inefficiency, and disregard of "the

---

1. Marvin Fisher has written the Whitman section and Willis J. Buckingham the Dickinson.

rules of decorum and propriety prescribed by a Christian Civilization." Loving does not believe that suppression or censorship was
the root issue in Whitman's dismissal but that this became Harlan's
defense after O'Connor raised the issue in *The Good Gray Poet*
("Whitman and Harlan: New Evidence," *AL* 48:219–22).

Several articles take up the subject of Whitman's sexuality without offering much that is new. Edward F. Grier offers "circumstan-
tially convincing evidence" of Whitman's capacity for heterosexual
relationships by tracing a possible liaison with Mlle. Sophie Farvar-
cer, an "artiste" from whom he may have contracted a "bad disorder"
("Whitman's Sexuality," *WWR* 22:163–66). Two others react to what
the authors consider the overemphasis on homosexuality in the CBS-
TV special on "Song of Myself" (Jerome M. Loving, "Walt Whitman: Is He Persecuted?" and Joseph Jay Rubin, "Plea to the Media,"
both in "The Bicentennial Walt Whitman: Essays from *The Long
Islander*," 24 June, ed. William White, reprinted as Supplement to
WWR 22:25–26 and 29–30).

Deborah S. Kolb compares Whitman's actual experience in the
American South with references in his prose and his poetry, conclud-
ing that he considerably exaggerated his degree of familiarity to en-
hance his claims as poet of all America ("Walt Whitman and the
South," *WWR* 22:3–14). Writing about Whitman's housekeeper,
Harold Aspiz says that, despite her own failing health and financial
sacrifice, Mary O. Davis felt it a privilege to serve the poet ("Mrs.
Davis's 'Drab Love,'" *WWR* 22:162–63).

c. **Criticism: General.**   Floyd Stovall provides an easy blend of ex-
trinsic and intrinsic criticism and biography in an essay that would
be a delight for the interested nonspecialist ("Walt Whitman as
American," *Four Makers*, pp. 43–63). But even the specialist would
find Harold Bloom's "Emerson and Whitman: The American Sublime" rather tough going (*Poetry and Repression*, New Haven, Conn.:
Yale Univ. Press, pp. 235–66). Bloom's highly technical, frequently
arcane vocabulary and reference to Kabbalistic models have the effect
of explaining the poetry in terms more obscure than the poem and
treating the Emerson-Whitman relationship in Bloomian terms of
"precursor" and "ephebe." The only full-length book on Whitman
is Ivan Marki's *The Trial of the Poet: An Interpretation of the First*

Edition of "Leaves of Grass" (New York: Columbia Univ. Press).
Marki argues for the superiority of the first edition. He has read the
critics and cites them frequently and respectfully. The argument,
however, might be better suited to an essay than a book. The section
on the 1855 preface is a 90-page amalgam of historical information,
psychosexual conjecture, and rhetorical analysis, but it seems longer.
The same pace characterizes the confident but plodding explication of
the poetry.

Several articles deal with Whitman and democratic concepts of
self and society. Depending a bit too heavily on Tocqueville's views
as contrapuntal to Whitman's, when, in fact, Tocqueville virtually
prophesied Whitman's advent, Donald D. Kummings describes
Whitman's vernacular perspective, his development of a new diction, and the emergence of a vernacular hero whose international
character transcended his American origins (*CRevAS* 7:119–31). Considering Whitman's prose as much as his poetry, Alfred Kazin discusses how his vision of democracy made possible his self-discovery
as a poet and his recognition of his subject matter in himself. But
democracy's promise for the future was largely vitiated by the scan-
dal and corruption of the Gilded Age, and Kazin suggests a correlation between the apparent failure of democracy and "America's failure to make the fullest possible use of Walt Whitman" (*Commentary*
61:52–58). In "Whitman and the Emancipated Self" Richard J. Fein
parallels Whitman's concept of the ego with Tocqueville's and Georg
Simmel's—the common idea being "that in a democratic society the
individual is thrown back upon himself for his identity, whereas in
an aristocratic . . . society the individual [looks] beyond his subjectivity to a communally sponsored identity" (*CentR* 20:36–49).
M. L. Rosenthal's "The Idea of Revolution in Poetry" (*Nation* 223:
117–19) uses Whitman's "To a Foil'd European Revolutionaire" as a
reflection of his nonconformist conservatism and his darkening idealism. Rosenthal finds that "our greatest poets" have recognized the
uncompleted and unexplored "revolution in the quality of our lives
as in our politics."

In a very cautious way Stephen L. Tanner writes of "Whitman as
Urban Transcendentalist" (*SDR* 14:6–18). He recognizes that Whitman's transcendentalism was rooted in rural nature and in bringing
it to bear on city scenes, he "does not offer us much help in coping

with the complexity of urban life." Because he believed that material
progress foreshadowed spiritual progress, Whitman proceeded to
mythologize the city, but the concurrent pastoral myth overshadowed
the urban myth "just as spirit tends to swallow up matter." Retracing
the route of "the machine in the garden," Roger Asselineau charts the
love-hate relationship of American poets to the city in "From Whitman's 'Yawp' to Ginsberg's 'Howl' or the Poetry of Large Cities in
American Literature" (*RLV* 42, U.S. bicentennial issue:23–35). Instructed by Emerson in acceptance and transcendence, the poets from
Whitman to Ginsberg (Hart Crane, W. C. Williams, Dreiser, Anderson, Sandburg, Eliot, and Dos Passos) struggle to see "beyond tragic
and disappointing appearances," past urban horror and suburban
smother, to that state of love and holiness every commuter aspires to.

    In "Walt Whitman and the Woman Reader" (*WWR* 22:102–10)
Lottie L. Guttry reasons that because Whitman rejected both the
feminine stereotype of helpless dependence and the masculine stereotype of stern self-sufficiency, women readers responded favorably and
male readers often censoriously. Whitman's ability to adopt a female
persona further illustrates his empathy with women and their need to
widen their life experience and gain self-esteem.

    A number of critics argue that Whitman knowingly or unknow-
ingly utilized ideas from science, philosophy, and, of course, Eastern
religions. Eugene Chesnick sees Whitman using new theories of
evolution to fuse older philosophies and religions that emphasize the
soul with modern science and its explanation of cosmic energies
("Whitman and the Poetry of the Trillions," *WWR* 22:14–22). James
E. Mulqueen, on the other hand, sees in Whitman's poetry a prefiguration of Spengler's theory of history from *The Decline of the
West*—Whitman bringing together the elements of culture and warning against the approaching stage of civilization and decay ("Walt
Whitman: Poet of the American Culture-Soul," *WWR* 22:156–62).
Massud Farzan illustrates the affinity between *Leaves of Grass* and
the Persian Sufi poets, culminating in the 1891 poem "A Persian Lesson" ("Whitman and Sufism: Towards 'A Persian Lesson,'" *AL* 47:
572–82). From a vantage point even further east, Morgan Gibson
argues that although Whitman may have had only a casual understanding of Buddhist ritual, his references in several poems indicate
knowledge of the Buddha's experiences as a youth and the consequent

discoveries of the awakened self. Both men "were great liberators" and "compassionate contemplatives" whose beliefs were largely compatible though not fully identical ("Whitman and the Tender and Junior Buddha," *EigoS* 122:264–68).

d. **Criticism: Individual Works.** After an apt comparison of Wordsworth's *Prelude* and "Song of Myself," Chaviva Hošek demonstrates that speaker, subject, and reader of Whitman's poem are renewed with each reading, so that the poem "dramatizes its own creation, enacting the speaker's transformation into a poet, the process of finding a subject matter, and the creation of a new kind of reader" ("The Rhetoric of Whitman's 1855 'Song of Myself,'" *CentR* 20:263–77).

Thomas W. Ford makes a case for "Excelsior" as something considerably less than "Song of Myself" or "Out of the Cradle" but remarkably illustrative, nevertheless, as a poetic microcosm of Whitman's major themes and technical devices, and in its several revisions as a reflection of his changing attitudes ("Whitman's 'Excelsior': the Poem as Microcosm," *TSLL* 17:777–85). Writing of "I Sing the Body Electric," Robert Coskren, also admits apologetically that while it is not one of Whitman's better poems, it provides Whitman's detailed commentary on the central concept of the indissolubility of body and soul ("A Reading of Whitman's 'I Sing the Body Electric,'" *WWR* 22:125–32). Douglas A. Noverr concentrates on "Our Old Feuillage" to explain the physical, political, and spiritual implications of the flower-leaf-bouquet image ("Poetic Vision and Locus in Whitman's 'Our Old Feuillage,'" *WWR* 22:118–22).

Two lesser-known works are discussed by Robert E. Abrams and George H. Soule. Abrams finds a sketch published in March 1842 noteworthy for its early experiment in "hallucinatory imagery" and distortion of reality in dream-vision ("An Early Precursor of 'The Sleepers': Whitman's 'The Last of the Sacred Army,'" *WWR* 22:122–25). Soule sees in "Pictures" (first published in 1925) Whitman's attempt to counter the influence of Tennyson's poetic and political ideas ("Walt Whitman's 'Pictures': An Alternative to Tennyson's 'Palace of Art,'" *ESQ* 22:39–47).

e. **Relationships, Influences, and Reputation.** Among the studies of relationships this year are some that merely stress parallels without arguing for direct knowledge or influence, some comparisons that deal more deeply with similarities and differences with stronger implications of influence, and some contrasts that imply only a relationship of difference.

Randolph Ian Gordon cites several parallels between Whitman's world view and that of St. Francis, arguing that Whitman sought to make the "Scientific Model as emotionally satisfying as . . . the Medieval Construct," and arriving at the unsurprising conclusion that the "Medieval Model" was more theocentric and the "Scientific Model" more anthropocentric ("Whitman as a Franciscan within the Modern Universal Construct," *WWR* 22:36–42). Using "Tintern Abbey" and "Out of the Cradle" as representative expressions of each poet's imagination, Gary Simon notes similarities and differences between the art and times of Wordsworth and Whitman ("Craft, Theory, and the Artist's Milieu: The Myth-Maker and Wordsworth," *WWR* 22: 58–66).

Several articles discuss aspects of Whitman's relation to his early and later contemporaries. G. Thomas Couser finds that Emerson's and Whitman's attitudes toward the past and toward the creative process strengthen the tie between the two, but that the distance between their designated audiences constituted a major difference ("An Emerson-Whitman Parallel: 'The American Scholar' and 'A Song for Occupations,'" *WWR* 22:115–18). On the other hand, Suzanne Poirier uses "A Song of the Rolling Earth" to illustrate the differences in the transcendental beliefs of Emerson and Whitman, particularly in regard to the didactic role of nature and poetry ("'A Song of the Rolling Earth' as Transcendental and Poetic Theory," *WWR* 22:67–74).

Of a more conjectural nature are two articles that consider Whitman's relationship to Whittier and to Dickinson. Lewis E. Weeks, Jr., asks, "Did Whittier Really Burn Whitman's *Leaves of Grass?*" and suggests that the anecdote is either apocryphal or greatly exaggerated (*WWR* 22:22–29). And in "Emily Dickinson's Awareness of Whitman: A Reappraisal," Walter H. Eitner suggests that despite the disclaimer in her 1862 letter to Higginson, she could have encountered a Whitman poem in an 1860 *Atlantic Monthly* or several in the Springfield *Daily Republican* in 1871 and *Harper's* in 1874 (*WWR* 22: 111–15).

In "Jack London et Walt Whitman," Roger Asselineau cites a passage from *Martin Eden,* indicating that London intended to write an epic with grass as its subject. He then tries to explain why London never got to it (*Europe: Revue Littéraire Mensuelle* 561–62:76). In a more extensive article he finds a strain of transcendental romanticism in American literature from Whitman's time to the present, citing instances from such varied fiction writers as Twain, Dreiser, Anderson, Hemingway, Updike, Kesey, and Bellow, as well as in the work of some notable 20th-century poets (" 'Dreaming in the Grass' ou la constante transcendentaliste de la littérature américaine," *EA* 29:331–40).

Two articles consider Whitman's influence or relation to artists in other fields. Henry Golemba levels the curious charge that Whitman may have been partially responsible for Charles Ives's loss of creativity through Ives's discovery of Whitman's darker side ("Charles Ives' Whitman," *ATQ* 29:36–39). Without suggesting overt influence, Barry K. Grant cites a number of parallels or similarities in "Whitman and Eisenstein" (*LFQ* 4:264–70). They include each man's experience of war or revolution, their use of montage and catalogue, their belief in "the epic quality of the masses," and their attempt to celebrate all individuals together rather than any specific individual.

Additional 20th-century writers linked to or contrasted with Whitman include Stein, Frost, Eliot, Roethke, Henry Miller, and William Carlos Williams. G. Thomas Couser lists a number of similarities between Whitman and Gertrude Stein and then discusses works of each as prophetic or idealized autobiography ("Of Time and Identity: Walt Whitman and Gertrude Stein as Autobiographers," *TSLL* 17:787–804). Focusing on the poet's acceptance of the invitation of the thrush in "Lilacs" and his rejection in Frost's "Come In," Thomas W. Ford argues that the differing responses are indicative of the diverging world views of the two poets ("Invitation from a Thrush: Frost versus Whitman," *WWR* 22:166–67). According to Jenijoy La Belle, Roethke's *Meditations of an Old Woman* has significant similarities to Eliot's *Four Quartets* because they have a common source in Whitman ("Out of the Cradle Endlessly Robbing: Whitman, Eliot, and Theodore Roethke," *WWR* 22:75–84).

Clive Bemrose notes that the first two verses of "For You O Democracy" were adapted by the headmaster and founder of Abbots-

holme School for use as the school song ("A Whitman Poem and
an 1890 English School's Song," *WWR* 22:168–70).

The American bicentennial year was in part the occasion for the
increased number of studies of Whitman's reputation. F. Lannom
Smith provides a detailed summary of critical opinion from the first
appearance of *Leaves* to Dr. R. M. Bucke's *Walt Whitman* ("The
American Reception of *Leaves of Grass*: 1855–1882," *WWR* 22:137–
56). Larry W. Cook looks at what a later group had to say about
Whitman ("The New Critics' Estimate of Walt Whitman," *WWR*
22:95–101) and concludes that their comments were more revealing
of their own values than of Whitman's poetry.

Ward B. Lewis and John Hess examine two segments of German
opinion of Whitman. Lewis surveys the Whitman criticism produced
by writers and critics who fled the Third Reich in the 1930s and published *Decision* in New York and *Deutsche Blätter* in Santiago ("Message from America: the Verse of Walt Whitman as Interpreted by
German Authors in Exile," (*GL&L* 29:215–27). Hess reviews the
"Reception of Whitman in the German Democratic Republic" (*WWR*
22:30–35), finding that Whitman is much appreciated in the GDR
for his identification with the working class, his hatred of war, and
his realistic portrayals of individuals and society.

The special issue of *The Long Islander*, reprinted as a supplement to *WWR* contains four reputation studies, moving outward
from the American college campus to Europe, Africa, and India. Jane
D. Eberwein, discussing "Whitman on Campus," reports that he remains popular for different reasons than in the past, with more emphasis on his humaneness, egalitarianism, sexual frankness, and
commitment to poetry (pp. 19–20). Roger Asselineau's report on
"Whitman in France in 1976" is not as sanguine (pp. 13–14). The
reasons are several: the unpopularity of lyric poetry, the unavail-
ability in French of *Specimen Days* and "Democratic Vistas," and
the preference for the "New Novel." Maurice Pollet finds that students of American literature in Senegal much prefer novels by Twain,
Steinbeck, and Hemingway ("Whitman in Dakar," p. 27). And
Amritzit Singh assures us that Whitman made his passage to India
in good shape and that his reputation is secure: not only is Whitman
influential on major poets in India, but there are also more doctoral
dissertations on Whitman than on any other American author ("Walt
Whitman in India: 1976," pp. 31–33).

ii. Dickinson

Major studies of Emily Dickinson having just been published, 1976 was a time for retrospection and for criticism on a smaller scale. Some of the most thoughtful contributions this year appeared as review articles, among which, to mention but one, an untitled essay by Nina Baym was particularly vigorous and astute (*JEGP* 75:301–7). In outlining some of the work that still remains, Baym notes that Dickinson "has not been approached from a women's studies point of view," that we still lack an overview of the *kinds* of poems she wrote, and that more "should be done on the analytic questions raised by her texts: the variants, for example, or the arrangement of her poems within the sewn packets." There was, in 1976, discernable movement in only the first of these directions.

a. **Bibliography, Editing.**   Having recovered the copy-text used for the first publication of an 1881 Dickinson letter, Barton Levi St. Armand and George Monteiro take us one step closer to the missing manuscript by publishing a facsimile of the printer's text in "On Behalf of Emily: Dickinson Letters and Documents (1891–1892)" (*RALS* 6:191–98). They also furnish the now hard-to-obtain 1892 article on Dickinson in which the letter first appeared as well as some correspondence related to that article by the poet's surviving sister, Lavinia. Recovery of another letter, this from Hamlin Garland to the poet's niece, Martha Dickinson, allows Monteiro and St. Armand to confirm an earlier suggestion (*ALS 1974*, p. 71) that the smartly dressed poetess Garland met at a party in 1902 and mistook for Emily Dickinson was, of course, not the aunt but the niece ("Garland's 'Emily' Dickinson—Identified," *AL* 47:632–33). The only bibliographical compilation this year is the listing by Shelia Taylor and Tsuyoshi Omoto of 133 diverse English and foreign-language items on Emily Dickinson published during the last decade ("Annual Bibliography—1975," *EDB* 30:55–65).

b. **Biography.**   Three discussions of the poet's life this year have much in common. Written by women who are themselves poets as well as critics, they propose that the single most important fact about Dickinson is that she was a female in a male-dominated environment. In the past, when it has been claimed that she chose her seclusion deliberately, the better to exercise her genius, the argument has usually assumed a kind of psychic frailty requiring protection from those day-to-day encounters in the real world which would otherwise have dulled or drained away her powers. Now the assumption is not so much that Dickinson had to conserve her energies as that she had to conceal them from a patriarchal culture. At least this is the reasoning, eloquently espoused, in Adrienne Rich's "Vesuvius at Home: The Power of Emily Dickinson" (*Parnassus* 5,i:49–74). The poet's enormous creative power, Rich suggests, must have threatened her sense of identity as a woman, for only men, in her day, were accorded the strength of mind Dickinson knew herself to possess. Thus the childlike pose sometimes observable in the poems and letters can be understood as an effort to counter or disguise, from herself perhaps as much as from others, her potentially desexing capacities: "The woman who feels herself to be Vesuvius at home has need of a mask, at least, of innocuousness and of containment." Mistaking "self-diminutization" as a confession of weakness, Rich says, has blinded critics to the many self-confirming expressions of power in her work and has prevented them from realizing that the masculine lover and god by whom she is possessed in the poems may refer to the terrific force of her poetic daemon. A poem like "My life had stood—a Loaded Gun—", for example, may indicate that while the poet, once enthralled, could not live without her masculine Muse, she nevertheless felt ambivalent about the risks of power incidental to womanhood in her society.

That society forced Dickinson to choose between being an "artist" and a "woman" is also Suzanne Juhasz's contention in " 'A Privilege So Awful': Emily Dickinson As Woman Poet" (*SJS* 2:94–107; reprinted, with some additional material in Suzanne Juhasz, *Naked and Fiery Forms: Modern American Poetry by Women, A New Tradition* [New York: Harper and Row], pp. 7–32). "Lively, popular, and attractive," Dickinson nevertheless refused the traditional feminine roles in order to find a place where she could be in control and maintain her self against potentially annihilating pressures from outside. That Dickinson explored, in her mind's inviolable space, numerous intimicies and extremities is, as Juhasz readily admits, not a new insight. What she interestingly suggests, however, is that not only did Dickinson solve issues which still affect women poets, she did so knowing fully the measure of her victory. "Sitting in the [expansive] world of her room, of her mind," Juhasz writes, Dickinson could "gently mock the traditional woman's restricted life and self in comparison with her own."

In a recorded essay, "Emily Dickinson as a Woman Poet" (Deland, Fla.: Everett/Edwards [1975], Cassette Lectures no. 5519), Virginia Terris similarly argues that as a gifted woman in a repressive society, Dickinson avoided insanity and suicide by turning to the creation of art. What principally interests this critic are the large number of Dickinson's poems which take as their subject other women or herself as a woman. Her cultural situation helps us understand how, in the latter case, the self Dickinson pictures is often helpless, starved, diminished, and dying. Nevertheless, and here Terris's argument appears to deny the common wisdom, Dickinson was as much a product of her genteel society as she was a critic of it. Not only did she accept and even cultivate a childlike, dependent life, she acceded to her society's expectation that women write only short lyrics, "serious" poetry being reserved for men. Her poems are short, moreover, because in performing the woman's role, she had to fit their composition between domestic tasks. Finally, Terris reminds us that in their ideality, in their didactic and melancholy tone, in the rhetoric of piety which colors them, and in their preoccupation with such themes as social ritual, home, love and marriage, death and eternity, Dickinson's poems reflect the inescapable social structure in which she lived. Taking a more specifically sociological approach, Barbara Welter arrives at a similar conclusion in *Dimity Convictions: The American Woman in the Nineteenth Century* (Athens: Ohio Univ. Press, pp. 8, 202, 203). Noting especially the poet's fear of growing up and the assumption in some of her love poems of new status achieved through marriage, Welter believes that Dickinson exhibits a whole cluster of 19th-century attitudes toward a woman's coming of age.

The literary side of that cultural situation particularly concerns Ellen Moers, who argues that a major influence on Dickinson's life was the women's literature of her day (*Literary Women* [Garden City, N.Y.: Doubleday], pp. 55–62, passim). Dickinson's "confident use of female experience and female accessories" derives, Moers says, from her admiration for Elizabeth Barrett Browning and other women writers whose work interested her more than writing by men. Moers thus confirms Terris's judgment that Dickinson was decisively influenced by her reading of women, from whose work she boldly fashioned her own unmistakably female poetic voice. Even female "littleness" (in physical comparison with males) is reflected in Dickinson's small-looking poems, though as Moers valuably reminds us, the poet's sportive handwriting fills her manuscript pages "with a sense of confident power that is drained away in print." In thus underscoring both Dickinson's conventional femaleness and her unconventional power, Moers allows us to see that the insights of these seemingly divergent understandings of Dickinson as a woman are not finally contradictory.

To turn from feminist accounts of Dickinson's life to the implied phallocentricity of Dorothy Waugh's *Emily Dickinson's Beloved: A Surmise* (New York: Vantage Press), is to experience a considerable jolt. The dust cover of this monograph promises to bring to light "a man not previously considered as he who probably inspired many of the world's great love poems." The man is Richard Salter Storrs Dickinson, a distant relative and friend of one of the poet's second cousins. Emily Dickinson could have met him during her three-week trip to Philadelphia in 1855 but since no correspondence between the two survives, much must be supposed—and is. In conjecturing a romance from fragments of the poems and letters, but without adding new facts, Waugh's volume is reminiscent of the 1930s, when every few years a new biography would put the same pieces of the puzzle together in a different way and behold, a new lover would emerge. The problem with this approach is not only that it yields few insights into the poetry, as William White observes ("Dickinson's Biography and Criticism of Her Art," *EDB* 30:66–76), but also that it can be made to promote virtually any nominee as *the* lover—male or female, friend or acquaintance. While there must have been real and fantasy people "behind" some of the poems, their identity will remain conjectural until and if ever we have new information. To straighten Dickinson's slant-wise words so as to make them point to a single person as their sufficient cause and explanation seems, at the present point in Dickinson studies, a strange atavism.

Readers of these pages are no doubt already familiar with William Luce's *The Belle of Amherst*, a one-woman drama based on the poet's life and performed, on the stage and for television, by Julie Harris. The play has been so successful that it constitutes a popular biography of sorts and is likely to influence perceptions of Dickinson for some time. For this reason, Luce's prefatory remarks in the published version of his play (Boston: Houghton Mifflin) may be instructive. His purpose in *The Belle of Amherst*, Luce says, was to portray "the humanity and reasonableness" of the poet: "The essential Emily of my play is secretly saying to the audience, 'Pardon my sanity.' " What Luce notably does not imply—in his Preface or in the play—is that Dickinson's life *would* have been irrational had it not been for her poetry. Rather, he insists, she was a woman living a cogent and deliberate life, who happened also to write.

c. Criticism: General. Changes of fashion betrayed in biographical approaches to Dickinson are, if anything, only more abundant and various when we turn to critical estimates of her work. Many of them are ably surveyed in Paul J. Ferlazzo's *Emily Dickinson* (TUSAS). A kind of "Reader's Guide," this slim volume is intended mainly for those who wish to begin intelligent study of the poet, though it is sound and thorough enough to be helpful to more advanced readers as well. Although the author compares legends with the facts of Dickinson's life, and while he also considers her prose and the effects she has had on later writers, his major effort is to provide an overview of five areas where Dickinson criticism has not yet achieved resolution. Dealing with these problem areas thematically (faith, mortality, love, sanity, nature), Ferlazzo's method is to depend largely on explications of key poems, though he occasionally (as in the chapter on sanity) also surveys the relevant scholarship. None of these discussions is intended to be exhaustive, but they gather in the range of possibilities on each issue with such clarity, modesty, and good sense that the volume as a whole provides the best brief, general introduction to Dickinson currently available.

Less interested in a range of possibilities is Ronald Lanyi, who attempts to expose the poet's "vein of Calvinist piety" by showing that some of her lines (never whole poems) reflect five of Calvin's most important doctrines ("'My Faith That Dark Adores—': Calvinist Theology in the Poetry of Emily Dickinson," *ArQ* 32:264–78). Unfortunately the complex problem of Dickinson's beliefs cannot be

resolved so simply, particularly when passages are taken out of poems
which, if quoted in full, would appear to express dissent from, rather
than satisfaction with, Calvinist principles. Since to disregard context
is to disregard meaning, the author's use of evidence here cannot fail
to result in a partially trumped-up conclusion.

Other interpretative studies of Dickinson this year focus on clusters of imagery. The best of these is Nancy Lampert's "Dew Imagery
in Emily Dickinson's Poetry" (*EDB* 29:44–53) in which she discusses
the contrast in many poems between morning and night, on the one
hand, and day (especially "noon") on the other. Dew thus often functions to symbolize fecundity and rest, both of which are vulnerable
to the "drying-up" of daytime bustle and commotion. Typically for
Dickinson, this day-night cycle, observable in minutest things, has
diverse implications, and Lampert's article is careful not to over-
simplify. Spiders and bees occupy the attention of two other contributors to *EDB* 29. JoAnne De Lavan Williams believes that Dickinson's spiders sometimes stand for the artist who spins out of herself
a pure and self-sufficient beauty more often than not incongruous in
the everyday world of housewives and their brooms ("Spiders in the
Attic: A Suggestion of Synthesis in the Poetry of Emily Dickinson,"
pp. 21–29). Reading Dickinson more transcendentally, but ignoring
some of the poet's playfulness, Steven K. Hoffman argues that her
bees often signify an important manifestation of divinity ("Emily
Dickinson's Bees: Development of an Agglutinative Symbol," pp.
30–35). Through the bee's Christ-like intercession, Hoffman says of
one poem, Dickinson found at least "the possibility of achieving religious satisfaction in the face of inherent mortal limitations."

Images associated with journeys and voyages are studied by Leslie H. Palmer but this large subject is treated too cursorily to yield
new conclusions ("Emily Dickinson's 'Father's Ground—The Travel
Motif of a Recluse Poet," *EDB* 30:95–104). More satisfying is Mary
Ann C. McGuire's study of bare feet in the poems ("A Metaphorical
Pattern in Emily Dickinson," *ATQ* 29,ii:83–85). She points out that
both Victorian prohibitions and biblical analogues inform Dickinson's use of this image and that it often functions to suggest a speaker
who is without social ease or assurance. Nevertheless, since Dickinson saw the conventions of her day as "impediments," she "defiantly
chose barefootedness" as a means of securing, in her role as outcast,
personal and artistic freedom.

d. **Criticism: Individual Works.** Among poems given separate study this year, two deal with the theme of self-isolation. In one, "From Cocoon forth a Butterfly," Audrey S. Eyler notes that the speaker remains strangely, almost eerily detached both from the heedless, "Romantic" world of nature and from the workaday, "Utilitarian" world of man ("An Explication of Poem 354," *EDB* 29:40–43). Butterfly and man, merriment and care, the poem darkly suggests, equally face extinction. In "Dickinson's 'What Soft—Cherubic Creatures'" (*Expl* 35,i:5–6), Robert Franicevich deftly refutes a claim made recently (*ALS 1975*, p. 101) that the speaker includes herself as one of the cherubs of the divan satirized in the poem. Clearly, context requires that "Brittle Lady" (in line 12) refers to the "Gentlewomen" and not to the poet herself. However pale and unexamined her neighbor's religious beliefs may have been, Dickinson's own struggle with faith could be harrowing, as Marcus K. Billson III points out in his elaborate, existential reading of "Me prove it now—Whoever doubt" ("Drama of Doubt, Dialectics of Pain," *EDB* 30:83–94). The author draws on Kierkegaard to show that in this poem, as in others, the courage to doubt serves as the necessary but paradoxical precondition for faith. A lesser paradox, but one receiving considerable attention, occurs in "As by the dead we love to sit." Is Dickinson saying here that death makes us value more highly the living who remain, or does she more perversely mean that so momentous do the dead become, the living are temporarily eclipsed? Nat Henry prefers the former interpretation (*Expl* 35,ii:26–27), while Edgar F. Daniels recommends the latter (*Expl* 35,ii:10–11), thereby confirming a view taken earlier by Laurence Perrine (see *ALS 1975*, p. 101).

Dickinson's thoughts on eternity are the focus of several other explications. In "Dickinson's 'Of Death I try to think like this'" (*Expl* 35,ii:18–19) Nancy McClaran argues, on the basis of parallels with the *Aeneid*, that Dickinson's poem affirms belief in a sort of pre-existence to which the spirit returns at death: "The soul, like Aeneas, after its journey through life, leaps the stream and 'resettles' in Hesperia—immortality—the motherland—the place it formerly inhabited." Laurence Perrine, on the other hand, sees in "As Watchers hang upon the East" only further evidence that Dickinson believed paradise, once gained, would be something of a letdown, no matter how enticing it had seemed from a distance (*Expl* 35,ii:4–5). A more transcendental Dickinson is reflected in Elizabeth Buzzelli's "An Explica-

tion: 'A Wife—at Daybreak I shall be'" (*EDB* 29:36–39). She argues
that Dickinson speaks here of going from mortal life to eternal "co-
existence with God." While some poems, like this one, yield easily to
cosmic interpretation, others have to be forced, as E. Miller Budick
amply demonstrates in " 'I had not minded—Walls—': The Method
and Meaning of Emily Dickinson's Symbolism'" (*CP* 9,ii:5–13).
Budick contends that the poem pictures hostile, disintegrating uni-
verses, and that what the poet fears is not separation from her beloved
but imprisonment "in a total and unalleviated materialism." Pushing
metaphors far beyond their own references in the poem, this reading
reflects more the fevered exhalations of a metaphysician gone ape
than a responsible attempt to engage the text.

Finally, two analyses reflect on Dickinson's relationship with other
poets. In "Emersonian Echoes in Dickinson's 'These Are the Signs'"
(*ATQ* 29,i:2–3), Lee J. Richmond finds in the poem a "Transcendental impulse to see a central unity and design in nature." Using a close
reading of "Our journey had advanced—" to demonstrate "rhetorical
disjunction," Harold Bloom finds that Dickinson anticipates Wallace
Stevens in her use of antithetical images "to make the visible a little
hard to see" ("Poetic Crossing, II: American Stances," *GaR* 30:787–
90).

e. **Affinities and Influences.** In "The Influence of Latin Poetics on
Emily Dickinson's Style" (*CLS* 13:214–29), Lois A. Cuddy thoughtfully proposes that Dickinson's intricate metrical designs may have
their sources in classical prosody, particularly as enunciated in a
Latin grammar used by her at Amherst Academy. Relevant to the
much-vexed problem of Dickinson's notation is Cuddy's belief that
the poet's "internal dashes function like the caesura in Latin verse
and are therefore essential for the rhythm and voice heard in these
poems." Classical texts, as they may have affected Dickinson's use of
"structure, epigram, cathartic verse, and elegiac perception" are further considered in the author's thesis, "Elegy and the American Tradition: Subjective Lyrics On Life and Experience" (*DAI* 37:273–
74A). Without dwelling on classical sources, Ronald Allan Sudol
considers the same subgenre in his thesis, "Elegy in the Poetry of
Emily Dickinson" (*DAI* 37:1557–58A).

An influence much closer at hand, of course, was Emerson, whose
conception of the self as flowing consciousness, James McIntosh says,

found its way into the work of Dickinson as among other 19th-century American writers ("Emerson's Unmoored Self," *YR* 65:232–40). Mary Janice Rainwater considers more extensively Dickinson's reaction to Emerson and to five other writers contemporary with her (the Brownings, the Brontës and George Eliot) in "Emily Dickinson and Six Contemporary Writers: Her Poetry in Relation to Her Reading" (*DAI* 36:4479A). As for her "disgraceful" contemporary, Walt Whitman, Walter H. Eitner believes that Dickinson may have known more of his work and have liked it better than has generally been thought ("Emily Dickinson's Awareness of Whitman: A Reappraisal," *WWR* 22:111–15). He shows that a considerable amount of Whitman's poetry was published after 1862 in the newspapers and periodicals to which her family subscribed. In a densely written but occasionally rewarding essay, M. M. Khan notes parallels between Dickinson's perceptions and the thought of Henri Bergson ("Intuition of Time, Eternity, and Immortality: Emily Dickinson and Bergson," *HJP* 14: 35–39). Khan's application of Bergson to "Because I could not stop for Death—" is especially useful.

Though Pound and Eliot were less than impressed by Dickinson when they first read her in Conrad Aiken's 1924 English edition of her *Selected Poems*, W. H. Auden, making her acquaintance at the same time, appears to have responded enthusiastically. That is the conclusion of A. S. T. Fisher, who notes that Auden liked her "oracular epigrams" well enough to write at least one poem clearly imitative of her style ("Auden's Juvenilia," *N&Q* 21[1974]:370–73). Robert E. Morsberger finds the Amherst poet more remotely situated in "Emily Dickinson On Kilimanjaro" (*EDB* 30:105–6). There are similarities in thought, he says, between Hemingway's story and two Dickinson poems. We can be certain that Theodore Roethke read Dickinson with pleasure, for as Jenijoy La Belle demonstrates, not only does he borrow from her, his poem "No Bird" was intended as a tribute to Dickinson (*The Echoing Wood of Theodore Roethke* [Princeton: Princeton Univ. Press], pp. 13–16). George Lensing and Ronald Moran urge that Dickinson's "There's a certain Slant of light" helps to clarify William Stafford's poem, "Level Light" (*Four Poets and the Emotive Imagination* [Baton Rouge: La. State Univ. Press], p. 214). However, comparison of two related poems, Dickinson's "Just lost, when I was saved!" and Sylvia Plath's "Lady Lazarus," convinces Jeffrey Steinbrink that while there are some initial similarities between the two poets, they approach death with quite different expectations ("Emily Dickinson and Sylvia Plath: The Values of Mortality," *W&L* 4:45–48).

Whatever the case with Plath, important parallels exist between Dickinson and a modern Brazilian poet, Henriqueta Lisboa—in their lives as well as in their themes and techniques—according to Blanca Lobo Filho, whose "The Poetry of Emily Dickinson and Henriqueta Lisboa" (*PPNCFL* 26[1975]:150–53) is an abbreviated version of an earlier essay by the same title and in the same journal (20[1969]:103–12). Finally, Dickinson's striking influence on a younger woman poet, Jay Macpherson, is observed in considerable detail by David Bromwich ("Engulfing Darkness, Penetrating Light," *Poetry* 127:234–39). He finds that Macpherson has absorbed and made her own even some of the most idiosyncratic features of Dickinson's language, rhythms, and punctuation, but above all, he says, both poets share "the conviction that self-scrutiny, an act of unswerving authority and intensity, is the way to self-possession in art."

Arizona State University

6. Mark Twain

Louis J. Budd

Since the first volume of *ALS*, this chapter has had only two curators
—John C. Gerber and Hamlin Hill. I would be happy to carry on
without change, but subjective colorings are inescapable. Hill's liveliness will disappear, for example, because I am inclined to be solemn
in Mark Twain's presence and so avoid any comparison between his
gift for humor and mine. Also, because *ALS* has been declared over-
weight, this essay will become more selective, will usually pass over
the weakest items that will soon sink under the torrent of fresh print.
The chapter can slim down anyway because scholarship about Mark
Twain has lessened in recent years though he seems as popular as
ever—especially with admen.

A positive reason for selectivity is that Thomas A. Tenney will
be updating annually in *ALR* (starting in November 1977) his *Mark
Twain: A Reference Guide* (1977), which deserves immediate mention because of its centrality. When Tenney's updatings are supplemented—if that is possible—with *AL*, *PMLA*, *MissQ*, *WAL*, *Mid-
America*, and the MHRA listing, there is no need for this chapter to
function as a catchall. (Does any other writer appear in the specialized bibliographies for southern, midwestern, and western literature?
Would Clemens also be included for New England?) Nor does this
chapter need to notice every item in the *Mark Twain Journal*, which
has clearly improved but still runs the gamut of quality, or in the
Twainian, which should be watched for a trickle of primary materials.
Finally, dissertations will be ignored because I would merely be
rehashing *DAI* entries.

i. Bibliographical and Textual

No matter how much the CEAA and CSE irritate some freewheelers,
close textual work keeps proving useful. In "Editorial Intrusion in

Pudd'nhead Wilson" (*PBSA* 70:272–76) Sidney Berger shows that
somebody, probably not the author, cut enough words out of the last
eight pages to save the wobbly American Publishing Company the
cost of a whole new signature. Not important but pleasant for brows-
ing is Virginia Haviland and Margaret N. Coughlan's *Samuel Lang-
horne Clemens, A Centennial for Tom Sawyer: An Annotated, Selected Bibliography* (Washington, D.C.: Lib. of Congress), got up
for an exhibition of his books "most widely read by young people."
Its plentiful illustrations are taken from foreign as well as American
editions. We have been far too slow to study Mark Twain's illustrators
and their impact on not only the buying public but on him.

The dust jacket for *The Mammoth Cod and Address to the Stom-
ach Club* (Milwaukee: Maledicta Press) promises the "key into the
hermetically sealed lock" of Clemens's later years. G. Legman's introduction does help to authenticate a little-known piece of bawdry
in 1901. Contending that impotence set in around the age of fifty, he
is also worth reading for his postmortem on Clemens's sexuality.
"Opening Remarks" by Kurt Vonnegut, Jr., for *The Unabridged Mark
Twain* (Philadelphia: Running Press) is worthwhile but disjointed;
the offbeat news here is the book itself—a three-pound paperback of
1,289 pages, over two and a half inches (or, for posterity, 6.6 cen-
timeters) thick, that reprints "from his first editions" the "best one-
third of Mark Twain's writing." This tome overshadows still another
anthology from Maxwell Geismar, *The Higher Animals: A Mark
Twain Bestiary* (New York: Crowell), a good-natured selection that
starts with "A: Alligators."

In importance and quality the real blockbuster was Paul Fatout's
688-page *Mark Twain Speaking* (Iowa City: Univ. of Iowa Press).
Nobody but Fatout has earned the right to prepare the texts—from
print, manuscripts, and eye-witness accounts—of Mark Twain's stunning variety and number of appearances before an audience. Fatout
himself is careful to admit that his texts may well be flawed, even
when based on a holograph version, and to list many speeches for
which he could find no version at all. Likewise, his concise introduction and headnotes could come only from a seasoned expert. Though
some of Mark Twain's speeches misfired and others became formulaic,
Fatout warns us that he was, of course, most effective when heard and
seen, that indeed a "large part of his technique—perhaps the larger
part—does not show in print." Still, what does show is often mighty

good, and *Mark Twain Speaking* is as enjoyable as it is indispensable.
Mark Twain as platform artist is an endlessly faceted subject.
While adding nothing startling, Frederick Trautmann's "The Twins
of Genius: Public Readings by George Washington Cable and Mark
Twain in Pennsylvania" (*PH* 43:215–26) dredges up further details
about the stage dress, program, audiences, and reviews of the tour of
1884–85; convincingly, Cable emerges again as the more tolerant and
adaptable of the "twins." Through hard-to-find newspapers Harsharan
Singh Ahluwalia, "Mark Twain's Lecture Tour in India" (*MTJ* 18,iii:
4–7), recovers some localized openings for his readings and some ad
lib comments—a form of placer mining usable for many of his platform appearances. In " 'It Is Unsatisfactory To Read to One's Self':
Mark Twain's Informal Readings" (*QJS* 62:49–56) Alan Gribben
concludes that Clemens's passion for reading aloud to family and
friends "helped develop the flexible narrative voice he strove to re-
produce in his fiction," whose "daily output" he liked to test for the
sound of sense. Mapping the metaphorical or allusive subtleties of
his prose must reckon better with his deliberated oral nuances. Is it
scholarly to mention *The Adventures of Tom Sawyer* (Argo Stereo,
ZSW561–3) in which Bing Crosby proves that the prose can hold,
even bewitch the listener for long stretches?

ii. Biography and General Criticism

In "Joseph P. Ament—Master Printer to Sam Clemens" (*MTJ* 18,ii:
1–6), Ralph Gregory rounds off by speculating sanely about what
Clemens learned from his nearly nine years in printing shops. With
too much anecdotage William V. Kahler, "Mark Twain: Adult Hero
of Daniel Carter Beard" (*MTJ* 18,iii:1–4), recounts how the illustrator for three of Mark Twain's later books became a lasting friend.
To be sure, interpreting the facts is the higher activity, especially
crucial—argues Hamlin Hill, "The Biographical Equation: Mark
Twain" (*AHumor* 3,i:1–5)—for separating the man from the persona
that co-opted him, sometimes even privately. Hill ends with a set of
jarring questions. Satisfied that Hill recently gave some fresh answers,
David E. E. Sloane, "A Revisionist Perspective on Mark Twain"
(*SAmH* 2[1975]:135–39), insists that the "family portrait" in *Mark
Twain: God's Fool* has exposed Albert Bigelow Paine's self-seeking
pieties and has thrown "corrective" light from Clemens's later domes-

tic tensions on the "preceding life and canon." Since Paine is not alive
to respond I will guess that he would be even more caustic and Victorian than in his verdict on Van Wyck Brooks—set down on December 30, 1928, for Cyril Clemens, who now reproduces it (*MTJ* 18,iii:
back cover): "He selected from my book things that seemed to support his case. I suppose you can prove anything by any book, in that
way, even by the Bible. Anybody that knows anything of Mark
Twain's mother and wife knows that he owed more to them than to
all other influences that came into his life." Such Mariolatry would
have also resented Robert R. Sears, "Episodic and Content Analysis
of Mark Twain's Novels: A Longitudinal Study of Separation Anxiety" (*LCP* 199–206). After carefully laying out his method Sears—
a professor of social sciences in psychology at Stanford—chooses one
trait and determines that Mark Twain's eighteen novels reveal his
lifelong "fear" of the withdrawal of love, especially by his wife and
especially around the times of the births and deaths of their children.
Neither knee-jerk hostility nor genuflection will make sense here,
even when Sears rounds out his clinical analysis.

Alan Gribben's " 'I Kind of Love Small Game': Mark Twain's
Library of Literary Hogwash" (*ALR* 9:65–76) leaves us wondering
about the psychic reason for crowing so gleefully over pieces of ex-
ecrable writing; to say they qualify as "camp" would not explain
much. Out of his Ph.D. dissertation Gribben has quarried a set of
authoritative essays, perhaps the most suggestive of which is " 'Good
Books & a Sleepy Conscience': Mark Twain's Reading Habits" (*ALR*
9:295–306); besides showing that Clemens read doggedly, it reveals
he paradoxically linked books with laziness and self-indulgence.
Surely some psychological critic should make more of this. In "Mark
Twain and Robert Ingersoll: The Freethought Connection" (*AL* 48:
183–93) Thomas D. Schwartz suggests that the candor of the Great
Agnostic may have lacerated Clemens's feeling that he had often
truckled to public opinion. Schwartz mainly studies how Ingersoll
may have shaped his attacks on Biblical fundamentalism—a valuable
line of analysis that needed to take broader account of his other reading. Still, it is on such specialized articles that the generalizing essays
have to depend while giving credit, as does Leon Dickinson's "Mark
the Twain: The Double Vision of Samuel Clemens" (*RLV* 42, U.S.
bicentennial issue: 81–91), which returns to Clemens's bracketing

of experience in opposites, from the pairing of characters to the broadest metaphysical incongruities.

Both solidity and richness are achieved in four other basic essays, though Larzer Ziff, "Authorship and Craft: The Example of Mark Twain" (*SoR* 12:246–60), creates thin historical props for discussing how Mark Twain's prose style "gained its strengths and its limitations from his sense of the writer as craftsman and writing as the trade that elevated one socially," that won esteem but an esteem continually subject to renewal by popularity and therefore eventually stultifying. Deploring approaches that dull his brilliance by setting him within some larger tradition, David Karnath, "Mark Twain's Implicit Theory of the Comic" (*Mosaic* 9:207–18), argues with more intricacy than any précis can indicate that comedy is the art of facing up to man's fictionizing; thus the ending of *Adventures of Huckleberry Finn* "confesses its own unreality, erasing what it has created"—a sophisticated reading that may puzzle those not used to hearing that the favorite (and presumably the highest) subject of literature is the literary process. However, other Twainians cannot help orienting his ideas toward a more widely shared world, especially that of moral values. Stanley Brodwin caps his fine work in this area with "The Theology of Mark Twain: Banished Adam and the Bible" (*MissQ* 29:167–89), which proves that in spite of Clemens's overt rejection of the Bible it remained dynamic for him in many ways. More specifically, Brodwin cuts to the heart of his fascination with Adam, Eve, and Satan, a trinity who "personified his loss of innocence" and his attempts to "return to an Eden imagined or real." The shape of his religion is truly complex, which may be why it has mostly been sketched rather than surveyed. In "Mark Twain's Rebellion against God: Origins" (*SwAL* 3[1973]:27–38), John Q. Hays tests the commonplaces about his late pessimism by taking a more precise case history of the Hannibal years, particularly within the heterodox family circle. The first durable book-length study of his religious ideas is yet to come. It should be at least respectful, according to a professor of philosophy—Philip E. Davis, "Mark Twain as Moral Philosopher," *SJS* 2,ii:83–93—who decides that Clemens did regularly try to reason out his beliefs and attain a "theoretical and general" perspective.

Of course the chief critical event was William M. Gibson's *The Art of Mark Twain* (New York: Oxford Univ. Press). Long in gestation, it is fully formed and informed. Leaving biography and the sociocultural context aside as best he could, Gibson set out to determine how Mark Twain's literary magic operates in his "truly . . . best works." While Gibson acclaims success along a range of genres —Mark Twain was "more of a man of letters in the traditional sense . . . than anyone has yet argued"—he holds that the "brilliant best" shines in the shorter pieces. *The Art of Mark Twain* opens bravely with a chapter on "one of the great styles of literature in English"; its biggest surprise is an entire chapter (out of seven) on the Pudd'nhead Wilson maxims as a triumph of "apothegmatic statement"; refreshingly it tackles *Huckleberry Finn* with an emphasis on the "total character of the work as comedy," especially as "false pathos"; it closes with "Dreams and the Inner Life," evaluating "The Chronicle of Young Satan" as "partly finished, roughly unfinished, unfinished" yet close to "greatness." Throughout, Gibson tries no Tom Sawyerish stunts, strives for elucidation rather than density, and keeps out of his own way. His book does about as much as possible in 225 smallish pages and will wear very well.

iii. Early Works

When the Iowa/California Edition of the early tales and sketches comes out one of these years, it will set off a burst of critical activity. But for 1976 little was written about them except Stephen Fender's " 'The Prodigal in a Far Country Chawing of Husks': Mark Twain's Search for a Style in the West" (*MLR* 71:737–56), a major inquiry into whether the western years educated Clemens in a "style of living as well as of writing." After demonstrating how his humor mediated between gentility and freedom, Fender concludes that in the West he "first looked over the brink, first confronted the possibility that he was, and would be, nothing; that not only he, but perhaps human society itself, was finally nothing." Fender reasons with both precision and force though he can hardly be said to have settled the question of what Virginia City was really like under its bluster and rawness.

A special issue on Mark Twain in the 1870s (*SAmH* vol. 2, no. 3) has, as premise, the observation that the 1870s deserve far more study than they get, relatively. Because I was the guest editor I will merely list its contents: David E. E. Sloane, "Mark Twain's Comedy: The

1870s," pp. 146–56; Robert Regan, " 'English Notes': A Book Mark
Twain Abandoned," pp. 157–70; Alan Gribben, "The Formation of
Samuel L. Clemens' Library," pp. 171–82; Howard G. Baetzhold, "Of
Detectives and Their Derring-Do: The Genesis of Mark Twain's 'The
Stolen White Elephant,' " pp. 183–95; Stanley Brodwin, "The Useful
and the Useless River: *Life on the Mississippi* Revisited," pp. 196–
208; Sherwood Cummings, "Mark Twain's Theory of Realism; or The
Science of Piloting," pp. 209–21. Another article that starts from the
1870s is Louise Schleiner, "Romance Motifs in Three Novels of Mark
Twain" (*CLS* 13:330–47). Small touches betray that she is not a
Twainian nor perhaps even a first-rate critic (since she calls David
Wilson a "rounded character"). Nevertheless, she amply shows that
despite Mark Twain's fondness for parodying the plots and handling
of motivation in prose romances, he went and did likewise in *The
Gilded Age, The Prince and the Pauper,* and *Pudd'nhead Wilson.*
What remains debatable is whether she defines the romance too
sweepingly while ignoring the sentimental-domestic novel. Garry
Wills might also object that she slights the realistic-mimetic mode;
for "Our Best Political Novel" (*NYTBR* 6 Jun:7) acclaims *The Gilded
Age* for making the "tie between politics and private life vivid in a
way no other fiction has."

iv. *Tom Sawyer* and *Huckleberry Finn*

Currently, interpretive critics often bracket the two major "boy"
novels instead of displaying *Tom Sawyer* as a warm-up sketch,
though nobody goes so far as to proclaim it the greater work. Outside
Huck Finn's company it comes off stronger than ever, as in Aidan
Chambers's "Letter from England: A Tale of Two Toms" (*Horn
Book* 52:187–90), which matches it with *Tom Brown's School Days*
as a vibrant paradigm of its society, and in Evelyn Geller's "Tom
Sawyer, Tom Bailey, and the Bad Boy Genre" (*WLB* 51:245–50),
which sees it as boldly extending Thomas Bailey Aldrich's break with
current stereotypes. Adding to these two forebears three later novels
—Edward Eggleston's *Hoosier School-Boy,* Booth Tarkington's *Pen-
rod,* and Salinger's *Catcher in the Rye*—Robert L. Coard, "Tom
Sawyer, Sturdy Centenarian" (*MQ* 17:329–49), compares them for
overall merit. His good-humored, unpretentious but graceful essay
judges that Mark Twain created the most "variegated" and persuasive

exemplar of the Not So Bad Boy; though Coard faces up to the flaws in *Tom Sawyer* he predicts that in 2076 it will enjoy a "vigorous bicentennial."

From his meticulous research into Clemens's reading, Alan Gribben, in "How Tom Sawyer Played Robin Hood 'By the Book' " (*ELN* 13:201–4), identifies another literary source for *Tom Sawyer*. But here the headline event was the unplanned debate between Clifton Fadiman—"A Second Look: A Centennial for Tom" (*Horn Book* 52: 139–44)—and Tom H. Towers—" 'I Never Thought We Might Want To Come Back': Strategies of Transcendence in *Tom Sawyer*" (*MFS* 21:509–20). Having asked why youngsters still read *Tom Sawyer* "even when it is forced upon them by teachers," Fadiman eloquently decides that they find in it a "hymn to freedom," a way out from the "technoculture," a "lyric *yes* that affirms the right of the boy to seek the identity that takes its shape out of idleness, out of dreams, out of fantasy." Without caring to discuss the waverings of tone, Towers pursues a "dark unity" of "profound despair" as Tom's attempts to rise above the spiritually dead society bring him a "sense of absolute and unrelievable loneliness," from which he flees not to the Territory but to conforming with the adults. In neither of the boy novels are "freedom and community or love really compatible." If Towers is right about *Tom Sawyer*, our junior-high PTA's have been asleep at the switch.

Seemingly guileless, *Huckleberry Finn* continues to be ransacked for its secrets. Even the briefest articles can end with a new theory, as in Maureen T. Krevec's launch from the guess that Huck was named after Fin MacCool, the hero of the Ossian forgeries—"Huckleberry Finn's Aristocratic Ancestry" (*MTJ* 18,ii:19–20). Steadier is a liftoff from the comments on John Bunyan's Christian—Alfred Bendixen, "Huck Finn and *Pilgrim's Progress*" (*MTJ* 18,iii:21). Refreshingly substantive is Carol Colclough Strickland's "Emmeline Grangerford, Mark Twain's Folk Artist" (*BNYPL* 79:225–33), which shows with the help of fine reproductions that Mark Twain described masterfully the "conventional mourning picture produced by amateur female artists" before he moved on to travesty its "sentimental romanticism" and "false piety." Under too broad a title Janet H. McKay, " 'Tears and Flapdoodle': Point of View and Style in *The Adventures of Huckleberry Finn*" (*Style* 10:41–50), anatomizes one brief passage to discover how its "vernacular and colloquial features" are webbed "to create the impression of an untutored narrator, while simultaneously developing a sophisticated, innovative" style or—more concretely—just how language is used to characterize Huck while making readers "believe in the reality" of his vision. I hope that McKay follows up her sensitive approach.

Three interpretive essays search directly for the ultimate secret. In a clearly stated case that jibes with Karnath's theory of humor Brent Keetch, "Mark Twain's Literary Sport" (*MTJ* 18,ii:7–10), proposes that *Huckleberry Finn* "burlesques its own fictional 'reality' which is a copy of the historical South which in turn is a parody of romantic literature." Likewise the "evasion" sequence burlesques Jim's original flight, thus implying "there is no freedom anywhere that will satisfy completely." Billy G. Collins, "Huckleberry Finn: A Mississippi Moses" (*JNT* 5[1975]:86–104), praises the ending because the "kindly Christian people of the Phelps farm who use the Bible to justify slavery" mirror the society of the opening chapters. This hardly new argument merges into a close drawing of parallels with Exodus, so close as to make Huck out "in effect . . . the very spirit of Moses." Trying to extend rather than trump previous criticism, Edward J. Piacentino's "The Ubiquitous Tom Sawyer: Another View of the Conclusion of *Huckleberry Finn*" (*CimR* 37:34–43) charts the tone of the novel primarily through Huck's underlying attitude toward Tom, which can question his antics while respecting his authority; indeed, Huck never does stop following Tom, the instigator of the plan to light out for the Territory. Well before these three essays, Winfried Fluck found it worthwhile to do a taxonomy of the criticism—before offering his own reading, as we would expect in—*Ästhetische Theorie und Literaturwissenschaftliche Methode / Eine Untersuchung Ihres Zusammenhangs am Beispiel der Amerikanischen Huck Finn-Kritik* (Stuttgart: J. J. Metzlersche, 1975). However, I am cribbing from Frank Bergmann's review (*ALR* 10 [1977]:221–23) of a schematic and polemical dissertation.

The Dramatic Unity of "Huckleberry Finn" (Columbus: Ohio State Univ. Press) by George C. Carrington, Jr., lies behind the warning about my biases. Looking ahead in *ALS 1975*, Hill saluted it as "brilliant," and his review elsewhere has rated it, modestly, as "probably the most exciting volume on Mark Twain to appear in the last decade" (*ALR* 9:381–83). Carrington's electric and learned mind, which reaches for the import of every physical or verbal gesture,

leaves me embarrassed at how many details I had not pondered before. But he is a born-again structuralist who finds previous gospels
misguided. To recover the true deep meaning he sets up a "situation"
theory of behavior and develops his own usage for "dramatic"—the
quality or trait of gaining control of one's world by turning experience into "events" or "drama." For an enriched summary of how
these terms are applied, Hill's review is the best place to go. I will
add only that Carrington joins the critics who can respect the ending
of *Huckleberry Finn*: though still dominated by his chum, Huck triumphs in becoming the artist-author who limns the Toms of this
world and its "indifference" toward its nonwhite victims.

Paul Delaney's "You Can't Go Back to the Raft Ag'in Huck Honey!: Mark Twain's Western Sequel to *Huckleberry Finn*" (*WAL* 11:
215–29) avoids the mistake of treating "Huck Finn and Tom Sawyer
among the Indians" as an epilogue. Ironically, taking it on its own
terms becomes the best way of letting it cast light on the masterpiece itself. Huck's creator, Delaney finds, had blundered into confronting him with insights his innocent eye could not reflect and,
after the Indians raped a girl, with sexual knowledge that Tom Sawyerish antics could not laugh away. Billy G. Collins, it should be
noted, had gone on to *Tom Sawyer Abroad*, though with the shaky
thesis that a "large share" of its purpose was to "make people aware
of biblical parallels in *Huckleberry Finn* that had previously been
only imperfectly observed, if at all."

v. Late Writings

The area between *Huckleberry Finn* and the "Great Dark" materials
was explored less than usual. For *A Connecticut Yankee in King
Arthur's Court* I found only the section (pp. 202–15) of John F. Kasson's *Civilizing the Machine: Technology and Republican Values in
America, 1776–1900* (New York: Grossman) and three compact passages in Kenneth M. Roemer, *The Obsolete Necessity: America in
Utopian Writings, 1888–1900* (Kent, Ohio: Kent State Univ. Press).
With crispness and finesse Kasson comes out on the dystopian side
of the *Yankee* as revealing "how a powerful, supposedly human-
itarian republican leader may betray his own ideals as he seeks to
extend control over a weaker, undeveloped nation through essentially aggressive use of his technology." The fact that the author him-

self, W. D. Howells, and other friends and reviewers saw it as a manifesto for natural rights "only reveals how deep-seated the Yankee's capacity for violence and for the self-deception that supported it was shared by society at large." More gently Roemer also strums the dark chords of the *Yankee*, which magnified "all the weak spots and sore spots in the utopian concept of history" and betrayed deep fear about leadership by an "Everyman-Superman." Clark Griffith, whose long essay in 1975 summed up the *Yankee* as "nihilistic," has moved on to *"Pudd'nhead Wilson as Dark Comedy"* (*ELH* 43:209–26). Accepting the much-patched novel as totally responsive to a firm intention, Griffith elicits a dialectic between comedy and tragedy before turning grim ("Twain's own descent into the Great Dark was finished—and final") because "in a world ruled by darkness" the patterns of comedy prove "worthless."

It is a long time since anybody rated *Personal Recollections of Joan of Arc* as an integrated triumph of any sort. Don Harrell, "Mark Twain's Joan of Arc: Fact or Fiction?" (*MarkhamR* 4[1975]:95–97), helpfully suggests that Joan was treated as a "surrogate Tom Sawyer" until history broke the doting author's control by demanding that she be burned at the stake. Much more ambitiously, William Searle devotes a third of *The Saint & The Skeptics: Joan of Arc in the Work of Mark Twain, Anatole France, and Bernard Shaw* (Detroit: Wayne State Univ. Press) to the paradox that Clemens "adopted from his Catholic sources an idolatrous version of Joan's career which was wholly out of keeping" with his freethought and "ended by representing her, in effect, as a saint in a world without God." After a portrait of him as (Goethe's) Faust—a tortured intellectual who has despaired of his own salvation—Searle's courage grows stark when he diagnoses a severe Oedipal complex, a "desire to atone to the mother without asking forgiveness of the father" that impelled the gut worship of the girl-Joan. An appendix mounts to intrepidity by deducing that Clemens's pervasive sense of guilt was exacerbated by his most probably having stolen that fifty-dollar bill he acquired in 1856. At least Searle offers a basis for serious debate about *Joan of Arc* in place of pained condescension. Factual beyond cavil is Coleman O. Parsons's "Mark Twain: Traveler in South Africa" (*MissQ* 29:3–41), which traces the daily movements of Clemens, his wife, and daughter Clara during ten weeks in 1896. He is a veteran tracker of Clemens, dependable and useful here for *Following the Equator.*

Interest keeps rising in the final works, particularly the rough-hewn fragments. James D. Wilson, " 'The Monumental Sarcasm of the Ages': Science and Pseudoscience in the Thought of Mark Twain" (SAB 40[1975]:72–82), makes good use of "The Secret History of Eddypus" for Clemens's hardening rejection of science and even the glories of technology, though we incline nowadays to graph his lowest moods after 1895 (and then extrapolate backward into his brighter years). Similarly, after Nancy Pogel, in "Mark Twain and the Clock" (MidAmerica 3:123–34), identifies a recurring detail or motif, she is quick to transmute his irritation with faulty timepieces into a matured "distrust of belief in a well ordered universe." In modest hope of adding insights for another fragment, Daryl E. Jones, "The Hornet Disaster: Twain's Adaptation in 'The Great Dark'" (ALR 9:243–48), plumbs the fact that in 1898 Clemens reread his scoop of 1866 about a nightmarish ordeal at sea. Jones kept mercifully aware that no such comparing of details can be erected into iron proof. With "Anatole France and Mark Twain's Satan" (AL 47:634–35) Alan Gribben—whose total number of articles for 1976 surely sets a record —still more judiciously goes no further than "similar" when singling out a passage in Le Crime de Sylvestre Bonnard on reality as imagined dream that precedes the crucial revelation in "No. 44, The Mysterious Stranger." All three versions of that tale are collated responsibly for ideas in Paul Delaney, "The Dissolving Self: The Narrators of Mark Twain's Mysterious Stranger Fragments" (JNT 6:51–65), which stresses the attitudes of the explicit narrator and their drift toward agreement with young Satan. Delaney also points up a choice between the elderly persona as a "thought" which imagines a life in our solid world and as a basically normal identity prone to bursts of solipsism. The "Mysterious Stranger" texts are repaying close study, are even compounding the interest.

Next to structuralism the most evident trend of literary studies in the past five years has been the explication of autobiography. In Educated Lives Thomas Cooley contrasts Mark Twain most often with Henry Adams and Howells. Pegging him as demoralized after his loss of faith in technology, Cooley decides that the Autobiography is an "antiform," a "failed story of education" that found no "sequence of identities connecting the remembered world" of boyhood with the present. Cooley is more certain than I about what constiutes the autobiography and when Clemens began it, but his coordinates lead to fresh perspectives such as its essential freedom from self-blame. What is needed—and is on the way—is a scholarly edition of the complete autobiography. More of the notebooks are also nearing print, and Fender's essay gives samples from vital unpublished letters. Though the pace is stiff now, Mark Twain scholarship and criticism should be waxing again.

Duke University

7. Henry James

William T. Stafford

The old saw that James was one who chewed more than he bit off has often struck me as a more apt description of his critics than of James himself—but perhaps never before quite so forcefully. The unparalleled amount of criticism described in these pages last year continues unabated—eight books devoted to Jamesian matters rather than twelve, but innumerably more articles. Much of the criticism, to be sure, is very good; but some of course is not. I have consequently had to pick and choose and *exclude* in ways not quite necessary before. I hope that the resulting rationale for what is included and excluded is apparent in what follows.

i. Honors, Letters, Life, Lists, Texts

At high noon on 17 June in the Poet's Corner at Westminster Abbey a memorial stone was unveiled and dedicated to Henry James, marked simply "New York 1843/London 1916." Tributes from England and France were respectively offered by Stephen Spender and Roger Asselineau with the major address, "Homage to Henry James," presented by Leon Edel. His gracious text, published the next day as "Henry James in the Abbey" (*TLS* 18 June:741), refers to James as a "Shakespeare of the novel" and recounts his various and extended ties to England whose honored recognition of those ties is said to reside in this final accolade of "benign articulate silence." Relevant to this memorial is "A Henry James Centenary" (*GaR* 30:34–52) wherein Charles R. Anderson presents his extended rationale for having successfully proposed that James be thus memorialized, seeing in his fiction from *A Passionate Pilgrim and Other Tales* of 1875 through *The American* of 1876 a kind of cultural independence paralleling the political one of a century earlier as the crucial steps leading to James's debut as an "international author."

Much less graceful, I fear, is the exchange between Christoph Lohmann and George Arms, on one side, and Leon Edel, on the other, in "Commentary" (*NCF* 31:244–51), wherein Lohmann and Arms detail a substantial number of inconsistencies, omissions, and inaccuracies between a selected number of holograph James letters and those same letters as printed in Volumes 1 and 2 of Edel's recent edition. Edel's reply takes issue with some of their contentions, admits human error about others, thanks Lohmann for having first privately pointed out his findings, but concludes by describing the publication of those findings at this late date "as a gratuitous act." Less crucial news about James's letters is in Franciszek Lyra's "The Letters of William James to Wincenty Lutoslaswki" (*YULG* 51:28–40), many of which have recently been acquired by the Yale Library and some of which are said to include some comments by William on Henry's fiction. Robert L. Gale's "An Unpublished Letter from Henry James to F. Marion Crawford" (*RLV* 42:179–82) is prefaced by a well-documented account of James's low opinion of Crawford's various potboilers as contrast to an ambigiously phrased letter of praise to Crawford.

Millicent Bell's "Jamesian Being" (*VQR* 52:115–32) is a much more intriguing biographical item—speculation on the possible effects an advocacy of "being" over "doing" had on various members of the James family—on Henry James, Sr., the mother, Rob, Wilky, and Alice, and, of course, on William and Henry. Each of their lives is briefly sketched in terms of the effects of this advocacy, with Henry finally described as having successfully merged being with doing through his solitary writing career.

Two book-length "lists" of Jamesian items deserve only the briefest attention. Elizabeth Morse Walsh Hunking's *The Picturesque English of Henry James: A Collection of Quotations* (Philadelphia: Dorrance and Co.) is nothing more than its subtitle declares, a random selection of quotations, most of them quite brief, from the random works of Henry James—his fiction, letters, essays, plays—with nothing more methodical or intelligible guiding the selection than what for Hunking *is* presumably "picturesque." Glenda Leeming's *Who's Who in Henry James* (New York: Taplinger), Leon Edel's brief Foreword on the importance of James's names notwithstanding, is both limited and redundant—limited in that its list of characters is restricted to the novels and five *nouvelles*, redundant in that Robert

Gales's *Plots and Characters in the Fiction of Henry James* (1965) covers the same ground, and a good deal more. Leeming's inclusion of unnamed characters, her listing two dogs and Maisie's doll, and her somewhat fuller descriptions of each character, often in James's own words, hardly justify another compilation of this particular sort.

Truly momentous, in contrast, is the fascinating facsimile, *Henry James* The American: *The Version of 1877 Revised in Autograph and Typescript for the New York Edition of 1907* (London: Scolar Press) and Rodney G. Dennis's brief introduction recounting its history. Although there are apparently "many variants" between the revisions here available and the text of the New York Edition—a result of still continued revision during the proof-correcting stage—what we do have available in this facsimile is by far the best example yet of literally "seeing" the revision process: the huge pasted-up sheets of the first edition with James's meticulous, expansive, audacious, balloon encircled insertions, mostly in autograph but with some type-written replacements, all on the page before one. Only with the original could one possibly feel any "closer" to the process. Also an important text is Alfred Habegger's edition of *The Bostonians* (Indianapolis: Bobbs-Merrill) with its fine introduction touching upon sources, composition, publishing history, Boston at the time, and the woman's movement. There is also a textual note, James's correspondence on the novel, and an annotated bibliography.

For three brief additional bibliographical or biographical notes I refer interested readers to the names D. Seed, Charlotte Alexander, and Jill Colaco in the *MLA Bibliography*.

ii. Sources, Parallels, Influences

Two critics dominate source studies this year. As has been the case during the past few years, the most expansive, eclectic, and prolific of these is the amazing Adeline R. Tintner, who had in print during 1976 eight different source studies exclusive of several reviews of Jamesian items. Her high point this year for me is her "Landmarks of 'The Terrible Town': The New York Scene in Henry James' Last Stories" (*Prospects* 2:399–435), a knowledgeable demonstration of how the impact of the city is reflected in such late stories as "The Jolly Corner," "Julia Bride," "Crappy Cornelia," "A Round of Visits," even the chapter "The Married Son" that James wrote for that composite novel *The Whole Family*—how its skyscrapers, museums, Central Park, and hotels function as iconographic metaphors and symbols in this fiction. Drastically more limited but equally fascinating in its information is her "Henry James at the Movies: Cinematograph and Photograph in 'Crappy Cornelia'" (*MarkhamR* 6:1–8), which contends that James's viewing of two early primitive movies (one of the Corbett/Fitzimmons championship prizefight in 1898, the other a Biograph short purportedly of the Boer War in 1900) provided him with some fresh and startling cinematographic imagery that is invidiously contrasted to the photographic imagery in this tale. Her " 'High Melancholy and Sweet': James and the Arcadian Tradition" (*CLQ* 12:109–21) traces both the literary and pictorial channels through which the Arcadian tradition is said to work in James's fiction—most completely, it is maintained, in *The Ambassadors*, but also in various ways in such earlier works as "The Europeans," *The Portrait*, and *The Sacred Fount* and in the later *The Wings of the Dove*. And her *"The Golden Bowl* and Waddesdon Manor" (*Apollo* Aug.: 106–13) finds in James's demonstrated familiarity with Baron Ferdinand de Rothchild's estate and its great 18th-century art collection many explanations for various metaphors in James's late novel—especially one complex figure of speech having to do with snuff boxes and pug dogs. She also sees some suggestive parallels between the Baron and Adam Verver and reproduces here one of James's rare attempts at verse which the novelist had playfully recorded in the Baron's guest-book. Of Tintners's remaining four pieces, all relatively brief notes, I will mention here only "Isabel's Carriage Image and Emma's Day Dream" (*MFS* 22:227–31), for its perceptive insight into James's possible use of Emma Bovary in some aspects of his concept of Isabel Archer.

The other source critic worthy of special attention is Robert Emmet Long. His "Henry James's Apprenticeship—The Hawthorne Aspect" (*AL* 48:194–216) is a tale-by-tale analysis of purportedly direct borrowings and transformation from Hawthorne in Jamesian tales beginning with "The Story of a Year" of 1865 through "Benvolio" of 1875 that is especially impressive with the early international tales. His subsequent "James's *Roderick Hudson*: The End of the Apprenticeship—Hawthorne and Turgenev" (*AL* 48:312–26) traces the ways the novel is both a tribute and a farewell, especially to the Hawthorne of *The Marble Faun*. Long is equally good here with

Turgenev, who is said to have begun replacing Hawthorne as an influence in *Roderick Hudson* but who was not to become prominently a model until *The American* and subsequent fiction of the next decade. Finally, Long's "Transformation: *The Blithedale Romance* to Howells and James" (*AL* 47:552–71) emphasizes how the long-recognized ties between Hawthorne's novel and *The Bostonians* is more significantly a transformation when viewed through James's use of Howells's *The Undiscovered Country* as a kind of stepping-stone "romance-novel" necessary to James's "fully achieved novel of manners."

Two provocative essays that link series of short fiction to events in James's own life oddly touch, at least in part, on the same event—James's relation with Constance Fenimore Woolson. "The poor sensitive gentleman" and "an equally sensitive but more aware woman" that Rayburn S. Moore locates in "The Beast in the Jungle," "The Jolly Corner," and "The Bench of Desolation" (in his "The Strange Irregular Rhythm of Life: James's Late Tales and Constance Woolson [*SAQ* 41,iv:86–93]) are seen as providing a spectrum of that relationship, with the problem set forth in the first tale, its "ideal solution" in the second, and a somewhat hyperbolic view of the poor gentleman's need in the last. Ellen Tremper, in her "Henry James's Altering Ego: An Examination of His Psychological Double in Three Tales" (*TQ* 19,iii:59–75), finds in "The Aspern Papers," "The Beast in the Jungle," and "The Jolly Corner" parallels to James's successive "love" relations with Ms. Woolson, Hendrik Anderson, and Jocelyn Persse. Both contentions result in neatly linked readings of the tales, but the speculative nature of the rooting of those readings in events in James's own life adds, for me at any rate, nothing very meaningful about the tales or the life.

The remaining source study of note, Sara Stambaugh's "The Aesthetic Movement and *The Portrait of a Lady*" (*NCF* 30:495–510) is thoughtful enough in seeing not only the movement generally but Oscar Wilde and his mother, Lady Wilde, in particular back of some aspects of James's conception of Osmond and his sister Countess Gemini.

The most important parallel study of the year, especially of James and other American writers, is John Carlos Rowe's difficult *Henry Adams and Henry James: The Emergence of a Modern Consciousness* (Ithaca, N.Y.: Cornell Univ. Press). But because its title indicates adequately enough its subject, to some extent even its thrust, I will do no more here than refer readers to my longish review of it in *JEGP* 76[1977].

Remaining studies of James and other Americans are a mixed bag. Better than most is Leland S. Person's "Aesthetic Headaches and European Women in *The Marble Faun* and *The American*" (*SAF* 4: 65–79) wherein European women are seen as a kind of generic incarnation of "the American's relationship to European culture and to the problems inherent in the creation of art." The resultant reading of Newman's engaged and disengaged relationship to Claire de Cintré is one of the most suggestive which I have seen in a long time. But somewhat strained is Elsa Nettles's " 'A Frugal Splendour,' Thoreau and James and the Principles of Economy (*CLQ* 12:5–13) in its attempt to link these two writers through their concepts of consciousness, "of art as the expression of the character and temperament of the creator," of their mutual distrust of others as a basis for judgment. Perhaps somewhat better is W. R. Macnaughton's "Maisie's Grace under Pressure: Some Thoughts on James and Hemingway" (*MFS* 22:153–64), a comparative analysis of *What Maisie Knew* and *The Sun Also Rises* as radically different novels that nonetheless render positive values flourishing in valueless, corrupt worlds. More is expected than forthcoming in Marcia Jacobson's "Popular Fiction and Henry James's Unpopular *Bostonians*" (*MP* 73:264–75), a study of James's allegedly cold and clinical view of the effects of the Civil War and of the battle of the sexes as contrasted to sentimental views of the subject in the popular fiction of the day. And Thelma J. Shinn's "The Art of a Verse Novelist: Approaching Robinson's Late Narratives through James's *The Art of the Novel*" (*CLQ* 12:91–100) is much, much too sweeping in its locating in the prefaces of the novelist and the narratives of the poet shared themes and mutual concepts of psychological realities, romance and realism, characterization, and dramatic structure. Finally, William B. Stone's "Idiolect and Ideology: Some Stylistic Aspects of Norris, James, and DuBois" (*Style* 10:405–25) places *The Ambassadors* in a context with *The Pit* and *The Souls of Black Folk* by way of discussing a Jamesian style that is described as a "shielding process" for a central concern with money, that style also giving only an "illusion of Freedom" to what in fact is determined.

Peter Brooks's *The Melodramatic Imagination: Balzac, Henry*

James, Melodrama, and The Mode of Excess (New Haven, Conn.: Yale Univ. Press), a contextual study of the same high quality as Rowe's book on Adams and James, is probably more centrally concerned with what the fiction of James and Balzac can contribute to his study of melodrama than what it can do for our understanding of that fiction. Even so, its contribution to one's understanding of James is considerable, for Brooks's is a convincing demonstration of how at least one "locus" of James's (and Balzac's) "true drama" is indeed the " 'moral occult,' " that "domain of spiritual forces and imperatives that is not clearly visible within reality, but which they believe to be operative there, and which demands to be uncovered, registered, articulated." Their consequent "recourse to the demonstrative, heightened representations of melodrama" thus becomes their mode. This is not the place to treat Brooks's intricate thesis on the role of the melodramatic imagination in both high and low examples of contemporary culture. But it is the place to note that his long chapter on James (pp. 153–97) is a remarkably persuasive exhibition of varied Jamesian uses of the melodramatic mode as it is transformed into establishing "moral integers," preserving "romantic" values, becoming the very form of surfaces whose significances are all "behind." Resulting readings of *The American, The Awkward Age,* and, most importantly, *The Wings of the Dove* are good indeed; for Brooks's book is clearly the most important overall demonstration of this aspect of James's fiction since the earlier studies of Jacques Barzun and Leo Levy whose works Brooks knowledgeably cites—and here significantly extends.

Of three remaining parallel studies worthy of mention, the most provocative is Jean Ashton's "Reflecting Consciousness: Three Approaches to Henry James" (*LFQ* 4:230–39), a good analysis of how Peter Bogdanovich's "irreverent" film adaptation of *Daisy Miller* and Claude Chabrol's "reverent" adaptation of "The Bench of Desolation" are successively less Jamesian in any good sense than Jacques Rivette's *Céline et Julie vont en bateau* and its "oblique" use of *The Other House.* Much less persuasive is Benjamin Beit-Hallahmi's "*The Turn of the Screw* and *The Exorcist*: Demoniacal Possession and Childhood Purity" (*AI* 33:296–303) in its description of the film, whatever the considerable qualifications, as "a modern version" of the tale. But Djelal Kadir's "Another Sense of the Past: Henry James's *The Aspern Papers* and Carlos Fuentes' *Aura*" (*RLC* 4:448–54) is a neat little contrastive study of attitudes toward time and consequently of the accessible past in these two remarkably similar stories by two remarkably dissimilar authors.

The only influence study of consequence is Sara deSaussure Davis's "Two Portraits of a Lady: Henry James and T. S. Eliot" (*ArQ* 32:367–80), a well researched case for enriching one's understanding of the poem through recognizing how much its technique, substance, and attitude owe to James's novel and to his fictional achievements in general.

iii. Criticism: General

Squarely atop the year's best general studies is Ruth Bernard Yeazell's superb *Language and Knowledge in the Late Novels of Henry James* (Chicago: Univ. of Chicago Press). It establishes in five beautifully succinct chapters the ways the language of the last three novels, through its syntax, its metaphors, its dialogue, creates characters in strange, disquieting worlds, characters who themselves create worlds in constant conflict with intrusive oppressive fact from which the creative had been established to avoid and yet finally, more inclusively, comes to enclose. The book is rich throughout, but I was especially intrigued with the analysis of some of the often bizarre metaphors of the late work—Maggie as a wet spaniel, for example, or the famous pagoda image of *The Golden Bowl*—metaphors whose contrary thrusts become in unexpected yet apposite ways a new kind of discovering. Her use of the unfinished *The Ivory Tower* as a kind of gloss on *The Golden Bowl* is also a fresh view. And the part of her chapter on "Talking in James" that appeared in *PMLA* (91:66–77), aside from its intrinsic virtues in its attention to such matters as the need "of creating one's own fact" or "of choosing finally to act on one's own fictions," was otherwise sufficiently provocative to elicit from Daniel J. Schneider, in the Forum section of *PMLA* (91:922–24), some reservations about Yeazell's describing the final morality of *The Golden Bowl* as "irreducibly ambiguous." His contrary contention that a study of image patterns confirms a view of Maggie's "spiritual aspiration" is more than amply refuted, it seems to me, by Ms. Yeazell's reply (in the same issue). But whatever one's view of this particularity, all good Jamesians should read Yeazell's book.

The remaining book-length study of the year, Manfred Mackenzie's difficult *Communities of Honor and Love in Henry James* (Cambridge, Mass.: Harvard Univ. Press), I can describe only as an exercise in structuralist psychology, centrally concerned, as Mackenzie puts it, with setting forth "a series of formulas that will both cope with the many aspects of James's work and amount to a coherent theory of his psychology." Neither aim, it seems to me, is satisfactorily achieved. In fact, the resulting formularizing strikes me generally as being much more centrally concerned with the viability of its own considerable intricacies than with its ostensible subject. To be sure, the patterning itself is very useful with Jamesian ambivalence, with repeated sets of unacceptable alternatives, with quests for unrealized "communities" (both inside and outside the international schemes), with techniques of compensatory "doubles," with secrets and conspiracy, with exposure and shame—all "to acquire or simply to recover identity." But even achieved identity and honor become "ambiguous," become ultimately dehumanizing. Hence, a "spiritual value" named love is said to emerge, most unequivocally in the post-dramatic years, a value "that is above identity and honor," one that in its "saintly" manifestations is said to have nothing above it. These formulas have their undeniable uses—as in the early story "Adina" as a "paradigm situation," or in *The Princess Casamassima* if it "were a Jamesian norm," or even the doubling formula in such disparate works as *Roderick Hudson* and "The Lesson of the Master." But there are defects in the virtues, most glaringly for me, perhaps, in the final chapter on *The Golden Bowl*, said to be "James's greatest novel," but then also described as being so unquestionably positive in its celebration of love and so schematically indifferent to that love's cost that the novel as finally revealed I could not help describing, from an admittedly different perspective, as both didactic and sentimental. Mackenzie is a subtle and knowledgeable critic. I simply wish for a schema of a more inclusive kind.

Of the handful of articles of general criticism that appeared during the year, at least four strike me as exceedingly good and deserving of much more attention than I can afford here. On top of that group is James E. Miller's "Henry James in Reality" (*CritI* 2:585–604), a brilliant, eloquent case for the variety of ways James's theories are open to infinite kinds of good fiction. Baruch Hochman's "The Jamesian Situation: World as Spectacle" (*UDQ* 11:48–66) is noteworthy not only for its carefully qualified sweep of the Jamesian

canon but for the way it sees character in James's best fiction crystallized when integrity is threatened and, indeed, for the ways it also
sees *threatening* characters restrictively but effectively revealed.
Mark L. Krupnick's "Playing with the Silence: Henry James's Poetics
of Loss" (*ForumH* 13,iii:37–42) is a closely argued and provocative
study contending that James's late fiction is characteristically organized around, structured, and given texture and shape by void,
silence, absences, spaces, and losses. Branching out into other works
from "The Altar of the Dead," it utimately confronts such basic conflicts as those between the "artistic" value of rendered losses and
those of "real" presences. Finally, attention should be called to the
availability of Leo Bersani's "The Jamesian Lie" (in his *A Future for
Astyanax: Character and Desire in Literature* [Boston: Little, Brown],
pp. 128–55), although my high views of its worth are adequately
spelled out in *ALS* 1969:101, where I reviewed its appearance in article form.

Remaining general studies are not so impressive. David Mogen's
"Agonies of Innocence: the Governess and Maggie Verver" (*ALR*
9:231–42) pairs these two Jamesian women and the contrasting responses they have evoked as pointed examples of modern "distaste"
for Victorianism, "especially the sentimental idealization of womanhood so central to the culture." George Sebouhian's "Henry James's
Transcendental Imagination" (*EIL* 3:214–26) makes perhaps as good
a case as can be made for seeing James as Emersonian, expressly so,
he contends, in James's autobiographical volumes, *The American
Scene*, and other nonfictional works, but also in the fiction. "Henry
James's 'Indispensable Centre': The Search for Compositional Unity"
(*EIL* 3:97–104) is said by Charles W. Mayer to have been found,
among the novels, only in *The Portrait, The Spoils*, and *Maisie*, for
only in those works did he achieve "a reflecting consciousness that is
a fused center of [both] command and interest" that contributed so
much to the late international fiction. Finally, James is throughout
both an example and a subject in Mary Doyle Springer's *Forms of
the Modern Novella* (Chicago: Univ. of Chicago Press, 1975). Several of James's tales aid her in categorizing various forms of the genre,
but she is at her best with the relationship of pathos to irony in
"Daisy Miller," especially as she relates it to *Washington Square* and
"The Beast in the Jungle."

iv. Criticism: Individual Tales

The year's few instances of individual studies of individual tales are marked by polarities of method, purpose, and quality. For example, Cathy N. Davidson, in her "'Circumsexualocution' in Henry James's *Daisy Miller*" (*ArQ* 32:353–66), goes far too far, it seems to me, in her citations of all kinds of sexual play in the allusions, names, and purported puns of the tales, although one would hardly argue that "sex" indeed "is perpetually on the minds of all the major characters in the story."

Three studies of "The Aspern Papers," on the other hand, are all quite good. Daniel J. Schneider's "The Unreliable Narrator: James's 'The Aspern Papers' and the Reading of Fiction" (*SSF* 13:43–49) is a compelling refutation of Wayne C. Booth's reading of the tale in *The Rhetoric of Fiction* by way of seeing Juliana as much an acquisitive and selfish predator as is the narrator. John W. Crowley, in contrast, in his "The Wiles of a 'Witless' Woman: Tina in 'The Aspern Papers'" (*ESQ* 22:159–68) pairs the niece with the narrator as one eager to exploit—even as he pairs them at the end as mutually foiled. But for Rosemary F. Franklin, in her "Military Metaphors and the Organic Structure of Henry James's 'The Aspern Papers'" (*ArQ* 32:327–40), the issue of interest is the tale's coherent structure via its display of military images and dramatic unities.

Mary E. Rucker's rather intricate "James's 'The Pupil': The Question of Moral Ambiguity" (*ArQ* 32:301–15) points to the enriched tensions resulting from the narrator's discreet point of view in its conflicts with the "moral action" of the characters. Edward Stone's more important "Edition Architecture and 'The Turn of the Screw'" (*SSF* 13:9–16) persuasively contends that mere length, rather than theme or symmetry of contents, was James's inadvertent but crucial consideration in placing the ghost story where he did in the New York Edition. Both James W. Gargano's "James's Stories in 'The Story in It'" (*NMAL* 1:item 2) and William McMurray's "Reality in Henry James's 'The Birthplace'" (*Expl* 35:10–11) are brief explications, the first by way of how characterization both embodies and transcends the literary stereotypes "talked" about in the story, the other by offering still another rationale for Gedge's elaborate lies. And in William Nance's "'The Beast in the Jungle': Two Versions of Oedipus"

(*SSF* 8:433–40) both "myth" and "complex" are utilized to describe the conflict between the "human potential" Marcher misses and the "fixed," "reductive" cypher he in fact is.

v. Criticism: Individual Novels

Unlike studies of individual tales, this year's attention to individual novels is almost overwhelming, in number and for the most part in quality. Although brief, James W. Gargano's "*Washington Square*: A Study in the Growth of an Inner Self" (*SSF* 13:355–62) is persuasive enough in its account of the details of Catherine's growth under the pressure of her varied ordeals. And Sallie J. Hall's "Henry James and the Bluestockings: Satire and Morality in *The Bostonians*," in *Aeolian Harps*, pp. 207–25, makes the very good point that it is "cultural stereotyping" of *both* sexes that is the target of James's satiric thrust in the novel.

Predictable studies of *The Portrait* continue to work over that already much worked-over novel. Nina Baym's "Revision and Thematic Change in *The Portrait of a Lady* (*MFS* 22:183–200) is a spirited defense of the early version in terms of the "woman question" by way of its there calling into question the then-current pallatives of love and marriage—a thrust not nearly so important in the internalized version of the revision. Martha Collins's "The Narrator, the Satellites, and Isabel Archer: Point of View in *The Portrait of a Lady*" (*SNNTS* 8:142–57) works out in exceptionally fine detail the developing relationships of the novel's various perspectives. Point of view in a way is also the point of William J. Krier's "The 'Latent Extravagance' of *The Portrait of a Lady*" (*Mosaic* 9,iii:57–65), in this case James's said-to-be happy decision not to go into Isabel's consciousness at the end of the novel and thus allow her, as it were, to begin "to become her own author."

Perhaps not so predictable is the plethora of studies, at least six, on *The Princess*, only three of which I will mention here. The best in my view is Paul J. Dolan's "James: The Aesthetics of Politics," in his *Of War and War's Alarms* (New York: Free Press), pp. 70–95, because of the range of subjects he sees the novel encompassing, from "the relationship of the aesthetic to the economic, political, and moral aspects of human experience" to the ways "the sexual, the domestic, the private worlds of Hyacinth" are seen reflecting those more encompassing issues. G. K. Girling's "On Editing a Paragraph of *The Princess Casamassima* (*Lang&S* 8[1975]:243–63) *may* also be important, at least to the student of stylistics; for it is a highly technical, copiously graphed and tabled illustration of stylistic elements involved in the changes James made in a single paragraph (the first paragraph of chapter 15) from manuscript holograph through serial and subsequent book-publication stages. Finally, I should perhaps mention James Walton's "A Mechanic's Tragedy: Reality in *The Princess Casamassima* (*ESColl* ser. 1,no. viii,20 pp.)—a strange new form of publication: you buy individual articles separately by special order. I am not at all sure I understand its lengthy and obscure reading of the novel as a sort of personal, highly parodied allegory of the conflicts among the aesthetic consciousness, the real world, and the processes that connect or disconnect the two.

Two studies of Maisie view her as a kind of artist. Carren Osna Kaston's "Houses of Fiction in 'What Maisie Knew'" (*Criticism* 18: 27–42) equates her "growing up" with "an act of authorship"; having successfully gone beyond the "fictions" her parents, stepparents, even Mrs. Wix have set up for her, she is now ready "for fictions of her own." Rather neat. William A. Nance's "*What Maisie Knew*: The Myth of the Artist" (*SNNTS* 8:88–102) sees the travels to, in, and from France as a kind of "monomythic plot of departure, initiation, and return" which is significantly controlled to define both artistic and personal maturity.

Two studies of *The Sacred Fount* are similarly obsessed with the processes of fiction as the subject of fiction. The more impressive of the two is William F. Hall's "The Meaning of *The Sacred Fount*: 'Its own little law of composition'" (*MLQ* 37:168–78). Although seeing as many have that the narrator "has made the general error of confusing what he has made with the reality," Hall is more attentive than most to such elements as the symbol of the fount itself, the allusions to Egeria, and the uses of some techniques of the *commedia dell'arte*. Joanne Feit Diehl's "'One Life within Us Abroad': The Subverted Realist in *The Sacred Fount*" (*JNT* 6:92–100) is notable only in its attempt to draw some distinctions between the narrator who remembers and writes the book and the remembered narrator in the process of testing his hypothesis.

Of the year's three studies of *The Ambassadors* only in Judith Wilt's "A Right Issue from a Tight Place: Henry James and Maria

Gostrey" (*JNT* 6:77–91) is much wit at play. It engagingly ties
Strether's and Maria's final confrontation to some distinctions in the
Preface as a kind of "appendix" to reveal some suggestive, dramatical-
ly intense implications about how the "artist" might be said to move
"irresistibly toward Lambert Strether" while the "story heads straight
for Maria Gostrey." But Allen F. Stein's "Lambert Strether's Cir-
cuitous Journey: Motifs of Internalized Quest and Circularity in *The
Ambassadors*" (*ESQ* 22:245–53) and T. B. Tomlinson's "Henry
James: *The Ambassadors*" (in his *The English Middle-Class Novel*
[New York: Barnes and Noble], pp. 148–65) are also both good.
Stein sees a special kind of "pathos, humor, and quiet courage" implicit in the novel when its "seemingly banal and studiously 'realistic' "
subject is read under a rubric of "the internalized quest romance."
Tomlinson's fresh emphasis is on the novel's simplicity, candor, and
forthrightness, especially in its characterization of Americans; for the
novel as a whole is said to be "concerned at least as much with the
shock of discovering unbridgeable gulfs between Europe and America as with anything the two may have in common."

   Sister Stephanie Vincec's " 'Poor Flopping *Wings*': The Making of
Henry James's *The Wings of the Dove*" (*HLB* 24:60–93) is extremely
important for the new material it reveals about the compositional
and publication history of the novel, in spite of an unfortunate conclusion that the more ignorant one is of "the circumstance of its composition, the more subjective will be one's critical conclusions."

   Possibly the most sensitive, yet contentious, essay on James's last
finished novel, Mark L. Krupnick's "*The Golden Bowl*: Henry James's
Novel about Nothing" (*ES* 57:533–40), sees the affirmed values of
the work so much "an idealization of . . . [James's] own imagination"
that his attempts to free the novel from the "intrusiveness of the
omniscient narrator" ironically eventuate into reinstating "authorial
dominance to a greater degree than ever." Donald D. Kummings'
"The Issue of Morality in James's *The Golden Bowl*" (*ArQ* 32:381–
91) is a somewhat abstract case for a concept of morality defined as a
true appreciation of our own "intuitions and impulses" as the necessary requisite to a desired concept of "otherness." And Bryan Red-
dick's "The Control of Distance in *The Golden Bowl*," (*MBL* 1:46–
55), although brief, is a fine, lucid analysis of the variety of ways the
language and techniques of the novel simultaneously put one in *and*
take one out of the story.

Finally, Alan W. Bellringer, in "*The Ivory Tower*: The Cessation of Concern" (*JAmS* 10:241–55), persuasively locates the reason for James's failure to finish the novel in the incompatibility of his already-worked-out role for Gray Fiedler, "its non-combatant hero, the 'happy Hamlet of the Newport lawns,'" to James's newly acquired consciousness of the world as it was at the outbreak of World War I.

Purdue University

8. Pound and Eliot

Stuart Y. McDougal

i. Pound

a. **Textual and Bibliographical.** With the publication of *Collected Early Poems of Ezra Pound*, edited by Michael King with an introduction by Louis L. Martz (New York: New Directions), Pound's youthful work is at last available in an accurate edition, with textual variants and bibliographical notes. Included are the contents of six early volumes, *A Lume Spento* (1908), *A Quinzaine for This Yule* (1908), *Personae* (1909), *Exultations* (1909), *Canzoni* (1911), and *Ripostes* (1912). Over fifty other poems are gathered from notebooks and periodicals. Pound later disavowed much of this verse, but it is invaluable in helping us to chronicle his development as a poet. The volume is too expensive for students, but all libraries should own copies. Hopefully, New Directions will now issue *Personae* (1926) in paperback.

b. **Biographical.** The most ambitious biographical work is C. David Heymann's *Ezra Pound, The Last Rower: A Political Profile* (New York: Viking Press). Heymann is the first scholar to have combed the F.B.I. files on Pound, now available due to the Freedom of Information Act, and he has unearthed material of considerable interest and importance. Rather than emphasize the "political profile" of Pound, Heymann has felt compelled to provide a context for his material. So, relying mainly on the earlier biographies of Charles Norman and Noel Stock, Heymann has written his own full-scale biography. He would have been better served by focusing exclusively on Pound's later years, where his materials are germane to the course of Pound's life. Heymann might also have avoided making literary judgments, where he is often on weak ground, as when he states that *Mauberley* "is almost certainly the high point of Pound's entire literary career." Such judgments mar a very useful work. Included in the appendixes are Pound's letters to Benito Mussolini, which Heymann had earlier published in *Encounter* (46,v:35–41).

Thirteen of "Ezra Pound's Letters to William Butler Yeats" have been collected by C. F. Terrell (*Antaeus* 21/22:34–49). Written between 1914 and 1958 (the last four to Mrs. Yeats ["Jarge"]), these letters deal both with personal and professional matters. Pound's later political problems are foreshadowed when he writes Yeats from France in 1924 requesting legal documents which would enable the Pounds to visit Ireland. Pound asks for "a real Irish Passport" noting that "an american passport in Europe is like a seven years itch in Bagdad."

Pound's early years are documented in detail in *Ezra Pound's Pennsylvania*, by Noel Stock (Toledo: Friends of the Univ. of Toledo Libraries). As Stock acknowledges on the title page, the materials were "compiled for the most part from Mr. Carl Gatter's researches into original sources and documents." Mr. Gatter, an amateur historian residing in Pound's old home in Wyncote, Pennsylvania, has collected a number of fascinating photographs, newspaper clippings, and local facts which help recreate the milieu of Pound's youth. The book is ponderously written and not sufficiently selective in its choice of materials, but it does illustrate what Pound meant when he spoke of his youth as a "surburban life."

Two shorter and more specialized studies of the same period also appeared. In "Caviar and Bread: Ezra Pound and William Carlos Williams" (*JML* 5:383–406) Geoffrey H. Movius examines the years from 1902, when Pound met Williams at the University of Pennsylvania, until 1914, when Williams published "The Wanderer" in the *Egoist*. Movius clarifies the growing estrangement between the poet who went abroad and the one who stayed at home, but his article would have been improved by a closer examination of their literary divergences as well. A more illuminating study along the same lines is B. J. Sokol's "What Went Wrong Between Frost and Pound" (*NEQ* 49:521–41). Sokol chronicles Frost's meeting with Pound in 1913 and elaborates upon the situation of each at the time. He summarizes Pound's review of *A Boy's Will* (*Poetry*, May 1913), suggesting that the review had a political side to it ("Frost's talent had been criminally scorned by editors until Frost at last escaped from the American cultural desert"), as well as an aesthetic side ("Frost was a back-woods, even a barnyard poet, to be praised mainly for simplicity and directness"). Pound was delighted to have published the first American review of Frost, and attempted to bring Frost within his orbit of influence. But Frost was displeased with the review, and strove to remain independent of Pound.

Robert W. Corrigan considers the war and postwar period of Pound's life in "Literature and Politics: The Case of Ezra Pound Reconsidered" (*Prospects* 2:463–82). Corrigan stresses Pound's political problems, noting that "there is little need for yet another intricate route through that much surveyed ideomatic jungle he called his *Cantos.*" But in fact, this is precisely what we do need. Corrigan adds little that is new to the political discussion, especially in view of Haymann's more exhaustive treatment of the subject, and his study suffers from inaccuracies of fact (Pound arrived in London in 1908, not 1909 as in paragraph one) and interpretation ("having exhausted Kensington's supply of literary sparring partners, Pound moved on to Paris").

c. Criticism: Books. Donald Davie has distilled his perceptions of Pound's life and work in a concise and luminous study for the Modern Masters series (*Ezra Pound,* New York: Penguin). Davie avoids the comprehensiveness of a study like Spender's of Eliot (reviewed below), and instead provides new approaches to Pound's work. His two suggestive chapters on the *Cantos* are an excellent point of departure for the new reader and will be of considerable interest to the seasoned reader as well. Davie argues that the *Cantos* must be read in large sections, in order to appreciate the rhythms of the work, even at the expense of the comprehension of details. And in "Ideas in the *Cantos*" Davie follows Allen Upward in defining an idea as an "outthrow . . . the imagination of a thing not yet there" rather than as a fixed opinion. Davie's book is sure to stimulate debate and discussion, and is strongly recommended.

In *The Genesis of Pound's Cantos* (Princeton, N.J.: Princeton Univ. Press), Ronald Bush has written an excellent study of Pound's early cantos which clarifies the nature of the *Cantos* as a whole. Bush focuses primarily on the years between 1915, when Pound completed the first three cantos, and 1925, when *A Draft of XVI. Cantos* was published. He gives us a good picture of the intellectual and cultural milieu of London and examines with considerable skill the varied influences on Pound at this time, especially Wyndham Lewis, whose "radicals in design" form a model for the early cantos, but also Allen Upward, Remy de Gourmont, Henri Gaudier-Brzeska, T. S. Eliot, Henry James, Flaubert, and Laforgue. The pages on Allen Upward, whose importance Davie also stresses, should help restimulate interest in this nearly forgotten figure. This book illuminates an important period in the history of modernism.

d. Criticism: Articles. Because of the ever-increasing size of ALS, specialized journals will no longer receive the detailed treatment they have been accorded in the past. This is unfortunate, because most of the criticism of Ezra Pound now appears in the pages of Paideuma. No university library should be without this beautifully produced journal, which is now in its fifth year of publication.

Although Paideuma dominates the field of Pound scholarship, several important articles appeared elsewhere. "Ezra Pound's Literary Criticism" (DQ 11,i:1–20), René Wellek's chapter on Pound from the fifth volume of his forthcoming History of Modern Criticism, is a rather severe assessment of the writer Wellek finds to have "a totally unphilosophical and untheoretical mind." Wellek surveys Pound's literary opinions and outlines his "concept of criticism." He notes that Pound "broke resolutely with the rhetorical tradition and defined a new taste." "There was genuine merit in Pound's fight against English provincialism," Wellek states, and "great merit in Pound's generous support of new writing." He concludes with a highly qualified statement: "If one of the functions of criticism is the discovery of new talent, a prediction of the new course of literature, then Pound was an important critic in his time."

Two studies of Pound's translations appeared this year. In "Ezra Pound as Translator of Italian Poetry" (SA 19–20:201–36) Glauco Cambon offers a very perceptive analysis of Pound's translations from Italian, and, in particular, his versions of Cavalcanti which Cambon views "as a milestone in his creative itinerary, a mark by and from which to assess his overall achievement." Cambon highlights Pound's accomplishment by comparing it with the translations from Italian of Robert Lowell and Joseph Auslander, concluding that "Pound's versatility as a translator, who can range from the archaic depths of language to the freshest surfaces, is the versatility of a master poet."

Michael Alexander's study of "Ezra Pound's 'Seafarer'" (*Agenda*, 13,iv/14,i:110–26) examines Pound's work as translation, interpretation and adaptation. Although Alexander does not make as detailed a comparison with the original as S. J. Adams's study of a year ago (see *ALS 1975*, p. 135), it has the virtue of considering Pound's work within an historical context. Thus, Alexander observes that "Pound's editing ... if bold, was not unreasonable in view of scholarly attitudes standard in his day." For Alexander, Pound's poem is perhaps best considered "as a translation of the experience of reading a 'Seafarer.'"

The only discussion of the *Cantos* to appear outside of *Paideuma* is Leon Surette's informative study, "Ezra Pound's John Adams: An American Odyssey," (*Prospects* 2:483–95). Surette presents a selective reading of the Adams Cantos (62–71), focusing primarily upon Adams's two trips to Europe, since they "best elucidate Adams's colonial experience." Surette clearly demonstrates why Pound was attracted to Adams, and how Pound utilized Adam's experience.

ii. T. S. Eliot

a. **Biographical.** In "Quest for a Frenchman" (*SR* 84:465–75), George Watson provides answers to many of the questions about Eliot's relationship with Jean Verdenal. Verdenal was a medical student in Paris during the year Eliot spent there (1910–11) who shared Eliot's interests in literature and music, and helped introduce Eliot to the intellectual life of Paris. He did not die at sea, but on land, and therefore is an unlikely candidate for "Phlebas the Phoenician." Watson states that "the sexual explanation, in short, is reductive; and I object to it not only because it is unproven but because it is trivial."

b. **Criticism: Books.** Several very good books on Eliot appeared in 1976. In *T. S. Eliot* (New York: Penguin), Stephen Spender surveys Eliot's life and career as a writer. Spender writes with grace and verve, and his book is marked by penetrating insights. At times, notable in his too brief discussion of *Four Quartets*, Spender's study suffers from the limitations of the series. But his book is an outstanding introduction to Eliot, and will be of value to all students of the period.

Balachandra Rajan has produced a more specialized study of Eliot's poetry in *The Overwhelming Question* (Toronto: Univ. of Toronto Press). This is a very tightly argued consideration of the "remarkable power of wholeness" in Eliot's verse. Rajan expects from his readers a good knowledge of Eliot's poetry, for his analysis makes frequent use of paraphrase and allusion. He convincingly argues that Eliot's work "is not simply a series of individual excellences but a totality fully experienced and almost painfully lived through. The movement suggested here, the carefully built trajectory of understanding, the attainment of enlightenment under conditions that compel the quest to be re-enacted, the circle closed and yet forever open, all point to a design too subtle and too organic to be planned." Rajan's book provides suggestive readings of individual poems and clarifies the contours of Eliot's oeuvre.

A book with a more limited focus is Derek Traversi's *T. S. Eliot: The Longer Poems* (New York: Harcourt, Brace, Jovanovich). Traversi writes in a leisurely, appreciative manner about *The Waste Land*, *Ash Wednesday*, and *Four Quartets*. Unfortunately Traversi conveys the impression that Eliot's work has been colonized and brought under control, but in returning to the poetry one realizes that this is simply not so. However he presents a good overview of these poems.

Two additional books have chapters on Eliot. A. C. Partridge devotes three chapters to Eliot in *The Language of Modern Poetry: Yeats, Eliot, Auden* (London: Andre Deutsch). Partridge applies "the time-honoured canons of Renaissance rhetoric" to the work of these poets with somewhat mixed results. This book is largely an attempt at classification but his discussions of the lexical features of individual poems are good. It is finally more of a handbook to be dipped into than a work to be read through. George Bornstein provides a provocative and original chapter on Eliot in his *Transformations of Romanticism in Yeats, Eliot and Stevens* (Chicago: Univ. of Chicago Press). Bornstein's study of "The Anti-Romanticism of T. S. Eliot" is of major importance. In a close reading of Eliot's work, Bornstein demonstrates how Eliot's imagination repeatedly opposes the "anti-romantic thrust of his intellect." Bornstein concludes his chapter by noting that Eliot "was a romantic against the grain, illustrating in his own career the contention of his essay on Baudelaire that in a romantic age a poet could not be anti-romantic except in tendency."

c. **Criticism: Articles.** The *T. S. Eliot Review*, now in its third year of publication, has changed its format and seems to be including articles and reviews of greater length and substance. It is also inaugurating what promises to be a useful series of monographs, the first of which will be a supplement to Mildred Martin's *A Half-Century of Eliot Criticism* (1972).

One of the best of this year's articles is George T. Wright's "Eliot Written in a Country Churchyard; the *Elegy* and *Four Quartets*" (*ELH* 43:227–43). Wright shows that Gray's *Elegy* is a "possible base from which Eliot evolved *Four Quartets*," and he cites many verbal echoes and similarities in theme. It is an illuminating comparison which enhances our readings of both works.

Another perceptive study is Jeffrey Hart's "Frost and Eliot" (*SR* 84:425–47). Hart demonstrates that "each [poet] complements the other. They are related dialectically, and the achievement of each is enhanced by that relationship." Hart chronicles Frost's "private war with Eliot," and shows how much is gained by considering Frost's volume, *New Hampshire* (1923), as a response to *The Waste Land.* He compares the poetic strategies of each, concluding that "if the Frostian mode characteristically keeps things separate, insisting on their differences, the central impulse of Eliot's poetry is to achieve coherence by perceiving identities."

Two studies of Eliot's *Four Quartets* examine the poem in the context of Eliot's romantic forebears, but neither with the success of Bornstein's approach. Christopher Clausen, in "Tintern Abbey to Little Gidding: The Past Recaptured" (*SR* 84:405–24) argues that "much of the most important Victorian and twentieth century English poetry . . . is a poetry of loss—loss above all of the spontaneity, spiritual wholeness, and naive energies of childhood." Clausen sees Eliot's poem as "the achievement of the quest" beginning with Wordsworth and continuing through Tennyson, Arnold, Hopkins, Hardy and Housman. In "Four Quartets as Poetry of Place" (*DR* 56:526–41), J. M. Reibetanz analyzes the shift in Eliot's poetry from a generally literary and mythical use of landscape to the realistic use of landscape in *Four Quartets*. Her consideration of the function of landscape is perceptive, but her application of the greater Romantic lyric to *Four Quartets* is somewhat forced.

Four Quartets is the ultimate focus of Richard O. Hocks's study of " 'Novelty' in Polarity to 'The Most Admitted Truths': Tradition and the Individual Talent in S. T. Coleridge and T. S. Eliot" (*Evolution of Consciousness*, pp. 83–97). Hocks examines the concept of polarity in Coleridge and Eliot and concludes with a discussion of polarity in *Four Quartets*.

Two studies consider Eliot's use of time in his poetry. In "*The Waste Land* and *The Sound and the Fury*: To Apprehend the Human Process Moving in Time" (*SLJ* 9,i:13–21), Mary E. McGann compares the "respective visions of the two works . . . [as] variations on the theme of time and death as concurrent tensions in the human process." Certainly there are parallels here, but in McGann's hands they become rather forced. Vincent Miller considers in some detail Eliot's exploration of the meaning of time, relating it to his Christian beliefs, and concluding that "Eliot decided that time exists as an essential and unending purgation" ("Eliot's Submission to Time," *SR* 84:448–64). Miller also offers a perceptive comparison of Eliot and Pound in the context of their discussions of "beliefs" in the thirties.

In "Sketches and Preludes: T. S. Eliot's 'London Letters' in the *Dial*" (*PLL* 12:366–83), Nicholas Joost and Ann Risdon survey the eight "London Letters" published in 1921 and 1922 and show how this material is "representative of the major preoccupations—themes, images, revelations of hints that inspired and directed [Eliot] as poet and critic." The authors successfully demonstrate how themes and images from this material were incorporated into Eliot's poetry, especially *The Waste Land*.

J. I. Morse covers the same period of Eliot's life in "T. S. Eliot in 1921: Toward Dissociation of Sensibility" (*WHR* 30:31–40), but he explores the autobiographical basis of Eliot's ideas. He is particularly interested in Eliot's "professional oedipus complex" with Matthew Arnold, who was one of the "great precursors" of the idea of the dissociation of sensibility. Morse interprets this idea as personal therapy: "The theory of the dissociation of sensibility was born out of . . . the individual anguish of a poet whose life served language; its function was to permit the poet to transcend his anguish." His assertions are unconvincing.

Sara de Saussure Davis expands what could have profitably been a short note in her study of "Two Portraits of a Lady: Henry James and T. S. Eliot" (*ArQ* 32:367–80). She compares the similar "cultural heritages" and themes in the two works of James and Eliot. While the general parallels are valid, Davis overstates the case and minimizes other influences which are equally important.

In "'Our mad poetics to confute': The Personal Voice in T. S. Eliot's Early Poetry and Criticism" (*OL* 31:208–23), Ronald Schuchard argues that "at the same time he [Eliot] was developing a theory of depersonalization in the creative process, he was defining a method of repersonalization for the critical process." Schuchard examines this voice and concludes that "the personal voice in Eliot's Laforguean poems reveals the emotional center of his intellectual-spiritual life at that time more than any biographical material or study of influences."

The remaining articles are all notes, with the exception of the first, which is an inflated note. In "Some Further Correspondences Between the 'Proteus' Section of James Joyce's *Ulysses* and *The Waste Land*" (*ES* 57:227–38), P. Barry amplifies on an earlier article by Giorgio Melchiori by noting the extensive parallels of theme between the two works. Barry's study would be of greater interest if he had also examined the facsimile of *The Waste Land*, which was not available to Melchiori. James F. Loucks identifies a one-line allusion to Browning's "How It Strikes a Contemporary" in "Burbank with a Baedeker: Bleistein with a Cigar," which "gives added emphasis to the theme of poetic vision" ("A Second Browning Allusion in Eliot's 'Burbank' Poem," *N&Q* 221:18–19). In "T. S. Eliot's 'A Cooking Egg': An Echo from Thomas Hood" (*N&Q* 221:299–300), James F. Loucks attributes the "Sidney/kidney" rhyme in stanza three to the same rhyme in a stanza of "A Lament for the Decline of Chivalry." He notes that "the echo from Hood serves to remind us that, despite his critical devaluation of the Romantic and Victorian poets, Eliot was apparently well acquainted with even the minor ones." A. V. C. Schmidt cites Dante's treatment of Tiresias in *Inferno XX* as a fourth source for Eliot's Tiresias in "Eliot, Swinburne, and Dante: A Note on 'The Waste Land,' Lines 215–248" (*N&Q* 221:17–18). Schmidt stresses the importance of the context of the passage in Dante: "For Dante's Tiresias is in the fourth circle of Hell, the region where soothsayers are tormented in a grotesquely appropriate manner." Finally, Richard F. Patteson's "An Additional Source for 'The Waste Land'" (*N&Q* 221:300–301), cites Madison Cawein's poem "Waste Land" published in *Poetry* (January 1913) as a possible source for the title as well as the imagery of Eliot's poem.

University of Michigan

9. Faulkner

Panthea Reid Broughton

Faulkner criticism this year shows the same weaknesses as in the past: too much of it is uninformed and redundant; too much is devoted to major, too little to minor works. But 1976 was also a very exciting year in Faulkner studies; the year's work suggests how much insight biographical knowledge and new critical approaches can offer.

i. Bibliography, Editions, and Manuscripts

For the past several years *MissQ*, under the careful editorship of James B. Meriwether, has brought into print a number of previously unpublished works by William Faulkner. This year's publication, "The Priest" (*MissQ* 29:445–50), was written early in 1925 as one of the "Mirrors of Chartres Street" series, but apparently was rejected by the editors of the *Times-Picayune* Sunday magazine section because of its subject—the desires and uncertainties of a young man the night before he is to be ordained (though "confirmed" is the word Faulkner uses) a priest. This prose sketch reveals Faulkner as a young artist in technical control of his medium, but timid about taking liberties with it; he does not try to capture the flow of consciousness, nor does he attempt extravagant or even very interesting metaphoric language. For Faulkner scholars, the special interest of "The Priest" is thematic and psychological; the same choice between celibacy and sexuality that the priest's vocation forces upon him is also the choice that Faulkner, at least in his early works, imaginatively projected onto the artist's vocation. Paradoxically, despite assuming a dichotomy between the life of the flesh and that of the spirit, Faulkner in "The Priest" describes spiritual achievements, as elsewhere he describes artistic achievements, in sexual terms. Finally, then, to us, "The Priest" is less interesting as art than as an index of

Faulkner's mental set in 1925 regarding sex and, by implication, art.

The publication of Thomas L. McHaney's *William Faulkner: A Reference Guide* (Boston: G. K. Hall) is a significant event in Faulkner studies. John Bassett's *William Faulkner: An Annotated Checklist of Criticism* (see *ALS 1972*, p. 115) preceded McHaney's survey by four years, but Bassett's book is now largely superseded by McHaney's. McHaney does not annotate as many reviews as Bassett does, but instead he annotates an impressive amount of foreign criticism. His organization is chronological; it begins in 1924 and continues by year to list and annotate all significant writings on William Faulkner. This organization offers its own implicit narrative line and avoids the redundancy that clogs Bassett's book. It is not, however, so easy to use as Bassett's. McHaney attempts to compensate by indexing all entries by authors, titles, titles of Faulkner's works, names of people and places, and by subject, theme, and types of critical approach, and by a system of careful cross-referencing. McHaney's text is characterized by insight, by scrupulosity, by thoroughness and conscientiousness, and by objectivity. In short, *William Faulkner: A Reference Guide* is a first-rate critical tool.

ii. Biography

Conservative of his genius, William Faulkner did not squander it on casual writing, certainly not on many of the letters collected in *Selected Letters of William Faulkner*, ed. Joseph Blotner (New York: Random House). Most of these letters seem to have been written out of obligation or necessity. Obligations were personal in the early years and both public and personal later. But whether writing to mother, wife, mistress, or the USIS, Faulkner seems to have presented a guarded face. Writing to agents and publishers, he often came closer to dropping that public mask; out of necessity (once he did not even have $15 to pay the electricity bill) he had to acknowledge his financial straits and, at least implicitly, something of his emotional plight. Reading these letters, one realizes, despite the masks, how poor Faulkner really was at self-protection. Personally and financially, he had a way of setting himself up for misery. Yet, as these letters show, even if he did not know how to protect himself, he knew how to protect his art. The best of these letters are about that art: the letters to Ben Wasson about editing *The Sound and the Fury,* the letter of appreciation to Warren Beck, the letters to Malcolm Cowley about *The Portable Faulkner*, and the letter to Joan Williams about his "amazing gift."

Since the letters to Cowley are aready available in *The Faulkner-Cowley File* and since Blotner has already made use of passages from a number of other letters in his biography, this collection of selected letters does not answer a pressing need. We have more of Faulkner's correspondence, but we do not have enough. Blotner has omitted some of the letters to which he had access because he considered them redundant, but I would like to know how often a particular concern appeared in Faulkner's letters. I am prevented from knowing because Blotner has omitted letters which he says "treat material covered in other letters or which constitute substantially the same type of letter already represented." I also cannot find in Blotner's annotations certain information which would be helpful. He tells us that some letters were written on the versos of particular typescripts, but he gives no indication of whether or not other copies of these letters were actually mailed. He tells us that the stories "Moonlight" and "Snow" are unpublished, but not where they may be found. He provides no note at all about the story "Black Music." And his notes about the publication of "The Wishing-Tree" do not finish the story they begin.

Blotner footnotes every reference to an individual in the letters except, by my count, one: to Faulkner's request that Bennett Cerf send a "copy of Wild Palms to Mrs Wolfgang Rebner" Blotner provides no note at all. That omission suggests that his feelings toward Mrs. Rebner (Meta Carpenter) are less than objective. Or perhaps Blotner is still trying to protect Estelle Faulkner's memory by insuring that we know as little as possible about the other women in Faulkner's life. If so, that intent raises a real problem. Blotner could not edit the complete letters of William Faulkner simply because numbers of the letters in private collections were not made available to him. But he claims that his *Selected Letters* is nevertheless "representative rather than inclusive." It may represent the types of letters Faulkner wrote, but it does not fully represent their contents, for almost all the letters to women that Blotner collects are spoiled by ellipses. Some of these omissions were made by the addressees; some were made by Blotner himself, but he does not indicate which are which. In fact, Blotner does not even distinguish between Faulkner's ellipses and his own; for he assumes "it will be clear to the reader at which points the ellipses appeared in the original." Blotner does acknowledge that he has deleted "intimate passages" from the letters. (He even inexplicably deletes those implicitly intimate passages from the letters to Joan Williams which he already printed in the biography.) He explains primly but none too coherently that "Some of these omissions are of the sort to be found in the published letters of James Joyce." (I take this to mean that the material he omits is of the sort included in Joyce's published letters and that he assumes we know what "sort" he means.) Blotner insists that the letters he collects reveal "different facets of the man," but he seems to have taken it upon himself to conceal at least one particular facet of William Faulkner's personality; thus his selection of letters cannot be termed "representative."

Since Blotner himself makes the comparison between the published letters of Joyce and of Faulkner, I think it fair to remark how disappointing this collection is when compared to Richard Ellmann's *Selected Letters of James Joyce.* Ellmann wants Joyce to be accessible to our understandings. Blotner, on the other hand, seems to want data about Faulkner available but the man himself to remain inaccessible. I think that Blotner's difficulty both as biographer and editor is that he is still trying to maintain Faulkner's distinction between public and private selves, without realizing that if we continue, after a person's death, to honor his opinions and protect his privacy, we tend to deify him and thereby preclude the possibility of understanding him. William Faulkner was too great a genius to be traduced even in the names of the very values he honored. The biographer's and editor's job is not to reify Faulkner's value system, but to make it comprehensible.

Another book published this year does tell us something about that very "facet" of Faulkner's personality Blotner would like to keep hidden. *A Loving Gentleman: The Love Story of William Faulkner and Meta Carpenter* by Meta Carpenter Wilde and Orin Borsten (New York: Simon and Schuster) is, as its title makes clear, the story of a love affair. Mostly, the book is a narrative of the Faulkner/Carpenter relationship set against an on-going sequence of films (Ms. Carpenter was a script girl for Howard Hawks when she and Faulkner first met), of historical events, and of Faulkner's home life and Ms. Carpenter's marriages. Writing a trade book account of her own love affair, Meta Carpenter need not pretend to objectivity or attempt analysis. But Carpenter does have a good sense of where analysis is needed. She wonders why Faulkner wanted to idealize her as an innocent girl-child, why he always felt a pull to be where he was not, and of course why he would rather continue an unhappy marriage than end it. Reading *A Loving Gentleman,* one cannot help wondering how much writing, for Faulkner, was sublimated sex, how prone Faulkner was to set himself up so he could never have what he said he wanted, and how much, for him, love and suffering were the same thing. By writing this book Carpenter has made Faulkner's personality more comprehensible. But in putting erotica (poems, drawings, and letters from Faulkner) under lock and key in the Berg collection of the New York Public Library until 2039, she has prevented several generations of Faulkner scholars from knowing all they might. Fourteen years after Faulkner's death, we do not want to judge him, much less to gossip about him, but we do want to understand him. Biographers, editors, intimates, and collectors could help by recognizing that the time for protecting Faulkner's privacy and that of his intimates has just about passed.

Three items reviewed elsewhere have some bearing on Faulkner's biography. *Some Time in the Sun: The Hollywood Years of Fitzgerald, Faulkner, Nathanael West, Aldous Huxley, and James Agee* (New York: Scribner's) (see chapter 20) includes a 70-page chapter on Faulkner's time in Hollywood, which Tom Dardis, the book's author, adds up as cumulatively four years. Though Dardis suggests that few accounts to date have dealt insightfully with Faulkner's "time in the sun," he does not correct that imbalance. He adds little to Blotner's work in the biography, and he shies away from the crucial question of how much Hollywood marked Faulkner as a writer. In "'The Giant Killer': Drink and the American Writer" (*Commentary* 61,iii:44–50) Alfred Kazin treats Faulkner as one of many alcoholic modern American writers. Kazin's comments are too oversimplified to offer any insight into Faulkner's biography. In "Faulkner, Hemingway, and the American Family," (*MissQ* 29:483–97) Earl Rovit considers Faulkner's stay in Paris, not for its biographical, but for what he considers its "mythic import." Rovit speculates about the probabilities of Faulkner and Hemingway meeting in 1925 and regrets (without recognizing that isolation may work positively) that Faulkner remained apart from celebrated Parisian artistic circles.

iii. Criticism: General

a. **Books.**   *Fifty Years After "The Marble Faun,"* ed. George H. Wolfe
(Tuscaloosa: Univ. of Ala. Press) is a collection of eight essays originally delivered at a symposium at the University of Alabama in October of 1974. Two years in press diminish the book's timeliness; poor
proofreading interferes with its readability. As a collection the book
has little unity except that five of the essays deal with what Lewis
P. Simpson terms Faulkner's literary novitiate. As a sort of paradigm
of Faulkner criticism though, the book as a whole suggests interesting
proportions; two essays are reductive thematic criticism; three are
rather limited treatments that broach real questions and fail to answer
them, and three are significant documents in Faulkner studies.

   Sally R. Page's "Faulkner's Sense of the Sacred" borrows heavily
from Abraham Maslow. Page's sweeping generalization about the
"search for wholeness of Being" in Faulkner's characters ignores their
failure to achieve such wholeness. In "Habet: Faulkner and the Ownership of Property" Floyd C. Watkins proves that Faulkner does not
share Isaac McCaslin's conviction that ownership should be held in
common. Determining that the good people in Faulkner's fiction own
but do not exploit property, Watkins provides a distressingly neat
evaluative system by which Jewel's love of his horse is proper and
Isaac McCaslin is nearly as irresponsible as Anse Bundren. Page's and
Watkin's essays disregard the fiction's multivalence. Both read as reductive attempts to use Faulkner's fiction to justify a value system.

   In "Sole Owner and Proprietor" Joseph Blotner promises to suggest something of how Faulkner projects himself into the fiction, but
Blotner basically just reviews the career. The essay reads like a speech
that could be given to almost any audience; it adds nothing to the
work Blotner has already done. Richard P. Adams's "Faulkner: The
European Roots" offers yet another corrective to the image of Faulkner as rustic unlettered genius. Speculating about the preponderance
of allusions to European sources in Faulkner, Adams sees these allusions as instances of Faulkner's determination that the local and particular be connected with the eternal and universal. Unfortunately,
the late Richard P. Adams did not in this speech investigate fully the
ways in which allusions resonate in Faulkner. In "William Faulkner
and William Butler Yeats" Cleanth Brooks suggests parallels not between men but between their cultures. Brook's conversational tone is

appropriate for a talk, but the essay is loose and Brooks tends to punt rather than deal with the very significant affinities between these two artists themselves.

Fifty Years After also includes three essays which neither reduce nor punt. James B. Meriwether's "Faulkner's Essays on Anderson" examines both extant essays (a third one went unpublished and apparently is lost) to discover what each tells us about Faulkner. Meriwether's close reading of the 1953 essay offers an especially interesting analysis of a Faulknerian exercise in criticism; for Faulkner read Anderson's story about trying to swap a horse for a night's sleep as a parable about Anderson's art. Meriwether, in turn, sees Faulkner's essay as a parable of the relation of a young writer to an older one and an expression of Faulkner's attitude toward art. Meriwether's own essay is an important clarification.

In "William Faulkner: The Discovery of a Man's Vocation," Louis D. Rubin, Jr., raises a number of questions about Faulkner's psychosexual makeup and its impact on the fiction. Rubin points out how Faulkner's discussion of art was often couched in sexual terms. Rubin too easily assumes that the dichotomy Faulkner first saw between sexuality and sensitivity was resolved in his later life and art; nevertheless, the essay is an important revelation of Faulkner's way of thinking and a reminder that psychobiographical criticism can shed light on Faulkner studies.

The collection includes another important essay—Lewis P. Simpson's "Faulkner and the Legend of the Artist." This learned study traces Faulkner's evolving sense of the artist's identity. Reviewing the development of the "modern literary priesthood," Simpson shows how the modern artist strives to write in history and yet to recapture, through identification with Pan, a mythic dimension. He is concerned with Faulkner's literary novitiateship which ended with *The Sound and the Fury* and with the creation of Quentin Compson. Simpson sees Quentin as a type of the world historical poet embodying Faulkner's dilemma and that of the modern artist. This essay is a significant document in intellectual history as well as in Faulkner studies.

If the eight essays in *Fifty Years After* suggest something of the range typical of Faulkner criticism, so too do the four books reviewed in the remainder of this section. Myra Jehlen's *Class and Character in Faulkner's South* (New York: Columbia Univ. Press)[1] is filled

1. My more extensive review of Jehlen's *Class and Character*, Levins's *Faulk-*

with egregious errors which alone make it untrustworthy. (Jehlen thinks Jason is the eldest Compson brother. She also thinks that Thomas Sutpen, who was born in 1807, landed in Haiti before 1791). Furthermore, Jehlen's Marxist-oriented study reduces all moral dilemmas to matters of class conflicts and rates the novels according to how honestly she thinks Faulkner faced up to the injustice of an aristocratic class system. The critical sins Jehlen commits are legion, but using criticism to attack a class system is inherently no more repugnant than using criticism to defend one. We need literary criticism which objectively examines the structure of Faulkner's values and the meaning—in terms of both origin and implication—of that structure. Jehlen cannot provide it, though she does suggest something of the manner in which class values influence Faulkner's imagination. Mostly *Class and Character in Faulkner's South* suggests that the topic calls for better, polemic-free criticism.

Warren Beck's *Faulkner* (Madison: Univ. of Wis. Press) is a collection of essays written over a period of more than thirty years. It begins with the three seminal essays on Faulkner Beck published in 1941 and ends with review-essays of *The Mansion* and *The Reivers* first published in 1960 and 1962. Between these essays occur nearly 600 pages of previously unpublished material, roughly 350 pages on *Go Down, Moses*, alone; despite the book's organization, I suspect—principally on the basis of style—that this material was written after the 1960 and 1962 pieces. Here Beck is prolix and diffuse. He seems to organize by free association. He does offer sound insight into theme and technique in *Sanctuary* but even this (the best of his new material) is marred by turgidity. Also he seems still to be fighting old battles against "lingering indifference or antipathy to Faulkner." For Beck's early insistence upon the morality of Faulkner's vision and the technical virtuousity of his art, we must be grateful. It is a pleasure to see these early essays collected together. But the new material, by contrast, lacks sharpness. It suggests the need for both an editor and a proofreader.

Lynn Gartrell Levins's *Faulkner's Heroic Design: The Yoknapatawpha Novels* (Athens: Univ. of Ga. Press), is limited by failures of conception and imagination. Levins defines heroism merely as accomplishing one's obligations despite extreme difficulties. By "heroic design" she means Faulkner's use, through allusion and analogy, of other heroic literatures. Levins provides insight into the uses of genre in *Absalom, Absalom!*, but that material was already published (see *ALS 1970*, p. 125). Her book is handicapped by a one dimensional approach that refuses to acknowledge multivalence in meaning or tone.

Albert J. Guerard's *The Triumph of the Novel: Dickens, Dostoevsky, Faulkner* (New York: Oxford Univ. Press) is an important study for several reasons. First, it makes a significant contribution to a growing critical insistence that the novel has been too narrowly defined as inherently mimetic. Secondly, it explores meaningful affinities between these authors. And thirdly, it provides valuable readings of particular novels and suggests how much insight technical and psychological approaches can offer.

Guerard finds in each of these novelists certain recurrent psychological oddities (often expressions of psychosexual taboos) which he sees as a fascination with "forbidden games." The essential question is whether or not these psychic oddities enriched or weakened the novelists' art. With Faulkner, Guerard sees the forbidden game as misogyny or an "imaginative distaste for normal sexuality." More specifically, "the ultimate and repugnantly forbidden game to the Faulknerian imagination was normal intercourse with a woman of marriageable age." Guerard suggests how Faulkner's misogyny influences incident and character throughout the fiction; then he presents a detailed treatment of *Sanctuary* (also printed *SoR* 12:215–31). Guerard's thesis is that misogyny gives form—through selection and compression—to the vision of evil in *Sanctuary*. He makes a significant correction to certain naive assumptions about Faulkner's regard for women, and he suggests something of how an unsound perspective can redeem itself by creating sound art. Nevertheless, I find this the weakest of the Faulkner chapters because Guerard does not address himself to the question of disparities between Faulkner's attitudes and those of his characters; furthermore, he assumes without enough explanation that a warped vision may focus and intensify an aesthetic achievement.

Guerard's remaining two Faulkner chapters offer aesthetic approaches. One entitled "Faulkner: Problems of Technique" presents a fine account of what materials and techniques Faulkner finds con-

genial, what uncongenial. Convincingly, Guerard treats *The Hamlet*
not as social realism but as exuberant imaginative play in which,
through a variety of imaginative distortions, mode and rhetoric are
successfully modulated. Guerard's last chapter "*Absalom, Absalom!*:
The Novel as Impressionistic Art" treats that novel in its own terms—
insisting, as the novel's form does, upon the primacy of imaginative
creation. Guerard's expertise on Conrad resonates throughout the
chapter as he compares the two novelists' use of narration by conjecture. This book is a sensitive and insightful study of Faulkner's art
and of the workings of the imagination within the novel form.

b. Articles. Other than three of the essays collected in *Fifty Years
After* (see above) there are no essays which succeed in generalizing
about Faulkner's work. Joan S. Korenman, in "Faulkner and 'That
Undying Mark'" (*SAF* 4:81–91) comes closest to succeeding. Her
thesis is that only after *Absalom, Absalom!* does Faulkner's time-
consciousness express itself as a craving for immortality. Though her
citations from manuscript and text revisions are limited, they do suggest an increasing concern with human immortality, But Korenman
hampers her argument by implying that this is an entirely "new facet
of an old concern." The basic problem with her essay though is that
it calls for, but does not offer, biographical analysis. In *Dimensions
of Detective Fiction*, ed. Larry N. Landrum, Pat Browne, and Ray B.
Browne (Bowling Green, Ohio: Popular Press) there are two essays
on Faulkner. One, by Mick Gidley, is a reprint (see *ALS 1973*, p.
140). The other, Douglas C. Tallack's "William Faulkner and the
Tradition of Tough-Guy Fiction" (pp. 247–64), is a diffuse study
which aims at placing *Sanctuary* in its entirety and *Light in August*
at least partially within the tradition of tough-guy fiction. Faulkner's
use of popular fictional genres merits critical attention, but both Gidley and Tallack tell more about the "tradition" under consideration
than about Faulkner. And Hunter McKelva Cole's "Welty on Faulkner" (*NMW* 9:28–49) is of more use to Welty readers than to Faulkner scholars or readers.

iv. Criticism: Special Studies

a. Ideas, Influences, Intellectual Background. Three publications
this year speak to Shreve McCannon's query: "*Tell about the South.*

What's it like there[?]." In "The Oxford *Eagle*, 1902–1962: A Census of Locations" (*MissQ* 29:423–31), James B. Lloyd lists locations for each run of the local paper not on microfilm. This is a helpful list for the scholar who wants to read contemporary local accounts of the material which served as background to Faulkner's writings. More appropriate to the layman is James W. Silver's "Faulkner's South" (*SHR* 10:301–12). This rambling reminiscence by a historian who knew Faulkner carries a minimum of biographical interest, but its main purpose is to establish, in a generalized, casual fashion, Faulkner's departures from traditional southern mythology—particularly Faulkner's moderate stance on the race question.

Calvin S. Brown's glossary, on the other hand, presents Faulkner's world as an entrée to his writing. In *A Glossary of Faulkner's South* (New Haven, Conn.: Yale Univ. Press) Brown's intent is to gloss every reference in the Yoknapatawpha fiction unclear to readers in times and places other than Faulkner's. This book is an invaluable aid to reading Faulkner because, as Brown points out, all Faulkner readers now are to an extent Shreves unfamiliar with some aspect of Faulkner's South. Brown glosses every phrase or reference which is southern. He even risks offending textual critics by glossing what seem to him to be errors and by suggesting how he thinks a passage should have been printed. In all of this, he is careful to indicate when his interpretation is tentative. Brown's introduction provides a cogent and clear explanation of the discriminations he has made; in an appendix he addresses himself to the question of the relationship between Yoknapatawpha and Lafayette Counties. Since Brown willingly acknowledges that Faulkner took many liberties with his source, this discussion seems to me to disarm those critics who feel that Brown argues for too close a resemblance between Jefferson and Oxford. Brown's thoroughness, judiciousness, and honesty will make *A Glossary of Faulkner's South* a significant source for the Faulkner student, translator, and scholar as well.

Three other essays reviewed in this section deal not with the social but with the intellectual background of Faulkner's fiction. In "Beardsley and Faulkner" (*JML* 5:339–56) Timothy K. Conley promises to go far beyond what other critics have said about the influence of decadent art, particularly Beardsley's, on Faulkner, but instead Conley does little more than review Faulkner's references to Beardsley and the comments of other critics on the subject. Printed with the essay are drawings by both Beardsley and Faulkner which themselves illustrate Faulkner's indebtedness to Beardsley. But Conley's text stops where it should have begun; in the last paragraph he speaks of a vision of the world in decay and a capacity to make the bizarre credible which Faulkner had in common with Beardsley. That vision and that capacity should have been the focus of his paper. Margaret M. Culley bases her "Judgment In Yoknapatawpha Fiction" (*Renascence* 28:59–70) on a distinction between apocalyptic eschatology and what Rudolf Bultmann terms a "realized eschatology." Culley's discussion of the fiction deals with familiar material, but cogently explains the moral conflict for such characters as Isaac McCaslin and Temple Drake Stevens in terms of its theological dimensions. This essay is a helpful corrective to criticism that sees Faulkner's vision as merely backward-looking and doom-conscious. Glenn O. Carey's "Faulkner and His Carpenter's Hammer" (*ArQ* 32:5–15) is a naive, platitudinous attempt to establish that Faulkner wrote out of a moral or Christian background to expose the presence of evil in the twentieth century.

b. **Language and Style.**   Unfortunately, 1976 saw few publications concerned primarily with Faulkner's language or style, though among full-length studies Albert J. Guerard's *The Triumph of the Novel* does offer real insight into Faulkner's departures from a realistic style (see section iii). Only three essays approached individual works primarily through attention to language and style. Two by Joseph M. Garrison were *As I Lay Dying* and "That Evening Sun" (see sections vi and ix); one by May Cameron Brown is also on "That Evening Sun" (see section ix).

c. **Race.**   In 1976 only Donald A. Petesch's "Faulkner on Negroes: The Conflict between the Public Man and the Private Art" (*SHR* 10: 55–63) dealt exclusively with the question of race. Petesch presents a cogent review of Faulkner's major comments on race and classifies the startling inconsistencies in Faulkner's comments. Petesch makes a persuasive explanation of these contradictions as symptomatic of a general disparity in Faulkner's thinking—a tendency to see in terms of a radical distinction between what is actual and familiar and expedient and what is ideal. Also Myra Jehlen's book (section iii above) and James W. Silver's article (section iv,a above) have some bearing on this topic.

v. Individual Works to 1929

This year Faulkner's early work received very little critical attention. In "*Soldier's Pay* and Virginia Woolf" (*MissQ* 29:339–46) Emily Dalgarno concentrates on the seemingly minor point that both authors make heavy use of parentheses. Dalgarno avoids the major point that both authors were experimenting with parenthetical contrasts because they found the interior monologue too inflexible and restricted a perspective. This essay fails to provide an adequate analysis and interpretation of its own material. Cleanth Brooks, in an essay entitled "Faulkner's *Mosquitoes*" (*GaR* 31:213–34), writes something of a defense of *Mosquitoes*, explaining what it has to tell us about Faulkner's personality and his aesthetics. Brooks sees the young Faulkner ambiguously hovering in *Mosquitoes* between allegiance to romanticism and antiromanticism, local and universal standards, but gradually moving toward the latter poles. The interrelationship between these two sets of poles is left unexplored, as are a number of other significant issues which Brooks seems to want to point out now and leave to other scholars to investigate later. In "Hardy, Falls, and Faulkner" (*MissQ* 29:435–36) William Miller sets out to go beyond the merely "speculative proof" of Hardy's influence on Faulkner. Miller's data is convincing enough but hardly more valuable or conclusive than the more speculative studies he disparages.

Once again *The Sound and the Fury* claimed a remarkable amount of critical attention—including one full-length study. André Bleikasten's *The Most Splendid Failure: Faulkner's "The Sound and the Fury"* (Bloomington: Ind. Univ. Press) derives its title from Faulkner's comments about writing *The Sound and the Fury*. Bleikasten takes these remarks at face value, since he wants to make use of the word "failure," but he sometimes uses the word so loosely that when we read "Caddy's beauty is the beauty of failure" we do not know whether he refers to Caddy's failure or Faulkner's. *The Most Splendid Failure* offers an approach which its author characterizes as "undogmatic and pluralistic," but it seems to be predominantly psychoanalytic and structuralistic. Bleikasten elucidates the psychic patterns each Compson brother displays, and he illustrates how these patterns are an integral part of the novel's structure. Referring to Barthes's notion of "*suspended* meaning," Bleikasten refuses either to affirm or deny Christian or transcendent values in *The Sound and the Fury.* Thus he ignores the significance of Dilsey's existence and treats the Reverend Sheegog as only a type of the artist rather than the preacher as well. Bleikasten might properly say that he is concerned with psychological and aesthetic meanings and that theological meanings lie beyond the province of his method; but he should not deny the existence of theological implications. Nevertheless, in reminding us that both *The Sound and the Fury* and *As I Lay Dying* are written around a "primal gap," Bleikasten offers significant insight into the psychological and aesthetic implications of that gap. *The Most Splendid Failure,* like John T. Irwin's *Doubling and Incest/ Repetition and Revenge* (see *ALS 1975,* pp. 146–48), makes available meanings hitherto neglected in Faulkner criticism. And this book has the advantage of being less schematic and more attentive to the text than Irwin's.

In addition to Bleikasten's book, the year's work on *The Sound and the Fury* included seven full-length articles and one note. Douglas B. Hill, Jr.'s "Faulkner's Caddy," (*CRevAS* 7:26–38) is an insightful and psychologically suggestive study of Faulkner's means of characterizing Caddy. Hill presents telling evidence that Faulkner's imagination, at the time of writing *The Sound and the Fury,* suffered from the same block the Compson brothers experience; they cannot accept Caddy's maturing or mature sexuality, and Faulkner cannot convey it except through stereotypes typical of male fantasies. Because Hill is scrupulously conscious of narrative voice, this very careful essay skirts successfully the pitfalls which open whenever a critic speaks of the workings of an author's mind. Hill also offers a convincing aesthetic explanation for the power of Caddy's felt presence in the novel which transcends the stereotypical presentations of her as a pubescent girl and sexually mature woman.

Another fine essay on *The Sound and the Fury* is Stephen M. Ross's "Jason Compson and Sut Lovingood: Southwestern Humor as Stream of Consciousness" (*SNNTS* 8:278–90). Ross offers a useful distinction between Jason's mode of speaking and Faulkner's manner of presentation. Ross explains the paradox of southwest humor—that it makes morally depraved behavior comic—and convincingly places Faulkner's portrayal of Jason within that tradition. This essay offers a worthwhile corrective to those who would allow their pleasure in Faulkner's characterization to blur into an exoneration of Jason's character.

Philip M. Weinstein has found in Proust's *La Fugitive* an incident which so closely parallels the "sister" episode in *The Sound and the Fury* as to suggest a borrowing. In "Caddy *Disparue*: Exploring an Episode Common to Proust and Faulkner" (*CLS* 14:38–52), Weinstein offers to compare not only the discrete episodes but also the imaginative worlds of their authors. It is unfortunate that he does the former very well, but the latter hardly at all. Two other essays on *The Sound and the Fury* serve only to reiterate, with slightly altered focus, what we already know about the novel. Isadore Traschen's "The Tragic Form of *The Sound and the Fury*" (*SoR* 12:798–813) imposes his definition of the four phases of tragic form onto the four sections of *The Sound and the Fury*. Traschen confuses the manner of Jason's presentation with its matter; otherwise, his reading is sound enough, but already familiar. Mary E. McGann's "*The Waste Land* and *The Sound and the Fury*: To Apprehend the Human Process Moving in Time" (*SLJ* 9,i:13–21) is yet another comparison between these two seminal works of the 1920s. McGann expands the now familiar parallels in order to see equivalence between the ending of the poem and the novel. To do so she must ignore the meaning of the order Jason restores. Other than that strained association, her reading is not so much wrong as it is old hat.

Lil Brannon's "Psychic Distance in the Quentin section of *The Sound and the Fury*" (*PAPA* 2,ii:11–18) is an awkwardly written treatment which offers no new insight into Quentin's psychology. Edward D. Clark, Sr.'s "Private Truth in *The Sound and the Fury*" (*CLAJ* 19:513–23) applies Anderson's theory of the grotesque to Quentin and Jason Compson. Clark is apparently unaware that any critic other than Michael Millgate has pursued the problem before. Nor is he aware that making abstract "truths" into "falsehoods" is a tendency not unique to Quentin and Jason. In "Jaybirds as Portents of Hell in Percy and Faulkner" (*NMW* 9:24–27), Barbara B. Sims gives a slightly fuller account than Brown (see section iv) of the folkloric legends about jaybirds which are referred to in the fourth section of *The Sound and the Fury*, as well as in Percy's *The Moviegoer*.

vi. Individual Works, 1930–39

Joseph M. Garrison, Jr.'s "Perception, Language, and Reality in *As I Lay Dying*" (*ArQ* 32:16–30) is not only this year's best article on this novel but one of the significant essays for 1976. It departs from the sorts of questions critics have been debating for at least the last twenty years and approaches the novel's meaning through close attention to language. Garrison's analysis of Darl's language indicates how linguistic dislocation and rigidity express Darl's increasingly helpless sense of his own incapacity to shape events. In projecting from Darl to the other Bundrens, Garrison does not have (or take) space and time for similar attention to the other characters' language. He particularly needs to attend to Cash's language and to offer his own thesis as refutation of the dichotomy Addie sees between words and deeds. Nevertheless, Garrison offers an excellent analysis of Faulkner's subtle use of linguistic patterns to characterize and convey meaning. Also, Garrison illustrates how a linguistic approach can reveal structure and meaning in a Faulkner novel.

In "Dilemma in *As I Lay Dying*" (*Renascence* 28:71–81) Gary Lee Stonum too takes note of the discontinuity in the novel's imagery; he finds it indicative of an either/or structure which is thematically central to the novel. This essay is an insightful investigation of the way the Bundren's mental set creates their experiential dilemma. Michael White in "Inverse Mimesis in Faulkner's *As I Lay Dying*" (*ArQ* 32:35–44) suggests parallels between the novel and Greek tragedy, but because he sometimes finds duplications, sometimes inversions of the Greek pattern, he forces his analogy. Furthermore, he ignores most previous work on his topic and fails to speak of the significance of what he believes to be Faulkner's intentional use of Greek materials.

The year's most impressive work on *Sanctuary* was in the fifth chapter of Albert J. Guerard's *The Triumph of the Novel* (see section iii). In "Character Parallels in *Crime and Punishment* and *Sanctuary*" (*GSlav* 2,i:5–14), Richard L. Chapple enumerates, rather literal-mindedly, specific parallels of incident and character between the novels. Chapple strains his analogies almost to imply that Faulkner rewrote Dostoevsky, but all the essay really does is to remind us of how much the novels have in common. Margaret Yonce's " 'His True Penelope was Flaubert': *Madame Bovary* and *Sanctuary*" (*MissQ* 29:439–42) likewise promises more than it delivers. Yonce does not talk of style, as her title implies she will, but only notes several similar descriptions in the novels and suggests that a more thorough study should be made. Clearly the question of influence does call for thoughtful investigations which do not simply cite similarities but instead discuss the significance of the echoes, in Faulkner, of the literature of other times and places.

The all-too-typical note on Faulkner takes a minor and trivial observation and inflates it into a dictum. I have ignored many such notes, but three items found in the same publication serve to suggest something of the range in quality among published notes. One item—James E. Mulqueen's "Horace Benbow: Avatar of Faulkner's Marbel [*sic*] Faun" (*NMW* 9:88–96)—is no more informative than its misspelled title would suggest. A second item, "A Note on Faulkner's Title, *These Thirteen*" (*NMW* 9:120–22) by H. K. Showett, is based purely on unsubstantiated supposition, but the note is nevertheless acceptable because it makes no pretentious claims to be anything other than speculation. Also, Showett makes his theory at least plausible. A third note—Mario L. D'Avanzo's "Doc Hines and Euphues in *Light in August*" (*NMW* 9:101–6)—is a much more detailed and convincing item suggesting how appropriately Eupheus Hines was named from John Lyly's *Euphues: Or the Anatomy of Wit*. D'Avanzo ignores certain ironies in *Euphues* (namely that Euphues's disgust with women appears only after his mistress has jilted him) and does not explore the analogy further, but D'Avanzo does make an interesting suggestion about the meaning of "light" in the novel's title. Clearly, a note may be informative or speculative, but it should contribute to our understanding. Too many notes published on Faulkner fail to meet even that simple criterion.

The year's work on *Light in August* is disappointing. Both the following essays are too thesis-ridden to acknowledge the complexity of the issues considered; both treat unawares material that has already received much more insightful attention. Doreen F. Fowler's "Faith as a Unifying Principle in Faulkner's *Light in August*" (*TSL* 21:49–57) offers no new insight, nor does it supply (as she asserts) the missing link to *Light in August*'s unity; nor finally is the rubric "faith" an adequate description of the phenomenon she considers—a coercive power which (both for good and evil) the mythic consciousness possesses. In "William Faulkner's Joe Christmas: A Rage for Order" (*ArQ* 32:61–73), Charles E. Davis ignores previous criticism and proves himself oblivious of the important psychological reasons for Joe's obsession with order.

Absalom, Absalom! fared much better than *Light in August* since it received insightful close readings in Albert Guerard's study of the novel (see section iii) and in several fine critical essays. Richard Forrer's "*Absalom, Absalom!*: Story-telling As a Mode of Transcendence" (*SLJ* 9,i:22–46) is a soundly researched article which provides real insight into some of the novel's difficulties. Especially impressive is Forrer's attention to the voice of an omniscient narrator whose comments serve throughout *Absalom, Absalom!* as commentary and corrective to the characters' hypotheses and to their limited understanding of what they themselves are doing in recreating Sutpen's story. Forrer's excellent study works on several planes at once to show how attention to technical matters can elucidate aesthetic and thematic issues.

In "The Re-creation of the Past in *Absalom, Absalom!*" (*MissQ* 29:361–74), Carl E. Rollyson, Jr., provides another careful reading of the question of how Quentin and Shreve know what they know. Rollyson offers a persuasive hypothesis that Quentin and Shreve work by intuition from models and patterns that they do know to make the imaginative breakthrough which occurs in chapter 8. Rollyson also argues less convincingly that Quentin learned of Bon's black blood from Clytie, but he fails to incorporate this argument into his basic thesis.

A third fine article is T. H. Adamowski's "Children of the Idea: Heroes and Family Romances in *Absalom, Absalom!*" (*Mosaic* 10,i: 115–31). Adamowski sees Sutpen's quest for autonomy in terms of the prototypical fantasy termed by Freud a "family romance." Adamowski's point is not that Sutpen "had" a family romance but that the novel's narrative structure is patterned on the structure of that fantasy. Distinctions between fact and conjecture in the novel are simply not relevant to this way of seeing, for Adamowski is concerned not with how Quentin and Shreve know what they know, but rather with how certain mythic patterns shape the terms in which Sutpen, Charles, and Henry lived and Quentin and Shreve conjecture. This article, which is buttressed by a skilful interweaving of literary criticism, philosophy, and psychology, offers a fine illustration of the way in which a slightly different angle of vision toward familiar material can yield up new and significant meanings.

In "Anderson's *Poor White* and Faulkner's *Absalom, Absalom!*" (*MissQ* 29:437–38), J. B. Rosenman suggests that the manner of Sutpen's death may have been suggested to Faulkner by Anderson. Unfortunately, Rosenman wants not just to associate an incident, but also to transpose an allegorical value system from *Poor White* onto *Absalom, Absalom!*. Sanford Pinsker in "Thomas Sutpen and Milly Jones: A Note on Paternal Design in *Absalom, Absalom!*" (*NMAL* 1:15–18) grants careful attention to the text and the chronology—which offer different versions of Milly Jones's date and place of birth —but he diminishes the force of some of the issues he broaches by using his evidence to support a thesis whose implications he ignores.

The annual Faulkner number of *MissQ* includes a worthy article on *The Unvanquished*. In "Sartoris Ludens: The Play Element in *The Unvanquished*" (*MissQ* 29:375–87), A. James Memmott bases his analysis on Johan Huizinga's *Homo Ludens* to show how action in *The Unvanquished* is structured by game theory. The essay would have profited if Memmott had made a clearer distinction between harmful and healthy game playing, but otherwise it is a fine essay. In "Faulkner's *The Unvanquished*" (*Expl* 34:item 49), John J. Roberts and R. Leon Scott, Jr., suggest more than they have space to explain or defend in this note.

Only one article on *The Wild Palms* appeared in 1976, and it adds nothing to our understanding of that novel. Theodore Colson's "Analogues of Faulkner's *The Wild Palms* and Hawthorne's 'The Birthmark'" (*DR* 56:510–18) is a strained attempt to associate not only Charlotte's scar and Georgiana's birthmark, but also Charlotte's pregnancy and Georgiana's birthmark. This essay skirts the real issues of sin and pride and sees analogies only in a literal and limited sense. Also, Colson does not distinguish between "Wild Palms" and *The Wild Palms*.

vii. Individual Works, 1940–49

Albert J. Guerard's *The Triumph of the Novel* (see section iii) offers an insightful treatment of *The Hamlet*. Larry Marshall Sams's "Isaac McCaslin and Keats's 'Ode on a Grecian Urn'" (*SoR* 12:632–39) shows how Keats's ode echoes through the thematically central tension between evanescence and eternality in the Isaac McCaslin stories. But though he reaches again the now standard conclusion about Isaac's failures, Sams does not note the cause and effect relationship between Isaac's desire for static permanence and his failure in the human world. Mark R. Hochberg in "The Unity of *Go Down,*

Moses" (*TSL* 21:58–65) makes another rather simplistic attempt to establish the unity of that novel. He reviews plots, but fails to consider imagery or the interrelationships with other themes. A better treatment is Weldon Thornton's (see *ALS 1975*, p. 163). As it is, Hochberg is not so much wrong as superfluous, as also Warren Beck largely is in his lengthy treatment of *Do Down, Moses* in his *Faulkner* (see section iii). The last item on this novel is John T. Hiers's "Faulkner's Lord-to-God Bird in 'The Bear'" (*AL* 47:636–37). This note provides interesting naturalistic and folkloric information about the bird who seems to be a harbinger for Old Ben.

By far the most valuable article in this section is Carol R. Rigsby's "Chick Mallison's Expectations and *Intruder in the Dust*" (*MissQ* 29: 389–99). Rigsby offers a significant corrective to those critics who see this novel as a polemic in which Gavin Stevens speaks for Faulkner. She also answers Cleanth Brooks's objections to the plot by giving feasible explanations for Crawford Gowrie's actions and by suggesting that in writing *Intruder in the Dust* Faulkner became less interested in writing a "whodunit" than in exploring more profound questions; thus Chick learns more about himself and his fellow man than about crime solving. Rigsby points out that a significant part of Chick's initiation is his disillusionment with his uncle whose legalizing and moralizing and self-lacerating all finally sound "phony." Such a sensible and sensitive reading of one of Faulkner's more neglected works is welcome.

viii. Individual Works, 1950–62

Only two articles treat works written during this period. Eileen Gregory's "The Temerity to Revolt: Mink Snopes and the Dispossessed in *The Mansion*" (*MissQ* 29:401–21) considers western myths which have shaped the dreams of those who are exploited or dispossessed. Gregory knows the traditions she uses, the history of *The Mansion*, and Faulkner criticism, but she seems less acquainted with narrative voice in the Snopes trilogy. She thinks, therefore, that Snopeses are a "truly demonic force" and regrets that only Ratliff comprehends the "unequivocal evil" embodied in Flem. She fails to note that Ratliff wants to see Snopes as an evil plague and that through their own rapacity and sexual hypocrisy the non-Snopes inhabitants of Yoknapatawpha County are accessories in whatever advantage

Flem takes of them. Nevertheless, Gregory makes an interesting discussion of the way Faulkner made use of Greek, Christian, and modern analogues for this novel of retribution and redemption. We do not
have to accept the Manichean universe Gregory projects in the first
part of her essay to appreciate with her the way *The Mansion* resonates with analogues from *The Oresteia*, the Christian myth, and
the Marxist myth.

The only other item in this section is Gale Tanner's "Sentimentalism and *The Reivers*: A Reply to Ben Merchant Vorpahl" (*NMW*
9:50–58). Unfortunately cast as a half-hearted rebuttal to another
article, this essay lacks a thesis of its own.

ix. The Stories

Little work on Faulkner's stories was published in 1976, but the two
finest pieces, both on "That Evening Sun," rest their analysis on close
attention to the language of the story. Joseph M. Garrison, Jr.'s "The
Past and the Present in 'That Evening Sun'" (*SSF* 13:371–73) is an
extended note which examines a subtle distinction between what
Quentin's narrative tells about the past and what he thinks he has
told. May Cameron Brown's "Voice in 'That Evening Sun': A Study
of Quentin Compson" (*MissQ* 29:347–60) is a much fuller treatment
than Garrison's, appropriately based upon knowledge of the story's
textual history and of past criticism. Brown argues that in the three
versions of "That Evening Sun" Faulkner's revisions served to enhance the artistic possibilities of narrative voice. She very persuasively bases her analysis upon careful attention to imagery and syntax.
In "Faulkner's Cry for a Healing Measure: 'Dry September'" (*ArQ*
32:31–34), John V. McDermott attempts to see that story as parable
without adding anything substantive to what we already know about
the tale. Alma A. Ilacqua's "An Artistic Vision of Election in 'Spotted
Horses'" (*Cithara* 15,ii:33–45) must be mentioned only to warn
against it. Ilacqua sees trees, houses, barns, animals, and people all
as symbols. Then she compounds folly with pride and proceeds to
divide not only sheep and goats but people, buildings, and vegetation
as well into the elect and the damned.

In a year in which so much of value in Faulkner studies has been
published, it is unfortunate to end this review with attention to an
essay which distorts Faulkner and mistakes the role of criticism. But

I think the pride in that article serves as a warning to us all. Humility before the man Faulkner would be inappropriate. But humility before his art is mandatory. If we are to understand his work, we must approach it with the same "alert respect" that he paid to language, art, and his own "amazing gift."

Louisiana State University

10. Fitzgerald and Hemingway

Jackson R. Bryer

This has been what might be termed a "quiet" year in Hemingway and Fitzgerald studies. We had no new full-length study of either writer, no collections on either writer, and very little exciting new critical material. In addition, the 1976 *Fitzgerald/Hemingway Annual* was delayed and was unavailable at the time this survey was written.

But, as always, there were some noteworthy and pleasant surprises. Chief among these was a special issue of the new journal, *Linguistics in Literature* (vol. 1, no. 2), devoted to studies of Hemingway's "Experiments in Structure and Style." In one of these essays, Barbara Sanders makes an observation which well could stand as a maxim for future students of both these writers: "Good interpretation of literature should begin with an examination of the smallest parts of the text (words) and describe how the parts 'work' in relation to each other, and then show how this relationship indicates a larger structure. . . . This type of critical analysis is more inductive than deductive; it moves from knowns to unknowns and never assumes a theme without previous textual indications."

i. Bibliographical Work and Texts

Although the tardiness of the 1976 *Fitzgerald/Hemingway Annual* is reflected most strikingly in the relative dearth of material in this category, we do have two very good examples of bibliographical and textual study used to provide illuminating literary criticism. Michael S. Reynolds's *Hemingway's First War: The Making of "A Farewell to Arms"* (Princeton, N.J.: Princeton Univ. Press) is as detailed an account as we are likely ever to get of the composition of a Hemingway novel. Reynolds ranges widely, dealing with how, when, and where Hemingway worked on the book, with the novel's historical accuracy, with the sources he probably used to achieve that accuracy, and with the real-life models he may or may not have used for his characters, (chapter 7 includes the text of a long 1971 interview with Agnes Von Kurowsky, long thought to be the prototype for Catherine, but Reynolds concludes she "contributes little to Catherine Barkley other than her presence and her physical beauty"). There is a lot of interesting new material here, including Fitzgerald's suggestions about revisions in the manuscript, most of which Hemingway ultimately ignored; and Reynolds's method does enable him to make some plausible contentions regarding the novel's structure and style, as for example when he observes that Hemingway plotted the book episodically and that thus it reads like "five tightly interrelated short stories." Reynolds's critical approach is similar to those in Grebstein's and Wagner's recent books in his focus on technique. He finds three principal techniques employed in *Farewell*: foreshadowing, "the echo scene," and "the technique of reversing roles between characters." His delineation and exploration of these is complete and convincing. His conclusion —that the novel is not principally about "war, love or initiation," but is "a study in isolation"—grows directly out of his examination of structure and methods of composition and thus has considerable authority. While Reynolds's study does seem poorly integrated at times and may strike some as redundant and overwritten in its determination to cover every conceivable angle of its subject, it is nonetheless a highly suggestive and valuable piece of scholarship and criticism.

James L. W. West III and J. Barclay Inge examine "F. Scott Fitzgerald's Revision of 'The Rich Boy'" (*Proof* 5:127–46). They trace the compositional history and enumerate Fitzgerald's changes. Their major concern is with how these changes affected the story's central figure, Anson Hunter, as he is viewed by the narrator. They show convincingly that Fitzgerald's revisions had the effect of portraying Anson as "more isolated, less charming, and less popular" and "incapable of the emotion of love." They are somewhat less persuasive in their contention that these changes show that the narrator "is a biased, unsympathetic, middle-class observer who cannot properly understand Anson or Anson's class"; and their inconclusive speculations as to whether the narrator is or is not Fitzgerald seem not only impossible to determine (as they admit) but also unimportant. Despite these reservations, this too is a meticulously researched piece which effectively weds bibliographical scholarship and critical inquiry.

Brief mention should also be made of West's review-essay on the SCADE edition of *The Great Gatsby* (see *ALS 1974*, pp. 139–40) and the *Gatsby* facsimile (see *ALS 1973*, p. 151). What is most valuable here is the case West makes against Matthew Bruccoli's choice, in the SCADE *Gatsby*, of the first-printing text over the manuscript as the copy-text for the novel. His conclusion ("if one follows the principles of Greg—and of the CEAA—one must use a multiple or shifting copy-text for this novel, with the manuscript as the base document and unrevised or revised galleys as alternative copy-texts when the manuscript passages do not qualify") is effectively supported by detailed examination of the changes made in the extant versions.

There are three essays on Hemingway's reception abroad. In the most carefully researched of these, "Zuckmayer, Hilpert, and Hemingway" (*PMLA* 91:194–205), Wayne Kvam offers, as a footnote to his *Hemingway in Germany* (see *ALS 1973*, p. 153), interesting material on Carl Zuckmayer and Heinz Hilbert's 1931 stage adaptation of *A Farewell to Arms*, entitled "Kat." Working from a typescript (the play has never been published), Kvam traces the similarities and differences between drama and novel. He also looks briefly at Zuckmayer's life and other works in attempting to account for his interest in Hemingway, drawing comparisons between *Farewell* and several of Zuckmayer's novels. The other two articles deal with Hemingway in Russia. In "Ernest Hemingway in Ukrainian Literature" (in *Proceedings of the Comparative Literature Symposium—Modern American Fiction: Insights and Foreign Lights* (Texas Tech University), 5[1972]:67–76), Yar Slavutych examines the "translations, critical comments, and poetical tributes" that reflect the significant impact of Hemingway on Ukrainian literature. Slavutych pays particular attention to the careful translations of Hemingway (which began with "The Killers" in 1946) and to the censorship which has heavily influenced the nature of the critical commentary on Hemingway in the Ukraine. Soviet censorship is also the subject of Julius Telesin's "How to Improve Hemingway (Moscow Style [sic])" (*Encounter* 46,vi:81–86), which focuses on the Russian edition of *For Whom the Bell Tolls*. A comparison with the 1973 Penguin edition reveals seventeen cuts and alterations.

In "F. Scott Fitzgerald Appraises His Library" (*Pages* 1:83–89), book-collector Anthony Rota presents a facsimile listing of part of his library which Fitzgerald prepared, apparently in the hopes of selling it to raise money. Fitzgerald placed values opposite all the titles; and Rota's commentary is concerned mostly with the prices these books would bring today.

Although no new Fitzgerald or Hemingway texts were uncovered this year, Scribner's did reissue a revised edition of Fitzgerald's play, *The Vegetable* (originally published in 1923). In an excellent introduction Charles Scribner III traces the history of the play's composition, includes Maxwell Perkins' suggestions for major changes, and provides Fitzgerald's own notes on the play. As appendices, the publishers have included scenes cut from the manuscript, as well as a list of "corrections and addenda" which Fitzgerald inserted in the final acting script. Altogether, this edition represents an unusually generous gesture towards the needs of scholars by a major American commercial publisher who has often been criticized by the scholarly community for his disregard of those needs. We can only hope that it signals the beginning of a new direction in commercial but scholarly editions of American authors.

ii. Letters and Biography

While no new Fitzgerald or Hemingway letters were published this year, four essays deal in various ways with the correspondences of the two authors. In the most significant of these, "The Hemingway Letters" (*SatR* n.s. 4,i:2 Oct.), Norman Cousins summarizes the contents of two groups of Hemingway letters in the University of Maryland Library. The first, an exchange between Hemingway and Fitzgerald biographer Arthur Mizener, is subtitled by Cousins, "I Loved Scott Very Much but . . ." The letters thus complement the Fitzgerald chapter in *A Moveable Feast* by viewing him, according to Cousins, as "a charming, cheerful companion when sober," "completely undisciplined," "extremely difficult because of his relationship with Zelda," and a hero-worshiper whose heroes were "Hemingway himself, Tommy Hitchcock, and Gerald Murphy." Cousins also reports Hemingway's opinions on Fitzgerald's work—he thought *Tender Is the Night* his best book—and on other contemporaries such as Edmund Wilson, James Joyce, and Gertrude Stein. The second batch of letters, written between 1923 and 1925 to short story anthologist Edward O'Brien, deal more directly with his writing then in progress and with his efforts to sell his work to magazines and publishers, and seem less personal than the later ones to Mizener.

Fitzgerald's relationship with Gerald and Sara Murphy is the focus of Linda Patterson Miller's " 'As a Friend You Have Never Failed Me': The Fitzgerald-Murphy Correspondence" (*JML* 5:357–82). Miller here prints 19 new letters and three telegrams from the Murphys to Fitzgerald, asserting that these materials "display in vivid and sympathetic terms the crucial role that Gerald and Sara Murphy played in confronting Fitzgerald, as man and artist, with himself." Miller suggests fruitful new areas for future investigation of the bases and effects of the Fitzgerald-Murphy friendship.

Another of Fitzgerald's "heroes," at least early in his literary career, was H. L. Mencken; and in "The Mencken-Fitzgerald Papers: An Annotated Checklist" (*PULC* 38:21–45), James L. W. West III calls for attention to the personal side of their relationship. As an aid and encouragement to this sort of study, West provides an annotated checklist of the primary materials currently available which bear on this relationship. The majority of these are letters, notes, and telegrams exchanged between the two; but also included are inscriptions in books, Mencken's diary entries, and letters about Fitzgerald which Mencken wrote after his friend's death. All items are fully described and their present location is given. This listing will make some scholar's future research a great deal easier. In contrast, Andrew B. Myers's " 'I Am Used to Being Dunned': F. Scott Fitzgerald and the Modern Library" (*CLC* 25:28–39) probably gives far more than we will ever need to know about a minor episode in Fitzgerald's career, the inclusion of *The Great Gatsby* in Bennett Cerf and Donald Klopfer's Modern Library. Myers's stylistically turgid account reprints a good deal of the correspondence between Cerf and Klopfer and Fitzgerald; but otherwise it is of little interest or importance.

In a year devoid of much exciting critical comment on Fitzgerald or Hemingway, the most significant publication was Mary Welsh Hemingway's long-awaited autobiography, *How It Was* (New York: Alfred A. Knopf). It is, we should note, Mary's biography, so we have an excellently written account of her childhood in Minnesota logging country and her early years as a journalist in Chicago and London.

Many things point to the mutual attraction of Mary and Ernest: their upper middle-class, midwestern backgrounds, early careers as journalists and a desire to pursue them abroad, and an interest in the outdoor life. Mary Hemingway does violate her husband's prohibition against publishing letters, but the excerpts she uses are in fact mostly love letters written when the two were separated and so there is nothing of a literary nature. In fact, throughout most of this book, it is often difficult to keep in mind that Hemingway was a professional writer, so infrequent are the references to his writing and working habits. Of course, there were squabbles—many of them quite violent —and there were other women (largely glossed over); but, for the most part, theirs seems to have been a marriage with much understanding and affection. The book is frequently episodic, disjointed, and disappointing in its too frequent avoidance of feelings; but it makes fascinating reading for both scholar and general reader.

If Mary Welsh was the last great love of Hemingway's life, Sheilah Graham apparently was the same for Fitzgerald. In *The Real F. Scott Fitzgerald: Thirty-Five Years Later* (New York: Grosset & Dunlap), she attempts—with her third full book on the subject—"to tell the accurate story . . . of what he himself told me of his whole life and what I remember personally." In fact, this book does differ from *Beloved Infidel* (1958) and *College of One* (1967) in that it is not simply an account of time spent with Fitzgerald but is rather a compendium of material about him and from him gathered from their time together. Arranged in topical chapters which deal with, successively, Scott as husband, Scott as father, Scott as drinker, Scott as lover, Scott as writer, *The Last Tycoon*, Scott as educator of Sheilah, and Scott's death, the book does rehash a good deal of old information; but it includes some new material. The amount and importance of the latter, however, do not justify an entire new book.

While we have probably heard too much by now from Sheilah Graham, heretofore we had not heard at all from Hemingway's youngest son. Gregory H. Hemingway's *Papa: A Personal Memoir* (Boston: Houghton Mifflin) is a strange wisp of a book. Written out of admittedly ambivalent feelings towards its subject, it is, like Mary Welsh Hemingway's autobiography, more interesting for what it does not state explicitly than for what it does. To be sure, there are some engaging vignettes—chasing German subs aboard the *Pilar*, Gregory making his father beam by tying for the shooting championship of Cuba at age eleven; and some good interviews with such people who knew Hemingway as boxer George Brown and millionnaire Mike Lerner. But our belief in the accuracy of the book is strained by the length and number of conversations with his father that Gregory renders verbatim; and we can only guess why father and son were estranged during the last decade of the father's life. It is, nonetheless, interesting to compare Gregory and Mary on a few of the episodes they both describe, such as the visit to Cuba of Adriana Ivancich, a lovely young Italian noblewoman with whom Ernest was obviously infatuated. In general, Gregory is far crueler about his father's last years than Mary is, noting at one point, "It's fine to be under the influence of a dominating personality as long as he's healthy, but when he gets dry rot of the soul, how do you bring yourself to tell him he stinks?" If his book were not suffused with this attitude, it might have been more valuable as biography; as it is, it does tell us a great deal by implication about the relationship of Hemingway and his youngest son, without providing much in the way of explanations.

Fitzgerald's only child, now Mrs. Frances Scott Fitzgerald Smith, apparently bears none of the resentment towards her father that Gregory Hemingway does towards his. In the latest of innumerable interviews she has granted in the last decade, Mrs. Smith speaks mostly of her father's writings and themes, dwelling at length on his sense of and interest in American history. She does admit to interviewer Christine Johnson, in "Daughter and Father: An Interview With Mrs. Frances Scott Fitzgerald Smith, Washington, D.C., August 29, 1973" (*EA* 29:72–75), that she wishes her father had "addressed himself more seriously to the problems of the time, instead of writing exclusively about the very rich."

Two final biographical items are primarily redundant. In "Hadley: An Engaging Person" (*LGJ* 4,i:27–30), Lawrence Broer quotes from an interview with Hemingway's first wife, who contributes little that is new to our picture of her husband and their relationship. Similarly, in his *Hanging On In Paradise* (New York: McGraw-Hill, 1975), Fred Lawrence Guiles gives detailed accounts of Fitzgerald's sojourns in Hollywood, paying considerable attention to the scripts he worked on during those trips; but he adds almost nothing to this already well-researched area.

a. **General Essays.** The general essays this year are neither as numerous nor as worthwhile as those covered in the recent surveys. The best of a meager lot on Fitzgerald is Ruth Prigozy's " 'Poor Butterfly': F. Scott Fitzgerald and Popular Music" (*Prospects* 2:41–67), which contends that Fitzgerald, more than most writers of his time, "was shaped by movies, by musical comedies, and not least by popular music." Specifically, Prigozy presents a chart of the popular songs in Fitzgerald's works and then examines how popular music is utilized—as an "analogue for a character's mood," as background, and as a means of developing his themes and commenting often ironically, on the action. Although her approach is somewhat unexciting, Prigozy's examples are suggestive and her thesis convincingly argued.

In "F. Scott Fitzgerald's St. Paul: A Writer's Use of Material" (*Minnesota History* 45:141–48), Patricia Kane sees Fitzgerald's St. Paul as "more symbolic than actual." Examining *Gatsby*, "The Ice Palace," "Winter Dreams," and several Basil Duke Lee stories, she concludes, not surprisingly, that Fitzgerald's "use of the city corresponds in part to his experience of it, but he freely altered or reinterpreted his perceptions to suit the characters and themes of his fiction."

Difficulties in defining key terms weaken the two other general essays on Fitzgerald. Douglas Robillard's "The Paradises of Scott Fitzgerald" (*EAS* 4[1975]:64–73) offers opinions on many of Fitzgerald's major works; but never really centers on what appears to be its main argument about the different sorts of paradises depicted in Fitzgerald's fiction. Robillard seems too intent on asserting a great deal of "waste in Fitzgerald's writing." Similarly, Edward Marcotte, in "Fitzgerald and Nostalgia" (*MQ* 17:186–91), begins with a definition of nostalgia as "a fixation on the past—but the past evoked in a special way," citing several "evocations" of this in *Gatsby* and Fitzgerald's notebooks; but then he jumps inexplicably from "nostalgia" to the mythic sense of Eden/America, calling Eden "the prototype of all nostalgia." This essay succeeds neither as definition, which it apparently intends to be, nor as literary criticism.

The general essays on Hemingway this year are characterized by a tendency to cover familiar territory, albeit from slightly different points of view. In "Hemingway and Revolution: *Mankinde* not Marx" (*Renaissance and Modern*, pp. 143–59), Joseph M. DeFalco focuses on Hemingway's writings between 1937 and 1940 as "works of a transitional phase in Hemingway's underlying assumptions about human life and values." Emphasizing *To Have and Have Not* and *For Whom the Bell Tolls*, DeFalco sees a "shift from self-concern to the concern for others." After Robert Jordan, then, "the Hemingway hero is no longer fettered by the egocentrism that marked many of the early heroes." DeFalco's argument is clearly presented and persuasive; but it is too similar to those offered by earlier critics, most recently Fredrik C. Brøgger (see *ALS 1975*, p. 181). Roger Whitlow seems to be dealing with basically the same pattern in Hemingway's works in "The Destruction/Prevention of the Family Relationship in Hemingway's Fiction" (*LitR* 20:5–16). Whitlow notes that in the fiction through *For Whom the Bell Tolls*, normal family life is impossible; but, in *The Old Man and the Sea*, affirmation occurs when Santiago reaches out to Manolin, thus creating a father-son relationship, and also when Santiago recognizes his brotherhood with all living creatures.

Hemingway's view of women and the Hemingway code are two other oft-studied topics which receive attention again this year. In "Ernest Hemingway's Conception of Love and Womanhood" (*BP* 19[1972; pub. 1974]:37–47), S. T. Kallapur repeats many of the clichés: the role of woman in Hemingway's fiction is "to keep her man comfortable"; all Hemingway heroines are basically the same; "whether it is lust or passion, love rarely rises above the biological level in Hemingway"; and "women are not individuals with their own existence—they are more like dream projections of an adolescent." Philip Durham is on slightly more original ground, in "Ernest Hemingway's Grace Under Pressure: The Western Code" (*PHR* 45: 425–32), when he suggests that Hemingway's reading of mystery writer Raymond Chandler and western fictionist Ernest Haycox is behind the code adhered to by the Hemingway hero. After examining *For Whom the Bell Tolls* at length and several short stories more briefly, Durham concludes, "The true Hemingway hero—although he may fight wars in Italy, climb mountains in Spain, shoot lions in Africa—is the same hero who walked the mean streets in Chandler's fiction and rode through the western mountains and deserts of the Haycox novels." The comparison, while intriguing, ultimately seems not to be productive of much additional insight into Hemingway's writings.

The issue of *Linguistics in Literature* (Spring 1976) which is entirely devoted to "Hemingway's Experiments in Structure and Style" includes a general essay by Bates Hoffer, "Hemingway's Use of Stylistics" (1,ii:89–121), among its studies of specific Hemingway stories (these items will be discussed below). In a very detailed and technical essay, Hoffer uses passages from Hemingway's fiction to illustrate each of the "linguistic elements which may be stylistic features." These include orthography, phonology, syllable structure, vocabulary (general vs. specific, name vs. pronoun, parts of speech, lexical density, imagery), sentence level (length or type), and higher level devices (symbol, allegory, matrix). Such analysis, Hoffer contends, "reveals a wide range of stylistic experiments, often while he retained the impression of simple, straightforward, realistic prose." In terms of his criteria, Hoffer concludes that "there isn't a single Hemingway 'style'; rather, there is a wide variety of styles coupled to structure and content." This is often a very difficult article to follow; but it rewards close attention.

In a briefer note on Hemingway's use of imagery, "How Ernest Is the Image: Hemingway's Little Animals" (*CEA* 37,iii[1975]:5–8), Patrick W. Shaw points out that it is not lions, sharks, and bulls which dominate Hemingway's fiction but a number of nonviolent smaller domestic animals. He discusses Frederic Henry as a "prime example of a Hemingway man whose character and life are exemplified by [domestic] animals and animal imagery." This is a slight but clearly developed piece.

Again this year we have the usual number of essays which compare Fitzgerald or Hemingway with other writers. The only one on Fitzgerald does at least offer a new name as a possible influence. In "Stephen Leacock: An Early Influence on F. Scott Fitzgerald" (*CRevAS* 7:5–14), Ralph Curry and Janet Lewis find Fitzgerald imitating Leacock in "Jemima" and see traces of Leacockian humor in later work like "The Cruise of the Rolling Junk." Their conclusion, that "the unprejudiced eye of the humorist stood Fitzgerald in good stead as he went on to write his criticism of society," is urged gently; and it reminds us that we have too few studies of humor in Fitzgerald's work.

Poe scholar Burton R. Pollin suggests an influence in "Poe and Hemingway on Violence and Death" (*ES* 57:139–42). Although Hemingway specifically denied being influenced by Poe (in *The Green Hills of Africa*), Pollin asserts that, "However and whenever the 'discovery' of Poe by Hemingway took place, it seems to me that the theme of violent death, the overcoming of fear, and the stress on sensations, all frequent and powerful in Poe, may have descended to Hemingway not only as part of the tradition but also as a direct part of his own personal reading."

The influence of Conrad, already much-studied with respect to Fitzgerald, is suggested with respect to Hemingway, in a short essay by Peter L. Hays, "Conrad and Hemingway" (*AN&Q* 14:87–88). Hays (whose name is misspelled Hayes in the journal) cites striking similarities between passages from Conrad's Preface to *The Nigger of the Narcissus* and Hemingway's famous comment on learning to write in *Death in the Afternoon*. Finally, despite its title, Earl Rovit's "Faulkner, Hemingway, and the American Family" (*MissQ* 29:483–97) deals less with Faulkner and Hemingway specifically than with them as emblematic of the post-World War I "lost generation."

b. **Essays on Specific Works: Fitzgerald.** Despite the publicity in 1976 surrounding the cinema adaptation of yet another Fitzgerald novel, *The Last Tycoon*, critical commentary on *The Great Gatsby* continued seemingly unaffected by this popular focus on Fitzgerald's last novel. The imbalance is even more striking than in previous years. Of twenty-two essays and notes on specific Fitzgerald works, 17 deal with *Gatsby* and 5 with *Tender Is the Night*. Again perhaps due to the delay in the publication of the *Fitzgerald/Hemingway Annual*, we have no studies of either any of the stories or of the other three novels. To make matters worse, most of the new material on *Gatsby* is slight and unoriginal in focus.

Studies of time, structure and style, Fitzgerald's dual vision, religion and myth, and eye imagery in the novel—all previously studied —dominate this year's *Gatsby* items. In what is the best of the structure and style pieces, "Structural Imagery in *The Great Gatsby*: Metaphor and Matrix" (*LNL* 1,i[1975]:53–75), Barbara Gerber Sanders, through detailed and, at times, highly technical, analysis, endeavors to find the "covert meaning" of *Gatsby*. Her technique is linguistically oriented but is also concerned with the structure and form of the novel. She finds a great deal of evidence that a "birth metaphor" is at the center and that it is used as "a standard by which to interpret" the characters. Her conclusion is that this interpretation makes Nick and his "awakening" the true subject of the novel. Unlike a good deal of linguistic criticism, this essay is coherent and convincing and does lead directly into areas where less technical literary criticism might prove rewarding. In " 'The Unreality of Reality': Metaphor in *The Great Gatsby*" (*Style* 11:56–72), Leonard A. Podis deals with the different kinds of metaphors in the novel, asserting that metaphor destroys the wall between reality and the world of imagination, thereby ideally projecting the combined romantic/realistic vision of *Gatsby*. Like Sanders, Podis focuses on Nick, citing "dead metaphors," "rationally analogical metaphors," and three classes of "radically subjective" metaphors. His examples do support his conclusion that a "close study of metaphor in *The Great Gatsby* . . . reveals that it is . . . central to the expression of the entire range of meaning conveyed in the novel."

Of the three studies of time in *Gatsby*, the best of a weak group is Paul Melebeck's "Time and Time Structure in *The Great Gatsby*" (*RLV* 42,U.S. bicentennial issue:213–24). Melebeck dates every event in the novel and then shows how time in the novel is double in nature: it is both material and visible and also psychological and emotional. Ultimately, Melebeck notes, the novel does what Gatsby could not do, it controls the past and imposes the order of art upon time. In "The Temporal Location of Fitzgerald's Jay Gatsby" (*TQ* 18,ii[1975]:122–30), R. Michael Sheffield also see two different sorts of time operating—quantitative and qualitative. Sheffield contends that Fitzgerald's technique is to study Gatsby quantitatively, first by rehearsing the events of his life and then to emphasize the qualitative aspects—most prominently his affair with Daisy in Louisville, which "eventually became the center of his entire being." This is at times a confusing essay which probably has little that is highly original to reward a careful reader. Robert Ian Scott's approach, in "A Sense of Loss: Entropy vs. Ecology in *The Great Gatsby*" (*QQ* 82[1975]: 559–71), is at least more original. He views the novel as an illustration of the second law of thermodynamics: time and wealth destroy the reality on which human relationships and hope depend. Scott cites the many forms of entropy in *Gatsby*—boredom, confusion, a sense of loss (particularly of the past)—and makes the rather obvious point that only Gatsby is great enough to see the hopelessness and yet determine to retain hope.

In what is the best new essay on *Gatsby* this year, "Love, Death and Resurrection in *The Great Gatsby*" (*Aeolian Harps*, pp. 273–89),

Robert J. Emmitt makes some intriguing suggestions as to how the Grail legend, the waste land myth, and "the ancient Semitic and Egyptian resurrection myths" became for Fitzgerald "a central armature around which he modeled the novel, as well as a resource for much of the elaborative symbolism which adorns it." Although Emmitt's analogies may seem far-fetched at first, his careful reading of such obviously central elements of *Gatsby* as its use of color, its symbols of seasonal change, and the death and rebirth pattern, in conjunction with his knowledge of how these same elements function in the myths he uses, make this a surprisingly original and even seminal essay on a subject which one might think exhausted in what now appear to be superficial previous studies. By comparison, Jeffrey Hart's "Reconsideration—*The Great Gatsby* by F. Scott Fitzgerald" (*NewRep* 174,xvi:31–33) is very flimsy indeed. Hart claims that although the novel is defined in religious terms, they are not those of Christianity but rather of magic and witchcraft. A "sense of strange transformation pervades the book," in which Gatsby, as divinity, changes his name, appearance, and dwelling, all through the magical power of the dollar; but he cannot annihilate time and proves a "false Christ," a "great doomed magician."

As its title suggests, Vasant A. Shahane's "F. Scott Fitzgerald's Dual Vision in *The Great Gatsby*" (*Indian Studies*, pp. 153–62) offers little new in its discovery of Gatsby's "sense of commitment to the ideal as well as his subtle awareness of the inevitable failure of that ideal" or in its observation that Gatsby's dream "destroys him but at the same time it gives him a new lease on life." By contrast, Paul A. Scanlon's modestly argued "The Great Gatsby: Romance and Realism" (*AntigR* 27:37–41) presents some new ideas on Jay Gatsby as a medieval chivalric knight. Scanlon's specifics are striking, especially his depiction of the courtship of Daisy as being in the best courtly tradition.

Ryan LaHurd, in "'Absolution': *Gatsby's* Forgotten Front Door" (*CollL* 3:113–23), seemingly is ignorant of the previous work on this subject; and his point about the importance of seeing Rudolph in the story as a preadolescent Jay Gatz, while it is explored more fully here, is not very original. Don Graham's "The Common Ground of *Goodbye, Columbus* and *The Great Gatsby*" (*ForumH* 13,iii:68–71) makes a good case for the influence of Fitzgerald's novel on Roth's, pointing out numerous connections, but observing that, while *Gatsby* "is essentially an elegy for a lost America," *Goodbye, Columbus* is "a dark comedy. The elegaic mood comes to us in parodic terms."

Strangely, four of this year's five notes on *The Great Gatsby* deal with an aspect of eye imagery in the novel. In *"The Great Gatsby*: Myrtle's Dog and Its Relation to the Dog-God of Pound and Eliot" (*AN&Q* 14:88–90), Michael Pottorf suggests that "sightless eyes incorporated within a dog-God motif was a metaphor common to Eliot, Fitzgerald, and others [who used it] as a vehicle to the perception of the materialistic demise and the moral disintegration of the jazz age." But the parallels he points out between *Gatsby* and *The Waste Land* have, for the most part, been noted previously. Sanford Pinsker's observation, in "Seeing *The Great Gatsby* Eye to Eye" (*CollL* 3:69–71), that Fitzgerald incorporated the eyes of Dr. T. J. Eckleburg into the novel as "an accident" after seeing a proposed dust jacket for the forthcoming book which Maxwell Perkins sent him in the summer of 1924, has been noted by earlier critics and is certainly open to conjecture (see Matthew J. Bruccoli's Introduction to his *Gatsby* facsimile [Washington, D.C.: Microcard Editions, 1973], pp. xvi, xviii).

Two critics attempt to establish the identity, real or symbolic, of the character Owl Eyes. In "Who Is 'Owl Eyes' In *The Great Gatsby?*" (*AN&Q* 13[1975]:72–74), David Savage views him as a contrast to Eckleburg, the "dead, unfeeling god of the waste land." Owl Eyes, the only party-goer to appear at Gatsby's funeral, "typifies the American capacity for compassion" and kindness. In asserting that Fitzgerald wanted him "to be associated with the best in moral and conservative America," Savage is investing a relatively minor character with a greater burden of significance than he should be asked to bear. Riley V. Hampton, in "Owl Eyes in *The Great Gatsby*" (*AL* 48:229), is far more restrained in offering Ring Lardner, who had been called "Owl Eyes" by a fellow sportswriter, as a possible "real-life prototype" for the character in *Gatsby*.

Finally, in what is the most worthwhile of the notes on *Gatsby*, "The Death of Rosy Rosenthal: A Note on Fitzgerald's Use of Background in *The Great Gatsby*" (*N&Q* 23:22–23), Dalton H. Gross observes that the gangland murder of Rosy Rosenthal outside the Metropole actually took place in 1912 and was given wide publicity; thus, Meyer Wolfsheim's allusion to it in the novel is, both for Nick and for the reader, "a chillingly realistic introduction to Gatsby's world."

Between July 1949 and April 1950 novelist Malcolm Lowry and his wife Margerie worked on a movie adaptation of *Tender Is the Night*, ultimately producing a 455-page script (now held by the University of British Columbia Library and "for copyright reasons" unpublishable) which was never filmed, and several pages of "Notes" on their version of Fitzgerald's novel. Prefaced with an engrossing introduction by Paul Tiessen, which traces the Lowrys' interest in *Tender* and explains the fate of their script, as well as relating the adaptation to Lowry's novel *Under the Volcano*, these notes have been published as *Notes on a Screenplay for F. Scott Fitzgerald's "Tender Is the Night"* (Bloomfield Hills, Mich.: Bruccoli Clark). Obviously, this material was not intended for publication; further, it has been left largely unedited and uncorrected. The result is a kind of shorthand stream-of-consciousness style which is frequently hard to follow. Although there is some analysis and criticism of *Tender* here, more often the comments concern the Lowrys' screenplay, which in turn is their interpretation of Fitzgerald's novel and thus should be used with caution.

The most substantial new essay on *Tender Is the Night* is Marjory Martin's "Fitzgerald's Image of Woman: Anima Projections in *Tender Is the Night*" (*ESColl* ser. 1,no.6,17 pp.). Martin disagrees with those previous critics who regard Fitzgerald's women characters as shallow, narcissistic, and inhuman, arguing that in *Tender Is the Night* they are aesthetically valid when one sees them as anima projections of Dick Diver and then recognizes that, as anima projections, they must be analyzed in terms of archetypal associations. In a full and clearly illustrated piece, Martin examines the female characters in the novel as illustrations of various archetypal figures: goddess, priestess, temptress, Kore maiden, Madonna, and purely sexual creature. This essay suggests fruitful further study of this topic.

In "Physician in the Counting House: The Religious Motif in *Tender Is the Night*" (*ELWIU* 2[1975]:192–208), Barry V. Qualls suggests that *Tender* is "essentially a religious drama, its very structure suggesting a pilgrim's progress," but an inverted one; for we witness the dissolution of Dick's religious sense in the face of the "fair world of the moneyed leisure class." Qualls is on firm ground when he shows how language and structure "stress what happens when the psychiatrist degenerates into a magician-entertainer" through irony and inversion; but, with all the previous analyses of Dick as a prototypical Fitzgerald "spoiled priest," this is not an overly original essay.

Alan S. Wheelock's "As Ever, 'Daddy's Girl': Incest Motifs in *Day for Night*" (*GyS* 2[1975]:69–75) is concerned far more with Truffaut's film than with Fitzgerald's novel, although it does suggest an "affinity" between them which Wheelock feels indicates Truffaut's "acknowledgement" of the book. The parallels cited—"both works exploit a Riviera setting," both "introduce husband characters whose professional speciality is psychiatry," both "employ the automobile accident as a symbol of impending disaster," and both "use the puerile lover . . . as a measure of the falling-off in human values inherent in the act of adultery"—are striking. A more literary relationship is proposed by George Monteiro, in "Henry James and Scott Fitzgerald: A Source" (*NConL* 6,ii:4–6). Monteiro points to the episode in *Tender Is the Night* in which Dick Diver, bicycling through Europe, unexpectedly runs into Nicole Warren, as having been influenced by James's *Daisy Miller*. Fitzgerald's debts to James have been noted often; and Monteiro's note is plausibly and unpretentiously argued.

c. **Essays on Specific Works: Hemingway.**   Primarily because of the special issue of *Linguistics in Literature* alluded to above, there is a disproportionate number of essays this year on Hemingway's short stories; but the novels continue to receive considerable attention as well. We have no less than nine essays on *The Sun Also Rises*. Several of the best endeavor, in different ways, to emphasize the optimism of the novel. In "*The Sun Also Rises* On Its Own Ground" (*JNT* 6:224–32), W. J. Stuckey rejects the orthodox reading of the novel as "a prose version of *The Waste Land*," insisting that actually Hemingway's "imagination and intellect and mode of life were in many ways the antithesis of Eliot's." Stuckey feels that the attitude which underlies the novel says, "with chin up and lowered eyes, that we are all bitched from the start but that we must live with the knowledge of death and extinction, taking what pleasure we can from the sensuous contemplation of that fact and some little comfort in the permanence of nature itself." This is a well-argued and clearly presented point of view which needs to be placed alongside the numerous earlier articles that see *Sun* in more negative terms.

Working within a more limited scope, Donald A. Daiker, in "The Affirmative Conclusion of *The Sun Also Rises*" (*McNR* 21[1974–75]: 3–19), comes to much the same conclusion as Stuckey. Daiker's focus is on book 3, with glances back to books 1 and 2. His point is that Jake, influenced by Romero and Mippipopolous, gains by the end of the novel "the strength and self-control to end once and for all his destructive relationship with Brett," thereby making the conclusion "quietly and deeply affirmative." This is a beautifully written and sensible piece of analysis. David Henry Lowenkron's "Jake Barnes: A Student of William James in 'The Sun Also Rises'" (*TQ* 19,i:147–56) also is concerned with Jake and also rejects previously held negative views of him. Lowenkron's approach is through William James's pragmatism, an "openness to philosophical change and the facts of existence that would cause a rationalist to be disgusted by its thingness, and the stoic to sneer, annoyed by its optimism." He then shows convincingly how Jake rejects, in the course of the novel, four other "systems or codes" which "he tries to absorb in order to give structure to his universe." These are Catholicism, hedonism, economics (the idea that you pay for what you receive in life), and professionalism (the example of Romero and Montoya). This essay is more persuasive in demonstrating Jake's rejections of these systems than it is in convincing us that he embraces pragmatism.

W. R. MacNaughton involves Hemingway with William James's brother Henry, in "Maisie's Grace Under Pressure: Some Thoughts on James and Hemingway" (*MFS* 22:153–64); but again the comparison is used to convince us that Hemingway's vision in *The Sun Also Rises* is basically affirmative. MacNaughton compares *Sun* with *What Maisie Knew*, concluding that, in both novels, "within the waste land worlds, values exist which, however evanescently, can transform games of war into games of love." While more attention is paid to James here than to Hemingway, the article is yet another in what seems to be a strong reaction in recent criticism against viewing *Sun* against a background of *The Waste Land*, an approach which has prevailed for so long. Charles C. Walcutt, in "Hemingway's *The Sun Also Rises*" (*Expl* 32[1974]:item 57), sounds an early note of this reaction by rejecting James Twitchell's characterization (Dec., 1972 *Explicator*) of Bill, Jake, and Brett as adolescents. Walcutt sees them rather as spiritually damaged people making the best they can out of a messy world.

In a well-documented and sound essay, "One More River to Cross: The Bridge Motif in *The Sun Also Rises*" (*CEA* 37,ii[1975]:21–22), David L. Vanderwerken notes that "a bridge crossing marks each step of Jake's pilgrimage from the corruption of Paris to the purity of Burguete" and contends that each crossing symbolizes a shift in Jake's physical or psychological state. Vanderwerken's article is too brief to do more than suggest the workability of this notion; but it is successful in doing this. Also brief but suggestive is Gerald T. Gordon's "Survival in *The Sun Also Rises* (Hemingway's Harvey Stone)" (*LGJ* 4,ii:10–11,17) which reassesses Stone, who is usually dismissed simply as a "vulgar lying drunk" or a "case of arrested development." Gordon points out Stone's affinities with Jake as well as his similarities to and differences from Robert, asserting that "Stone's only asset is his perseverance—his ability to hang on the ropes in the face of defeat," adding that "there is something suspiciously reassuring in that."

If Eliot is falling out of favor as a writer with whom to pair Hemingway, replacements new and old are available. Martin Light, in "Sweeping Out Chivalric Silliness: The Example of Huck Finn and *The Sun Also Rises*" (*MTJ* 17,iii[1974–75]:18–21), takes the assertions of Earl Wilcox (see *ALS 1971*, p. 137) that Huck and Jake and Tom and Robert be linked as realists and romantics, respectively, one step further by placing all four "in a matrix derived from Cervantes' *Don Quixote.*" Thus, Tom/Robert reflect Don Quixote and Huck/Jake reflect Sancho; and both novels invoke the formula of a character who reads romantic literature and is impelled to adventures where he "tests society, rights wrongs and quests for a beloved lady." Light's arguments seem a justifiable extension of Wilcox's, although they are far from startlingly original. Eben Bass's "Hemingway's Women of Another Country" (*MarkhamR* 6:35–39) is more original but probably less convincing than Light's essay. Bass's focus is on Robert Cohn, a man dominated by women, who is insufficient both as a Hemingway male (who should know he must survive without women) and as the Jewish Machiavelli of Marlowe's "Jew of Malta." The article also contains a long and rambling comparison of Robert and the Esau-Jacob-Isaac story in the Bible.

Like many of the essays on *The Sun Also Rises*, the three articles on *For Whom the Bell Tolls* all stress the upbeat and regenerative final impression which the novel leaves. Ironically, two of the pieces arrive at this conclusion from what seem to be diametrically opposed points of view. David E. Zehr's "Bourgeois Politics: Hemingway's Case in *For Whom the Bell Tolls*" (*MQ* 17:268–78) evaluates Hemingway's "political response and commitment" in the novel, contending that, at the beginning of the book, Robert Jordan is "emotionally alienated, [a] pragmatic instrument of those who are conducting the war." At the end, Hemingway has not shown us a disillusioned Jordan but rather he has restored his "ability to function as a political man" which is awakened by his contact with the partisans. What he realizes is that, ultimately, men must combat both fascism and power politics "in the name of such simple human virtues as individual freedom and dignity."

In "*For Whom the Bell Tolls* as Mythic Narrative" (*DR* 56:52–69), John J. Teunissen begins with the assertion that "the basic theme of *For Whom the Bell Tolls* is not a political one." Instead, he sees Jordan as going through the mythic process of "de-individuation," whereby he is ritually initiated into mythic *tempus* and *locus*. The going gets a little heavy as Teunissen develops his thesis; but it is clear that he is calling for a view of the novel which places it in the American tradition of romance and ritual, as opposed to previous critics who have insisted on perceiving it through political, historical, or sociological perspectives.

Like Zehr and Teunissen, Gary K. Elliott, in "*For Whom the Bell Tolls*: Regeneration of the Hemingway Hero" (*CEA* 38,iv:24–29), sees Jordan as renewed at the end of the novel. Elliott's perspective is that of religion, noting that Robert "establishes and sustains faith in his work as a substitute for orthodox religious faith, one that emphasizes man's responsibility to men and, ultimately, a man's responsibility to himself." As so many critics have found recently, with respect to *For Whom the Bell Tolls*, Elliott locates the optimistic ending of the book in Jordan's growing awareness of and faith in "community action," his oneness with others.

The most valuable new material on *A Farewell to Arms* is to be found in Michael S. Reynolds's book, which has already been discussed. But two essays are also worthy of mention. William Adair's "Time and Structure in *A Farewell to Arms*" (*SDR* 13,i[1975]:165–71) is a modestly argued study of two aspects of the theme of Time in the novel. Adair emphasizes the first of these, the manner in which the passage of Time "finds poetic embodiment in an almost constant *movement along lines*: walking along, and perhaps more important, the passage of vehicles—metaphorically, vehicles of Time—along various 'lines': streets, roads, tracks, bridges, shorelines, and hallways." As a "counter-theme," Adair proposes "Frederic's attempt to impose a sense of order and control on the movement of Time and the consequent flux of circumstances." His discussion is specific and stresses his contention that images embodying these themes intensify markedly at the three moments of "violent disruption" in the novel: Frederic's wounding, the arrest and desertion, and Catherine's death. Next to this unpretentious piece, Judith Fetterley's "*A Farewell to Arms*: Hemingway's 'Resentful Cryptogram'" (*JPC* 10:203–14) seems shrill and overly insistent, albeit coherent and well written. Fetterley is the latest in a long line of critics to take Hemingway to task for his female characters. She sees Hemingway as immensely hostile to women and further as disguising that hostility in this novel through a "disparity between its overt fabric of idealized romance and its underlying vision of the radical limitations of love."

In the better of two recent essays on *The Old Man and the Sea,* Georges Bataille's "Hemingway in the Light of Hegel" (*Semiotext[e]* 2,ii:5–15), Hemingway's moral vision is likened to Hegel's "dialectic of master and slave." In this system, masters were those who confronted death, slaves those "who preferred loss of liberty to loss of life"; and thus Hemingway's morality is that of the masters. In *The Old Man and the Sea,* Bataille sees Santiago's struggle with the fish as that of a master fighting for recognition by an equal in a confrontation with that equal in a life or death struggle. In comparison with this carefully worded essay, Krishna Nandan Sinha's "*The Old Man and the Sea*: An Approach to Meaning" (*Indian Studies,* pp. 219–28) is trivial and unoriginal with its emphasis on the "Christian analogy" of the novel.

The one new essay on *Islands in the Stream,* Stephen L. Tanner's "Hemingway's Islands" (*SWR* 61:74–84), stresses the way nostalgia functions in the novel, showing that it counterpoints the action in part 3 and finally unifies the book structurally. Tanner sees Thomas Hudson's last nostalgic recollections as serving two basic functions: "they provide a lull or breathing spell in the action, a contrast which frames the final violent incident" and they "bring the high points of the first two parts to bear on the conclusion, illuminating and intensifying its meaning." Hardly a startling insight, but useful.

The tendency, in criticism of the last few years, to see a unity or a pattern in *In Our Time* continues with E. D. Lowry's "Chaos and Cosmos in *In Our Time*" (*L&P* 26:108–17). Although Lowry depends too heavily on the biographical fact of Hemingway's own wounding on the Italian front as the event which shaped the writer's "mind and art," he is persuasive in finding the book's "narrative technique" in "the systematic interruption and resumption of Nick's story —but always on a new plane, with a new and different Nick"—as part of an overall "rhythmic interplay of life and death, destruction and renewal, chaos and cosmos." T. G. Vaidyanathan, in "The Nick Adams Stories and the Myth of Initiation" (*Indian Studies*, pp. 203–18), is intent on disproving a pattern. He denies that, in the Nick Adams stories, "there is a continuum of cumulative experiences, strung in a convenient linear order, all of which contribute to Nick's education." By examining several of the individual stories, Vaidyanathan shows in rather pedestrian fashion that many of them constitute full units in themselves rather than part of a continuous developing story of Nick's education.

Because many of the essays on individual Hemingway stories this year appeared in the special issue of *Linguistics in Literature* and because each of those pieces discusses a different story but from basically the same sort of perspective, they will be dealt with together here rather than comparing them with the other essays on Hemingway's short fiction.

As might be expected, the nine essays are uneven. Three are quite good, two are very bad, and four are undistinguished but useful. In general, however, the approach of analyzing the style and structure of Hemingway's short stories through linguistically oriented criticism is one which ought to be encouraged. In one of the best, Mary Kay Willis's "Structural Analysis of 'The Battler'" (*LNL* 1,ii:61–67), an examination of "the lexical density of adjectives" used to describe the three main characters of the story leads to a plausible interpretation of the meaning of the story. Willis sees it as illustrating "a learning experience as to the meaning of friendship and the role of violence and even perhaps the blows a battler must face in life." In this view Nick is himself the battler who "moves forward to the new experiences which await him." In "Structural Matrix: A Stylistic Analysis of 'The End of Something'" (*LNL* 1,ii:53–60), Jessie C. Gunn, through a study of vocabulary, key "lexical items," symbol sets, and analogies, makes three very interesting and convincing observations about this story: "Hemingway set up in this story a comparison between Nick and Marjorie's love affair and the lumber mill"; "the love affair is as dead as is the old lumber town"; and "regeneration is the key to the development of Nick and is, indeed, the key to the story." Barbara Sanders's "Linguistic Analysis of 'Cross-Country Snow' " (*LNL* 1,ii:43–52) is a dense but rewarding critique which contends that the "structural-thematic scheme" of the story is "a completely balanced set of opposites and depends on tension." To illustrate this she examines word repetition, the similarity between the beginning and the ending of the story, the shifting of tenses within sentences, and the recurrence of certain images such as the skiers.

Two of the other essays in this special issue also find patterns of analogies. In "Symbolic Motifs in 'A Canary for One' " (*LNL* 1,ii:35–41), Trisha Ingman sees the train as epitomizing "the emotional journey of the characters." Thus, the "view outside the train windows parallels the change in the couple's relationship," as the "domestic setting of the red brick house disintegrates into an uninhabited area" and the sea, "the life-giver," is at first visible clearly, then only occasionally, and then not at all. Similarly, a burning farmhouse, passed by the train, is "like the couple's marriage, laid bare in front of many spectators," having "gone up in smoke." But Ingman's essay tends to fall apart in its second half when she draws numerous parallels between Hemingway's own marital situation at the time he wrote the story and that of the fictional couple. Leslie Miller's " 'Cat in the Rain' " (*LNL* 1,ii:29–34) similarly focuses on Hemingway's "use of contrasting images, symbols, and irony to convey his complex ideas in a minimum of space." The cold, unkind husband is contrasted with the benevolent hotel-keeper; the growing darkness of the day is contrasted with the artificial light illuminating the square. Parallel images Miller cites include the empty square as equated with "the hollowness and sterility of the couple's marriage" and the war monument in the square as representative of their past relationship.

Barbara Maloy, in "The Light of Alice's World" (*LNL* 1,ii:69–86), finds parallels also, but hers are between Hemingway's "The Light of the World" and *Alice in Wonderland* and *Through the Looking Glass*. These startling comparisons, which Maloy presents in a chart as an appendix to her essay, are interspersed with somewhat more convincing and helpful material about images of Hell in the story. Ray Lanford's "Hemingway's 'My Old Man'" (*LNL* 1,ii:11–19) is an interesting study of how our view of the story's meaning can shift as we become aware of different levels of interpretation. Lanford begins with the obvious surface theme of the story—Joe's sudden and brutal entry into an adult world—and with the structural devices employed to reinforce this interpretation; but then he shifts to an examination of how the reader and Joe have been misled into drawing false conclusions about Joe's father. To do this he focuses on a pattern of "reversals; the items which Joe somehow misunderstands, the items which, after their first appearance in the story, come to be seen differently by the time of the story's end," leading to a revised conception of the father as a noble figure.

In an incoherent and poorly argued piece, "'The Gambler, the Nun, and the Radio'" (*LNL* 1,ii:21–28), Donna Pearson relies too heavily on number symbolism which is at best questionable, as well as on sentence length, jargon, and vocabulary, as evidence for her interpretation of the story: "the idea that people live life in different ways, some very successfully, and some tragically." Lois Brackenridge's "Analysis of 'Today Is Friday' by Ernest Hemingway" (*LNL* 1,ii:1–10) seems too forced in its attempts to find exact parallels between characters in Hemingway's story and figures in the Biblical passion narrative. Her approach is not as systematic as it should be and her conclusions are not convincing.

Not surprisingly, we have our yearly essay on the waiter's speech controversy in "A Clean, Well-Lighted Place." C. Harold Hurley, in "The Attribution of the Waiter's Second Speech in Hemingway's 'A Clean, Well-Lighted Place'" (*SSF* 13:81–85), maintains that the lack of identifying tags does not conceal the fact that Hemingway meant to present "two different kinds" of waiters, because he used a simple pattern for differentiating between them: the younger waiter asks the questions, while the older one gives terse answers in keeping with his advanced awareness of the nihilism to which the younger waiter has not yet had much exposure. Surely there is more to the matter than this proposal which Hurley offers. Lawrence Broer's "The Iceberg in 'A Clean, Well-Lighted Place'" (*LGJ* 4,ii:14–15, 21) also dwells somewhat redundantly on the nihilism of the older waiter, although he does range more widely in comparing this character to other Hemingway heroes and in examining the "images of isolation and aloneness" in the story.

The usage of parallel and contrasting images, which pervades so much recent commentary on Hemingway's short stories, is the main point of one of the two new essays on "The Snows of Kilimanjaro," Alfred Kolb's "Symbolic Structure in Hemingway's 'The Snows of Kilimanjaro'" (*NMAL* 1:item 4). Kolb notes two sets of symbols which frame the story, the leopard and the hyena, and the mimosa tree and the airplane, and examines both of these closely, observing that each symbol "encompasses both positive and negative elements," suggesting that Hemingway "consciously invested his symbols with ambiguities and that these very ambiguities point up his intent." The other essay, Gennaro Santangelo's "The Dark Snows of Kilimanjaro" (in *The Short Stories of Ernest Hemingway: Critical Essays*, ed. Jackson J. Benson [Durham, N.C.: Duke Univ. Press, 1975], pp. 251–61), which, unfortunately, was omitted from last year's survey, is more general in its concerns, offering a view of Harry as a "failed artist," Hemingway's fictional embodiment of the unsuccessful writer who works "too close to life." In this view, the leopard becomes an "ironic counterpart" to Harry—"he is everything Harry is not"—and Harry's wife is seen as a basically "good-natured, bland woman who likes to please her husband" and is treated with "unwarranted cruelty" by him. Although this interpretation of the story is certainly debatable, Santangelo presents it clearly and coherently.

Of the two new essays on "The Short Happy Life of Francis Macomber," one, Warren Beck's "The Shorter Happy Life of Mrs. Macomber: 1955, 1975" (*MFS* 21[1975]:363–85), is a long footnote (pp. 377–85) to an earlier essay, here reprinted, which contended that Mrs. Macomber wanted to save her husband and felt that he was worthy of being saved. Beck defends his position against Mark Spilka's 1961 attack on it, noting that Spilka's piece was not as closely tied to the text of the story as Beck's had been. Robert Morsberger's "That Hemingway Kind of Love: Macomber in the Movies" (*LFQ* 4:54–59) compares the story with the movie adaptation, *The Macomber Affair* (which Morsberger calls the "most nearly faithful and successful screen version of a Hemingway short story"). His conclusion is that, despite "its fidelity to detail and dialogue until the end," the film is unable to capture the story's interior monologues and its "carefully crafted narrative-descriptive prose." Further, the film "sentimentalizes" the relationship between Wilson and Margot by having Wilson genuinely care for her; and it also tacks on a conclusion to the original which is totally false. This is an interesting piece which obviously is of only marginal interest to literary scholars.

Two of the remaining new essays on short stories offer worthwhile original viewpoints. John J. Roberts' "In Defense of Krebs" (*SSF* 13:515–18) points out that Krebs is traumatized not so much by the war as by "the Midwestern view of war, not [by] the truth of death but the lie of life." Significantly, although Krebs retreats from social interaction and commitment, his story ends with his journey to Kansas City, signifying a continuing search for psychic and spiritual restitution. In " 'The Killers' As Experience" (*JNT* 5:128–35), W. J. Stuckey disputes the conventional reading of the story as an initiation into evil for Nick assisted by code hero Ole Andreson. Stuckey shows plausibly that Ole is "a failed code hero . . . [whose] passive surrender to death is unacceptable to Nick."

In "Irony and Allusion in Hemingway's 'After the Storm' " (*SSF* 13:374–76), Robert G. Walker cites the parallel between the narrator of Hemingway's story who discovers a ring-bedecked corpse on a wrecked liner but cannot get inside to the treasure or the person and the myth of Gyges, told to Socrates by Glaucon in *The Republic*. In the myth, Gyges does get the ring, thus gaining for himself the powers of invisibility which he uses to murder the king and usurp his throne. Knowledge of this myth does help us understand the ironic use Hemingway makes of it in his story. Similarly, argues James F. Barbour in " 'The Light of the World': The Real Ketchel and the Real Light" (*SSF* 13:17–23), knowledge of the difference between the fictional fighter argued over by the two whores in the story and the real fighter on whom he is based suggests ultimately that reality—and truth arrived at through physical experience—is far superior to conjured romantic beliefs in god-like men who never existed.

d. **Dissertations.** Doctoral research on Hemingway decreased somewhat this year. We have only one dissertation totally on Hemingway, with two others partially on him. Fitzgerald, on the other hand, was the sole subject of six dissertations. Two of these were restricted to

The Great Gatsby, but two others were entirely about the short stories. Moreover, the titles of three of the dissertations on Fitzgerald—"The Dynamic of Image and Theme in the Novels of F. Scott Fitzgerald"; "*The Great Gatsby*: A Stylistic Analysis"; and "Image Patterns in the Novels of F. Scott Fitzgerald"—imply that we may have some interesting criticism to consider in future surveys.

University of Maryland[1]

1. This essay could not have been completed without the research assistance of Jane DeMouy and Ruth M. Alvarez.

Part II

11. Literature to 1800

Robert D. Arner

Highlighted by Kenneth Silverman's *Cultural History of the American Revolution*, the year 1976 was an extremely good one for early American studies. One striking development was that Jonathan Edwards was virtually ignored, but this phenomenon was more than offset by other valuable contributions made during the year. In addition to Silverman's book, which simply cannot be praised too highly, there were a number of fine interdisciplinary essays by Richard Crawford, Roger B. Stein, and J. A. Leo Lemay. Lemay also edited a solid collection of essays on Benjamin Franklin, while other scholars provided editions of a number of primary texts: Everett Emerson gave us his collection of *Letters from New England* and Edward W. Clark edited John Williams's popular *Redeemed Captive*. A year marked by special bicentennial issues of *SCN*, *AQ*, and *SLitI* and by several festschriften and other collections of essays, notably Calvin Israel's *Discoveries & Considerations* and John W. Eadie's *Classical Traditions in Early America*, produced as well a host of good articles by Cecelia Tichi, Virginia Bernhard, David Smith, Donald T. Siebert, Jr., and Lewis P. Simpson, among others literally too numerous to mention. As usual, a few pieces probably did not merit publication, but overall the picture for colonial scholarship was a bright one.

i. Edward Taylor

Two articles deal with the Taylor-Stoddard controversy. First is James W. Barbour's "The Prose Context of Edward Taylor's Anti-Stoddard Meditations" (*EAL* 10[1975]:144–57). Arguing that "Taylor's prose—over a period of thirty years—establishes the necessary context for reading the anti-Stoddard meditations" (2.102–11), Barbour centers his discussion on "the consistency of Taylor's thought and imagery" during that period, including the striking and impor-

tant image of the "wedden garment." His approach illuminates some
tricky passages in Taylor's poems and in general succeeds very well
in establishing his thesis. A second article on this same subject is
David L. Parker's thoughtful "Edward Taylor's Preparationism: A
New Perspective on the Taylor-Stoddard Controversy" (*EAL* 11:
259–78), which takes issue with the standard designation of Taylor
as the conservative and Stoddard as the liberal in this ecclesiastical
debate. As Parker sees it, the crux of the controversy was Taylor's apparent assignment of "an efficacious element" to the preparationist
stage of conversion, a stage which for Stoddard remained a non-
efficacious part of the morphology of conversion. "Taylor was no
Arminian," Parker cautions, "but his expansive view of the significance of preparation illustrates the tendency of New England conversion theory that would culminate in the Arminian spectre com-
batted by Jonathan Edwards."

Among studies of Taylor's sources and imagery, Thomas M. Davis
and Arthur Forstater's "Edward Taylor's 'A Fig for thee Oh! Death' "
(*Discoveries & Considerations*, pp. 67–81) explores the possibility
that Edward Pearce's *The Great Concern* might have inspired some
of the imagery of Taylor's poem , but the resemblances are too general to be entirely convincing. Much better is the discussion of how
Taylor moved beyond conventional *descriptio mortis* and unified his
poem through intricate puns connecting sex and death; Davis and
Forstater also print the "Manuscript Book" version of the poem.
The same funereal imagery is discussed in Donald E. Stanford's "The
Imagination of Death in the Poetry of Philip Pain, Edward Taylor,
and George Herbert" (*SLitI* 9,ii:53–67). A serious literal belief in
Revelation and in a final apocalyptic event, says Stanford, gives "Tay-
lor's imagination of death an emotional intensity . . . lacking in the
less dogmatic Herbert and Pain."

An image study of another kind is Cheryl C. Oreovicz's "Edward
Taylor and the Alchemy of Grace" (*SCN* 34:33–36), which notes the
proliferation of alchemical imagery throughout Taylor's meditations
and stresses the point that most of his references to alchemy are positive in nature. A different sort of scientific imagery is discussed in
William J. Scheick's " 'That Blazing Star in Joshua': Edward Taylor's
'Meditation 2.10' and Increase Mather's *Kometographia*" (*SCN* 34:
36–37); Scheick focuses on how Taylor's interpretation of "cometlike
Joshua" differs from *Kometographia* in viewing comets as prognostic

both of good and evil and he clarifies the typological and scientific backgrounds of the image.

In the final piece on Taylor for 1976, Thomas M. Davis examines "Edward Taylor's Elegies on the Mathers" (*EAL* 11:231–44), recovering from the "Manuscript Book" and the "Poetical Works" four versions of a late elegy on Increase Mather and a 35-line fragment which, Davis conjectures, may be Taylor's lost elegy on Richard Mather.

ii. Puritanism

As usual, the Yankees have cornered the critical market again this year. Everett Emerson edited a judicious selection of *Letters from New England* (Amherst: Univ. of Mass. Press) covering the years 1629–38; the letters are arranged so as to provide not only an historical overview of the development of the Bay Colony but also to reveal insights into the personalities of the men who built Massachusetts. Many of the letters are familiar enough to students of early American literature—the letters of Francis Higginson (perhaps Emerson should have distinguished more exactly between private and public letters) and John Winthrop, for example—but others, such as John(?) Pond's and John Eliot's, have not previously been so easily available.

The response of the first wave of Plymouth settlers to the American Indian is the subject of Frank Shuffleton's "Indian Devils and Pilgrim Fathers: Squanto, Hobomok, and the English Conception of Indian Religion" (*NEQ* 49:108–16), which investigates the cultural reasons for the Pilgrims' failure to understand the element of shamanism in Indian religion and, therefore, for their misassignment of motives to Hobomok and Squanto. A general article of a different sort is Phyllis Jones's "Biblical Rhetoric and the Pulpit Tradition of Early New England" (*EAL* 11:245–58), which rather unimaginatively points out that first-generation ministers were influenced in their preaching styles not only by sermon manuals but also by Biblical examples, particularly by the example of St. Paul; the argument should have more thoroughly considered 17th-century English sermon style also.

In a wide-ranging study of "The Apocalyptic Sensibility of Seventeenth-Century Puritan New England Verse" (*SCN* 34:50–52), Cecelia Tichi offers a quick and mostly disappointing survey of her subject; the essay does, however, make two points: that both layman and minister were drawn toward apocalyptic imagery and that the expectation of the Apocalypse "was an intensely personal Puritan conception which allowed a subjective individuation within the orthodox Puritan mold." Less broad in scope is Harold S. Jantz's "American Baroque: Three Representative Poets" (*Discoveries & Considerations*, pp. 3–23); Jantz identifies three early New England poets—Edward Johnson ("in poetic rhythm and diction"), John Fiske ("in poetic form and contextuality"), and Edward Taylor ("in poetic imagery and lyric ductility")—whose works, taken together, help to focus the main critical problems of American baroque.

Individual Puritan poets treated this past year include David Dunster, who, according to Harrison T. Meserole's "New Voices from Seventeenth-Century America" (*Discoveries & Considerations*, pp. 24–45), deserves "to rank well up the scale in the canon of early American literature"; but the evidence, to this reader at least, is unconvincing, and we shall have to await a full view of the verse before we can tell whether Meserole's enthusiasm is justified. Richard Steere is the topic of Donald P. Wharton's valuable "The Poet as Protester: Richard Steere's 1695 Defense of Liberty of Conscience" (*SCN* 34: 46–50), which relates how Steere, a General Baptist, joined forces with the Rogerenes of New London, Connecticut, in a vain protest against harassment and property confiscation by the Congregationalists. Richard Crowder's "'The Day of Doom' as Chronomorph" (*JPC* 9:148–59) says some perceptive things about the popularity of Wigglesworth's New England epic, attributing its powerful emotional force to "narrative point counterpoint" developed by "multiplicity of synchronous action." Finally, in a brief note on another minor poet, Leo M. Kaiser presents an annotated text of "Early American Latin Verse: 'Epigram on an Earthquake' by Peter Bulkeley" (*SCN* 34:68–69).

Two articles on Anne Bradstreet round out the offerings on Puritan poetry for the year. Robert D. Arner's "The Structure of Anne Bradstreet's *Tenth Muse*" (*Discoveries & Considerations*, pp. 46–66) argues that Bradstreet's poems are organized around a progressively self-assertive feminine voice and an intensifying *vanitas vanitatum* theme. But Arner's hypotheses and conjectures—in fact, all criticism of Bradstreet's poetry—are implicitly challenged by Joseph

R. McElrath's "The Text of Anne Bradstreet: Biographical and Critical Consequences" (*SCN* 34:61–63), which reminds us that no one knows for certain whether either the 1650 or the 1678 edition of her verses possesses authorial authority and that, consequently, critics cannot really speak about her developing artistry or changing personal attitudes. All of which reminds me of something Jonathan Edwards once said about the universe, that even though it is all mind, we may still speak of it in the same old way, as if it were matter.

Studies of individual Puritan prose writers start with Robert J. Gangewere's "Thomas Morton: Character and Symbol in a Minor American Epic" (*Discoveries & Considerations*, pp. 189–203), a tight survey of literary versions of the story of the invasion of Merry Mount. John J. Teunissen and Evelyn J. Hinz contribute two fine articles on another early outcast, Roger Williams; in "Roger Williams, Thomas More, and the Narragansett Utopia" (*EAL* 11:281–95), they start from the proposition that Williams may have been predisposed to view the Indians in a positive light, convincingly demonstrate how Sir Thomas More's *Utopia* may have helped to shape Williams's *Key into the Language of America*, and then differentiate between More's and Williams's Utopian visions. And in "Anti-Colonial Satire in Roger Williams' *A Key into the Language of America*" (*ArielE* 7,iii:5–23), Teunissen and Hinz argue that subtle contrasts between primitivism and overcivilization lie at the heart of that work. Also on the subject of colonial satire, Jean F. Beranger's "Voices of Humor in Nathaniel Ward" (*SAmH* 2[1975]: 96–104) asserts that *saeva indignation*, the traditional motive of the satirist, is not the only impulse underlying Ward's *Simple Cobler*. Beranger's point about Ward's changing voices is well taken, I believe, though it is not always clear what makes these voices comic or how they help to make Ward's book an early example of American humor.

Teunissen and Hinz's discussion of Roger Williams's Utopian vision finds a counterpart in Cecelia Tichi's "Edward Johnson and the Puritan Territorial Imperative" (*Discoveries & Considerations*, pp. 152–88), though her concern is with Johnson's modernism rather than with his reaction against it. She identifies Johnson's "salient achievement" in *Wonder-Working Providence* as the successful fusion of "a bifocal world of earth and spirit in a literary weld of scriptural authority and 17th-century technics, all in the spirit of practicable utopianism." Johnson's faith in technology as evidence of spiritual achievement, Tichi seems to be thinking but does not explicitly state, is but another of those traits of mind bequeathed us by the Puritans, one that would in time foster the commonplaces of American optimism and call forth the scathing satires of Hawthorne's "Celestial Railroad" and Melville's *Confidence-Man.*

Colonial women other than Bradstreet also came in for some attention in 1976, commencing with Laurel Thatcher Ulrich's "Vertuous Women Found: New England Ministerial Literature, 1668–1735" (*AQ* 28:20–40), a survey of Puritan attitudes toward women as indicated by the virtues most praised by Puritan ministers; "in a very real sense," Ulrich concludes, "there is no such thing as *female* piety in early New England," since what distinguishes a saint from a sinner turns out to have no reference to gender. But Ulrich does not bother to record what Cotton Mather had to say about Hannah Duston in his *Magnalia,* and she also misses the chance to talk about another remarkable woman, who is, however, the topic of Ann Stanford's "Mary Rowlandson's Journey to Redemption" (*ArielE* 7,iii:27–37). Stanford characterizes Rowlandson as a "pious, capable, ruggedly self-reliant" frontierswoman whose story of her own captivity during King Philip's War must be understood on three levels: allegorically, as "a descent into hell and a redemption and a return"; ritualistically, as a rite of passage into a new identity, part savage, part civilized; and symbolically, as the story of a "growing awareness of the self in its relation to other." Yet another remarkable woman whose journey was, however, quite different from Rowlandson's is Sarah Kemble Knight, whose comic observations on New England rustics are treated in Faye Vowell's "A Commentary on *The Journal of Sarah Kemble Knight*" (*ESRS* 24,iii:27–37), probably the best account yet published of Madam Knight's humorous narrative.

Madam Knight's Boston neighbor, Judge Samuel Sewall, raised quite a ruckus with *The Selling of Joseph,* an antislavery tract examined by William Bedford Clark in "*Caveat Emptor!*: Judge Sewall vs. Slavery" (*SLitI* 9,ii:19–30). Characterizing Sewall's pamphlet as "a personal, compulsive, and largely intuitive outgrowth of its author's troubled Christian conscience," however, seems to me erroneously to play down the deliberate rhetorical strategies Sewall employed in this work, though Clark is quite right to note that the Judge's stand against slavery must in some ways be regarded as an adjunct to his hopes that America might one day become the site of the New Jerusalem. Sewall's Latin scholarship also receives brief notice in Leo M. Kaiser's "On Sewall's Diary" (*EAL* 11:279), which helpfully annotates four sources not identified in M. Halsey Thomas' fine edition of the *Diary* (1973) and corrects one of Thomas' mistranslations (on 2.682). Finally, one of Sewall's friends, the Rev. John Williams, has been graced with a good modern edition of his *The Redeemed Captive*, ed. Edward W. Clark (Amherst: Univ. of Mass. Press), the editorial apparatus of which is above reproach.

This year as last, Leo M. Kaiser continues to perform as John Leverett's unofficial literary executor, editing "*Prae Gaudeo, Prae Lucta*: The First Commencement Address of President John Leverett" (*HLB* 24:381–94). Then there is Pope Solomon Stoddard, subject of two good essays in 1976. In an important article ("Solomon Stoddard's 'Arguments' Concerning Admission to the Lord's Supper," *PAAS* 86:75–112), Thomas M. Davis and Jeff Jeske edit Edward Taylor's transcription of Stoddard's sermon on the Half-Way Covenant, an argument to whose contents Increase Mather's "Confutation" had previously provided the only clue. The document demonstrates that as late as 1688, Stoddard had not adopted the extreme and unorthodox position that the Lord's Supper was a converting ordinance; that change came rather suddenly sometime between June 1688 and October 1690.

In an attempt to put Stoddard into a broader and yet more specific intellectual perspective than is provided by Perry Miller's well-known analysis, Karl Keller deftly pulls together the good and (infrequently) debatable points made in five recent published and unpublished studies of Edwards's grandfather ("The Example of Solomon Stoddard: A Review-Essay," *SCN* 34:58–61). Keller stresses the political implications of the "piety of sensation," Stoddard's resemblances to Roger Williams, and his influence on Edwards and American religion before the Revoluton.

All three generations of the Mather family came in for comment in the year just passed. It seems a strange thing, to begin with, for a man to write a book about someone of whose accomplishments he appears to feel contemptuous, but such is the case with B. R. Burg's *Richard Mather of Dorchester* (Lexington: Univ. Press of Ky.). Perhaps the problem is that Burg is a better historian than he is a biographer, for in all fairness his two chapters on Mather's role in formulating the Cambridge Platform and fighting for the Half-Way

Covenant are both excellent discussions; but by that time the reader
has waded through so much bad writing ("an aspiring would-be Calvin"), so many superficial attempts at psychology, and so many annoying (and almost uniformly unsupported) conjectures about Mather's weak-willed personality and conniving political motivations that
he is out of all patience with the study, and not even the final chapters
can entirely redeem it.

As for Richard's most famous son, William L. Joyce and Michael
G. Hall describe three of his previously undescribed documents in
"Three Manuscripts of Increase Mather" (*PAAS* 86:113–23). The
first of these is the committee report of the Synod of 1679; it reveals
the Synod's thinking on the issues of communion and conversion before those matters were debated and the Synodical stand modified by
Solomon Stoddard's arguments. The second writing, a quarto manuscript of 7 sheets, represents Mather's attempt to refute the heresies
of Habbakuk Glover, a "Particular Baptist" living with the rest of the
heretics in Rhode Island, while the third document, a 69-page manuscript, is clearly the most important of the three; entitled "A discourse
concerning the glorious state of the church on earth under the New
Jerusalem," it was probably written in 1682 and reveals Mather's continuing (and unfashionable in the post-Restoration period) insistence
upon a literal interpretation of the scriptural promise of a New Heav-
en and a New Earth.

A fine essay on Cotton Mather is Virginia Bernhard's "Cotton
Mather and the Doing of Good: A Puritan Gospel of Wealth" (*NEQ*
49:225–41), which measures Mather's treatise against the standards
set by Richard Baxter's *How to Do Good to Many* and Robert Nelson's
An Address to Persons of Quality and Estate and concludes that
Mather's work emerges "as a statement from a distinctively American
society" that is both less class conscious and more optimistic than
English society about the possibilities and rewards of doing good;
the root contradiction of Mather's argument, one which Mather never
discovered, was that his "instructions for getting on in the world contributed to the very [social] fragmentation" that he sought to avoid.
Far less significant than Bernhard's article is Leo M. Kaiser's short
note "On Mather's *Christian Philosopher*" (*EAL* 11:280), which identifies seven allusions and the meter of five other Latin phrases in one
of Mather's late works. And Kenneth Silverman's "Cotton Mather
and the Reform of Puritan Psalmody" (*SCN* 34:53–57) treats only

Psalterium Americanum and *The Accomplished Singer*, noting Mather's attempts to effect minor reforms in music and text, pointing out
how the minister's own translations tended to work against the reforms he proposed, and then considering Mather's liturgical revisions.
Of related interest is Karl Josef Höltgen's "Francis Quarles, John Josselyn, and the Bay Psalm Book" (*SCN* 34:42–46), a study of the probability that Quarles was indeed the translator-poet of psalms 16, 25,
51, 88, 113, and 137; Höltgen concludes that these six psalms may
quite possibly have been translated by Quarles, but that Quarles's
habit of paraphrasing ran directly counter to the Puritans' wishes and
that, consequently, his efforts were rejected by Cotton.

One final note on the Puritans is a bibliographical entry, Edward
J. Gallagher and Thomas Werge's reference guide to *Early Puritan
Writers: William Bradford, John Cotton, Thomas Hooker, Edward
Johnson, Richard Mather, and Thomas Shepard* (Boston: G. K. Hall),
certainly an enterprise worthy of note even though I was unable to
pry loose a review copy and so cannot comment on the usefulness of
the entries.

iii. The South

Probably the best piece of writing to date on George Alsop is Ted-
Larry Pebworth's "The 'Character' of George Alsop's *Mary-Land*"
(*SCN* 34:64–66), which establishes Alsop's indebtedness to the popular "character of a country" subgenre; these were mostly satirical,
somewhat scatological characters, though their general tone was, as
Pebworth observes, at odds with Alsop's promotional purposes: hence
Alsop's shift to the Susquehanna Indians at the end of the book, since
the savages allow his satiric wit free play without endangering his
praise of "civilized" Maryland.

Another satirist of a later generation is Ebenezer Cooke, the subject of Robert D. Arner's "The Blackness of Darkness: Satire, Romance, and Ebenezer Cooke's *The Sot-weed Factor*" (*TSL* 21:1–10).
Arner argues that the romance provides an aristocratic social and
linguistic norm against which the sotweed factor's pretensions are
measured and that the overall effect of the satire is to deprive readers
of a "consistently moral, consistently ethical point of reference within
the poem" and to make the reader himself a victim of the speaker's
confidence game. Thomas Cradock, another early Maryland poet of

some stature, is discussed in David Curtis Skaggs's "The Chain of Being in Eighteenth-Century Maryland: The Paradox of Thomas Cradock" (*HMPEC* 14:155–64). Skaggs examines Cradock's sermons and compares them with the minister's satires on upper-class freethinkers and deists, corrupt clergymen, and immoral planters and overseers; on the one hand, Skaggs concludes, Cradock "sought to uphold the social synthesis learned in his catechism and on the other, his incisive, often satirical commentary on those charged with maintaining that cosmology contributed to its downfall in the American revolutionary era." And in "Elegy and Mock Elegy in Colonial Virginia" (*SLitI* 9,ii:79–93), Jack B. Wages assesses the contributions of other early southern poets, including the authors of the elegies on Sir John Randolph, Miss Molly Thacher, Evelyn Byrd, and the mock "Elegy upon Walter Dymocke [John Robertson]."

The author of the elegy on Evelyn Byrd was, of course, her famous father, and in "William Byrd of Westover as Augustan Poet" (*SLitI* 9,ii:69–77), Carl Dolmetsch analyzes some of Byrd's other verses to conclude that Byrd "may be an 'Augustan poet' in name only," since his modes of poetic expression hearken back to an earlier age of Restoration wit. Byrd is also discussed in David Smith's excellent "William Byrd Surveys America" (*EAL* 11:296–310), an analysis of the symbolic importance of the survey and the dividing line itself as a "singularly intense and penetrating symbol [of] the whole vision of America's territorial destiny." Smith finds in Byrd's record expressions of "some deep-seated, archetypal yearning for contact with the territory of the unbounded . . . a latent homosexuality and an embracing of an alien Indian culture," even though the public aim of the expedition, paradoxically, was to further the establishment of orderly settlements and fence out the wilderness.

Another first-rate article on Byrd is Donald T. Siebert, Jr.'s "William Byrd's *Histories of the Line:* The Fashioning of a Hero" (*AL* 47:535–51), which examines the implications of Byrd's adoption of the persona of "Steddy" in "The Secret History," draws parallels between Byrd's ideal gentleman and the public personality projected in the life and writings of Sir William Temple, and relates the *Secret Diary* to Byrd's lifelong effort to preserve steadiness as a social ideal: in the diaries, says Siebert, "Byrd is Steddy by the fiat of the pen. He has created himself in his own ideal image."

The first attempt at an analysis of the work of Byrd's brother-in-law, Robert Beverley, is Robert D. Arner's "The Quest for Freedom: Style and Meaning in Robert Beverley's *History and Present State of Virginia*" (*SLJ* 8,ii:79–98). Arner discusses the implications of Beverley's posing as an Indian as the posture relates to the attempt to write a plainer prose than any then current in English literature and to make that prose the touchstone of his attack on a series of self-seeking royal governors.

iv. Franklin and the Enlightenment

The year's major contribution to Franklin scholarship is *The Oldest Revolutionary: Essays on Benjamin Franklin*, ed. J. A. Leo Lemay (Philadelphia: Univ. of Pa. Press), an outstanding collection of papers which pays tribute to the memory of Theodore Hornberger. The title is a bit curious, since none of the essays has much to do with Franklin's career as a revolutionary, but in the initial piece in the volume Lewis P. Simpson explores the political implications of "The Printer as a Man of Letters: Franklin and the Symbolism of the Third Realm" (pp. 3–20). Simpson is interested in Franklin's crucial contributions to the emergence in America of the "Republic of Letters . . . from the Republic of Christ," the triumph of modernism in an "Age of Print" which demanded, among other things, a new stylistic "strategy of intimacy" that Franklin brought to near perfection in the *Autobiography* and elsewhere. Franklin's "assertion of the moral and intellectual power of the Republic of Letters," Simpson says, "is integral to its evolvement into world historical meaning in the Revolution and the founding of the new nation."

The next two essays, Bruce I. Granger's "Franklin as Press Agent in England" (pp. 21–32) and Percy G. Adams's "Benjamin Franklin and the Travel-Writing Tradition" (pp. 33–50), are in a sense companion pieces, good overviews of Franklin's antiministerial writing and of his awareness of the political possibilities exploited by travel writers in the late 17th and early 18th centuries. Paul M. Zall's "A Portrait of the Autobiographer as an Old Artificer" (pp. 53–65) is likewise a solid study of Franklin's craftsmanship as indicated by the manuscript of the *Autobiography* at the Huntington Library, one that, however, finally seems to shy away from the larger critical questions about the overall structure of that book. Another piece on the *Autobiography*, David L. Parker's "From Sound Believer to Practical Preparationist: Some Puritan Harmonics in Franklin's *Autobi-ography*" (pp. 67–75), is perhaps the most tentative piece in the volume; it examines Franklin's project for arriving at moral perfection in terms of the stages of the Puritan conversion experience, finding (and sometimes forcing) parallels in vocabulary and terminology to argue its case. Although Franklin's Poor Richard has often been the subject of critical commentary, Cameron C. Nickels's "Franklin's Poor Richard's Almanacs: 'The Humblest of his Labours' " (pp. 77–89) adds to our understanding by tracing Poor Richard as a character who "changes over twenty-six years from a rather indolent but affable stargazer to a pompously didactic almanac maker who likes to see himself as an eminent author." And in "The Text, Rhetorical Strategies, and Themes of 'The Speech of Miss Polly Baker' " (pp. 91–120), J. A. Leo Lemay scrutinizes yet another of Franklin's familiar personae; he argues the provenance of the *Maryland Gazette* text over the more frequently followed *General Advertiser* text on the basis of the *Gazette*'s stylistic superiority and its greater accuracy of reference to colonial American institutions and customs. Lemay then anatomizes the rhetorical divisions of the Speech, concluding that "nothing said by Polly Baker attempts to reply to the actual law" and that Franklin deliberately created her as "an ironic, obtuse persona," but on that point I remain unconvinced.

Lemay's collection of essays closes with two contributions which offer 20th-century perspectives on Franklin's life and career. In "Franklin's Sanity and the Man Behind the Mask" (pp. 123–38) John Griffith claims that Franklin achieved a kind of "American work-ethic folk mysticism"; he did not feel "driven or caught or alienated" from the activities he engaged in and experienced no sense of tragic inadequacy to the roles he was called upon to play in history. The other essay, William L. Hedges's "From Franklin to Emerson" (pp. 139–56), is nearly as strong as Simpson's opening one, tracing the surprising number of connections between two men who are often thought of as occupying antithetical positions in the history of American ideas.

Other publications on Franklin include Morton L. Ross's "Form and Moral Balance in Franklin's Autobiography" (*ArielE* 7,iii:38–52); Ross believes that the structure of Franklin's self-portrait, leaving out the brief fourth section, depends upon a calculated opposition between self-advertisement in the first two segments and self-effacement in the third. Critics who charge Franklin with initiating only an "overweening concern for the appearance of respectability" have failed to understand how he "completes the pattern by offering a series of anecdotes . . . which illustrate the responsible use of wealth and leisure." And in a final piece on Franklin, Katalin Halácsy ("The Image of Benjamin Franklin in Hungary," *HSE* 10:9–25) surveys Franklin's reputation as physicist, public figure, freedom fighter, reformer, capitalist and citizen, historical figure, and private person (Halácsy's categories) from 1756 to 1975.

More general studies of the American Enlightenment are to be found in a special issue of *American Quarterly*, which opens with Joseph Ellis's "Habits of Mind and an American Enlightenment" (28: 150–64). After surveying some of the generalizations about that phase of American intellectual activity, Ellis calls for a more careful scrutiny of the language of the Founding Fathers in order to determine just what emotional and psychological complexities are involved in their use of terms like "moral," "virtue," "natural law," and repetitive metaphors of balance. D. H. Meyer follows up Ellis's observations in "The Uniqueness of the American Enlightenment" (28:165–86) with an analysis of the *Federalist* designed to illustrate American assimilation and oversimplification of European thinking; "provincialism, democracy, and nationalism worked together to filter ideas, blur their sharpness, and mellow their impact." One process whereby foreign thought arrived in the colonies is the subject of David Lundberg and Henry F. May's "The Enlightened Reader in America" (28:262–71); the authors use booksellers' lists, sales catalogues, and private library holdings to chart the popularity of European writers (excluding novelists and dramatists) during four key chronological periods: 1700– 76; 1777–90; 1791–1800; and 1801–13. Another study of a similar sort is Edwin Wolf's "The Classical Languages in Colonial Philadelphia" (*Classical Traditions*, pp. 49–80). Wolf is convinced that, apart from a few accomplished classicists like James Logan and Isaac Norris II, most early Philadelphians who knew Greek and Latin at all knew only the most familiar quotations and that, therefore, classical influence did not play a very large part in shaping America's Revolutionary mentality (but see below, pp. 35–36).

Also of general interest is Linda Kerber's "The Republican Mother: Women and the Enlightenment—an American Perspective" (*AQ* 28:187–205), an examination of the extremely limited perspectives on female equality and political action offered by Locke, Montesquieu, Condorcet, Rousseau, and Lord Kames and of the ways in which Judith Sargent Murray, Susanna Rowson, Benjamin Rush, and Charles Brockden Brown (whom Kerber treats far too cavalierly) contributed to an expansion of those limited points of view. Finally, one last contribution to research on writers of this period is Rose Marie Cuttings's *John and William Bartram, William Byrd II, and St. John de Crèvecoeur: A Reference Guide* (Boston: G. K. Hall), which must be used with caution, since even a casual look at its contents discloses that Cutting has failed to include several important essays.

v. Edwards and the Great Awakening

All but ignored this past year, Jonathan Edwards was treated in only one article, Robert Lee Stuart's "Jonathan Edwards at Enfield: 'And Oh the Cheerfulness and Pleasantness . . .'" (*AL* 48:46–59), and even Stuart merely manages to remind us that when we read "Sinners" we should be alert to the words of consolation that Edwards wrote into that infamous sermon. For the rest, there is only J. M. Bumsted's "Emotion in Colonial America: Some Relations of Conversion Experience in Freetown, Massachusetts, 1749–1770" (*NEQ* 49:97–108); Bumsted presents nine brief conversion narratives composed by seven women and two men who gained admission to Silas Brett's Freetown church. These, Bumsted claims, help to bring the modern reader closer to the sense of guilt and of release actually experienced by newly awakened individuals of no particular intellectual pretension, though he also says, somewhat contradictorily, that the narratives were edited by Brett to some unascertainable degree.

vi. Revolutionary and Early National Periods

Though next to nothing was written about American Tories in 1976, the year did provide several British perspectives on the American war effort. Major James C. Gaston finds from scanning important London magazines and dailies in "Richard Prescott and Mud Island: Epitomes of the American Revolution as Seen by London's Poets" (*EAL* 11:147–55) that many English poets (a good number of them members of the Whig opposition, though Gaston does not note this) found in the recapture of Major General Richard Prescott and the stalwart American defense of Fort Mifflin on Mud Island symbolic evidence "that the whole scheme of coercion in America was wrong and potentially catastrophic to England." In the same vein, Peter J. Stanlis's "British Views of the American Revolution: A Conflict over the Rights of Sovereignty" (*EAL* 11:191–201) presents an admirably concise summary of the three chief positions taken in England on "the question of sovereignty over America" during the years 1763–83: those who, like Horace Walpole and Josiah Tucker (though for a variety of complex and different reasons) argued for American independence; those who agreed with the king, the North ministry, Samuel Johnson, and, initially at least, the public at large that America should be kept an English dependency by force of arms if necessary; and those who followed Lord Rockingham and Edmund Burke in arguing that America would have to be conciliated. Yet another historical perspective is provided by Paul J. Archambault's "From Alliance to Great Schism: France in America, 1763–1815" (*PLL* 12: 339–65), a lengthy and mostly historically oriented study of the changing relationships between America and France, both officially and unofficially, from the Treaty of Paris through the administrations of Washington, Adams, and Jefferson.

A reply to Edwin Wolf's contention that classical thought was not very influential in forming political attitudes in America (see above, p. 32) comes from James McLachlan, who in "Classical Names, American Identities: Some Notes on College Students and the Classical Tradition in the 1770s" (*Classical Traditions*, pp. 81–98) reminds Wolf that classical culture need not be either perfectly articulated or extensively cited by the Founding Fathers in order to be considered formative in Revolutionary ideology; his discussion of classical costuming and the Greek and Roman names assumed by members of Princeton's Cliosophic Society suggests that classical models were a very important part of the "underthought" of the era. Incidental support for this thesis may be found in George Kennedy's "Classical Influences on *The Federalist*" (*Classical Traditions*, pp. 119–38), a sound study which is particularly good at discerning several sorts of classical influence—general, specific, and formal—in the styles of Hamilton, Madison, and Jay.

In another general study of the mind of America on the eve of the Revolutionary War, Lewis Leary isolates "Literature in New York,

1775" (*EAL* 11:4–21) a tight summary of divided New York loyalties in the days just before Lexington and Concord. Only the visitors Alexander Hamilton and Philip Freneau, he says, really gave the city any literary distinction, but he also treats Tory and patriot verse and reprints a poem that appeared, strangely, in the Loyalist *Rivington's New-York Gazetteer*, verses lamenting the defection of Dr. Benjamin Church of Boston from the patriot's side.

By far the year's best study of colonial and Revolutionary mentality, however, is Kenneth Silverman's *A Cultural History of the American Revolution, 1763–1789* (New York: Thomas Y. Crowell). Not the least virtue of the book is its narrow historical focus upon a period during which America experienced a notable outburst of artistic activity, although perhaps only in the visual arts, with the emergence of Copley and West, did the country produce any genuinely first-rate talents. Silverman's time span is not so short, however, that it excludes consideration of several generations of American poets (Nathaniel Evans to Freneau, Barlow, and Dwight), playwrights (Thomas Godfrey to Royall Tyler), and painters (John Hesselius, John Smibert, John Wollaston, and Jeremiah Theus through West and Copley to Ralph Earl, Mather Brown, and Gilbert Stuart). Thematically, the book is unified by Silverman's "Excursus" on "Whig Sentimentalism," which in 18th-century America provided a political frame of reference able to unite heroic endeavor and simple domestic virtue and which for Silverman provides the chief critical background for sensitive discussions of works as diverse in discipline and genre as William Billings's *New-England Psalm-Singer*, Godfrey's *Prince of Parthia*, Dwight's *Conquest of Canaan*, and William Hill Brown's *Power of Sympathy*. There are also good treatments of popular culture, together with ample documentation from colonial newspapers and literally dozens of informative treatments of forgotten minor figures. Withal, the book is written in a graceful and lively style, especially in the sections dealing with the pageants honoring the ratification of the Constitution and the Inauguration of Washington. If there is one problem with it, it is that Silverman insists too much on noting firsts (some of which are inaccurately claimed also), but that will not trouble all readers and is amply compensated by the richness of his discussions.

The distaff side of Silverman's centrally important American family is the topic of Wendy Martin's "Women and the American Revolution" (*EAL* 11:322–35), but, frankly, I am growing bored with studies that really contribute little to our understanding of the dilemma of American women at any given historical moment except the fact that, whatever men might have thought, some women possessed minds and talents of their own. More specific work of the sort offered by Edmund M. Hayes's "Mercy Otis Warren: *The Defeat*" (*NEQ* 49:440–58), which also reprints the play, seems to me what really is needed. For similar reasons, I find George Rigsby's article on "Form and Content in Phillis Wheatley's Elegies" (*CLAJ* 19 [1975]:248–57) also disappointing, since in this piece the phrase "black consciousness" serves merely as a convenient term for making even the most drably conventional of Wheatley's images worth our attention.

A. Owen Aldridge's "The Concept of Ancients and Moderns in American Poetry of the Federal Period" (*Classical Traditions*, pp. 99–118) is another general study which attempts to establish that "American poets of the Federal Period revealed neoclassical traits in . . . rhetoric and structure . . . but anti-classical tendencies in their ideology" and that "the verse and critical writings of these poets contain close parallels with concepts in the European quarrel between ancients and moderns"; but the first of these points is so much a commonplace that it scarcely seems worth arguing, and the second fails to distinguish adequately between those American authors who merely anticipated another Ovid or Homer in America and those who were certain that American bards would surpass their classical prototypes.

Among individual poets of the period, Philip Freneau received most attention, though not always to his (or our) advantage. Poorly written, uninformative, and critically naive, for example, Mary Weatherspoon Bowden's *Philip Freneau* (TUSAS, 260) reinvokes all the clichés about the poet's position in literary history—transitional poet, pre-Romantic, etc., etc.—but examines none of them. Sometimes Bowden thinks Freneau is a successful poet because he handles Gothic and Romantic material very well; sometimes she blames these elements of his verse for his failures. She tosses around a generalized vocabulary of commendation but never descends to particulars and apparently does not feel it necessary to support her subjective evaluations with anything more than the flimsiest of reasons; she says nothing about metrics, linguistic patterns, recurrent images, or all the rest of the usual stock in trade of poets. What we are left with, then, is a book which argues only the case for another book on Freneau.

And maybe Lewis Leary will give us just that—again. His "The Dream Visions of Philip Freneau" (*EAL* 11:156–82), at any rate, represents yet another article in his continuing effort to qualify certain overly negative judgments on Freneau in *That Rascal Freneau: A Study in Literary Failure* (1941), and in this one Leary presents a reading of the 1779 "House of Night" as "an extraordinarily personal poem . . . revealing tensions not yet resolved between what war required and what poetry demanded"; it is not only, says Leary, "a young man's farewell to war, it is a young poet's attempt to redeem what he could of his craft." An appendix to the article also reprints a facsimile of the earliest version of Freneau's poem.

The work of one of Freneau's predecessors, Nathaniel Evans, was republished in 1976 as *George Washington's Copy of 'Poems on Several Occasions' by Nathaniel Evans: A Facsimile Edition* (New York: Fordham Univ. Press), which features a 59-page introduction by Andrew B. Myers detailing the difficulties that Provost William Smith met in getting the edition together and commenting on the relationship between Evans and Elizabeth Graeme; Myers also speculates on the question of how Washington received the book.

From poetry to political prose. Taking up once again the issue of Jefferson and slavery, John P. Diggins, in "Slavery, Race, and Equality: Jefferson and the Pathos of the Enlightenment" (*AQ* 28:206–28), perceptively isolates Jefferson's intellectual "tragedy" as an inability to "fully recognize that the mind imposes its own categories on nature. Once the question of equality was posed in naturalistic terms, the ideal of equality could no longer be regarded as a moral protest against nature." "In his natural rights philosophy," Diggins says, "Jefferson tried to establish an ethical assumption upon a scientific foundation. Conceiving equality as an empirical proposition, he looked to the natural world to confirm an idea that actually had its origins in the moral world . . . failing to find evidence for universal equality, he would not allow his mind to make demands upon nature."

Far too long for what it says is William S. Howell's "The Declaration of Independence: Some Adventures with America's Political Masterpiece" (*QJS* 62:221–33), in which Howell recounts in droning

detail the "brilliant" stroke of deductive logic he employed to cer-
tify his intuition that William Duncan's *Elements in Logic* could have
influenced Jefferson's choice of a syllogistic structure to construct "an
eloquent political argument that measured up to the austerities of
Science." The connection is, of course, William Small, who taught
Jefferson at William and Mary and who studied under Duncan in
Scotland.

Two other political writers of the Revolution are the subjects of
A. Owen Aldridge's "Paine and Dickinson" (*EAL* 11:125–38), an
essay that demonstrates that in their faith in natural rights and laws,
in their self-defined Federalism, and in their regard for each other's
writings, the two men, though more often contrasted than compared
in scholarly writing, held important ideas in common. Paine's career
is also studied in Eric Foner's *Tom Paine and Revolutionary America*
(New York: Oxford Univ. Press); Foner believes that Paine's achievement as a political pamphleteer lay principally in his development
of "a rhetoric aimed at extending political discussion beyond the narrow bounds of the eighteenth-century's 'political nation,' " though he
is largely unsuccessful in his efforts to define that style in any meaningful way. His socioeconomic analysis of Revolutionary Philadelphia, on the other hand, his discussion of Paine's ideological similarities to and differences from the Philadelphia artisan constituency,
his assessment of Paine's role in framing the Pennsylvania Constitution of 1776, and his explanation of Paine's connections with the
Girondins (or, for that matter, of Paine's unlikely alliance with the
elitist Robert Morris on the issue of the Bank of North America in
the late 1780s) are first-rate.

In his study of "Crèvecoeur as New Yorker" (*EAL* 11:22–30),
Thomas Philbrick concentrates chiefly on one of the seven *Sketches
of Eighteenth Century America*, "Landscapes," the one which features most references to New York scenery. The sketch "supplies a
sobering insight into the individual suffering, the injustice, and the
masked ambition and greed that attend the noblest of great historical
events" and anticipates "the ironic awareness that later and better
writers would bring to their awareness of the American Revolution."
Another member of the Revolutionary generation, of peripheral interest to literary students, is Dr. Thomas Young of Boston, whose political career is admirably surveyed in Pauline Maier's "Reason and
Revolution: The Radicalism of Dr. Thomas Young" (*AQ* 28:229–

49). And, finally, Bruce Granger deals with prose writers in general, and Hugh Henry Brackenridge and Francis Hopkinson in particular, in his "The Addisonian Essay in the American Revolution" (*SLitI* 9,ii:43–52).

Francis Hopkinson was also favored with Paul M. Zall's edition of the *Comical Spirit of Seventy-Six: The Humor of Francis Hopkinson* (San Marino, Calif.: Huntington Library), which features a sound introduction. Yet another welcome edition of an early writer is William E. McCarron's *A Bicentennial Edition of Thomas Godfrey's 'The Prince of Parthia, A Tragedy'* (1765), the first edition of Godfrey's drama in over 50 years (Colorado Springs, Colo.: U. S. Air Force Academy, Dept. of English and Fine Arts).

A number of essays studied the later reputations of several prominent Revolutionary figures. Robert D. Arner's "The Death of Major André: Some Eighteenth-Century Views" (*EAL* 11:52–67) examines the popular response to André's execution as reflected in literature of the period and hypothesizes that André's story owes its currency to its adaptibility to sentimental and heroic idioms on the one hand and, on the other, to displaced feelings of fratricidal and patricidal guilt from which the fictional André absolves Americans. In "John Adams and Hawthorne: The Fiction of the Real American Imagination" (*SLitI* 9,ii:1–17), Lewis P. Simpson analyzes Hawthorne's "My Kinsman, Major Molineux" against an historical background of Adams's distrust of human rationality, and in "Their Kinsman, Thomas Hutchinson: Hawthorne, the Boston Patriots, and His Majesty's Royal Governor" (*EAL* 11:183–90), Peter Shaw approaches the same story as an oblique study of the guilt, remorse, and personality transference that afflicted the leading Boston patriots who ousted Thomas Hutchinson. More conventional is James M. O'Toole's "The Historical Interpretations of Samuel Adams" (*NEQ* 49:82–96), which ignores altogether what could have been the fascinating subject of Adams's portrayal in American literature and focuses instead on the various interpretations of Adams's Revolutionary role as advanced by Tory, Whig, Progressive, Consensus, and New Left historians. By contrast, John McWilliams's "The Faces of Ethan Allen: 1760–1860" (*NEQ* 49:257–82) explores fictional treatments of Allen in Daniel Thompson's *The Green Mountain Boys* and Melville's *Israel Potter*, among other works; Allen, McWilliams contends, was rescued from "the disfiguring pieties" of early 19th-century historians by the romancers' transformation of him into a democratic hero, nature's nobleman, but it was Allen himself who made this transformation possible by "forever . . . [submerging himself] behind the public selves he had created."

Several essays to go along with Kenneth Silverman's interdisciplinary study are Irma B. Jaffe's "Contemporary Words and Pictures: Drawings (1782–1810) by John Trumbull" (*EAL* 11:31–51) and J. A. Leo Lemay's exemplary study of "The American Origins of 'Yankee Doodle'" (*WMQ* 33:435–64); all but impossible to summarize, Lemay's article employs virtually every kind of scholarly methodology in attempting (successfully, I think) to prove its central thesis: that "'Yankee Doodle' is an American folk song, reflecting American traditions and American self characterization." The year's work in this period is rounded out by two excellent editions of Revolutionary popular culture, Mason I. Lowance's and Georgia Bumgardner's *Massachusetts Broadsides of the American Revolution* (Amherst: Univ. of Mass. Press) and George C. Carey's interesting *A Sailor's Songbag: An American Rebel in an English Prison, 1777–1779* (Amherst: Univ. of Mass. Press), an edition of popular and bawdy songs from a manuscript by Timothy Connor.

vii. Brown and Contemporaries

Just when it was beginning to seem that *Wieland* was indeed a puzzling novel—see, for example, the synopsis of articles in *ALS* (1975) —along comes Michael D. Butler to tell us, in "Charles Brockden Brown's *Wieland*: Method and Meaning" (*SAF* 4:127–42), that the old critics had the book figured out all along: in the survival of Clara Wieland the novel affirms the triumph of human rationality. In order to reach this conclusion, Butler rather cavalierly dismisses the "psychological implications" of Clara's dreams, does not really consider the possibility that her insistence on finding rational explanations for every event may mask a fear of her own inner darkness and in any case is frequently contradicted by her actions, and neglects to mention that her powers of deduction lead her to blame Carwin alone for the entire catalogue of horrors that beset the Wieland family. Butler also revives Larzer Ziff's thesis (*PMLA* 77[1962]:51–57) that *Wieland* is deliberately intended as a criticism of the sentimental novel—here his argument seems more solidly based but still fails to convince entirely—and that this element of parody "imposes a necessary order upon the novel."

Along much the same lines Patricia Jewell McAlexander, in "*Arthur Mervyn* and the Sentimental Love Tradition" (*SLitI* 9,ii:31–41) presents an interesting but finally unconvincing argument that "in portraying Arthur's son-pupil relationship" with Achsa Fielding, Brown is simply following a convention of the sentimental tradition; Arthur's dream of a vengeful first husband, she says (ignoring all the other ambiguous paternal and maternal patterns in the book), arises from the guilt he feels at manipulating Achsa, trying to possess her knowledge of sin and suffering without paying the price himself, and attempting to elevate himself through passionate love above the common race of mortals.

Another early American novelist, Susanna Haswell Rowson, is treated in Patricia L. Parker's "*Charlotte Temple*: America's First Best Seller" (*SSF* 13:518–20), a vapid summary of the plot of the novel which argues that Rowson may be considered mildly feminist in her views. That thesis is extended in Dorothy Weil's *In Defense of Women: Susanna Haswell Rowson (1762–1824)* (University Park: Pa. State Univ. Press), the first full-length study of Rowson's writing. Somewhat weak on the general area of early American culture which provided the context for Mrs. Rowson's career, Weil's book also has surprisingly little to say about *Charlotte* but more than makes up for that deficiency by its excellent coverage of Rowson's other works. Particularly good is Weil's discussion of Mrs. Rowson's ambivalent feelings about the sentimental tradition which she herself exploited.

The anonymous author of an early short story receives praise in Jack B. Moore's "Making Indians Early: The Worth of 'Azakia'" (*SSF* 13:51–60), which makes the general point that serious fiction about Indians before Cooper is worthy of study and proves his case by a detailed analysis of "Azakia," a story which, judging from its frequent reprintings, enjoyed wide popularity among early American readers.

In "Timothy Dwight and the American Landscape: The Composing Eye in Dwight's *Travels in New England and New York*" (*EAL* 11:311–21), John F. Sears offers an account of how Dwight made use of the Burkean sublime and William Gilpin's writings on the picturesque to distance himself psychologically from the unpleasant realities of the American wilderness; but Sears is wrong, I think, to contrast William Bartram with Dwight as a "romantic primitivist," since Bartram's landscapes reveal nearly as strong a tendency to avoid the negative implications of the American wilderness. In any case, Sears's thesis appears overly simplistic when set beside Cecelia Tichi's brief but absolutely splendid treatment of American landscape in "The American Revolution and the New Earth" (*EAL* 11: 202–10), which discusses not only Dwight's *Travels* but also selected passages from Joel Barlow and David Humphreys in describing how (in Barlow's battle between Hesper and the Frost Spirit in *The Columbiad*) Americans found literary images, poetically inept though they might have been, to join "the battle for liberty . . . with the battle for the environment" and assert a crucial, millennially based "relationship between the Revolution and the freeing of vast continental acreage to man's reforming hand."

Two essays consider the problem of early American drama. In "Theatre Versus Drama: Popular Entertainment in Early America" (*Discoveries & Considerations*, pp. 131–51), Julian Mates reminds us that literary critics need not necessarily be good judges of the cultural value of drama, since "it is frequently in nonliterary ways that drama makes itself felt"; he then presents an overview of comic opera, melodrama, and the minstrel show in late 18th- and early 19th-century America, arguing that these performances, which in the absence of a deeply rooted native tradition of serious theatre achieved an easy preëminence and came to be identified with theatre itself, gave to America "not merely an escape but a picture of itself." And in "Shakespeare in America: Great Shakespeare Jubilee, American Style" (*Shakespeare and English History: Interdisciplinary Perspectives*, ed. Ronald G. Shafer [Indiana, Pa.: Indiana Univ. of Pa. Press], pp. 83–100), Harrison T. Meserole takes a look at Shakespeare's reputation in early America and at the 1823 Jubilee which Boston promoters modelled on Garrick's 1769 celebration.

viii. General and Miscellaneous

An interesting contribution to go with the interdisciplinary studies cited earlier is Richard Crawford's "Watts for Singing: Metrical Poetry in American Sacred Tunebooks, 1761–1785" (*EAL* 11:139–46), which notes that William Billings is virtually unique in providing unfamiliar texts (such as his own "Chester") to underlay new tunes

and that most other early American composers (and even Billings to
a significant degree) preferred to set the familiar lyrics of Watts's
Hymns and Spiritual Songs and *Horae Lyrica*; even so, despite the
dependence of American composers on English texts, Crawford believes that sacred singing is worthy both of literary and historical
study because "sacred sung poetry fosters experience both broad and
deep" in that "God's power and mercy, Jesus' sacrifice for sinful man,
death and its terrors, and life after death all represent [ontological
and universal] ideas close to the forefront of colonial consciousness."
And in the realm of early American art, Roger B. Stein's "Copley's
Watson and the Shark and Aesthetics in the 1770s" (*Discoveries &
Considerations*, pp. 85–130) provides an excellent discussion of the
cross-fertilization of artistic disciplines and European and American
artistic traditions.

American racial attitudes during the early Federal period are
commented upon in David S. Wiesen's "The Contributions of Antiquity to American Racial Thought" (*Classical Traditions*, pp. 191–212),
which briefly explores the Americanization of Aristotle's doctrine of
innate inferiority through an examination of the writings of Thomas
Jefferson, Samuel Stanhope Smith (who opposed Aristotle's views),
and, later, George Fitzhugh. Another study of classical thought in
early America is Martin D. Snyder's "The Hero in the Garden: Classical Contributions to the Early Image of America" (*Classical Traditions*, pp. 139–74), which attempts to establish that classical literature provided two contradictory paradigms, the myth of the
Elysian Islands/Golden Age and the prototypical adventurer-hero
Jason, to serve as definitions of the American experience; but Snyder's
quotations are far too randomly selected and too superficially examined to lead to any new conclusions or cause us to rethink any
old ones.

An uninteresting overview of American biographical writing from
Cotton Mather through Mason Locke Weems to William Wirt and
John Pendleton Kennedy, Richard Hankins's "Puritans, Patriots, and
Panegyric: The Beginnings of American Biography" (*SLitI* 9,ii:95–
109) contends that American biographers gradually became more
objective and balanced in their approaches to their subjects, no longer indulging in conscious myth-making as Mather had done.

In some ways W. Howland Kenney's edition, *Laughter in the
Wilderness: Early American Humor to 1783* (Kent, Ohio: Kent State

Univ. Press), is a welcome contribution to colonial studies, for, as he points out in his introduction, too many critics still overlook the early American's capacity for laughter and, missing that, they also fail to understand something essential about the colonial's humanity. One may take issue with Kenney's overly rigid distinction between the Puritans and colonial southerners, with his repeated and annoying assertion that Nathaniel Ward wrote *The Simple Cobler* only for a London audience, or, for that matter, with the very familiarity of his anthologized offerings. On the other hand, Kenney does include snippets from colonial newspapers, passages from Dr. Alexander Hamilton's *Itinerarium,* and some lesser-known Revolutionary satires (though he probably should have added something from *M'Fingal*), so that overall this edition should help to set thinking straight about the early American's sense of humor.

Noteworthy for its treatment of those "other" early American cultures so often and so shamelessly overlooked—in this case the Spanish culture—is William Felker's "The New World is Lonely: Reflections on the '*Epístola a Belardo*' by the Amarilis Indiana" (*SCN* 34:70–72). Felker can add no evidence that Amarilis really was a Peruvian nun and not another pseudonym for Belardo (Lope de Vega) or one of his friends, but, he says, hers are exactly the sentiments we should expect to hear coming back to the Old World from the New in the early 17th century. The heavy Spanish baroque style of the poem, Felker adds, "may certainly have been a most satisfying means to express the tremendous multiplication of previously unimagined facts and experiences."

Bibliographical studies during the past year are headed by George Selement's "A Check List of Manuscript Materials Relating to Seventeenth-Century New England Printed in Historical Collections" (*BNYPL* 79:416–34), which will undoubtedly, as he claims, save scholars "weeks of sifting through volume after volume." Far less valuable is Jayne K. Kribbs's "Seventeenth-Century American Literature: A Survey of Scholarship, 1970–74" (*SCN* 34:72–77), which is much too selective to be of use to anyone but a neophyte colonialist. Then there is Harrison T. Meserole's bibliographical chapter on "American Literature," pp. 268–326 in F. W. Bateson and Meserole's *A Guide to English & American Literature,* 3rd. ed. (London: Longman), much of which is of course devoted to writers beyond the pale of early American literature; the "Bibliographical Guide and Handbooks" section inexplicably fails to list J. A. Leo Lemay's *Calendar of American Poetry,* but otherwise the chapter strikes me as entirely useful and as complete as such things can reasonably be expected to be. One interesting development is Meserole's elevation of Cotton Mather to the status of a major writer, a development long overdue.

It also seems fitting to include here two review essays of Richard Slotkin's *Regeneration Through Violence: The Mythology of the American Frontier, 1600–1860* (1973). Honored with practically every academic publishing award and highly praised by colonialists because it made use of early primary materials which other studies of the frontier had neglected, the book has already come in for some reappraisals. First there was Michael J. Colacurcio's careful evaluation of the strengths and weaknesses of Slotkin's thesis (*EAL* 9 [1975]:333–36), which focused upon the inadequacy (not to say the banality) of Slotkin's handling of 17th-century captivity narratives and the tentativeness and oversimplification that plague the treatments of Melville and Hawthorne. Now there is John Seelye's "Ugh!" (*SCN* 34:37–41), a reëxamination of Slotkin's study as "an exercise in assertion rather than the assembly of proof." Pointing out, like Colacurcio before him, how deeply indebted Slotkin's argument is to D. H. Lawrence's idea of blood consciousness and echoing Colacurcio's charge that the "treatment of the earlier period is both arbitrary and ill-informed," Seelye also takes issue with a fundamental failure to establish and maintain a distinction between truly mythic and merely popular literary expressions of the American theme of violence against "'the spirit of the wilderness,'" with Slotkin's caricature of the Puritan and his failure to take into account the complexity of the Puritan's response to the wilderness, and, most especially, with the absence of Captain John Smith from Slotkin's study. Smith, Seelye argues, "not only anticipates but discredits Slotkin's emerging 'myth' [of Daniel Boone]," both "taking away some of Boone's uniqueness and considerably diminishing the blame placed on the Puritans for the Indians' tragic fate."

University of Cincinnati

12. 19th-Century Literature

Warren French

Two thematic studies appropriately frame the bicentennial year offering of 19th-century scholars. Paul John Eakin's *The New England Girl* traces an American inspirational dream's collapse into disillusioning workaday reality; Alan Rose's *Demonic Vision* conversely illustrates the amelioration of regional nightmare into the same drab reality. Eakin shows how Hawthorne, Harriet Beecher Stowe, Howells and Henry James "drew upon a well-established assumption of nineteenth-century American society," which saw Woman functioning "as an all-purpose symbol of the ideals of the culture, the official repository of its acknowledged moral code, and . . . a redemptive figure in the fiction of the era" (p. 5). Rose, on the other hand, shows how the parallel antebellum southern white racial vision of Negroes, and even more frequently Indians, "was shaped by the formal imagery already associated with the archetype of the devil" (p. 10).

Thus, much of the major fiction of the first century of our national history drew upon (a pun here is unavoidable) black-and-white images—the kind of thought characteristic of childhood—that in the significant fiction of our second century have merged into the despairing grayness of unwilling adulthood. Eakin suggests that the dream faded first, that even Mrs. Stowe recognized the New England girl's "capacity for the religious sublime" as "a kind of sickness and bondage" (p. 47), so that even as early as Howells's *April Hopes* (1888), this former heroine had become "the principal impediment to the hero's moral development" (p. 117). The nightmare persisted, Rose maintains, until the 20th century, so that it is only in works like Flannery O'Connor's *Wise Blood* that we find "the exhaustion of the demonic tradition" (p. 124).

These two potently documented theses suggest ways in which the alienation and exhaustion characteristic of Modernist American fiction may be only the last violent reactions to a disillusionment that has been developing for a century—not with things as they are, but with their failure to be as easily categorized as good or evil as we would like them to be. Certainly the most striking criticisms of particularly popular 19th-century literature during our festival year illustrate ways that these writings may be perceived as symptoms or diagnoses of our chronic, psychosomatic naivete.

i. General Studies

A most useful aid to the difficult process of digging out the materials for study of an early phase of this history is *Indices to American Literary Annuals and Gift Books, 1825–1865*, comp. E. Bruce Kirkham and John W. Fink (New Haven, Conn.: Research Publications, 1975), an oversized 625-page guide to the 469 occasional volumes listed in Ralph Thompson's *American Literary Annuals and Gift Books, 1825–1865* (1936), now generally available on 58 reels of microfilm. Data on individual volumes are followed by indices of editors, publishers, stereotypes, titles, authors, and engravings. The result is an inexhaustible reference book that deserves our boundless thanks.

M. E. Grenander's "The Heritage of Cain: Crime in American Fiction" (*AAAPSS* 423:47–66) is such a sweeping consideration of artists' attitudes toward social and cultural problems, written in an almost telegraphic style, that one can only share some of the author's tentative, but unsurprising conclusions: "Literature for a mass audience tends to confirm accepted values. Critical examination of these values in such fiction serves as a warning signal that sizable numbers of people are already beginning to doubt them . . . At a more fundamental level, high art diagnoses cancers in the body politic still unnoticed by most people" (p. 66).

Of extremely specialized interest is the only other of the year's surprisingly few general period studies, Robert L. Bloom's "The Battle of Gettysburg in Fiction" (*Pa. Hist.* 43:309–27), which discusses at length the historical accuracy of a number of generally obscure works and reaches the conclusion that "the better novelists come as close as do historians in providing a credible picture."

ii. The Age of Elegance—Irving Cooper, and Their Contemporaries

Appropriately, the Bicentennial has been a banner year for our first internationally acclaimed fictionist, Washington Irving, especially so far as resource works are concerned. Haskell Springer's *Washington Irving: A Research Guide* (Boston: G. K. Hall) provides not only a chronological account year-by-year of "scholarship, criticism, reviews, and miscellaneous commentary" published between 1807 and 1974, but also objective annotations about the contents of rare and difficult-to-locate works. *A Century of Commentary on the Works of Washington Irving*, ed. Andrew B. Myers (Tarrytown, N.Y.: Sleepy Hollow Restorations) supplements Springer's work by reprinting the whole text or portions of 45 of the most important of the critical pieces from William Cullen Bryant's 1860 eulogy to Philip Young's celebrated 1960 essay on the mythic aspects of "Rip Van Winkle." After a lapse of several years, publication has also resumed on the new collected edition of Irving's work by a new publisher. The first volume to appear, *Astoria, or Anecdotes of an Enterprise Beyond the Rocky Mountains*, ed. with intro. by Richard Dilworth Rust (Boston: Twayne) is scheduled to be followed quickly by several other long-awaited texts.

Materials are certainly here to facilitate the new critical consideration of Irving that is surely needed if this year's vapid productions indicate the state of current scholarship. Martin Roth's misleadingly titled *Comedy and America: The Lost World of Washington Irving* (Port Washington, N.Y.: Kennikat Press) deals only with the writings through *The History of New York*, which Roth sees as "not a short-lived exercise in the adaptation of various strains of English and European comedy to America, but a coherent, though intuitive, attempt to create an American literature" (p. ix). This attempt resulted in what Roth calls "burlesque comedy," a category differing from satire and humor in that "all moral reference is lacking" (p. 5). Although Irving was able "to generate the first deeply charged American narrative voice," it was "the voice of a childish neurotic and solipsist" (p. 30) that was silenced when his impulse toward "burlesque comedy" dried up.

The importance of the two most famous tales in Irving's *Sketch Book* to the development of an American literature is also reviewed. Eugene Current-Garcia's " 'Soundings and Alarums': The Beginning of Short Fiction in America" (*MQ* 17:311–28) makes the sound, but obvious, point that before 1800 generally the moral of the short tale "*was* the story," but that Irving marked a turning point from primitivism toward the promise of aesthetic maturity because his work "imparted a feeling of life-likeness and immediacy." Walter Shear's

"Time in 'Rip Van Winkle' and 'The Legend of Sleepy Hollow' " (*MQ* 17:158–72) makes the more complicated point that "while both Rip and Ichabod are in a sense betrayed by history" and separated from their societies, Irving articulates through the stories the idea that "the historical fate of such culturally absurd people as the American could be taken seriously," because "without the continuity of class structures," "everyday citizens can see their notions of fame, happiness, and contentment . . . distributed capriciously by a random Eternal Justice."

Kathryn Sutherland's rambling and anecdotal "Walter Scott and Washington Irving: 'Editors of the Land of Utopia' " (*JAmS* 10:85–90) adds up to the observation that the "kindred minds" of the writers are shown by the fact that while Irving was much indebted to Scott (as has been widely recognized), Scott was also obligated to Irving for similar developments in the use of the story-telling persona.

The year's two best articles provide insights into Irving's feeling towards his work. In "The New York Years in Irving's *The Life of George Washington*" (*EAL* 11:68–83), Andrew Myers, editor of the recent "miniaturized" version of the biography, gives a sense of the feelings that Irving brought to the writing of the original five-volume work in which he sought to present Washington as not a demigod, but a flesh-and-blood general and president. Earl Harbert follows up a recent study of the formal problems posed by one of Irving's most difficult-to-classify works (*ALS 1974*, p. 196) with "Irving's *A Chronicle of The Conquest of Granada*: An Essay in the History of Publication, Revision, and Critical Reception" (*BNYPL* 79:400–15), which relates the complicated history of the differing English and American original editions and Irving's efforts to make the 1850 revision a better book than either.

Early poetry attracts scant attention. Curtis Dahl's "Ezra Styles Ely (1786–1861): Three Notes and a Query" (*PBSA* 70:116–21) supplements and corrects present bibliographies of this controversial Presbyterian minister and pamphleteer and then supplies extensive evidence for identifying him as the author of *William and Ellen: A Poem in Three Cantos*, a pedantic narrative of love and seduction, published anonymously, probably in 1811. Two essays return to one of William Cullen Bryant's best-known poems. Gerald J. Smith's "Bryant's 'Thanatopsis': A Possible Source" (*AN&Q* 13:149–51) points out the similar tone and imagery of the Funeral Oration of Pericles as recorded by Thucydides. E. Miller Budick's " 'Visible' Images and the 'Still Voice': Transcendental Vision in Bryant's 'Thanatopsis' " (*ESQ* 22:71–77) defends the poem as representing a valiant and successful attempt to define precisely, and without the excesses of facile Romantic rhetoric, the constituent complexities of man's apprehension of transcendent truth in natural images. Bryant's "central achievement," Budick believes, is a "tough-minded and yet eloquent portrayal of the process whereby nature imparts to man her vision of transcendence."

Influences upon Cooper—one of the first American writers for whom the demons destroyed the dream—continue to be rewardingly studied, especially in Blake Nevius's *Cooper's Landscapes: An Essay on the Picturesque Vision* (Berkeley: Univ. of Calif. Press). In a very modest space Nevius deals competently and felicitously with the relationship between those who paint landscapes with brushes and with words and also with the way in which "Cooper's European experience altered his mode of viewing and representing the American landscape" (p. x). The heart of the book is an analysis of one of Cooper's "most perplexing romances," *Wyandotté*, as "understandable perhaps only in terms of Cooper's attempts to mediate between irreconcilable visions of the good life" (p. 85). Nevius explains that Cooper described three stages in the progress of society in a new country—a clearing, leveling stage; a second symptomized by a "struggle for money, power, and position;" and a third in which a uniform civilization is achieved" (pp. 82–83). In *Wyandotté*, Captain Willoughby eliminates the second stage, "with its attendant social evils," so that miraculously his knoll passes quickly from wilderness to civilization. Yet even this achievement proves dishearteningly short-lived.

Cooper's references to the impact of European conventions upon another art are also examined in Joel R. Kehler's "Architectural Dialecticism in Cooper's *The Pioneers*" (*TSLL* 18:124–34). Kehler finds the urbanism of Templeton in the novel symptomatic of a manic "desire to appear *Europeanized*." Such pseudoclassicism, however, "proves singularly unadaptable to American materials, climates and uses," whereas Natty Bumppo's humble hut "is one of a long line of primitive literary refuges" and its destruction by his own hand marks the victory of "civilization" over nature in America. This action of Natty's is viewed in the same light by Rosemary F. Franklin in her more comprehensive "The Cabin by the Lake: Pastoral Landscapes of Poe, Cooper, Hawthorne, and Thoreau" (*ESQ* 22:59–70). Franklin first generally points out that "the pond and the cabin are microcosms of the two counter-forces of the pastoral wilderness and city, but they embody only the positive and complementary aspects of these poles, not the destructive and divisive." Turning to Cooper, then, she sees the burning of the only cabin Natty ever possesses as the author's setting his own imagination free "for his future novels of the series which will increase in their Romantic and primitivist qualities."

Further evidence of Cooper's self-liberation is revealed in David T. Haberly's "Women and Indians: *The Last of the Mohicans* and the Captivity Tradition" (*AQ* 28:431–43), which describes Cooper's problem as reconciling "his own ideas—the beauty of the American wilderness, the glory of the Westward movement and goodness of at least a part of Indian America—with the powerful captivity tradition of horrendous barbarities committed on the western frontiers by Indians unspeakably vile." Cooper resolved these antitheses, Haberly maintains, through his handling of the role of white women, whose "intrusive, destructive power must be removed before the ideal harmony of the frontier can exist once more," even though their removal leads to the pairing of what D. H. Lawrence called "childless womanless men of opposite races." While these can produce "no real issue," they lead to such fictional offspring as Huck and Jim and the Lone Ranger and Tonto.

Whatever the fictional consequences of this novel, Michael D. Butler argues in "Narrative Structure and Historical Process in *The Last of the Mohicans*" (*AL* 48:117–39) that Cooper traced in it "a historical process in which a physical, masculine, red culture" embodied in futureless bachelorhood, "gives way to a more spiritual, more feminine, white culture." In general, Butler theorizes, the novel embodies "a theory of human progress," illustrated by "the three most crucial developments in our nation's past": the decline of both Indian and European on this continent and the consequent creation and rise of the American.

Terence Martin succeeds in resolving these seemingly incompatible interpretations of Cooper's views in the novel as retrogressive and progressive in "Surviving on the Frontier: The Doubled Consciousness of Natty Bumppo" (*SAQ* 75:447–59), by arguing brilliantly that while experience usually destroys frontier innocence, Cooper in the Leatherstocking Tales "works toward a strategy of making experience serve innocence." His "master stroke," Martin maintains, is to double Natty's consciousness to include that of the savage Chingachgook, "without diminishing the separateness or integrity of the two characters." Since Natty can comprehend deeds of his dark double that he need not compromise himself by performing physically, he becomes a figure of "fulfilled innocence."

The last of these provocative bicentennial speculations about Natty Bumppo, Edwin Haviland Miller's "James Fenimore Cooper's Elegiac Comedy: *The Prairie*" (*Mosaic* 9,iv:195–205) deals with the mortal end of this deathless figure. Miller feels that approaching the novel as an elegiac comedy enables us to explain its affirmative conclusion in a way that epic and mythological parallels cannot, since Natty becomes "the 'father' who reestablishes the cornerstone of civilization, the family," for the others that he sends back to civilization. In creating an affirmative end worthy of his beloved, however, Miller believes that Cooper came close to confusing Natty's role because the frontiersman became also—as Haberly argues—"the boy-man of our literature" and the "father" of other boy-men like Huck Finn and Billy Budd.

The Bicentennial has also inspired critics to look beyond the Leatherstocking saga. In "Cooper and the Revolutionary Mythos" (*EAL* 11:84–104), James Franklin Beard observes that a powerful influence on Cooper's novels about the Revolution was his saturation in this mythos, "that elusive but distinctive coherent cluster of ideas, values and attitudes . . . that enabled reflective citizens of the early Republic to comprehend the awesome circumstances that brought them to their independence." By the time Cooper wrote *Wyandotté*, however, Beard feels—as Blake Nevius does—that while the novelist's personal commitment to the mythos was unchanged, he was persuaded that the "pseudo-patriotism" of opportunists had brought about a series of publicly unacknowledged Constitutional crises that had gradually transformed a "sincere" government into an "insincere" one.

Similar conclusions about Cooper's attitude toward the Revolution and its aftermath are reached by a somewhat different route in H. Daniel Peck's "A Repossession of America: The Revolution in Cooper's Trilogy of Nautical Romances" (*SIR* 15:589–605). Peck's theory is that Cooper understood the Revolution as the event that opened America to the full force of history. *The Pilot* and *The Red Rover* describe "different stages of America's adolescent rebellion," but the last and most mythical of the trilogy, *The Water Witch*, describes the land's innocent childhood. Cooper believed that if revolution introduced social and political disorders, "it was necessary to return to the 'past.'"

Concentrating on just one of these books, Jeffrey Steinbrink in "Cooper's Romance of the Revolution: *Lionel Lincoln* and the Lessons of Failure" (*EAL* 11:336–43) comments on the abortive project to write a series of "Legends of the Thirteen Republics." Steinbrink thinks that Cooper abandoned this scheme after the failure of the first novel because its lesson was that "he could incorporate only so much historical material into his work and that some times his fiction simply collapsed under the weight of his respect for the past," because he never recognized "the difference between accuracy and authenticity."

While the Bicentennial has resulted in a preoccupation with Cooper's early American tales, J. Gary Williams carries us to quite another theater of his concern in "Cooper and European Catholicism: A Reading of *The Heidenmauer*" (*ESQ* 22:149–58), which argues that despite demurrers of previous critics, the novel is "*about* the Reformation—its cause, the manner in which it spread, and its effect." Cooper's "lesson" in this work, Williams argues, is that "Roman Catholicism is not an orgre and that neither Catholics nor Protestants have exclusive holds on truth, virtue, or piety."

Although William Gilmore Simms has never rivaled Cooper as a writer of international stature, resurgent southern scholarship makes writings about this regional favorite bulk nearly as large as those about the New Yorker. The fall, 1976 issue of *MissQ* is devoted almost entirely to Simms. Charles S. Watson introduces the four papers from a seminar at the 1975 MLA meeting with "Simms and the American Revolution" (29:498–500), which describes Simms's subject as "the warfare in the South Carolina low country from 1780 to 1782, when the colony bore the major burden of the war" and briefly reviews the limited previous scholarship about these works. C. Hugh Holman's "Simms's Changing View of Loyalists during the Revolution" (29:501–13) points out that while Simms supported the war,

he recognized in early works that "Whig fanaticism and brutality
had contributed strongly to the stand taken by many Loyalists," who
were largely poor whites. Later, however, reacting adversely to Lorenzo Sabine's adverse criticism of South Carolina in *The American
Loyalists* (1847), Simms made the preponderance of Tories in his
later works, *The Forayers* and *Eutaw*, "knaves, villains, and other
comic buffoons" in the folk tradition of southern frontier humor.
Miriam J. Shillingsburg's "The Influence of Sectionalism on the Revisions in Simms's Revolutionary Romances" (29:526–38) also reviews Simms's angry response to Sabine but observes that when the
novelist came to revise his early Revolutionary novels in the 1850s,
"he did not vent his hostilities toward the North," since his purpose
was "to record an exciting period in South Carolina's history" and
not to grind political axes.

Narrowing the focus to a single novel and shifting from political
to aesthetic criticism, L. Moffitt Cecil argues in "The Design of William Gilmore Simms's *The Kinsmen*" (29:514–25) that despite the
patronizing attitude of many critics who feel that Simms's work
"could hardly stand serious dissection," a careful study of this novel
reveals him as "an ingenious and skillful craftsman." Elsewhere Roger
J. Bresnahan also assesses "William Gilmore Simms's Revolutionary
War: A Romantic View of Southern History" (*SIR* 15:573–87). After
pointing out that Simms's friends discouraged his interest in the Revolution as "a topic barren of meaning for the present generation,"
Bresnahan explains that Simms saw his role as one of uncovering
regional riches and "arranging them in conformity to a developing
world view and a deepening understanding of their permanent values
in the cultivation of a Southern consciousness."

Richard C. Shaner in "Simms and the Noble Savage" (*ATQ* 30 pt.
1:18–22) takes a dim view of the kind of consciousness that Simms
helped to develop. Pointing out that *The Yemassee* is not historically
accurate, Shaner explains that it does foreshadow and justify the government policy that Indian removal to the West was desirable—
"whites deserved the land because they were a greater race and would
make proper use of it," while Indians were safer and happier away
from civilization.

Critiques of other works are scattered. Mary Ann Wimsatt suggests in "*Ivanhoe* and Simms's *Pelayo*" (*SSL* 12[1975]:250–69) that

in this first novel on a Spanish theme, the numerous resemblances to Scott's novel suggest that Simms's indebtedness "extends far beyond the fragmentary borrowings previous writers on the subject proclaim." Dennis Gendron's "A Source for Simms's *The Yemassee*" (*AL* 48:368–70) points out that the novel has similarities not only to James Nelson Barker's play *The Indian Princess*, as previously noted, but also to Barker's verse tragedy, *Superstition*. James W. Dewshap reveals Simms's own aspirations as a dramatist in "William Gilmore Simms's Career as a Playwright" (*MissQ* 29:149–66), but points out that although Simms considered drama his *forte*, only one of his plays, *Michael Bonham*, was ever produced and that ran only three performances in March 1855 in his native Charleston.

Charles S. Watson comes up with two accounts of Simms's reaction to Harriet Beecher Stowe: "Simms's Review of *Uncle Tom's Cabin*" (*AL* 48:365–68) locates at last this anonymous attack in the *Southern Literary Messenger* (Oct. 1852); and "Simms's Answer to *Uncle Tom's Cabin*: Criticism of the South in *Woodcraft*" (*SLJ* 9,i: 78–90) points out that Simms should not be regarded as just a defender of the South, since he attacks also many aspects of its culture, especially the wastefulness and indolence of many planters and the violent irresponsibility of the poor whites.

Two bibliographical resources for the study of Simms have become available: James E. Kibler, Jr.'s *Pseudonymous Publications of William Gilmore Simms* (Athens: Univ. of Ga. Press) provides a guide to the incredible number of pen-names that Simms used over a span of 48 years, especially when publishing poems; and Betty Jo Strickland's "The Short Fiction of William Gilmore Simms, A Checklist" (*MissQ* 29:592–608) provides an exhaustive catalog of all such works to appear during the writer's life.

A particularly sobering contribution to the critical literature of our bicentennial year is Richard M. Rollins' "Words as Social Control: Noah Webster and the Creation of the American Dictionary" (*AQ* 28:415–30), which points out that although virtually everyone has believed that the dictionary was a nationalist tract, it was "stimulated by much more than patriotism" and reflected through revisions Webster's change "from an optimistic revolutionary in the 1780s . . . to a pessimistic critic of man and society." It finally exhibited "the values and beliefs of the evangelical movement of the early nineteenth century whose major emphasis was limiting human action, not of the nationalistic fervor of the late eighteenth century." The demons were dispelling the dream.

iii. Popular Writers of the American Renaissance

Although often the subject of attacks like Simms's, Mrs. Stowe marches on; and during this bicentennial year she eclipses both the frontier humorists and Fireside Poets as a subject for critical reconsideration of popular antebellum writing. Her further pursuit will be greatly aided by Margaret Holbrook Hildreth's *Harriet Beecher Stowe: A Bibliography* (Hamden, Conn.: Archon), which provides a comprehensive listing of not only her works in many forms published in this country, but abridgments and translations of *Uncle Tom's Cabin*, as well as songs and books inspired by her works, along with criticisms of them.

The shortcomings of many past accounts of her life are illuminated in E. Bruce Kirkham's "Harriet Beecher Stowe: Autobiography and Legend" (*Portraits*, pp. 51–69) which points out that most are plagued with corrupt texts of letters and other inaccuracies. Kirkham blames many of these on Mrs. Stowe herself as a result of presenting the world as she wished to see it in the first biographical account that she dictated to her son. (This book also contains articles on Lyman and Catherine Beecher and other members of this influential clan.) Edwin Fussell's "Mrs. Stowe's Income from the Serial Version of *Uncle Tom's Cabin*" (*SB* 29:380–82) straightens out the record on one long contested point by establishing $400 as the correct figure for the total amount paid her by Gamaliel Bailey of the *National Era*.

Meanwhile a new line of attack, opened by Thomas P. Riggio's "*Uncle Tom* Reconstructed: A Neglected Chapter in the History of a Book" (*AQ* 28:56–70), examines the novel's ambivalence towards blacks as preparing the way for the racist vision of "New America" in southern Reconstruction fiction, particularly the work of Thomas Dixon (whose novel *The Clansman* served as the basis for D. W. Griffith's film *The Birth of a Nation*). Riggio explains how Dixon in *The Leopard's Spots* resurrects Mrs. Stowe's villainous Simon Legree and turns him into an exploiter of southern poor whites, "crucified both psychologically and economically by the black man under the tutelage of an industrialized Simon Legree."

An earlier imbroglio that saw Mrs. Stowe widely attacked is recalled in Jean Willoughby Ashton's "Harriet Stowe's Filthy Story: Lord Byron Set Afloat" (*Prospects* 2:373–84). Mrs. Stowe had hoped, by calling attention in "The True Story of Lady Byron's Life" to the poet's mistreatment of his wife and incestuous relationship with his sister, "to rescue the new generation of readers from uncritical worship" of the profligate poet. Instead she was widely attacked by contemporary hypocrites for "bringing to the surface what had been only gradually and with relief buried" and for intentionally catering "to the salacious tastes of the masses."

A less well-remembered antislavery novel than Mrs. Stowe's is described in Michael K. Simmons' "*Maum Guinea*: or, A Dime Novelist Looks at Abolition" (*JPC* 10:81–87), an account of the "double" dime novel (selling for 20 cents) published by Mrs. Metta V. Victor in 1861. Simmons calls this tale "the most significant" of the dime novels dealing with slavery. Ostensibly an account of the Christmas celebrations on a Louisiana plantation with an innocuous plot, the novel contains interpolated stories "calculated to portray an insensitive, wicked white society subjugating fellow human beings."

Unusual insights into the conditions surrounding the publications of Mrs. Stowe and other popular women writers of the period is afforded by Susan Geary's "The Domestic Novel as a Commercial Commodity: Making a Best Seller in the 1850s" (*PBSA* 70:365–93), which explains the technological improvements that—along with the spread of literacy and a growing populace—made large sales of books possible. Geary points out the increasing role that advertising also played in promoting writers and novels but notes that few works of fiction sold over 100,000 copies, though larger sales were possible during the period.

One of the few men cited in this study as a popular novelist before the Civil War is Joseph Holt Ingraham, and fresh information about one aspect of his varied and still somewhat mysterious career comes to light in Robert W. Weathersby, II's "Joseph Holt Ingraham and Tennessee: A Record of Social and Literary Contributions" (*THQ* 34[1975]:264–72), which chronicles his often surprising movements and activities during the final years of his life as a Protestant Episcopal minister.

After a brief revival, writing about the once-beloved Fireside Poets has tapered off again. Nothing during the Bicentennial matches John B. Pickard's edition of Whittier's letters (*ALS 1975*, p. 245), but

the same editor has prepared, in collaboration with Donald C. Free-
man and Roland H. Woodwell, a charming companion piece, *Whittier and Whittierland: Portrait of a Poet and His World* (North An-
dover, Mass.: Trustees of the J. G. Whittier Homestead), which, as
the editors announce, uses "contemporary photographs, illustrations,
and facsimile reproductions" to present virtually all aspects of Whittier's life as "editor, politician, abolitionist, and poet."

Attention shifts from Longfellow to those around him. John J.
McAleer's "Schoolcraft's Vulnerable Red Men" (*ATQ* 30, pt. 1:13–
18) discusses an attempt to reconstruct the Indian originals that Longfellow drew upon for *Hiawatha* in a book published five months after
the poem and dedicated to the poet by a writer angry with the distortions of early Romantics and proud of his faithfulness to his material. McAleer reasons that Longfellow's handling of the materials
was more popular because in Henry Rowe Schoolcraft's report the
legends were often more exciting and violent "than most readers of
the romantic era were ready for."

iv. Henry Adams and the Romantic Historians

Although popularizations of history flooded the market for the bicentennial year, less attention than in recent years was accorded the
first great generation of American historians. Henry Adams's personal writings, however, continued to fascinate speculative scholars.
While the much-debated matter of his self-confessed "failure" will
continue to provoke comment, John Carlos Rowe's *Henry Adams and
Henry James: The Emergence of a Modern Consciousness* (Ithaca,
N.Y.: Cornell Univ. Press) provides a thoughtful resolution likely to
satisfy those who have remained abreast of recent scholarly dialogue.
Although the book couples two writers, it is largely about Adams and
the accounts of his work and James's are easily separable.

Viewing Adams's thought as a foreshadowing of the existentialist
vein in modern literature, Rowe finds that *Mont St. Michel and Chartres* and *The Education of Henry Adams* "describe a modern figure
who uses the failure of his own effort and the chaos and discontinuity
of his own experiences as the means for surviving in a maddeningly
modern world" (p. 48). "The man who refuses to recognize his alienation and accept responsibility for the world," Rowe concludes, "is
the prisoner of the modern situation" (p. 233). Adams, however,

"does not remain paralyzed by his failure," but rather uses his art "to question the nature of all signification." "The failure" that he describes is "the impossibility of man transcending the limits of his own consciousness" (p. 240).

Several shorter accounts by others reach substantially the same conclusion independently. Eric Mottram's "Henry Adams: Index of the Twentieth Century" (*American Literary Naturalism*, pp. 90–106) argues, for example, that "power is the unifying theme of the *Education*, the two novels, and everything else that Adams wrote: how not to be at the mercy of entropic forces. His own sense of failure is presented in terms of failure to control and influence the point at which the atomic self intersects the cultural field" (pp. 97–98)—something that would surely require man's transcending the limits of his own consciousness. Mottram, like Rowe, feels that "there is a human care in Adams which stems from the most crucial understanding in his work" (p. 105).

Two similar essays start from the same geographic point. S. A. Burns's "Henry Adams: On the Steps of Ara Coeli" (*AN&Q* 14: 116–19) points out that "the unsought, unrecognized truth that young Adams met on the steps of the [Roman] 'Gate of Heaven' is that in this life men must seek to discover the undiscoverable solution to the eternal question and that the search must end in some relative truth taken on faith." L. S. Mansfield's "Henry Adams's Longest Journey: From Santa Maria Di Ara Coeli to Notre Dame de Chartres" (*CentR* 20:197–218) presents Adams's position most vehemently. Although Adams had a devoutly religious nature, Mansfield maintains, neither rationalism nor irrationalism had supplied him with a personal religion. As an old man he concluded that "if the old religion was dead and its successors offered no deity equal in love and compassion for man to Notre Dame de Chartres," he would defiantly reject all of them and maintain his self-respect.

Thomas Cooley makes what appears to be the same point less effectively in prefatory remarks to his chapter on "The Dissolving Man: Henry Adams" in *Educated Lives* (pp. 27–49): "Inclined to conceive of the self as the product of constant change, Adams and his generation were forced in their abdication of religious faith to search their self-recollections for universal values and lasting hopes" (p. 22). In the company of these analyses, Patrick Wolfe's "The Revealing Fiction of Henry Adams" (NEQ 49:399–426), which argues that for understanding Adams none of his works are so important as his novels because they reveal "the forces that caused him to adopt his famous life-style of pessimism and despair," seems superficial and behind the times.

William Prescott's views toward Indians are examined in Donald G. Darnell's "Cooper, Prescott and the Conquest of Indian America" (*ATQ* 30, pt. 1:7–12). Darnell finds the two writers' viewpoints similar in: (1) their development of the myth of inevitable conquest and dispossession, (2) "a reciprocal vision of providential force sending white men in the vanguard of progress," (3) their strict observance of the Romantic literary conventions employed to depict the noble savage. Darnell believes that they differed, however, in that Prescott viewed the two cultures as mutually exclusive, while Cooper in his last novel about the Indians, *The Oak Openings*, found beneficial effects for them in white civilization. Elsewhere Wayne R. Kime's "The American Antecedents of James de Mille's *A Strange Manuscript Found in a Copper Cylinder*" (*DR* 55:280–306) cites Prescott's *History of the Conquest of Mexico* as one of the American influences on the Canadian writer's anti-Utopian novel.

v. The Local Color Movement

The most promising dissertation chronicled during the bicentennial year and the most promising hope for a welcome revitalization of local color studies is Susan Stone Prevost's "The Local Colorists and the Early William Dean Howells: The Social Ideal" (*DAI* 37:1552A–53A), written under the direction of Louis A. Rubin, Jr., whose own contributions to this revitalization will be mentioned below. Prevost's thesis is that the prominent eastern local colorists "all evidenced, to some extent, a Howellsian belief in social compromise" and "acceptance of the contemporary business ethic" and that western authors looked to the East for cultural studies, concluding that "interregional tensions could be solved only if the East imposed its rigid morality on the free and self-indulgent West." If sound, these arguments would indicate that the local color movement was a reinforcement of the *status quo* rather than a dynamic movement to raise readers' consciousness of significant sectional differences. Prevost's position would, therefore, do much to explain the superficiality of the writings usually designated as "local color."

Sarah Orne Jewett continues to command most attention among the eastern local colorists, but attention shifts from her best known works to the novel *A Marsh Island*. Randall R. Mawer argues in "Setting as Symbol in Jewett's *A Marsh Island*" (*CLQ* 12:83–90) that even though Jewett's most enthusiastic critics have said little about this work, it is a successful blending of story and setting, in which "every scene bears directly or symbolically upon the action" that illuminates its theme of "the hard-won triumphs of loyalty to house and home" that will keep the island Edenic for at least another generation. Mawer's "Classical Myth in Jewett's *A Marsh Island*" (*AN&Q* 14: 85–86) reveals an even subtler pattern in the work—the mention of the Greek god Vulcan in a simile suggests both the sexual nature and the universality of the provincial romantic triangle depicted. Philip B. Eppard's " 'Dan's Wife': A Newly Discovered Sarah Orne Jewett Story" (*CLQ* 12:101–2) locates this short account of domestic conflict in *Harper's Bazaar* for August 2, 1889.

Attention continues to focus also on the writer who remains the South's most significant contributor to the local color movement. In fact, Louis D. Rubin, Jr.'s previously unpublished "Politics in the Novel: George W. Cable and the Genteel Tradition" (*William Elliott*, pp. 61–81) suggests—as have other recent accounts—good reasons for placing Cable among the pioneering social realists of the late 19th century rather than with the local colorists. Largely, however, Rubin's account of *John March, Southerner* is a depressing analysis of Cable's failure to transcend his artistic origins.

Donald A. Ringe, in "The Moral World of Cable's 'Belle Demoiselles Plantation' " (*MissQ* 29:83–90), also reads this familiar fable as a less conventional work than it is usually considered: as an exemplification of "the ideal of Christian charity," in which the last representatives of a dying family "find in their human need a greater good than either of them had sought or imagined."

Especially in the light of Rubin's speculations, C. James Trotman's "George W. Cable and Tradition" (*TQ* 19,iii:51–58) is superficial and out of date. Trotman maintains that the "uniqueness" of Cable's fiction, which is its social consciousness, "disappeared when he became famous"—an explanation that fails to take into account Rubin's revelation of the problems that Cable had with genteel eastern editors in his later years. New light on the developments that led to these relations with the eastern establishment is found in Richard Crowder's "A Note on George Washington Cable" (*AN&Q* 14:103), which prints a message from Edward King, a free-lance writer visiting the South, that led to the friendship that opened for Cable the pages of the nationally popular *Scribner's Magazine*. William Evans explores one effort to find Cable a wider audience in "Cable, Poquelin, and Miss Burt: The Difficulties of a Dialect Writer" (*LaS* 15:45–60). Evans shows how at a schoolteacher's suggestion, Cable revised his story "Jean-ah Poquelin" (1875) in 1898 in order to make the dialect passages more comprehensible to junior high school readers.

Catherine Sherwood Bonner McDowell, who wrote under the name of Sherwood Bonner, is often recalled only as Longfellow's amanuensis (*ALS 1975*, p. 245), but William L. Frank's *Sherwood Bonner* (TUSAS 269), the first book-length study of her life and works, makes a case for her importance as the first contributor of Negro dialect stories to a northern journal in 1876, three years before Joel Chandler Harris began to publish his Uncle Remus tales. Had she lived more than 34 years, Frank speculates that she might have made a contribution to the movement from Romantic local color toward Naturalism. More than half the book is devoted to Frank's arresting presentation of the struggle of an ambitious and talented young southern woman growing up in ravaged post-Civil War Mississippi and breaking through traditional barriers to support herself by writing; but the following critical chapters are tedious and inconclusive, mostly plot summaries of obscure stories in random order.

Consistently better handled is Beverly R. David's "Visions of the South: Joel Chandler Harris and His Illustrators" (*ALR* 9:189–206), which discusses Harris's great pleasure at finding at last in Arthur B. Frost an illustrator whose work helped make Harris's tales his own and who impressed upon many readers' minds a lasting "vision of the South." David prefaces the account of this rewarding collaboration with a history of Harris's earlier frustrating relationships with an artist who "never could penetrate the world of Uncle Remus and his friends." Michael Flusche's "Underlying Despair in the Fiction of Joel Chandler Harris" (*MissQ* 29:91–103) presents an uncustomarily dark view of this world. Flusche maintains that while Harris's overt message is cheerful, "just beneath the surface lies a world in which every man is an island with few bonds to other members of society." Harris had, Flusche believes, "no conception of an organic society that could provide a genuine bond between people."

Louis A. Rubin, Jr., includes also in *William Elliott* a respectful study of another often misunderstood Georgia artist. Surveying, in "The Passion of Sidney Lanier" (pp. 107–44), the whole of the poet's unfulfilled career, Rubin argues that Lanier's views really agreed with those of the later southern Agrarians, but that the 20th-century regionalists were offended by "the superficial, emotional form" in which Lanier advanced these ideas. While Lanier wrote little important poetry, Rubin thinks that he traveled away from the southern community and directly identified his situation with nature in the manner of the Transcendentalists, so that his achievement was that "even while paying his respects to the outward forms of poetry of the dominant genteel tradition, he stretched them to new limits and actually managed to force new vigor and life into them."

The West is represented among local color studies this year by David B. Kesterson's *Bill Nye: The Western Writings* (WWS 22), a disappointing account that offers many examples of Nye's dated wit and little critical analysis of it. Kesterson praises Nye for "bold, honest examinations of life," manifested in a respect for the "genuine fibre and simplicity" of Western life that he defends satirically against the joyless East; but he fails to consider the extent to which Nye's one-liners may merely have exploited comic conventions of his period to draw transient laughter from a mindless audience. We need studies that probe beneath the surface appeals of humorists to learn if there are any consistent social or political positions that may have influenced their choice of targets.

The pious tracts of Victorian America are, of course, not necessarily local color writings (though some like E. P. Roe's *Barriers Burned Away* are), but their facile optimism matches that quality in much local color writing so that this is the appropriate place to call attention to Elmer F. Sudermann's "Religion in the Popular American Novel: 1870–1900" (*JPC* 9:1003–9), a wittier piece than one might expect on the subject. The main conclusions that Sudermann draws from the 150 specimens he dissects are the not surprising ones that "the urge to improve society is based on a sentimental view of man" and that the novels "are dull because the authors do not show any great interest in the craft of the novelist."

vi. William Dean Howells and Genteel Realism

Much of *ALR* in 1976 is devoted to biographical and bibliographical notes about Howells and Hamlin Garland that supplement standard reference works. Also if there are those who wish to appear well-informed about Howells without bothering to read his works, there is now George C. Carrington, Jr., and Ildikó de Papp Carrington's *Plots and Characters in the Fiction of William Dean Howells* (Hamden, Conn.: Archon), part of a series of books that summarize the stories of various authors and provide a finding list to the actors in them. Meanwhile people do keep reading Howells himself; it requires more than 300 pages for Clayton L. Eichelberger to chronicle *Published Comment on William Dean Howells Through 1920: A Research Bibliography* (Boston: G. K. Hall).

The studies are still coming, too, with an unusual number appearing in *AL* during the bicentennial year. Robert Emmet Long argues in *Transformations: "The Blithedale Romance* to Howells and James" (*AL* 47:552–71) that Howells's *The Undiscovered Country* and Henry James's *The Bostonians* "occur in something like a direct line of descent" from Hawthorne's romance, but Long makes a significant distinction: while James's novel is "an anti-democratic satire of manners" that "illuminates the fallacies behind the 'truths' which a particular culture regards as absolute," he finds that Howells's novel "works towards a reconciliation to community and finds sanity and health in normality and the democratic average."

Other critics, however, show Howells moving later towards James's position. Sidney H. Bremer's "Invalids and Actresses: Howells's Duplex Imagery for American Women" (*AL* 47:599–614) suggests that, especially in *April Hopes* and the long obscure *Mrs. Farrell*, "Howells's imagery of invalids and actresses . . . represents a significant break from the established literary convention of associating women with transcendent angels, sprites, devils, and goddesses." Uniquely important to an understanding of the evolution of the Howells woman are Paul John Eakins's observations in *The New England Girl*. Too complex to summarize here but essential reading for anyone interested in American culture, they trace Howells's gradual shattering of the angelic image that he had himself fostered.

Isolating a much less frequently explored aspect of Howells's work, Thomas Cooley provides evidence in "The Wilderness Within: Howells's *A Boy's Town*" (*AL* 47:583–98) to support the speculation that "Howells's preference for the common daylight of realism over the moonlight of romance owed a great deal to his early knowledge of the havoc that moon-bathed fantasies can produce in some hypersensitive minds" and his consequent fear of questioning too closely the subconscious mind from which dreams arose. (A fuller version of this essay appears in *Educated Lives*, pp. 73–99.) One of Howells's hesitations about confronting what Cooley calls "the painful social and sexual realities informing the realism of Crane, Norris, and Dreiser" is explored in William L. Andrews's "William Dean Howells and Charles W. Chesnutt: Criticism and Race Fiction in the Age of Booker T. Washington" (*AL* 48:327–39). Andrews documents the way in which Howells moved from "a thorough and responsive evaluation of Chesnutt's literary art in his first book of short stories" to a review of *The Marrow of Tradition*, which is "illustrative of a larger problem which faced the Afro-American writer as he came into his maturity"—viz, the critic's tendency to ignore the novel "as literature in order to respond to the psychological and social implications of the novelist's temperament and perspective," which Howells found to be justified in Chesnutt's case, but too "bitter."

Other signs appear of a shift in critical winds that reassigns Howells—who has generally been receiving sympathetic treatment recently—his old role of whipping boy for the anti-Victorians.

Robert Gillespie's "The Fictions of Basil March" (*CLQ* 12:14–28), striking a new note in a hitherto usually genial journal, reviews the novels and short stories in which Howells's most persisting spokesman appears and judges March "not satisfying as a narrator or a character." Describing March as "a mild voyeur stuck with a sexually unresponsive wife and a dull life," Gillespie goes on to say that what's wrong with the character may also explain "what's wrong with much of Howells's fiction"—both author and character "equate the marriage state and the cultured aristocracy with abstract virtue and literary realism with caring about people." In a more rambling attack, "Nineteenth-Century American Humor: Easygoing Males, Anxious Ladies, and Penelope Lapham" (*PMLA* 91:884–99), Alfred Habegger, before turning to Howells, explores the long-standing American tradition "that women have, or ought to have, a basic incapacity for humor or wit," along with some exceptions to it like

Marietta Holley's once-popular Samantha Allen. Although Habegger maintains that Howells generally operated in the tradition that American humor was masculine, the critic insists that the novelist should be granted credit for creating in daughter Penelope, in *The Rise of Silas Lapham*, "the first humorous heroine of an American novel." Proper Bostonian society, however, Habegger argues, could not long accommodate Penelope and Howells "could not bring himself to blame society for exiling the democratic colloquial humorist." Penelope represented "a way of seeing, thinking, and talking that the enormously successful author had stifled in himself."

Habegger treats a similar problem in "W. D. Howells and the 'American Girl'" (*TQ* 19,iv:149–56), describing "the secret of Howells's ladies" to be "strict, irrational, life-denying discipline," while his "manly men" are "casual, easygoing, and hard working." Habegger's main point, however, is that in novel after novel, Howells was concerned with unaggressive men and women struggling to be independent but doomed to wander about aimlessly "in the no person's land between the masculine and feminine domains." Still further charges of complacency are launched against the younger Howells in Rita K. Gollin's "The Place of Walden in *The Undiscovered Country*" (*TSB* 137:7–8), which points out that the visit of the novel's hero to Walden Pond (after the Civil War a resort for summer pleasure-seekers) establishes the goal that he and the heroine will share of seeking "fulfillment within the bounds of married love in a Boston suburb."

A hopeful corrective to this growing tendency to consign Howells once again too exclusively to the ranks of the fuddy-duddies is the first edition in many years of the shockingly neglected *The Leatherwood God*, ed. David J. Nordloh (A Selected Edition of W. D. Howells, [Bloomington: Ind. Univ. Press]). Eugene Pattison's introduction stresses the historical background of this extraordinary tale, published in 1916 when Howells was nearly 80, of a self-proclaimed Messiah on a violent frontier. Perhaps this welcome resurrection will help the novel achieve the classic stature it deserves as the archetypal fable of midwestern naivete and irrationality—the surrender to demons in a land without dreams.

A welcome complement to this new edition, timed exactly right, is William Baker's "The Little Miami River Heritage of William Dean Howells" (*AR* 34:405–16), which recalls Howells's only other novel about the Ohio of his boyhood, *New Leaf Mills* (1913) and describes its inspiration in the year that Howells as a boy of 14 spent during 1850–51 in a log cabin. That Howells, for all his Boston refinement, remained a tough businessman is suspensefully illustrated by William J. Scheick's "William Dean Howells to Bret Harte: A Missing Letter" (*ALR* 9:276–79), which shows Howells's mastery in calling the arrogant Harte's hand in his negotiations with the *Atlantic Monthly*. Howells is also credited with a subtlety not always recognized in his work in W. R. MacNaughton's "The 'Englishmen' in *The Rise of Silas Lapham*" (*MTJ* 18,ii:11–12). Through recording a slip of the tongue, MacNaughton suggests, Howells implies to careful readers that the supposed Englishmen involved in a questionable deal are actually "blatantly dishonest conspirators in a peculiarly American type of evil."

Two writers for *SAF* also find in even some of Howells's early works darker shadows than many recent readers have seen. Kenneth Seib contemplates Basil March and Howells's first novel in "Uneasiness at Niagara: Howells' *Their Wedding Journey*" (4:15–25) and argues that the seeds of the novelist's later despair "were there from the very beginning of his literary career." "At Niagara, America's premier symbol of marital and national harmony," Seib maintains, "Basil and Isabel March, and, one suspects, Howells himself, found not harmony but a profound disunity, not national identity but irreconcilable diversity, not a smiling satisfaction but a terrifying uneasiness." Similarly Rosalie Murphy and Seymour Gross, in "Commonplace Reality and the Romantic Phantoms: Howells' *A Modern Instance* and *The Rise of Silas Lapham*" (4:1–14), review two of the author's best known works and find that "his 'true to life' characters, for all their American innocence, often lead lives of quiet desperation; novels which should unfold the glorious possibilities of American life are strangely melancholy and ambiguous."

Howells also figures largely in Kenneth M. Roemer's *The Obsolete Necessity: America in Utopian Writings, 1888–1900* (Kent, Ohio: Kent State Univ. Press), in which the author provides the larger context for his recent accounts of various Utopian schemes put forward at the end of the 19th century. (The tendency to create Utopias flourished especially during these years because of the desperate efforts to exorcise the demons that still beset our culture and to find some way of embodying the religious sublime.) Roemer makes extensive comparisons between the solutions advanced in these proposals and winds up with a fascinating reconstruction of "The Simplicity and Unity of a Day in Utopia." Pointing out, however, that "the overt celebration of infinite progress and the not-so-covert longing for a static state is the most glaring contradiction in the utopian concept of history" (p. 28), he describes much of his book as a critique of the frightening limitations of Utopian thought "that survive still and influence American beliefs and behavior" (p. xiv).

As the renewed condescension towards Howells indicates, attention generally is shifting from the genteel realists to the decadent Naturalists, although Sybil Weir bucks the tide in "*The Morgesons*: A Neglected Feminist *Bildungsroman*" (*NEQ* 49:427–39) by making a plea for closer attention to one neglected work. She describes Elizabeth Drew Stoddard's 1862 novel as a unique 19th-century work in which *a woman* "undertakes the voyage of self-discovery and firmly rejects the established social institutions." Weir is less well disposed toward a better-known woman novelist. In "Southern Womanhood in the Novels of Constance Fenimore Woolson" (*MissQ* 29:559–68), she maintains that "Woolson's ambivalence about the South emerges in her portrayal of Southern women," since, with rare exceptions, mature women in her novel are northern, while "the self-indulgent, irresponsible women" are southern.

While on the subject of women authors, I should note that the greatest surprise in Dee Garrison's "Immoral Fiction in the Late Victorian Library" (*AQ* 28:71–89) is the revelation that when "public librarians made a bold attempt in 1881 to define the best-selling fiction that offended genteel sensibilities," 10 of the 16 offenders proved to be sentimental domestic writers, "writing chiefly for women and about feminine experience," and including such great favorites as Mrs. E. D. E. N. Southworth and Augusta Jane Evans Wilson. More surprises await in another article that no one concerned about American popular culture should miss, Thomas H. Pauly's "In Search of 'The Spirit of '76'" (*AQ* 28:444–64), the unlikely history of the multiple "originals" of Archibald Willard's celebrated patriotic work.

Two studies examine aspects of Hamlin Garland's career. Robert Bray argues in "Hamlin Garland's *Rose of Dutcher's Coolly*" (*GrLR* 3,i:1–14) that in this novel the author "gave the Midwestern woman in fiction a new psychological reality, a new sense of intellectual and creative integrity and a different sensibility," so that it still stands "virtually alone in its hopeful attitude toward human growth among the women and men of the Midwest." During the following decade, Bray believes that Garland relied strongly "on the developing conventions of the western to avoid treating the substantial aspects of his subjects." Robert Gish examines the works in question in *Hamlin Garland: The Far West* (WWS 24) and finds that "the message at work to one degree or another" in them is that "character is a reflex to environment" (p. 27). Although, as Gish observes, "Garland was generally credited with an innovative, first-hand, compassionate treatment of the Indians," his problem remained "how to allow the Indian his dignity and heritage and still assume the necessity that he must follow the white man's trail" (pp. 38–39). Although Gish calls Garland's attitudes "ambivalent," one leaves his useful guide with the feeling that Garland's fiction was confused—as Habegger finds Howells's was—by an inability to reconcile a compassionate nature with a yen for respectability in conventional Boston.

Eberhard Alsen identifies thinking of a much less popular kind in one of the earliest post-Civil War realistic novels in "Marx and De-Forest: The Idea of Class Struggle in *Miss Ravenel's Conversion*" (*AL* 48:223–28). Although Alsen doubts that DeForest even knew who Karl Marx was, he cites parallels to urge strongly that DeForest was influenced in shaping his concept of the Civil War as "a class struggle between Southern aristocrats and Northern working men" by Marx's theories as transmitted through editorial writings in the *New York Daily Tribune*.

vii. The Ironic Vision of Stephen Crane

After the remarkable stride forward last year in Crane criticism by Frank Bergon's *Stephen Crane's Artistry*, this year's scattering of speculations and complaints is generally thin and retrogressive; but it takes a while for a new approach to sink in.

Most regrettable is the space wasted on Paul Breslin's "Courage and Convention: *The Red Badge of Courage*" (*YR* 66:209–22), which again inadequately reads the novel as an "initiation story," even though Breslin puzzles about its being "unique" in "the absence of any social context" (surely a clue in itself that this is *not* an initiation story). Such labeling helps Breslin, however, reach the dubious conclusion that the novel is a "subversive" work that tells us that "courage can exist without a great soul" and that "brave men often cannot afford great souls," though he feels that Crane was only half-conscious of the implications of his treatment.

A good antidote to Breslin's condescension is James Nagel's "Stephen Crane's Stories of War: A Study of Art and Theme" (*NDQ* 45 [1975]:5–19), a somewhat disjointed overview arguing that the shorter war pieces contain "subtle innovations" that refute Thomas Gullason's generalization of them as "essentially miniatures of *The Red Badge*." The best of them, Nagel feels, "surpass even *The Red Badge* in artistic control and thematic richness," since "the mode of Crane's best work" is "the recurrence of small and initially unimportant details in circumstances which make them of vital importance to the thematic developments of the story."

Other tributes to Crane's quite conscious control of his narrative effects are Thomas Bonner, Jr.'s "Crane's 'An Experiment in Misery' " (*Expl* 34:item 56) and Herb Stappenbeck's "Crane's 'The Open Boat' " (*Expl* 34:item 41). Bonner points out that Crane underscores the animalistic quality of Bowery life in his sketch by giving a beggar the characteristics of the blood-sucking assassin bug, and Stappenbeck looks once more at the correspondent's relationship to the poem he recalls from childhood and argues that it carries him "beyond brotherly feelings for the three men who may save his life," through self-pity, to "a profound and perfectly impersonal comprehension of his obligation to suffer with his fellow man." Even more ingenious, yet quite credible is Margaret P. Anderson's suggestion in "A Note on 'John Twelve' in Stephen Crane's 'The Monster' " (*AN&Q* 15:23–24) that Crane uses this unusual name for one of the respectable gentry who visit Dr. Trescott in order to relate the behavior of the group to that of the Pharisees whose hypocritical behavior after the raising of Lazarus is unmasked by Jesus in the Biblical book of St. John, chapter 12.

Bryant Mangum and Ryoichi Okada, however, press doubtful cases too far in other ingenious speculations about possible sources for Crane's "red badge." Mangum's "Crane's Red Badge and Zola's" (*ALR* 9:279–80) suggests that Crane may indeed have read Zola's *The Downfall* before writing his novel, since it contains the phrase "red badge," while Okada suggests "Another Source of Crane's Metaphor, 'The Red Badge of Courage' " (*AN&Q* 14:73–74) in a reference to scalping in *The Last of the Mohicans*. Somewhat problemat-

ical also is Frank Sadler's "Crane's 'Fleming': Appellation for Coward
or Hero?" (*AL* 48:372–76), which analyzes the eight references to
Henry's surname to argue that Crane delayed its appearance in the
novel "to heighten the reader's understanding of Henry's self-deception and eventual moral triumph."

The most considerable essay about Crane to come along since
Bergon's book is Thomas A. Gullason's "Stephen Crane: In Nature's
Bosom" (*American Literary Naturalism*, pp. 37–56), a competent,
but unsurprising survey of Crane's whole life and works, apparently
intended as an introduction for new readers. Similarly sound but
limited is Malcom Foster's "The Black Crepe Veil: The Significance
of Stephen Crane's 'The Monster'" (*IFR* 3:87–91), which reads the
story as a metaphorical protest of "the general dehumanization of
black people in the United States after the Compromise of 1876."

Gullason's position is supported by Charles W. Mayer's "Two
Kids in the House of Chance: Crane's 'The Five White Mice'" (*RS*
44:52–57), a complex argument that while in Crane's early work contradictions may result from an uncertain emphasis on both self-
reliance and "the moving ox" of necessity, later works give "full
credence to the possibility of significant human actions" and associate
Crane with not just Naturalism, but with Howells and Henry James.

Another effort to lift a limiting label from Crane is Bert Bender's
"Hanging Stephen Crane in the Impressionist Museum" (*JAAC* 35:
47–55), which points out the great differences between Crane's work
and that of the French impressionist painters with whom he has often
been associated. It concludes that far from "recreating impulses of
the realist-impressionist movement," Crane "anticipated the new art
of the twentieth century."

Two pieces explain the support that Crane received from prophets
of this new art. G. Thomas Tanselle's "Addenda to Stallman's *Crane*:
Thomas Wood Stevens" (*PBSA* 70:416–19) identifies favorable references to Crane's distinctive poetry and imitations of it in Stevens's
avant-garde literary magazine, *The Blue Sky*. Joseph J. Kwiat's "Stephen Crane and Frank Norris in the Magazine and the 'Revolt' in
American Literature in the 1890s" (*WHR* 30:309–21) provides for
general audiences an account of the familiar ways in which both popular and experimental magazines provided the young writers with
outlets.

Finally, two contributions to *SAF* provide new materials that will merit consideration in future studies of Crane. Lillian B. Gilkes's "The London Newsletters of Stephen and Cora Crane: A Collaboration" (4:174–201) straightens out the problems of who contributed what to these reports that the Cranes attempted to sell American newspapers in an effort to raise funds, while Stanley Wertheim's "Stephen Crane Remembered (4:45–79) reprints hitherto overlooked memoirs that provide "significant new information about an important phase in Crane's life" by Nelson Greene, Walter Parker, Mark Barr, and Cora Crane.

viii. Frank Norris and the 1890s: Naturalism and Decadence

The necessary summing-up period appears to have arrived in Kate Chopin studies with a great deal of background material and a number of the many recent essays about *The Awakening* collected in a new edition of the novel edited by Margaret Culley (New York: Norton) that has appeared along with *Edith Wharton and Kate Chopin* (Boston: G. K. Hall), a reference guide edited by Marlene Springer.

Fresh criticism has been limited largely to short pieces in the *Kate Chopin Newsletter*, although one interesting new approach is Elaine Jasenas' "The French Influence in Kate Chopin's *The Awakening*," (*NCFS* 4:312–22), which identifies Baudelaire's influence as profound, yet not essentially different from Maupassant and Flaubert's, since "all three represent not a tradition, but forms of estrangement."

Meanwhile interest rises once again in one of the earliest and bitterest voices of American decadence. Sidney J. Krause properly leads off *American Literary Naturalism* with "Edgar Watson Howe: Our First Naturalist" (pp. 11–36), which reads *The Story of a Country Town* (1884) as presaging the fictional demolition of genteel pretensions during the next decade. "The key to Howe's Naturalism," Krause finds, "lies in the very substance of the unnaturalness which we see in Jo Erring's progressive annihilation of his well-being, his marriage, his wife and himself." The analysis leads to the unsettling question, "What happens if we . . . *accept* the Freudian implication that ultimately all of life is sick; or . . . the implication, which Howe would like us to entertain—that perhaps Jo Erring is not really all that mad?" (pp. 32–33).

Charles W. Mayer's "Realizing 'A Whole Order of Things': E. W. Howe's *The Story of a Country Town*" (*WAL* 11:23–31) usefully supplements Krause's speculations by suggesting that the novel, despite criticism to the contrary, possesses an "extraordinary unity of effect" through the use of two major plots "modulated to reinforce the significance of one another," internal commentators who provide "integrating power," and "a carefully developed 'devil' motif that externalizes an inner psychological condition, becoming an effective correlative for intense jealousy, hate, and neurotic frustration."

Samuel Coale's "Frederic and Hawthorne: The Romantic Roots of Naturalism" (*AL* 48:29–45) impressively identifies the major problem of another "Naturalistic" classic, *The Damnation of Theron Ware*, as the *disunity* of its point of view. Coale traces the powerful effects of Hawthorne upon the conception of the novel and argues that "Frederic was trying to forge a new 'romanticism,'" but failed because "the elements of Hawthorne . . . just do not fuse with the historic realism of the novel." Nonetheless he thinks that *The Damnation* is most adequately viewed "not as an example of literary naturalism but as the midpoint between Hawthorne's allegories and Faulkner's myths," which "accomplish finally the convergence of social and mythic patterns in the American psyche." In the light of Coale's theory that Frederic sensed this convergence but could not articulate it, one can understand the puzzlement of one of the most judicious reviews of the novel at the time that it appeared, rediscovered by Don Graham in the San Francisco *Wave* and reprinted in "'A Degenerate Methodist': A New Review of *The Damnation of Theron Ware*" (*ALR* 9:280–84). The anonymous reviewer concludes a detailed, but bewildered review with the observation that Frederic "has left too many riddles."

Other essays investigate influences of Frederic's native New York state on his work. John Rees's "'Dead Men's Bones, Dead Men's Beliefs': Ideas of Antiquity in Upstate New York and *Theron Ware*" (*AmerS* 16,ii[1975]:77–87) points out that in the novel Frederic "makes his upstate setting reflect what his birthplace region . . . conveyed in reality to those that lived there—a sense that their young towns and farms had been built, as in the Old World, 'on the ruins of something else,'" here the burial sites of the vanished Indian mound-builders. T. F. O'Donnell's "Oriskany, 1877: The Centennial and the Birth of Frederic's *In the Valley*" (*NYH* 57:139–64) traces the origins of another novel to the impressive celebration of the centenary of the Battle of Oriskany that Frederic witnessed.

A disputed point is apparently set to rest in Matthew C. O'Brien's "Ambrose Bierce and the Civil War" (*AL* 48:377–81), which affirms that extant documentary material refutes the contention of Bierce's biographers that he served in the Carolina campaign under General Sherman. The biographers mistakenly assumed that the later diary of another man in a notebook that had originally belonged to Bierce was also his.

But another literary legend remains under investigation. W. T. Lhamon, Jr., asks in "Horatio Alger and American Modernism: The One-Dimensional Social Formula" (*AmerS* 17,ii:11–27) why so many of our best novelists from James and Faulkner to Ellison and Baraka have been influenced to write in Alger's vein? He suggests that a partial explanation is the dream of an open society that Alger fostered was for his predominantly middle-class readers, "a necessary logomachy—prompted by their position, their guilt, and their competition with a vital working-class subculture." Gary F. Schornhorst in "The Boudoir Tales of Horatio Alger, Jr." (*JPC* 10:215–24) goes beyond the hundred-odd tales for boys that Alger wrote and provides one of the rare glimpses into the eleven novels he wrote for adults between 1857 and 1869. A reading of these, Schornhorst maintains, shows that "Alger wrote essentially American morality fables, not business tracts . . . The hero earns success and happiness by his virtue, especially by his charity, never by business acumen," clearly an assuagement of bourgeois guilt.

Consideration of middle-class values also dominates William B. Stone's long-winded "Idiolect and Ideology: Some Stylistic Aspects of Norris, James, and DuBois" (*Style* 10:405–25), which is built on the theory that a writer's ideology conditions his style. The main point about Norris seems to be that his "stylistically manifested emphasis upon environment" could mistakenly be "taken as both inherent to Naturalism and subject to the approbation of a Marxist critic." Not so, however, for Stone finds it rather a form of escapism —"through a relative deemphasis of the social, or class forces, as opposed to the physical environment, involved in the struggles the novels portray."

Glen A. Love also thinks that we may generally have mistaken the relationship between characters and settings in Norris's novels;

but his point in "Frank Norris's Western Metropolitans" (*WAL* 11: 3–22) is that California's Pacific slope has been from the beginning primarily an urban rather than a rural region, and that, whereas our study of western literature "has found its primary archetype in the solitary individual set against a wilderness landscape," "Norris's novels reveal an attempt to combine the primitivistic and sensate qualities of western life with a complex urban society which he saw as the product of an inescapable evolutionary advance."

Joseph R. McElrath, Jr., believes we have also been misreading one of Norris's most controversial works. In "Frank Norris's *Vandover and the Brute*: Narrative Techniques and the Socio-Critical Viewpoint (*SAF* 4:27–43), he reads the novel "not as a moralistic tale," but as "a Naturalistic tale of degeneration in which Norris uses the basic degeneration-tale structure to psychologically explore the root causes of Van's self-destructive life vision." McElrath sees the novel not as an attack on Vandover, but rather an attack on "nineteenth-century morality and the archaic life-vision of a world of fixed certainties which informed it."

The most important new speculations about Norris and the relationship of his landscapes to Naturalism are found in James K. Folsom's "The Wheat and the Locomotive: Norris and Naturalistic Esthetics" (*American Literary Naturalism*, pp. 57–74), which argues that the success of Norris's best work is linked to his "ability to transcend the sterile symbolic moral polarities of 'good and evil' and 'right and wrong' and the system of philosophical hierarchies which such polarities imply," because "the unconscious does not think in moral terms but in symbolic ones." "The landscape of the naturalistic novel," Folsom perceives, "at its best bears a remarkable similarity to the landscape of a dream," a backdrop "more true to the interior reality of the dreamer's psyche than to the exterior reality of day to day life."

A similar point is made about the long neglected poetry of Frederic Goddard Tuckerman. His singularity as a precursor of the decadents is evident from Eugene England's "Tuckerman's Sonnet 1:10: The First Post-Symbolist Poem" (*SoR* 12:323–47), which maintains that the poet "challenged the nineteenth century with high modernistic metaphors, diction, and use of partial rhyming." England provides a more detailed reading than that recently granted many 19th-century poems (except Whitman's and Dickinson's) in order to show that this work is "not simply a meditation on death," or a reverie—"It is not thinking *about* something but *rethinking* it by way of selected and empowered verbal imagery."

A. H. Rosenus's "Joaquin Miller and His 'Shadow'" (*WAL* 11: 51–59) also suggests that, in view of the growing interest in the decadent literature of the 1890s, closer attention to another midcentury precursor of this sensibility might be rewarding. Rosenus describes *Unwritten History: Life Among the Modocs* as Miller's "finest prose work," which succeeds in expressing his "ambivalent feelings (and remorse) about his relations with the Indians." Rosenus doubts, however, that Miller's *persona* really undergoes any moral regeneration because "there is no point at which the mutually destructive sides of his nature acknowledge each other and work upon each other to effect a change of attitude or 'recognition.'"

Finally, a poet who, in contrast to Tuckerman, was popular in his own time and is nearly forgotten today is the subject of the most entertaining piece of literary criticism to come along in some time, William R. Linneman's *Richard Hovey* (TUSAS 263). Actually "criticism" is a misnomer; the most engrossing part of the book is the long, biographical opening chapter about the short and unlikely life of this descendant of New England's founding Puritan fathers as proto-hippie. Linneman is wise enough to keep subsequent comment to a minimum and let Hovey speak for himself through his rousing, but superficial vagabond lyrics about "outlaws and rebels," the sort of people not usually invited into genteel homes.

No demons beset Hovey's lyric world, but he seeks to create no Utopia either; the force that conquered a continent has transformed itself after the closing of the frontier into vagabondage. Yet it is pleasant to read about an idle dreamer at a time when the best criticism of the literature of our 19th-century concentrates upon the demon-beset figures of James Fenimore Cooper and the fin-de-siècle decadents.

Indiana University–Purdue University at Indianapolis

13. Fiction: 1900 to the 1930s

David Stouck

A large number of the essays I read this year were written for the observance of an author's centenary. Sherwood Anderson, Ellen Glasgow, and Jack London were the subjects of centennial essays, some of which appeared in special numbers of journals and others in volumes of collected criticism. Going through these collections, I was struck by their similarity in format and by their limitations as scholarship. These articles, with but a few exceptions, did not present stimulating revaluations or suggest new approaches to the author's work. One problem is that veteran scholars are invited to make reassessments when their current interest is elsewhere. Another problem is that the editors, concerned to establish their author's continuing relevance, invite contributors to take up topics of current interest when these are not very relevant to the author. The result is a proliferation of essays that are redundant and of marginal value. With the possible exception of Jack London, these authors have not been served well by centennial studies. The irony here is that the editors invariably begin by lamenting their author's poor treatment by critics in the past, but take pride in the healthy state of scholarship at present. This seems to be the old confusion of quantity with quality.

i. Sherwood Anderson

Anderson's centenary in 1976 saw the publication of two volumes of essays. *Sherwood Anderson: Dimensions of His Literary Art*, ed. with an intro. by David D. Anderson (East Lansing: Mich. State Univ. Press), is a collection of essays by veteran Anderson scholars. Several of the papers are of limited value or interest. William V. Miller's "Portraits of the Artist: Anderson's Fictional Storytellers" (pp. 1–23) is misleadingly titled since only the final pages focus on the artist. There Miller lists and doggedly illustrates obvious character-

istics of the artist such as "capacity for growth, talent with and respect for language, involvement yet detachment, an especially active
imagination," etc. The bulk of the essay is an encyclopaedic account
of the character types in Anderson's fiction. In "The Warmth of Desire: Sex in Anderson's Novels" (pp. 24–40) Ray Lewis White tries to
account for his embarrassment when reading Anderson's novels by
examining the author's treatment of sex. He concludes that where
Anderson could brilliantly capture the effects of sexual adventure
and frustration in his short stories, he moralized and sentimentalized
sexuality in his novels until the matter was didactic and overblown.
Welford Dunaway Taylor takes up the question of reputation in "Anderson and the Problem of Belonging" (pp. 61–74); he points out
that critically Anderson has never fared well with the "New York
Intellectuals," but has found support in the broader-based humanists who bring a spirit of detachment and "a minimum of ideological
predilection" to their criticism. Two essays approach matters of form.
Linda W. Wagner's "Sherwood, Stein, the Sentence, and Grape Sugar
and Oranges" (pp. 75–89) discusses Stein's influence on Anderson.
Wagner rightly dismisses *Tender Buttons* as an influence (Anderson
never experimented with the purely formal dimensions of prose) and
focuses attention on *Three Lives*, looking for its resonance in Anderson's writing. Wagner lists her findings under the headings of
mood, incremental adjectives, figurative language and refrain, and
yet on close scrutiny these amount to little more than the familiar
point about repetition. In "Anderson's Theories on Writing Fiction"
(pp. 90–109) Martha Mulroy Curry sorts through Anderson's many
contradictory statements about form and concludes that moments
of "inspiration" come as close as anything he said to accounting for
the formal success of his short fiction. William A. Sutton, in "Anderson's Letters to Marietta D. Finley Hahn: A Literary Chronicle" (pp.
110–117), gives a bibliographical account of his personal acquaintance with Anderson's friend and of his preparing to publish Anderson's letters to Mrs. Hahn.

Only two of the essays represent fresh and vigorous scholarship.
In "Talbot Whittingham and Anderson: A Passage to *Winesburg,
Ohio*" (pp. 41–60), Walter B. Rideout examines carefully the fragmentary "Talbot Whittingham," a story about a boy from an Ohio
town who becomes an artist, and shows how this unpublished novel
anticipates at many points scenes and characters in *Winesburg, Ohio*.

He points out that while the manuscript was not publishable it contained many things, including a vision of the grotesque, which had persistent psychic value for Anderson and that it stands midway between the promise of the first two published novels and the artistry of *Winesburg, Ohio.* In "Anderson and Myth" (pp. 118–141) David D. Anderson sees Anderson's life as one with the destiny of America and locates three significant myths in his writing. In the early works he finds the myth of escape and the quest for fulfillment. This escape, he says, which at its heart is a rejection of materialism, is subtly repudiated in Anderson's middle works where he celebrates the artist as craftsman and attempts to recapture childhood in both its innocent and brutal aspects. He sees in the late works a final mythical figure emerging, a worker who has the strength to fuse the values of the past with the industrial-material complex of the future.

Sherwood Anderson: Centennial Studies, ed. Hilbert H. Campbell and Charles E. Modlin (Troy, N.Y.: Whitson Pub. Co.) is another commemorative volume with limited rewards. The book is divided into two parts. The first, titled "source materials," contains some previously unpublished Anderson letters, an interview with Eleanor Anderson, and some notes on the Anderson collection at the Newberry Library, including a catalog of Anderson's library at Ripshin. The second part consists of critical essays. Six of the essays explore Anderson's relationship with other artists including George Borrow, Edgar Lee Masters, Henry Adams, Alfred Stieglitz, Louis Bromfield, and J. J. Lankes. The substance of two of these essays appears in print elsewhere: David D. Anderson's "The Search for a Living Past" (pp. 212–23) is an extension of "Anderson and Myth" (cited above) drawing an analogy with Louis Bromfield's career, while Robert E. Ned Haines's "Anderson and Stieglitz: A Fellowship of Sayer and Seer" (pp. 202–211) makes the same suggestion as his article, "Turning Point: Sherwood Anderson Encounters Alfred Stieglitz" (*MarkhamR* 6:16–20), namely that Stieglitz's affirmation of human innocence may have had an influence on Anderson in the years 1923–24 and on the writing of *A Story Teller's Story*. Probably the most interesting essay which relates Anderson to another artist is John W. Crowley's "The Education of Sherwood Anderson" (pp. 185–201) in which Crowley compares *A Story Teller's Story* with *The Education of Henry Adams.* He finds that where Adams uses his life to exemplify failure, "Anderson offers his life as a model of a successful education, leading not to despair but hope." What saves Anderson according to Crowley is his view of art as an act of sympathy.

Only two other papers in the collection are worth noting here. In "The Ambiguous Endings of Sherwood Anderson's Novels" (pp. 249–63), Nancy L. Bunge notes that most of Anderson's novels conclude optimistically with the hero beginning a new relationship which he hopes will liberate him. These relationships, says Bunge, are by implication doomed, but she feels Anderson could not bring himself to cynicism and despair, even if it meant his novels were aesthetically weakened. Probably the best essay in the collection is Glen A. Love's "Horses or Men: Primitive and Pastoral Elements in Sherwood Anderson" (pp. 235–48). Love argues that Anderson is more accurately described as a pastoral writer than a primitivist because the characters in his fiction try to understand their dilemma rather than simply escape into the world of nature, childhood, and horses. Love's essay focuses on the race-track story "I Want to Know Why," where the boy narrator says at the outset that he wants "to think straight and be OK."

France and Sherwood Anderson: Paris Notebook, 1921, ed. Michael Fanning (Baton Rouge: La. State Univ. Press) makes available in print another of the fragmentary manuscripts from the Anderson collection at the Newberry Library. The editor has devised a book consisting of three chapters. The first chapter provides a historical context for the notebook, describing the events leading up to Anderson's trip to Paris in 1931 and some of the significant places and people he encountered there. Chapter 2 is the notebook itself which Fanning has transcribed without corrections in spelling, punctuation or grammar, thereby retaining the integrity of its workbook form. The notebook consists of random observations of Parisian life, reflections on aesthetics, and some impressionistic story outlines. The third chapter relates the notebook to some of Anderson's other writings and ideas, particularly to *A Story Teller's Story*. Fanning is concerned to formulate Anderson's ideas on art and ponders Anderson's attraction to Chartres Cathedral, Rembrandt, Saint-Chapelle, and the writing of Gertrude Stein. He stresses that Anderson's view of writing as a craft was reinforced by being in France and surrounded by so many objects of excellent craftsmanship; he also explores Anderson's concern with the indissoluble role of fancy and fact in writing. Fanning's discussion of the notebook text, however, is not comprehensive in any way; another editor might have discussed more fully the France-America contrast as an aspect of the American theme in Anderson's writings, or examined carefully the story outline of the servant girl which can be seen as an analogue, if not an early outline for, one of Anderson's finest stories, "Death in the Woods."

Douglas C. Rogers's *Sherwood Anderson: A Selective, Annotated Bibliography* (Metuchen, N.J.: Scarecrow Press) provides the Anderson student with an efficient and useful bibliographical guide to both primary and secondary Anderson works. Rogers has not designed the volume as a complete bibliography; he focuses on English and American editions and criticism, and refers students wishing information on translations and foreign criticism to the bibliographical work of Ray Lewis White. Perhaps the greatest value of this volume lies in the annotations to the entries of criticism. These comprehensive summaries will help students, scholars, and teachers to locate critical information and opinion quickly.

In a 16-page essay, *The Revision of "Seeds"* (Ball State Monograph, 25; Muncie, Ind.: Ball State Univ.), William A. Sutton examines three extant versions of the story, including a newly available manuscript, and concludes that Anderson was not the spontaneous writer he wishes us to believe. Joan Zlotnick's "Of Dubliners and Ohioans: A Comparative Study of Two Works" (*BSUF* 17,iv:33–36) is a superficial comparison of Joyce's and Anderson's stories. Finally, Anderson scholars will want to look at the September issue of *American Notes and Queries*, 15,i, a centenary number which contains several brief items, again by well-known Anderson critics.

ii. Jack London

Centenary essays on Jack London appeared in special numbers of *Modern Fiction Studies* and *Western American Literature*. These essays, along with shorter pieces in the *Jack London Newsletter*, proved on the whole to be more vital and interesting than those published on Anderson—perhaps because several of the London essays focus on specific works. *Martin Eden* received the most attention. Sam S. Baskett's "*Martin Eden*: Jack London's Poem of the Mind" (*MFS* 22:23–36) is a substantial study of the novel as London's portrait of the artist. Baskett argues that "in this novel London is primarily concerned with the quest of the writer to order experience." He believes that London was unsure of the outcome of such a quest and "consequently he gave several different portraits of the artist, rejecting each in turn." In a different vein George M. Spangler's "Divided Self and World in *Martin Eden*" (*JLN* 9:118–26) argues that the novel refutes Nietzsche because individualism is an abstract element of Martin's rhetoric, not an integral part of his being. Spangler illustrates in some detail the division within both Eden and the structure of the novel. In "The Transformation of Material in Mimetic Fiction" (*MFS* 22:9–22), Gordon Mills attempts to measure the success and failure London met in transforming autobiography into fiction when writing *Martin Eden*.

Following the Marxist literary approach of Robert Weimann, Nathaniel Teich in "Marxist Dialectics in Content, Form, Point of View: Structures in Jack London's *The Iron Heel*" (*MFS* 22:85–99) demonstrates how the dual narrative perspective in *The Iron Heel* functions in London's indictment of capitalism and how point of view is always an integral part of a novel's political content. In "*The Iron Heel* and *Looking Backward*: Two Paths to Utopia" (*ALR* 9: 307–14), Gorman Beauchamp points out that, while both London and Bellamy envision utopias dependent on the efficiency of machines, they disagree diametrically on the means by which utopia will be achieved. For Bellamy, writes Beauchamp, "socialism will establish itself by the sheer force of reason" whereas London foresees the necessity of a long and bloody struggle to achieve utopia. The socialist utopia of *The Iron Heel* is important to Carolyn Willson's " 'Rattling the Bones': Jack London, Socialist Evangelist" (*WAL* 11:135–48) which reviews London's active participation in socialism.

One of the best essays published on London during his centenary is Marie L. Ahearn's "*The People of the Abyss*: Jack London as New Journalist" (*MFS* 22:73–83). This fine study in literary genre shows how London's description of the poor in London, England, has the immediacy of the reporter but also the intensity of the novelist who uses devices like the coronation parade of Edward VII to expose the great gulf between rich and poor. Ahearn also suggests some of the models that might have served for *The People of the Abyss* and she points to books of "new journalism" such as Mailer's *The Armies of the Night* and Tom Wolfe's *The Pump House Gang* that have followed in this tradition. Considering the same book, Andrew Sinclair's

"A View of the Abyss" (*JLN* 9:86–95) gives a balanced account of the strengths and weaknesses in London's emotional portrayal of life in the East London slums.

The liveliest facet of London criticism turns currently on questions of sexual attitudes and the myth of the masculine hero. In "Androgyny in the Novels of Jack London" (*WAL* 11:121–33), Clarice Stasz examines London's fictional protagonists in terms of self-development and the thwarting system of sex roles. Stasz believes that London recognized how society represses the full development of personality through narrow definitions of masculine and feminine, but admits that he did not break with sexist values in his own life. Similarly, Robert Forrey in "Three Modes of Sexuality in London's *The Little Lady of the Big House*" (*L&P* 26:52–60) argues that the novel's strident heterosexuality is a false front, that Dick Forrest's strongest sexual feelings are for his friend Evan Graham and that his wife's affair with Evan is bisexual in nature. Dick Forrest is a highly successful rancher and Forrey suggests that the novel's real value is to "illustrate the tendency of sexually troubled or impotent men to rely on the power of technology and machines to prove their manhood." Charles N. Watson, Jr., in "Sexual Conflict in *The Sea-Wolf*: Further Notes on London's Reading of Kipling and Norris" (*WAL* 11:239–48), takes an approach similar to Forrey's and argues that Humphrey goes through a homosexual phase in his achievement of manhood. Watson also argues that the plot and characters of *The Sea-Wolf* might owe something to Kipling's *Captains Courageous* and Norris's *Moran of the Lady Letty*. Watson feels that Norris's novel with its bisexual heroine might have particularly influenced London since he has his hero attracted in turn to both a man and a woman.

London the man is carefully scrutinized in a series of articles. Earle Labor views the author in a positive light. In "From 'All Gold Canyon' to *The Acorn-Planter*: Jack London's Agrarian Vision" (*WAL* 11:83–101), Labor sees London as a Transcendentalist at heart whose agrarian novels are concerned with finding the right moral attitude to the land. Labor is concerned to erase the picture of London as a dissolute rancher and to show that London's agricultural dream was not an escapist pastoralism but a prophetic vision of technology's potential to convert the sword into the plowshare. In the very opposite vein Jon A. Yoder in "Jack London as Wolf Barleycorn" (*WAL* 11:103–19) contends that whether he committed suicide or not, London "had been destroying himself both physically and psychologically from the time he adopted an impossible concept of manly success." He points out that while alcohol boosted in London a strong sense of masculinity, it slowly destroyed him. And in a letter to the editor (*MFS* 22:595–99) Robert Forrey denounces the special London issue for continuing to foster the machismo myth. Earl Labor and his critics, writes Forrey, managed to exclude serious discussion of London's alcoholism, racism, homosexual and suicidal leanings. This, laments Forrey, is "to perpetuate the uncritical attitudes that have always stood in the way of an appreciation of London the artist." Labor's reply follows (*MFS* 22:599–602). Forrey must nonetheless have been sympathetic to Clarice Stasz's "The Social Construction of Biography: The Case of Jack London" (*MFS* 22:51–71), which compares the various biographies of London and shows how a sexist London mythology has evolved, one which presents London as the vigorous male who sought achievements but who was destroyed by women and lack of self-control. Stasz points out that the feminine side of London's nature and his radical politics have been persistently played down in favor of the more acceptable values of his masculinity and rugged individualism. Richard Etulain's "The Lives of Jack London" (*WAL* 11:149–64) is an objective and useful description of the London biographies which points out that a definitive biography of London is yet to be written.

Myth colors London's biography, and it is also fundamental to his fiction. In "Jack London's Wild Man: The Broken Myths of *Before Adam*" (*MFS* 22:37–49), Jon Pankake examines the mythic character of one of London's less frequently discussed works. Pankake believes that the novel's tripartite vision of human potential and man's struggle to achieve civilization gives the book a lasting dynamic, but he feels that ultimately the book fails because London does not show the necessity of man coming to terms with the beast or "wild man" in himself and his culture before he can realize his true humanity. The second chapter of James Glennon Cooper's thesis, "A Womb of Time: Archetypal Patterns in the Novels of Jack London," has been excerpted for *JLN* 9:16–28. In this article Cooper lists the characteristics of the hero as described by Joseph Campbell, Otto Rank, and Lord Raglan, and shows how the elements of the hero tale appear in virtually every London story and generally in the same order as described by the scholars of myth.

In a brief bibliographical essay entitled "London in France" (*ALR* 9:171–77), Mary Sue Schriber finds that French critics have generally viewed London as the archetypal American in the Horatio Alger vein, and have evaluated the various facets of his writing in that light. But this is not the case in a recent double issue of *Europe* (nos. 561–62) devoted to London criticism by French critics. These articles range from literary sources and influences to London's works in translation and on the screen, but a majority focus on London's socialism and on *The Iron Heel*. The special European interest in London is also documented in Olga Orechwa's "Recent Soviet Publications Commemorating the Centennial of Jack London's Birth" (*JLN* 9:78–80). Finally, there is a review by Marlan Beilke (*JLN* 9:114–17) of Rolf Recknagel's *Jack London: Leben und Werk eines Rebellen* (Berlin: Verlag Neues Leben), a book not yet available in English. Beilke writes that while as biography Recknagel's book is "sometimes unnecessarily encumbered with politicized interpretations and socialistic side-commentary," the volume as a whole is informed by viewing London's best work through a literary genre, *Abenteuerliteratur*, the literature of adventure.

iii. Willa Cather

The interest in Willa Cather generated by her centenary in 1973 is reflected in the large number of articles that continue to be published on this author. Several of the articles focus on individual novels. In an excellent essay entitled "The Mysteries of Ántonia" (*MQ* 17:173–85), Evelyn Helmick gives a mythic reading of Cather's best known novel. Helmick asserts that Cather's "ability to evoke such strong responses [lies in] the conscious connection of her art with the eternal themes of myth." Many scenes in *My Ántonia*, writes Helmick, have mythic dimensions but book 5, "Cuzak's Boys," "recreates in both meaning and structure the Eleusinian Mysteries observed by the Greeks before the eighth century, B.C." This, I feel, is an important article which gives depth and resonance to our reading of Cather's classic book. In "Cather's Last Stand" (*RS* 43[1975]:245–52), Marilyn Arnold argues that *Sapphira and the Slave Girl* is a wholly escapist novel, that Cather turned to her Virginia childhood as a place of refuge where peace and order might be assured. Arnold points out that the plot of the novel turns on the slave girl's escape and that "tension felt in the book is generated by the characters' attempts to evade confrontation and conflict." Less satisfactory than these two essays is Eugenie Lambert Hamner's "Affirmations in Willa Cather's *A Lost Lady*" (*MQ* 17:245–51), which argues that because Niel Herbert, like Captain Forrester, ultimately accepts rather than judges Marian's behavior, the Captain's values do survive and the novel therefore has a positive dimension. The weakness of this argument lies in Hamner's failure to analyze the Captain's values to see if they are a worthy legacy for Niel. Cather made the Captain a complex character whose weaknesses are as striking as his strengths.

Two articles examine Cather novels in the light of musical analogues. In "The Art of *Shadows on the Rock*" (*PrS* 50:37–51), John J. Murphy likens Cather's Quebec novel to a six-part musical composition wherein each book contains all the major themes in varying degrees, but develops only one to its dramatic height. Murphy argues that dramatic intensity is achieved by an interweaving technique of comparisons and contrasts without any one theme concluding until the final pages of the novel. The six themes around which Murphy sees the composition constructed include the themes of order, family, self-denial, the wilderness, national identity, and maturity. In "The Contrapuntal Complexity of Willa Cather's *The Song of the Lark*" (*MQ* 17:350–68), Robert Roulston asserts that in *The Song of the Lark* Cather exhibits an imagination of Wagnerian power and he shows how the author's basic themes, set forth at the beginning of the novel, "undergo permutations similar to the process whereby Wagner's *leitmotifs*, as they wend their way through the harmonic maze of the *Ring*, are transformed into new musical phrases." Like Murphy, Roulston explores a richness in Cather's narrative which accrues through juxtaposition and antithesis rather than dramatic conflict.

Two essays are concerned with image patterns in Cather's work as a whole. In a fine piece entitled "The Image of the Rock and the Family in the Novels of Willa Cather" (*MarkhamR* 6:9–14), Frank W. Shelton demonstrates the intimate connection between these two pervasive images in Cather's fiction. Cather viewed the family, Shelton points out, as both a trap and a necessity, and in several of her novels her central character trades his or her personal family for the larger, permanent community represented by the ancient civilization of the rock. But, says Shelton, Cather also viewed this as a denial of life, a quest after an abstraction, and in *Shadows on the Rock* she reconciles the quest for a permanent ideal with something fully human by portraying a living civilization on the rock. In "Through the Looking-Glass with Willa Cather" (*SN* 48,i:90–96), Mona Pers argues that the numerous window scenes in Cather's fiction present the author's tragic view of life—the longing for the unattainable. Pers examines several window scenes where "outsiders" symbolically wish to get inside and belong, while "insiders" yearn for freedom and independence. The window, says Pers, which gives one a glimpse into the world of one's dreams, thus becomes a Cather symbol for the human predicament.

Ellen Moers has a high regard for Cather and in *Literary Women* (Garden City, N.Y.: Doubleday) refers to her as one of the "great writers." At one point (pp. 189–92) she suggests that Cather may owe a literary debt to her admired George Sand, for in both Sand's *Consuelo* and Cather's *The Song of the Lark* operatic performance serves to show off a woman's artistic genius. In a section examining literary heroines (pp. 230–42), Moers asserts that the Electra story informs many of Cather's portraits of women, that the fiction from her greatest period centers on the death of a mother-figure or aging female tyrant, and is viewed with ambivalent anguish by the novel's central consciousness. In the last chapter of the book (pp. 257–63) Moers posits that in the Panther Cañon section of *The Song of the Lark* Cather has created "the most thoroughly elaborated female landscape in literature" and that there is a mystical dimension to her prairie and desert landscapes that is curiously akin to the landscapes of other women writers, such as the Brontës' Yorkshire moors and Isak Denisen's African Highlands. The sexual implications in Cather are also touched upon in "The Limits of Passion: Willa Cather's Review of *The Awakening*" (*W&L* 3,ii[1975]:10–20) by Sharon O'Brien who shows how Cather's negative review of the Chopin novel reflects the distrust of sexual love in her own fiction. O'Brien points out that the young Cather referred to Edna Pontellier's passion as "individual" and "self-limited," which is to say subjective and self-gratifying, where Cather herself believed that true happiness could be found only through self-abnegation, by identifying with something larger than oneself.

Cather's empathy for different cultures is central to two articles. In spite of its gimmicky title, Benjamin George's "The French-Canadian Connection: Willa Cather as a Canadian Writer" (*WAL* 11:249–61) articulates nicely the Canadian-American cultural contrasts which can be extrapolated from a reading of *Shadows on the Rock*. George points to Cather's concern for tradition in the New World, her image of hostile nature surrounding Quebec, and her picture of the woodsman hero who retains his ties to society as all characteristic of the Canadian cultural experience. In "Willa Cather and the Indian Heritage" (*TCL* 22:433–43), David Stouck posits an undercurrent of thought and feeling in Willa Cather's fiction "which turns away from the American dream of selfhood toward the richness and complexity of the perceptual world, and which views art not as the product of self-expression but as a process of sympathy for people, places, and events." This less familiar aspect of Cather's art, Stouck believes, found its fullest expression in her interest in the Indians of the Southwest, for whose cultures she had such a great affinity. Stouck shows how the Indians' communal way of life, their respect for the environment, and their organic art forms informed both the shapes and themes of Cather's art, especially in *O Pioneers!*, *The Song of the Lark* and *Death Comes for the Archbishop*. Of related interest is S. M. Bennett's "Ornament and Environment: Uses of Folklore in Willa Cather's Fiction" (*TFSB* 40[1974]:95–102). Bennett first makes clear that for studying folklore in literature one must know that the author derived the folk materials not from reading but from "an oral or customary tradition." Bennett writes that the folk material Cather gathered from the immigrant neighbors of her childhood—such details as food, burial customs, Christmas decorations—are used ornamentally in the Nebraska novels to embellish character or to color incident, but in her historical novels, *Death Comes for the Archbishop* and *Shadows on the Rock*, the folk materials she gathered from her travels, local stories of saints and martyrs are used to create the entire fabric of the novel's environment. Finally, Robert A. Martin in "Primitivism in Stories by Willa Cather and Sherwood Anderson" (*MidAmerica* 3:39–45) draws a comparison between "Neighbour Rosicky" and "Death in the Woods." The comparison is somewhat gratuitous but Martin points out that the narrators of both stories find something complete and beautiful in the death of the central figure, a death which is the fulfillment of the "natural," rural life in contrast to the sophisticated life of city men.

iv. Theodore Dreiser

In this period of American literature the outstanding book of criticism for 1976 is Donald Pizer's *The Novels of Theodore Dreiser, A Critical Study* (Minneapolis: Univ. of Minn. Press). What is impressive about this study is that Pizer has approached works of naturalist fiction largely from an aesthetic point of view, and in so doing demonstrates that Dreiser, while often prolix and self-contradictory, was nonetheless a writer with a powerful imagination. In a preface Pizer states his purpose as twofold: "to establish the facts of the sources and composition of each of Dreiser's novels and to study the themes and forms of the completed works." Pizer's achievement as regards his first purpose is especially worthy. By examining with care all extant manuscripts he has been able to describe in detail the stages and process of each novel's composition. Most interesting perhaps is Pizer's discovery that Dreiser's friend, Arthur Henry, had a much greater influence on the composition of *Sister Carrie* than was previously known. Pizer found that Henry not only encouraged Dreiser but actually helped in the writing and editing of the novel. Pizer observes that Dreiser's principal resources as a novelist were his research and his family memories. In the Cowperwood trilogy, writes Pizer, research was paramount while in works like *Jennie Gerhardt*, the autobiographical element was strongest. Dreiser's best books (*Sister Carrie* and *An American Tragedy*), continues Pizer, were a skillful blend of the two.

In his study of the themes and forms in Dreiser's fiction, Pizer is determined not to examine the books from an overriding theme or direction. Some readers may feel Pizer's book as a whole lacks focus, but there is a richness in the consideration of each novel which would likely be lost in a more schematic approach. Where Pizer does take an overview is in an introductory chapter entitled "A Summer at Maumee," which concerns itself with four stories Dreiser wrote in 1899. Pizer believes these stories exemplify the significant characteristics of Dreiser's fiction. "The Shining Slave Makers," writes Pizer, contains the three strands of Dreiser's Darwinism: life seen as an animal-like struggle for existence, life with evidence of moral behavior, and life seen as chaotic but beautiful. The stories, says Pizer, also exhibit in embryo some of the structures central to Dreiser's novels: the circular structure with the quester returning to where he started, the dramatic structure where authoritarian parent and romantic youth are in conflict until a seducer figure takes the youth away, and the parody structure wherein sentimental or hackneyed narrative patterns are employed ironically and with unexpected reversals. At relevant points Pizer shows these patterns recurring in the novels. Pizer's chapters on *Sister Carrie* and *An American Tragedy* are both masterful studies, but perhaps the most informative and interesting chapter is the one on *Jennie Gerhardt*. Pizer not only carefully documents the novel's source in relation to Dreiser's family history, but illuminates its themes and structures in a fine defense of the novel's artistic merits. Pizer's book is an original and very substantial contribution to Dreiser scholarship which also provides the teacher and scholar of Dreiser with a splendid compendium of information.

Vera Dreiser did not intend her book, *My Uncle Theodore* (New York: Nash Publishing Corp.), to be viewed as a work of scholarship. In the Prologue she states that her aim is to write for the general reading public and "to acquaint the youth of today with Theodore Dreiser, the uncle I knew." The book as a whole does little to change our picture of Dreiser. A psychologist by profession, she puts forth the thesis that Dreiser was emotionally and sexually crippled by an attachment to his mother, that he may have been latently homosexual. She is concerned to "set right" certain disputed biographical matters such as the composition of "On the Banks of the Wabash." Theodore did a rough sketch of the first verse, she tells us, but his brother Paul Dresser polished that verse, wrote the music, and added more verses and a chorus. She also gives a vigorous defense of Dreiser's first wife, replacing the image of a prudish school teacher with that of a shy but warm-hearted woman who wanted and was denied children. One feels the truth probably lies somewhere in between. Vera Dreiser's account of her uncle naturally reflects the biases and self-interests of a member of the family, but scholars will enjoy and value these further additions to the complex image of Dreiser and his world.

Philip L. Gerber's "Dreiser's Stoic: A Study in Literary Frustration" (*LMonog* 7[1975]:85–164) follows the composition of *The Stoic* from its conception in 1913 to its publication in 1947. Gerber has worked closely with the unpublished correspondence in the Dreiser Collection at the University of Pennsylvania and is able to document the many pitfalls, including quarrels with publishers, the criticisms of friends, which beset the project. He also shows how closely Dreiser kept to the facts of Yerkes's life and how Helen Dreiser, with her interest in Indian philosophy, shaped the ending of the novel. One of the best articles I read during the year is Leon F. Seltzer's "*Sister Carrie* and the Hidden Longing for Love: Sublimation or Subterfuge?" (*TCL* 22:192–209). In this original and highly perceptive essay Seltzer suggests that Carrie's yearning throughout the novel is a desire "for love and emotional relatedness." He argues that Dreiser was incapable of appreciating the possibilities of human intimacy himself and consequently he either idealizes Carrie's feelings as "emotional greatness" or explains them away mechanistically as sexual drive. Seltzer believes the power of the novel lies in its depicting the tragedy of human loneliness and that Dreiser never fully understood what he had created. In "Dreiser's *Trilogy of Desire*: The Financier as Artist" (*CRevAS* 7:151–62), Carl F. Smith tries to show where artist and financier significantly overlap in the characterization of Frank Cowperwood. He points out that Cowperwood, like an artist, has the drive and desire to shape the modern city, but that his production, a financial empire, cannot be judged on artistic grounds. Smith believes that Dreiser was trying to show that material crassness in America was a necessary precondition for spiritual refinement.

Two short essays consider *An American Tragedy* and matters related to Clyde's guilt. In "Innocent or Guilty: Problems in Filming Dreiser's *An American Tragedy*" (*ConnR* 9,ii:33–40), Lilian R. Furst points out that none of the film versions maintains Dreiser's ambivalence on the question of Clyde's guilt. She reminds us that Eisenstein's scenario would have Clyde innocent and American society responsible for Roberta's death, while Sternberg's and Stevens's films envisage Clyde as a guilty though likeable figure. With a strictly literary interest, Charles N. Watson, Jr., in "The 'Accidental' Drownings in *Daniel Deronda* and *An American Tragedy*" (*ELN* 13:288–91), suggests that the ambiguous mixture of conscious intent and timely accident in Dreiser's rendering of Roberta Alden's death may owe something to his reading of George Eliot's similar handling of Grandcourt's death in *Daniel Deronda*.

v. Edith Wharton

Margaret B. McDowell's *Edith Wharton* (TUSAS 265) is a very good survey of the Wharton canon. Faced with such a massive *oeuvre* McDowell has wisely chosen to focus on the major novels and stories and to see other works as stages in Wharton's growth as a writer. The heart of this study is in the discussion of the major novels, which are each given a separate chapter. McDowell sees two main themes in *The House of Mirth*—Lily's destruction by society and her victory over self-centered motives—and accordingly she finds that Wharton presents Lily both as victim of circumstances, like the heroine of a Naturalistic novel, and as a woman acting freely, struggling between good and evil. Throughout the study McDowell pays attention to the development of Wharton's literary technique and in her chapter on *The Custom of the Country* she shows the extent Wharton matured as a skillful satirist. McDowell is especially good on *The Age of Innocence*, which she believes is Wharton's masterpiece. Here she argues among other things that May Welland is a more vital person than her virginal exterior would suggest. She shows us that May understands and forgives Archer and suggests that her inner strength is reflected in her enjoyment of athletics. The last chapters are a vigorous but objective defense of Wharton's late works. McDowell points out that after age 60 Wharton wrote a credible war novel, two satirical fantasies on the rootless people of the 1920s and two novels about the growth of an artist's consciousness, and she reminds us that these were all new themes for the aging author.

There were also three excellent articles on Edith Wharton in 1976. Cynthia Griffin Wolff's "*The Age of Innocence*: Wharton's 'Portrait of a Gentleman'" (*SoR* 12:640–58) is a highly sophisticated study of Wharton's New York masterpiece, defending the novel against charges of escapism and nostalgia. Wolff argues that *The Age of Innocence* is really a *Bildungsroman* and that old New York is important because the growth of Newland Archer's character is rooted in the society into which he was born. Wolff feels that Wharton, after the holocaust of World War I, was seeking like Archer an identity and maturity which would stand up against the chaos of time. Dealing with the same novel is James A. Robinson's "Psychological Determinism in *The Age of Innocence*" (*MarkhamR* 5:1–5). In this finely tuned essay Robinson shows that Archer is controlled by his New York culture, but argues that the conventions and values of that society are quietly affirmed because they constitute what is fundamentally decent and best in Archer. The deeper tragedy of the novel, says Robinson, is that Archer does not fully appreciate the culture that produced him, nor his life with May. Another first-rate study is "Fairy-Tale Love and *The Reef*" (*AL* 47:615–28) by Elizabeth Ammons, who shows how a buried pattern of fairy-tale motifs underpins this novel's concern with "deluded female fantasies about love and marriage." Ammons sees sexually repressed Anna Leath circumscribed by the story of Sleeping Beauty and economically dependent Sophy Viner as defined by the Cinderella story. Both women, says Ammons, dream of life being transformed by a man, by Prince Charming, but Wharton shows that the love of a man, George Darrow, who views women as property, cannot rescue or awaken the heroines.

A secondary bibliography on Edith Wharton has been published. In the Preface to *Edith Wharton and Kate Chopin: A Reference Guide* (Boston: G. K. Hall) Marlene Springer, compiler, does not claim her bibliography of writings about Edith Wharton to be fully comprehensive or definitive, but scholars will find this book a valuable tool nonetheless. The major omission, explains Springer, is in the area of reviews because Wharton's canon was so large and her reputation international. The entries are annotated to give the scholar direction in locating critical information.

vi. Gertrude Stein

In *Gertrude Stein* (TUSAS 268) Michael J. Hoffman's special interest is in studying the ways that Stein in the early works progressively omits from her writing the traditional elements of narrative. He sees the process as tied to her belief that personality does not change so that a writer need only be concerned with a character's present, not his past. The repetitive style and the present tense, writes Hoffman, reflect her view of "life as composed of continuously repeated actions and reactions." Hoffman describes Stein's style in *The Making of Americans* as a "cinema technique" where images are repeated but always with a subtle variation, the way each frame in a moving picture changes slightly. Hoffman's other chief concern is to show how Stein adopted the conventions of painting to the medium of writing. He points out that, like the Cubist painters, Stein made meaning internal, not referential, and in a book like *Tender Buttons* she shifted the focus from people to things.

Hoffman is less interesting when looking at the later works. He tells us that in a piece like *Lucy Church Amiably* setting, not the human drama, takes the foreground, but he does not really explain why. In surveying Stein's work in various genres he repeatedly points to the author's irreverence for convention, but that is hardly significant commentary on these works. Hoffman probably fell victim to the limitations of the Twayne format, or perhaps, like Stein, he grew tired of the book he was working on! But on the whole this is a good introduction and I recommend it as such.

vii. Glasgow, Cabell

Ellen Glasgow: Centennial Essays, ed. M. Thomas Inge (Charlottesville: Univ. Press of Va.) suffers the worst faults of centenary-inspired collections. All the contributions are by veteran Glasgow scholars. In a cranky prologue entitled "Northern Exposure: Southern Style" (pp. 7–21) Howard Mumford Jones laments that Glasgow has been unjustly ignored by the critics and reviews a number of American literary histories in which Glasgow is either not mentioned or given only brief consideration. This is not an inspiring lead article for the book. Two of the essays focus on Glasgow's less important works. In "The Earliest Novels" (pp. 67–81) Howard Mumford Jones describes the plots of *The Descendant* and *Phases of an Inferior Planet* and shows how these novels are derivative from books by other writers rather than from life. But he also notes in these apprenticeship novels such aspects of style as the balancing of phrases and the theme of inner victory which characterize Glasgow's best fiction. Frederick P. W. McDowell's "The Prewar Novels" (pp. 82–107) is a comprehensive discussion of *The Deliverance, The Miller of Old Church,* and *Virginia.* McDowell believes these are novels of considerable artistic merit and feels that *Virginia,* with its consistent ironic vision, can stand comparison with the late comedies of manners. Two other essays focus on Glasgow's portraits of men and women. Blair Rouse's essay, "Ellen Glasgow's Civilized Men" (pp. 131–66), is a lengthy study of a subject difficult to define—namely, the nature of being "civilized." Rouse uses Glasgow's phrase "the heart in the intellect" as a touchstone and examines five of her characters—Tucker Corbin, Marmaduke Littlepage, General David Archbald, John Fincastle, and Asa Timberlake—to see whether in their lives reason and emotion are mutually informing. In "Ellen Glasgow as Feminist" (pp. 167–87) Monique Parent Frazee assesses both Ellen Glasgow and her fictional creations from a feminist point of view. She points out that Glasgow was not interested in such issues as sex, family, work, professional success, economic and political responsibility, but rather that the core of her feminism rested in the intellectual and emotional emancipation of women. Frazee writes that Glasgow believed in a woman's right to happiness according to her own choice and shows how Glasgow's fictional women demonstrate courage and fortitude that men lack. The failure of the Glasgow centenary to inspire a fresh evaluation of her work is reflected in the fact that the two most important essays in this volume have appeared in print before: C. Hugh Holman's "The Comedies of Manners" (pp. 108–28) appeared previously as "April in Queenborough: Ellen Glasgow's Comedies of Manners" (see *ALS 1974*, p. 245); Edgar E. MacDonald's "An Essay in Bibliography" (see *ALS 1972*, p. 240) has been revised for its inclusion here.

Elsewhere C. Hugh Holman published "Ellen Glasgow and History: The Battle-Ground" (*Prospects* 2:385–98), in which he argues that Ellen Glasgow began by writing a form of historical novel and ended by writing contemporary novels of manners. For *The Battle-Ground*, he says, she did a substantial amount of research, reading newspaper files from the Civil War period, traveling over the physical settings of the novel in addition to recalling from memory old family stories. He points out that her real concern was with social history and the rise of the middle class in Virginia and consequently her focus is not on military movements and battles but on a way of life that was being radically altered.

In "Cabell and the Mabinogion" (*Kalki* 26:47–50) Maggey Mateo pursues some of Cabell's possible sources of inspiration in Welsh legend, while in " 'Some Ladies' and 'Jurgen' " (*Kalki* 26:51–57) Paul Spencer examines the growth of *Jurgen* out of the short story "Some Ladies and Jurgen," first published in *Smart Set*, July 1918. *Kalki* reports the publication of a new Cabell bibliography which I have not seen—*James Branch Cabell: A Complete Bibliography*, compiled by James N. Hall, with a Supplement of Current Values of Cabell Books by Nelson Bond (Brooklyn, N.Y.: Revisionist Press). According to this review, the bibliography "is filled with nearly everything that anybody could want to know about the printing and binding of Cabell's volumes, and his many other excursions into fine print."

viii. John Dos Passos

In "John Dos Passos' *Three Soldiers*: Aesthetics and the Doom of Individualism" printed in *The First World War in Fiction: A Collection of Critical Essays*, ed. Holger Klein (London: Macmillan), Stanley Cooperman argues that Dos Passos was not engaged with the horrors of machine warfare, but with "cultural naivete, and the essential mindlessness of mass organization." Dos Passos, writes Cooperman, uses the political and military situation as a metaphor for 20th-century civilization and sees the mobilization of an entire civilization as "the supremacy of what Henry Adams termed 'The Dynamo' over all individual action or reaction." In a brief overview entitled "The Riddle of Dos Passos" (*Commentary* 61,i:63–66), Joseph Epstein suggests that Dos Passos's political move to the Right was disastrous for his fiction because, whereas in his early novels he not only expressed anger at the enemy but sympathy for the victims, in his late fiction he became chiefly a pamphleteer with no sympathy for any of the characters. Epstein points out that without sympathetic interest in the destiny of his characters a novelist will fail to engage his readers.

Two other articles deal more specifically with literary technique. In "Narration in the Making of *Manhattan Transfer*" (*SNNTS* 8: 185–98) Lois Hughson convincingly shows how Dos Passos's discontinuous narrative technique creates a continuity of emotion in *Manhattan Transfer*. When we glimpse minor characters at crucial moments in their lives, says Hughson, we are learning something indirectly about the fate and emotions of the central characters. If, writes Hughson, we see the sufferings of the legless man, Anna Cohen, Dutch, and Ellen as embodiments of Jimmy Herf's feelings, then we can understand fully his judgment on the city and his decision to leave. Similarly, she adds, we feel more powerfully the spiritual defeat and frustration of those who remain trapped. In "Auto-biographical Elements in the Camera Eye" (*AL* 48:340–64), James N. Westerhoven authenticates the details of the Camera Eye sections in *U.S.A.* as being Dos Passos's personal memories. Westerhoven feels this research will give the Camera Eye technique greater credibility and will serve as a useful guide to readers distracted by references in *U.S.A.* to unfamiliar persons and places. Of related interest is "The Poetry in American Fiction" (*Prospects* 2:513–26) in which Linda W. Wagner shows succinctly how the principles of Imagism such as concreteness, simplicity, and directness of presentation influenced the prose writers of the same generation. Wagner focuses on the work of Hemingway, Dos Passos, and Faulkner, giving specific examples of the Imagist style in fiction.

ix. B. Traven

Last year when I reviewed Donald O. Chankin's *Anonymity and Death: the Fiction of B. Traven* (see *ALS 1975*, pp. 290–91), I classed Traven as a proletarian writer, but Michael L. Baumann in *B. Traven: An Introduction* (Albuquerque: Univ. of New Mexico Press) argues that Traven protests not so much against capitalism as against all institutions which deprive the individual of his freedom. He argues in turn that Traven is more accurately viewed as an anarchist, influenced by the writings of Max Stirner. Baumann describes his book as an introduction to specific problems surrounding Traven and inevitably one of the problems is the question of Traven's identity. Baumann approaches the question through language and style. He agrees with the East German critics that Traven was once the German anarchist Ret Marut, but he also supports the *Erlebnisträger* theory that the fiction narrated by Gerard Gales was not Traven's own but that he borrowed and translated it from an American living in Mexico. Baumann lends support to this theory by examining Traven's style, which he demonstrates is not idiomatic in either German or English. If Traven were translating an American writer's novels into German, he says, this would explain the materials set in America and Mexico at a period when Traven was apparently living in Germany as Ret Marut and would explain the stylistic infelicities and Americanisms in the texts. Baumann focuses his study of style and theme throughout on *The Death Ship*.

In the last chapter of his book Baumann takes up the question of Traven being classified as an American writer. He demonstrates the similarities between Traven and writers like Melville, Poe, Twain, and how Traven exhibits the American preference for solitude, male companionship, and preoccupation with death, which give his fictions "an American feel that is genuine." Baumann's introduction to problems surrounding both the mysterious life and the significant writings of Traven stirs one's interest afresh.

x. Women and Women Writers

The continuing interest in women's studies is reflected in the number of articles that examine the portrayal of women in fiction. In "Early Feminist Fiction: The Dilemma of Personal Life" (*Prospects* 2:167–91), Nan Bauer Maglin examines 21 novels about women from this period and finds that while these novels explore a woman's relationship to the world through work and politics, they do not handle the range of personal issues—sexuality, love, marriage, women's relations with women—from a feminist perspective. Maglin singles out Cather's *My Ántonia* as unique for suggesting, in the close relationship of Lena and Tiny, an alternative for marriage. Barbara Meldrum's "Images of Women in Western American Literature" (*MQ* 17:252–67) is a survey of numerous fictional women around the familiar thesis that women characters, usually identified with the East, act as civilizing forces on the frontier, and their ideals, in conflict with those of the Western male, often provide dramatic tension in the novels. Meldrum also examines several women characters in terms of their achievements and self-realization. More original and probing is Nancy Bunge's "Women as Social Critics in *Sister Carrie, Winesburg, Ohio* and *Main Street*" (*MidAmerica* 3:46–55). Bunge shows how the heroines of these novels seek love and beauty in a world committed to the male values of competition and efficiency. These heroines, Bunge argues, find the social order alien and ally themselves with the larger order of nature; but at the same time, she says, these women need love and this becomes a tragic necessity because it returns them to the alien world of men.

There were also some articles of note on minor women novelists. Most of an issue of *American Literary Realism* (9:95–169) is devoted to California writer Gertrude Atherton. Charlotte S. McClure has prepared the only existing checklist of Atherton's writings and in a brief introductory essay suggests that Atherton's creation of the "advanced" California girl—intellectual and adventurous—deserves attention today. Similarly Thomas H. Landess in "The Achievement of Julia Peterkin" (*MissQ* 29:221–32) urges that this author's work be carefully reviewed. Her stories and novels, he says, were once considered sensational because of their treatment of blacks and their exploitation of the grotesque and violent, but should now be viewed on purely literary grounds. Margaret Anderson's editorial career is sympathetically reviewed in Abby Ann Arthur Johnson's "The Personal Magazine: Margaret C. Anderson and 'The Little Review'" (*SAQ* 75:351–63). The best treatment of a minor woman writer is in T. E. Blom's "Anita Loos and Sexual Economics: *Gentlemen Prefer Blondes*" (*CRevAS* 7:39–47), which argues, contrary to general opinion, that Loos's novel "is a classic American satire." Blom says that in Lorelei Loos created the archetypal dumb blonde of American culture, but also introduced into American fiction a new kind of character—the female rogue-picaro. She is an instrument of satire, he writes, because she mirrors faithfully "a society which, in worshipping her, worships its own acquisitiveness." Adds Blom, she also points up the inadequacy of the American male who fears sexuality and must have it packaged in the guise of blonde innocence.

Simon Fraser University

14 Fiction: The 1930s to the 1950s

Margaret Anne O'Connor

For writers who came into prominence in the thirties and forties, 1976 has been a year of reëvaluation. Critics have rediscovered Christopher Morley, Erskine Caldwell, and James T. Farrell, while Margaret Mitchell seems to be developing an appreciative academic audience that she never previously enjoyed. David Peck's "Salvaging the Art and Literature of the 1930's: A Bibliographical Essay" (*CentR* 20:128–41) outlines the thirties revival in television and current films and heralds the end of what Peck terms "the Anti-1930s" attitudes of the war and postwar years. Peck reviews booklength works of the last decade which treat the period as a whole and, while he does not deal with scholarship on individual writers, Peck traces the changes in critical attitudes toward such figures as Clifford Odets as evidence of the new interest in writers of the thirties. It is the current interest in the documentary and New Journalism that accounts for the revived popularity of the socially conscious art of the 1930s in Peck's view. In a feisty overview of the period Leslie Fiedler gives his reasons for abandoning earlier plans to write a critical appraisal of the 1930s. In "Fiction of the Thirties" (*RLV* 42, U.S. bicentennial issue: 93–103), Fiedler finds the proletarian writers—who would have been his major interest ten years ago—to be "overrated" today. Since the "mythology of race-fear and genteel Fascism" forming "the undermind of the Southern Agrarians" has little credence in the mid-seventies, they too are hardly worthy subjects of extended criticism. In a final inflammatory jibe Fiedler terms Marshall MacLuhan "the last spokesman for Southern Agrarianism." Only the popular writers of the period, principally Edgar Rice Burroughs and Margaret Mitchell, receive Fiedler's praise. Fiedler devotes several pages of his brief survey of the period to a perceptive reading of *Gone With the Wind*, arguing that it is one of the few novels of the 1930s that retains its power upon a rereading. Fiedler's appraisal reflects his long-held interest in women writers, best-sellers, and the popular reading audience. As usual he is provoking—at times even thought-provoking.

Several book-length works of general reference offer information on many writers of this period. *Literary New York: A History and Guide* (Boston: Houghton Mifflin), by Susan Edmiston and Linda D. Cirino, is both a useful research tool and a fine companion to take along on a visit to New York City. Completed under an NEH grant, the volume offers far more information than do similar works. The authors treat the literary histories of the city's districts in individual chapters and provide keyed street maps and directions for walking tours through the haunts of New York's literary visitors and residents. Commentaries on individual authors such as Carson McCullers, Thomas Wolfe, Henry Roth, and Edna Ferber make excellent use of autobiographical writings and authoritative biographical and critical sources. A second volume of general interest is the Fourth Series of *Writers at Work: The "Paris Review" Interviews*, ed. George Plimpton (New York: Viking). This volume contains conversations with Conrad Aiken, Eudora Welty, and Vladimir Nabokov which have appeared in the *Paris Review* over the last fifteen years. The entry on John Steinbeck is of dubious value. The editors of this section have excerpted comments on the craft of fiction made by Steinbeck in various Viking publications, most notably *Steinbeck: A Life in Letters* (see *ALS 1975*, p. 297). The "composite essay" seems a weak substitute for an interview, and I wonder why Steinbeck was included at all.

i. "Art for Humanity's Sake"—Proletarians and Others

a. **The Proletarian Writers.**   Several critical surveys covering a time span much greater than the confines of this chapter are treated by Michael Hoffman in his essay in this volume of *ALS* and should not be overlooked in assessing the treatment of proletarian writers in 1976. One of the most important of these works is Sylvia Jenkins Cook's *From Tobacco Road to Route 66* (Chapel Hill: Univ. of N.C. Press) which includes lengthy discussions of the fiction of Erskine Caldwell, John Steinbeck, and James Agee. Malcolm Cowley's "Georgia Boy: A Retrospect of Erskine Caldwell" (*Pages* 1:62–73) is a second important treatment of Caldwell's work published this year. Cowley's essay is primarily biographical, but a significant point which he makes is that "it is the early books—say the first three novels and the stories up to *Georgia Boy* (1943)—on which Caldwell's reputation will stand or fall." The success of *Tobacco Road* and *God's Little Acre* changed the focus of his writing—not for the better.

Jesse Stuart contributes an autobiographical essay treating his Kentucky childhood and college career in "Three Teachers and a Book" (*Pages* 1:90–101). Informative as the essay is, the strongest impression it leaves with its readers is that modesty is not one of Stuart's gifts. Stuart lauds the prescience of several of his early teachers who recognized his writing talents, but he still seems to be smarting from the sting of low grades received in a graduate course he took at Vanderbilt under Robert Penn Warren. Barbara L. Baer's "Harriette Arnow's Chronicles of Destruction" (*Nation* 222:117–20) includes a record of an interview with the Kentucky-born writer. Baer focuses her attention on Arnow's Kentucky trilogy—*Mountain Path* (1936), *Hunter's Horn* (1949), and *The Dollmaker* (1954)—and champions the works on the grounds of the "coherent vision" the three novels display. Though only *The Dollmaker* is currently in print, Baer argues that Arnow is not a one-book author; all three novels chronicling the poor white class are written "in the best tradition of American fiction."

The John Steinbeck Society (headquartered at Ball State University in Muncie, Indiana) and its energetic executive director Tetsumaro Hayashi are responsible for the vast majority of criticism on Steinbeck appearing this year. Hayashi himself edited two book-length works, coedited a monograph, and as editor of the Society's *Steinbeck Quarterly* and Steinbeck Monograph Series, he oversaw the publication of an additional monograph and twenty articles in 1976. As editor of *John Steinbeck: A Dictionary of his Fictional Characters* (Metuchen, N.J.: Scarecrow), Hayashi alphabetizes lists of characters submitted by six contributors—each of whom covers one or more of Steinbeck's works—and compiles a bibliography of recent secondary materials as an appendix. Most entries merely identify figures physically and summarize their role in the works in which they appear; longer entries, however, present virtual interpretations of individual works. The contributors, all regulars in the pages of *StQ*, have done a very creditable job of covering the material. Robert E. Morseberger on characters in *The Grapes of Wrath* and John F. Slater on those in *Tortilla Flat* go far beyond the rather pedestrian format of the *Dictionary* as a whole in their contributions. In *A Study Guide to Steinbeck's "The Long Valley"* (Ann Arbor, Mich.: Pierian Press), Hayashi reprints thirteen essays originally appearing in *StQ* which present readings of individual stories. Two new pieces consider often neglected stories in *The Long Valley*; Robert Benton deals with "'Breakfast' I and II" (pp. 33–40) and Katherine M. and Robert E. Morseberger collaborate on "'The Murder'—Realism or Ritual" (pp. 65–71). The Morsebergers's essay is of particular value now that Norton's ubiquitous anthology, *The American Tradition in Literature*, includes this puzzling story as one of its two Steinbeck selections. Noting the cursory treatment the story has received in book-length studies, the Morsebergers argue that the striking surface story has hidden the more provocative level of ritualized murder from most critics' attention. Each essay is followed by a series of discussion questions, not only complementing the preceding interpretive essay but leading to other issues in the story as well.

The two monographs published under the auspices of the Steinbeck Society are assessments of Steinbeck's accomplishments as a writer. In *Steinbeck's Prophetic Vision of America: Proceedings of the Bicentennial Steinbeck Seminar* (Upland, Ind.: Taylor University), Hayashi and Kenneth D. Swan collect the nine evaluative papers and tributes paid the author at a meeting held in May 1976. *Steinbeck's Literary Achievement* (Steinbeck Monograph Series, 6) by Roy S. Simmonds treats his major themes, sense of humor, style, sources, and influences in five brief chapters and concludes with a positive appraisal of his influence and career. Simmonds finds Steinbeck "guilty . . . not of prostituting his art, but rather of immense artistic courage" (p. 39). A disinterested observer might prefer that Steinbeck's merits be considered by a less biased judge and jury than either of these monographs provides.

Several of the articles in *StQ* deserve particular mention. *StQ* began the year by devoting its winter issue to papers delivered at the Steinbeck Seminar at the 1974 MLA. Warren French, Peter Copek, Donald Pizer, and Alan Henry Rose all consider the question of Steinbeck's naturalism in this group of papers. A fifth participant in the forum—John Ditsky—presents an expanded version of his paper in "*The Winter of Our Discontent*: Steinbeck's Testament on Naturalism" (*RS* 44:42–51). Roy S. Simmonds's "Steinbeck's 'The Murder': A Critical and Bibliographical Study" (*StQ* 9:45–51) is more bibliographical than critical. Simmonds's observations, drawn from collating the two magazine versions of the story and that in *The Long Valley*, are useful guides to Steinbeck's intent at the various stages of writing, but Simmonds stops short of giving a reading of the work. It is a good companion piece to the Morsebergers's treatment of "The Murder" in *A Study Guide to Steinbeck's "The Long Valley,"* however. *StQ* continues its interest in Steinbeck's depiction of female characters in two articles in 1976. Mimi Reisel Gladstein finds the main female character in *The Pearl* to be "a composite of all the best qualities of the archetypal feminine" in "Steinbeck's Juana: A Woman of Worth" (9:20–24). Robert E. Morseberger looks at another stereotype in "Steinbeck's Happy Hookers" (9:101–15).

Steinbeck's depiction of female characters was of interest outside the pages of *StQ* as well. In "Steinbeck's Strong Women: Feminine Identity in the Short Stories" (*SWR* 61:304–14), Marilyn L. Mitchell develops a comparison suggested by Peter Lisca in *The Wide World of John Steinbeck* (1958) between Steinbeck's female characters and those of D. H. Lawrence. Elisa Allen of "Chrysanthemums" is a "warm three-dimensional character" compared to Mary Teller of "The White Quail" who is "a virtual caricature of the selfish, castrating female" often found in Lawrence's work.

Steinbeck's work as a screenplay writer and the adaptation of his own novels to the film was the subject of three articles in 1976. In "'To Tom, Who Lived It': John Steinbeck and the Man from Weedpatch" (*JML* 5:151–94), Jackson J. Benson identifies the man referred to in the second dedication of *The Grapes of Wrath* as Thomas A. Collins, manager of the California migrant labor camp where Steinbeck researched material eventually included in the novel. Upon the recommendation of Steinbeck, Collins served as a technical advisor when the film was made. The "Tom who lived it" is more akin to Casy in temperament and personality than to Tom Joad. Benson suggests that Steinbeck's admiration for Collins and his idealism accounts for the positive portrait of life in government-sponsored camps in the work. Benson's contribution to this number of *JML* does not end with this article, however. It is in three parts and—taken as a whole—could be an addendum to *The Scholar Adventurers*. After completing the first article Benson discovered more about the mysterious Tom Collins. Eventually Benson located an unpublished autobiographical novel by Collins written under a pseudonym; the book concerns his life in the migrant camp and his contact with Steinbeck. Benson outlines his search for these materials in the second section of *JML* (5:195–210); this section in turn serves as an introduction to Benson's third contribution, a portion of Collins's manuscript. "From *Bringing in the Sheaves* by 'Windsor Drake'" (*JML* 5:211–32) concerns Collins's contact with Steinbeck (who is referred to by name) and how his work on the novel and film led to the destruction of his career with the Farm Security Administration. Benson's work suggests there is much more to be done on the sources of *The Grapes of Wrath* and Steinbeck's models for his characters.

In a second article bearing on Steinbeck's career as a film writer, Robert E. Morseberger discusses his first screenplay in "Adrift in Steinbeck's Lifeboat" (*LFQ* 4:325–38). The 1944 movie *Lifeboat*, directed by Alfred Hitchcock, was greeted with mixed reviews and many of the film's detractors argued that the screenplay was "soft" on Nazism. Refuting Steinbeck's responsibility for this real or imagined "softness," Morseberger notes that while the scenario grew from an unpublished story by Steinbeck, the final screen version reflected "an uneven conglomeration of Hitchcock suspense, Steinbeck philosophy and [collaborator Jo] Swerling situation and dialogue." Morseberger cites evidence beyond the screenplay to clarify Steinbeck's attitude toward Nazism. A final article on Steinbeck's screen work is John Ditsky's "Words and Deeds in *Viva Zapata!*" (*DR* 56,i:125–31). In his "cinematic and literary" consideration of the work, Ditsky concludes that three character types predominate—the articulate but ineffectual, the silent men of action, and the most admirable of all, the men who combine word and deed to accomplish great things. The same paradigm might well be found in many of Steinbeck's works of fiction.

Published criticism on James Agee in 1976 centered on his sense of form—in his poetry, documentary writings, and fiction. Victor A. Kramer publishes the text of a 1928 manuscript in "Agee's Early Poem 'Pygmalion' and his Aesthetic" (*MissQ* 29:191–96) and relates the stages of its revision to Agee's overall method of composition. William J. Rewark's "James Agee's *Let Us Now Praise Famous Men*: The Shadow Over America" (*TSL* 21:91–104) defends the work against charges of formlessness leveled by both its contemporary reviewers and more recent critics. Rewark's article is valuable for its thorough treatment of the work's critical reception but the "form"

Rewark outlines for the work is vague if not incomprehensible. Stated succinctly in the abstract Rewark provides for the essay, Agee's form is "a complex fusion of the horizontal, organic process of life and the vertical simultaneity of life and death." The essay itself fails to make this abstraction more concrete. Joseph O. Milner is more successful in his attempt to resolve a critical debate in "Autonomy and Communion in *A Death in the Family*" (*TSL* 21:105–13). Citing conflicting 1970 interpretations of the work offered by Gene W. Ruoff and George and Panthea Reid Broughton, Milner suggests that both articles have more than a grain of the truth in them. Agee does write of the need for community as Ruoff claims, but he is equally intent upon presenting the value of self-reliance and individualism as the Broughtons argue. According to Milner, it is the tension between these equally revered qualities that is the central focus of the work. As their title suggests, Charles Gregor and William Dorman write not so much of Agee himself as of "The Children of James Agee" (*JPC* 9:996–1002). Joan Didion, Norman Mailer, Tom Wolfe, Gail Sheehy, and Gay Talese are all seen as practitioners of the school of New Journalism founded on the principles of documentary writing attributed to Agee. Like Agee, the "New Journalist uses the ideas, the language, and the techniques of fiction. His style is filled with metaphor and simile, anecdotes, characterization, subjectivity, conclusions, intuition, and thematic organization."

Among proletarian writers of city life, James T. Farrell received the lion's share of critical attention in 1976. In "James T. Farrell: An Essay in Bibliography" (*RALS* 6:131–64), Jack Salzman updates Edgar M. Branch's thorough 1957 bibliography of primary sources but concentrates his attention on secondary materials. Salzman finds Farrell underrated, not so much by critics as by publishers who have permitted many of his works to go out of print. He also calls for a definitive biography and a paperback collection of Farrell's essays and reviews. His request is answered in part by Jack Alan Robbins's hardbound edition of *James T. Farrell: Literary Essays, 1954–74* (Port Washington, N.Y.: Kennikat), which Robbins views as a continuation of Farrell's collection, *Reflections at Fifty*, published in 1954. Despite Robbins's claim in his Introduction that critics are mistakenly ignoring Farrell's late career as a fiction writer and critic in favor of concentrating their attention on the earlier *Studs Lonigan* series, there is little in the present volume to arrest the attention of readers from their concern with his earlier work. The essays, reviews, and memoirs included fail to show the matured vision Robbins admires in his Introduction; in part, this is due to their extreme brevity. While Farrell offers some valuable insights over a broad range of topics, the volume's staccato pace does not give it the impression of being a sustained piece of literary scholarship.

Twentieth Century Literature devotes its first number in 1976 to a consideration of Farrell and his work, and Farrell himself contributes two previously unpublished pieces to the issue. Farrell's interview with Dennis Flynn and Jack Salzman, as well as his assessment of his own career in "Farrell Looks at his Writing," begin the special issue, and eight critics treat his major works of short fiction, criticism, and novels in the following essays. While several essays are tributes rather than interpretations or assessments, three essays seem of particular importance. Edgar M. Branch appraises the author's current reputation in "James T. Farrell: Four Decades after *Studs Lonigan*" (22:28–35) and concludes that Farrell "has a prominent place within a distinctly American tradition of art and thought." Barry O'Connell praises the sociological insights of Farrell's treatment of the Irish on the South Side of Chicago in "The Lost World of James T. Farrell's Short Stories (22:36–51). Joseph W. Slade discusses with obvious admiration the writer's latest and "most ambitious" novel cycle which has received little attention from other critics in " 'Bare-Assed and Alone': Time and Banality in Farrell's *A Universe of Time*" (22:68–79).

Leonard Kriegel gives a personal response to Farrell's work in "Homage to Mr. Farrell" (*Nation* 223:373–76). Despite the weaknesses Kriegel finds in Farrell's work—including his twenty-fourth novel *The Dunne Family* (Garden City, N.J.: Doubleday), weaknesses that include his inability to move beyond the thirties for a setting for his works and his use of dated slang in dialogue—Kriegel states that "no one has written better of what motivates young men in the city than has Farrell." Most of the persuasive defenders of Farrell's fiction continue to base their standards on his grasp of the social situation of the thirties, not on his style or techniques.

William Freedman's "A Conversation with Henry Roth" (*LitR* 18[1975]:149–57) is one of several interviews with the author of *Call It Sleep* published in the last few years. This interview took place in Israel in 1972, and Freedman focuses his questions on Roth's purposes in writing his lone novel. When Roth describes his hero David Schearl as "an innocent victim of social forces," a surprised Freedman asks for further clarification. Roth then contradicts himself somewhat by stating that *Call It Sleep* is "certainly not a proletarian novel. Even the Jewishness isn't very important." Roth is more concerned with the more universal themes developed in the work, as well as his use of Freudian psychology in his characterizations.

b. **Liberals in the Cold War.** Diana L. George treats an often-anthologized short story in "Thematic Structure in Lionel Trilling's 'Of This Time, of That Place'" (*SSF* 13:1–8). She bases her reading largely on Trilling's comments on the story made in *The Literature of Experience* (1967). The story embodies one of the great conflicts of the 20th century in George's view: "Science is the villain, totally correct but abominably immoral." Chrysostom Kim delineates Trilling's moral stance as a critic in "Lionel Trilling on 'The Self In Its Standing Quarrel with Culture'" (*ABR* 27:332–56).

Lillian Hellman's memoir *Scoundrel Time* (Boston: Little, Brown) expresses her disappointment with America's intellectual community during the McCarthy era. Gary Wills's excellent introduction trenchantly describes the political tensions affecting the arts of the late forties and early fifties and is a vital part of the success of the volume as a whole. As in her two previous volumes of memoirs, *An Unfinished Woman* (1969) and *Pentimento* (1973), Hellman does not simply move chronologically through a certain period in her life; instead she organizes her work around portraits of the figures who have left a lasting impression with her. *Scoundrel Time* begins as Hellman receives a subpoena requiring her to appear before the House Committee on Un-American Activities to testify about her political affiliations. Her long-time companion Dashiell Hammett's earlier encounter with the committee had led to months in federal prison for contempt of court charges when he refused to testify. The threat of a similar fate hangs in the air for the rest of the volume as Hellman moves forward and backward in time presenting her view of the relationship between the anti-Communist government campaign and the writers and artists of the period. Norman Cousins, Lionel and Diana Trilling, Clifford Odets, as well as Hollywood figures Elia Kazan, Louis Mayer, Samuel Goldwyn, and Harry Cohn are criticized for their vacuous "liberalism" which disappeared under government

pressures put upon them. To Hellman these figures are more villainous than the predictable Joe McCarthy, Richard Nixon, or committee counsel Robert Stripling, who prosecuted the government's
case. Beautifully written, *Scoundrel Time* chronicles a personal and
national period of crisis deeply affecting the literary community in
America.

c. Social Iconoclasts—West and Salinger.   Two recent bibliographies of Nathanael West, both comprehensive through 1974, are surprisingly good companions, rather than competitors to each other.
William White culminates twenty years of publishing bibliographic
checklists of West in various periodicals with *Nathanael West: A
Comprehensive Bibliography* (Kent, Ohio: Kent State Univ. Press,
1975). Though secondary sources receive adequate treatment, the
annotated entries on primary sources form the major strength of this
volume. His descriptive bibliography of book-length works traces the
history of various printings, including foreign publications and translations. Briefer entries on original and subsequent publications of
West's short stories and essays are augmented by a discussion of
West's screenplays and unpublished plays. White also reprints the
title page of each of West's book-length works and appends a group
of occasional writings which were originally published in small newspapers and journals. White's treatment of primary sources is so thorough that, rather than duplicate his effort, West's second recent bibliographer, Dennis P. Vannatta, simply lists West's works in a brief
appendix and directs his readers to White's volume for more detailed
information. Vannatta's *Nathanael West: An Annotated Bibliography*
(New York: Garland) is a carefully researched, thoroughly annotated
list of secondary sources on West, the most recent of which is White's
bibliography. While White rarely annotates secondary sources in his
volume, Vannatta often finds it valuable to annotate his entries several times. If there is a flaw in this excellent bibliography, it is in the
format. Vannatta begins with a "Master Checklist" of 507 items arranged chronologically under separate headings—books, chapters in
books, brief mentions, critical articles, reviews, theses, and dissertations. Occasionally items are annotated here but more frequently a
reader is sent to one or several of the eleven topic sections of the
volume which represent to Vannatta the various approaches to West's
work that have been undertaken. Beyond biography and bibliogra-

phy, Vannatta isolates studies under categories such as influence, genre, comparative, historical, sociological, or source studies. Thus a comprehensive work such as Jay Martin's *Nathanael West: The Art of His Life* (see *ALS 1970*, pp. 245–46) is annotated 15 times under different headings and subheadings and each citation begins with a repetition of the complete bibliographic entry. Ironically, the amount of cross-referencing makes the book unwieldy to use. Vannatta might, indeed, have gone beyond the demands of the standard bibliography in this work, but its complexity and the consequent difficulty in its use makes White's more traditional bibliography a useful research tool to use in tandem with Vannatta's study.

In addition to the two bibliographical studies, Nathanael West prompted a dissertation and several articles worthy of note, three ranging broadly over West's work and two treating aspects of *Miss Lonelyhearts*. Jacques Cabeau covers some now-familiar territory in "Humour noir et surréalisme dans les romans de Nathanael West" (*EA* 29:429–36) but emerges with some new conclusions. Like the surrealists, West uses black humor as a method for denouncing the horror of daily living and for transfiguring it into "poetic surreality"; this transfiguring power is radically opposed to romantic metaphor which, by finding "correspondences," offers the vision of a reassuringly harmonious world. "Black humor is not a mediator, like metaphor, but a detonator," Cabeau posits. While West owes much to the techniques of the surrealists, he was suspicious of the surrealist programs and in this respect he was probably more faithful to Dada than to surrealism.[1] A second comparative study finds affinities between "Nathanael West and the Theatre of the Absurd" (*SHR* 10: 225–34). Frank W. Shelton sees many stage metaphors in West as evidence of his ties to surrealism, the Dadaists, and continental absurdist drama. All the characters in West's novels "are actors, poseurs" as are the stage characters in Samuel Beckett, Eugene Ionesco, and Jean Genet. Reviewing West's novels chronologically, Shelton claims that "a striking and not merely coincidental congruence of theme and technique can be traced" between West and the absurdists. J. A. Ward investigates the same quality of characterizations but attributes them to a different source in "The Hollywood Metaphor: The Marx

1. I am indebted to Thomas J. Cousineau of the Department of French, St. Ann's Episcopal School, Brooklyn Heights, N.Y., for his commentaries on this and the four other French language articles reviewed in this essay.

Brothers, S. J. Perelman and Nathanael West" (*SoR* 12:659–72). Both Perelman and West use Hollywood as a metaphor for all America and as the Marx brothers satirized society's public self in social events—dinner parties, a night at the opera, a day at the races— Perelman and West show how society in general practices the "show business" of Hollywood. "Hollywood *is* reality" for Perleman and his brother-in-law West, in Shelton's view.

In "Miss Lonelyhearts and the Detached Consciousness" (*Paunch* 42/43[1975]:21–39), Bruce Clark compares the main character in West's novel to the archetype of the *uroboros* described by D. H. Lawrence. The coiled snake, "Him with his tail in his mouth," cannot escape from the solipsistic trap of egotism, and Clark sees Miss Lonelyhearts's detached game-playing as a symptom of the self-involvement which makes him an emotional cripple in the novel. In a similar vein, Ronald J. Palumbo briefly discusses Biblical allusions in "Stone and Rock in West's *Miss Lonelyhearts*" (*AN&Q* 14:74–75) which underscore the portrait of Miss Lonelyhearts as one of the failed "priests of twentieth century America."

While the body of the text of Warren French's second edition of *J. D. Salinger* (TUSAS 40) remains substantially unchanged from the 1963 edition, French has updated his annotated bibliography of primary and secondary sources and added a fine essay as a preface evaluating Salinger's current critical reputation. After reviewing changes in the reading public which account for a renewed interest in Salinger's work, French concludes that "today's readers are turning to his books not for his scathing condemnation of the 'phony' society that he and his contemporaries hated but for his embodiment in fiction of principles of the contemplative life that they seek to enter" (p. 12). Recent favorable appraisals of Salinger's work by critics such as Robert Coles and Ernest Ranly lead French to suggest that Salinger—despite his apparent decision not to add to the canon of his work—is still a vital force in American literature of the mid-seventies. Mireille Tabah compares Salinger's disaffection with society as seen in *The Catcher in the Rye* with that of a contemporary East German writer in "*Die neuen Leiden des jungen W.*: Ulrich Plenzdorf entre Goethe et Salinger" (*EG* 30[1975]:335–44). The plot of Plenzdorf's 1973 novel is borrowed directly from Goethe's *Werther*, while the verbal style of the narrator shows the obvious influence of Salinger's Holden Caulfield. In each of these works the common element is the portrayal of the asocial hero who refuses a life without purpose or meaning in a society where he cannot satisfy his deepest needs. Tabah judges that Plenzdorf has avoided the psychological and existential depth of his models in deference, perhaps, to the official attitude toward such a personal withdrawal held by the East German Communist Party. Plenzdorf's novel is comparatively superficial because it merely underlines the political dimensions of its hero's life, which is treated with simplified optimism. Richard Lettis joins the debate over the "meaning" of the main character's name in "Holden Caulfield: Salinger's 'Ironic Amalgam'" (*AN&Q* 15:43–45). Lettis emphasizes the birth overtones of *caul* in suggesting that the "catcher in the rye," with his baseball glove, wants to *hold in the caul field*, or retain his childish innocence and that of those around him. Lettis's interpretation is certainly as plausible as other explanations reviewed in this brief note.

ii. Expatriates and Émigrés

Richard McDougall's *The Very Rich Hours of Adrienne Monnier* (New York: Scribners) succeeds admirably in presenting "an intimate portrait of the literary and artistic life in Paris between the wars," which it promises on its book jacket. Adrienne Monnier was the owner of the bookshop La Maison des Amis des Livres which formed, with Sylvia Beach's English language bookshop, Shakespeare and Company, the center of a truly international group of artists during this period. Many of the eighty essays McDougall translates in this collection were published in literary magazines Monnier distributed through her shop and the essays—or *gazettes* as Monnier termed them—seem like chatty, exuberant letters to friends rather than literary commentary. McDougall begins the collection with a long biographical essay emphasizing Monnier's prominent role in the literary world of her time and concludes with commentary on individual essays explaining their contexts. His translations retain the unique phrasing and literary skills he attributes to Monnier's original French essays and make the volume sheer pleasure to read. The selections included range from philosophic discussions of the nature of France or the influence of Americans in Paris to more immediate concerns such as her reaction to seeing Marlon Brando play Mark Antony in the film version of *Julius Caesar*. A scholar might wish that the index were comprehensive, rather than selective, but such a short-coming is trivial compared to the enormity of McDougall's accomplishment in the volume.

Djuna Barnes was of particular interest in 1976. In addition to two dissertations surveying her entire career, described in *DAI*, two book-length works appeared. Douglas Messerli's *Djuna Barnes: A Bibliography* (New York: David Lewis) is the product of extensive research and a very useful source of information not only on Barnes but on the expatriate community of which she was a part. Despite Messerli's claim that the work is "aimed at the scholar and student of Barnes, rather than the bibliographer," the technical data provided on editions of her book-length works makes the bibliography useful to all. Messerli's list of primary sources includes book-length works, poetry, short fiction, drama, and journalism, and he carefully records all reprintings of these materials. Journalism and nonfiction articles are annotated, as are entries on secondary sources. His thoroughness in noting even passing references to Barnes and her work in memoirs and critical studies is commendable, as is the inclusion of foreign language materials.

James B. Scott's *Djuna Barnes* (TUSAS 262) is less successful in fulfilling its aims than is Messerli's bibliography. Intended as a critical introduction for the reader unfamiliar with Barnes's work, Scott follows the Twayne format and begins with a brief—a too brief—biographical sketch and treats her major book-length works in separate chapters. Scott terms Barnes "an inverted naturalist," a description based on his idiosyncratic definitions of the world views of naturalists and existentialists. He is at his best discussing Barnes's verse drama *The Antiphon* (1958), but his chapter devoted to *Nightwood* (1936) also offers a lucid summary of the novel and a perceptive discussion of its experimental structure and prose style. The annotated list of 11 secondary sources in the "Selected Bibliography" is woefully inadequate, however. Since Scott's volume is the first book-length treatment of Barnes's work, one would have hoped for a more thorough and even treatment of her life and writings.

Nightwood received two additional treatments in 1976. Michael Vella's perceptive discussion of the surrealistic movement as it permeated the artistic community of Paris in the twenties and thirties gives a context for his reading of the novel in "Djuna Barnes Gains Despite Critics' Pall" (*LGJ* 4,i:6–8). He finds "irrational juxtaposition" the major structural technique of the novel while Freudian sexual symbolism is the major source of imagery. The novel is not mimetic; instead it is "a surreal collage of identities" which requires a different set of expectations from its critics than does the traditional novel in Vella's view. In "Style's Hoax: A Reading of Djuna Barnes's *Nightwood*" (*TCL* 22:179–92), Elizabeth Pochoda argues that appreciating the wit in the novel is a key to understanding its meaning. She finds it "a tremendously funny book in a desperately surgical way." Noting that the novel is more acclaimed among creative writers than critics, she suggests affinities in the work with those of John Hawkes and Thomas Pynchon, authors who share with Barnes "a writer's suspicion of the morality of writing itself."

Under the Sign of Pisces includes several papers delivered at the Anaïs Nin Seminar at the 1975 MLA in its second number of 1976. One of the best of these is Fred Watson's "Allegories in 'Ragtime': Balance, Growth, Disintegration" (7,ii:1–5). Watson terms the work a collection of fragments which Nin structures upon the Freudian model of the workings of the mind. The female narrator functioning as the conscious mind is almost oblivious to the figure of the ragpicker operating in the disruptive unconscious. A second article worthy of note in the same issue is Suzette Henke's "Anaïs Nin: Bread and the Wafer" (7–17), which compares the themes and structures of the *Diaries* to *Cities of the Interior*. Nin's *Diaries* are also the subject of Valerie Carnes's "Author Tries Distillation of Anaïs Nin's Voluminous Diary" (*LGJ* 4,i:11–13,21). "For Nin the diary became the symbolic equivalent of Virginia Woolf's room of one's own: it furnished the necessary interior space to be alone, think her own thoughts" in Carnes's view. Unlike autobiography, the diary captures life in process and Carnes argues that Nin's success with the diary form has created a new and separate genre of literature. Jean Normand is no less enthusiastic when he proclaims Nin's *Diary* "the most extraordinary of contemporary documents on the human psyche and the birth of a personality" in "Anaïs Nin ou Le Labyrinth Radieux" (*EA* 29:478–86). Normand sees in Nin the case of an author who succeeded in transforming negative experiences (resentment, feelings of abandonment, and humiliation) into a positive personality and a great literary work. He investigates the image of the labyrinth recurring in many of her works and, as support for his interpretation of its importance, appends a facsimile of a 1975 letter (in English) from

Nin responding favorably to an early draft of his essay. Nin terms the image of the labyrinth "my favorite symbol" and lauds Normand's interpretations of her work as "exact."

Clearly someone thought that the time was right for an anthology of racy passages from ten of Miller's works, so we have the right title, catchy but not raunchy (*Genius and Lust: A Journey through the Major Writings of Henry Miller*); the right publisher (Grove Press); and the right editorial guide through all this (Norman Mailer). Mailer intersperses his selections with nine essays which rival the master in salty, vivid language and scatological metaphors. Though Mailer's admiration for Miller's work is sincere and the commentaries often illuminating, the volume seems designed for a popular market rather than a critical academic audience.

Mailer's volume ends with an updating of two chronologies of Miller's life appearing earlier, and the final entry notes the publication of Miller's *Book of Friends* (Santa Barbara: Capra Press), a disappointing collection of brief sketches of Miller's friends and acquaintances. Leon Lewis comments on one of these friendships in "Henry Miller's Portrait of Walter Lowenfels" (*LGJ* 4,ii:16–17,20). As the model for Jabberwhorl Cronstadt in *Black Spring*, Lowenfels can be considered responsible for the "positive view of expatriatism" which the character presents in the work.

Critical assessments of Miller's work in 1976 have all been quite positive, suggesting that his reputation as an artist is rising. In a group of random reflections on poetry and fiction in contemporary America, Ronald Sukenick suggests that "Henry Miller is for American novelists what Whitman is for American poets" ("Thirteen Digressions"; *PR* 43:90–101). Jacques Lefebvre is no less complimentary in the company he chooses for Miller in "Jeux et masques dans l'oeuvre d'Henri Miller" (*LanM* 70:189–95). Commenting on Miller's works as a whole, Lefebvre notes that Miller's preferred image of himself is that of the clown. He mentions Miller's childhood fondness for burlesque and vaudeville which nourished his continuing vision of life as a spectacle, a ritual, as an enormous joke. Through his vision of himself as an inspired clown, Miller is able to regard the world from the vantage point of a Shakespearean fool who has achieved the divine laughter of Nietzsche. In a third positive assessment of Miller's achievement, Bertrand Mathieu terms *The Collossus of Maroussi* (1941) "a neglected American classic" in "Henry Miller and the

Symboliste Belief in a Universal Language" (*AntigR* 27:49–57). "The language of the heart" Miller seeks in this work is akin to the "Speech of the Angels" of Swedenborg and the universal language sought for by Baudelaire and Rimbaud.

Felice Flannery Lewis offers a new perspective on a famous controversy in "*Tropic of Cancer* on Trial: The Correspondence of Henry Miller and Elmer Gertz" (*Pages* 1:297–303). Lewis includes in their entirety the letters and telegrams exchanged by Miller and his Chicago lawyer during the 1961 court battle. Her introductory comments on the Chicago case and the friendship begun between the two men enhance earlier treatments of the legal battle made by E. R. Hutchinson and Charles Rembar. Lewis also announces that she has an edition of the complete correspondence between Miller and Gertz forthcoming from the Southern Illinois University Press.

L. L. Lee's *Vladimir Nabokov* (TUSAS 266) is the latest in a series of brief introductions to the work of America's most illustrious émigré. Lee's volume differs from those of Douglas Fowler and Donald E. Morton (see *ALS 1974*, pp. 263–64) in its inclusion of substantial treatments of Nabokov's early Russian novels and stories. Individual discussions expand the thesis Lee first presented in a 1964 article (see *ALS 1964*, p. 163) that proclaimed the spiral Nabokov's primary structural image. Unfortunately, Lee's attempt to be all-inclusive—not only in the works he chooses to cover but in criticism on these works as well—makes for tight, complex commentaries that are often as perplexing as the texts under scrutiny. The attempt to combine disparate readings of *Pale Fire*, for instance, leads to a series of compromises that warp the arguments of critics discussed and does little to unravel the complexities of the novel itself. A narrower, but more satisfying treatment of Nabokov in a book-length work appears in Elizabeth W. Bruss's *Autobiographical Acts: The Changing Situation of a Literary Genre* (Baltimore: Johns Hopkins Univ. Press). Bruss argues for a new set of criteria by which autobiographies should be judged, one growing from the "speech act" concepts expounded by J. L. Austin and John Searle. Rejecting the strictures of Roy Pascal on modern autobiography, Bruss contends that Nabokov—and by extension, other modern autobiographers—never intended to represent "the whole man" in autobiography. Nabokov permeates the entire volume as Bruss discusses John Bunyan, James Boswell, and Thomas De Quincey to prepare readers for a consideration of the "almost

Olympian impersonality" of Nabokov's autobiography *Speak, Memory* and his "burlesque of autobiography in *Lolita*" (p. 18). Bruss's perceptive readings of the two works are a fine contribution to Nabokov scholarship as well as convincing support for her assertions on the present state of a literary genre.

Periodical criticism of Nabokov focused on his novel *Lolita* in 1976. Samuel Schuman offers "a new source of allusion and illusion" in "A Tempest in a Fleshpot" (*Mosaic* 10,i:1–5) as he demonstrates that Nabokov builds parallels to *The Tempest* in *Lolita*. Schuman's brief but illuminating note extends the seemingly infinite number of allusions to be found in the work, a task also undertaken by Thomas H. Miles in "Lolita: Humbert's Playful Goddess" (*NConL* 4,v:5–7). Miles finds similarities between Nabokov's preteen nymph and Lalita, a goddess in Tibetan-Tantric Buddhism. He makes such a convincing case for these ties that his suggestion that the similarities are "apparently coincidental, yet significant" seems both contradictory and unnecessary.

Three substantial articles treat Nabokov's late novels. In "'The Viewer and the View': Chance and Choice in *Pale Fire*" (*SAF* 4: 203–21), David Walker gives a lively reading of the novel stressing Nabokov's belief that "the essence of art lies not in its 'text but in its texture'" as John Shade's poem contends. Walker approaches *Pale Fire* as "a three-dimensional game of chess" composed of "the story, the real story, and the real, real story." Walker's graph of the 3D checkerboard plots might reveal the complexities of the work better to an undergraduate audience than would a week of lectures. Claude Mouchard's "Le Docteur Froid" (*Critique* 32:311–16) concerns Nabokov's attitude toward Freud and Freudians, particularly as seen in his novel *Ada* (1969). Mouchard contends that the Freud who is attacked by Nabokov is a caricature, the purveyor of a form of systematic knowledge which is either absurd or obvious. He is critical of Nabokov's view of Freudianism because it leads him to ignore the real question Mouchard believes Freud's insights pose to writers, i.e., does psychoanalysis mean the death of literature? A final essay by Richard F. Patteson treats "Nabokov's *Transparent Things*: Narration by the Mind's Eyewitness" (*CollL* 3:102–12). Comparing the 1972 novel to the earlier *Pnin* (1957), Patteson finds that though the two works are superficially very different, they are alike in narrative structure. In both cases the structure is spiral, not circular as has been argued. Patteson, then, supports the reading of the work in Lee's volume described earlier in this essay.

iii. The Southerners

Michael Hoffman treats six book-length studies of southern literature in his chapter of *ALS 1976* and most devote substantial chapters or essays to writers in the 1930s to 1950s period. The most controversial of these works is Walter Sullivan's *A Requiem for the Renascence: The State of Fiction in the Modern South*. Sullivan tolled the death knell for the Southern Renascence in October 1974 when he delivered the four essays included in his collection as part of Mercer's University's Lamar Memorial Lecture Series. The leader of the Loyal Opposition on the issue, Louis D. Rubin, Jr., responds to Sullivan's pessimistic assessment of contemporary southern literature in a provocative essay answering the question "Is the Southern Literary Renascence Over?" in *The Rising South*, ed. Donald R. Noble and Joab L. Thomas (University: Univ. of Ala. Press), I,72–91. Rubin characterizes the opposing arguments as Sullivan's "Vanderbilt Apocalyptic School of Southern Literary Interpretation" and Rubin's own "Chapel Hill Pollyanna School of the same." While he personally cannot agree with Sullivan that literature of the contemporary American South has lost the regional distinctiveness of the work of the Vanderbilt Fugitives, Faulkner, Porter, McCullers, or O'Connor, Rubin suggests it is time for the question to be considered by a new generation of critics: "We had better be honest enough to recognize that the new writing of the 1960's and 1970's does not and can not hold the interest and offer the excitement of discovery to us that the writing of our own generation was able to do." He calls for "a moratorium, not on the continued criticism of the contemporary southern literary scene, but on its continued criticism in terms of Is the Southern Renascence Over?" Chapel Hillian C. Hugh Holman enters the debate from a different angle in "The Southern Novelist and the Uses of the Past" (*SHR* 10,bicentennial issue:1–12) as he reviews the qualities which have traditionally distinguished southern fiction, principally the southern writer's "sense of the tragic implications of life and history" growing from the unique southern experience of the Civil War and Reconstruction. Holman forecasts no end of a literary era; his essay stresses the continuity of southern literary traditions from the work of Caroline Gordon and Margaret Mitchell through Margaret Walker's *Jubilee* (1966). Identifying Faulkner as the great figure of southern literature and Robert Penn Warren as a close second, he cites William Styron as one of several fine contemporary inheritors of this tradition.

A contributor to the Agrarian manifesto *I'll Take My Stand* (1930) is the subject of Robert G. Benson's "The Excellence of John Donald Wade" (*MissQ* 29:233–39). This brief biography and appreciation of Wade's contribution to the Agrarian movement is followed by Gerald J. Smith's "John Donald Wade: A Bibliographical Note" (*MissQ* 29:241–44), which lists 29 items to be added to M. Thomas Inge's comprehensive bibliography of primary sources appended to his 1969 edition of Wade's biography of Augustus Baldwin Longstreet.

The fiction of Fugitive poet Allen Tate figures prominently in the October issue of the *Southern Review* devoted to an assessment of Tate's career. Walter Sullivan's *"The Fathers* and the Failures of Tradition" (*SoR* 12:758–66) suggests that Tate's thesis in the 1938 novel might be paraphrased as "the South would have been better off had it been formed along medieval lines." It is Tate's longing for a white rather than black peasantry and Catholic rather than Protestant religion for the region which supports Sullivan's view that "the mythology around which southern civilization was organized was wrong" in Tate's view. George Core argues that Tate's criticism and fiction are as integral a part of southern literature as is his poetry in "Allen Tate and the South (*SoR* 12:767–75). Lynette Carpenter also treats Tate's single novel in "The Battle Within: The Beleaguered Consciousness in Allen Tate's *The Fathers*" (*SLJ* 8,ii:3–23). Making use of the recently published correspondence between Tate and Donald Davidson (see *ALS 1974*, pp. 339–40), Carpenter offers a close reading of the novel focusing on Lacy Buchan as the main character. As "a poet's novel," *The Fathers* profits from such close scrutiny. Taken with the assessments of the novel in *SoR*, Carpenter's article argues convincingly for a more prominent place in literary study for the novel than it has previously held.

Robert Penn Warren's "A Conversation with Cleanth Brooks" (*The Possibilities of Order: Cleanth Brooks and his Work*, ed. Lewis P. Simpson, Baton Rouge: La. State Univ. Press, pp. 1–124) records the thoughts of both men on subjects of common interest to them since their association began at Vanderbilt in the mid-twenties and forms a document of major importance on American literature's most revered literary collaborators. Marshall Walker considers Warren as a critic and creative writer in "Making Dreams Work: The Achievement of Robert Penn Warren" (*London Magazine* 15,v:33–46). Terming Warren "an enlightened conservative Southerner," Walker defends the author against the criticism of academics who he feels are suspicious of Warren's popularity. Published criticism appearing in 1976 suggests that such a defense is no longer necessary, however. The lion's share of critical attention focused on Warren's best-seller, *All the King's Men* (1946), but his world view as seen in less familiar novels is also a topic this year. In one minor note, "A Key to Robert Penn Warren's 'When the Light Gets Green'" (*CEA* 38,ii:16–18) Patrick W. Shaw develops parallels between the story and Andrew Marvell's "The Garden," which Warren and Brooks included in the 1938 edition of *Understanding Poetry*. Two critics dealing with different novels come to the same conclusion about Warren's use of naturalism. In "Warren's *Night Rider* and the Issue of Naturalism: The 'Nightmare' of Our Age" (*SLJ* 8,ii:41–61), Richard Law asserts that *Night Rider* is "a philosophical novel in the best sense of the term." While the protagonist Perse Munn accepts the doctrine of naturalism, his belief in its deterministic doctrines gives him a convenient excuse for inaction. Through the novel Warren argues the existence of "a pragmatic inadequacy in naturalism; it offers Munn nothing he can use, nothing he can live by." A similar rejection of naturalism occurs in *Band of Angels*, according to Alma A. Ilacqua's "Amanda Starr: Victim of Her Own False Assumptions" (*HSL* 8: 178–89). In this instance the novel's protagonist considers and then rejects determinism as an approach to life.

Four recent articles on *All the King's Men* approach the work in a variety of ways. James A. Grimshaw's useful "Robert Penn Warren's *All the King's Men*: An Annotated Checklist of Criticism" (*RALS* 6: 23–69) is complete through 1972 with occasional later entries. The descriptive annotations are helpful and the index to critics makes the chronological checklist even more valuable. Richard Hannaford elevates a minor character to membership in a triumvirate he sees at the center of the novel in "Sugar-Boy and Violence in *All the King's Men*" (*NConL* 4,iii:10–13). Though Sugar-Boy is less articulate than Willie Stark or Jack Burden, as their chauffeur he is in physical control of their movement. His centrality underscores the chaos of the modern age that entraps Stark and Burden according to this provocative reading of the novel. Dennis M. Welch defends the novel against charges that politically the work is superficial and simplistic in "Image Making: Politics and Character Development in *All the King's Men*" (*HSL* 8:155–77). Citing current political science textbooks as evidence of the importance of "personality cults" to the success of politicians, Welch terms Warren's treatment of Willie Stark's image-making evidence of the political sophistication of the work. The opposing critics cited by Welch, however—such as Saul Maloff, Jonathan Baumback, Orville Prescott, Wallace Douglas, Alfred Kazin, and Roger Sale—base their judgments on a wide variety of observations suggesting the novel does not concern itself with the intricacies of the political process. If one were to refute these critics' assertions, it would have to be done on a sounder basis than the single one Welch chooses. Robert E. Snyder treats *All the King's Men* as one of four novels based on the figure of Huey Long in "The Concept of Demagoguery: Huey Long and His Literary Critics" (*LaS* 15:61–83). Snyder reviews the reception of Hamilton Basso's *Sun in Capricorn* (1942), Dos Passos's *Number One* (1943), Adria Locke Langley's *A Lion is in the Streets* (1945), and Warren's novel to demonstrate that the public accepted these fictional works as factual accounts of Long's personality and career. Of the four works, Warren's is the most successful artistically, but Snyder devotes his attention to Basso's novel as the most offensive in terms of its interpretation of Long: "Of the four writers . . . Basso was the only one to openly and consistently grind his ideological axe against Longism," in Snyder's view. Snyder's unstated thesis seems to be that fictional interpretations of historical figures, in this case of Huey Long, are unfair tactics to use for political commentary.

There are two books on Thomas Wolfe, issued by subsidy publishers. In *Thomas Wolfe: A Study in Psychoanalytic Literary Criticism* (Ardmore, Pa.: Dorrance), Richard Steele chooses to ignore biographical information completely in favor of equating Eugene Gant and Thomas Wolfe in this reading of *Look Homeward, Angel*. There is general disservice both to the study of Wolfe and to psychoanalytic literary criticism in this confused volume. Elaine Westall Gould's *Look Behind You, Thomas Wolfe: Ghosts of a Common Tribal Heritage* (Hicksville, N.Y.: Exposition Press) is an unintentionally entertaining defense of the Westall family in response to unfavorable portraits of individual members drawn in many of Wolfe's works. The only Westall denigrated in Gould's consideration is Wolfe's mother, whose "lack of good breeding" stands in contrast to that of the rest of the Westall brood in Gould's opinion.

In the brief monograph, *The Wolfe Family in Raleigh* (Raleigh, N.C.: Wolf's Head Press), Richard Walser investigates the weak linkage between Thomas Wolfe's family and Raleigh. When Walser cites sexually explicit legal documents in describing W. D. Wolfe's divorce from his first wife, he reveals new portions of family history. Walser's monograph deserves a wider audience than the limited edition of one hundred copies can accommodate.

Wolfe's North Carolina ties are also the subject of Louis D. Rubin, Jr.'s "Thomas Wolfe and the Place He Came From" (*VQR* 52:183–202). In one sense, this article is a reconsideration of statements Rubin made in print in 1953 which emphasized Wolfe's affinities to recognized southern writers. At that time Rubin felt Wolfe's identity as a southern writer was in question and so he tried to show what made Wolfe's work similar to that of other southern writers; today Rubin is interested in what makes Wolfe different from them. Wolfe's stature as a major writer of the South requires an expanded definition of who and what a southern writer is. In contrast to Rubin's affirmation of Wolfe's stature as a writer, Nigel Hampton claims that "a sense of shame hovers over Wolfe's work" in "Who's Ashamed of Thomas Wolfe?" (*CEA* 38,i:18–20). We never get a clear definition of "sense of shame," and so we never quite understand the question posed in the title. Apparently Wolfe's major flaw as a writer was "the shame of extravagance."

Several brief notes and an article consider specific aspects of individual works in 1976. Charmian Green underscores Wolfe's interest in Carlyle by comparing passages from the conclusions to *Look Homeward, Angel* and "The Everlasting Yea" section of *Sartor Resartus* in "Wolfe, Carlyle, and 'the Imprisonment of the Actual'" (*AN&Q* 13:118–20). The title of Robert McIlvane's discussion of Wolfe's choice of family name gives both his thesis and best supporting evidence—"Thomas Wolfe's GarGANTuan Family" (*NConL* 6,i:2–5). Elizabeth Evans contributes a more substantial essay on "Music in *Look Homeward, Angel*" (*SLJ* 8,ii:62–73), which outlines Wolfe's allusions to popular, classical, and folk music in his most famous work. Her treatment does not lead to any broad conclusions on the topic, however; instead she is content with enumerating instances of "Wolfe's conscious use of musical experience for specific purposes in the novel." Evans also writes of "Thomas Wolfe: Some Echoes from Mark Twain" (*MTJ* 18,ii:5–6) and finds evidence in *Of Time and the River* and "The Web of Earth" of the same image patterns contrasting light and darkness to be found in *Huck Finn.*

Robert F. Kiernan's *Katherine Anne Porter and Carson McCullers: A Reference Guide* (Boston: G. K. Hall) provides a much-needed annotated checklist of secondary sources on both southern writers. Kiernan's checklist is complete through 1973 with occasional later entries on both figures; his succinct introductions to the two sections of the volume summarize the critical response to their work documented in the volume as a whole. Kiernan's annotations are precise and amazingly inclusive, considering the necessary brevity of each entry. His abstracting skill is particularly evident in his treatment of book-length works.

Charles W. Smith's "A Flaw in Katherine Anne Porter's 'Theft': The Teacher Taught" (*CEA* 38,ii:19–21) argues that "even very talented writers make mistakes." His suggestion that the opening sentence of Porter's story be doubled in length to make it grammatically correct and easily understood ignores other considerations the author might have had in mind in constructing the sentence. In a feminist consideration of "Katherine Anne Porter and the Ordeal of Southern Womanhood" (*SLJ* 9,i:47–60), Jane Flanders approaches Porter biographically as a woman with "no acceptable models of womanhood" during her childhood and whose fiction is filled with female characters who, like herself, must struggle with "the restrictions of the role of Southern Womanhood." Focusing on the Miranda stories in *Pale Horse, Pale Rider,* Flanders delineates a prominent character in Porter's fiction, a woman "committed to flight, to withdrawal from experience and evasion of human ties."

In "Carson McCullers' 'Proletarian Novel' " (*SIH* 5:8–13), Joan S. Korenman agrees with Leslie Fiedler's description of *The Heart is a Lonely Hunter* as "the last of the 'proletarian novels,' a true Depression book" (*Love and Death in the American Novel*). Her brief discussion notes anticapitalistic overtones particularly prominent in imagery surrounding characters who "can be judged by the way they handle money." Edgar E. MacDonald has a more formidable project in mind in "The Symbolic Unity of *The Heart is a Lonely Hunter*" (*A Festschrift for Professor Marguerite Roberts*, ed. Frieda Elaine Penninger [Richmond, Va.: Univ. of Richmond Press], pp. 168–87). Responding to critics such as Ihab H. Hassan who see a "failure of form" in the novel, MacDonald delineates an "elaborate and occult symbolism" underlying "an almost mathematically determined" structure he finds in the novel. "For Carson McCullers, knowledge obviously means *freedom*" and her novel's structure, built as it is on Gnostic cosmology, ends with an affirmation of life in MacDonald's view. This careful reading of the work successfully challenges many accepted interpretations of the novel and should be taken into consideration in any future treatment of the work.

In a brief note James Missy discusses "A McCullers Influence on Albee's *The Zoo Story*" (*AN&Q* 13:121–23). Ties between the two writers go beyond their acquaintance when Albee adapted *The Ballad of the Sad Cafe* to the stage. Missy compares "A Tree. A Rock. A Cloud" to *The Zoo Story* and suggests the authors share the same attitude toward love. In a second article more directly commenting on McCullers's works adapted to other media, Louis D. Giannetti's "*The Member of the Wedding*" (*LFQ* 4:28–38) declares this work "a neglected minor masterpiece of the American theater." While his primary subject is the film version of the work, Giannetti discusses the novel and stage versions as well, noting that the essentials of plot and characterization remain substantially unchanged in all three forms.

Eudora Welty discusses her use of history, folklore, and southern humor in her first novel in *Fairy Tale of the Natchez Trace* (Jackson: Miss. Historical Society, 1975) and much of the most informative commentary on Welty's work in 1976 shares this preoccupation with her historic and mythic sources. Originally presented as a lecture to the historical society in March 1975, Welty's essay cites a Grimm fairy tale as the basis of *The Robber Bridegroom* (1942) but also emphasizes the local folklore and legends of the area she incorporates into the novel. Despite its brevity, the essay is useful not only for its discussion of the genesis of this single novel but for its delineation of a method of incorporating myth and historic fact present in many of her works. Hunter McKelva Cole annotates 27 recorded statements made by Welty from 1949 to 1973 on her fellow Mississippian in "Welty on Faulkner" (*NMW* 9:28–49). Cole terms the writers "complementary geniuses."

Though three dissertations treating broad themes in Welty's novels and stories were completed in 1976, the single book-length work published is Victor H. Thompson's *Eudora Welty: A Reference Guide* (Boston: G. K. Hall). Thompson annotates criticism on Welty's work since the publication of her first short story in 1936 and continuing into 1975. Useful as the volume is, it could have been of even more service with a more detailed index and a brief listing of primary sources for the convenience of readers. In his Introduction, Thompson notes the dearth of book-length works on Welty; only four full-length books and two monographs have appeared in the 34 years of Welty criticism he reviews.

Thompson's observations on the present state of scholarship on Welty make one aware of how piecemeal her works are usually studied. Continuing the trend, several valuable but brief articles approach single stories from a single perspective. Despite its title, Gary Carson's "The Romantic Tradition in Eudora Welty's *A Curtain of Green*" (*NMW* 9:97–100) concerns only the title story of Welty's first collection, not the entire volume. Carson seems to draw his conclusions from a wider sampling of Welty's work, however, when he asserts that in this story "the perspectives of the visionary and the innocent seem hopelessly at odds, a typical situation in Welty's fiction." A second story from *A Curtain of Green* is the subject of two brief notes. Jeanne R. Nostrandt cites an old Norse tale anthologized widely in textbooks in use in Mississippi during Welty's childhood as a source for the characterization of Phoenix Jackson in "Welty's 'A Worn Path'" (*Expl* 34:item 33). Frank R. Ardolino's "Life out of Death: Ancient Myth and Ritual in Welty's 'A Worn Path'" (*NMW* 9:1–9) is far less precise than Nostrandt's article in its investigation of the theme of rebirth in the story. Ardolino finds support for a positive interpretation of Phoenix Jackson's unfinished journey through a brief survey of rebirth myths in Greek, Roman, and Christian cultures. Too much ground is covered for adequate support, but fortunately the interpretation is so common that few critics need persuasion.

In "Aaron Burr in Eudora Welty's 'First Love'" (*NMW* 8:75–83),

Victor H. Thompson traces the author's use of historical materials in the story and suggests that personal history and the public record converge through the interaction of the main characters. John M. Warner presents a slightly different reading of the same work in "Eudora Welty: The Artist in 'First Love'" (*NMW* 9:77–87). Viewing the story as "a parable about art," Warner also discusses the historical basis for Welty's characterization of Aaron Burr and attributes the negative portrait of Burr to Welty's reading of McCaleb's *The Aaron Burr Conspiracy* (1902; 1936). A final article on Welty's use of history and myth treats the story "Circe" from *The Bride of Innisfallen* (1955). In "Eudora Welty's Circe: A Goddess Who Strove with Men" (*SSF* 13:481–89), Andrea Goudie compares the story to its Homeric analogue and notes the compassion Welty displays toward the goddess who cannot understand the ways of men.

Three substantial articles take a broader look at several of Welty's works. In "Eudora Welty: The Three Moments" (*VQR* 51[1975]: 605–27), John A. Allen finds that Welty's feminine perspective permeates her depiction of heroism in her major works. Making light of "the posturing male hero-adventurer," Welty often models her protagonists after the Perseus figure as she does in *The Golden Apples*: "In the first moment of the heroic stroke, the hero wields the sword; in the second moment, he becomes the victim of that stroke. In the third moment he achieves some measure of gain in understanding which leads to self renewal." Feeling and perception are required of heroes in Welty's work, according to Allen. R. J. Gray's "Eudora Welty: A Dance to the Music of Order" (*CRevAS* 7:57–65) argues that "movement from order to confusion is characteristic of Welty's fiction." Gray presents readings of "A Memory" and *Delta Wedding* to support his assertion that Welty subtly criticizes "traditionalism, regionalism and Southern-ness" in these and other works. A final article on Welty treats two volumes that have been ignored by academic critics since they received accolades from reviewers when they first appeared. In "Eudora Welty and the Children's Hour" (*MissQ* 29:109–18), Jeanne Rolfe Nostrandt sees Welty's 1964 children's book, *The Shoe Bird*, as a direct offspring of experiences recorded in Welty's photographs of the early thirties eventually published in *One Time, One Place* (1970). The children's pageant at a black church seen in the photos first appeared in Welty's writings in her 1943 essay "Pageant of Birds." In *The Shoebird* the personal experience of the thirties is realized in fiction. This intriguing article traces the movement of a visual image into art.

iv. Popular Fiction

Biographies of Christopher Morley and Raymond Chandler offer perspectives on the American reading public in the thirties and forties that are augmented by broader based studies of American writers as reflectors of the American popular culture of this period. Alfred Kazin suggests that a desire for popularity itself caused the dependence of many writers on alcohol in " 'The Giant Killer': Drink and the American Writer" (*Commentary* 61,iii:44–50). Kazin posits the thesis that "only in America have first-class novelists been driven to 'prove' their acceptability by also becoming best-sellers" as can be seen in the careers of John O'Hara, J. P. Marquand, Dashiell Hammett, John Steinbeck, and Thomas Wolfe, among writers of the thirties and forties. Kazin's conclusion that "the drive for success of every kind, the hunger for prestige, fame and money" eventually "drove all these writers to drink" seems a simplistic interpretation of a complex problem.

a. **The Best-Sellers.**   Earl F. Bargainnier reviews a century of southern popular literature in "The Myth of Moonlight and Magnolias" (*LaS* 15:5–20). Bargainnier sees *Gone With the Wind* as a pivotal work in the rise and fall of a vision of the old South, which C. Vann Woodward termed "one of the most significant inventions of the new South." Margaret Mitchell's novel signals the decline of the force of the myth by focusing attention on four main characters, rather than two. It is the energy of the vigorous characters of the new South, Rhett Butler and Scarlett O'Hara, that attracts attention from the representatives of the old South, Ashley and Melanie Wilkes, who fade into the background full of "moonlight and magnolias." Bargainnier's brief but incisive review of scholarship on the development of the myth makes this essay particularly valuable. Richard Harwell's edition of *Margaret Mitchell's* Gone With the Wind *Letters, 1936–1949* (New York: Macmillan) offers more information on the novel and its author than any single work published in the last 40 years. Harwell has chosen over 300 letters written by Mitchell to correspondents all over the country concerning the writing, publication, and success of the novel and its 1939 film version. Mitchell's letters are lively and entertaining, as well as informative. In his Introduction Harwell describes the large collection of letters, manuscripts, and memorabilia in the Margaret Mitchell Marsh Collection at the University of Georgia Libraries (over 50,000 items in all), and if Leslie Fiedler's high praise for the novel discussed in the introduction to this chapter is a sign of growing critical interest in her work, there is a wealth of primary material available to scholars.

Christopher Morley, one of the foremost arbiters of popular taste in America from the mid-twenties to the mid-fifties, is the subject of two critical biographies, after a decade of virtual neglect in published criticism. As one of the founders of the *Saturday Review of Literature* and a judge for the Book-of-the-Month Club selections for 30 years, Morley left his mark on the literature of the entire period. In *Christopher Morley* (TUSAS 278), Mark I. Wallach and Jon Bracker approach Morley as a literary promoter, one whose own early fiction endowed the bookselling trade with the romance and excitement Morley himself found there. The authors treat Morley's essays, poetry, and fiction chronologically within chapters devoted to each genre and, following the format of the Twayne series, include a chronology of his life, notes, and an annotated bibliography of primary and secondary sources. The authors have done an excellent job of providing an overview of Morley's work and its popular reception. Frequent references to materials in the large Christopher Morley Collection at the University of Texas add a great deal to the value of the study.

The second volume on Morley takes its title from the literary club he founded rivaling the more acerbic gatherings at Alexander Woollcott's Algonquin Round Table. While Wallach and Bracker give only the broadest outline of Morley's private life, Helen McK. Oakley pictures Morley in the context of his family and the literary community he was so much a part of in *Three Hours for Lunch: The Life and Times of Christopher Morley* (New York: Watermill Publishers). Describing herself in the Foreword as "a housewife from Manhasset," Oakley traces Morley's "love affairs with cities" but stresses his life in the Long Island community of Roslyn that was his home for 37 years. As president of the Christopher Morley Knothole Association in the Roslyn-Manhasset area, Oakley uses collections of the author's materials in local libraries and augments these with letters and interviews with his associates. Her opening judgment of the man rings true at the end of her study: "Today, his importance lies not so much in his own writing, solid achievement though that was, as in the part he played in the world of books" (p. xi). Both studies of Morley argue convincingly that popular tastes and *belles lettres* meet in the life and works of Christopher Morley.

Two short articles investigate James Thurber's brief sojourn in Paris in a special issue of the *Lost Generation Journal* (3,i[1975] devoted to Thurber. Richard C. Tobias's "Thurber in Paris: 'Clocks Kept Different Time'" (pp. 2–6) notes that "in bulk Paris provided him with less than five percent of his material." In several of his early essays, however, Thurber presented Paris as a contrast to the very "natural" Columbus of his youth. Thurber approaches Paris with occasional sarcasm and, like Mark Twain's innocents going abroad, makes light of the hallowed shrines of the European world. The remaining articles in the special issue have nothing to add about Thurber in Paris. Peter A. Scholl's "Thurber's Walter Ego: The Little Man Hero" (pp. 8–9,26) identifies the most successful Thurber hero—a Walter Mitty or John Monroe—as "a part-time chump, klutz, and neurotic schlemiel." Phyllis Braunlich's brief "Hot Times in the Catbird Seat" (pp. 10–11,30) outlines the "serious side" of Thurber through his comments on politics and art. Two final articles review Thurber manuscript holdings. Robert Tibbetts's "The Thurber Collection at Ohio State University" (pp. 12–15) describes materials in the collection of this O.S.U. alumnus; and Lewis Branscomb, in "James Thurber and Oral History at Ohio State University" (pp. 16–19), describes the tapes and transcripts of interviews with family, friends, and contemporaries.

Several critics reconsider popular novels and argue for their literary merit. In "*The Bridge of San Luis Rey Revisited*" (*TQ* 19,iii: 76–79), Victor White calls for a reissuing of Thornton Wilder's 1927 novel, terming it "clearly a masterpiece." Jeanette W. Mann gives a reading of the first novel of Jean Stafford in "Toward New Archetypal Forms: *Boston Adventure*" (*SNNTS* 8:291–303). Despite the Pulitzer Prize Stafford won in 1970 for her collected short stories, she has been neglected by critics in Mann's view. Mann suggests that a new consciousness is needed to read Stafford, one not limited by masculine archetypal constructs. Her interpretation of *Boston Adventure*

(1944) relies heavily on Erich Neumann's *The Great Mother: An Analysis of the Archetype* (1956) and is presented as a model of such studies.

b. **Detective Fiction.** Despite its promising title, M. E. Grenander's "The Heritage of Cain: Crime in American Fiction" (*AAAPSS* 423: 47–66) fails to confront the "heritage" because of an arbitrary choice of materials treated. Grenander avoids a discussion of the detective novel by asserting: "I have slighted popular literature which reflects the prevailing ethos, in order to concentrate on enduring works, which subject their culture to searching criticism." In an extended essay which attempts to generalize about crime in 19th- and 20th-century American literature, Grenander's stance leads to the exclusion of pertinent materials and thus runs the risk of distorting the conclusions. Grenander examines attitudes toward crime, the apprehension of criminals, trials, and punishment in the works of Poe, Hawthorne, Melville, and Mark Twain and extends her study into the 20th century by including less arguably "enduring works" by Willard Motley, Herman Wouk, and Rex Stout. The absence of commentary on the works of Hammett, Chandler, or Ross Macdonald is difficult to justify considering the inclusion of these even less recognized 20th-century novelists.

In *The Life of Raymond Chandler* (New York: E. P. Dutton), Frank MacShane terms the Nebraska-born product of an English public school "one of the most important writers of his time" (p. 267). Although Chandler achieved popular success in America, in England he was lionized as a major force in contemporary letters. To the English, Chandler was an innovator who elevated the detective novel to the level of literature. In quotations from the voluminous correspondence, MacShane finds convincing evidence of Chandler's high aims and serious intent; but most readers, I believe, will dislike MacShane's disturbing habit of lauding Chandler at the expense of other writers and of making other wild, gratuitous claims. But there is far more biographical information here than in Philip Durham's admirable critical study (see *ALS 1963*, pp. 157–58), and MacShane's careful consideration of individual works is his best support for his high assessment of Chandler.

Armchair Detective revised its format in 1976 and while it looks more professional and polished, it has not sacrificed its admirable in-

formality or special features such as its yearly checklist of detective
fiction and criticism that have made it both useful and a pleasure to
read. In "Where have all the Values Gone?: The Private Eye's Vision
of America in the Novels of Raymond Chandler and Ross Macdonald" (9:128–31), Etta C. Abrahams argues that Raymond Chandler's
high moral stance continues in the novels of Macdonald. She sees
Macdonald's Lew Archer as an inheritor of the traditions of the old
West, an environmentalist who decries the corruption of the natural
environment much as Chandler's Philip Marlowe attacked the moral
corruption of "America in the guise of Hollywood." William F. Nolan
updates his annotated bibliography of 1973 in "Revisiting the Revisited Hammett Checklist" (9:292–98, 324–29). Nolan's current
checklist begins with a contribution by William Godshalk, who describes the Dashiell Hammett papers at the University of Texas.
Another useful feature of Nolan's list of primary and secondary materials published since 1973 is the addition of citations to the radio
scripts Hammett wrote. In a chatty postscript, Nolan offers some
clues for locating other, as yet unlisted materials and announces that
Steven Marcus and William Godshalk are in the process of writing
full-length biographies of Hammett while Richard Layman is preparing a descriptive bibliography of his works for the University of
Pennsylvania Press.

c. Science Fiction.   Two 1976 volumes attest to the growing scholarly respectability of science fiction. Brian Ash's *Who's Who in Science
Fiction* (New York: Taplinger Publishing Co.) contains 400 brief
biobibliographical entries on writers, editors, screenwriters, and di-
rectors of importance in the field of science fiction. In an introduction Ash briefly surveys the history of the genre beginning with Francis Godwin's *The Man in the Moone* of 1638, but he finds the roots
of contemporary science fiction to grow more directly from the early
19th-century awareness of the social possibilities—both positive and
negative—of technological advancement. Ash also provides a list of
pulp magazines of the twenties and thirties specializing in science
fiction and a chronological listing of all figures included in the volume
to suggest their historical position in the development of the genre.
While entries are less complete than they could be—no publishers are
listed for books and only works in science fiction are included in individual biblographies—Ash does offer a starting point for future

work. *Who's Who in Science Fiction* is most useful for its identification of the major figures in an area of popular culture with which few literary scholars are familiar.

Thomas D. Clareson's *Voices for the Future* (Bowling Green, Ohio: Bowling Green Univ. Popular Press) includes eleven original essays on science fictionists "whose careers had begun by the end of World War Two." A final essay considers the work of Kurt Vonnegut, who has gained the "academic attention" Clareson feels is due many of his precursors. In the first essay of the collection, "The Years of Wonder" (pp. 1–13), science-fiction writer Jack Williamson reviews his early years of publishing in pulps in the late twenties and thirties. He credits Hugo Gernsback, editor of *Science Wonder Stories*, with coining the term *science fiction* in 1929 and speaks of the talented group of writers of *Amazing Stories*, *Weird Tales*, and Gernsback's magazine in much the same terms Frank MacShane lauds the detective writers of the thirties who contributed to *Black Mask*. Clareson's collection identifies the major writers of this period as Jack Williamson, Olaf Stapleton, Clifford D. Simak, Isaac Asimov, Robert A. Heinlein, Ray Bradbury, and Arthur C. Clarke, but he suggests that a projected second volume of essays will add writers to this list. While all of the essays included argue the literary merit of these neglected writers, the most persuasive of them is Maxine Moore's "Asimov, Calvin, and Moses" (pp. 88–103). Moore attributes "an elaborate metaphorical structure" to Asimov's best works "that combines New England Calvinism with the Old Testament Hebraic tradition of the 'Peculiar People' to set forth a highly developed philosophy of mechanistic determinism with a positive ethic to justify it." Moore delights in Asimov's Nabokovian word play and her treatment of his conscious artistry is convincing evidence of his concern for both form and subject matter in nine of his novels. The entire collection heralds the long overdue arrival of academic respectability to the study of this area of popular literature.

d. **Western Fiction.** Mary Beth Crain compares Walter Van Tilburg Clark's most famous novel with its film version in "*The Ox-Bow Incident* Revisited" (*LFQ* 4:240–48) and concludes that William Wellman's film "is not a faithful representation of the actual spirit of Clark's book." While *The Ox-Bow Incident* "is an existentialist novel," Wellman's film is merely "an indictment of mob rule," which was a more palatable message for the film audiences of the thirties than the harder lessons embodied in the novel. "The book leaves the reader in despair for mankind; the film, while exposing man in his sordid reality, still leaves hope for justice and those who carry it out" in Crain's view.

Two articles on novels by Frank Waters are examples of approaches taken by differing "schools" of literary criticism. Frances Malpezzi suggests the need for an expanded role for the feminist critic in "A Study of the Female Protagonist in Frank Waters's *People of the Valley* and Rudolfo Anaya's *Bless Me, Ultima*" (*SDR* 14,ii: 102–10). While many feminist critics have limited themselves to outlining the disparaging portraits of women in literature, Malpezzi finds a more productive purpose to be that of identifying positive treatments of women as she does in the characterizations of Maria in Water's 1939 novel and Ultima in Anaya's 1973 work. Since both novels "portray a stereotypically machismo culture," Malpezzi sees it as ironic to find "positive images of women in respected positions of authority and power" in these works. Christopher Hoy gives a Jungian reading of Waters's 1942 novel in "The Archetypal Transformation of Martiniano in *The Man Who Killed the Deer*" (*SDR* 13,iv:43–56), which traces the main character's movement from "arrogant individuality" to an acceptance of the collective will of his Indian people. Corrupted by the patriarchal values of white society, Martiniano must adapt himself to the matriarchal pueblo culture he wishes to enter. Hoy justifies the superimposition of Jungian thought on the novel by citing Waters's own references to the work of Jung, particularly in *Masked Gods* (1950), and thus makes a strong case for the relevancy of Jung's archetype of the Great Mother to this novel.

As a final item on Western writers, the existence of a new cassette tape series of introductory lectures on individual authors should be noted. Joseph Flora's *The Works of Frederick Manfred* (Deland, Fla.: Everett/Edwards) is one of several 1976 additions to the series that includes lectures on Willa Cather, Walter Van Tilburg Clark, Vardis Fisher, Frank Waters, Harvey Fergusson, and John Steinbeck—each contributed by a noted authority on that author's work. In *The Works of Frederick Manfred*, Flora gives a brief biographical portrait describing Manfred as "a Midwesterner who has preferred to face West" in his work. Like the most successful of the other tapes in the series, Flora's lecture considers the broad issues in his subject's fiction but also devotes attention to a close reading of texts. This and other series from Everett/Edwards on Twentieth Century American Writers, Women's Studies, and Southern American Writers offer useful pedagogical tools for treating many authors included in this review essay.

University of North Carolina, Chapel Hill

15. Fiction: The 1950s to the Present

James H. Justus

The year's work on contemporary fiction offers no surprises and yields no firm trend. A slight decline in the number of books is matched by a similar decline in essays; meretricious work still accounts for too much of the latter, and a middling quality marks most of the books. The most impressive theoretical criticism of the year turns out to be on the nonfiction novel, and, despite its cultist air, the best concentrated work on an individual author is a collection of essays on Pynchon. Critical interest in Mailer and O'Connor remains at about the same high level that these authors have enjoyed for nearly a decade; scholarship in Updike, Roth, and Styron has leveled off; last year's decline in interest in Heller continues; and for the first time in several years there is no major work on either Hawkes or Kesey. There has also been a slight decline in the number of completed dissertations reported—reflecting perhaps the general state of graduate education in English—and their subjects tend to corroborate those found in books and articles: Mailer, Malamud, Coover, Vonnegut, Bellow, Barth, Pynchon.

i. General Studies

a. **Overviews and Special Topics.** The theoretical claims for the validity and importance of the nonfiction novel find their most persuasive expression in *The Mythopoeic Reality: The Postwar American Nonfiction Novel* (Urbana: Univ. of Ill. Press) by Mas'ud Zavarzadeh, who traces those intellectual developments in physics and psychology responsible for smudging the boundary between stable facts and illusory fictions before he proceeds to a formal analysis of the genre. The nonfiction novel spurns the transformation of stark actualities into a "safe zone of unified meaning," explains this critic; it is "transcriptional" rather than interpretive, and it is "bireferential" (i.e., containing a balanced ratio between external and internal referents). Zavarzadeh explicates in separate chapters the three major narrative situations of the nonfiction novel: *exegetical* (Capote's *In Cold Blood*), *testimonial* (Mailer's *The Armies of the Night*), and *notational* (Warhol's *a*). Despite heavy theorizing, the style of *The Mythopoeic Reality* is remarkably clear and forceful—even at times assertive; indeed, some readers may object to Zavarzadeh's uncompromising advocacy when he calls for a scrapping of restrictive taxonomies which distribute narratives into fictional and factual categories according to the types of "reality" they contain, or when he dismisses as "neo-escapist" Bellow, Malamud, Updike, and most nonexperimentalists. This strong book may provoke opposition, but it cannot be ignored.

A special supplement on the "New Journalism" (*JPC* 9[1975]: 95–249), edited by Marshall Fishwick, consists of 17 brief pieces of varying merit, including those by James Green on Hunter Thompson (pp. 204–10); Kent Jackobson, who locates the freakiness of New Journalism in the "radical forms of alienation" in American culture (pp. 183–96); John Brady, who relates the fascinating account of the birth of *Playboy* (pp. 153–61); and Ronald Weber on the attraction of New Journalists to the astronauts and space exploration (pp. 142–52). Two of the more thoughtful essays are Robert J. Van Dellen's analysis of the New Journalists' preoccupation with style, their tendency to collapse subject matter and form, and their systematic elimination of critical distance between fact and fiction (pp. 219–31); and Michael L. Johnson's discussion of how its ironies, comic and satiric devices, and "epistemological paradoxes" make the form "inevitably subversive" (pp. 135–41). Still another attempt at definition and discrimination is "The Children of James Agee" (*JPC* 9:996–1002), in which Charles Gregory and William Dorman insist that the ultimate quality of the New Journalist is his integrity and that his text must be judged by the same criteria as the novelist's or poet's.

Although her critical insights are unoriginal, Josephine Zadovsky Knopp isolates a central theme in *The Trial of Judaism in Contemporary Jewish Writing* (Urbana: Univ. of Ill. Press) which links such Jewish-American writers as Bellow, Roth, and Malamud, to I. B.

Singer and the novelists of the Holocaust; she demonstrates that this "trial" takes three forms: of God, of Jewish tradition, and of the Jews themselves. Knopp includes separate chapters on Singer, Elie Wiesel, Malamud, Bellow, and the chroniclers of the Holocaust.

In a special number on "The Anti-Hero" Melvin J. Friedman recapitulates some familiar traits in his definition of "The Schlemiel: Jew and Non-Jew" (*SLitI* 9,i:139–53). Unhappily, in the more interesting segment, he is less than satisfactory in suggesting "something of the nature of these non-Jewish or quasi-Jewish schlemiels"; he thinks Pynchon's Benny Profane "less a schlemiel" than the protagonists of Mark Harris, but no reasons are given.

In a random sampling of contemporary humorous fiction, Charlotte T. Whaley contrasts "Black and Bright Humor: Comic Vision in the Modern Short Story" (*SWR* 61:370–83) and finds, to nobody's surprise, that "bright" humorists (traditionalists who tend to confirm an order "either within the individual or in the world without") are harder and harder to find. "The Ethics of Contemporary Black Humor" (*ColQ* 24:275–88) is an unpretentious and honest piece by Mathew Winston, who contrasts satire (which is normative and judgmental) with black humor (which uses our standards of behavior only to upset them). Although destructive in impulse, black humor paradoxically increases our sense of complexity "by revealing the limits of our ability to know."

The subversion of the prevailing stoical moralism of the 1950s is the subject of Morris Dickstein's "Seeds of the Sixties: The Growth of Freudian Radicalism" (*PR* 43:501–23), which is built around the personal and intellectual influence of Herbert Marcuse, Paul Goodman, and Norman O. Brown. While Dickstein denies wanting to reduce complexities in such books as *Life Against Death* and *Eros and Civilization* "to moments in my private history," his very thesis is predicated on that linkage.[1] "Marxism and the Writing of Fiction" (*MinnR* 5:98–103) is Scott Sanders's no-nonsense manifesto in which

1. The special Paul Goodman double number of *New Letters* (42,ii–iii) contains a generous sampling of the fiction (which Goodman once described as "expressionist"); two tributes by Meyer Liben and Geoffrey Gardner; Colin Ward's "The Anarchist as Citizen" (pp. 237–45), which complements Dickstein's account; Michael True's "Paul Goodman and the Triumph of American Prose Style" (pp. 228–36), which finds Goodman heir to Thoreau's "antitradition"; and Tom Nicely's "Notes Toward a Bibliography" (pp. 246–53).

Marxism is offered as an alternative to the Modernist notion that
human nature is permanently flawed: "anthropological optimism,"
which sustains faith in the "human potential for creation."

"The Middle-Aged Man in Contemporary Literature: Bloom to
Herzog" (*CLAJ* 20:1–13) is a fairly pointless exercise in which Sam
Bluefarb looks at a random group of characters who suffer *à la* Le-
opold Bloom. Under the rubric of "The Madman as Hero in Contemporary American Fiction" (*JAmS* 10:257–69), Michael P. Woolf sees
an effort by Kesey, Roth, Kerouac, Heller, Pynchon, and others to
reinvent the possibility of heroic action through characters who, despite their gloomy fates, are "profound nonrealists defying the
recognized limits of the possible." In "Conceptions Literary and
Otherwise: Women Writers and the Modern Imagination" (*Novel*
9:141–50), Donna Gerstenberger, a sane voice among the often shrill
feminists, declares that the task facing women writers is that faced
by all modern writers, "the exploration of conceptual limits and
modes."

In "Literature and the Police Function: A Theoretical Perspective" (*The Police in Society*, pp. 123–29), Barry A. Marks contrasts
American popular culture, and its perfectionist tendency, with serious
literature, which communicates a sense that the world is ambiguous,
its problems "unsolvable, and yet finally acceptable." Theodore Ziolkowski's "The Telltale Teeth: Psychodontia to Sociodontia" (*PMLA*
91:9–22) is an entertaining romp through the history of "human
attitudes toward teeth," especially their relation to organismic conceptions of the state. Though Norris's McTeague is curiously missing
in his rollcall of dentists, Ziolkowski cites "philosophers of decay" in
Henderson the Rain King, Couples, V., and *Mother Night.*

From Maurice Friedberg's "The U.S. in the U.S.S.R.: American
Literature through the Filter of Recent Soviet Publishing and Criticism" (*CritI* 2:519–83), crammed with informative statistics, publishing priorities, critical receptions, and the status of ideological
differences, we learn that the tradition of social realism is still highly
prized in Russia, and among contemporary Americans, John Cheever,
William Styron, and Harper Lee are favorites. According to Steven
J. Rubin's "Contemporary American Ethnic Literature in France"
(*JEthS* 3,i[1975]:95–98), French interest in black and Jewish writing, feminist literature, and the work of contemporary American Indians is more sociological than literary.

Checklists of both primary and secondary items for 136 authors, 80 of them American, appear in Alfred F. Rosa and Paul A. Eschholz's *Contemporary Fiction in America and England, 1950–1970: A Guide to Information Sources* (Detroit: Gale Research Co.). The editors also provide a convenient directory of journals hospitable to work on contemporary fiction and a four-sectioned checklist of "Studies and Reference Works" with annotations. Specialists will want to check authors' listings carefully, for although the editors claim "comprehensiveness," a spot-check in the entries under Agee and O'Connor reveals the omission of a few articles.

b. The New Fiction: Theories and Modes. The subject of Tony Tanner's "Games American Writers Play: Ceremony, Complexity, Contestation, and Carnival" (*Salmagundi* 35:110–40) is the contemporary tendency to turn "modes of discourse into objects of discourse," especially the "carnivalization" of recent fiction, which is defined as "an enactment of life freeing itself from old rigidifying forms . . . and releasing an energy of regeneration." In this richly implicative essay, Tanner focuses on three representative novels: Gass's *Willie Masters' Lonesome Wife*, Barth's *Chimera*, and Pynchon's *Gravity's Rainbow*. "Games and Play in Modern American Fiction" (*ConL* 17:44–62) is the result of Robert Detweiler's analysis of 60 novels and short story collections, most of them since 1965, for the purpose of "shaping a literary criticism based on the structure of games and play."

Jerome Klinkowitz's "Poetry in the Novel: American Fiction of the Last Eight Years" (*PAus* 59:61–69) is the best apology for the new fiction yet written. Crisply, cogently, and with only minor hectoring of the traditionalists, Klinkowitz discusses the three characteristics of the fiction beginning in 1967: a penchant for formal experimentalism, self-conscious artistry, and a belief in the "imaginative transformation of reality" *pace* Wallace Stevens and W. C. Williams.

In "Structuralism and the Reading of Contemporary Fiction" (*Soundings* 58[1975]:281–306), R. E. Johnson emphasizes not a specific methodology but ideas which can contribute to "non-linear, even non-spatial" definitions of form which in turn can make sense of such writers as Gass, Barthelme, and Coover. Especially pertinent in this piece of applied criticism is Johnson's analysis of the "exchange structures" of "The Pederson Kid," which point to repetition of patterns as a replacement for plot and character development. Philip Stevick uses examples from Borges, Pynchon, and Barthelme to illustrate his distinctions among "Lies, Fictions, and Mock-Facts" (*WHR* 30:1–12). The mock-fact, because it alters the "traditional equipoise" between the empirical world and the novelist's, makes fiction which denies its own impulses; it conflates the factual and the fictive in its pretense of making statements about the actual world while internally admitting their falsity; and its function is to convert rhetorical possibilities into sprightly invention.

In "*Surfiction*: Plunging into the Surface" (*Boundary* 2 5:153–65), a long critique of Raymond Federman's recent volume (see *ALS 1975*, p. 454), Doris L. Eder objects to those postmodernists who insist upon using multimedia techniques arbitrarily, make a cult of cinematic presentness, assert incoherence and meaninglessness, and pretend that language is not linear and temporal. After listing the progressive stages of the modern distrust of language, Brigitte Scheer-Schäzler, in "Language at the Vanishing Point: Some Notes on the Use of Language in Recent American Literature" (*RLV* 42:497–508), concentrates on the most recent views (that rhetoric is "perverted" and that language is "a control instrument") in Barth, Pynchon, and Nabokov, and in the most radical of these writers, William Burroughs, who advocates the destruction of what he calls "diseased verbal systems." Scheer-Schäzler calls for a new "*aesthetics of the negative*" to deal with style "that defines itself by its absence, by its felt omissions."

Forms of knowledge, cognition, and verification in fiction, and the problems of dealing with a received language are the related subjects in a give-and-take among Donald Barthelme, William Gass, Grace Paley, and Walker Percy in "A Symposium on Fiction" (*Shenandoah* 27,ii:3–31). Perhaps Gass sums up the aim of the new fictionists generally when he declares that poets, like mathematicians, are interested in "formal coherence," not truth.

ii. Norman Mailer

The most flamboyant of the three books on Mailer this year is Jonathan Middlebrook's *Mailer and the Times of His Time* (San Francisco: Bay Books). Stylistically, it is swinging confessional prose; structurally, a conventional sequence of chapters on the major works; substantively, a farrago of cliché, meaningless digression, and congratulatory egocentrism. Of no value to any seasoned scholar of Mailer.

When his subject is in focus, Middlebrook's Mailer is an artist of "constant imagination," and each book is yet one more version of that sensibility. In two other studies the "process of growth" is the emphasis. In *Existential Battles: The Growth of Norman Mailer* (Athens: Ohio Univ. Press), Laura Adams glosses this theme by concentrating on three books, each of which she sees as a culmination of one phase of Mailer's efforts to expand the consciousness and explain the subconscious: *Advertisements for Myself, An American Dream,* and *The Armies of the Night;* a final phase is still "in progress." Similarly, in chronological sequence, Stanley T. Gutman, in *Mankind in Barbary: The Individual and Society in the Novels of Norman Mailer* (Hanover, N.H.: Univ. Press of New England, 1975), traces Mailer's search in his fiction for effective ways to deal with the "limitations on man set by nature and the malfunctions of society"—from mere endurance (*The Naked and the Dead*) and "humanistic socialism" (*Barbary Shore*) to artistic creation (*The Deer Park*) and radical new modes of perception (*An American Dream, Why Are We in Vietnam?*). Along the way Adams places Mailer in the mainstream of American literature by relating his work to "visionaries" rather than "craftsmen," especially in the national penchant for dealing with dualities. She covers Mailer's mayoralty campaign as a serious enterprise, gives considerable attention to the films (especially *Maidstone*), and sees *Of a Fire on the Moon* as a descendant of *Moby-Dick.* One should not be put off by Adams's claim that her approach is "adventurous criticism," an unhappy term which better describes Middlebrook's effort; *Existential Battles* is solid, perceptive, and commonsensical. The weakest aspect of Gutman's study is a tendency to restate earlier observations (e.g., on the sexual component in man's drive for power; the political allegory of *Barbary Shore*; the pivotal importance of "The White Negro"); but the general level of *Mankind in Barbary* has a judicious solidity, and certain specific segments are freshly realized: the relevance to Mailer's temperament of Emersonian and Wordsworthian romanticism, the significance of totemic magic in *An American Dream,* and the clear-eyed assessment of authorial schizophrenia in *The Armies of the Night.*

Observing that Mailer has always been fascinated by characters whose attitudes have been shaped by national myths, Benjamin T.

Spencer ("Mr. Mailer's American Dreams," *Prospects* 2:127–46) examines the writer's efforts to translate a persistent concern with "national mission" into appropriate fictive correlatives. Spencer's most
compelling segment is on the ambiguous conclusion of *An American
Dream*, in which Rojack finds no spiritual alliance with the urban
black but flees west; this failure is redeemed by "the gumption of
Western humor" in *Why Are We in Vietnam?* and the nonfiction, in
which Mailer scraps the White Negro as hero and becomes his own
protagonist for testing his existentialism. This superb essay is also a
corrective to Mailer's more fashionable apologists—i.e., Richard
Poirier and Leo Bersani—who read the fiction "as a mere release of
feelings or a playful display of verbal tactics."

In "Norman Mailer" (*JPC* 9[1975]:174–82), Donald Fishman
observes that Mailer's recent writing incorporates three personae:
the public celebrity, social critic, and the American Writer. Don
Anderson's "Norman Mailer: Man Against the Machine" (*Cunning
Exiles*, pp. 165–97) is mostly a derivative survey of Mailer's use of
the cancer metaphor, his "synoptic imagination," his Manicheanism,
and the "energetic effect" of the voice heard in the journalistic pieces.

iii. Flannery O'Connor

Last year John R. May was pleading for consensus among critics still
arguing about the tension between O'Connor's art and belief (see
ALS 1975, p. 335). This year readers may feel that his terms for mediation in *The Pruning Word: The Parables of Flannery O'Connor*
(Notre Dame, Ind.: Notre Dame Univ. Press) are too loaded: that
"the word of revelation spoken or the gesture of judgment seen" constitutes the dramatic core of O'Connor's fictions, which are "scriptural
in inspiration and parabolic in effect." The New Testament parable *is*
the form of "Revelation," as May convincingly demonstrates; he skillfully shows how the dialogue and diction make such stories as "A
Stroke of Good Fortune" and "The Artificial Nigger" ideal hermeneutic texts. But many of the stories resist such categorizing, and in
fact May often forgets O'Connor's "appropriated form" when discussing works which are not quite parables. *The Pruning Word* is also
notably skimpy in its treatment of the novels: 103 pages are devoted
to the stories, both uncollected and those in the two volumes, and

only 25 pages concern the two novels, where the hermeneutic pattern is less immediately perceptible. In a more detached theological study, "The Heterodoxy of Flannery O'Connor's Book Reviews" (*FOB* 5:3–29), Ralph C. Wood concludes from a survey of her reviews that O'Connor admired people who lived at "the edge of spiritual extremity" (St. Catherine of Siena, Madame Guyon, Karl Barth) and held in low esteem secular humanism, the youth cult of Zen Buddhism, the "empty faith" of Catholic liberals (Eugene McCarthy, Dorothy Day) and the "candied piety" of Catholic conservatives (mostly Irish-American). But Wood's study is most valuable in showing the writer's developing attitude toward Teilhard de Chardin: from advocacy of his scientific mysticism (in 1960), to tempered enthusiasm (in 1961), to unqualified assent to the Vatican's warning of the faithful to beware of Teilhard's theology (in 1963).

If O'Connor's work constitutes a critique rather than a vindication of Teilhard's efforts to reconcile nature and grace, it is also, according to Marion Montgomery, a "corrective to the Manichean confusions" which plague many of Faulkner's characters (and perhaps their creator's vision as well). "Some Reflections on Miss O'Connor and the Dixie Limited" (*FOB* 5:70–81) is a rich but shapeless essay. In "L'Ecriture Catholique de Flannery O'Connor" (*RFEA* 1:125–33), Maurice Lévy delivers less than promised in his thesis: that O'Connor's fiction conveys Catholic truths not directly through themes but obliquely through style.

In "Flannery O'Connor's Devil Revisited" (*SHR* 10:325–33), Preston M. Browning, Jr., contends that the function of O'Connor's devil figure, beyond that as devourer of souls, is to deflate the complacently pious. Patricia D. Maida examines the theme of sight in most of O'Connor's works in "Light and Enlightenment in Flannery O'Connor's Fiction" (*SSF* 13:31–36), settling on the relationship of three recurring images: the tree-line, the sun, and the color purple. In "Flannery O'Connor's Sense of Place" (*SHR* 10:251–59), John F. Desmond finds that the novelist uses Florida as a "topographical symbol for man's attempt to deny the Fall, his link with the natural order and history, and by extension his need for a divine redeemer."

Thomas LeClair argues in "Flannery O'Connor's *Wise Blood*: The Oedipal Theme" (*MissQ* 29:197–205) that Haze's blinding is not

contrived, as some have claimed, since it resolves the Oedipal as well
as the religious theme. Through imagery and allusion, Constance
Pierce shows how "The Mechanical World of 'Good Country People'" (*FOB* 5:30–38) encompasses all three females ("mechanical
people playing at being human") as well as Pointer, who at least
"lives by his perversion." Daniel Walden and Jane Salvia, in "Flannery O'Connor's Dragon: Vision in 'A Temple of the Holy Ghost'"
(*SAF* 4:230–35), believe that the unnamed child is the author's alter
ego, whose story confirms the necessity for accepting mystery—the
basis of both creative genius and religious faith.

     Gabriele Scott Robinson argues for an imagistic and moral affinity
between O'Connor and Joyce through a comparative reading of
"Araby" and "A Temple of the Holy Ghost." "Irish Joyce and Southern O'Connor" (*FOB* 5:82–97) is only partly convincing because
Robinson so deëmphasizes Joyce's aesthetic bias—the single greatest
difference between the two writers—that the impressive similarities
are distorted. David Aiken in fact finds in "Flannery O'Connor's
Portrait of the Artist as a Young Failure" (*ArQ* 32:245–59) that the
satiric object of at least one story—"The Enduring Chill"—is Stephen
Dedalus; O'Connor attempts to "correct" Joyce's failure in judgment
(in giving his hero a man-centered epiphany) but in the process
loses control of her "fine tension between seeing and believing."

     One hopes that Maryat Lee's sprightly "Flannery, 1957" (*FOB* 5:
39–60) is only a segment of a longer memoir in progress. A generous
selection of letters from O'Connor shows both wit (in observing the
social scene) and reverence (in observing the dictates of Christianity). "The Manuscripts of Flannery O'Connor at Georgia College"
(*FOB* 5:61–69) is Robert J. Dunn's lucid account of the provenance
of the papers, a history of their ordering, and a description of the
filing system for the most extensive O'Connor manuscript collection.
Based on narrative development of the fragments, the present ordering in 892 folders eliminates "misleading interpretations or conjectural reconstructions" of the writer's early intentions, though Dunn
warns that precise dating cannot be determined until letters and publishers' records are generally available. Those interested in film versions of O'Connor's work will be interested in two separate pieces by
Patrick Neligan, Jr., and Victor Nunez, "Flannery and the Film Makers" (*FOB* 5:98–104).

iv. Saul Bellow, Bernard Malamud, and Philip Roth

It is perhaps appropriate that alienation is the rubric by which we identify so much of Bellow, the quintessential novelist of the 1950s; but even when articulated by such a serious interpreter as Peter Bischoff (*Saul Bellows Romane: Entfremdung und Suche* [Bonn: Bouvier, 1975]), its implications are predictable, including the sound distinction between alienation as a socially shaped condition and alienation as an inner, private ailment. One of the many shrewd observations here, however, is how Bellow comes full circle with his alienated hero: his Gerontion, Sammler, is just as much a marginal man as predraftee Joseph. Despite his contention that the Bellovian hero's search for personal identity is ontological rather than social, Bischoff devotes nearly twice as many pages to the social forces confronting such diverse protagonists as Herzog, Henderson, and Leventhal than he does to the more crucial inner quests. For all the reality instructors, abstract behavioral models, and grail-like searches, the gritty social texture is finally the interesting ingredient in Bellow's fiction—which many commentators tend to undervalue.

One of the best attempts to show the "Americanness" of Bellow is M. A. Klug's "Saul Bellow: The Hero in the Middle" (*DR* 56:462–78). While Bellow rejects the polar extremes of optimism and pessimism which much of American literature swings between, his protagonists are shaped by such extremes. Characteristically they pursue an ideal self "by willfully restraining" their imagination and intellect. Whereas Klug's essay is firmly grounded in a knowledge of national traits, "Saul Bellow's Henderson as America" (*CentR* 20:189–95) is a kind of bicentennial rhapsody by Eusebio L. Rodrigues: Henderson represents a technological America transfigured by an "unquenchable and radiant power of the human spirit." Alfred Kazin's "From Sweden to America: Mr. Bellow's Planet" (*NewRep* 175,xix:6–8) is simultaneously a tribute to the recipient of the Nobel Prize and an attack on the young innovative fictionists who scorn his traditionalist methods and humane vision.

Ethical dualities in Bellow are the subject of two fine essays. Ralph Berets's "Repudiation and Reality Instruction in Saul Bellow's Fiction" (*CentR* 20:75–101) is an overlong but solid survey of the tensions between alternatives, a major structuring device in all of the novels:

the hero must decide whether to conform to received patterns or to explore new possibilities. Although his focus is on one novel, J. R. Raper fits it into an overall scheme in "Running Contrary Ways: Saul Bellow's *Seize the Day*" (*SHR* 10:157–68). He notes that variations of the "Spirit of Alternatives" occur in six out of eight novels and inform the theme "that a man's character develops by running contrary ways." In *Seize the Day*, the climactic coffin scene marks the beginning of a process by which Tommy may discover that the sources of his fantasies "lie in the collective mind of man and, through this realization, free himself of their destructive personal influence."

Ralph C. Hainer adds "The Octopus in *Henderson the Rain King*" (*DR* 55:712–19) as a symbol of death to the other well-explicated symbols of pig, frog, and lion: the reverberations from the encounter at the French marine station never recur in the last third of the novel and indicate that Henderson's growth has been complete. "Artistry and the Depth of Life: Aspects of Attitude and Technique in *Mr. Sammler's Planet*" (*AWR* 25,lvi:138–53), despite Roger Jones's claim that the key to the novel is Bellow's 1967 essay, "Skepticism and the Depth of Life," is mostly a familiar general analysis which finds that the "philosophical, essay-like, sometimes speechifying, aphoristic, speculative" bits are all unified in Bellow's vision of contemporary reality.

In their edition of *Bernard Malamud: A Collection of Critical Essays* (Englewood Cliffs, N.J.: Prentice-Hall, 1975), Leslie A. and Joyce W. Field include an interview with the novelist, a chronology, a selected bibliography, and ten essays, three of which are new with this volume. In "An Interview with Bernard Malamud" (pp. 8–17), we hear the novelist's opinions on the fictional use of *schlemiels* ("Willy-nilly, it reduces to stereotypes people of complex motivations and fates"), the term *Jewish-American*, which he considers reductive, and teaching. Despite Malamud's suspicions about the term, Leslie Field's own contribution, "Portrait of the Artist as Schlemiel (*Pictures of Fidelman*)" (pp. 117–29) is yet another attempt to define the type and its application to Malamud's book, which Field describes as a combination of the picaresque and the *Bildungsroman*.

Sam Bluefarb finds diverse strands of influence in "The Syncretism of Bernard Malamud" (pp. 72–79): proletarian, realistic, psychological, mythic. Richard Astro's contribution is the prize of this volume: "In the Heart of the Valley: Bernard Malamud's *A New*

Life" (pp. 143–55). Though he makes no great claims for the novel (he finds it too dependent upon Leslie Fiedler), Astro notes the literal parallels from Oregon State that went into this *roman à clef* and discusses both themes—the flawed dream of the mythic west and a Jew's uneasy journey to human dignity.

Going beyond the sexual diagnosis of Roth's most popular novel, Gene Bluestein, in *"Portnoy's Complaint: The Jew as American"* (*CRevAS* 7:66–76), stresses the political and cultural dimension; the main thrust of the novel, he argues, is "to question the assumptions of Jewish exceptionalism." His description of the consequences of the breakdown of liberal theology and values makes this Roth's "most important contribution to American literary tradition."

Naseeb Shaheen's "Binder Unbound, or, How Not to Convert the Jews" (*SSF* 13:376–78) points out that in this story, which begins with a Jewish scene and ends with a Christian one, the Rabbi's conversion is temporary because of "duress." In "The Myths of Summer: Philip Roth's *The Great American Novel"* (*ConL* 17:171–90), Ben Siegel insists that Roth's humor, more surrealistic and obsessive since *Portnoy's Complaint*, is self-conscious and moralistic in its exposure of the disparity between a professed idealism and the underlying grossness in American society. Pierre Michel describes that obsession as the "sublimation of experience to the actualities of the extravagant" in "Philip Roth's Reductive Lens: From 'On the Air' to *My Life as a Man"* (*RLV* 42:509–19). He believes the "level of language" in the three-fold narrative of *My Life as a Man* suggests that Roth is content to interpret life as a "deterministic and unexplained sequence of accidents on which no conscious patterning can have any effects."

v. John Barth and Thomas Pynchon

David Morrell says that his *John Barth: An Introduction* (University Park: Pa. State Univ. Press) is for "lay people as opposed to academics," and certainly his method has an unpretentious pattern: plot summary and account of each work's genesis, critical reception, and interpretation. Lay and professional readers alike should object to having a dominant Barthian theme tossed off as "self-knowledge is generally bad news," which is to vulgarize a drama that in Barth is already perilously close to being boring. Generally, however, Morrell is sensible and perceptive. He gives detailed comparison of the two versions (1956, 1967) of *The Floating Opera*,[2] and he makes sense out of the relationship between the themes of nihilism and relativism in the first novel and the second. If he too readily accepts Robert Scholes's *fabulation* for Barth's kind of fiction, he is surely right in dismissing *black humor* as the proper term. He also contends that Barth's verbal extravagance parallels Hemingway's spare style in reflecting visions of reality: whereas Hemingway's focus on things in their ordered places can be a refuge from thought, Barth's focus on language can be a "refuge from the complexity of things"—mutability and multiplicity. Though informative, the last two chapters—on Barth's biography and writing habits—are annoyingly chatty.

Zoltán Abádi-Nagy's "The Principle of Metaphoric Means in John Barth's Novels" (*HSE* 9[1975]:5–31; 10:73–94) is an exhausting and reified two-part analysis of the types and function of metaphor in Barth's works. The key term is Barth's, meaning an author's investiture with emblematic value of every aspect of his fiction—not only the form or point of view, but also the genre and the "fact of the artifact itself." Abádi-Nagy is clearest when glossing the geometric motifs: the symbolic use of interlocking triangles in *The Floating Opera*, the "compressed triangle" in *The End of the Road*, the circle in *The Sot-Weed Factor*, and the spiral in *Perseid* and *Chimera*.

In "Todd Andrews, Ontological Insecurity, and *The Floating Opera*" (*Crit* 18,ii:34–50), Charles B. Harris investigates the connection between Todd's fear of death and the "defensive" and "desperate" form of the novel. Bodily pleasures are couched in images of decaying flesh, which point to Todd's irrational fear of the human body. Despite Barth's broadly comic regard for most "modern intellectualisms," Freudianism is at the "center" of the first novel: this is Eugene Korkowski's view in "The Excremental Vision of Barth's Todd Andrews" (*Crit* 18,ii:51–58), an anatomy of "anal etiology." Korkowski makes much of the "anal psychodynamic" puns (crap game), analogies (the famous pickle jars become an equation of Todd's filing system), behavioral patterns (daily paying of hotel bills), innocent dialogue (Osborn is "relieved" when he confesses to eavesdropping), and acts (Todd wipes his glasses with toilet paper).

---

2. See also Enoch P. Jordan, *"The Floating Opera* Restored" (*Crit* 18,ii: 5–16), another systematic and thorough study of the revisions, which goes further than Morrell in interpreting the effects of those revisions on the unity and coherence of the novel.

Less fun than Korkowski's piece is "Desire and Disease: The Psychological Pattern of *The Floating Opera*" (*Crit* 18,ii:17–33), in which Dennis M. Martin contends that the novel is an enactment of its protagonist's consciousness of his sexual impotency (probably caused by gonorrhea) and his endeavor to conceal from both the reader and himself the significance of his symptoms.

Martin suggests that Todd's false candor comes from Barth's lack of artistic control, but Inger Aarseth, in "Absence of Absolutes: The Reconciled Artist in John Barth's *The Floating Opera*" (*SN* 47[1975]: 53–68), sees Barth totally in control, so much so that he anticipates the narrators of the later novels who transcend the dictates of both reality and literary conventions. Aarseth is especially acute in discussing the "calliope music" chapter and the relationship between Todd's "self-inquiry" and the actual writing of the novel.

Manfred Puetz discusses the problems involved in creating mythic worlds in "John Barth's *The Sot-Weed Factor*: The Pitfalls of Mythopoesis" (*TCL* 22:454–66). Through both Eben and Burlingame, Bath suggests that "converting the specifics of world, history, and self into freely permutable elements of imaginative creation implies the danger that the imagination may get lost in a maze of fictions within fictions without exit," themes which Barth confronts directly in the later work.

Charles B. Harris argues in "George's Illumination: Unity in *Giles Goat-Boy*" (*SNNTS* 8:172–84) that the novel affirms "'ways of speaking' as, quite simply, the only way *to* speak"—i.e., the narrative impulse. Although the analysis of the hero motif, the Jungian parallels, the allegory, and the *Bildungsroman* form helps to clarify Harris's thesis, the major point here is the importance of the final 40 pages. The most interesting part of S. C. Fredericks's "Science Fiction and the World of Greek Myths" (*Helios*, n.s. 2[1975]:1–22) is on the "prefigurative technique" of such mythological fiction as *Giles*; yet Fredericks observes that Barth's final point is that myths in fact "do *not* establish patterns of universal validity for human action."

In "*Lost in the Funhouse*: 'A Continuing, Strange Love Letter'" (*Boundary 2* 5:103–16), William J. Krier believes that Barth uses "existential love" ("a love union which provides knowledge of one's existence, but does not provide any clear sense of one's essence") as his basic metaphor for the act of writing and reading, which allows the reader to discover his own fundamental importance to the book.

Using the three protagonists as variant examples of the same ailment in "John Barth's *Chimera*: A Creative Response to the Literature of Exhaustion" (*Crit* 18,ii:59–72), Jerry Powell argues convincingly that "the process of writing about writer's block transcends the problem" suggested in Barth's famous essay; this work is both about the problem and the solution to it. For Ursula MacKenzie the use of myths to transcend actuality is the resolution to this novel. "John Barth's *Chimera* and the Strictures of Reality" (*JAmS* 10:91–101) is a firmly reasoned essay, though one observation—that in returning to the "roots of story-telling," this work avoids the "too strong" fantasy in *Giles*—is questionable. In "The Circuitous Journey of Consciousness in Barth's *Chimera*" (*Crit* 18,ii:73–85), Patricia Warrick relates the dominant image (the spiral) to "the fall" into self-consciousness as a recurring journey for the artist, whose act of making fictions is "the definitive human act." In her structural study, "'The Key to the Treasure': Narrative Movements and Effects in *Chimera*" (*JNT* 5[1975]:105–15), Cynthia Davis describes the tension which results from two kinds of framing (suggesting strict control) and the tentative tone (suggesting uncertainty), a tension which she suggests is a "metaphor for the relationship between the artist and his tradition."

"Pole-Vaulting in Top Hats: A Public Conversation with John Barth, William Gass, and Ishmael Reed" (*MFS* 22:132–51), lightly edited by James McKenzie and dominated by Barth, is a three-way intellectual celebration of "arbitrary complexity," which, claims Barth, is not ugly, sterile, or decadent: "It's fun."

Joseph Weixlmann updates and expands his earlier checklist (see *ALS 1972*, p. 296) with his *John Barth: A Descriptive Primary and Annotated Secondary Bibliography, Including a Descriptive Catalog of Manuscript Holdings in United States Libraries* (New York: Garland Publishers). In addition to critical commentary on Barth's work, this book lists the Library of Congress collection, including notes, chronologies, maps, and character lists as well as holographs and typescripts.

Refusing the implications of Pynchon's original title for *Gravity's Rainbow*—*Mindless Pleasures*—George Levine and David Leverenz call their gathering *Mindful Pleasures: Essays on Thomas Pynchon* (Boston: Little, Brown). The core of this collection of 11 pieces is last year's special *TCL* number (see *ALS 1975*, pp. 343–44); five essays are new. The editors' useful introduction, gingerly cautious lest their whole enterprise may be a Pynchon-prepared trap; a fascinating summary by Mathew Winston of what is now known about the reclusive author ("The Quest for Pynchon," pp. 251–63); and Bruce Herzberg's supplement (1972–75) to Joseph Weixlmann's 1972 bibliography complete the volume. In his own stylish contribution, "Risking the Moment: Anarchy and Possibility in Pynchon's Fiction" (pp. 113–36), Levine speculates on the curious mixture of decadence and innovative challenge in Pynchon's language: the style must "sustain the uncertainty it is structured to deny, to imply what cannot be articulated in language." Leverenz, on the other hand, analyzes interminably his own interpretive difficulties in "On Trying to Read *Gravity's Rainbow*" (pp. 229–49); after three readings, he thinks the novel is a "dualistic melodrama" between the forces of order, transcendence, and evil and those of disorder, death, and redemptive human feeling.

While he feels that a full theory of encyclopedic narrative must wait, Edward Mendelson nevertheless describes its formal properties and how Pynchon's novel contains them in his "Gravity's Encyclopedia" (pp. 161–95). This superb generic study also considers, among other sources and parallels, the influence of Max Weber, Joyce, and popular forms.[3] "Pre-Apocalyptic Atavism: Thomas Pynchon's Early Fiction" (pp. 31–47) is Catherine R. Stimpson's modish lament over Pynchon's "sexual conservatism." In "Brünnhilde and the Chemists: Women in *Gravity's Rainbow*" (pp. 197–227), Marjorie Kaufman tries to answer the question that most serious readers never bother to ask: does Pynchon give "a fair shake to his women characters, to the female sex?" The answer: a grudging "Yes." Between them, Stimpson and Kaufman claim a whopping 46 pages in this collection, which should strike most critics as a self-indulgent irrelevance. Except for this imbalance—and a concentrated dosage of all the words we have come to expect in the Pynchonist lexicon (*interface, preterite, entropy, paranoia*)—*Mindful Pleasures* is a distinguished book.

3. Mendelson's contribution to Pynchon's studies last year (see *ALS 1975*, pp. 344–45) has elicited comment from Thomas Hill Schaub, who in his "Open Letter in Response to Edward Mendelson's 'The Sacred, the Profane, and *The Crying of Lot 49*'" (*Boundary 2* 5:93–101), accuses Mendelson of locating "meaning" in a particular set of Pynchonist structures; as a corrective he stresses the ambiguity of Oedipa's efforts "fraught with maybes, dim visions, poor lighting. . . ."

In a lively style composed of the very elements he finds in post-modern fiction, James Rother not only describes the work of the "tortuously self-conscious writers" named in his "Parafiction: The Adjacent Universe of Barth, Barthelme, Pynchon, and Nabokov" (*Boundary 2* 5:21–43); he also defines what he calls the proper term for the "new marginalism." Postmodernism, he argues, was inspired by neither Dadaism nor surrealism, since both were nourished by "centrism." *Parafiction* rejects centrism in all its forms.

vi. William Styron, Walker Percy, James Dickey

The imaginative scholarship of Philip W. Leon's "*The Lost Boy* and a Lost Girl" (*SLJ* 9,i:61–69) establishes the influence of Thomas Wolfe (the death of Grover in *Look Homeward, Angel*) on characterization, situation, and tone of *Lie Down in Darkness*, through an early short version written when Styron was at Duke.

One of the more fruitless exercises on Styron's first novel is Catherine Trocard's "William Styron and the Historical Novel" (*Neohelicon* 3,i–ii[1975]:373–82). Doggedly applying the insights of Lukács to a work which resists such efforts results in the observation that *Lie Down in Darkness* has a wealth of allusions to historical moments and the conclusion that the novel has "imaginary characters, but no imaginary events." From its very first sentence ("All Styron's characters are aspects of Styron himself"), this essay dashes all hope that its author might probe the meaningful relationship of history and imagination in Styron's vision.

Ardner R. Cheshire, Jr., has more success in his application of Gabriel Marcel's theories of reflection and recollection in human experience to the ending of Styron's most controversial novel. "The Recollective Structure of *The Confessions of Nat Turner*" (*SoR* 12: 110–21) explores Nat's meditation up to his "redemption," the moment when his recollection shows him he loved Margaret Whitehead. For those who missed the contretemps the first time around, two essays on certain black writers' objections to *Nat Turner* have surfaced: Okon E. Uya's "Race, Ideology and Scholarship in the United States: William Styron's *Nat Turner* and Its Critics" (*AmerSI* 15,ii:63–81), and Ernest P. Williams's "William Styron and His Ten Black Critics: A Belated Mediation" (*Phylon* 37:189–95).

James L. W. West, III, comes up with a refreshing variation on the interview form, asking questions which future textualists would want answered. In "A Bibliographer's Interview with William Styron" (*Costerus* 4[1975]:13–29), Styron talks about his habits and methods of composition, his treatment of texts before publication, his use of textual alterations after publication, and his working relationship with his editors.

In *A Requiem for the Renascence*, Walter Sullivan remarks that after a solid beginning, Walker Percy's work "moved farther and farther away from reality." Mark Johnson, however, believes that one aspect of that reality—place—is gradually more integral to the theme in novels after *The Moviegoer*. In "The Search for Place in Walker Percy's Novels" (*SLJ* 8,i[1975]:55–81), Johnson finds that in *Love in the Ruins* Percy succeeds in tying the concepts of "abstraction and angelism-bestialism" to a sense of place, and More comes full circle "in his return to the church and to the Slave Quarters."

Richard Pindell, in "Basking in the Eye of the Storm: The Esthetics of Loss in Walker Percy's *The Moviegoer*" (*Boundary 2* 4 [1975]:219–30), discusses the way in which Binx contrives "to like the corner into which he has painted himself"—i.e., how the "humor of frivolity" and the "sadness of misery" may be accommodated. The last three pages of this essay are a beautiful stylistic analysis of how that achieved balance is communicated to the reader. In a belabored semisemiotic essay, "Title as Microtext: The Example of *The Moviegoer*" (*JNT* 5[1975]:219–29), Simone Vauthier spends excessive time studying the title, though the game is broadened considerably when she uses "extraneous" information—how our impression of the title as "emblematic of an existential posture" is reinforced if we know Percy's essay "The Man on the Train," and how our knowledge of Percy's first choice of a title (*The Confessions of a Moviegoer*) complicates our generic expectations. Barbara B. Sims's "Jaybirds as Portents of Hell in Percy and Faulkner" (*NMW* 9:24–27) is self-explanatory.

Is *Deliverance* a literal or ironic expression of the wilderness mystique? Two critics take opposing views. Charles E. Davis sees James Dickey's only novel as a critique, rather than a recrudescence, of those notions engendered in the early 19th century. The novel is a tissue of multiple ironies, he says in "The Wilderness Revisited: Irony in James Dickey's *Deliverance*" (*SAF* 4:223–30), which casts doubt on any modern attempt to undergo a "moral cleansing" in the woods or any other aspect of nature. Rosemary Sullivan, in "*Surfacing*

and *Deliverance*" (*CanL* 67:6–20), attempting to find "national differences in the imaginative preoccupation of two cultures," compares
the American novel, which she reads as Dickey's search for authenticity within the cult of sensation, with Margaret Atwood's *Surfacing*.
The Canadian view, she concludes, is ironic and the myth of violence
"internalized" into masochism and victimization; the American concern for wilderness is nothing more than the "mythification of violence" in which problems of human motive and social responsibility
are evaded.

vii. Kurt Vonnegut and Joseph Heller

Between inevitable plot summaries in *Kurt Vonnegut, Jr.* (TUSAS
276), Stanley Schatt makes some pertinent observations on the novelist's use of father figures, on the influence of *The Pilgrim's Progress* as
a contrasting text for *Slaughterhouse-Five*, and on the way Alain
Robbe-Grillet's theories turned *Breakfast of Champions* into an "anti-
novel." Schatt's knack for connecting his subject with larger intellectual traditions is a refreshing approach: *The Sirens of Titan* becomes
a "revolutionary novel" as ideological as *The Grapes of Wrath*; the
stylistically unusual *Cat's Cradle* is really a "comic investigation of
epistemology." Schatt devotes separate chapters to the short stories
and plays, and he writes interestingly about the uninteresting George
M. Helmholz stories which Vonnegut wrote for the *Saturday Evening
Post* in the 1950s. It may be that by abandoning his narrative masks
in the later works Vonnegut "appears to be moving on the same path
that Norman Mailer has traveled," but when Schatt identifies Vonnegut's burden as "love for all humanity," he sets in relief the considerable space separating the two writers on that path.

    Unlike most Vonnegut buffs, Jerome Klinkowitz sees *Breakfast of
Champions* as a significant departure from his previous work. In "Kurt
Vonnegut, Jr.'s Superfiction" (*RFEA* 1:115–23), Klinkowitz sees hints
of Ronald Sukenick and Steve Katz in that novel, which he attributes
to Vonnegut's friendship with other writers (Vance Bourjaily, Donald Barthelme) and the reading of "innovative" writers (Céline).
Robert W. Uphaus, however, finds authorial frustration in *Breakfast
of Champions* in his exploration of the relationship between the fiction ("which essentially defies problem solving") and the reader's

conventional expectation of finding meaning in that fiction. In "Expected Meaning in Vonnegut's Dead-End Fiction" (*Novel* 8[1975]: 164–74), Uphaus shows how the novelist's narrative conclusions emerge out of and preserve a complex awareness of the interplay between the "inner space of imagination" and the "outer space of history."

Two complementary essays examine Vonnegut-as-character in his most popular novel. In his succinct "*Slaughterhouse-Five*: Kurt Vonnegut's Anti-Memoirs" (*ELWIU* 3:244–50), Maurice J. O'Sullivan, Jr., feels an ideological and temperamental distinction between Billy Pilgrim and the authorial persona who dominates the first chapter and intrudes periodically thereafter. While Billy finally adopts a philosophy "which justifies his purposelessness," the author, like Coleridge's Mariner, is driven to "relive his story by retelling it," and his story thus becomes "fictional autobiography." In "Time, Uncertainty, and Kurt Vonnegut, Jr.: A Reading of *Slaughterhouse-Five*" (*CentR* 20:228–43), Charles B. Harris investigates discrepancies in chronology and relates them to metaphors centering upon linear time and death, aesthetic patterns devised by the author-as-character to combat his fears.

Most of what Iwao Iwamoto says in "A Clown's Say—A Study of Kurt Vonnegut, Jr.'s *Slaughterhouse-Five*" (*SELit* Eng. no. 1975:21–31) will be familiar to American readers, but a useful observation is his notion of war as a stage on which "human follies are enacted" by clowns such as Billy Pilgrim (who transcends such follies to become a "clown-saint") and Roland Weary (whose exaggerations satirize the illusory heroics of war). Dolores K. Gros Louis makes a similar distinction between Billy and his creator in "The Ironic Christ Figure in *Slaughterhouse-Five*" (*Biblical Images in Literature*, ed. Roland Bartel and others [Nashville, Tenn.: Abingdon Press, 1975], pp. 161–75). Vonnegut rejects his "resurrected survivor" and his "extraterrestrial gospel"—i.e., his complacent Tralfamadorian values—because it leads away from moral responsibility. Gros Louis also contributes to the same volume "Christ Figures in Modern Literature: An Annotated Bibliography" (pp. 176–78). As an anatomist of Folly, Vonnegut writes in the tradition of "fools' literature," according to A. Swerew's "Kurt Vonnegut. Von der Vorausschau zur Wirklichkeit" (*KuL* 24:296–321), and his target is technocratic consciousness. John

D. Haskell, Jr., confirms a previously unverified Vonnegut story in "Addendum to Pieratt and Klinkowitz: Kurt Vonnegut, Jr." (*PBSA* 70:122).

Among the handful of items on Heller is the high-decibel "Eros and Thanatos in *Catch-22*" (*CRevAS* 7:77–87) by Mike Frank, who sees Milo's "thanatotic American morality" representative of a much larger enemy—the Protestant ethic with its fanatic "profit motive." Carol Pearson's useful pedagogical piece, "*Catch-22* and the Debasement of Language" (*CEA* 38,iv:30–35), proposes that this novel attacks "the destructive power of language" when it manipulates rather than communicates. H. R. Swardson's "Sentimentality and the Academic Tradition" (*CE* 37:747–66) is a strong blast at teachers who, having abandoned their New Critical principles, have canonized *Catch-22*, the "phony" heir to the "sentimental religion" of the 19th-century midwest, which placed primary value on "righteous emotions." "Something Always Happens on the Way to the Office: An Interview with Joseph Heller" (*Pages* 1:74–81) is a discursive profile by Alden Whitman in which the novelist talks mostly about his slow writing habits and the difficulties of defining humor.

viii. John Updike, Joyce Carol Oates, and James Purdy

Alice and Kenneth Hamilton argue that "The Validation of Religious Faith in the Writings of John Updike" (*SRC* 5:275–85) occurs as early as *The Poorhouse Fair*, with its position between a "culturally dominant humanism and 'other-worldly' Christianity" dramatized in the clash of Hook and Conner; it is extended in *Couples*, which they read as an exposé of the shallowness of "immanence and self-realization" that humanists were so fond of in the 1960s.

In a more simplistic piece, "*Eros* and *Agape*: The Opposition in Updike's *Couples*" (*Renascence* 28:83–93), Linda M. Plagman isolates one aspect of that humanism which creates despair: the characters choose *eros*, which is death-seeking, over Christian *agape*, which is "acceptance of death." The notion of love is as elusive in Plagman's essay as it is in the novel itself. W. W. de Grummond sees the "Classical Influence in *The Poorhouse Fair*" (*AN&Q* 13:21–23) —mostly the use of Greek and Latin roots for characters' names—as Updike's effort to underscore thematic significance.

Following Joyce Carol Oates's own observation on Harriette

Arnow's *The Dollmaker*, James R. Giles finds the lack of wealth "a determinant of spirituality" for this chronicler of "contemporary American spiritual history." "Suffering, Transcendence, and Artistic 'Form': Joyce Carol Oates's *them*" (*ArQ* 32:213–26) is a particularly good discussion of "psychic suicide" in Loretta, a survivor only because she accepts the very values which have dehumanized her.

In "'Don't You Know Who I Am?': The Grotesque in Oates's 'Where Are You Going, Where Have You Been?'" (*JNT* 5[1975]:66–72), Joyce M. Wegs points out how the use of debased religious imagery anticipates the entrance of Arnold Friend, a symbolic Satan who also functions as the incarnation of Connie's erotic desires in "uncontrollable nightmare form." "A Study in Counterpoint: Joyce Carol Oates's 'How I Contemplated the World from the Detroit House of Correction and Began My Life Over Again'" (*MFS* 22:213–24) is a no-nonsense explication by Sue Simpson Park, who rearranges the author's skillful disarrangement to show the contrapuntal design of motifs and verbal echoes based on "place"—urban vs. suburban Detroit.

Like most admirers of James Purdy, Stephen D. Adams laments the paucity of critical interest in his subject and in *James Purdy* (New York: Barnes and Noble) attempts to show through evolving themes the steady progress of this underrated "Christian existentialist." Adams concentrates on the child-parent bond and the fate of words in a commercial culture, especially the loss of meaning "at the point where they have become mere 'memorials' of the spirit they claim to house." Adams is fine in his analysis of *Malcolm,* but he is even better in handling the deceptive realism of *The Nephew*; he also sees broader perspectives beginning with *Cabot Wright Begins* and *Eustace Chisholm and the Works.* Purdy's major achievement, says Adams, is in invoking ancient human feelings—a collective past—through a linguistic imagination. From a structural analysis, Marie-Claude Profit in "Lecture(s) de *Malcolm*" (*RFEA* 1:135–43) concludes that Purdy's most famous novel is a work-in-progress reflecting the canons of the French *nouveau roman.*

ix. Donald Barthelme, Robert Coover, and Other Innovators

Two essays attempt to disengage Barthelme from the kind of free-form game fiction celebrated in some of the essays in Raymond Federman's *Surfiction*. In " 'Bees Barking in the Night': The End and Beginning of Donald Barthelme's Narrative" (*Boundary 2* 5:71–92), R. E. Johnson, Jr., focuses on the "linguistic realism" of Barthelme's fiction: his dialectic establishes the priority of the imagination, realizing itself in language forms both old and new, "at once creative and decreative." Alan Wilde's "Barthelme Unfair to Kierkegaard: Some Thoughts on Modern and Postmodern Irony" (*Boundary 2* 5: 45–70) is a mini-history of irony (from technique to autonomous vision), as well as a defense of Barthelme's work against those who see it as nonreferential. The ludic strain in his work, says Wilde, persists "not as a denial of meaning, of referentiality, but as an assertion of the artist's privilege to create meaning."

Pierre-Yves Petillon's "Fictions d'Amerique: Donald Barthelme" (*Critique* 32:626–42) is a kind of summary for French readers of the "mechanical" language used to capture lives composed of "trash," the reliance upon "fragments" as form, the Lewis Carroll kind of humor, the influence of Borges, and the literalization of nursery rhymes. Despite impressive charts of representative verbs, rhetorical anaphora, and parallel constructions, Sally Allen McNall's " 'But Why Am I Troubling Myself About Cans?': Style, Reaction, and Lack of Reaction in Barthelme's *Snow White*" (*Lang&S* 8[1975]:81–94) is a purely clinical examination; the only venturesome conclusion is that Barthelme's "juggling act" is "too interesting to be called empty." Clinical too is Daniel A. Dervin's "Breast Fantasy in Barthelme, Swift, and Philip Roth: Creativity and Psychoanalytic Structure" (*AI* 33: 102–22), but, surprisingly, Barthelme's breast ("The Balloon") turns out to be medium for perceiving the greater world outside the ego rather than a symptom of "fixation or overdependence."

In addition to defining metafiction and tracing its origins in "Robert Coover, Metafiction, and Freedom" (*TCL* 22:210–27), Margaret Heckard argues that the endings of Coover's fictions are affirmative because of their stress on freedom—from literary conventions, myths, notions about human nature—from anything "that prevents the individual from becoming conscious of his own consciousness." In "The Dice of God: Einstein, Heisenberg, and Robert Coover" (*Novel* 10: 49–58), Arlen J. Hansen draws a parallel between the atomic physicists who are conscious that "*things* and *names* are not the same" and Coover, whose work shows how perception is governed by the language we use to think with.

"Against the Grain: Theory and Practice in the Work of William H. Gass" (*IowaR* 7,i:96–107) is a smartly written critique by Ned French, who finds a discrepancy between Gass's theory (that nothing exists except what the page contains) and the actual writing, and suggests that the theory is only a "corrective" for Gass's tendency toward overwriting. In "The Fortunate Fall in William Gass's *Omensetter's Luck*" (*Crit* 18,i:5–20), Richard J. Schneider uses the mythic fall to dramatize the quarrel between philosophy and fiction as well as that between other basic human conflicts. In Gass's first novel, the fall consists of tragic separations, and Furber's theology amounts to "inferred literary criticism."

Although "The Sacrificial World of William Gass: *In the Heart of the Heart of the Country*" (*Crit* 18,i:36–58) is a series of perceptive related readings by Bruce Bassoff of all the stories in this volume, "The Pederson Kid" occupies a central position: in its resemblance to Hemingway's fiction, the association of two characters with Christ, and in its "recursive" quality.

What Gass describes as his "essay-novella" is the subject of two essays. In this "virtual casebook of literary experimentalism," Larry McCaffery observes in "The Art of Metafiction: William Gass's *Willie Masters' Lonesome Wife*" (*Crit* 18,i:21–35) that Gass's use of typography, paper quality, and graphics suggests the parallels between reading and sexual intercourse. In "The Grotesque as Structure: 'Willie Masters' Lonesome Wife'" (*Criticism* 18:305–16), Reed B. Merrill sees this work as an "aesthetic conglomeration" of ideas from Plato, Wittgenstein, Nietzsche, the Symbolists and other aestheticians. He stresses the relevance of the grotesque and irony in Gass's principles of creativity, an art-for-art's-sake notion of infinite value.

Jeffrey L. Duncan is the tactful conductor of "A Conversation with Stanley Elkin and William H. Gass" (*IowaR* 7,i:48–77), in which the two writers talk about movies, the definition of the short story, and some of their contemporaries. Larry McCaffery contributes "A William H. Gass Bibliography" (*Crit* 18,i:59–66).

"John Hawkes and the Elements of Pornography" (*JPC* 10:150–55) is about simultaneous attraction and repulsion central to Gothic and decadent literature, qualities which Helen S. Garson thinks much of Hawkes's fiction shares with pornography. Although he concentrates on *The Lime Twig* in "Nature et fonction de narrateur dans les romans de John Hawkes" (*RFEA* 1:101–14), Pierre Gault generalizes on the intricate relationship among author, narrators, and other characters in Hawkes's fiction.

In "Journey to Ixtlan: Inside the American Indian Oral Tradition" (*ArQ* 32:138–45), Carl R. V. Brown deals with those teachings of Don Juan Matus which correspond directly to "ways of thinking and perceiving observable in the American Indian oral tradition generally." Carlos Castaneda's shaman is an obvious influence in *Out* and 98.6, according to "Tales of Fictive Power: Dreaming and Imagination in Ronald Sukenick's Postmodern Fiction" (*Boundary* 2 5:117–35), in which Daniel C. Noel links an archaic shamanlike practice with a postmodernist's use of self-consciousness; both are able to "psychosynthesize fresh worlds."

x. Others

a. **Thomas Berger, J. P. Donleavy, and Stanley Elkin.** According to Fred M. Fetrow, "The Function of the External Narrator in Thomas Berger's *Little Big Man*" (*JNT* 5[1975]:57–65) is to satirize Americans' racial arrogance and cultural moralism through a character at once gullible and astute. Admirers of *Little Big Man* will be interested in two complementary articles: Paul A. Hutton's "From Little Bighorn to Little Big Man: The Changing Image of a Western Hero in Popular Culture" (*WHQ* 7:19–45) is a fascinating study of Custer's shifting reputation; and in "The Martyrdom of General George Armstrong Custer, U.S.A." (*Prospects* 1[1975]:297–311), Bruce A. Rosenberg sees the Last Stand as a folk narrative in the same league with the stories of Roland, Saul, and Davy Crockett.

In *J. P. Donleavy: The Style of His Sadness and Humor* (Bowling Green, Ohio: Bowling Green Univ. Popular Press, 1975), Charles G. Masinton sees a fairly steady decline in this author's fiction after *The Ginger Man*, partly because the pleasure principle—the inventiveness and raw energy behind his most notable hero—succumbs to a preoccupation with dejection and death. Masinton finds several instances of black humor in *The Ginger Man*, as well as the influence of Henry Miller and Kingsley Amis; he is perceptive in his discussion of the double in three novels and the "earthy female" in *The Saddest Summer of Samuel S.* One chapter is devoted to the works after 1968. Similarly, in "The Tragic-Comic Novels of J. P. Donleavy" (*MichA* 9,i: 15–24), John Johnson stresses the dark vision, noting that in the pattern of the failure of satisfying love or family relationships, only male friendships and brief sexual encounters become threads of meaning which bind Donleavy's characters to the world.

In his essay on Stanley Elkin's *The Dick Gibson Show*, Raymond M. Olderman characterizes "The Six Crises of Dick Gibson" (*IowaR* 7,i:127–40) as a "one-man cultural history" of American consciousness from the Great Depression to the Vietnam War. Central to Elkin's notion is the "false belief that the individual can somehow be extraordinary through an extraordinary embrace of the ordinary."

b. **E. L. Doctorow and John Gardner.** In "Surviving McCarthyism: E. L. Doctorow's *The Book of Daniel*" (*MR* 16[1975]:577–87), Barbara L. Estrin perceptively traces the generic permutations of this "orphan novel" through Doctorow's theme of the futility of innocence and the circularity of evil: though Daniel begins as an innocent victim of society (i.e., the Old Right of the 1950s and the New Left of the 1960s), he ends as a victimizer himself. In "Doctorow and Kleist: 'Kohlhaas' in *Ragtime*" (*MFS* 22:224–27), Walter L. Knorr persuasively contends that Coalhouse Walker's story derives from Heinrich von Kleist's greatest protagonist, the wronged 16th-century horsetrader who becomes the scourge of Saxony. "In adopting Kohlhaas as a model," says Knorr, "Doctorow transforms the theme of class discrimination of the Reformation to that of racial discrimination in our era."

Both Judy Smith Murr and Susan Strehle emphasize the functional use of confrontations in Gardner's works. In her fine "John Gardner's Order and Disorder: *Grendel* and *The Sunlight Dialogues*" (*Crit* 18,ii:97–108), Murr shows how "an adherent to forms and a believer in magical chaos" conduct a search to determine if life is nothing more than a series of comical, meaningless exercises; affirmation comes only in the recognition of our "ridiculousness and indignity and of the unkillable power of love." In "John Gardner's Novels: Affirmation and the Alien" (*Crit* 18,ii:86–96), Strehle concentrates on the same two works, as well as *The Wreckage of Agathon*, and finds the source of tension in the opposition of an alien, an artist manqué, pitted against representatives of complacency and righteousness. After establishing, on somewhat shaky evidence, a compositional chronology of "early" and "later" works, Strehle concludes that *Grendel* is Gardner's most satisfyingly experimental work.

c. **Popular and Science Fictionists.** In *Jack Kerouac: Prophet of the New Romanticism* (Lawrence: Regents Press of Kans.), Robert A. Hipkiss argues that the Beat writer was the most uncompromising of the postwar Romantics. One chapter is devoted to a comparison of Kerouac with J. D. Salinger, James Purdy, John Knowles, and Ken Kesey. Of the six chapters which trace themes and techniques, only the one on "Spontaneous Prose" is original, partly because it accounts for the origins of Kerouac's prose and persuasively outlines its intended effects; more often than not, Hipkiss is reluctant to examine in any detail how Kerouac's distinctive style works, even in *The Subterraneans*. A final chapter proposes that because of his "visionary idealism" (a syncretistic mixture of French Canadian Catholicism and Mahayana Buddhism). Kerouac's particular quest for ecstasy and oneness with God led to an incorrigible loneliness, "the final position of the quintessential Beat."

Kerry Ahearn's "More D'Urban: The Texas Novels of Larry Mc-Murtry" (*TQ* 19,iii:109–29) is a frank appraisal of the decline "to success" of a popular novelist; the increasing lack of psychological depth and aesthetic refinement can be attributed to "that peculiar Eastern parochialism which views the Great Plains only as a place, denying it the complexity of reality." Janis P. Stout is less devaluative in seeing McMurtry's progressive loss of regional identity. In "Journeying as a Metaphor for Cultural Loss in the Novels of Larry McMurtry" (*WAL* 11:37–50), Stout examines in all five novels the aimless journey as an appropriate archetype for the "radical dissociation from a culture."

"Memoryscape: Jean Shepherd's Midwest" (*ON* 2:357–69) is Joseph F. Trimmer's astute evaluation of a writer whose best work (*In God We Trust, All Others Pay Cash*) mixes realistic detail with comic hyperbole, but whose later work is dominated by a Mencken-like observer of contemporary lunacies. Like Mark Twain's later writings, Shepherd's recent work is haunted "by the madness of dreams rather than the magic of memories."

In "John D. MacDonald: The Liabilities of Professionalism" (*JPC* 10:38–53), Thomas Doulis finds the Travis McGee novels paradoxically flawed because they were so "deeply felt" that they could not be accommodated to the formulaic patterns of most of MacDonald's work. Joseph Browne's "The Greening of America: Irish-American Writers" (*JEthS* 2,iv[1975]:71–76) deals with Jimmy Breslin, Mark

Costello, Joe Flaherty, Tom McHale, and Pete Hamill and the traits they share: alienation of sons from fathers and a tendency toward Manicheanism. Dwight C. Smith, Jr., finds that at least 300 paperback books using the Mafia theme have surfaced in the wake of Mario Puzo's *The Godfather.* "Sons of the Godfather: 'Mafia' in Contemporary Fiction" (*ItalAm* 2:191–207) is in general an interesting and solid study in popular culture, but Smith's claim that Puzo's influence and the times "converged to create a new art form" is patently extravagant.

"A Future Issue" (*NewRep* 175,xviii:31–41) is the general title of a clutch of brief essays on the nature of science fiction: Mark Rose defines the subgenre and looks into its origins in "What is Science Fiction Anyhow?"; Ursula K. Le Guin's "Science Fiction as Prophecy" is on Philip K. Dick; Frederic Jameson's "Science Fiction as Politics" is on Larry Niven; Robert Scholes's "Science Fiction as Conscience" is on John Brunner and Le Guin; and Derek de Solla Price's "Science Fiction as Science" is on the nonstylish fiction of the pulps in the 1930s.

Mark Rose's introduction to his *Science Fiction: A Collection of Critical Essays* (Englewood Cliffs, N.J.: Prentice-Hall) emphasizes generic properties ("the characteristic romance form of the scientific age") and links the present popularity of the form to a general interest in "uncanonical" literature. Rose reprints eleven essays and excerpts from books. In an exacerbated style, John Rothfork, in "NASA, the Sixties, and the American Hero" (*ColQ* 24[1975]:102–12), describes the evolution of science fiction into "speculative fiction"—a growth which he ascribes to the closing of the frontier. Criticism of the form is now sustained by a cultural context in which "childlike dreams become respectable."

John Hollow would agree with Rothfork when he claims that science fiction is really "a way of coping with the much closer problem of death." His "*2001* in Perspective: The Fiction of Arthur C. Clarke" (*SWR* 61:113–29) is a first-rate analysis and overview of this famous fictionist and of the Stanley Kubrick film based on his work. "The Lost Canticles of Walter M. Miller, Jr." (*SFS* 3:3–26) is David N. Samuelson's biocritical sketch of the "technophilic" author who mysteriously stopped writing in 1959. Robert Plank's "Ursula K. Le Guin and the Decline of Romantic Love" (*SFS* 3:36–43) stresses the depiction of her "grim" world where ambisexuality is institutional-

ized. In his unique study of historical linguistics in science fiction,
"The Future History and Development of the English Language"
(*SFS* 3:130–42), Walter E. Meyers concludes that these writers are
"more inventive with photons than with phonemes."

The diverse images of Faust and Frankenstein are generative
figures in science fiction; in "Robinsonade und Science Fiction"
(*Anglia* 94:140–62), Ulrich Broich argues for the reincarnation of
Defoe's Robinson Crusoe in the work of such writers as William
Golding and Robert Heinlein. Questioned by Robert Boyers and
Maxine Bernstein, Susan Sontag speaks forthrightly about science
fiction and its "authoritarian imagination," along with low culture,
high culture, conservatism, and the relationship of art to the moral
sense in "Women, the Arts, and the Politics of Culture: An Interview
with Susan Sontag" (*Salmagundi* 31–32:29–48).

d. **Miscellaneous.**   " 'In That Time and at That Place': The Literary
World of Elizabeth Spencer" (*MissQ* 28[1975]:435–60) is an inter-
view in which the novelist talks to Charles T. Bunting about other
women writers, her own habits of composition, and the relation of her
work to the Southern Renascence. A full biographical note on this
Mississippian now living in Montreal is attached to "An Elizabeth
Spencer Checklist, 1948 to 1976" (*MissQ* 29:569–90), compiled by
Laura Barge. John C. Calhoun's "Borden Deal: Mississippi Novelist"
(*NMW* 9:63–76) consists mostly of plot summaries of a "good mid-
level popular novelist" done in a manner that succeeds in being both
clotted and elliptic. As Calhoun says of one of Deal's novels, "if there
is anythings [*sic*] of lasting value in the Southern novel, then along
with things like Capote's *Other Voices* and O'Conner's [*sic*] *Sad
Cafe* [*sic*] this is it."

A traditionalist observes in "Time's Prisoners: An Interview with
Wallace Stegner" (*SWR* 61:252–67) his postmodernist colleagues,
whose reflexive self-consciousness he attributes to the lack of a stable
society; he also talks to David Dillon about his regionalism and that
of southerners and the role of Bernard DeVoto in the depiction of
western sensibilities.

Robert D. Harper singles out "Wright Morris's *Ceremony in Lone
Tree*: A Picture of Life in Middle America" (*WAL* 11:199–213) as
the culminating work in this novelist's depiction of the Midwest, an
effort which fuses three major strains: the frontier, the Gothic, and

the sentimental. One segment of this essay is on Morris's fictive technique, which Harper identifies as a combination of internal monologue and objective reporting.

For the first time since George Garrett's brilliant essay (see *ALS 1964*, p. 170), John Cheever's fiction gets the perceptive criticism it deserves with Scott Donaldson's authoritative "The Machines in Cheever's Garden" (*The Changing Face of the Suburbs*, ed. Barry Schwartz [Chicago: Univ. of Chicago Press], pp. 309–22). Surveying most of the fiction, Donaldson sees Cheever as "the Jeremiah of our suburban age" whose dispiriting profile of a culture with no future (and which has repudiated the past) is vivified by transportation symbols (railroads, airlines, freeways) which "shrink space, distort time, and confuse perceptions" of alienated suburbanites.

In "Laughin' Just to Keep from Cryin': Fariña's Blues Novel" (*JPC* 9:926–34), Gene Bluestein demonstrates that *Been Down So Long It Looks Like Up to Me* is a text of its time—1966—but he fails to explain why it deserves further attention. Max Byrd's choice for "Reconsideration" (*NewRep* 175,xvii:29–31) is Peter DeVries's *The Mackerel Plaza*, but this crisp little piece is also a general retrospective of DeVries's comedies, which "are always turning imperceptibly" into tragedies.

Landon C. Burns analyzes the symbolism and structure of Calvin Kentfield's first novel in "Man as Mariner: Kentfield's *The Alchemist's Voyage*" (*Crit* 18,i:92–104); and D. B. Graham's "Naturalism and the Revolutionary Imperative: Yurick's *The Warriors*" (*Crit* 18,i:119–28) is on Sol Yurick's novel about adolescent street gangs in New York City. In "Survey Courses, Indian Literature, and *The Way to Rainy Mountain*" (*CE* 37:619–24), Kenneth M. Roemer proposes Scott Momaday's book as an introduction to the varieties of Indian literature because it dispels certain stereotypes.

Ted L. Estess's "Elie Wiesel and the Drama of Interrogation" (*JR* 56:18–35) is the first significant attempt to place this Holocaust writer more centrally into the "broader currents of contemporary sensibility." Wiesel's characteristic vision—the willingness to question—antedates World War II. In "Seeing and Blindness: A Conversation with Isaac Bashevis Singer" (*Novel* 9:151–64), the Yiddish writer talks theology with Grace Farrell Lee; the subjects are skepticism and belief, God as tempter, the nature of the Devil, free will, Cabalists and Hasids, and Spinoza.

In "Les Images dans *Trout Fishing in America* de Richard Braut-igan" (*RFEA* 1:39–53), Marc Chénetier finds four categories of imagery both reflecting conventional iconography and commenting on the circularity of discourse. Stephen R. Jones's "Richard Braut-igan: A Bibliography" (*BB* 33:53–59) is both primary and secondary, described as reasonably complete "through late 1975."

Indiana University

16. Poetry: 1900 to the 1930s

Richard Crowder

There was an increase in activity during the last year. *Explicator* articles have moved from four to seven; dissertations from 13 to 20; books from 9 to 13.

David Perkins's *A History of Modern Poetry: From the 1890s to the High Modernist Mode*, vol. 1 (Cambridge, Mass.: Belknap Press of Harvard Univ. Press) brings the story of our poets to the mid-1920s. A second volume promises to carry the reader into the modern age. This study of the period as a whole considers both British and American poets since there has been unceasing mutual influence. The Americans are treated in some excellent passages: ten pages devoted to Robinson, an entire chapter to Frost (discussing such topics as "The Spoken Language" and "Unsaying the Romantics"). Some 125 pages spell out the contributions of Americans to "Popular Modernism." There are other important considerations: "The New Poetry of America," "Imagism," "Poetry for a Democracy," "Conservative and Regional Poets of America," and "Black Poets of America: The First Phase." One chapter studies the early work of Stevens; his later poems and the poetry of Hart Crane and E. E. Cummings (figures usually discussed in this chapter) will be analyzed in volume 2. Perkins's book brings into focus the entire age, giving it definition and limits, going well beyond the studies of individual writers which have dominated our criticism in recent years. *A History of Modern Poetry* has achieved a significant breakthrough.

i. Frost

Frank Lentricchia's contribution to Frost scholarship this year is *Robert Frost: A Bibliography, 1913–1974* (Metuchen, N.J.: Scarecrow Press), compiled with Melissa Christensen Lentricchia. It fills a surprising void in Frost studies—a "working" bibliography, and adds importantly to work done by W. B. Shubrick and Charles Green, Reginald L. Cook, and Uma Prameswaram. The primary materials are identified in part 1: the major publications, recordings and films, books of letters, and an anthology of interviews. These are followed by the names and addresses of 21 libraries with significant manuscript holdings. Part 2, on secondary materials, gives information on reviews, books, and parts of books on Frost, scholarly and popular articles (both arranged alphabetically within decades), articles in foreign languages, bibliographies and checklists, and titles of doctoral dissertations. Three appendices supply a bibliographical history of the poems, a list of selected anthologies containing Frost poems, and a directory of the first publication of the uncollected poems (44 of them). An index of authors of secondary materials concludes this indispensable reference book.

Robert Spangler Newdick, former professor of English at Ohio State University, struck up a close friendship with Robert Frost in 1934 and continued to see him and correspond with him for five years until Newdick's death at age 40 in 1939. Except for some of Frost's letters, which Mrs. Newdick has sold, the materials from Newdick's files have been edited and published by William A. Sutton in *Newdick's Season of Frost: An Interrupted Biography of Robert Frost* (Albany: State Univ. of N.Y. Press). The 13 short tentative chapters of the professor's Frost biography cover 81 pages. The remainder of the book (to page 454) consists of research materials. A long section by the editor (part 2) traces the five years of the Frost-Newdick friendship through notes, letters, anecdotes, and such, the last item being a Frost letter to Mrs. Newdick written late in December 1953. There follows a record of 36 "Items" (136 pages) headed "Newdick's Research Findings," including first-hand accounts of the professor's encounters with the poet and recollections of Frost's friends and acquaintances. Eight "Appendixes" supply various data such as Appendix E: "Notebook Sent to Newdick by Frost in 1935" and Appendix H: "Text of Robert Frost's Longhand Table of Contents for *Recognition of Robert Frost*, September, 1937." The substantial index (34 pages) should be of enormous assistance to a scholar wanting to locate details in this valuable book.

Though not stated openly, Dennis Vail's *Robert Frost's Imagery and the Poetic Consciousness* (Lubbock: Tex. Tech Press) appears to be a printing of his dissertation, directed by Arthur Mizener. Dwelling on how the poet's lyric imagery works, Vail follows the course of several images (particularly of woods and trees as "the best example"). He works out such ideas as "Art . . . like anything else, is subject to misappropriation and exploitation," and he considers at length the relation of love to art. The writing is good, and the development of concepts is interesting (more than a cut above the average thesis).

Frost: Centennial Essays II, ed. Jac Tharpe (Jackson: Univ. Press of Miss.) is the sequel to *Frost: Centennial Essays*, reviewed in *ALS 1974*, pp. 328–29. Only a little over half the size of its predecessor, the current volume publishes 22 essays divided by the editor into five groups: "Frost Country" (the title of the first essay, by Warren French), "Religion," "Method and Theory," "Play," and "Background and Biography." Among the authors are such well-known critics and scholars as Marie Boroff, George W. Nitchie, Marion Montgomery, Laurence Perrine, Perry Westbrook, and Stearns Morse, whose essay on "The Subverted Flower" (pp. 170–78) is of central importance. Other experienced essayists are included, of course, as well as several younger students of Frost's poetry. It would take half this chapter to review the articles adequately, but it must be said that the entire book, like the 1974 volume, is well worth the investment. Treatment ranges from close readings to broad views; topics are varied: from "animal anthropomorphism" to "politics in theory and practice," from "triangulation" to "thematics of imagination." According to the index, poems the authors find most frequently useful are "After Apple-Picking" and "The Trial by Existence," though several others are discussed four or five times. Even if some of the ideas may sound familiar, all in all, it would be a mistake to overlook this book.

At least four articles link Frost with other poets. B. J. Sokol discusses "What Went Wrong between Robert Frost and Ezra Pound" (*NEQ* 49:521–41), in a narrative account of the meetings between the two poets in England and Pound's reviews of Frost's books. Frost in the early days felt insecure as a poet but knew that he could not submit to Pound. The two men were friendly only about four months in 1913, after which Frost began escaping the Pound influence through "humor and indirection."

Two studies bring Frost together with Robert Lowell. Michael Folsom, in "Poets and Presidents: Frost and Lowell" (*New Orleans Review* 5,i:21–26), concludes that neither man fulfills Whitman's promise of a poet who will use "weapons with menacing points" to serve as a check on presidents and other leaders. Robert G. Twombly compares the two poets in "The Poetics of Demur: Lowell and Frost" (*CE* 38:373–92). Frost, he finds, is even "confessional" in the sense of being self-centered in grief or shame. Frost is close to Lowell in being vulnerable or gruff, in indulging in "self-biting irony or . . . hasty demur." In both poets the paradox is the final "turning away into silence" as "the most compelling gesture of obligation." Often they imply the transmutation of love "into aggression or malice." This is a thoughtful article linking New England poets of different generations.

"Frost and Eliot" is the title of an essay by Jeffrey Hart (*SR* 84: 425–47), in which the author notes the need for "truly first-rate Frost criticism." He sees these two poets as complementing each other and having a dialectical relationship. In spite of many differences, there are similarities: e.g., the central theme of metaphysical desolation and the conservative point of view. Hart traces Frost's "literary guerilla warfare against Eliot" from the time of *New Hampshire* (1923), in which he felt constrained to reply to *The Waste Land*. (There are definite divergences, as in Frost's insistence on differences and Eliot's impulse toward identities.) In his turn, says Hart, Eliot in "The Dry Salvages" makes reply to Frost and America. The author interprets "Directive" (1947) as a return to Frost's quarrel with Eliot; by the end of the poem we see Frost as pure poet, not as "national hand-holder." Sociologically, he remains "resolutely individualistic," whereas Eliot inhabits a "community" (his neighbors being Juliana of Norwich, George Herbert, et al).

Frost's commitment to individualism and to differences is further explored in two articles in *CEA* 38. Julian Mason, in "Frost's Conscious Accommodation of Contraries" (iii:26–31), sees the poet as advocating largeness of spirit in facing the facts of opposites: polarities are to be met, not succumbed to. Arnold G. Bartini maintains that Frost is essentially indifferent to the perspective of morality: it is individual "existential choice" that gives definition to life. His essay is "Robert Frost and Moral Neutrality" (ii:22–24). Furthering Bartini's idea, Thomas K. Hearn, Jr., in "Making Sweetbreads Do:

Robert Frost and Moral Empiricism" (*NEQ* 49:65–81), finds no sure guide in the poems, but sees Frost as calling us to appreciate nature with all our individual sensitivity in order to achieve moral insight and maturity. Poetry is a way toward such awareness.

Mordecai Marcus has published two Frost studies. "Motivation of Robert Frost's Hired Man" (*CollL* 3:63–68) puts Silas at the center of the famous poem. Marcus traces the hired man's "faint residue of pride" and his small remaining "sense of self-worth." In his other essay, Marcus studies the relationship between "The Witch of Coös" and "The Pauper Witch of Grafton," published together in 1923. "The Whole Pattern of Robert Frost's 'Two Witches': Contrasting Psycho-Sexual Modes" (*L&P* 26:69–78) concludes that the Coös witch is socially more conventional than the frank and less savory Grafton witch. In the two poems Frost is being ironic about society's inability to make accurate sexual, societal, and moral judgments.

William H. Pritchard shows by example a close link in Frost between manner of speaking and communication of emotional drive. "Metaphor is it and the freshness thereof." His essay is entitled "The Grip of Frost" (*HudR* 29:185–204). Quoting poems attributed to Frost in his high school *Bulletin*, 1890–92, Andrew J. Angyal and Kent Ljungquist—"Some Early Frost Imitations of Poe" (*PoeS* 9:14–16)—support the thesis that Poe was more than just marginally influential at the beginning of Frost's career.

Robert F. Fleissner, in "Frost on Frost . . . at Midnight" (*SIH* 5:32–38), claims "Acquainted with the Night" to be directly indebted to Coleridge's "Frost at Midnight" much more than to Æ, whose statement "The time is not right" did, however, affect Frost. (Fleissner mistakenly calls George William Russell "A. E. Russell.") In seven pages Fleissner treats the reader to 42 footnotes—pretty cautious going toward what has to be a minor point. Another Fleissner note is "Frost's and Yevtushenko's 'Irreverent' Poems" (*NConL* 6,i: 14–15), which relates "Forgive, O Lord" to Yevgeny Yevtushenko's "An Attempt at Blasphemy" (both seriocomic). He issues the obvious warning to distinguish between "face-value meaning" and ultimate intention. Further, adding a point to his essay in *Frost: Centennial Essays* (1974), Fleissner, in "Frost and Tennyson: Factual as Well as 'Archetypal'" (*AN&Q* 14[1975]:53–55), tells how Frost, in a talk at Breadloaf, "in virtually the same breath," discussed the relation of the lore of number to poetry, to Tennyson, and to his own poem, "The

Gold Hesperidee," all patently linked in his thinking. Developing
more thoroughly the Tennyson connection, Edward Proffitt traces
through the collected poems Frost's maturation from the Victorian
(Tennysonian) "mode (and mood)" of gloom (evening, darkness,
autumn) of A Boy's Will in the direction of affirmation in the later
poems. In "Frost's Journey from Gloom (RS 44:248–51), Proffitt examines "Come In" (1942), in which stars have become bright, positive emblems rather than the earlier symbols of nothingness.

Two brief items in ELN 13 are not without interest. George Monteiro, in "Frost's Quest for the 'Purple-Fringed'" (204–6), lays out
the editorial and critical problems caused by the poet's confusion of
orchid and gentian in a poem of 1901. Anya Taylor's "A Frost Debt
to Beddoes" (291–92) points to the similarity between "The woods
are lovely, dark and deep" and the Beddoes line "Our bed is lovely,
dark, and sweet" in "The Phantom Wooer." Beddoes's conclusion,
however, stops short of Frost's call to duty. John Ciardi in "Ghosts in
an Inscription" (SatR, Aug. 21:52) reports discovery of an inscription on a stone wall in Inch, Ireland, dated 1907, that parallels the
concluding lines of "Stopping by Woods on a Snowy Evening," written some years later.

Archibald MacLeish has contributed "Robert Frost and New
England" (NG 149:438–44). Frost, he maintains, discomfits his
readers because he is not in all ways the Yankee poet they might
expect. His irony, for example, goes beyond New England dissem-
bling into disturbance by tragic, even savage implications. It is Frost
who speaks in his poems, Frost who selected New England as his own.
Born and reared in the city, he moved into the "real," "country" New
England only when he was 26. MacLeish interprets the "road less
traveled by," not as the life of poetry, but as "the way to the art of
poetry," e.g., the move to the New Hampshire farm. It was then that
"New England became an all-including metaphor." In "The Pasture"
Frost encourages his reader to look beyond the thing, in other words
to see.

Following MacLeish's essay DeWitt Jones presents "A Photo
Portfolio: Look of a Land Beloved" (NG 149:144–67). This is a selection of pictures of New England's land and people accompanied
by quotations from Frost. The pictures help the viewer to "see"
Frost's territory.

ii. Stevens

It is a fine thing when a university press gives us a single book on a poet, but Bucknell has provided us with two very interesting full-length studies: Alan Perlis's *Wallace Stevens: A World of Transforming Shapes* and Thomas J. Hines's *The Later Poetry of Wallace Stevens: Phenomenological Parallels with Husserl and Heidegger* (Lewisburg, Pa.: Bucknell Univ. Press).

Taking off from a 1952 essay by Sister Bernetta Quinn, Perlis restates the core idea that Stevens reshapes his perceived world into "imaginary constructs." Fresh *explications de texte* develop and broaden Quinn's view. Perlis also points out relationships between her stance and that of critics who think Stevens feels unable to encapsulate the object world accurately. Perlis's point is that Stevens, while recognizing the futility of life, faces it nevertheless, with a saving poise and even with a broadly comic tone. The book concludes with a three-page selective bibliography and a well-constructed index. It is an engaging, sound contribution to Stevens studies.

The Hines book is of equal interest in a different direction. "Parallels" is the key word in the title. The author makes no pretense of finding in the works of Edmund Husserl or Martin Heidegger any source material for the poetry of Stevens. He seeks rather to show how the poet used "meditational processes and . . . visionary forms" similar to those in the work of these two philosophers. He finds in the poet's early epistemological approach many parallels with the methods of Husserl. Later the parallels are with Heidegger: recognizing that Being and beings are after all different. Being is "the center and source of both the mind and the world." Throughout, Hines insists that Stevens's vision is not that of a philosopher but of a poet. The book demonstrates, with patient lucidity, how an understanding of relevant parts of the work of Husserl and Heidegger will make the mind of Stevens and the "aesthetic adequacy" of his work more accessible to the willing reader.

The other two Stevens books compare and contrast him with other poets. Both studies, like the Perlis book, give at least initial attention to the process of transforming reality. George Bornstein's book is indeed entitled *Transformations of Romanticism in Yeats, Eliot, and Stevens* (Chicago: Univ. of Chicago Press). Beginning with explications of two Stevens poems, "Of Modern Poetry" (which serves as both example and definition) and "Man and Bottle" (which relates Romanticism to Modernism), the author then formulates the Romantic theory of creative imagination, defines the "Greater Romantic Lyric," and studies the "manipulations of imagery, speaker, and rhetorical strategy." He examines the anti-Romantic attitudes of the New Critics and others and reviews works that have more recently opposed and rectified their vogue.

After chapters on Yeats's "Last Romanticism" and Eliot's "Anti-Romanticism," Bornstein turns to "The New Romanticism of Wallace Stevens" (pp. 163–230), exploring (1) the poet's changes in Romantic theory and the way it affected his poetry and (2) his form of "mental action," which evolved as his poetry matured. Bornstein follows a generally chronological order in unfolding the development of Stevens's peculiar brand of Romanticism, quoting from "Notes Toward a Supreme Fiction" (section X of "It Must Give Pleasure") to show the final requirement, that the mind "can never be satisfied." This is, on the whole, an audacious study, bearding some pretty fierce critical lions and coming through victorious.

On the other hand, Helen Regueiro appears to go beyond Bornstein in *The Limits of Imagination: Wordsworth, Yeats, and Stevens* (Ithaca, N.Y.: Cornell Univ. Press). After suggesting that Wordsworth finds balance between imagination and nature and that Yeats, in his early work, chooses a world constructed by the imagination (though not solipsistic), she presents a section on Stevens (pp. 147–218) which, more or less in order, traces the "change in his attitude toward the imagination." At first he sees it as transforming chaos (reality) into order ("a habitable place"). But, as he grows older, he finds a destructive power in the imagination and tries to return to "the plain sense of things," using paradoxically the language and the self-conscious attitude that separates poetry from the world of reality. He acknowledges, in other words, the inadequacy of the imagination (which may perhaps be the cause of Bornstein's constantly dissatisfied mind). Regueiro finds ultimate rejection of metaphor, a pushing of "the poem into the silence of mere being . . . into the presence of reality." This is a perceptive study, based on breadth of learning and depth of intellect.

"Wallace Stevens: Reduction to the First Idea" (*Diacritics* 6,iii: 48–57) is drawn from Harold Bloom's forthcoming book. The author traces in Stevens the Idea of Firstness, an attempt "to see earliest," from the 1918 poem "The Death of a Soldier" through a number of later works. Bloom offers an elaborate close reading of "The Snow Man," getting at such problems as the difference between "regard" and "behold" and the significance of listening to the wind. He concludes that, though Stevens could not maintain the High Romantic vision in the first books, his later poetry nevertheless relies more on "chant" than "regardings" and "beholdings." Bloom, by the way, admires Regueiro's book. It will be profitable to study his coming book and *The Limits of the Imagination* together.

Bloom's colleague, J. Hillis Miller, has written a two-part essay, "Stevens' Rock and Criticism as Cure" (*GaR* 30:5–31; 330–48). As a starting point the author dissects four lines from "The Rock" which use a form of the word *cure* five times. In this poem Stevens again and again takes a simple word and plays with it until it becomes very complex. Miller here borrows a phrase from heraldry, *mise en abyme*. A still more complicated *mise en abyme* is the interweaving, juxtaposed, and superimposed "figurative terminology" in baffling repetitions and increments. Miller sees each scene in "The Rock" as equal to all others, resulting in "a chain of chains . . . articulated . . . around the verb 'to be.' " The labyrinth of the poem goes back through Milton all the way to the whole family of Indo-European languages, inviting ceaseless commentary. The second part of the essay looks at Paul de Man, Harold Bloom, Geoffrey Hartman, and Jacques Derrida as critics who question the ground ("rock") of literature. As one would expect, Miller's essay is full of suggestions for scholars to pursue.

Stevens makes a connection between his own affinity for aphorism and his belief in the possibility of perceiving reality only in fragments. This is Beverly Coyle's theme in "An Anchorage of Thought: Defining the Role of Aphorism in Wallace Stevens' Poetry" (*PMLA* 91:206–22). The poems bear witness to Stevens's opposing tendencies: to seek a unity by centering on a self-sufficient experience but at the same time to testify to the great variety of experience, rich and conflicting.

Samuel Jay Keyser turns to structural analysis in "Wallace Stevens: Form and Meaning in Four Poems" (*CE* 37:578–98). Each discussion links formal analysis with content and meaning. For example, in the final stanza of "The Death of a Soldier" the total meaning is made clear as "phonological, morphological, and imagistic chiasmus all converge relating form and content in an integral fashion." Too often linguists have been satisfied with essays in structuralism. This article demonstrates how hitherto mostly separated disciplines can be brought together for greater richness of literary experience.

John N. Serio contends that "The Comedian as the Letter C" is the conjunctive unit of Stevens's first book. He sees "Sunday Morning" and "Peter Quince at the Clavier," among others, moving, with "The Comedian," in the direction of the poet's lifelong obsession with the problem of achieving reconciliation between reality and the imagination. Serio would support Perlis and Bornstein when he points out how transforming "banal suburb" into "Olympia" is for Stevens necessary to freedom. His essay is " 'The Comedian' as the Idea of Order in Harmonium" (*PLL* 12:87–104).

Sharon Cameron, in " 'The Sense Against Calamity': Ideas of a Self in Three Poems by Wallace Stevens" (*ELH* 43:584–603), emphasizes as a diminishing factor separation from profundity of experience. In poems like "The Snow Man" or "The World as Meditation" the reader recognizes himself. "Final Soliloquy" goes further by confronting such a question as "What is it we are when we let go of our preconceptions long enough to be anything?" and by proposing a possible alternative for the reader's life pattern.

Terrance J. King, in "Radial Design in Wallace Stevens" (*VLang* 9[1975]:25–46), claims that Stevens's pattern of typographical units, especially in the earlier work, are arranged so as to have numerical and sometimes geometric symmetry. For example, "Life Is Motion" (1919) uses "a stump" as its central unit (with eleven words, 19 syllables on each side of it) and "as a kind of fulcrum for the statement of the piece." Among others, King finds radial design in "Anecdote of the Jar" (1919). As he grew older, King observes, Stevens no longer exerted himself in this kind of "silent metaphor." This is an innovative article.

BSUF 17,ii, publishes three essays on Stevens. Sandy Cohen's article, "A Calculus of the Cycle: Wallace Stevens' 'Credences of Summer,' an Alternate View" (31–36), argues that in "Credences" Stevens is not looking for metaphysical transcendence but an intellectual yea-saying to nature—a "credence of summer" through analysis by means of "aesthetic calculus." It takes many impressions to realize what a summer day is. To make an effort at giving these sensuous images some kind of order is a necessary exercise in calculus.

Robert J. Bertholf, in "Renewing the Set: Wallace Stevens' *The Auroras of Autumn*" (37–45), compares *Auroras* with "Credences" in that it looks for appropriate images to record inevitable changes, here of fall. Innocence is now only "pure principle" and, as such, takes away from the aurora borealis any magic or anthropological wonder. Hence, it is important to believe in a fiction—a projection of the imagination. " 'Prologues to What Is Possible': Wallace Stevens and Jung" (46–50) makes a comparison with Jung in what the author, Janet McCann, finds is something like the "collective unconscious"—*de rigueur* for a commonly recognized reality, in the long run unachievable; so (Sandy Cohen would agree) "the totality of all appearances must be reality enough."

Kermit Vanderbilt—"More Stevens and Shakespeare" (*CollL* 2: 143–45)—sees relations and differences among "The Emperor of Ice-Cream" and closing speeches in some Shakespeare tragedies as they urge the audience to notice the dead but to realize the ongoing demands of life and empire. Michael Payne's "Taking Poets Seriously" (*CollL* 3:83–93) in its brief conclusion uses Stevens's "Of Modern Poetry" as "a synthesis of experience and cognition, a ground for our thoughts, a living memory of our past, and imaginative models for a world we are just beginning to create." These two articles may be useful as teaching aids, but are on the whole obvious and thin. On the other hand, Robert G. Goulet and Jean Watson Rosenbaum present a useful and thoughtful, if uncomplex, reading in "The Perception of Immortal Beauty: 'Peter Quince at the Clavier' " (*CollL* 2:66–72). They examine the dramatic situation, the narrative, and the commentary (Quince's remarks to demonstrate how he takes to myth in moving from sensation and desire to a realization that beauty is immortal).

iii. Cummings, Crane, Robinson, Lodge, Monroe, the Benéts

Gary Lane has written a sound book, *I Am: A Study of E. E. Cummings' Poems* (Lawrence: Univ. Press of Kans.), built around the poet's "dialectic of love, death, and growth," the core of unity in all his work. Explication of 25 poems progresses from love as seduction, through identity and appreciation of self, true death, false death to a "final unity" through transcendence of the limitations of the man and his world. A concluding chapter does not hesitate to point out the poet's weaknesses; but, all in all, Lane classes Cummings as a major poet with affirmative vision, highly developed discipline, and the touch of genius. This book is of significance for all readers of 20th-century poetry.

As we have remarked before, Cummings is an easy target for structural linguists. John M. Lipski applies his techniques to a few brief poems in "Connectedness in Poetry: Toward a Topological Analysis of E. E. Cummings" (*Lang&S* 9:143–63). To clarify his vocabulary and elucidate his practice, Lipski supplies some definitions, then explains that "topology is simply an axiomatic method for formally decomposing a given domain, and the domain upon which the topological structure is to be defined is known as a *space*." There follow two final definitions, scintillant with mystic symbols and technical phrases such as "*nonempty* sets." Having spent 13 pages setting up his scheme, with the illustrative assistance of a few brief Cummings poems, Linski devotes the next three pages to "decomposing" two of these poems, to prove that "human language, especially literary language" is akin to mathematics. He admits that his exercise is only exploratory and needs the cooperation of other scholars to check on its reliability and practicability.

Rushworth M. Kidder describes sensitively, even exquisitely, the economical, witty style of Cummings's drawings, 16 of which are reproduced to illustrate "'Author of Pictures': A Study of Cummings' Line Drawings in *The Dial*" (*ConL* 17:470–505). He says very little about the poems until, in the final paragraph, he points, in a general way, to delight, humor, economy, precision, movement, and life in both pictures and verse.

HLB 24 contains two Cummings items. Kidder (again) examines "'Buffalo Bill's': An Early E. E. Cummings Manuscript" (373–80). He gives a descriptive analysis of the manuscript (reproduced in three plates) and concludes that significant symbols came to the poet from "daily experience" expressed in "the exact rhythm and the perfect word." Richard S. Kennedy's "E. E. Cummings at Harvard: Studies" (267–97) surveys the poet's formal course work at college, where, among languages, he seemed to prefer Greek and Italian. He studied literature under distinguished professors, but had no training in aesthetic analysis so that his later written comments were impressionistic. Harvard's long tradition of writing worked to his advantage. This is a highly useful article, one that scholars interested in other poets might emulate—the contribution of college courses and of professors to the development of an artist.

J. Haule, in "E. E. Cummings as Comic Poet: The Economy of the Expenditure of Freud" (*L&P* 25[1975]:175–80), asserts that Freud theorized that the comic "originates from an economy of expenditure in thought." Haule analyzes "listen my children and you" to show that Cummings had comic quality in Freud's sense, though the two are not "a perfect fit." James E. Tanner, Jr., in "Experimental Styles Compared: E. E. Cummings and William Burroughs" (*Style* 10:1–27), points out that both writers catalogue, punctuate unconventionally, capitalize erratically, alter word classes, bury words, delete, and so on, though Cummings is the more revolutionary. His words and structures are dynamic, whereas Burroughs "retreats from the word" with a feeling of existential inadequacy.

Richard P. Sugg's *Hart Crane's "The Bridge": A Description of Its Life* (University: Univ. of Ala. Press) begins by defining the poet's aesthetics: *The Bridge* is the result of the imagination's giving form and meaning to itself by assimilation and unification of external reality. There follows a close reading of each section of *The Bridge* from "Proem" ("at once prior and posterior to the rest of the poem") to "Atlantis" (not only a conclusion but a signal for the commencement of fulfillment). Sugg has written a reasonable, straightforward interpretation of Crane's "epic," if not brilliant, at least clear and direct, certain to be useful to the classroom teacher and to the graduate student preparing for an examination.

Thomas Parkinson continues his discovery of an interesting literary relationship in "Hart Crane and Yvor Winters: *White Buildings*" (*SoR* 12:232–45), drawing from the 45 letters from Crane to Winters in the library at California—Berkeley. Here Parkinson quotes three of the letters and other documents to show Winters to have been useful and generous. Margaret Jennings, C.S.J., compares Crane's life and art to an arc in his climb from the conflicts of his youth to ecstatic heights back down again when, finding after all only a philosophy of despair, he committed suicide. She contrasts Crane's self-destruction with Sartre's means of "alternate survival" in "Parabola: Hart Crane and Existentialism" (*MarkhamR* 5:31–34).

Marc Simon studies Crane's worksheets and the poems of Samuel
B. Greenberg and discovers how influential Greenberg was in the
composition of "Voyages II." Simon's article is "Hart Crane's 'Greenberg MSS' and the Launching of 'Voyages II'" (*JML* 5:522–29). Z.
Zatkin-Dresner judges "Royal Palm" to be a fine work of art. His
comments are in "Levels of Meaning in Hart Crane's 'Royal Palm'"
(*Thoth* 15,i:29–37), in which he sees the tree as object to be described, as symbol of immortality and transcendence, as poetic imagination itself, and as embodiment of spiritual love. "A Defense of
Hart Crane's Poetic License" (*LWU* 9:182–88), by Reid Maynard,
relates phrases from "At Melville's Tomb" to *Moby-Dick*. Maynard
uses Crane's correspondence about the poem with Harriet Monroe.
He works especially hard to explain Crane's line "Frosted eyes there
were that lifted altars."

Richard Cary has compiled and edited *Uncollected Poems and
Prose of Edwin Arlington Robinson* (Waterville, Me.: Colby College
Press, 1975). The editor's narrative introduction is an account of the
poet's rejections and excisions (here published) from the final
"canon." Copious notes at the end of the volume describe first places
of publication and provide apt quotations from the biographies and
the poet's letters. The book also includes Robinson prose passages
both long and short ("Briefs"), suitably annotated, as well as a useful index. As usual, Cary has done Robinson scholars a great service.

In *CLQ* 12 appear four essays, three focusing on single poems,
the other discussing the last long narratives. R. Meridith Bedell, in
"Perception, Action, and Life in 'The Man Against the Sky'" (29–
37), cites several shorter poems as they confront "observed immediate reality," then turns to the ending of "The Man Against the Sky,"
which, Bedell asserts, is not a summons to suicide, but a call to
conscious decisions to determine appropriate responses. William V.
Davis points out that the twice-mentioned "Auld Lang Syne" in "Mr.
Flood's Party" fits into the doubling technique Robinson uses throughout (e.g., "two moons"). Davis speculates that the expression "enduring to the end" might suggest Matthew 10:22, which could lead to
Matthew 26:39—"let this cup pass from me," thus joining two Biblical
allusions ("doubling"). Davis's article is called "'Enduring to the
End': Edwin Arlington Robinson's 'Mr. Flood's Party'" (50–51).
Michael G. Miller—"Miniver Grows Lean" (149–50)—suggests that
Cheevy has "consumption" aggravated by alcoholism, a physical

wasting away parallel with his spiritual degeneration. Finally, Thelma J. Shinn discusses "The Art of a Verse Novelist: Approaching Robinson's Late Narratives through James's *The Art of the Novel*" (91–100). Her thesis is that what James's book says about dramatic structure, psychological portraiture, themes, the romantic and the real, and characterization (including *ficelles*) finds ample illustration in Robinson's stories. She finds in both writers emphasis on dramatic purpose and careful use of symbol.

In editing *Selected Fiction and Verse* by George Cabot Lodge (St. Paul, Minn.: John Colet Press), John W. Crowley publishes 69 pages of selected poems and verse plays for which he supplies textual commentary. In addition to a bibliography listing manuscripts, sources of published letters, poems in magazines, and books by Lodge, there is also an extended enumeration of secondary sources. An introduction details the poet's life and reviews both his poetry and his prose critically. Crowley admits that Lodge is minor, but defends the idea that he is worth reading as an example of a Conservative Christian Anarchist, fated to be, in his own view, an "alienated poet-warrior."

Abby Arthur Johnson, in "A Free Foot in the Wilderness: Harriet Monroe and *Poetry*, 1912 to 1936" (*IllQ* 37,iv[1975]:28–43), outlines Monroe's early life and career as poet and traces her influence through *Poetry*. The article reviews Pound's attitudes towards her and lauds her "substantial contribution" to the poetry of our time. Laura Benét has published a little book about growing up with her two brothers, who became well-known poets. *When William Rose, Stephen Vincent, and I Were Young* (New York: Dodd, Mead) is written in uncomplex narrative style without any attempt at deep analysis of relationships or causalities. The Library of Congress catalogue suggests "Juvenile Literature" as one classification for the book.

iv. Warren, Ransom, Tate, Jeffers, Lindsay, Masters, Sandburg

Peter Stitt claims Robert Penn Warren to be our best living poet, celebrating man's intellect and imagination and emphasizing the necessity of awareness of time and of a feeling for moral responsibility. Though his best poems range across time, they settle in a single personality—not in a solipsistic sense but in union with creativity in the universe. In "Robert Penn Warren, the Poet" (*SoR* 12:261–76) Stitt supports his opinion in detailed studies of *Incarnations, Audubon,* and *Or Else.* Sister Bernetta Quinn, O.S.F., in "Warren and Jarrell: The Remembered Child" (*SLJ* 8,ii:24–40), examines the 24 parts of *Or Else* and concludes that they are full of "new speculations." After discussing the work of Randall Jarrell, she opines that he and Warren celebrate childhood with unmatched genius in America. William Tjenos theorizes that Warren applies his consciousness to his experience to bring about a response to desire: the present must reform consciousness; the past must take its form from the present. In "The Poetry of Robert Penn Warren: The Art to Transfigure" (*SLJ* 9,i:3–12) Tjenos explicates "Homage to Emerson" to demonstrate his thesis, though he admits that no rigid formula is possible.

To a book centering on Frost (*Centennial Essays II*) Thomas Daniel Young contributes an account developed from his pursuit of facts for a biography of Ransom ("Our Two Worthies: Robert Frost and John Crowe Ransom," pp. 281–90). Young reveals that Frost's enthusiasm for Ransom's *Poems about God* (1919) helped push Henry Holt into publishing Ransom's first book. Young's narrative follows the vicissitudes of the two poets' friendship from that time through the Kenyon years. In another essay on Ransom, Young recounts the incidents of the debates based on *I'll Take My Stand* in various southern cities. Though Ransom did not always take active part in the discussions, he referred to them later as "larks," sources of great enjoyment. Young's account is "A Prescription to Live By: Ransom and the Agrarian Debates" (*SoR* 12:608–21). In fact, says Richard Gray, Ransom maintained that the only road to fulfillment and wholeness is through an agrarian and traditional life, though involving hard work, yet based on ritual and ceremony, necessary to civilization. Gray's "The 'Compleat Gentleman': An Approach to John Crowe Ransom" (*SoR* 12:622–31) explicates "Dead Boy" and "Antique Harvesters" in support of this view. Six letters from Ransom to Allen Tate, written between December 1922 and February 1927, have been published by Young and George Core, who suggest the theme of the letters in their title: "Art as Adventure in Form: Letters of John Crowe Ransom, 1923–1927" (*SoR* 12:776–97). Ransom mulls over the ideas of critical theory which eventuated in *The World's Body* (1938).

A garland of five essays in *SoR* 12 pays tribute to Allen Tate as poet. Cleanth Brooks leads off with "Allen Tate and the Nature of Modernism" (685–97), in which he says that Tate's poetry reveals a world near to destruction because man's "heart and head are hardly on speaking terms anymore." In spite of his unhappy vision, Tate is, in Brooks's opinion, a great artist, a sound critic, and a profound sage. The next essay, by Denis Donoghue, is entitled "Nuances of a Theme by Allen Tate" (698–713), that theme being "the relation of the imagination to the actual world." Faith and sensibility are indispensable to awareness, and Tate in his poems uses occasions and forms to gain "direct access to experience."

Allen Williamson discusses "Allen Tate and the Personal Epic" (714–32). Tate, he argues, has executed in poetry precisely what he adversely criticized in Hart Crane and Pound: a series of lyrics concentrating on self rather than presenting history as a whole: all his poems reflect his feeling of suffocation in the present. His late poems, however, show the effect of his conversion to Catholicism: he is willing now to let tradition guide him and provide him with "expansive possibilities." Related to this discussion is Radcliffe Squire's "Allen Tate and the Pastoral Vision" (733–43), in which the author sees Tate as longing for both the pastoral and the epical visions, but unable to achieve either fully. From "Cold Pastoral" (before 1922) onward he has found strength in both traditions. Finally, Louis D. Rubin, Jr., in "The Serpent in the Mulberry Bush Again" (744–57), reëxamines "Ode to the Confederate Dead" and finds in the serpent of the conclusion a symbol for "a continuity of experience" between past and future as man struggles with belief and meaning.

Four issues of *RJN* continue to supply solid information for students of the poetry of Robinson Jeffers: notices of new and old editions and related publications, reviews of new books, heretofore unpublished letters, descriptions of scholarly holdings in various libraries, titles and sometimes full summaries of dissertations, brief relevant biographies, as well as articles of explication and criticism. *RJN* 44:11–17 presents Henry Nuwer's "Jeffers' Influence upon Walter Van Tilburg Clark," which traces such imagery as the hawk and purification with water in early poetry and his later prose. Donnan Jeffers contributes "Portraits of Robinson Jeffers: A Preliminary List" to *RJN* 45:7–8. In *RJN* 46:5–6 Robert J. Brophy says that Mabel Dodge Luhan's pamphlet, *Robin and Una*, adds "insights into Una's first husband . . . , [a] vivid sense of the daily routine at Tor House,

and [an] analysis of Una's formative relationship with . . . Jeffers."
RJN 47 presents three unpublished letters of Jeffers and excerpts from
letters by Una. An essay by Edward A. Nickerson, "The Holy Light
of Jeffers' Poetry" (19–28), studies the symbolic significance of light
in its many aspects in the poems. "Being shines with the holy light
of renewal, but blackness also calls." Bill Hotchkiss (7–8) reviews
James Shebl's *In This Wild Water: The Suppressed Poems of Robinson Jeffers* (Pasadena, Calif.: Ward Ritchie Press). Jeffers's publishers asked the poet to omit these ten poems from *The Double Axe*
(1948). The book also includes letters exchanged between poet and
publishers as well as meaningful excerpts from Jeffers's original
preface.

Fraser Drew has written a biographical account of Una Jeffers's
Irish travels in 1912, of the visits of Una, Jeffers, and their sons in
1929 and 1937, of the trip in 1948 of husband and wife, and finally of
Jeffers's visit in 1956 (after Una's death) accompanied by his son
Donnan and family. In "Una and Robinson Jeffers at Lough Carra"
(*Éire* 9,iii:118–25), Drew says that the Jefferses were constantly referring to the work of George Moore, of which they were singularly
fond. Robert J. Brophy's excellent *Robinson Jeffers: Myth, Ritual,
and Symbol in His Narrative Poems* (reviewed in *ALS 1973*, p. 324)
has been reissued (Hamden, Conn.: Shoestring Press of Archon
Books) with corrections, updating, and appropriately sweeping and
dramatic illustrations.

Marc Chénetier champions Vachel Lindsay's poetry as multimedia
expression, growing from the poet's conviction that poetry has a social
responsibility. In " 'Free-Lance in the Soul-World': Toward a Reappraisal of Vachel Lindsay's Works" (*Prospects* 2:497–512), Chénetier claims that, though hedged in by many limitations, Lindsay must
be understood to have been an innovator, a man of daring imagery and
of important obsessions, a poet with a highly uncommon imagination.

In celebration of the Bicentennial, Western Illinois University at
Macomb has published *The Vision of This Land: Studies of Vachel
Lindsay, Edgar Lee Masters, and Carl Sandburg*, ed. John E. Hallwas
and Dennis J. Reader. It contains eight original essays by as many
hands. Blair Whitney ("The Garden of Illinois," pp. 17–28) points up
the reliance on the soil of all three poets in creating their imagery
and ideas. There are two essays on Lindsay. Dennis McInerny
("Vachel Lindsay: A Reappraisal," pp. 29–41) explains the poet's

ultimate pessimism ('excess" rather than "meanness of spirit"). In his second Lindsay essay this year, "Vachel Lindsay's American Mythocracy and Some Unpublished Sources" (pp. 42–54), Chénetier makes use of a number of unpublished manuscripts and letters to show Lindsay as something other than a participant in the higher vaudeville. Two essays on Masters follow. "Edgar Lee Masters: The Lawyer as Writer" by Charles E. Burgess (pp. 55–73) studies the complications of character in this man of two careers. Herb Russell, in "After *Spoon River*: Masters' Poetic Development 1916–1919" (pp. 74–81), looks at the poet's problems immediately after his rise to fame. Of the three Sandburg essays, two discuss the poetry and the third considers the Lincoln books. Charles W. Mayer, in *"The People, Yes*: Sandburg's Dreambook for Today" (pp. 82–91), begins with a portrait of Sandburg as two poets—of democracy and of evanescence. The author's argument is that Sandburg faced difficulties in being consistent in an affirmative view. On the other hand, Richard Crowder's "Sandburg's Chromatic Vision in *Honey and Salt*" (pp. 92–104) analyzes the extraordinarily abundant use of vivid color in the poet's last book and concludes that he maintained a basically vigorous interest in the objective world, an interest normally found in a much younger man. In "Sandburg and the Lincoln Biography: A Personal View" (pp. 105–13), Victor Hicken recalls his own reactions to Sandburg's personal appearances and juxtaposes Sandburg's story of Lincoln with the "facts," thus underscoring the "legendary" quality of the biography. *The Vision of This Land* is enriched by a group of photographs (pp. 12–16) and a checklist of "Criticism from 1950–1975" (pp. 114–128), compiled by the indefatigable William White.

Purdue University

17. Poetry: The 1930s to the Present

Linda Welshimer Wagner

i. General

The criticism of contemporary poetry in 1976 appears to be at a stage of consolidation. For the past four years, the number of dissertations and books increased year by year; 1976, conversely, saw only fifteen dissertations (four on Williams, two on James Dickey; others on Galway Kinnell, Howard Nemerov, Randall Jarrell, and several combinations of, particularly, women poets), and not many more books. There did appear to be more essays and reviews of new work by contemporary poets, with several important books announced for 1977, and David Perkins's wise and thorough *A History of Modern Poetry*, vol. 1 (Harvard Univ. Press) appearing this year. (Excellent in its consideration of both English and American work, Perkins's book gives important emphasis to currents sometimes forgotten in present critical enthusiasms—for example, the Chicago school in American poetry; because its second volume will relate more closely to the topics of this chapter, it will receive attention in subsequent years.)

Charles Altieri's "Objective Image and Act of Mind in Modern Poetry" (*PMLA* 91:101–14) continues the trend of last year's best criticism to define and locate distinctive qualities of the poetry being written today. Altieri stresses the common debt of both contemporary and modern poetry to early modern tendencies, despite the apparent emphasis in the more recent poetry toward "discovering the energies and possible moral forces inherent in acts of perception." By analyzing the change in the use of the image, and the author's varying "objective" or "subjective" stance toward it, Altieri takes the reader from the originally startling impact of Flaubert's *Madame Bovary*, through the work of Joyce, Eliot, and Williams, creating his own responsible definition of metonymy in the process. The ability to perceive and then recreate is the modern writer's gift to literary tradition, and some attempt to describe that gift is made in this important essay.

Robert Pinsky intends a similarly wide-ranging approach in his *The Situation of Poetry, Contemporary Poetry and Its Traditions* (Princeton, N.J.: Princeton Univ. Press), but his insights are undercut by what appears to be ignorance of previous critical work done in this area. His opening sentence sets the tone for much of his analysis: "Modern poetry was created by writers born about a hundred years ago."

Pinsky's book is useful in several ways, even if his premises are seldom clearly presented. He often groups poets regardless of chronological correspondences, as in the case of Thomas Hardy, John Crowe Ransom, and John Berryman or Louise Bogan and Frank O'Hara, breaking through the reader's established ways of thinking about the respective poets; and he does insist on the primacy of the single poem, so that many of his analyses are valuable. The chapters, however, are relatively loosely connected.

Much of the criticism focuses on the problem of the individual voice—how credible is that voice when it is specifically personal? How viable is what appears to be the poet's experience, for other readers? The usual answer to this set of questions is that the personal experience is only an image for the human condition, that even the most literal of voices is not exactly autobiographical. Hayden Carruth, however, in "The Art of Love, Poetry and Personality" (*SR* 84:305–13), contends that while such was the situation with the best of modern poetry, the contemporary use of the premise is mistaken. The best modern poets were "engaged in the conversion of crude experience into personality through metaphor . . . *personality* to mean the whole individual subjectivity, the spirit-body-soul," and the act of writing is a "deeply moral endeavor." For many more recent poets, however, the definition of *self* has become very limited, and the poetry that results is only self-indulgent. Paul Ramsey ("Image and Essence, Some American Poetry of 1975" (*SR* 84:533–41) comments on the sameness of the "disconnected" structures in poetry, as offering "not freedom but a trap that traps very much of the best talent of our time: every move means (very nearly) the same thing, and the poems have one principle and genre: mimetic disorganization."

Charles Molesworth answers both these objections in "'We Have Come This Far': Audience and Form in Contemporary American Poetry" (*Soundings* 59:204–25).

Bibliographically, several books have appeared which should make the always elusive study of contemporary literature somewhat more possible. Sander W. Zulauf and Irwin H. Weiser have compiled a new annual *Index of American Periodical Verse: 1973* (Metuchen, N.J.: Scarecrow), which lists single-poem publications by poet and title. Lloyd David and Robert Irwin have compiled a 3,400-entry listing of books of poetry published during the 1950s and 1960s. (*Contemporary American Poetry: A Checklist*, Metuchen, N.J.: Scarecrow, 1975), and Phillis Gershator has this year published *A Bibliographic Guide to the Literature of Contemporary American Poetry, 1970–1975* (Scarecrow). Not only is the reference very useful, divided into critical studies, biographical work, anthologies, and textbooks; but Gershator's long bibliographical essay about other sources for these kinds of materials is valuable to all readers of contemporary literature.

Gary M. Lepper's *A Bibliographical Introduction to Seventy-Five Modern American Authors* (Los Angeles: Serendipity Books) is another important contribution. Of poets, Lepper provides information about Ashbery, Berry, Blackburn, Bukowski, Di Prima, Levertov, Snyder, Wakoski, and many other writers whose publications are usually hard to find. This is a primary listing, with many obscure items listed: Ted Berrigan has 19 items listed, for example; Ed Dorn, 40. Lepper has worked with the cooperation of the poets (and fiction writers as well) and the items run through 1975.

Several anthologies of both poems and statements by poets should also be noted: Stephen Berg and Robert Mezey's second edition, *The New Naked Poetry* (Indianapolis: Bobbs-Merrill) with its useful section of poets' statements and completely revised table of contents; William Heyen's *American Poets in 1976* (Bobbs-Merrill), with essays by each poet in the context of which specific poems are read and discussed; and *The Third Coast: Contemporary Michigan Poetry* (Detroit: Wayne State Univ. Press), ed. Conrad Hilberry, Herbert Scott, and James Tipton. The latter is a strong collection of poetry, most of it by unknown poets, which suggests that poetry is, indeed, alive and well throughout the country.

ii. William Carlos Williams

Only essays (no books) on Williams appeared during 1976. Among the most interesting or innovative are Sherman Paul's "An Introduction to William Carlos Williams" (*Repossessing and Renewing*, pp. 179–94), with his emphasis on Williams's insistence on "playing out the drama of cultural allegiance" while his real interest was in the "interior drama of imagination." Paul chooses "St. Francis Einstein of the Daffodils" as being "modern" in both content and form; unlike Eliot, Williams was not searching for "personal distinction" but rather for a means of giving life to the unknown. As Paul concludes, "With him modernism incorporated organicism and expressed again the American wonder" (p. 192).

R. W. Flint's "America of Poets" (*Parnassus* 5,i:162–82) is more than a review essay of recent books on Williams, though it is that also. Flint discusses the reasons for Williams's importance and the difficulty in critics' seeing those reasons perceptively: he stresses Williams's concern with love of all kinds, and does some expert reading of *Paterson*, especially its language ("its polyphony and counterpoint," "true to a principle of vitality").

Del Ivan Janik ("Poetry in the Ecosphere," *CentR* 20:395–408) finds Williams similar to Roethke, Snyder, and D. H. Lawrence in that he recognizes the importance and independence of biocentric objects, without forcing all things into some human context. Geoffrey H. Movius treats the differences between Williams and Pound during the early years of their friendship ("Caviar and Bread: Ezra Pound and William Carlos Williams, 1902–1914," *JML* 5:383–406); M. L. Rosenthal ("The Idea of Revolution in Poetry," *Nation* 223,iv:117–19) thinks Williams—like most other great poets—is "political" in that he is concerned with people. Rosenthal reads "To Elsie" and sections of *Paterson* as illustration. Linda W. Wagner discusses Williams's use of allusion in comparison to that of Eliot in "Ohhh, That Shakespherian Rag" (*CollL* 3,ii:139–43). Kenneth Johnson discusses the Williams-Eliot situation in "Eliot as Enemy: William Carlos Williams and *The Waste Land*" (*The Twenties: Fiction, Poetry, Drama*, ed. Warren French [Deland, Fla.: Everett/Edwards, 1975] pp. 377–86).

Paul Mariani's "The Poem as a Field of Action & Guerilla Tactics in *Paterson*" (*IowaR* 7:94–117) is an important demonstration of aesthetic theory in practice in what Mariani feels is Williams's strongest work.

Norma Procopiow sees Williams as a "confessional poet" because of his use of "place names and concrete, domestic details" and a "prosody to imitate the contours of conversational language" (in "William Carlos Williams and the Origins of the Confessional Poem," *Ariel* 7,ii:63–75); and Linda W. Wagner stresses that "conversational language" as both idiom and structure in her introduction to *Interviews with William Carlos Williams: "Speaking Straight Ahead"* (Norfolk, Conn.: New Directions). Emily Mitchell Wallace surveys the 25-year friendship between Williams and Norman Holmes Pearson ("River Man, In Tribute to Norman Holmes Pearson," *WCWN* 2,i: 1); John Vernon relates Williams to David Ignatow ("A Crowd of Oneself," *Nation* 223:119–21); Linda W. Wagner speaks of Williams as humanist and educator in "William Carlos Williams' *The Embodiment of Knowledge*," *Nation* 222:282; Joseph N. Riddel discusses the book as an "anti-book" in "Dr. Williams' Anti-(Ante?)dote" (*Boundary 2*, 5:293–303); and Marvin Bell writes of Williams's importance to contemporary poets in two essays in *APR* (5,iii:31–33 and 5,vi: 10–13).

iii. Jack Kerouac, Kenneth Rexroth, Louis Zukofsky, Gary Snyder, Allen Ginsberg, Charles Olson, Robert Creeley, Robert Duncan, Fielding Dawson, David Antin, Jerome Rothenberg

John Tytell's *Naked Angels, The Lives and Literature of the Beat Generation* (New York: McGraw-Hill) treats Jack Kerouac, Allen Ginsberg, and the too often forgotten William Burroughs, both as personalities and as writers. For all his rich detail and good interpretive sense, Tytell's most important contribution is his accurate description of the "Beat" philosophy and movement, placing their roots, appropriately, in the milieu of the 1940s. This is also the best study of the work of these three writers, though Robert A. Hipkiss's *Jack Kerouac, Prophet of the New Romanticism* (Lawrence: Regents Press of Kans.) is also useful. Hipkiss discusses all of Kerouac's writing, poetry and prose, and compares his work with that of other contemporaries, J. D. Salinger, James Purdy, John Knowles, and Ken Kesey. If one does accept the category of "new Romanticism," this comparison is interesting; if not, the reader might wish Hipkiss had spent more time discussing Kerouac's work in depth.

Hipkiss's exposition of Kerouac's prose method is detailed further in "The Logic of Spontaneity: A Reconsideration of Kerouac's 'Spontaneous Prose Method'" by George Dardess (*Boundary 2*, 3:729–43). This essay is followed by a summary of Kerouac's own statements (743–45). Ronald Primeau presents convincingly the importance to Kerouac of the Midwest, especially in *On the Road*; his essay, "'The Endless Poem': Jack Kerouac's Midwest" (*GrLR* 2,ii:19–26) establishes mythic importance for location in Kerouac's work. Victor-Levy Beaulieu takes a more comprehensive perspective in a recent book, *Jack Kerouac: A Chicken-Essay*, trans. Sheila Fischman (Toronto: Coach House Press), which also surveys all the work.

Thomas Parkinson's major essay on "Kenneth Rexroth, Poet" (*OhR* 17,ii:54–67) stresses the importance of the poet's place in American letters—as poet, translator, and editor. Items of interest on Louis Zukofsky are Marcella Booth's *A Catalogue of the Louis Zukofsky Collection* (Austin: Univ. of Tex., Humanities Research Center) and Hugh Kenner's impressionistic "Bottom on Zukofsky" (*MLN* 90:921–22), both items from 1975.

Robert Steuding's *Gary Snyder* (TUSAS 274) is comprehensive and generally accurate, flawed only by a Messianic tone in places. Steuding describes Snyder's cultural role during the 1960s as being of as much significance as some of his poetry. More discerning critical readings are to be found in "Gary Snyder's Turtle Island: The Problem of Reconciling the Roles of Seer and Prophet" (*Boundary 2*, 4:761–77), in which Charles Altieri questions the very cultural role Steuding emphasizes, and Abraham Rothberg's "A Passage to More than India: The Poetry of Gary Snyder" (*SWR* 61:26–38).

Several interesting Ginsberg items add to a more credible identity for the poet than criticism has been presenting recently. Stephen Hahn's "The Prophetic Voice of Allen Ginsberg" (*Prospects* 2:527–67) is a sociopolitical study, with attention to the continuum of the poetry, and the poet's "commitment to art and life as mutually informing categories." Hahn emphasizes Ginsberg's use of various kinds of disjunction (*parataxis*) and ellipses as part of his vision. He also charts the changes in Ginsberg's 25 years of poetry.

To Eberhart From Ginsberg: A Letter About Howl *1956: An Explanation by Allen Ginsberg of His Publication* Howl *and Richard*

Eberhart's New York Times Article "West Coast Rhythms" Together with Comments by Both Poets (Lincoln, Mass.: Penmaen) shows both poets with candor.

Olson, The Journal of the Charles Olson Archives completes the feature "Olson's Reading," and includes 59 pages of early (1953–57) unpublished poems intended to be a part of *Maximus,* complete with notes by George Butterick (6:4–75). Volume 5 contains 65 pages of unpublished manuscript material, "Background to the Maximus Poems, Notes and Essays, 1945–1957." Thomas F. Merrill's essay, "'The Kingfishers,' Charles Olson's 'Marvelous Maneuver'" (*ConL* 17:506–28) discusses the centrality of that poem—both in theme and movement—to Olson's later work.

Parnassus 4,ii:243–76 includes three essays on Olson, Jonathan Williams's "Am-O" (pp. 243–50), a selection of unpublished letters; and Guy Davenport's "In Gloom on Watch-House Point" (pp. 251–59), in which he sees the third *Maximus* collection as the end of American literature that emphasizes America as promise. Olson "is our anti-Whitman. . . . He is a prophet crying bad weather ahead, and has the instruments to prove it" (p. 259). Paul Metcalf also reviews *The Maximus Poems: III* (pp. 260–74), finding in that collection Olson's final turn to a complete subjective identification with his material, "The Last of the Great nineteenth-century Romantics."

Jacob Leed's "Robert Creeley and *The Lititz Review*: A Recollection with Letters" (*JML* 5:243–59) includes correspondence and personal reminiscence from 1950, relating to Creeley, Cid Corman, and the author. Terry R. Bacon's informative interview with the poet, "How He Knows When to Stop: Creeley on Closure" (*APR* 5,vi:5–7) and Philip Milner's "Life at All Its Points: An Interview with Robert Creeley" (*AntigR* 26:37–47) continue the development of primary source material that seems most interesting to Creeley's readers.

One of the most comprehensive readings of Robert Duncan's work occurs in Charles Altieri's "The Book of the World: Robert Duncan's Poetics of Presence" (*Sun & Moon* [College Park, Md.] 1:66–94). Other useful items are George Butterick's *Fielding Dawson, A Checklist* (Univ. of Connecticut, Bibliography Series, no. 7); Shirley Kaufman's retrospective essay, "Charles Reznikoff, 1894–1976: An Appreciation" (*Midstream* 22,vii:51–56); and a special issue of Barry Alpert's *Vort,* 7 (1975) on David Antin and Jerome Rothenberg, including material by the poets as well as by Gil Sorrentino,

346 Poetry: The 1930s to the Present

David Bromige, Hugh Kenner, Kenneth Rexroth, Eric Mottram, and others.

iv. Theodore Roethke, John Berryman, Robert Lowell

Jenijoy La Belle's *The Echoing Wood of Theodore Roethke* (Princeton, N.J.: Princeton Univ. Press) has as theses the concept that Roethke's poetic innovation was rooted in a wide knowledge of earlier poetry, that he was basically a highly traditional and eclectic poet. La Belle perceptively correlates Roethke's poems with those of Wordsworth, Blake, Smart, Donne, Sir John Davies, Whitman, Yeats, Eliot, Dante and others; but this study is more than a search for sources (as some of her short essays—see previous volumes of *ALS* —would suggest). La Belle also explains several stages in Roethke's development, marked by the various ways in which he used his knowledge of poetry, even though, as she admits, Roethke himself "saw his literary tradition not as a series of periods but as a community of selected individual talents, somehow in touch with one another even as he was in touch with them" (p. 165). (Sections of the book appear this year in *WWR* 22:75–84 and *MLQ* 37:179–95. See also Nicholas Ayo's "Jonson's Greek Ode in Roethke," *AN&Q* 13:107.)

Stanley Kunitz records some useful literary history by publishing "Six Letters to Theodore Roethke" (*Antaeus* 23:165–72) and Jay Parini gives details on Roethke's early poems in "Theodore Roethke: The Poet as Apprentice" (*ibid.*, pp. 153–64). Charles Molesworth's "Songs of the Happy Man: Theodore Roethke and Contemporary Poetry" (*JBS* 2,iii:32–51) finds Roethke's work central to other poems because it emphasizes "the individuation of the poet," both in voice and theme. Molesworth sees Roethke as concerned with a search for origins, mystical and physical, and for beliefs, largely existential.

Gary Q. Arpin published *John Berryman: A Reference Guide* (Boston: G. K. Hall) in the introduction to which he divides the poet's work into three periods, and *Master of the Baffled House: The Dream Songs of John Berryman* (Rook Critical Monograph, 1; Derry, Pa.: Rook Society). The latter study includes an overview—partly biographical, partly critical—and a close analysis of the poetry's techniques and form, based on "a pattern of regularity and deviance, each highlighting the other" (p. 38).

A series of biographical essays, written by John Haffenden, serves informally as a near biography. "Paris and a Play" (*JBS* 2,ii:66–70) relates events from 1936; "Berryman in the Forties," in two parts, appeared in *New Review* 3,xxx; "A Year on the East Coast: John Berryman" (*TCL* 22:129–54) and "The beginning of the end: John Berryman, December 1970 to January 1971" (*Critical Quarterly* 18,iii: 81–90)—all essays are well documented and correlated with the poems being written at the respective times.

Jack Vincent Barbera stresses interrelation of theme, image, and myth in "Shape and Flow in *The Dream Songs*," (*TCL* 22:146–62), and describes the "plot" as being "of casual rather than necessary order—variations on the personality of Henry as he lives, remembers, and dreams at various times over the decade." Other essays that deal specifically with *The Dream Songs* are Susan G. Berndt, "Berryman's Baedeker: An Abstract," a study of the epigraphs (*JBS* 2,iii:68–69); Anne B. Warner, "Berryman's Elegies: One Approach to *The Dream Songs*" (*ibid.*, pp. 5–22) and Linda W. Wagner's "Berryman: From the Beginning," relating the poems to his critical study of Stephen Crane (*JBS* 2,ii:71–79). Ernest C. Stefanik, Jr., contributes "A Collation of Berryman's Early Poems, 1938–1948" (*ibid.*, pp. 87–108) by line, and Yuichi Hashimoto discusses "'Winter Landscape' and the Intentional Fallacy" (*JBS* 2,iii:23–29). A review essay by Joel Conarroe ("After Mr. Bones: John Berryman's Last Poems," *HC* 13,iv: 1–12) reminds us that his book on Berryman will be published next year by Columbia University Press.

Charles Molesworth discusses Berryman (as well as Anne Sexton, W. D. Snodgrass, and Sylvia Plath) in "'With Your Own Face On': The Origins and Consequences of Confessional Poetry" (*TCL* 22:163–78), finding that "Berryman's art, then, thrives on what we might call the 'dirty little secret' of our desire for fame," the tension between the secret and public, the contradictory desire to shield and expose.

The same observations could be extended to the poetry of Robert Lowell, whose work in 1976 prompted less criticism than usual. The most inclusive essay was by Irvin Ehrenpreis ("Lowell's Comedy," *NYRB* 28 Oct.:3–6) in which he views Lowell's reliance on comedy as a means to accurate representations of his ambivalences. Lowell's characteristic comparisons between human beings and animals, his own wry self-portraits, his liberties with formal poetic structures (in both his translations and sonnets), his use of theatrical settings, his use of incongruity—Ehrenpreis sees all of Lowell's work to reflect his fascination with the artist's ability to present paradox through a variety of technical means.

In Robert G. Twombly's "The Poetics of Demur: Lowell and Frost" (*CE* 38:373–92) his comparison is between Frost and Lowell's "poetics of stringent social decorum, of constraints thrown upon the reader *not* to respond in certain ways. It is a poetics of affect." Twombly's emphasis on the role of performance (and of the persona as performer) links the two writers' work. He discounts the terms "confessional" when applied to Lowell's writing, because it "means no more than that the incidents in many of his poems are the incidents in his life . . . and that the *I* of his poems accordingly stands bare." Edward Neill makes somewhat the same point in "Aspects of a Dolphinarium: Robert Lowell's Subjective Correlative" (*ArielE* 6,iv [1975]:81–108); and Philip Furia adds some information about the personal in Lowell's poems in " 'IS the whited monster': Lowell's Quaker Graveyard Revisited" (*TSLL* 17:837–54). In *Evolution of Consciousness* R. K. Meiners ("On Modern Poetry, Poetic Consciousness, and the Madness of Poets," pp. 106–20), locates the typical persona (at least in the poems of Lowell, Berryman, Jarrell, Schwartz, and Roethke) in "poet as sufferer," both contemporary and mythic. Meiners describes the "powerful sense of harassment and turmoil" in these poems of "the tragic generation," and finds that their particular "mode of poetic consciousness" reflects their "sense of acute mental and social crisis," of " 'the mind at the end of its tether.' " That Meiners sees what seems to be a fairly personal concern as the means to reach problems that plague all moderns is another step out of the confessional bind into which so much criticism of these particular poets has fallen.

v. Sylvia Plath

Several books and many essays mark the continuing interest in Plath's work. David Holbrook's *Sylvia Plath, Poetry and Existence* (London: Athlone Press) considers both her poetry and fiction, from a quasi-psychological approach. As Holbrook explains, his view of Plath's work is that it cannot be separated from her persona, that "she suffered a characteristic sense of existential insecurity in our world . . . she had, in her private phenomenology, a fatally false sequence in her logic: she believed that death could be a pathway to rebirth, so that her suicide was a schizoid suicide" (p. 1). Unfortunately, Holbrook's only "proof" of this contention is a phenomenological reading of "Poem for a Birthday," and attention to the poems he considers psychotic, "Lady Lazarus," "Sheep in Fog," "Balloons," "Child," "Nick and the Candlestick," "Elm," "The Applicant," with no sense of either technique or humor throughout.

Somewhat more moderately, Edward Butscher reaches some of the same conclusions in Sylvia Plath, Method and Madness (New York: Seabury). He points to essential conflicts between Plath's desire to please her parents and her driving personal ambition, the ego situation then complicated with her marriage to another poet. Butscher sees Plath, in the final poems, as "bitch goddess," and the last work, evidence of her psychic disintegration. Like Holbrook, his choice of poems as "proof" of his diagnosis is the weak link in his argument. One would like a more factual account and a more objective tone.

Several essays concern the problem of Plath's suicide as it relates to—or in some cases, is foreshadowed in—her work: Murray M. Schwartz and Christopher Bollas, "The Absence of the Center: Sylvia Plath and Suicide" (Criticism 18:147–72); Waltrand Mitgutsch, "In Search of the Centre of Being: Two Approaches in Modern Poetry (Sylvia Plath and Ted Hughes)" (RLV 42, U.S. bicentennial issue: 235–53); and Constance Scheerer, "The Deathly Paradise of Sylvia Plath" (AR 34:469–70), Saul Maloff laments the use being made of Plath's death, as the criticism described here so aptly illustrates, in "The Poet as Cult Goddess" (Commonweal 103:371–74).

Perhaps the most helpful work this year was Suzanne Juhasz's chapter on Plath in Naked and Fiery Forms (see vi) and Frederick Buell's essay, "Sylvia Plath's Traditionalism" (Boundary 2, 5:195–211) because—even though he begins by discussing The Bell Jar—Buell interprets the poems as coming from "the tradition of post-Romantic, symbolist writing," even though Plath—and this daring marks her greatness—went, finally, beyond those traditions. At their best (and Buell chooses most of the same poems that Holbrook and Butscher find "psychotic"), Plath's poetry shows that "those private experiences have been so completely absolutized that personal vision becomes also cosmic." That Buell sees Plath as a true artificer, dehumanized in the process of her art, counteracts the kind of pitfall most of the other criticism this year has succumbed to: readers seem surprised when a woman writer can be "so self-conscious, unspontaneous, and alienated." Plath needs to be read as a writer, not as a "woman writer," or, even worse, as a "psychotic."

Gene Ballif's sane reading of the late poems in conjunction with *Letters Home* is also refreshing ("Facing the Worst: A View from Minerva's Buckler," *Parnassus* 5,i:231–49). She is especially perceptive on the poem "Daddy," seeing it as a response to Ted Hughes rather than to Otto Plath.

vi. Marianne Moore, Denise Levertov, Helen Chasin, Adrienne Rich, Elizabeth Bishop, Diane Wakoski

Suzanne Juhasz's *Naked and Fiery Forms, Modern American Poetry by Women, A New Tradition* (New York: Harper and Row) is an excellent study not only of important 20th-century women poets, but also of the problems confronting them as artists. As Juhasz rightly conjectures, the woman artist must have assertive (masculine) qualities in order to pursue her art—"ego strength, independence, need for achievement." But she is also, most likely, "supra feminine" in other areas; and she is "set up to lose, whatever she might do. The conflict between her two 'selves' is an excruciating and irreconcilable civil war" (p. 2). Juhasz's remarks apply to the work produced as well as the life lived.

In addition to reading each poet's work carefully, Juhasz illustrates, chapter by chapter, the tactics each poet has used to meet her "double bind" situation. Emily Dickinson's withdrawal counters Marianne Moore's successful presence in the enemy camp (more attention to Moore's work may be forthcoming, now that the *Marianne Moore Newsletter* is published at 2010 DeLancey Place, Philadelphia 19103). Her three chapters on Denise Levertov, emphasizing that poet's reliance on, and creation of, ritual; Plath, a judicious answer to much of the criticism recorded here; and Anne Sexton, rich with the implications of the poet's own metaphor and simile, are each powerful and accurate essays which deserve to be read whenever the poet is studied. Her concluding chapters link Gwendolyn Brooks and Nikki Giovanni, representative of the black woman's experience, and Adrienne Rich and Alta, of the newly vocal feminist experience. Her concentration here is on new developments in both language and theme; and, as she concludes about the "new tradition": women's poetry speaks with "a voice that is open, intimate, particular, involved, engaged, committed" (p. 205).

Among the more informative essays on American women poets this year are Victoria Harris's analysis of Denise Levertov's progression to the late work, drawing from the moving—and often public —experiences of the recent decade ("The Incorporative Consciousness: Levertov's Journey from Discretion to Unity," *Explor* 4:33–48); Crale D. Hopkins's "Inspiration as Theme: Art and Nature in the Poetry of Elizabeth Bishop" (*ArQ* 32:197–212), a close study of Bishop's imagery as related to thematic concerns; and John F. Nims's survey essay, "Helen Chasin: An Appreciation" (*NewRep* 175,xv:35–37).

Margins, vols. 28–30, includes a "Symposium on Diane Wakoski," pp. 90–129, ed. Toby Olson. Many excellent photographs of the poet and poems written for her punctuate the text of some dozen essays by Olson, David Smith, Gloria Bowles, Michael Rossman, Rochelle Owens, Theodore Enslin, William E. Thompson, Andrea Musher, Carol Ferrier, Armand Schwerner, David Ignatow, George Economou, and James F. Mersmann. The latter's long essay, "Blood on the Moon: Diane Wakoski's Mythologies of Loss and Need" (pp. 116–28), is the kind of informative and accurate correlation of her poetry that we have had so little of. Mersmann identifies image patterns, explains their context and Wakoski's rationale for their choice, and helps in articulating her poetic mythology.

Adrienne Rich's *Of Woman Born, Motherhood as Experience and Institution* (New York: Norton) is of interest here party because of Rich's reputation as a firmly established poet, partly because the book —even though it may seem more sociological than literary—treats many of the problems Juhasz identifies in her study. Rich discusses many phases of the social and biological role of motherhood, including formative concepts about patriarchy and matriarchy, the evolution of myths relating to the feminine, and contemporary relationships among people. *Of Woman Born*, in some ways an extension of Virginia Woolf's 1928 *A Room of One's Own*, should be read by anyone interested in women writers because of Rich's commitment to expressing quandaries long unvoiced: "I realized I could only survive as a woman through a shared commitment with other women; I could only go on working as a writer if I could fuse the woman and the poet, the woman and the thinker. This book comes out of the double need to survive and to work. . . ."

vii. Robert Bly, James Wright, William Stafford, Louis Simpson

Four Poets and the Emotive Imagination: Robert Bly, James Wright, Louis Simpson, and William Stafford (Baton Rouge: La. State Univ. Press), by George S. Lensing and Ronald Moran, groups the four poets into a single helpful category, without slighting recognition of their many differences. Lensing and Moran emphasize the use of colloquial language (and matter-of-fact statement) in a poem heavily imaged, whose impact comes from a congruence of "timing, leaps, and muted shock." The poem's effect on the reader should parallel the seeming recognition of the poet in the process of writing: "The power of the Emotive Imagination rests with its capacity to transform subjects of lyric simplicity into a personal and subjective instant of emotion" (p. 11). And these poets share as well an interest in America as subject and source of myth, in mythic patterns and archetypal images. This useful book should begin to fill the need which grows more apparent each year for a new critical vocabulary that more accurately describes the kinds of poems being written today.

The Great Lakes Review (3,i:66–69) publishes Franklyn Alexander's bibliography of primary and secondary materials about Robert Bly. *Boundary 2* (4:677–726) includes both an interview with the poet, and an essay by Ekbert Faas in which many of Faas's comments parallel the concepts of Moran and Lensing. Kevin Power's "A Conversation with Robert Bly" appears in *TQ* 19,iii:80–94. Michael Atkinson discusses Bly's reliance on Jungian theory in "Robert Bly's Sleepers Joining Hands: Shadow and Self" (*IowaR* 7,iv:135–53), and Julian Gitzen sees much of the appeal of Bly's poetry to lie in its emphasis on "the region around Madison, Minnesota," not so much as natural scene but as inducement to the compelling personal state of mind Bly evinces ("Floating on Solitude: The Poetry of Robert Bly," *MPS* 7:231–41). Through this study of the poet's characteristic imagery, Gitzen concludes that he is as important a social critic as was W. H. Auden.

Jonathan Holden's *The Mark to Turn: A Reading of William Staf-*

ford's Poetry (Lawrence: Univ. Press of Kans.) is a thorough and accurate close reading of Stafford's major poems. Holden, himself a poet, is a good reader, and his contentions that Stafford's language is the source of his impact—its positioning in a seemingly artless structure—and other technical implications are well substantiated. The book is another in the series from Kansas which offer succinct, valuable, but short surveys of poets who have not yet received adequate critical attention.

viii. Frank O'Hara, John Ashbery, A. R. Ammons, Kenneth Patchen

Marjorie Perloff gives convincing reasons for the current interest in O'Hara in "Frank O'Hara and the Aesthetics of Attention" (*Boundary* 2, 4:779–806). She points to his innovative use of time shifts (consonant with his disdain for the temporal) and the employment of techniques of action painting no less than film in his verbal work. As with any innovative poet, readers must learn to distinguish structural and syntactic patterns instead of concentrating only on the themes of O'Hara's work. Fred Moramarco links Ashbery with O'Hara in the respect of their use of visual, graphic effects ("John Ashbery and Frank O'Hara: The Painterly Poets," *JML* 5:436–62), trying to create "a parallel verbal universe" corresponding to a visual one. Moramarco describes the biography of each man so that the reader can understand the affinities; he emphasizes that—of the two—"The painterly dimension of Ashbery's work is broader than of O'Hara's . . . and incorporates a painterly sensibility drawn from various periods of art history."

Anthony Libby ("O'Hara on the Silver Range," *ConL* 17:240–62) agrees with Perloff and Moramarco that the poet links American poetry and modern painting. Libby shows the comparison between Williams and O'Hara (especially in the latter's poem "Personism"), more evident in technique than in theme; and relates O'Hara to Jackson Pollock's art in his tendency to abandon the expected visual imagery.

Alvin Rosenfeld's discussion, "A. R. Ammons: The Poems of a Solitary" (*APR* 5,iv:40–41), stresses the meditative quality of the work, that evincing "the disciplined satisfactions of perception and reflection. . . . Seeing is the stimulus to thought in this poet's world, and thought a release into finer observations." Rosenfeld places Ammons in the context of Emerson, Dickinson, and Frost for many of the same reasons that Harold Bloom relates his work to that of the British Romantics (see Bloom's reprinted essays on Merwin, Ashbery, Strand, and Ammons in *Figures of Capable Imagination*, pp. 123–233) and D. E. Richardson relates his writing to that of the strongest southern poets (Ammons was reared in the South), in "Southern Poetry Today," *SR* 12:879–90.

R. W. Flint ("The Natural Man," *Parnassus* 4,ii:49–56) points to "thematic clusters" in the wide variety of Ammons's poems, and refuses to align him with any other American poet writing today. His strength is his *Diversifications*.

To conclude this year's survey of criticism, which necessarily and apologetically omits mention of much good writing, let attention fall on James Schevill's "Kenneth Patchen: The Search for Wonder and Joy" (*APR* 5,i:32–36), an essay about one of America's overlooked but seminal poets by another fine writer. In Schevill's blend of memoir and criticism, the reader catches sight not only of Patchen's energetic and celebratory writing but also of the truest impulse toward criticism, great admiration for the work being described, and for the writer whose creation that work is: "Patchen's poetry and art reveal an incredible dialogue between the world of his reality, his making, and the world that surrounded him with its distortions of war, illness, poverty, politics, death. Out of this dialogue, this search through fantastic realms of color, line, and verbal textures, comes a final triumph, the sense of a man of faith who conquers pain and disaster and finds his own world of love. . . ." [p. 35]

When the poems of writers as good as Patchen—and Williams and Plath and Levertov and Olson and countless others—exist, and when that work is dynamic and innovative—ears in 1976 still tuned to Ezra Pound's injunction to "Make it new!"—the need for searching and directive criticism becomes more and more apparent. As Theodore Roethke once suggested, the reader's task should be to "solve all the leaps of light."

Michigan State University

18. Drama

Winifred Frazer

There may be no landmarks of scholarship in American drama in this bicentennial year, but there is a volume by Richard Foreman, *Plays and Manifestos*, ed. Kate Davy (New York: N.Y. Univ. Press), illustrating and explaining his Ontological-Hysteric Theatre—a consciousness-altering drama, meant to be experienced rather than understood. Sharing Gertrude Stein's phenomenological esthetic, Foreman focuses on the moment-to-moment reality of things in a kind of "atomic" structure in 39 plays with such titles as *Sophia=(Wisdom) Part 3: The Cliffs*. Since he sees the nature of reality—ontology—to be made up of the "pieces of things" which the mind experiences, he breaks up the traditional conflict (hysteric) basis of drama into the momentary random fits and starts of the human consciousness. Since 1968 Foreman has produced 21 O-H plays in off and off-off Broadway theatres, using electronic music, tape-recorded cues, off-stage voices and spoken recorded "Legends," as well as an assortment of strange sound and lighting effects.

In contrast—fortunately, some will say—there is still interest in the well-made, proscenium-arch play, as is evidenced in the paperback reprint of George Pierce Baker's *Dramatic Technique* (New York: Da Capo). In his introduction to this Workshop 47 text of 1919, Harold Clurman calls Baker's advice modest and sensible. Tracing the precise steps in the development of a play from its seed idea to the completed script, the book in its teaching of method and craftsmanship is, according to Clurman, a "classic" which is, above all, "concrete." It should be noted that Clurman uses *concrete* as opposed to *theoretical* or *abstract*—not in the modern sense of concrete poetry, which, like the concrete O-H theatre, illustrates the phenomenon which is its subject.

Theatre criticism is the concern of two books. In *Persons of the Drama* (New York: Harper and Row), Stanley Kauffman has gathered a decade of his "theater criticism and comment" in a volume of reviews written for the *New Republic* and the *New York Times* and others delivered over PBS-TV in New York. He also includes articles from various journals—one critical of Joseph Papp, who by "the bulk and busyness of his career" has acquired an undeserved reputation. In a discussion of "Homosexual Drama and Its Disguises" Kauffman complains that three important American homosexual playwrights disguise homosexuality under the guise of marital arguments on stage —a practice he admits they are forced into by American mores. Covering American theatre from Foreman's Ontological-Hysteric to William Ball's American Conservatory Theater of San Francisco, Kauffman, who has previously published three books of film criticism, shows empirical but also idealistic judgment in his analysis of theatre people, of modes in modern drama, and of the theatre critic himself.

Roderick Bladel, in *Walter Kerr: An Analysis of His Criticism* (Metuchen, N.J.: Scarecrow), concludes that Kerr is an "impressionist and a relativist," interested in affective criticism, "the shock of delight" which an audience experiences when playwright, director, and actors intuitively create a tension that makes the audience feel a personal involvement in the "show." Besides captioning some 30 photographs of popular plays with Kerr's words, Bladel has pieced together Kerr's comments on various aspects of theatre, such as "acting," "design," and "the structure of playwriting," in an attempt to uncover Kerr's theory of the art of theatre. He concludes that Kerr, a successful playwright himself, is interested in discussing principles only in terms of plays. Condemned by esthetes and intellectuals as a "supercritic" wielding his power through the *New York Times* to extol the popular and condemn the classical and the experimental, Kerr in some 3,000 reviews and essays at least provides a vivid record of what the public responded to in mid-20th century American theatre.

The December issue of *Modern Drama* (vol. 19, no. 4) is a bicentennial number on American drama. Besides pieces on O'Neill, Miller, Williams, and Albee (see individual playwrights) and black playwrights, there are discussions of the past, present, and future of American drama. Editor Walter Meserve, in a Foreword, makes a brief case for greater study of the entire two hundred years. In "Birthday Mutterings" (pp. 417–21), Gerald Weales describes the condition of current American theatre as one in which "everyone is riding off in all directions." Finding regional, university, and off-Broadway theatres first producing the plays which later go to Broadway, the post-World War II playwrights no longer active, black playwrights writing for increasing numbers of black audiences, musicals less lavish, and traditional Broadway comedy less popular than in past decades, Weales dares make no positive generalizations about the future.

Thomas Grant in "American History in Drama: the Commemorative Tradition and Some Recent Revisions" (pp. 327–39) describes American plays which commemorate people and events, such as *Valley Forge, The Patriots, The Magnificent Yankee,* and, on the other hand, such revisionist plays as Robert Penn Warren's *Brother to Dragons,* Arthur Kopit's *Indians,* and Robert Lowell's *The Old Glory,* which redefine myths and old attitudes. Peter Shaw, writing on this year's revival of the last (" 'The Old Glory' Reconsidered," *Commentary* 61:64–67), denounces *The Old Glory* trilogy as agit-prop of the sixties, which he considers the age of rubbish. In "The-May-Pole of Merry Mount" Lowell makes the Puritans symbols of American greed and racism; in "Endicott and the Red Cross" he celebrates street violence and humiliation of the establishment; in "Benito Cereno," his Delano stands for vulgarity, involvement in business, and racial murder.

i. 18th and 19th Centuries

Theatre history in America is of interest to several researchers. In *Antebellum Charleston Dramatists* (University: Univ. of Ala. Press), Charles S. Watson describes the period from the 1790s to the Civil War, during which the Charleston theatre led other southern cities in original dramatic writing for the stage, its nearest competitors being New Orleans, Richmond, and Norfolk. From 1800 to 1825 only the northern cities of New York, Philadelphia, and Boston surpassed it in output. Providing evidence of Raymond Williams's theory of drama as a reflector of its period, Watson shows that the pro-French, pro-Republican nationalistic view of the late 18th century gradually gave way to a sectional view as the question of slavery emerged. Although playwrights like William Ioor and John Blake White made important contributions, Watson gives evidence that William Gilmore Simms, with his plays *Michael Bonham* and *Norman Maurice*, both of which favored admission of slave states to the union, was the outstanding playwright of Charleston.

Evidence of a traveling company of players is provided by Yashdip Singh Bains in "The American Company of Comedians in Halifax in 1768" (*DR* 56:240–46). From August through October the American Company of Comedians from Brunswick, North Carolina, under the leadership of an actor named Mills presented such plays as Smollett's *The Reprisal*, Lillo's *The London Merchant*, Fielding's *The Virgin Unmasked*, and Rowe's *The Fair Penitent*. Although the *Nova Scotia Gazette* published Puritanical letters protesting the presence in Halifax of this first company of professionals to visit Canada, the Players apparently portrayed Vice Punished and Virtue Applauded to the satisfaction of the audiences. Anti-British propaganda emerges in a short play reproduced from the *Boston Gazette* (May 23 and July 19, 1773) by Edmund M. Hayes in "Mercy Otis Warren: *The Defeat*" (*NEQ* 49:440–58). The second of three plays by Mercy Warren satirizing Governor Hutchinson as Rapatio, Bashaw of Servia, *The Defeat*, like the others, portrays him as a Judas, guilty of double-dealing with the British to betray the colonies.

George Winchester Stone, Jr., relates American to British drama in "Lag and Change: Standards of Taste in Early American Drama" (*ETJ* 28:338–46). In spite of the time lag between a British production and the presentation of the same drama in America, the cultural ties with England remained for many years after the political cord was severed, if theatre imports are any evidence. If a Britisher had attended the Baltimore theatre in 1782–83, he would have seen almost the same repertory as he had seen in London 20 years earlier: tragedies such as *Isabella*, *Richard II*, *The Roman Father*, *Zara*; comedies such as *The Gamester*, *The Wonder*, *The Clandestine Marriage*; and farces like *Catherine and Petruchio*, *Irish Widow*, and *High Life Below Stairs*. By 1856 in Baltimore he would have seen the kind of spectacle—*The Naiad Queen*, or *The Revolt of the Water Nymphs*—that he had enjoyed in London in 1802, whereas in London taste would have shifted from melodrama to sophisticated comedy and the beginning of the problem play. Until the 1860s London (granting the time lag) provided the basis for the American theatre.

Matthew Dolkey, in "Follies in Fashion: The Afterpiece in the

American Theatre" (*Players* 51:96–102), points out that from 1750 to 1860 the afterpiece was an expected part of an evening's performance following a full-length drama. These consisted of short, usually anonymous ballad operas, farces, pantomimes, and later melodramas and burlesques. As vaudeville, minstrel, and variety shows came in and as the performance was moved in mid-19th century from 6 to 8 o'clock, the afterpiece declined, to be revived only in the 20th century in the boisterous, escapist animated cartoon following a film.

ii. Late 19th, Early 20th Century

Several theatrical figures of the late 19th and early 20th century are the subjects of review. In "E. E. Rice and Musical Burlesque" (*Players* 51:154–66), Allan S. Jackson writes of one of America's most important theatrical producer-managers of musical extravaganzas— *Hiawatha, The Corsair,* and, for the Chicago Columbian Exposition, *1492.* Combining the talents of such stars as Lillian Russell and Fay Templeton, with huge choruses and lavish sets of ships, jungles, and palaces in musical numbers, some of which he wrote himself, Rice provided the public at the turn of the century with productions which pleased the American taste of the era.

Between the years 1905 and 1914 a thriving Italian theatre in the North Beach area of San Francisco produced grand opera, Shakespeare, Goethe, Dumas, Suderman, Otway, as well as *commedia dell'arte* and vaudeville sketches by the comic Farfariello, who portrayed for Italian immigrants the difficulty of adjusting to America. In "Antonietta Pisanelli Alessandro and the Italian Theatre of San Francisco: Entertainment, Education, and Americanization" (*ETJ* 28:206–19), Maxine Seller tells of the remarkable woman-singer and entrepreneur—whose productions, though in a limited locale, seem to have outclassed in quality those of more prominent American managers. Writing of a theatrical figure from across the continent, Richard Moody in "Edward Harrigan" (*MD* 19:319–25) finds this Dickens-like creator of the "Mulligan" plays in the 1880s, depicting immigrants of the Lower East Side, a playwright and director worthy of more notice.

As the leading serious American dramatist of the period, Herne is the subject of Patti G. Gillespie's "James A. Herne: A Reassessment" (*Players* 51:66–71). Her conclusion is that, in spite of Herne's innovative realism in characterization, diction, and setting, his plays are "episodic" and "out of balance" in construction.

iii. 20th Century

a. **Eugene O'Neill.** Nothing very new emerges in a half dozen articles and a book about O'Neill, but the continuing interest in new examinations of the Nobel Prize playwright testify to his importance. H. N. Levitt analyzes O'Neill's plays according to Alan Reynolds Thompson's classification of the six sources of laughter in "Comedy in the Plays of Eugene O'Neill" (*Players* 51:92–95) and concludes that although all examples show "verbal humor," only the late autobiographical plays show "comedy of ideas." Thomas P. Adler's "Through a Glass Darkly: O'Neill's Esthetic Theory as Seen through His Writer Characters" (*ArQ* 32:171–83) begins with the poet in *Fog* and extends through Edmund in *Long Day's Journey*, proving through nine writers that they can lift man through the fog to a region where "the truth of life's meaning is revealed." In an influence-of-Strindberg article, "*Miss Julie* and O'Neill" (*MD* 19:351–64), Egil Tornqvist points out similarities in the *Electra* trilogy and *Miss Julie*: Lavinia like Julie is boyish and Puritanical, proud and finally self-punishing; Christine's affair with Brant, "son of a servant," is like that of Julie's with Jean.

Three items are concerned with O'Neill and ritual: John H. Stroupe's "The Abandonment of Ritual: Jean Anouilh and Eugene O'Neill" (*Renascence* 28:147–54), James A. Robinson's "O'Neill's Grotesque Dancers" (*MD* 19:341–49), and Leonard Chabrowe's book *Ritual and Pathos: The Theater of O'Neill* (Lewisburg, Pa.: Bucknell Univ. Press). In the first, Stroupe claims that since the renunciation of the rituals established by society equals the renunciation of life, Anouilh's characters—Antigone, Becket, and Orpheus—perish, whereas some of O'Neill's—Nina Leeds, the inhabitants of Hope's Bar—accept social programming and survive, illusion itself becoming ritualized in *Iceman*. In the second, Robinson describes the bizarre dances and mechanical movements in O'Neill's expressionistic plays, leading to the grotesque mass movements of *Lazarus*. Leonard Chabrowe, in the last, has parlayed his very perceptive article of 1962, "Dionysus in *The Iceman Cometh*" (*MD* 4:377–88), into a whole book, thus giving wider exposure to O'Neill's theory of tragedy as ritual, and to his practice of learning from *Lazarus* how to get naturalistic choric effects in *Iceman*. Chabrowe further makes the case—hardly a new one but worth proving again—that O'Neill's great plays are cathartic in effect, moving the audience to the pathos which Nietzsche postulated as the esthetic effect of tragedy.

Perhaps the most ingenious of the O'Neill pieces is Lucina P. Gabbard's "At the Zoo: From O'Neill to Albee" (*MD* 19:365–74). In both *The Hairy Ape* and *The Zoo Story*, Gabbard sees the metaphor of man caged within himself and society as conformist, materialistic, and indifferent. Although four decades apart in time, both plays mirror "the increasingly suicidal nature of modern man and society," a major difference being O'Neill's strong hero in the tragic mode, in contrast to Albee's ineffectual protagonist in the ironic mode.

Besides the above, Ernest G. Griffin edits a collection of formerly published essays, *Eugene O'Neill: A Collection of Criticism* (New York: McGraw-Hill) in the Contemporary Studies in Literature Series. Many of the essays have not been reprinted in other *O'Neill* collections. William T. Going, in "Eugene O'Neill, American" (*PLL* 384–401), makes a well-documented case for O'Neill as a playwright in the mainstream of representative artists which include Hawthorne, Melville, and Frost.

Of interest to all scholars of O'Neill is the *Eugene O'Neill Newsletter*, appearing three times a year (Jan., May, Sept.) under the editorship of Frederick Wilkins, Suffolk University, Boston 02114. Included are an exchange of critical views, notes on various productions of O'Neill's plays, and information about Tao House, which may in time house a company to perform O'Neill's plays.

b. **Between the Wars.** One of the big success stories of the 1920s is that of the author of *Abie's Irish Rose*, who besides making millions as author and producer of the play, wrote numerous vaudeville sketches and 20 other plays. Doris Abramson and Laurilyn Harris relate her story in "Anne Nichols: $1,000,000.00 Playwright" (*Players* 51:123–25). In the world of the theatre an unknown can succeed and a known like F. Scott Fitzgerald can produce a flop. The latter's play, *The Vegetable* (New York: Scribner's), now in paperback reprint, was first published in 1923. Although reworked three times and emended with many suggestions from Edmund Wilson and Maxwell

Perkins, the produced play was a "frost." Satirizing the desire of every American boy to become president (otherwise he is a vegetable), Fitzgerald has his Jerry Frost go from President to postman—happily. An appendix of emendations may be of interest to the Fitzgerald scholar.

Concerning known playwrights of the period, Gerald Weales, in "The Very High Comedy of Philip Barry" (*Commonweal* 103:564–66), regrets that the republication of eight Barry plays last year (*States of Grace*, New York: Harcourt Brace) has not brought the revival that Barry admirers hoped for—either of his high comedies or of his religious-philosophical fantasies.

There is now a long-overdue volume on Maxwell Anderson in a standard series (TUSAS 279). With the help of Anderson's sister and son, Alfred S. Shivers has fashioned a useful biographical chapter and gives competent treatment to some 23 of Anderson's numerous published plays.

The entire December issue of *ETJ* (vol. 28, no. 4) consists of "A Self-Portrait of the Group Theatre." Edited by Helen Krich Chinoy, who interviewed the living members and gathered much personal information about deceased founders, the issue consists of reminiscences by Harold Clurman, Morris Carnovsky, Robert Lewis, Cheryl Crawford, Elia Kazan, Lee Strasberg, Mordecai Gorelick, and others. An important addition to Clurman's *The Fervent Years*, Chinoy's issue includes a chronicle of events between 1925 and 1940, some dozen pictures, and a general record of the experience which "marked the participants for life." Benjamin Appel, in "Odets University" (*LitR* 19:470–74), carries on the story of one important member of the Group theatre to 1951, when Clifford Odets was teaching playwriting at the Actors Studio. Called to appear before HUAC, Odets revealed the names of those he had known before the war as Communists, turning former friends against him and ending the "university," much to the regret of such students as playwright Appel. The story of the demise of the Federal Theatre Project in 1939 and the efforts of many of the country's leading actors and playwrights like Odets to get appropriations to keep it going is told by Patrick Chmel in "The Ignored Majority: Actors Respond to the Declining FTP" (*Players* 51:114–17).

Since her career as a playwright, Lillian Hellman has recently had a second, as a biographer of herself and her times. Her memoir, *An*

Unfinished Woman (1969) was followed by *Pentimento: A Book of Portraits* (1973) and this year by *Scoundrel Time* (Boston: Little, Brown), wherein she narrates the events of the McCarthy era and how the hearings affected her and Dashiell Hammett, who went to jail for refusing to name contributors to the Civil Rights Congress jail bond fund. Without vindictiveness she concludes sadly that Mr. Nixon later, with his Haldeman and Ehrlichman, made McCarthy's Cohn and Schine look like "cute little rascals from grammar school" and that America quickly hides its mistakes in forgetfulness, thereby learning little from them. In a tribute, "Lillian Hellman" (*NewRep* 175:25–27), John Hersey praises her for being "radically political while essentially remaining outside politics." Her response to McCarthyism was, "I simply will not do this indecent thing." In all her works and in herself, according to Hersey, "she gives us glimpses of *all* the possibilities of life on this mixed-up earth." From Cornelia Otis Skinner, another prolific woman writer of the theatre, comes *Life with Lindsay and Crouse* (Boston: Houghton Mifflin), an entertaining account of two theatrical giants and their collaborative efforts on such productions as *Life with Father, Arsenic and Old Lace*, and *Call Me Madam.*

c. Mid-Century—Inge, Miller, Williams, Albee. An item on Inge, Phillip M. Armato's "The Bum as Scapegoat in William Inge's *Picnic*" (*WAL* 10:273–82), relates Hal, the broad-shouldered buck who is cast out of town, to Captain America of *Easy Rider*, likewise used by aggressive residents as scapegoat for their own frustration. Another by Charles E. Burgess, "An American Experience: William Inge in St. Louis 1943–49" (*PLL* 12:438–68), gives a well-documented account of Inge's teaching and newspaper career preceding his successful plays of the 1950s.

Arthur Miller expresses his opinions in an interview at the University of Michigan between rehearsals of the premiere 1974 productions of Miller's work *Up from Paradise*, as recorded by Robert A. Martin and Richard D. Meyer in "Arthur Miller on Plays and Playwriting" (*MD* 19:375–84). There is now a second, updated edition of Hayashi Tetsumaro's 1969 *An Index to Arthur Miller Criticism* (Metuchen, N.J.: Scarecrow).

The life and plays of Tennessee Williams each year elicit a number of commentaries, frequently on his use of myth and symbol. Nancy

Baker Traubitz, in "Myth as a Basis of Dramatic Structure in *Orpheus Descending*" (*MD* 19:57–66), explains Williams's reworking of the play to include myths such as the loss of Eden, the battle of angels, the Crucifixion, the destruction of Orpheus, and possibly Adonis as the beloved—all the while never violating the naturalistic style. The first of two essays by Mary Ann Corrigan—"Realism and Theatricalism in *A Streetcar Named Desire*" (*MD* 19:385–96)—like Traubitz's article, treats of the conflict between the realism of the stage picture and the depth of agony revealed underneath by distortion of reality through symbol. The second, "Memory, Dream, and Myth in the Plays of Tennessee Williams" (*Renascence* 28:155–67), might well be titled "Time in TW": in his early plays, his characters are time-bound; in the 1950s they quest for what is timeless; in the plays of the next two decades they immerse themselves in time, rather than escaping or denying it.

Making a more thorough case in an encomium, John Satterfield in "Williams's *Suddenly Last Summer*: The Eye of the Needle" (*MarkhamR* 6:27–33) analyzes symbols, from the names of the characters to the sensual garden scene (emphasizing Williams's purpose in such puns as three times calling the pieces of metal, which the little cannibals play as they destroy Sebastian, "cymbals"). Overloaded as the play may be with ornate trappings and fantastic richness of "emotional components," it is a humpbacked camel which "forces an expansion of the needle's eye opening on artistic paradise."

Not quite such high praise is deserved by Williams's autobiography, *Memoirs* (Garden City, N.Y.: Doubleday, 1975), as it is a stream-of-consciousness account of his early life, his playwriting, his associates and friends, his breakdowns, and his triumphs. Williams obviously enjoys this confessional, having learned the technique of free-associational recall during periods of psychoanalysis. Along with the account of Williams's life by his mother, Edwina Dakin Williams (*Remember Me to Tom*, New York: G. P. Putnam's, 1963), *Memoirs* contains a lot of bits and pieces of interest to students of the playwright, as does Williams's semiautobiographical novel, *Moise and the World of Reason* (New York: Simon and Schuster, 1975).

Jenijoy La Belle has a new explanation of the title of Albee's "*Who's Afraid of Virginia Woolf?*" (*Expl* 35,1:8–9): Woolf's short story, "Lappin and Lapinova," portraying a couple who imagine themselves as king and queen of the rabbits, until Lappin, tiring of the game, explains that Lapinova has been caught in a trap and killed. In another note with the same title (*Expl* 35,ii:8–10) Leonard J. Leff points out that the Bette Davis film, *Beyond the Forest*, from which Martha quotes the line, "What a dump," has, like Albee's play, much naturalistic bitchery, verbal castration, and exposure of the illusions of a discontented wife. In "Albee's Festival Chant: *Who's Afraid of Virginia Woolf?*" (*MichA* 9:61–67), Grace Stewart Wurster asserts that it is certainly not George who is afraid. The spring rites of Albee's festival affirm for George the fertility of ritual, the purgation of the extraneous guests and of the son who might replace him, and the resurrection of his masculinity in the eyes of Martha. In "Death as a Mirror of Life: Edward Albee's *All Over*" (*MD* 19:67–77), Robbie Odom Moses claims that there is more life in the dying husband than in the living children, wife, and mistress and that, as Albee sees it, 20th-century family life is built upon "rancor, resentment, and rivalry."

d. **Contemporary.** If anyone doubts that the age of the WASPish Broadway play is past, he need look only at the varieties of regional and minority theatre dealt with in the following items. In "Hawaiian Pidgin Theatre" (*ETJ* 28:57–68), Dennis and Elsa Carroll relate the success of the Kumu Kahua group, which has moved from the University to a large professional theatre, with such plays as *Twelf Nite or Wateva!* With the great success of an improvisational pidgin group, Booga Booga, as well, such theatre may soon move to the mainland. *Contemporary Chicano Theatre* (Notre Dame, Ind.: Univ. of Notre Dame Press), edited by Roberto J. Garza, includes eight plays by Chicano playwrights, most of whom are connected with schools or colleges in the Southwest. Garza points out that from the social-realist mode of the Teatro Campesino of Luis Valdez in Delano, California, Chicano playwrights are moving toward a cosmic view of the human condition, as reflected in the variety of the eight plays in this collection.

An Italian-American playwright is the subject of Mario B. Mignone's "Mario Fratti and the Theatre of Entrapment" (*Players* 51: 46–53). Called an American Pirandello as well as an Italian Tennessee Williams, Fratti's many one-act plays (*The Cage*, 1962, being best known) are extremely popular in off- and off-off Broadway theatres. Through lively stage action, scenic ingenuity, spontaneous dialogue, as well as humor and biting satire, Fratti makes man aware of the political, social, and economic forces which may be his downfall, but which are part of the reality of life. Peter James Ventimiglia, in "Through Others' Eyes: The Image of the Italian-American in Modern Drama" (*ItalAm* 2:228–39), reviews characters in such plays as *They Knew What They Wanted, The Rose Tattoo* and *A View from the Bridge*, who are of historic interest to those Italians moving into the American mainstream.

The March issue of the *Drama Review* (vol. 20, no. 1), on the theme of "Theatre and Therapy," covers the Nuyorican (Puerto Rican) street theatre of New York, the Cell Block theatre of New Jersey state prisons, Anne Halprin's Therapy Workshop dance theatre of San Francisco, Robert Wilson's Movement Workshops, Zen training for the actor, and psychologists' use of Primal Theatre in therapy. The following issue for June (vol. 20, no. 2), headed "American Theatre," includes among others a description of Indian tribal ceremonies, theatre in America's Chinatowns, the Otrabanda Company traveling the Mississippi River by raft, Hispanic Oratorio in New York City, and Disneyland's Carousel Theatre performance, "America Sings."

Articles on two of today's well-known playwrights also testify to a theatre much changed from that of earlier decades. Charles R. Backman, in "Defusion of Menace in the Plays of Sam Shepard" (*MD* 19:405–15), tells of Shepard's use in 27 plays performed in the last ten years of such popular culture as grade-B movies, sci-fi, and horror films, to create potentially violent characters and forces, which he then defuses by avoidance of confrontation or by devices of audience alienation.

Tom Prideaux writes in praise of Preston Jones in "The Classic Family Drama is Revived in 'A Texas Trilogy'" (*Smithsonian* 7:48–54). Written for the Dallas Theatre Center, Jones's regional plays portray the three stages in the life of Lu Ann Hampton Laverty Oberlander, whose full name gives the middle play of the trilogy its title. She passes from cheerleader to divorcée through a second marriage and widowhood, supporting her daughter, caring for her old father, "salty and hard" but uncomplaining.

Indefatigable Ruby Cohn in *Modern Shakespeare Offshoots* (Princeton, N.J.: Princeton Univ. Press) describes several American plays derived from Shakespeare, including James Branch Cabell's

Hamlet Had an Uncle, Barbara Garson's *McBird,* Elmer Rice's *Cue for Passion* and Percy MacKaye's *Caliban by the Yellow Sands,* written for the tercentenary of Shakespeare's death.

e. **Film.** In a year when a lead article in *PMLA*—"Rosebud, Dead or Alive: Narrative and Symbolic Structure in *Citizen Kane*" (91:185–93)—is on a motion picture and when that article "applies traditional methods of literary criticism" to a well-known American film, it is perhaps time for *ALS* to include an annual section on this art form. Robert L. Carringer sees Rosebud not as mere "Hollywood gimmickry" but as part of a "subtle ironic design"—a symbol which, instead of explaining everything, serves in the film's complex narrative organization as an ironic comment on him who thinks it will explain everything. Books more numerous each year cover film criticism (some of them by critics of the stage), film history, film language, and semiotics. The TUSAS volume *Paddy Chayefsky* by John M. Clum is a welcome critical biography of a writer best known for his television and film scripts (recently *Network*) who also achieved successes with live theatre in *The Tenth Man* and *Gideon.*

iv. Reference Works

William C. Young has added to his previous volumes of *Documents of American Theatre History.* His *Famous American Playhouses* in two volumes, and *American Theatrical Arts: A Guide to Manuscripts and Special Collections in the United States and Canada* are followed by the two-volume *Famous Actors and Actresses on the American Stage* (New York: R. R. Bowker [1975]). The last includes evaluations of important actors by their contemporaries and the philosophy and practices which they applied to various roles. The indispensable compendium of annual statistics—*The Burns Mantle Yearbook,* now edited by Otis L. Guernsey, Jr. (New York: Dodd, Mead)—in this its 57th year includes a city-by-city directory of professional theatres around the country as well as a record of all off- and off-off Broadway productions, thus testifying further to an American theatre no longer confined to Broadway. Of the "ten best," moveover, only the two musicals originated on Broadway. Two of the dramas came from London, four from eastern regional theatres, and two from off-Broadway.

In an article, "Exhibition Catalogues: Critical Resources for Research in Theatre Art" (*ETJ* 28:389–97), Orville K. Larson lists some two dozen catalogs from important exhibitions of the theatre arts. Often an exhibition including the work of such figures as Robert Edmond Jones, Gordon Craig, Lee Simonson, and Kenneth Macgowan, has a catalog, which although not listed in bibliographies, is of great value to the scholar. *Performing Arts Resources* (New York: Drama Book Specialists), ed. Ted Perry, describes specialized theatre collections, mainly in various university libraries: for example, the Belknap Collection at the University of Florida, the collection at the Wisconsin Center for Theatre Research, and that at the Ohio State University Theatre Research Institute. The second volume emphasizes certain library collections of film, video, and radio materials.

The Research Libraries of the New York Public Library have issued *Catalog of the Theatre and Drama Collections, Part III: Non-Book Collection* (Boston: G.K. Hall) in 30 volumes with emphasis on production photographs, press clippings and program details. *American Drama Criticism, Supplement II* (Hamden, Conn.: Shoe String Press), ed. Floyd Eugene Eddleman, like the first volume and *Supplement I*, lists, under the name of the playwright, the location of reviews of all his produced plays. Included also are listings of the location of interpretive studies and articles on black women playwrights, writers known best for some other genre, and many reviews of off- and off-off Broadway plays, as well as those reviewed in cities other than New York. *Theatre World, 1975–76* (Philadelphia, Footnotes Press), ed. John Willis, has a 6,000-entry index of the Broadway and off-Broadway season with 950 photographs of plays, producers, casts, and other items.

University of Florida

19. Black Literature

Charles Nilon

Several excellent books devoted to single authors (Imamu Baraka, W. E. B. Du Bois, Chester Himes) and perhaps as many well-written autobiographies by writers have been published this year. The number of books published on black literature and ancillary topics (although those are not included here) is larger than the number published last year.

Interest in autobiography as a genre is growing and is clearly evident in the number of essays that are written on the subject as well as in the use of biographical material in a good many essays devoted to the study of other genres. This interest in black autobiography and biography, not only that of the writer, is not separate from a critical concern with evaluation and reevaluation of black literature.

Most of the writing about black literature mentioned here shows a distinct awareness of a black literary tradition that derives its validity from a use of black experience. This interest in literary and cultural history—early literary magazines, the Schomberg Reference Center, the beginnings and state of black bibliography, and the careful appraisals of the work of early authors and their environments —is related to this concern to discover what the black literary tradition is. Blyden Jackson's retrospective collection of his published essays and their introductions portray the activity and concern under stress of an older group of black critics who helped to keep that tradition alive. Many of the essays discussed here show how the black writer uses black music, folklore, and history as means to shape his art and to keep in touch with his tradition.

i. General Bibliography

Bibliographies of black literature are appearing in good number, and there is a need for more and better ones. Richard C. Tobias's "A

Matter of Difference: An Interim Guide to the Study of Black American Writing" (*Literary Research Newsletter* 1:129–46) describes the present state of black bibliography, and points to its neglect in standard bibliographies and to the patterns of organization in some bibliographies that make their use difficult. Tobias raises questions about the need for racially separate bibliographies and lists and evaluates bibliographies that he feels are especially useful to the student of black literature. His essay is sensible in its discussion and excellent in its content and tone. Its criticism of individual bibliographies is specific and constructive. Ester Spring Arata and Nicholas Rotoli contribute to satisfying the need that Tobias clarifies in their *Black American Playwrights, 1800 to the Present: A Bibliography* (Metuchen, N.J.: Scarecrow Press). They call their work a sourcebook and say that it is designed to assist in the study of black playwrights and their works. Their book contains an alphabetical listing of black playwrights and their works together with criticism and reviews of plays. Its third section is a general bibliography and section 4 is an index of play titles. Robert N. Glenn's *Black Rhetoric: A Guide to Afro-American Communication* (Metuchen, N.J.: Scarecrow) contains lists of black bibliographies, anthologies, and books that may guide the reader to find particular speeches and essays. In addition to these there is a bibliography of speeches and essays and a chronological list of speeches and essays.

Ernest Kaiser's "Recent Books" (*Freedomways* 16:67–78, 137–44, 205–9,266–72) is a quarterly annotated bibliography. Kaiser's annotations are useful, incisive, and honest. Annual bibliographies of black literature now appear in two journals. Virginia Barrett, Dorothy Evans, Lorraine Henry, Jennifer Jordan, and Vattel T. Rose's "An Annual Bibliography of Afro-American Literature, 1975. With Selected Bibliographies of African and Caribbean Literature" (*CLAJ* 20:94–131) contains primary and secondary works in black literature with entries under nine headings: anthologies and collections, autobiography and biography, bibliographies, indexes and checklists, drama, fiction, folklore, general literary criticism and history, poetry and miscellaneous. There are annotations and cross-references. "Studies in Afro-American Literature: An Annual Annotated Bibliography, 1975" (*Obsidian* 2,i:96–123), edited by Charles H. Rowell, is devoted to secondary sources for the study of black American literature published in the United States. The bibliography includes interviews, reports, general studies, studies in poetry, fiction, drama, autobiography, and studies of individual authors.

Oro Williams's "Works by and about Alice Ruth (More) Dunbar-Nelson: A Bibliography" (*CLAJ* 19:322–26) is a list of Dunbar-Nelson's published and unpublished works. James P. Hutchinson's "Fenton Johnson: Pilgrim of the Dust" (*SBL* 7,iii:14–15) is more important as a bibliography than it is as criticism. It lists and provides a description of Johnson's published poetry and summarizes the tendencies of his criticism. Alan M. Cohn's bibliographical note, "Additions to Dace's Le Roi Jones (Imamu Amiri Baraka)" *PBSA* 70:537–38) adds to Letitia Dace's bibliography (see *ALS 1972*, p. 348) six pieces that appeared in *Wild Dog*. The evidence used to identify these pieces as Jones's appears sound. They mention Diane di Prima, Allen Ginsburg, Gregory Corso, and other persons, and contain paragraphs on jazz. Cohn believes that the six pieces reflect Jones's gradual move toward "total identification with revolutionary causes."

Tom Quirk and Robert E. Fleming identify six pieces by Jean Toomer in "Jean Toomer's Contribution to the *New Mexico Sentinel*" (*CLAJ* 19:524–32) that are signed Nathan Jean Toomer. The pieces were published in the "New Mexico Writers" column of the *Sentinel* from July of 1937 to July 1938. There are five short essays and one poem—Toomer's first published poem since "Blue Meridan." The essays contain some biographical information, and the essays and the poem are printed in the article.

The history of black bibliography and other library resources is the subject of several essays. Robert L. Harris's "Daniel Murray and the Encyclopedia of the Colored Race" (*Phylon* 37:270–82), an essay about Daniel Murray, who was employed at the Library of Congress in 1871, is a detailed account of his and other early bibliography on the Afro-American. Murray's list of books on "Negro Literature" prepared for the Paris Exposition and his *Preliminary List of Books and Pamphlets by Negro Authors* were published in 1900. The multivolume encyclopedia on the black man that he announced in 1872 did not appear. By the provision of his will, his personal library of works by black authors was given to the Library of Congress and, with those volumes that were exhibited in Paris, once constituted the Library of Congress's "Colored Authors Collection." Otilla Pearson gives a brief description of the history of the Schomburg Collection and of the services that are provided to the scholar by the Center in

"The Schomburg and Black History—Participating Observer" (*Schomburg Center for Research in Black Culture Journal* 1,i:1–2, 4).

ii. Fiction

Two studies of black novels that are very different in purpose and execution, by scholars who are not Americans, deserve attention. Amritjit Singh's *The Novels of the Harlem Renaissance, Twelve Black Writers, 1923–1933* (University Park: Pa. State Univ. Press) is a study of 21 novels by Arna Bontemps, Countee Cullen, W. E. B. Du Bois, Jessie Fauset, Rudolph Fisher, Langston Hughes, Nella Larsen, Claude McKay, George Schuyler, Wallace Thurman, Jean Toomer, and Walter White. Singh discusses the intraracial issues of "self-definition, class, caste, and color in the works of these writers and judges aesthetic and sociocultural impulses." The first chapter of the book, "When the Negro Was in Vogue," is a brief history of the Harlem Renaissance, a discussion of the social, political, and cultural forces that were at work in the 1920s; and it describes the effort of Alain Locke, Charles S. Johnson, and others to develop a conscious movement of the black arts. Fritz Gysin's *The Grotesque in American Negro Fiction, Jean Toomer, Richard Wright, Ralph Ellison* (Bern: Francke, 1975) concludes that the grotesque turns out to be more than a copy of the black American's psychological estrangement; that it is a complex structural phenomenon and contains divergent thoughts, emotions, and experiences. By his definition of the grotesque, Gysin explains paradoxes in Toomer, the quest for the absolute in Wright, and the mastery of chaos in Ellison. The grotesque helps them to present "the black experience as a symbol of the complexity of human experience." The study exhibits good scholarship and gives persuasive interpretations of the novels.

a. Chesnutt, Du Bois, Dunbar.

The critics who write about Charles Waddel Chesnutt this year say more about the circumstances under which he wrote than they do about what he wrote. There is in almost all of the essays about him an attempt to determine the relation of circumstances to his success. Several Chesnutt bibliographies have been published during the year. The significant interest that was shown in his work last year continues.

William L. Andrews's essay, "William Dean Howells and Charles

W. Chesnutt: Criticism and Race Fiction in the Age of Booker T. Washington" (*AL* 48:327–39), contributes to an understanding of the relationship between Howells and Chesnutt and offers a reason for Howells's change in attitude toward Chesnutt's work. Howells, Andrews says, gave his critical approval and support to Chesnutt's early work because he thought Chesnutt's attitudes, political and social, were like Paul Laurence Dunbar's, Booker T. Washington's, and Frederick Douglass's. Howells's review of *The Marrow of Tradition*, in which he agrees with Chesnutt's logic but finds the novel—as a whole—bitter, is evidence of his changed attitude toward Chesnutt who, in that novel, preferred justice to mercy and was not conservative. The discussion of Howells's opinions of Douglas, Dunbar, and Washington is perceptive.

Rodney Barfield's "Charles Waddel Chesnutt" (*Crisis* 83:11–13) is an appreciation which praises Chesnutt's achievement. Mainly, the essay is a summary of Chesnutt's biography which shows him achieving against odds from the time he was nine until he moved from Fayetteville, North Carolina. Michael Flusche's "On the Color Line: Charles Waddel Chesnutt" (*NCHR* 53:1–24) is biographical and finds in Chesnutt's response to his racially mixed ancestry reasons for what he judges to be Chesnutt's minor success as an American author. Flusche says, "Chesnutt's career as an author seems paradoxically to validate the stereotype of the tragic mulatto," and that "by calling himself a 'near-white'" Chesnutt "assigned himself a tragic role in American society and doomed himself to a minor position in American letters." This, I believe, is not the opinion that is generally held of Chesnutt's success. Wendall Jackson probably gets closer to the reasons for Chesnutt's not continuing to write in the discussion that he presents in "Charles W. Chesnutt's Outrageous Fortune" (*CLAJ* 20:195–204). By dealing, in his fiction, with economic decay, ethical compromise, and prejudice in the South, Chesnutt found himself in conflict with a moralistic public—pressures which affected his artistry and his relationship with society. This essay also contains useful publication history. Wayne Mixon's essay, "The Unfulfilled Dream: Charles W. Chesnutt and the New South Movement" (*SHR* 10, Bicentennial Issue:23–33), supports Jackson's observations, although its main stress is on Chesnutt's failure to fulfill his dreams. Mixon says that Chesnutt criticized the New South's complacency toward its social ills, questioned its claims of economic revival, and declined to give to southerners the literary pablum that had long been served to them. "He refused to defend the region's shortcomings, hoping instead to excise them by facing them openly and presenting them realistically in his fiction." Chesnutt's novel, *The Colonel's Dream*, catalogues the South's ills and presents a vision of its new ideal.

In addition to his essay mentioned above, William L. Andrews has published two much-needed Chesnutt bibliographies. "Charles Waddel Chesnutt: An Essay in Bibliography" (*RALS* 6:3–22) and "The Works of Charles W. Chesnutt: A Checklist" (*BB* 34:4–52). The first of these, a bibliographical essay, is an almost complete list of Chesnutt bibliographies, which contains a careful annotation and evaluation of each entry included, and adds a general statement on the state of Chesnutt bibliography. The essay is divided into sections on editions, manuscripts and letters, biography, and criticism. The checklist provides the basic bibliographic information about Chesnutt's books, short fiction, poems, essays and articles, and miscellaneous writings. Reprints of his work are not included in it. Joan Cunningham's "Secondary Studies on the Fiction of Charles W. Chesnutt" (*BB* 33:48–52) is divided into two sections—a list of representative reviews of Chesnutt's books and a list of secondary studies.

A critical study of W. E. B. Du Bois's writing has been done by Arnold Rampersad that is called *The Art and Imagination of W. E. B. Du Bois* (Cambridge, Mass.: Harvard Univ. Press). This study gives careful attention to the form and content of Du Bois's writing. Rampersad believes that Du Bois's greatest gift was poetic in nature and that "his scholarship, propaganda and political activism drew their ultimate power from his essential poetic vision of human experience and from his equally poetic reverence for the word." This thesis seems particularly sound as Rampersad uses it in the explication of Du Bois's novels and other literary works. The overall approach to the discussion of Du Bois's fiction that is used in the application of Rampersad's thesis is necessarily eclectic and includes a discussion of the social purposes of the fiction as well as its aesthetic quality. Rampersad's discussions of the ideas and history that are part of the fiction are clear and sound.

Lovie N. Gibson judges Du Bois's work as a novelist in a narrower way in "W. E. B. Du Bois as a Propaganda Novelist" (*NALF* 10:75–77,79–83). She argues that it is as a propaganda novelist that Du

Bois's personal consciousness merges with his social consciousness and the true genius of his creativity arises. She says that he has definite ideas as to the composition and characteristics of a "good black novel" and that these characteristics raise the question of the value of propaganda in fiction. From his statements she argues that Du Bois believed every writer adopts a theory or view of life and his work becomes a conscious or unconscious effort to convince the reader of the plausibility of his ideas. Irene Diggs's essay "Du Bois and Children" (*Phylon* 37:370–99) shows Du Bois's interest in and concern for children, and some of the quotations in it come from his fiction.

Gregory L. Candela's "We Wear the Mask: Irony in Dunbar's *The Sport of the Gods*" (*AL* 48:60–72) is a careful analysis of Dunbar's use of irony in *The Sport of the Gods*, which places Dunbar inside the "black author's march toward literary realism." Candela's explanation of the Hamiltons' return to the South and its significance is perhaps not convincing. The return, however, is consistent with the irony of the novel's total situation. Perhaps a fuller sense of the implication of their return to the South may be gained by comparing it with the attitude that Dunbar expresses toward the South in *The Fanatics*.

b. **Fisher, Hughes, Hurston, McKay, Toomer.** The quality and significance of Rudolph Fisher's portrayal of lower-class characters is discussed by Thomas Friedmann in "The Good Guys in the Black Hats: Color Coding in Rudolph Fisher's 'Common Meter'" (*SBL* 7,ii:8–9), in which he says Fisher anticipates the notion of "Black Is Beautiful" and uses the blackness of a man's skin to indicate his goodness. He adds that "Common Meter" is a valuable source for those who look for early indications of change in black consciousness.

R. Baxter Miller discusses *Not Without Laughter* in "'Done Made Us Leave Our Home': Langston Hughes's *Not Without Laughter*—Unifying Image and Three Dimensions" (*Phylon* 37:362–69). His main idea is that the image of home unifies the novel and indicates a movement from innocence to experience. He shows convincingly that the image of home has meaning on three levels: mystical, historical, and social. Melvin G. Williams's "Langston Hughes's Jesse B. Simple: A Black Walter Mitty" (*NALF* 10:66–69) is an essay in which Thurber's character and Simple are compared for the purpose of showing that Simple's dreams are interesting and that unique fantasies grow out of his special situation.

Except for her short stories, which were published during the Harlem Renaissance, Zora Neale Hurston's fiction was written after that period. Robert Hemenway's "Folklore Field Notes from Zora Neale Hurston" (*BlackS* 7:39–46) is useful to the reader who is interested in the folk content in her fiction. Hemenway's brief introduction to several tales that Hurston collected and to some of her notes on folklore gives some understanding of what was characteristic of her as an anthropologist and as an artist. Because the source of much of her fiction was in folklore, the folk tales printed here give a reader examples of her writing that are useful in understanding some of her fiction. Peter Swallenberg suggests in "Time as Point-of-View in Zora Neale Hurston's *Their Eyes Were Watching God*" (*NALF* 10:104–7) that the effective way in which she portrays Janie, the novel's main character, is the result of her use of time as point-of-view.

James R. Giles's *Claude McKay* (TUSAS 271) is a careful, reliable study that explores the influences that shaped McKay's literary and political stance (Marxist economic theory, the Roman Catholic Church, and Jamaica). Giles's purpose, in part, is to overcome the oversimplification that has characterized much McKay criticism. He points out that McKay never accepted many of Du Bois's and Alain Locke's ideas, that his poetry was not uniformly militant, and that fiction is his major achievement. Some of the supporting evidence that Giles uses comes from McKay's essays and correspondence and from analysis of the content of McKay's published autobiography, *A Long Way from Home* (1937) and his *Harlem: Negro Metropolis* (1940). Throughout the study the reader is given some accounting of McKay's struggle to reconcile his views of art with his concepts of self, blackness, and the proletariat. Clarence Major describes two of McKay's unpublished novels and his unpublished memoir, *My Green Hills of Jamaica*, in "Claude McKay" (*APR* 4,ii[1975]:40–41). The essay is brief, but the descriptions are adequate, and the opinions are useful. There is brief comment in the essay about a McKay novel, *Color Scheme*, that publishers refused and which McKay destroyed. The two unpublished novels, *Romance in Marsailles* and *Harlem Glory*, are given reasonably full descriptions. The first of these novels was probably written during 1929 and 1930 and resembles *Banjo*.

Its central character, Lafala, is based on a real person who is described in a letter (13 Jan. 1928) in the James Weldon Johnson collection at Yale. The central character in *Harlem Glory* is a West Indian, and that narrative begins in Paris. Major believes that *My Green Hills of Jamaica* is more unfinished and the weakest of McKay's efforts at autobiography.

Several of the essays about the Harlem Renaissance are important because they show the continuing interest and the discovery of value in minor figures. This is true of Joseph Schuyler and Wallace Thurman. Michael Peplow argues in "Black 'Picaro' in *Black No More*" (*Crisis* 83:7–10) that *Black No More* is an attack on blacks and whites who are obsessed with color. He argues that the novel has been read wrongly as assimilationist fiction, because the main character, Matthew Fisher, has been misunderstood. Fisher, Peplow says, is a black "picaro" who passes as white to "put on ole Massa" and who by passing gives Schuyler's satire a different connotation. Huel D. Perkins's "Wallace Thurman" (*BlackW* 25,iv:29–35) is an estimate of Thurman as a writer, a critic, and an editor "who was like a mirror holding up to artists and would-be artists alike the image of themselves."

There continue to be, from year to year, a good number of journal articles in which appropriate critical approaches to Jean Toomer's *Cane* are explored. Kay R. Van Mol attempts this in an effective comparison in "Primitivism and Intellect in Toomer's *Cane* and McKay's *Banana Bottom*: The Need for an Integrated Black Consciousness" (*NALF* 10:48–52). These have a common thematic concern, that of cultural dualism, and both novels deal with the development of a black consciousness. The development of this consciousness, Van Mol argues, by comparing the development of characters in the two novels, is the product of reconciling or blending what may be called the "intellect" of the Western world and the "primitivism" of the African heritage. In a sense Odette C. Martin in "*Cane*: Method and Myth" (*Obsidian* 2,i:5–20) and Howard Faulkner in "The Buried Life: Jean Toomer's *Cane*" (*SBL* 1,i:1–5) are concerned to point out the method that Toomer used to show an integrated black consciousness, (though they do not claim that this is Toomer's purpose). Martin makes several useful observations about Toomer, his method, and his use of myth. She says that Toomer seemed to think of the poet (the writer) as a prophet who created reality through the power of his vision. That vision, she says, is presented in a collage, a method, or a device, which is complex enough to permit the development of "the many shadows and planes of reality" that Toomer wanted to show. Collage, as Martin uses it, means a variety of literary techniques and devices. *Cane* is, she says, a "pilgrimage novel" in which Toomer's journey in search of soul is "a journey ultimately into blackness, his own and America's lost blackness." Faulkner believes that Robert Bone (*The Negro Novel in America*) and Roger Rosenblatt (*Black Fiction*) "inadequately explicated" *Cane.* He finds a unity comparable to that in Anderson's *Winesburg, Ohio*: the buried life of Toomer's characters resembles the failure of Anderson's characters, and dreams are a form of release.

c. **Wright, Ellison, Baldwin.** The fiction of Wright, Ellison, and Baldwin—the order in which their writing careers began—continues to attract major critical attention, although there is still argument over the proper methods to use in judging them. In "Wright, Ellison, Baldwin—Exorcising the Demon" (*Phylon* 37:174–88), Jerry H. Bryant applies political and social criteria in analyzing *Native Son, Invisible Man,* and *Go Tell It on the Mountain.* The literary ghetto mentioned in the title of Louis H. Pratt's "James Baldwin and the Literary Ghetto" (*CLAJ* 20:262–72) affirms the position of John A. Williams in "Problems of the Negro Writer: The Literary Ghetto" (*SatR* 20 Apr. 1963, pp. 21, 40), in which he says the trend in white criticism of black writing is to label black writers, which serves to "limit severely the expansion of the talents of Negro writers and confine them to a literary ghetto." Pratt argues that the effects of this kind of criticism have resulted in Baldwin's being labeled a protest writer and spokesman for the black community. The implications of these designations, he says, ultimately serve to substitute social for artistic status and to deny the aesthetic achievement of Baldwin's writings. He specifies aesthetic qualities in Baldwin's work that he believes have been overlooked. Baldwin has of course been criticized for not being appropriately or sufficiently a social critic and a spokesman. Mark R. Daniels's "Estrangement, Betrayal, and Atonement: The Political Theory of James Baldwin" (*SBL* 7,iii:10–13) disagrees with Eldridge Cleaver's argument, as most critics do now, that Baldwin's work is void of a political, economic, or social reference. Daniels says that the political theory that can be drawn from Baldwin's works is that all men are estranged, though not estranged in nature, and that their estrangement is due to man's betrayal of his true nature.

Frequently Richard Wright has been looked at as a naturalist and as a protest writer and consigned to the literary ghetto that is mentioned in Daniels's discussion of Baldwin. That is not true in the several essays that are devoted to him this year. Except for Sylvia H. Ready's essay, "Richard Wright's Women Characters and Equality" (*NALF* 10:124–28), in which the author argues as other critics have that Wright's female characters are not full human beings but function as conveniences for the resolution or development of masculine dilemmas, the articles published this year find aesthetic quality in Wright's works or seek to correct earlier opinions of them. Jerry Wasserman compares Wright and Ellison in "Embracing the Negative: *Native Son* and *Invisible Man*" (*SAF* 4:93–103) to show that the American experience has made similar demands on the two authors. The historical reality of the American experience has demanded that the black writer or character create a legitimate identity for himself amid a dominant white culture that prescribes his existence in negative and contradictory terms. Both Bigger Thomas and Ellison's narrator discover "what might be termed an existential dilemma" and deal with it by embracing exactly and consciously the negative, stereotyped idea of "blackness" which the society has provided for them and, using the stereotype as a means, transcend it. Wasserman presents this transcendence as an existential process that is explained in the ideas of Laing, Sartre, and Kierkegaard. Genet and his play, *The Blacks*, are models of this kind of action, although Bigger is, because he has no sense of history and is inarticulate, different from Genet's characters and never transcends the white created role he chooses as his own. Some ideas that are related to Wasserman's position are discussed in "A Definition of Freedom in the Fiction of Richard Wright" (*CLAJ* 19:327–46). Here Anne O. Cauley says that Wright argues in his fiction, as Baldwin does, that "no one can demand more of life than that life do him the honor to demand that he learn to live with his fears, and learn to live, every day, within his limits and beyond them." Cauley says that Wright's recipe for freedom for blacks in America requires that literary artists create a system of values, separate from those of the majority of Americans, that is relevant to blackness and the black experience. Self-identity and mastery, she says, are achieved in active confrontation "with the re-

ality and passion of an oppressed state; a freeing of *spirit*, not necessarily a physical liberation." *Lawd Today, Native Son, The Man Who
Lived Underground,* and *The Outsider* are discussed in this essay.

Most of the essays about Wright's work discuss in some way his
use of aesthetic means. Barry Gross does this in "Art and Act: The
Example of Richard Wright" (*Obsidian* 2,ii:5–9), in which he asserts
that *Native Son* picks up where *Black Boy* leaves off—that *Black Boy*
is the portrait of the artist in origin and *Native Son* is the portrait of
the artist in process. Gross says, as an extension of this generalization,
that Bigger is a hero in the sense that Melville's Ahab is, and that the
white world is his white whale. He argues persuasively that, through
Bigger, Wright discovered his own myth—the myth of the inexorable
self—as Newton Arvin said Melville did.

Refuting appraisals of the novel made by David L. Cohn, James
Baldwin, Irving Howe, and Robert Bone, who claim that in books
1 and 2 of *Native Son* Wright was the "witless instrument of wild and
overpowering feeling over which he had no control," Dorothy S.
Redden argues convincingly against this view in her essay, "Wright
and *Native Son*: Not Guilty" (*NALF* 10:111–15). An interesting
reading of Wright's early work is provided in P. Jay Delmar's "Tragic
Patterns in Richard Wright's *Uncle Tom's Children*" (*NALF* 10:3–
12) in which, after providing a definition for contemporary tragedy,
Delmar shows that, at least potentially, each of the stories in this
collection is a tragedy. Delmar suggests that Edwin Burgum's opinion
of these stories (as a series of tragedies whose protagonists seek to
restore in themselves a sense of psychological equilibrium and unity)
is sound.

There are several interesting interpretations of Ralph Ellison's
Invisible Man. Philip G. Williams says in "A Comparative Approach
to Afro-American and Neo-African Novels: Ellison and Achebe"
(*SBL* 7,i:15–18) in which he compares *Invisible Man* and Chinua
Achebe's *Things Fall Apart,* that black authors may draw upon a
latent tradition which they themselves may not recognize as African
in origin. He supports his idea that there are residual African resources that may be drawn on by these writers in a discussion of
Miguel de Unamuno's concept of *intrahistoria.* This interesting suggestion of possibility, however, is not clearly developed in the comparison of the novels. Jeffrey Steinbrink shows that *Invisible Man*
is more than an exploration of the problem of identity in "Toward a

Vision of Infinite Possibility, A Reading of *Invisible Man*" (*SBL* 7,iii: 1–5). He argues that it is important for the reader to know this, because he may be led to believe falsely that Ellison's narrator knows who he is at the book's end. Steinbrink argues, finally, that the novel deals with ontology—with considerations that precede identification. On the other hand, Ardner R. Cheshire, Jr., uses Martin Buber's dialogical concepts in "*Invisible Man* and the Life of Dialogue" (*CLAJ* 20:19–34) to show that Ellison's narrator moves from monologue to dialogue and hence from invisibility to identity. E. M. Kist shows in "A Laingian Analysis of Blackness in Ralph Ellison's *Invisible Man*" (*SBL* 7,ii:19–23) that R. D. Laing's observations in *The Divided Self* and *The Self and Others* "shows how various aspects of the invisible man's experience cohere in a meaningful way." His comments on Trueblood, Tod Clifton, the grandfather, and the mad psychiatrist who is encountered at the Golden Day, are perceptive. Two useful notes provide interesting comment on Ellison's development of particular sequences in the novel. L. A. Ehlers's "Give Me the Ocular Proof: Othello and Ralph Ellison's *Invisible Man*" (*NConL* 6,i:10–11) shows that *Invisible Man* alludes to Shakespeare's *Othello*, and thereby underscores the blindness-perception theme and clarifies the relationship between the narrator, Brother Jack, and Tod Clifton. The parallel between the monkey and goat images in the episode at the Golden Day and Othello's mad line, "You are welcome, Sir, to Cypress.—Goats and Monkeys!" (IV.ii.276) and Iago's accusation that Desdemona and Cassio are "as prime as goats, as hot as monkeys" (III.iii.403) are used to show that Brother Jack is like Iago and that Tod Clifton and the narrator are deceived by him. Janet Overmeyer's "The Invisible Man and White Women" *NConL* 6,iii: 13–15) draws attention to the possibility of observing the narrator's growth in the way that he deals with the problems presented by white women.

Patricia Chafee's "Slippery Ground: Ralph Ellison's Bingo Player" *NALF* 10:23–24) and Pearl I. Saunders's "Symbolism in Ralph Ellison's 'King of the Bingo Game'" (*CLAJ* 20:35–39) comment effectively on Ellison's treatment of identity and personhood. Chafee says that the nameless bingo player is Everyman and that Ellison's view is more grimly negative in this story than in *Invisible Man*. Saunders explains that this negative view is effectively portrayed through the use of the bingo game and in the namelessness of the protagonist.

d. **Himes, Demby, Motley.** Since the interview that was done by John A. Williams in *Amistad I* (1970), Chester Himes has received increasingly serious critical attention and appears now to have achieved solid literary stature. *My Life of Absurdity*, the second volume of his autobiography which was published this year, increases the reader's knowledge of him and aids in understanding his fiction. Two good studies of his fiction have appeared—Stephen F. Milliken's *Chester Himes, A Critical Appraisal* (Columbia: Univ. of Mo. Press) and James Lundquist's *Chester Himes* (New York: Ungar). The first is thorough and perhaps more useful than the second. Both make considerable use of *The Quality of the Hurt*, the first volume of Himes's autobiography. The overall estimate that Milliken makes of Himes's craft and fiction seems sound, and his treatment of Himes's beginnings as a writer is done in a perceptive and well-organized chapter whose developed insights and generalizations are useful to him and to the reader throughout the book. Perhaps the best analysis in the study is of the autobiographical novels—*The Third Generation, Cast the First Stone,* and *The Primitive.* The chapter in which the detective novels are discussed is valuable in so far as it traces their origin and judges them as detective fiction. Lundquist's study is smaller, but it provides a good introduction to Himes's work. Significantly, he says that Himes's vision, "the fear that inhabits the minds of all blacks who live in America, and the various impacts of this fear," is objectified in his writing.

Lundquist calls *If He Hollers Let Him Go* and *The Lonely Crusade* war novels, which may mean that he wished to avoid calling them protest novels as Milliken does. The general effect of the discussion of Himes's fiction in these two books leads the reader to believe that it is not right to regard Himes as merely a naturalist or a writer of protest. A. Robert Lee defends this point in "Real and Imagined Violence in the Novels of Chester Himes" (*NALF* 10:13–22), an essay in which the eight detective novels are discussed. Lee believes that these novels are responsible for the new regard of Himes's work and that they confirm the reader's belief in the diversity of his ability, that they and his other novels "are addressed to the unflagging play of violence in America." The detective novels, which Lee says approach inspired surrealism, and his other novels which are not formulaic and angry, are really logical points of arrival for an author to whom violence is both the essential condition and abuse of the life before him. Lundquist says that violence becomes a form in all of Himes's novels. Himes denies that his detective fiction is innovative, but John M. Reilly argues in "Chester Himes's Harlem Tough Guys" (*JPC* 9:935–47) that it is. He finds new angles that mark important adaptations of the American Tough-Guy story which illustrate both the continuing possibilities of the genre for social commentary and the rich contribution to be made to yet another portion of popular American culture by the expression of an author's black experience. Reilly believes that the Harlem detective stories are an appraisal of the whole of American culture.

Critical interest continues in the work of William Demby and Willard Motley. In "William Demby's Fiction" (*NALF* 10:100–103), Joseph F. Connelly offers rather convincing reasons for believing that Demby's two novels are, to an extent, autobiographical and that they offer explanations for his not continuing to write fiction. James R. Giles and Karen M. Myers support their judgment that the thesis of *We Fished All Night* is not valid but that it has far-reaching implications which might have resulted in a work of enduring value in "Naturalism as Principle and Trap: Theory and Execution in Willard Motley's We Fished All Night" (*SBL* 7,i:19–22). They argue that artistic plausibility does not result from the novel's realistic proof. N. Jill Weygant's "Lyrical Experimentation in Willard Motley's Mexican Novel: *Let Noon Be Fair*" (*NALF* 10:95–99) shows that she has made a considerable effort to understand and judge all of Motley's fiction. Although her essay is not totally satisfying, it supports her opinion that his last novel was not "didactic, documentary, and conventional." Some of Weygant's opinions about Motley are probably less sound than her opinions about *Let Noon Be Fair*. Structurally this novel is different from Motley's earlier novels; in other ways, I am not certain that it is as different as she suggests.

e. Gaines, Kelley, Reed. Ernest Gaines's stories about black manhood are studies in William Burke's "*Bloodline*, A Black Man's South" (*CLAJ* 19:545–58). Burke says that the first five stories in the collection demonstrate their excellence in two ways; they are human and symbolic. Howard Faulkner shows in "The Use of Tradition: William Melvin Kelley's *A Different Drummer*" (*MFS* 21:538–42) that this novel permits the white readers to see themselves from the outside and that the novel's white characters are treated with accuracy. His observation that Kelley is kinder to rich whites than he is to those who are not is not supported.

The most rewarding discussion of Ishmael Reed's fiction is found in an essay by Michel Fabre that is discussed here in the section on criticism. Reed tells a good deal about his fiction himself in his conversation with Barth and Gass that is mentioned in the list of interviews. Lorenzo Thomas argues in "Two Crowns of Thoth: A Study of Ishmael Reed's *The Last Days of Louisiana Red*" (*Obsidian* 2,i: 5–25) that "Reed's study of our situation [the situation of black Americans] reveals a spiritual strain of our maroon Africanness that forms the basis of a major motif in both our folk and 'popular' arts." He tries to show the truth of this observation in his analysis of Reed's novel by examining the significance of the color red, tracing the sources of images to the Egyptian *Book of the Dead*, and comparing it with Jean Toomer's *Cane*.

iii. Poetry—Wheatley, Horton, Cullen, Hughes, McKay, Brooks, Harper, Hayden

The two essays about Phillis Wheatley are interesting primarily because they show that scholarly interest in her work continues. Chickwenye Okonjo Ogunyemi's "Phillis Wheatley: The Modest Beginning" (*SBL* 7,i:16–19) does not add significantly to Wheatley criticism. It is significant, however, that an African at the University of Ibadan is writing about her. Muphtar Ali Isani's bibliographical note, "The Original Version of Wheatley's 'The Death of Dr. Samuel Marshall' " (*SBL* 7,iii:20) identifies an unsigned version of the Marshall poem as it appears unsigned in the *Boston Evening-Post* for 14 October 1771 from the published 1773 version. Blyden Jackson's "George Moses Horton, North Carolinian" (*NCHR* 53:140–47) is a sympathetic evaluation of Horton and his verse and provides a clear portrait of him as a gifted man. Jackson says of Horton that "slender as his talent may well have been, George Moses still was sufficiently, to use his own term, 'gifted' to justify his consideration as more than a mere curiosity." In the essay Jackson praises Richard Walser's *The Black Poet* (see *ALS 1966*, pp. 145–46) as an excellent account of Horton's life and provides a list of black North Carolina poets.

Among the significant poets of the Harlem Renaissance, critical opinion differs most, perhaps, about Countee Cullen. Ronald Primeau's essay, "Countee Cullen and Keats's 'Vale of Soul-Making'" (*PLL* 12:73–86) explores further the acknowledged influence of Keats on Cullen. He says their common ground is always their persistent and almost obsessive drive to render poetically the realities of bittersweet human experience. Although he feels that Keats's influence became a burden that Cullen did not overcome, he also feels that Cullen's reading of Keats was most influential, not in what is sometimes called his "non-racial" verse, but rather in poetry he created, as a black poet, from his most personal experiences. Primeau suggests that other influences on Cullen's poetry—spirituals and other black poets—must be fully evaluated, and he believes that Cullen's talent is underestimated.

Onwuchekwa Jemi's *Langston Hughes: An Introduction to the Poetry* (New York: Columbia Univ. Press) is an excellent study of Hughes's themes and techniques in which Jemi interprets and judges the poetry from the perspective of the oral tradition and from those of the tradition of struggle and protest. Early in the text he discusses Hughes's essay, "The Negro Artist and the Racial Mountain," and selects from it part of what he calls Hughes's Black Aesthetic. Although his sense of the relationship of blues and spirituals is probably not sound, he is particularly convincing when he writes about the influence of blues and jazz on Hughes's poetry.

The things and persons that have influenced Hughes have been of concern to a good number of critics. Some critics have argued that Carl Van Vechten's influence on Hughes was not good. Faith Berry argues with good evidence in "Did Van Vechten Make or Fake Hughes's Blues" (*BlackW* 25,iv:22–28) that according to her judgment and Hughes's statements, Van Vechten's relationship with him was positive and in no sense an exploitation. Berry feels that Van Vechten was of less influence in the renaissance and on him than Charles S. Johnson, Jessie Fauset, and Alain Locke were. Lloyd W. Brown discusses "Children's Rhymes," "Harlem," and "Freedom's Plow"—three of Hughes's poems—in "The American Dream and the Legacy of Revolution in the Poetry of Langston Hughes" (*SBL* 7,ii:16–18) and concludes that Hughes does not explore the legacy of revolution in any "exhortatory" sense and that he does not espouse any concept of "a radically transforming revolution." Baxter Miller makes a rather rigid analysis of one poem in "A Mere Poem, 'Daybreak in Alabama,' A Resolution to Langston Hughes's Theme of

Music and Art" (*Obsidian* 2,ii:30–37) and concludes that the poem is Hughes's final and most aesthetic definition of music and art.

Claude McKay emerges from the efforts to judge his poetry as a rather atypical Harlem Renaissance writer. The reason for this is, partially, his Jamaican background. William H. Hansell says in "Jamaica in the Poems of Claude McKay" (*SBL* 7,iii:6–9) that although the Jamaican poems are aesthetically inferior to McKay's other poems, the portrayal of Jamaica in them is increasingly idealized. Hansell believes that in addition to nostalgia and escapism, which may account for McKay's idealization of Jamaican life, those poems compensate for his disillusionment and they counterbalance the portrayals of Negro life in his protest poems. Stanley Warren's "Reminiscences of Claude McKay" (*The Crisis* 83:345) is a brief account of the "reputation" and use of McKay's sonnet, "If We Must Die" as well as an indication that 'Harlem Renaissance poet' is not an entirely happy designation for McKay.

Barbara B. Sims provides a good analysis of a Gwendolyn Brooks poem in "Brooks' 'We Real Cool'" (*Expl* 34:item 58) in which she notices the economy of the poem and the way in which this economy parallels the lives of pool players. She comments on the changes in tone, diction, and rhythm that come appropriately in the last line of the poem. Constance J. Post in "Image and Idea in the Poetry of Robert Hayden" (*CLAJ* 20:164–65) says that any new directions that Hayden might have taken recently are ". . . primarily in the area of consolidation, if only to look at his old themes from a new angle." His search for new themes, she says, began in the middle of his career and is apparent in "Kodachrome of the Islands" a poem in *Words in the Mourning Time* (1972). She points out that struggle is a common theme in his poetry and that the star is his chief symbol for it. Often Hayden's use of oxymorons supports the theme of struggle and his tragicomic view of life.

The June issue of the *Hollins Critic* (13,iii:2–16) contains Robert B. Stepto's "Michael Harper's Extended Tree: John Coltrane and Sterling Brown," one of two essays that Stepto has published on Harper this year. The second essay, "Michael S. Harper, Poet as Kinsman: The Family Sequences" (*MR* 17:477–502), complements the first, in which Stepto discusses the poems contained in two of Harper's books—*Dear John, Dear Coltrane* (1970) and *Nightmare Begins Responsibility* (1976). In both of these volumes, his first and his most recent, Harper is concerned with the artist choosing his ancestors both in the sense of craft influences and in kinship relations. He honors John Coltrane (the musician) and Sterling Brown in these poems, acknowledges his relationship and indebtedness to them, and indicates the pervasive general influence of black music and the black literary tradition upon his art. Most of the poems in the second book examine Harper's "kinship" to a good and varied number of black writers. Stepto says that Harper ". . . is a non-Western poet in the all important sense that he rejects the Cartesian 'either/or' in favor of Animism, and because he is a leading example of the Afro-American artist who sustains through art that cultural tradition which," Harper calls, " 'the honoring of kin' or the learning of their names." The essay communicates Stepto's as well as Harper's admiration of and respect for Sterling Brown and includes an excellent estimate of his importance as an author. Stepto's second essay explains how kinship is for Harper a recurring metaphor for poetic process, the artist's obligations to traditions, and for living a life morally and well. Stepto is particularly interested in what he calls "kinship-in-process," which he finds in sequences of Harper's poems.

iv. Drama

Doris E. Abramson surveys the attitudes of white drama critics toward black theatre before the 1940s in "The Great White Way: Critics and the First Black Playwrights on Broadway" (*ETJ* 28:45–55). She concludes that black playwrights have paid a high price for success and arrives at her judgment by examining the words and tone of the critical reviews. Summaries of the critical reviews of Garland Anderson's *Appearances* (1925), Frank Wilson's *Meek Mose* (1928), Wallace Thurman's and William J. Rapp's *Harlem* (1929), Hall Johnson's *Run, Little Children* (1933), Langston Hughes's *Mullatto* (1935), and Hughes Allison's *The Trial of Dr. Beck* (1937) are used to support her opinions. Abramson notes in the essay that Kenneth Burke's criticism of Hall Johnson's play was exceptional in its lack of condescension and in its fairness. The essay contains short descriptions of the plays and of the circumstances of their production. Lorraine Hansberry's *Raisin in the Sun*, James Baldwin's *Amen Corner*, and Alice Childress's *Wine and Wilderness*, plays in which there are examples of a stereotype, are studied in Mary Louise Anderson's "Black

Matriarchy: Portrayal of Women in Three Plays" (*NALF* 10:93–95).
Using the characteristics of the mothers in these plays, Anderson defines a black matriarch as a woman who regards the black male as
undependable and who is frequently responsible for his emascula-
tion. She is quite religious, regards mothering as one of the important
things in her life, and attempts to shield her children from and to prepare them to accept the prejudices of the white world. The image of
the black woman is also the subject of Barbara Molette's "Black
Women Playwrights" (*BlackW* 26,vi:28–34). She studies Angelina
Grimké's *Rachel* (1916), May Miller's *Graven Images* (1929), Mary
Bunell's *They That Sit in Darkness* (1919), and more recent plays by
Alice Childress and Lorraine Hansberry and concludes that black
women have traditionally portrayed positive images of black motherhood and tried to promote mores that were humanistic in their plays.
Mary Arnold Twining's *"Heaven Bound* or *The Devil Play*: A Note
on Dichotomous Predicates" (*CLAJ* 19:347–51) is an attempt to trace
an African survival in Afro-American theatre. The essay traces the
survival and changes in a traditional African use of masks in dramatic
productions to its use in an American folk play, *The Devil Play*, which
was produced on John's Island, South Carolina. Although masks are
not used and the play is in many respects Western, Twining suggests
that *Heaven Bound,* a musical produced in Atlanta in the 1930s, is an
adaptation of the John's Island play because the two plays deal with
the same subject—the progress of the human soul between good and
evil—and the role of the devil is similar in both plays, although he is
not masked in *Heaven Bound.* She says "the dichotomous predicates
of Christian morality function to balance the world as do the masked
figures of West African societies."

Kimberly W. Benston's *Baraka, The Renegade and the Mask*
(New Haven, Conn.: Yale Univ. Press) has an excellent Foreword
written by Larry Neal and is the best critical study of Baraka's work
to be published. This is not to say that Theodore Hudson's *From
LeRoi Jones to Amiri Baraka* (see *ALS 1973*, pp. 351–62) is not a sound
and good study. Hudson and Benston do different things. The reference point of Benston's study is Baraka's drama. In an ordered way
he explores Baraka's themes and his attitudes toward culture. His
book is divided into two sections: one in which culture, nationalism,
art, black music, the Black Aesthetic, and Baraka's poetry are discussed; and, the second, in which Baraka's plays are discussed. The

first section of the book provides background for the second. Benston believes that "Baraka's aesthetic theory has evolved from a concern with 'standing somewhere in the world.'" He also believes that Northrup Frye's categories of literary structure provide a perfect model for the study of Baraka's development of dramatic form. He says that "Baraka's theatre, from *Dutchman* to *Slave Ship*, has clearly evolved from a concern with the individual cut loose from society to the community itself as victim, rebel, and finally, triumphant hero." Linda G. Latlin writes about *The Toilet, Dutchman, The Slave,* and *Baptism* in "Paying His Dues: Ritual in LeRoi Jones' Early Dramas" (*Obsidian* 2,i:21–31). She finds that Baraka concerns himself with the emptiness and sterility of black and white lives, and that he presents black and white people performing rituals that fail to sustain them or to reinforce their insecure positions because they possess little responsibility to themselves or to each other. Owen E. Brady argues in his essay, "Cultural Conflict and Cult Ritual in LeRoi Jones's *The Toilet*" (*ETJ* 28:69–77) that the play shows the difficulty that a black individual encounters in forging self-identity while living amidst antithetical cultural forces and experiencing the tension of double consciousness. Ritual, Brady argues with Latlin, takes the place of identity that is lost.

The importance of landscape, of world, in Ed Bullins's plays is discussed in Robert L. Tener's "Pandora's Box: A Study of Ed Bullins's Dramas" (*CLAJ* 19:533–44). Tener says that the spatial volume conceptualized by Bullins contains a basic dichotomy or a built-in element of opposition in which the lives of his characters are ordered by man, chance, and change and in which their dreams are determined by their frustrations.

"*Cities in Bezique*: Adrienne Kennedy's Expressionistic Vision" (*CLAJ* 20:235–44) is an interpretation of that play by Kimberly Benston that convinces the reader that Kennedy's expressionism is successful and a more appropriate technique for her purposes than naturalism. Benston believes that Baraka's *Four Revolutionary Plays* influenced the form of this play. *Cities in Bezique* is a dramatic distich that is composed of *The Owl Answers* and *A Beast Story* and organized around a cluster of themes that investigate black identity. Geneva Smitherman's "Ron Milner, People's Playwright" (*BlackW* 25,vi:4–19) is part interview and part essay and gives a rounded impression of Ron Milner who thinks of himself as a playwright for a people's theatre. Her piece discusses his dramatic theories (particularly their use of music and ritual), provides a biographical sketch, analyzes two of his plays (*Season's Reasons* and *What the Winesellers Buy*), and offers several perceptive generalizations about contemporary black theatre.

v. Criticism

From the essays and books that have been written this year it appears that the conception of what the Black Aesthetic is is becoming clearer, and the misunderstanding held by some readers—that those critics who accept the Black Aesthetic feel that literary form is of no importance—is disappearing. Much of this year's criticism stresses three overlapping needs for black historical perspective, for a knowledge of the black literary tradition, and an understanding of the black experience. The discussion among black critics, which is often healthily controversial, causes Rhett D. Jones to argue that black writers are unable to help in understanding black thought. He says in "Understanding Afro-American Thought: Can Black Writers Help?" (*SBL* 7,ii:10–15) that black writers are too much involved in trying to work out their own identities to be as helpful as they might in providing understanding. Jerry W. Ward raises questions about the concept of a national literature—an American literature—which does not give proper recognition to black literature and its tradition in "Poetry and History" (*Crisis* 83:364–65).

Whether the black writer can and does contribute to understanding Afro-American thought is answered affirmatively and well in *The Image of Black Folk in Literature*, a published typescript of the speeches and papers from three of the panels of the National Conference of Afro-American Writers which took place on the Howard University campus, November 8–10, 1974. Part 1 of the conference materials was edited by Stephen E. Henderson (Washington D.C.: Institute for the Arts and Humanities, Howard University). The papers in the collection include John O. Killens's "The Image of Black Folk in American Literature"; Samuel F. Yette's "Black Hero Dynamics and the White Media"; Sharon Bell Mathis's "Black Writers and Children: Lessons in Black Love"; Lorenz Graham's "The Task of Black Images Makers"; Jane Jordan's "Towards a Survival Literature for Afrikan Amerikan Children"; John Stepto's "On Writing Children's Literature"; Clay Goss's "The Creative Team"; Alice Childress's "Image and the Contradiction of Black Experience"; J. E. Franklin's "Common Theological Questions in Black Literature"; Ron Milner's "The 60's: Myth or Reality"; Eugene Perkins's "Black Theater as Image Maker"; and Richard Wesley's "New Directions for the 70's."

Eugene B. Redmond's *Drumvoices: The Mission of Afro-American Poetry, A Critical History* (Garden City, N.Y.: Anchor/Doubleday) is a history of Afro-American poetry. Redmond says that "the thesis of *Drumvoices* is simple: that God's trombones have historically blared through or soothed the harsh and stark realities of Afro-American experience; and that the sources (records) of these sooth-sayings, locked in cultural safe-deposit boxes of drums and the intricate acoustics of the folk, remain accessible to anyone desiring to tap them." Redmond attempts to show historically the pattern of development and the characteristics of Afro-American poetry.

In "Tradition in Afro-American Literature" (*BlackW* 25,iv[1975]: 20–35) Chestyn Everett says that the most solid roots of a Black Aesthetic are in the traditions of Afro-American literature and music, and he argues that the new in black literature must make a "truce" with the realities of the past. Pat M. Ryan raises important questions about what can be called the African content of the Afro-American tradition in "African Continuities/Discontinuities in Black American Writing" (*A-AS* 3[1975]:227–34). The essay describes the way in which Don L. Lee, Saunders Redding, Imamu Baraka, Richard Wright, William Melvin Kelley, William Demby, and John A. Williams have come to terms with Africa (use Africa in their writing). Ryan's discussion in "Pluriverse of Afro-American Poetics: Can You Dig the Music" (*A-AS* 3[1975]:227–34) explores another aspect of the tradition of Afro-American literature and is specifically concerned with the Black Aesthetic. He sees a relationship between decolonization and the resulting African independence and decolonization and blacks in the United States in their effects upon the black writers on the two continents. Although this parallel (or similar) effect is not fully developed, Ryan questions the reality, validity, and politics "of so-called black poetry since aesthetics should be secondary to propaganda." Insofar as Negritude is part of the content of the Black Aesthetic and the black literary tradition, he believes its cumulative effect upon Afro-American poetics has been negative. James Cone's "Speaking the Truth" (*BBB* 4,i:6–13) is a discussion of the black sermon. What he says about this genre is useful as a further indication of the importance of tradition in black literature. He says that the sermon uses the truth that comes out of black experience, that the sermon is poetic, and that it uses animal and folk tales and embodies a theology that results from an investigation of the socioreligious experience of black people "as that experience is reflected in black stories of God's dealings with black people in the struggle for freedom." Addison Gayle and Margaret Walker contribute toward a fuller understanding of the Black Aesthetic. Gayle in "Notes From an Arm Chair Philosopher" (*BBB* 4,ii:52–53) corrects the assumption that he believes literary form to be unimportant as is stated in Maria K. Mootry's "The Way of the New World" (*BBB* 4,i:37–48). Mootry's essay is a review of Gayle's study of the black novel. In effect Gayle says in his reply to her criticism that the Black Aesthetic does not deny the importance of form. Margaret Walker says in "Some Aspects of the Black Aesthetic" (*Freedomways* 16:95–102) that the Black Aesthetic derives its standard of beauty and cultural dynamism from folk patterns (African art, jazz, dance, rituals).

Michel Fabre's "Tendances du Roman Afro-Américan Contemporain: vers une Esthétique néo-vaudou" (*EA* 29:499–509) comments with significance and understanding on a large group of contemporary black novelists: John A. Williams, Ernest Gaines, Ronald Fair, Charles Wright, LeRoi Jones, William Melvin Kelley, Ishmael Reed, Samuel R. DeLaney, John Edgar Wideman, Cyrus Coulter, Henry Van Dyke, Clarence Major, Steve Cannon, and Melvin Van Peebles. He tries to find among this group of writers, whose traits are considerably different, a sense of the direction in which Afro-American fiction is developing. He finds LeRoi Jones (*The System of Dante's Hell*) and Charles Wright (*The Messenger* and *The Wig*) to be influential and the Preface to and the content of Ishmael Reed's anthology, *19 Nicromancers*, to give an indication of the direction away from realism and the importance of the mode of satire.

Ishmael Reed's fiction, which embodies his aesthetic, his use of voodoo and tradition, seems of most significance among the tendencies that Fabre writes about. He says "La fiction de Reed représente certainement le développement le plus original du nouveau romain afro-américain, non seulement parce qu'il anime l'école 'vaudou,' mais parce qu'il unit à une esthétique de la deconstruction par la parodie un projet de contre-mythologie que ses contemporains blancs ne peuvent formuler'" (p. 506). Although the essay is not specifically concerned with what is commonly called the Black Aesthetic, its rather full judgment of Reed's aesthetic does a good deal to clarify the role of tradition in the Black Aesthetic.

A good deal of the critical work that has been written during the year is important in the ordering and making of Afro-American literary history or in presenting the details that constitute the tradition of Afro-American letters. Thomas S. Hale's "From Afro-American to Afro-France: The Literary Triangle Trade" (*FR* 44:1089–96) shows how the African diaspora, or triangle trade, which resulted in the scattered communities of the New World, is a kind of metaphor for efforts of anglophone and francophone blacks on both sides of the New World to reestablish contacts among these dispersed communities "and to recreate, via literature a sense of ethnic identity and unity." Hale traces the relationship among authors and the influences that produced *La Revue du Mond Noir, Legitime Défense, L'Etudiant Noir, Tropiques,* and *Présence Africain.* Something of the influence of the Harlem Renaissance is suggested in Hale's article. Margaret Perry's *Silence to the Drums, A Survey of the Literature of the Harlem Renaissance* (Contribution in Afro-American and African Studies 18, Westport, Conn.: Greenwood Press) provides a useful survey of the writing and the ideas of the Harlem Renaissance period and is more valuable as a survey than as criticism.

Jabulani Kamu Makalani attempts to answer several sociological questions about the Harlem Renaissance in "Why Harlem" (*BlackW* 25,iv:4–13). Why should a cultural and artistic flowering be important for black people at that particular point in history? Who were the primary participants, and why did this event occur in a northern city? What factors facilitated a communications network among artists and the development of a self-conscious artistic movement? Although Mark Hebling's "Carl Van Vechten and the Harlem Renaissance" (*NALF* 10:39–47) is primarily an evaluation of Van Vechten's *Nigger Heaven,* it does attempt to show what his relation to the Renaissance was and is of some value in understanding some of the events of that period. Richard A. Long's "The Genesis of Locke's *The New Negro*" (*BlackW* 25,iv:14–20) is more valuable. Alain Locke's *The New Negro* is regarded by many historians and scholars as the "keystone" of the Harlem Renaissance movement. Long's essay, which is largely textual criticism, reveals the steps by which this anthology was compiled. He provides a careful documentation of the circumstances and of the persons who were involved in its publication.

Blyden Jackson's *The Waiting Years, Essays on American Negro Literature* (Baton Rouge: La. State Univ. Press) is an important and revealing book. It provides an example of what a black literary scholar and critic was and is from the 1930s to the present and shows the effects of American culture and repression on him and his writing. The book contains an autobiographical essay and fourteen of Jackson's critical pieces that have been published during several decades. The book makes clear the opportunities that existed for black scholars to publish during the 1930s and 1940s, the existence of a community of black literary scholars, the formation of the still predominantly black College Language Association, and the *CLA Journal*, which has now been published for more than 20 years. There are in his collection essays on Countee Cullen, Langston Hughes's Simple, Richard Wright, the minstrel mode, the Harlem Renaissance, the black novel, Jean Toomer's *Cane*, and others. The book is more than a portrait and a sample of Jackson's work; it presents a view of the critical world, assumptions, and standards of an older group of Afro-American critics.

An additional effort to provide a history of an Afro-American literary tradition is found in accounts of two journals. Mary Fair Burks's "The First Black Literary Magazine in American Letters" (*CLAJ* 19:318–21) is an account of the *Anglo-African Magazine* that was founded by Thomas Hamilton in New York in 1859 and was published through 1862. The essay contains a list of the authors and of the works that were published during those years. Walter C. Daniel's "*Challenge Magazine*: An Experiment That Failed" (*CLAJ* 19:494–503) is a study of the short life of *Challenge Magazine*, which began publication in 1934 and which was published for six issues from 1934 to 1937. The editor of the journal was not able, as she had hoped, to revive some of the literary interest of the Harlem Renaissance years and to discover new writers.

A good deal of the criticism written this year attempts to judge tendencies, general practices, and modes that are present in Afro-American literature. In "The Reversal of the Tainted Blood Theme in the Works of Writers of the Black Revolutionary Theater" (*NALF* 10:88–91), Willene P. Taylor notes an indication of the disappearance of the concepts of good and bad blood which frequently characterized the writing about miscegenation. She studies Jimmie Garrett's *And We Own the Night,* Imamu Baraka's *The Slave,* Herbert Stokes's *The Uncle Toms,* and Sonia Sanchez's *The Bronx* and finds that these authors reject Western values and have moved from the notion that black blood spoils to the notion that black blood improves. Although this essay is not well written, it treats an interesting subject. Trudier Harris's essay, "Ceremonial Fagots: Lynching and Burning Rituals in Black Literature" (*SHR* 10:235–47), judges with understanding and skill the episodes (rituals) of lynching that occur in the fiction of a good many black authors. She finds that, in black literature, lynchings and burnings have been adapted and altered to suit the purpose of individual authors, and that they are accessory devices, often ornamentations, to suggest the innate character of white society, such as its destructive nature, and do not contribute to the structural or thematic development of works in which they appear. William Couch, Jr., studies the treatment of the black soldier by black and white authors and concludes in "The Image of the Black Soldier in Selected American Novels" (*CLAJ* 20:176–84) that "not even the black novelist has fully discerned the black soldier's powerful and illuminating figure." He compares the portrayals of black soldiers in the novels of James Jones, Howard Odum, William Styron, Claude McKay, John O. Killens, and John A. Williams. Ronald Billingsley's "The Burden of the Hero in Modern Afro-American Fiction" (*BlackW* 25,vi[1975]:38–45,66–73) studies the characterization and the function of the Afro-American hero. Billingsley concludes from a reading of such works of fiction as Ted Poston's "The Revolt of the Evil Fairies," Wright's *Native Son,* Chester Himes's *If He Hollers Let Him Go,* Ernest Gaines's "Three Men," Ralph Ellison's "Flying Home," and James Cain's *Blueschild Baby* that the black hero is often engaged in a struggle to throw off old, negative definitions of himself, and to forge new and positive ones. He finds that, at the level of the individual, violence is a cleansing force and describes the psychic nature of the struggle which black men must wage for freedom. Each of these four essays contributes in a particular way to building an awareness of a black literary tradition.

Several critics study individual writers. Joel Roache's "What Made Him and What He Meant: The Politics of Wholeness in 'How Bigger Was Born'" (*Sub-stance* 15:133–44) is an attempt to judge the literary importance of Richard Wright's essay, "How Bigger Was Born." Roache says "the literary impact of the essay results largely from its dramatization of the creative process as an act of total engagement of the whole person with social reality" and he argues that the essay provides the reader with an awareness of the influence of socialism upon Wright's work and of a sense of his departures from the assumptions and directions of the familiar tradition of naturalism. Roache disagrees with Ellison's suggestion that Wright was the victim of the "much abused idea that novels are 'weapons.'" Theresa R. Love's "Zora Neale Hurston's America" (*PLL* 12:422–37) is a general evaluation of Hurston's language and purposes as a folklorist and a writer of fiction." Don N. Menchise describes Baraka's socialism in "Le Roi Jones and the Case of Shifting Identities" (*CLAJ* 20:232–34).

vi. Autobiography, Biography, Interviews

Biography, beginning with the slave narratives, has always had a significant place in black letters and in recent years the interest in the genre has increased. The biography of the black writer is of particular importance because of the light it sheds on the art of black writing, not only as a source for the content of the literary work, but more importantly because of what it may tell of the circumstances of the production and distribution of literary works, of the ideas and values of the authors, and of many details that contribute to a knowledge of a black literary tradition and its relation to the black experience.

Several essays examine the form. Roger Rosenblatt makes several thoughtful generalizations about it in "Black Autobiography: Life as the Death Weapon" (*YR* 65:515–27). He says that black autobiography exists as a special form of literature "because there are discernible patterns within black autobiographies which tie them together, and because the outer world apprehended by black autobiographies is consistent and unique, if dreadful." He comments on the ways in which the genre has changed, on the variety of the material and the similarity of the polemics. The two constants in black autobiography, he says, are the expressed desire to live as one chooses, as far as possible, and tacit or explicit criticism of external national conditions which work to ensure that freedom of choice is limited or nonexistent. Rosenblatt compares black fiction and black autobiography effectively. Paul John Eakin uses his essay "Malcolm X and the Limits of Autobiography" (*Criticism* 18:230–42) to examine certain of the possibilities of autobiography and is not primarily concerned with the special characteristics of black autobiography. His study of Malcolm X's autobiography suggests to him that the idea that the individual first discovers the shape of his life and then writes the life on the basis of this discovery, a natural and seemingly inevitable inference, is not necessarily true as it is tested in Malcolm's autobiography. Claudia C. Tate's "*Black Boy*: Richard Wright's 'Tragic Sense of Life'" (*BALF* 10:117–19) is both an attempt to discover why *Black Boy* is different from Richard Wright's actual experience and how Wright has used autobiography. She suggests that the black tragic view of life that colors the book may represent, to some extent, the influence of Wright's reading of Miguel de Unamuno's *The Tragic Sense of Life* in 1937. She finds that *Black Boy* may be a depiction of the boy Richard's attempt to establish himself as a distinct and fully conscious individual and more a portrait of Wright's developing personality and growth of consciousness than an account of his childhood experiences. Two critics discuss the first volume of Maya Angelou's autobiography. Liliane R. Arensberg says in "Death As Metaphor of Self in *I Know Why the Caged Bird Sings*" (*CLAJ* 20:273–91) that the style of the work seems a conscious defense against the pain that is felt when unpleasant memories are looked at. She explains that the book suggests a self as perpetually in the process of becoming, "of dying and being reborn," in all its ramifications. John Hiers's note, "Fatalism in Maya Angelou's *I Know Why the Caged Bird Sings*" (*NConL* 6,i:5–7) complements Arensberg's idea. He says that the autobiography is a study of fatalism as well as racism and that the fatalism never completely diminishes.

The third volume of Maya Angelou's autobiography, *Singin' and Swingin' and Gettin' Merry Like Christmas* (New York: Random House) and three other autobiographies of black writers have appeared this year—Lucile Clifton's *Generations, A Memoir* (New York: Random House), Chester Himes's *My Life of Absurdity, The Autobiography of Chester Himes*, vol. 2 (Garden City, N.Y.: Doubleday), and Julius Lester's *All is Well* (New York: William Morrow). James Baldwin's *The Devil Finds Work* (New York: Dial Press) contributes to his biography insofar as it shows, particularly during his early years, how he was influenced and affected by the movies he saw. In a more specific sense the book is a cinema chronicle, or film criticism, which presents a clear argument. The chapters contain racial and cultural clarifications and add to the reader's knowledge of Baldwin's life. Baldwin's questions about the truths that have not been present in particular films are searching.

Robert C. Twombly's "A Disciple's Odyssey: Jean Toomer's Gurdjieffian Career" (*Prospects* 2:437–61) is a careful study of the influence of Georgi Gurdjieff's teaching in Jean Toomer's life. Twombly argues convincingly that the Gurdjieffian influence was dominant in Toomer's life from the 1920s until his death. Because of this influence Twombly argues that Toomer was "hardly a 'new Negro.'" The essay contributes a good deal to understanding Toomer's quest and life.

Virginia W. Smith and Brian J. Smith in "An Interview with Linda Brown Bragg (*CLAJ* 20:75–87) provide an introduction to a young, not well-known poet who feels that she has been influenced by Robert Frost, Gwendolyn Brooks, and Don L. Lee, and who believes that it is important for a poet to make statements that people pay attention to. Charles H. Rowell's interview, "In Conversation with Dudley Randall" (*Obsidian* 2,i:32–44) is valuable for Randall's comments on his political background, on the Harlem Renaissance, on certain post-Renaissance poets, particularly on Melvin Tolson's scholarship, and on his own poetry. James McKenzie's "Pole Vaulting in Top Hats: A Public Conversation with John Barth, William Gass and Ishmael Reed" (*MFS* 22:131–51) is a report of a conversation that took place among these writers at the University of North Dakota Writers Conference, March 1975. In the discussion among the three authors, Reed explains how his novel, *The Free Lance Pallbearers*, began as a naturalistic novel about Newark, New Jersey, politics and then became a fantasy about an imaginary dictatorship. The conversation indicates Reed's feelings about language, his use of sculpture and the plastic arts, and his adaptation of movie techniques. The statement about his use of the myth of Antigone contributes to an understanding of his theory of myths. In addition to giving a good sense of the liveliness and of the critical quality of George Schuyler's mind, Richard A. Long's "An Interview with George Schuyler" (*BlackW* 25,iv:68–78) contains interesting observations about Harlem Renaissance personalities and other persons (Nancy Cunard, Chandler Owen, A. Philip Randolph, and Lonnie Aden). Charles H. Rowell's "Poetry, History, and Humanism: An Interview with Margaret Walker" (*BlackW* 25,ii [1975]:4–17) contains a description of Walker's humanism and several of her opinions. She feels that the role of the novelist is comparable to that of the historian. She admires Ishmael Reed and Sam Greenlee and finds Imamu Baraka, Don L. Lee, and Sonia Sanchez courageous and bold but not totally acceptable to her. John A. Williams gives a good account of his novel, *Night Song*, in Joseph T. Skerrett's "Novelist in Motion: An Interview with John A. Williams" (*BlackW* 25,iii:58–67,93–97). Generally, he appears in the interview to be a realist about social change.

Statements about their work or about themselves that are comparable to those found in interviews have been made by several writers. Ed Bullins's "Playwright's Journal 1975" (*Confrontation* no. 12:3–19), journal entries for a month conveys his interest in black Marxists and his pleasure in the public response to his recent writing. Several of the entries are about new plays that he is working on in which the poets Lucy Terry and Phillis Wheatley are the subjects. Clarence Major's "Open Letters: A Column" (*APR* 5,i:39–40) is an account of his experiences at the International Poetry Festival in Yugoslavia in 1975. It creates a scene, introduces several poets, and gives an account of a conversation with Lèopold Sìdan Senghor. Ishmael Reed's "The 'Liberal' in Us All" (*Antaeus* 21–22:149–54) is a summary of a keynote address that he delivered at the Third World Writers and Thinkers Symposium on Asian, Black, Chicano, and Indian writing at California State College, Sacramento, April 1975.

Jervis Anderson presents a portrait of Ralph Ellison as a person in "Profiles: Ralph Ellison" (*New Yorker* 22 Nov:55–108) that gives a clear impression of a strong man who is aware of his sources and who has remarkable integrity and humanity. Anderson observes and talks with Ellison and his friends when Ellison is visiting and being honored in Oklahoma.

Some of the material in James Presley's "Langston Hughes, War Correspondent" (*JML* 5:481–91) is also in Hughes's *I Wonder as I Wander*, but Presley's essay gives an added impression of Hughes and of his courage during the months that he was in Spain. References are made to black Americans who fought in the Spanish Civil War whom Hughes knew and saw while he was in Spain. Hughes's reports on the war were published in the *Baltimore Afro-American* from the summer of 1937 through January of 1938.

University of Colorado

20. Themes, Topics, Criticism

Michael J. Hoffman

This is the fourth year I have sat down to write this chapter after reading three- or four-score books. In *ALS 1975* I suggested that we might well be in an age of critical flowering and that the general level of publication in both literary criticism and in writings about American literature was high. I see no reason to revise my opinion downward, even though the number of outstanding books published in 1976 was fewer than that published the previous year. The level of even "run-of-the-mill" works remains high, and the variety is fascinating. It is quite clear, for instance, that certain fields such as women's studies have come of age with the appearance of a number of works of high quality. There were also a number of interesting overviews of American literature, one of which will almost surely go down as a classic.

i. American Literature

a. **Handbooks and Anthologies.** I shall begin this section by noting the publication of a number of handbooks and one anthology of American literature. Lewis Leary's *American Literature: A Study and Research Guide* (New York: St. Martin's) is a solid introduction to the field of American literary study which draws on Leary's lifetime of work in basic historical scholarship. The book contains a good survey of research materials as well as a brief history of scholarship in the field. Leary introduces the student to biographical and bibliographical resources, to works on American language and the various genres, to the schools of American criticism, and to basic works about each of almost 30 major American writers. He is a solid, tough-minded historical scholar, an ideal mind with which beginners should be asked to grapple. I recommend the book for both advanced undergraduates and beginning graduate students.

A different kind of introductory volume is provided by Martin S. Day in *A Handbook of American Literature: A Comprehensive Survey from Colonial Times to the Present Day* (New York: Crane, Russak). This history of American literature in survey form contains the many faults one might expect from one's person's attempting so vast a work. The scholarship is not poor, it is merely thin. The writing is lively but tends to slickness. The book might serve as a supplementary text in an introductory survey of American literature where serious scholarship is not an issue. Since the contents are crammed into one large paperback volume, the format tends to be unwieldy. Most serious of all is the historical imbalance. Scarcely one-fourth of the book covers the period to the Civil War. Most of the rest is concerned with the 20th century, and the inadequate treatment of the earlier period—in particular that of the American Renaissance— should warn the instructor to look the volume over carefully before assigning it.

Of the same genre but better than Day's book is a two-volume "Barnes & Noble Outline" by James T. Callow and Robert J. Reilly: vol. 1, *Guide to American Literature from its Beginnings through Walt Whitman: Summaries, Interpretations, and Annotated Bibliography*; vol. 2, *From Emily Dickinson to the Present* (New York: Barnes & Noble [1977]). This good introductory handbook is well written, succinct, and scholarly. The two volumes are of approximately equal length (the second one is about 30 pages longer), and the authors provide an adequate balance among periods, categories, and authors. As a supplementary text providing an historical overview, this inexpensive two-volume set would be a useful adjunct to historical surveys of American literature.

One of the most influential taste-making texts in American literary scholarship has been updated by Richard Ellmann in *The New Oxford Book of American Verse*, the first edition since F. O. Matthiessen's (1950). Any new edition of this work is an event in American letters. The history and even the format of the volume lend it a magisterial quality, suggesting its power to establish the basic canon of American poetry.

The format of the anthology is spare. It has no footnotes and a bare minimum of apparatus. The poems are attractively printed on the page, establishing the fact that the text is paramount. The brief introduction by Ellmann surveys American verse historically, with

Walt Whitman the first central figure and T. S. Eliot the next. There are generous selections from poets born in the 1920s and 1930s, who would have been in their teens and early adulthood when Matthiessen's edition was published. The previous version ended with Robert Lowell (b. 1917). There are few surprises in the recent selections, with poets like Ammons, Ashberry, Merwin, and Snyder appearing as the major poets of the period.

From the point of view of the history of taste, it is interesting to compare which poets from the earlier periods are new, which poems have appeared and disappeared in the course of the two publications, and which poets now seem more or less prominent than before. I should like to spend some space analyzing these phenomena by comparing this edition with the previous one.

In the colonial period Ellmann has chosen two new poets, Philip Pain (c. 1666) and Phillis Wheatley (?1753–84). The Edward Taylor selections are substantially the same as in Matthiessen, which indicates that the Taylor canon had been established by 1949.

In the 19th century the selections from Emerson have substantially increased, indicating the rising favor that poet has found in recent criticism. The same statement can be made of Melville's poetry, whose representation here has increased even more dramatically. In addition to more poems by Emily Dickinson, there is a new section entitled "Folk Songs and Ballads" as well as a large section (9 poems) by Frederick Goddard Tuckerman, who was unrepresented in Matthiessen. Edgar Lee Masters has been cut from 16 poems to 5, Edward Arlington Robinson from 22 to 14, and Trumbull Stickney from 6 to 2. Stephen Crane, whose poetry did not appear in the previous edition, is now represented by 3 poems.

In the 20th century Ellmann reflects the rising interest in William Carlos Williams by an increase from 17 to 26 of his poems. He has also enlarged the number of poems of H. D. and cut in half the number by John Crowe Ransom. Poets cut out altogether are Elinor Wylie, John Peale Bishop, Stephen Vincent Benét, Edna St. Vincent Millay, Phelps Putnam, and Howard Baker. Although one could make a case for individual poems by each of the above, the decisions seem defensible. More eccentric are the removal of W. H. Auden (because Ellmann considers him British down to the "bone") and Karl Shapiro, who was represented by no less than ten poems in Matthiessen and whose work is still more substantial than that of some of the poets

Ellmann has chosen to add, such as Jean Garrigue, Gwendolyn Brooks, and Yvor Winters. Other additions of poets born before Robert Lowell's 1917 birthdate are Langston Hughes, Theodore Roethke (a reminder of how late his reputation developed), Charles Olson, and John Berryman.

b. **General Studies.** In this section I shall discuss in roughly chronological order and by subject the books published on more general topics in American literature, beginning with a fine book by J. Martin Evans, *America: The View from Europe* (San Francisco: San Francisco Book Co.), part of a new venture called "The Portable Stanford Series." Intended as a set of high-level popularizations written by members of the Stanford University faculty, this work goes beyond that intention. It is, although short, a substantial book, a well-written, deeply felt study of the images by which Europeans have perceived America. Evans's deep feelings for the subject arise from the fact that he is an Englishman who has lived and has himself become Americanized during the past 12 or 13 years.

The book's historical perspective is strong and is in many ways a compressed version of the same material that appeared in Hugh Honour's *The New Golden Land*, reviewed in these pages last year. Evans traces the evolution of the idea of America throughout European history from the time of the Renaissance on. Divided into three sections entitled "American Myths," "American Values," and "American Character," the table of contents reveals how the book is organized: (1) "The Best of All Possible Worlds"; (2) "A Fool's Paradise"; (3) "The Open Society"; (4) "Sweet Land of Liberty"; (5) "The Ignoble Savage"; and (6) "The Mistress of Europe." Through this thematic breakdown Evans sets up some fascinating contrasts, particularly in the juxtapositions of chapters 1–2 and 5–6. The book also contains some excellent graphics.

On a similar theme is *America in Modern European Literature: From Image to Metaphor* (New York: N.Y. Univ. Press), by Richard Ruland. Ruland is concerned with demonstrating the influence that America has had on Europe, particularly on the works of six modern European writers in light of the use to which they put America in their writings. In his close readings of these authors Ruland emphasizes the creation ("invention") of America as a kind of myth ("image"). He covers basically the same ground as Evans in the beginning, but with emphasis on literature and philosophy rather than the plastic arts. There is more solid scholarship here than in Evans, but overall the book is rather dull. Evans's book is more succinct and well written, and for the reader who wishes to follow the general themes of the creation of the *idea* of America and its influence on Europe, I strongly recommend Evans.

More of a traditional literary study is Neal Frank Doubleday's *Variety of Attempt: British and American Fiction in the Early Nineteenth Century* (Lincoln: Univ. of Neb. Press). The thesis of this unpromisingly titled book is stated as an attempt to show how self-conscious craftsmanship developed on the part of writers in the early 19th century who were "thinking hard about the uses and the means of fiction" (p. 1). The result is really a loosely connected series of essays on British and American novels from about the year 1800 to the publication of Hawthorne's *The Marble Faun* (1860). The book is concerned with many minor writers as well as some major ones, but its connections are not well made. The critical techniques are old fashioned and Doubleday's attempt to mix literary criticism and literary history is unsatisfying.

A better work is the first full-length study of F. O. Matthiessen, *F. O. Matthiessen: The Critical Achievement* (Seattle: Univ. of Wash. Press), by Giles Gunn. One wonders what it says of American scholarship that we are now seeing the publication of books *about* our leading critics (I shall later discuss a book on Cleanth Brooks). Is it a sign that the study of American letters is coming to a new maturity or does it signify a turning of attention inward and away from the primary materials of literary study? Those considerations aside, however, the present book is an excellent, well-written assessment that stresses two major themes in Matthiessen's work: (1) its evaluative nature, and (2) its organic nature, particularly the attitude "that the critic must write for all the people instead of for a special coterie" (p. 5). The book is organized to lead up to and then away from Matthiessen's major achievement, *American Renaissance*. Gunn, who teaches both American studies and religion, is better at assessing Matthiessen's Christian orientation than his Marxist one. He is, in addition, very good at placing Matthiessen in his historical context, as part of the American radical movement and as part of the development of American literary studies in the American university. It is ironic that a book about a literary scholar should contain some of the best writing of the year about American literature.

Another fairly good book by an established writer heavily influenced by Matthiessen is Sherman Paul, *Repossessing and Renewing: Essays in the Green American Tradition* (Baton Rouge: La. State Univ. Press). This collection is centered on what Paul calls the "Emersonian" tradition in American letters, or the positive, "green" tradition, and on his own commitment to that tradition as a basic scholarly focus. The essays are united by a similar set of themes, although they do not really build to an overall thesis. Especially interesting are the chapters on John Jay Chapman, Paul Rosenfeld, Louis Sullivan, Gary Snyder, and Alfred Kazin.

In line with the books about American war literature discussed in last year's chapter is Peter Jones, *War and the Novelist: Appraising the American War Novel* (Columbia: Univ. of Mo. Press). This solid book is comparable in subject matter, and to some extent in theme, to the books I reviewed last year by Fussell and Aichinger, although it does not in any way reach the level of the former. The book has not so much a thesis as a thematic organization, which the author discusses on the first page. The author, a lieutenant colonel, focuses on post–World War II novels, although he uses three earlier war novels —*The Red Badge of Courage, Three Soldiers,* and *A Farewell to Arms*—as models. In the course of his discussions, Jones introduces us to certain novelists not so well known, such as Anton Myrer, whose *The Big War* the author esteems highly. Two other well-known books —James Gould Cozzens's *Guard of Honor* and James Jones's *From Here to Eternity*—are the author's favorite novels of the Second World War.

A contribution to the literature on regionalism is William Everson's *Archetype West: The Pacific Coast as a Literary Region* (Berkeley, Calif.: Oyez), a poet's meditation on the West as an archetype. The book is really an expansion of the provocative essay Everson published in *Regional Perspectives* (see ALS 1973, p. 438). Everson has expanded the essay to book length by increasing the number of examples and by extended expositions of certain writers. He builds his argument by accretion rather than by developing a careful thesis. His style is lively and highly personal, and he does his best to make an out-of-fashion subject interesting.

One of the finest books of this or any year is Irving Howe's *World of Our Fathers: The Journey of the East European Jews to America and the Life They Found and Made* (New York: Harcourt Brace), winner of the National Book Award. This marvelous book is basically a history, but it does have relevance for students of the last century of American culture and of the contributions made by East European Jews. Two large sections of the book, "The Culture of Yiddish?" and "Dispersion," in particular, give the reader a vivid sense of Yiddish-American artistic culture in the areas of language, theater, poetry, and fiction. The book is beautifully written, sensitive, and amazingly erudite—a classic of scholarship.

Another interesting book on a quite different subject is by Tom Dardis, *Some Time in the Sun: The Hollywood Years of Fitzgerald, Faulkner, Nathanael West, Aldous Huxley, and James Agee* (New York: Scribner's). This well-researched book tries to displace some old myths about these writers and their attitudes toward writing for the moving pictures. All these men had to adapt themselves to the collaborative aspects of film making, and some were more successful than others. Fitzgerald, who applied himself seriously to the craft of screenwriting, was one of the unsuccessful ones, and yet he was not as miserable in Hollywood as writers like Arthur Mizener have tried to suggest. Faulkner never saw the movies as much more than a way to make money, although he had some good instincts about films. Huxley had an artist's attitude toward films and did write two "classic" screenplays, *Pride and Prejudice* and *Jane Eyre*. About Nathanael West, Dardis adds little to the account given in Jay Martin's biography. It was James Agee who was most at home in films, for he had considered them a serious artistic medium ever since his student days. Dardis considers Agee to have written the most fully realized screenplays of all these authors, some of them—particularly *Night of the Hunter* and *The African Queen*—being classics of their kind. This is an informative book on a subject still in need of more research.

Another major manifestation of American popular culture is the automobile, which is the subject of Cynthia Golomb Dettelbach's *In the Driver's Seat: The Automobile in American Literature and Popular Culture* (Westport, Conn.: Greenwood Press). This is a clever, somewhat insubstantial study of how the automobile has served as a literary theme, a psychological and sociological object, a source of personal aspiration, a symbol, and an occasion for psychic projection in American literature as it reflects American culture. This is primarily a cultural study, using a mixture of sources from all levels of literary culture. Dettelbach's attempt is "to say something, if only tentatively, about the car's role in the larger dream/nightmare patterns dominating America life and thought" (p. 5). However, she only partially succeeds. The chapter titles indicate the basic themes of the book: "Fumbling for the American Dream," "Youth: Dreams of Innocence, Nightmares of Experience," "Dreams of Freedom, Nightmares of Constraint," "Dreams of Success, Nightmares of Failure," "Dreams of Possession, Nightmares of Being Possessed."

John Tytell's *Naked Angels: The Lives & Literature of the Beat Generation* (New York: McGraw-Hill) contains an excellent overview and insights into the whole Beat movement, placing it firmly in the tradition of the 19th-century movements from which it in large part emerged as well as within the contemporary scene in which its writers lived. Tytell mixes equal measures of biography, literary history, and critical insights. His three main authors are William Burroughs, Jack Kerouac, and Allen Ginsberg, on whom he writes two chapters apiece. The first of each pair is biographical, treating the life as symbolic of the movement. The second analyzes the books of each author chronologically and thematically. *Naked Angels* makes the best possible case for each of the writers as important literary figures. This is the finest book yet on the Beat movement; it may well be definitive.

c. **Southern Literature.**   The year saw a cluster of books concerned with southern literature, beginning with an edition of the proceedings of a 1972 conference on southern literature, edited by Louis D. Rubin, Jr., and C. Hugh Holman, *Southern Literary Study: Problems and Possibilities* (Chapel Hill: Univ. of N.C. Press, 1975). Better than many books of its kind, this one opens with four papers on major topics written by leading scholars in the field, Rubin, Richard Beale Davis, Arlin Turner, and Lewis P. Simpson. All four of these essays are worth reading, particularly the ones by Davis and Simpson, and all of them open up possibilities for further work in southern literature. Following them are 150 pages consisting of transcriptions of five topical discussion sections. There is also an appendix listing topics for further study. As one might expect, the book is a bit uneven and lacks the rigor of a more carefully prepared volume. It sometimes rambles, but it does have the occasional virtue of spontaneity. When read selectively, it gives one a good understanding of the possibilities available to the student of southern literature.

Louis Rubin has authored another book in this section, *William Elliott Shoots a Bear*, a collection of his own essays on southern literature that try to deal with the problem, "Why do southern writers write the way they do?" (p. ix). The essays cover a wide variety of topics and range from the early 19th century to the "problem" of William Styron. The title essay, which is concerned with a minor 19th-century, typically "southern" writer, gives a good sense of Rubin's version of the southern sensibility. There are first-rate essays on Thomas Wolfe, William Styron (two of them), and Joel Chandler Harris. The book is sensible and sensitive, and Rubin is quite optimistic about the prospects for contemporary southern literature.

Not so optimistic is Walter Sullivan, whose *A Requiem for the Renascence: The State of Fiction in the Modern South* (Athens: Univ. of Ga. Press) was originally given as the Mercer University Lamar Memorial Lectures, no. 18. Sullivan picks up from Lewis Simpson's *The Dispossessed Garden* (see *ALS 1975*, p. 450), but he is much more pessimistic. His thesis is that the southern literary flowering is past and that present writers are mining a dying tradition. He repeats much that is familiar about the "myth" of the South, and the ordering of his book into three chapters entitled "Myth," "Community," and "Rainbow's End" conveys the familiarity of his approach. He makes a weaker case then he might for his thesis because he tends to be moralistic and antimodernist. This vision causes Sullivan to espouse an almost reactionary point of view. A disappointing book.

Alan H. Rose's *Demonic Vision: Racial Fantasy and Southern Fiction* (Hamden, Conn.: Archon Books) is a fairly straightforward revision of a doctoral thesis. It traces the history and embodiment in literature of southern racial fantasy in such manifestations as blacks-as-devils. It goes from seriousness to irony in its literary subjects, from Thomas Dixon's *The Clansman* (on which *Birth of a Nation* was based) to Flannery O'Connor's *Wise Blood*. Rose uses psychoanalytic devices—primarily Jungian—to analyze his texts, which include the writings of George Washington Harris and William Faulkner, and Twain's *Tom Sawyer*, *Huck Finn*, and *Pudd'nhead Wilson*. There are few insights in this book that the reader has not encountered elsewhere in writings on southern literature.

A more solid piece of scholarship is *From Tobacco Road to Route 66: The Southern Poor White in Fiction* (Chapel Hill: Univ. of N.C. Press), by Sylvia Jenkins Cook, which deals with yet another southern stereotype, that of the poor white. The book traces the beginnings of interest in poor whites in the tradition of 19th-century literary humor. Cook traces the continuity of this tradition into the 20th century in the writings of Faulkner, Caldwell, and Steinbeck, showing the increasing seriousness with which the poor whites are taken as literary material even in humorous books. Cook traces the rise of a poor-white class consciousness through such episodes as the Gastonia Strike, and she focuses most heavily on the 1930s. A solid, informative book.

d. **Women in Literature and the Rise of Feminist Consciousness.** I begin this section with a discussion of two books that are not directly concerned with American literature but rather with the more general problem of women in literature, and conclude with a discussion of four books about women in American literature. The quality of works in this general field has improved dramatically in the past year, and although there are no major works reviewed in this section, there are a number of works of high quality.

Patricia Meyer Spacks's *The Female Imagination* (New York: Knopf, 1975) explores the problem of whether there is a feminine psychology or female imagination. Spacks's sources are primarily literary, and she draws from both female writers like Jane Austen and Virginia Woolf and male writers like Henry James and John Stuart Mill. Spacks writes about both well-known figures and less-known ones, such as Dora Carrington and Marie Bashkirtseff, whom she tries to resurrect. Her thematic categories will be made clear by a few selected chapter titles: "Power and Passivity," "The Adolescent as Heroine," "The World Outside," "Free Women." Although the book is not presented as a history of her subject, Spacks projects a strong historical consciousness. The weakness of this consistently interesting study lies, however, in Spacks's psychological generalizations. Her own consciousness seems too purely literary for this kind of analysis, and the book exemplifies some of the difficulties inherent in generalizing too readily from almost purely literary examples.

Ellen Moers has received much attention in the past year for her

Literary Women: The Great Writers (Garden City, N.Y.: Double-day), a book that shares some of the same weaknesses as Spacks's. It has a basically literary focus that attempts some generalizations about the nature of feminine literary consciousness, although fewer than Spacks's about the nature of women. Moers is concerned with what she considers to be the "major" women writers, whom we would read, she claims, whether or not we were concerned with the fact of their sex. This is then not a feminist book, although Moers has sympathy with and understanding of the situation of women writers and the contents of their books. Her approach, while categorical, demonstrates a fairly solid historical sense. Moers is a good scholar with a richly erudite sensibility, but she tends to be a bit unsystematic. As a result, the book we are given has weak theoretical underpinnings but covers familiar territory with a somewhat fresh point of view. There are, for instance, good readings of Virginia Woolf and Jane Austen, but a fairly ordinary one of Gertrude Stein. This is not as good as Moers's book on Theodore Dreiser or especially her book on the dandy.

Judith Fryer, in *The Faces of Eve: Women in the Nineteenth Century American Novel* (New York: Oxford Univ. Press), claims that the dominant image of women in 19th-century American literature was created by men until the coming of Kate Chopin, so totally was the culture dominated by males and "male" values. Fryer starts with the image of America as the Garden of Eden. Other writers, she claims, have treated of Adam in the Garden but have neglected to deal with Eve. In opening her discussion of the Garden by quoting from R. W. B. Lewis and Leo Marx, Fryer also quotes quite effectively from de Tocqueville on the essentially servile position of American women in the early part of the century. Like so many other writers on similar subjects Fryer likes to deal with her materials in such suggestive categories as "The Temptress," "The American Princess," "The Great Mother," and "The New Woman." Although these titles sound familiar, the book is more convincing than one might expect. The sources are predictable, including Hawthorne, Melville, Holmes, Howells, and especially James, but the readings are sharp and intelligent, the writing clear and unpretentious.

Another point of view on the same historical period lies in Barbara Welter's *Dimity Convictions: The American Woman in the Nineteenth Century* (Athens: Ohio Univ. Press). This is a cultural study

similar to Ernest Earnest's *The American Eve* (see *ALS* 1975, p. 449).
Welter, a professor of history, is concerned with the culturally dominant attitudes in that period toward such matters as womanhood,
the "American girl," and sexuality. She is concerned with how stereotypes about women were developed and fostered, and her documentary sources range widely in such places as novels, letters, speeches,
sermons, journalism, and diaries. Particularly interesting are the
chapters, "Female Complaints: Medical Views of American Women"
and "Mystical Feminist: Margaret Fuller: a Woman of the Nineteenth Century." The book is well written, the documentation excellent.

A more localized treatment of materials used by Fryer and Welter
occurs in Paul John Eakin's *The New England Girl: Cultural Ideals
in Hawthorne, Stowe, Howells and James* (Athens: Univ. of Ga.
Press). The book tries to answer the question, "Why did these writers connect their characterization of women with their ambition to
comprehend the moral reality of American life?" (p. 4). Eakin traces
the development of this interconnected theme through various manifestations and levels of sophistication in the four writers. As one
might easily guess, the most sophisticated use of the characters of
women as moral registers occurs in Henry James. This is a solid book
of the same quality as Fryer's, with which it might well be read in
tandem. The research is good and the readings of individual novels
convincing.

The last work treated in this section leaps forward almost a century. It is Mary Allen's *The Necessary Blankness: Women in Major
American Fiction of the Sixties* (Urbana: Univ. of Ill. Press), in
many ways the most strongly feminist work of the group. Its subject
matter is quite bleak. Allen uses the characterization of women in
the fiction of, in particular, Roth, Updike, Oates, and Plath to demonstrate the difficulty of being a woman with anything like independence of character and the freedom to develop properly in the American society of the 1960s. This is a grim, well-written adaptation of
a doctoral dissertation that hammers home its thesis relentlessly.
Within the lines drawn by the thesis, Allen's readings are convincing.
I am left, however, unsure at the end of her book that it has developed
much beyond the sense that it is a terrible thing to be a female character in contemporary American fiction. One might have hoped for
more.

ii. General Literary Works

a. **The Profession.** Two books by English professors taking an evaluative look at academia provide some thought-provoking insights. Richard Ohmann's *English in America: A Radical View of the Profession* (New York: Oxford Univ. Press) has received a mixed press, often stemming from varying attitudes toward the new and old structures of the Modern Language Association. Because Ohmann has publicly aligned himself with radical ideological positions (radical, that is, within the context of our profession), he has often been attacked ad hominem. The book contains essays written over the past decade that attack many attitudes about the humanities and particularly about the teaching of writing. While Ohmann tends to overuse some radical shibboleths (such as "elitism"), he often cogently analyzes a profession that is at the moment deeply in need of self-analysis.

Ohmann (for years the editor of *College English*) points out, often at too great length, how our universities and their writing and literature programs are agents of a middle-class society, hardly a surprising insight. Many reviewers have been troubled by Ohmann's prescription of the need for "socialist revolution." But he is vague in his argument, and he does not succeed in convincing the reader that such a revolution will either take place or would successfully cure the ills of the profession. One does not need, however, to accept the prescription in order to appreciate Ohmann's insights. He is a good adversary with whom to argue, often deft and witty, but tending unfortunately toward self-righteousness and solemnity.

Hazard Adams, in *The Academic Tribes: A Wry View of the American University—with a Dash of Bitters* (New York: Norton), has written some "confessions of a former administrator." A well-known critical theorist and former department chairman, Adams recently spent a few years as academic vice chancellor at the University of California, Irvine. On his return to teaching, he has decided to share his insights into the folkways of the American university, an institution more complex and certainly a lot stranger than most others in our society. Adams poses as an anthropologist examining a strange culture in order to figure out the behavior of the natives. The opening chapter, "A Primer of Academic Politics," provides a delightful set of insights into the tensions of university governance. It is as good a

short look into the subject as one could want. The rest of the book
does not quite meet those standards, however, although Adams manages to be entertaining throughout most of it, especially in a chapter
entitled "Bureaucriticism: What's Wrong and Why It Isn't Likely to
be Fixed." He is unfortunately least successful when he tries to be
most wry and parodic; but his sense of humor is more genuine than
Ohmann's and he does not have the former's sanctimoniousness.

b. **Collections of Essays.**   A number of well-known critical elder
statesmen have provided us with collections of essays which I shall
treat alphabetically. The first critic, Cleanth Brooks, is the occasion
rather than the author of a collection edited by Lewis P. Simpson,
The Possibilities of Order: Cleanth Brooks and His Work (Baton
Rouge: La. State Univ. Press). This festschrift uses Brooks's work
as its subject. A very long opening section consists of a transcribed
series of conversations on many subjects between Brooks and his
frequent collaborator Robert Penn Warren. It is a rambling dialogue,
not without interest but containing few insights not already there
in the writings of both men. Articles by Allen Tate and Robert Heil-
man are reminiscent and rambling. Essays by Walter Ong, Thomas
Daniel Young, René Wellek, and Monroe Spears deal with various
aspects of Brooks's work. The best pieces are by Wellek and Spears.
The former has written a thorough, scholarly study of Brooks's writings on other critics. Spears's essay is a balanced, clear assessment of
the nature of Brooks's achievement as a literary figure.

The prolific Northrop Frye published two books in 1976, one of
them a set of essays written between 1969 and 1975: *Spiritus Mundi:
Essays on Literature, Myth, and Society* (Bloomington: Ind. Univ.
Press). Divided into three sections—"Contexts of Literature," "The
Mythological Universe." "Four Poets"—the twelve essays explore various aspects of Frye's lifelong thesis, that "myths" embody the basic
core of belief that animates a culture and the writers who work within
it. There is a repetitive quality to these essays, embodied in their
continuous circling around the same basic theme and united by what
the author himself characterizes as an evangelical tone. Because he
has mined so many of the same ideas for years, Frye has honed his
writing style to the point that this book is much easier to read than
Frye's earlier, more basic works on Blake and the "anatomy of criticism." Especially interesting here are "The University and Personal

Life," "The Times of the Signs" (an essay on the Copernican revolution and its implications for modern mythology), "Spengler Revisited," "Charms and Riddles," and "Wallace Stevens and the Variation Form."

E. D. Hirsch, whose *Validity in Interpretation* created a stir about a decade ago, has published a collection of essays called *The Aims of Interpretation* (Chicago: Univ. of Chicago Press), a book that carries on his interest in the subject of hermeneutics. Hirsch defines hermeneutics as having two primary emphases: (1) defining meaning, and (2) defining significance. He is an antirelativist who opposes the currently fashionable theories of language evolving from the Heideggerian and French schools. The essays are divided into two sections that follow an introduction. The first, "Current Issues in Theory of Interpretation," is heavily hermeneutical and is disappointing because the author spends too much time defending and clarifying his earlier position without really advancing it very much. The second section, "The Valuative Dimension," is more concerned with defining the role and function of the critic. The last two chapters of this metacritical section, "Some Aims of Criticism" and "Afterword: Knowledge and Value," are excellent. Hirsch's style is a bit dry and his references are more philosophical than literary, but he does represent an important tendency in modern critical thought.

Morse Peckham has published another series of essays on his central subject, in *Romanticism and Behavior* (Columbia: Univ. of S.C. Press), stating and restating, and developing in a number of contexts the themes he has been evolving since *Beyond the Tragic Vision* and *Man's Rage for Chaos.*

The book is divided into three broad sections: "The Romantic Tradition," which contains essays on Romanticism and on the relationship of certain authors to that movement; "Critical Theory," which deals mainly with various problems in literary theory; and "Behavior, Education, and Society," which covers a wide range of topics emanating from the author's encyclopedic range of interest and reference. Like Frye, Peckham sees literature as only one avenue toward a comprehensive theory of humanity. Unlike Frye, however, Peckham's writing has become more abstract and difficult. Those who have not read his earlier work will not find these essays easy. At one point Peckham reveals that he is working on a book on the subject of human behavior. I can think of no other literary critic who has developed such a full-scale theory. Whether his theories will ever be widely accepted by literary people is, nonetheless, debatable. His orientation is behavioristic, certainly an unpopular one today. He is anti-Freudian and condescending to myth criticism. His gadfly pose, his cranky impatience with fools and his deliberately iconoclastic opinions are conscious signs to frighten off the unwary. I for one, however, eagerly await his book.

I. A. Richards, *Complementarities: Uncollected Essays*, ed. John Paul Russo (Cambridge, Mass.: Harvard Univ. Press) is another volume of yet uncollected works by this author, similar to the one published last year (see *ALS 1975*, p. 460). The astonishing chronology is 1919–75. These are almost exclusively literary essays, with a few that are autobiographical. Excluded are Richards's pieces on education, science, Basic English, and language training. Many of the papers are either book reviews or were originally inspired by the publication of new books, and the quality is surprisingly consistent. The long introduction by Russo presents a good overview of Richards's career and of the contents of the book. Richards enthusiasts will find much to be happy about in these pages.

Just before his death W. K. Wimsatt had seen through the press *Day of the Leopards: Essays in Defense of Poems* (New Haven, Conn.: Yale Univ. Press), a collection of pieces written during the last decade of his life. The title essay was composed as a defense of humanistic reason during the heat of the late 1960s. Almost all the rest of the book is concerned with literary topics. It is apparent from these pieces that Wimsatt is that anomalous creature, a nonsystematic theoretician. He is extremely intelligent, rational, and erudite, and he can be both testy and polemical. His essay on "Northrop Frye: Criticism as Myth," is devastating, but quite deliberately one-sided. Wimsatt returns to his old theme of the intentional fallacy in "Genesis: An Argument Resumed," a piece that has already been anthologized. It contains a fine discussion of the problem, in many ways better than the original essay. There is also an excellent survey of contemporary critical theory in "Battering the Object." Wimsatt's standards and his sinewy style remained first-rate throughout his life. I cannot help but think that toward the end he must have found himself slightly out of phase in a department containing the likes of Bloom, Hartmann, and Hillis Miller, although with his formidable witty intelligence Wimsatt did not, I am sure, lose many arguments.

c. **Folklore.** Three books generally about folklore came to my attention this year. Jan Harold Brunwand, in *Folklore: A Study and Research Guide* (New York: St. Martin's), has prepared a student handbook on the subject something like Richard Altick's on literary research. The book fills the need for such an introductory text in a field that is rapidly coming to a strong sense of independence from literature and anthropology where it has long functioned as a satellite. The text lays out the definitions of various terms, and it reviews the history of the discipline, avoiding a strongly partisan tone in a field where partisanship still runs high. There is also an excellent bibliographical essay. This is a good text for introductory folklore courses for either graduate students or advanced undergraduates.

The partisan tone in folk studies is nowhere better demonstrated than in a new collection of essays by one of its leading figures, Richard M. Dorson, *Folklore and Fakelore: Essays Toward a Discipline of Folk Studies* (Cambridge, Mass.: Harvard Univ. Press). It was Dorson himself who developed the concept of "fakelore" as contrasted to honest materials developed by the folk. Dorson's introduction is polemical, highly partisan, and a bit evangelical. His essays are quite diverse, ranging from heavily theoretical matters to studies of popular media and fakelore. As a theoretician Dorson is less systematic than he supposes. He is also heavily anecdotal about the battles he has had to wage in establishing the legitimacy of his discipline. He is always entertaining, however, and because Dorson is one of those who defines the field for folklorists, this is an important book.

American Folklife (Austin: Univ. of Tex. Press), ed. Don Yoder, is not about folklore as Dorson defines it, but about folk*life*, which Yoder defines as "regional ethnology" (p. 3). Regional ethnology studies the particulars of life, culture, customs, and mores in regional locales. This collection of essays by twelve authors attempts to develop a discipline designed to preserve and understand the specifics of regional subcultures. The quality is high for a collection of this type, and the contents range widely—studies of social change, studies of film documentation, studies of regional styles in home buildings. Regional ethnology walks a tight line between anthropology, history, culture studies, and sociology. There is little here in the way of specific literary content and concern, and yet there is an obvious potential for developing ways of applying the materials of this fledgling discipline to literary matters. It will be interesting to watch during the next few years to see how this kind of study blends with the existent concerns about regional studies to have an effect on the more traditional approaches to literature.

d. **Fantasy.**   Two books on the subject of fantasy deal with the same subjected treated in Tzvetan Todorov's work of the earlier 1970s (see *ALS 1973*, p. 418). Neither of them quite reaches Todorov's level of excellence, but both have a number of interesting insights.

Eric S. Rabkin's *The Fantastic in Literature* (Princeton, N.J.: Princeton Univ. Press) defines fantasy as follows: "The fantastic is a quality of astonishment that we feel when the ground rules of a narrative world are suddenly made to turn about 180°. We recognize this reversal in the reactions of characters, the statements of narrators, and the implications of structure, all playing on and against our whole experience as people and readers" (p. 41). Todorov defined the fantastic generically, whereas Rabkin sees it as a general set of psychological categories of stimulus and response. This is somewhat surprising to me in that Rabkin's previous book on narrative suspense (see *ALS 1973*, pp. 418–19) was a fairly straightforward work of structuralist generic criticism.

Rabkin is solid and literary but with an unfortunate penchant for jargon. His approach is dialectical in that things are seen in terms of opposites or seeming contradictions and mirror images. He has a fondness for discovering paradox. Along the way he has provocative things to say about such matters as the gothic, utopias, and perspective. Although a more flexible work than Todorov's (Rabkin mentions Todorov only once in a long footnote), Rabkin's book finally is not a very useful critical instrument.

Another way of treating the same subject appears in W. R. Irwin, *The Game of the Impossible: A Rhetoric of Fantasy* (Urbana: Univ. of Ill. Press). This is not really so much a "rhetoric" of fantasy as a study of its genres. Two of Irwin's definitions will give the reader some sense of how he uses the word: "A fantasy is a story based on and controlled by an overt violation of what is generally accepted as possibility" (p. 4) and "Fantasy relies on a discrimination between possible and impossible that is clearly conceived, even though it may not rely on evidence. Any obscuring of this discrimination precludes fantasy" (pp. 89–90).

The tone of the book is casually learned rather than systematic, which makes it an interesting contrast to Rabkin's. Irwin mentions Todorov, but his own nonsystematic approach does not make his work congenial to that of the French structuralist. While possessing a historical consciousness, Irwin prefers to deal with the general characteristics of his subject. More comfortable with his material than Rabkin, he is nonetheless more a writer of critical *aperçus* than creator of a critical tool that can be applied. In this regard, he is even less successful than Rabkin, although his book is not completely without interest.

e. **Theory of Fiction.** A surprisingly small number of books concerned themselves with the theory of fiction. The most substantial attempt in this area is by Norman Friedman, *Form and Meaning in Fiction* (Athens: Univ. of Ga. Press). The title itself gives away the dualistic focus of this collection of essays. Underlying it is the Aristotelian approach of the Chicago school of criticism that seeks meaning through form and genre.

The essays add up more to a coherent set of values than a systematic theory of fiction, especially since Friedman is by and large a common-sense rather than an ideological critic. There are many good individual essays, some of them theoretical, many of them readings of works and authors. The overall effect, however, is somewhat unsatisfying, perhaps because, since the book was written during such a long period of time, it now seems out of date. Most of the recent work on the nature of fiction has not affected Friedman's thinking.

A more impressive though less ambitious work of fictional genre theory is Mary Doyle Springer's *Forms of the Modern Novella* (Chicago: Univ. of Chicago Press), a book that is deeply influenced by Sheldon Sacks's *Fiction and the Shape of Belief.* Springer explicitly adapts Sacks's terms "action," "apologue," and "satire" early in the book and applies them throughout. Rather than coming up with a single definition of novella which can then be applied to individual novellas, Springer develops five categories within which she claims novellas operate: (1) the serious "plot of character"; (2) the degenerative or pathetic tragedy; (3) satire; (4) apologue; and (5) the example. She applies these categories throughout the book to many works of novella length.

As to the matter of length, Springer seems simply to accept it as a given and does not argue its intrinsic necessity. Her range of reference is quite wide, and her evaluative stance toward the novella as a form, although merely implied throughout most of the book, becomes quite explicit at the end, when she speaks of the best novellas as having "an emotional economy . . . which novels cannot match when they attempt the same kind of thing" (p. 157). She characterizes the novella as a "sleek thoroughbred" when compared to James's characterization of the Tolstoyan novel as a "baggy monster." This is the best treatment I know of the novella as a literary genre.

A less impressive work is a collection of essays on the short story as a form, edited by Charles E. May: *Short Story Theories* (Athens: Ohio Univ. Press). The focus here is primarily on the American short story, and the contents are a mixture of comments from both practitioners and literary scholars and critics. There is a dearth of serious critical writing on the nature of the short story, and this collection brings together much of what is worthwhile on the subject, from Poe's review of Hawthorne's *Twice-Told Tales* to Richard Kostelanetz's "Notes on the American Short Story Today." This is a useful book, limited not by the skill of the editor but by the lack of substantial writing that has yet to be done on the subject.

f. **Modernism.** I shall discuss three books that explore various aspects of the emergent culture of the 20th century. In the first, *Notes for a New Culture: An Essay on Modernism* (New York: Barnes & Noble), Peter Ackroyd, an English poet, presents a philosophical, personally committed discussion of Modernist culture. The book develops from a premise about the relationship of language and nothingness, a concept first explored by Mallarmé. Ackroyd uses humanism as the cultural base from which Modernism departs. It is his claim that English criticism does not fully partake of the Modernist spirit because it so stubbornly remains rooted in a humanist tradition.

Ackroyd's truly modernist culture is French, as one might suspect from his opening premise about language. True Modernism, for him, descends from Nietzsche, Husserl, and Heidegger, and is best expressed in modern French thought by the two Jacques, Lacan and Derrida. The book does not make invidious distinctions between Modernism and post-Modernism, but rather sees Modernist culture as an unbroken continuity. Aside from this salutary aspect, however, the book says little that is new and does not develop a viable theory of Modernism that goes beyond a few basically valid insights.

One of the influential but relatively unheralded movements in early 20th-century art and literature was Vorticism, which numbered among its adherents, at least for a time, such figures as Gaudier-Brzeska, Ezra Pound, and Wyndham Lewis. That movement has now received its fullest treatment in a two-volume study by Richard Cook, *Vorticism and Abstract Art in the First Machine Age* (Berkeley: Univ. of Calif. Press); vol. 1, *Origins and Development*; vol. 2, *Synthesis and Decline* (1977). This is an elaborate historical and critical analysis of the significance of this relatively short-lived movement. Anyone interested in the development of Vorticism, in the publication of such periodicals as *BLAST*, in the various manifestos published by the members, in the role of Pound and Lewis as both artists and publicists, and of the relationship of Vorticism to Cubism and Imagism must read this book. It is sumptuously published and very costly, but it is worth the expense, not only for the quality of Cook's text but because of the many excellently reproduced graphics. The publisher is to be complimented on producing so attractive a book.

On another Modernist literary and artistic movement, Surrealism, there is a new study by J. H. Matthews, *Toward the Poetics of Surrealism* (Syracuse, N.Y.: Syracuse Univ. Press). The first two chapters are more general in nature and thus more useful to nonspecialist readers. They contain good analyses of the affinities between Surrealism, Romanticism, and Naturalism (chapter 1), and on the emergence of Surrealism from the works and ideas of Guillaume Apollinaire and the Dada movement (chapter 2). The rest of the book contains essays on various related topics. Overall, the book presents a competent overview of the subject and complements Matthews's other books on Surrealism. The reader unversed in the subject might turn with even better results, however, to the books on Surrealism by Maurice Nadeau and Anna Balakian.

g. Miscellaneous. The following books appear in this section largely because they do not fit easily into any of the categories so far developed. I shall treat them alphabetically.

Northrop Frye begins this section with *The Secular Scripture: A Study of the Structure of Romance* (Cambridge, Mass.: Harvard

Univ. Press), a published version of the Charles Eliot Norton Lectures for 1974–75. Frye's thesis is contained in the following question and statement: "Is it possible, then, to look at secular stories as a whole, and as forming a single integrated vision of the world, parallel to the Christian and biblical vision?" "Romance is the structural core of all fiction: being directly descended from folktale, it brings us closer than any other aspect of literature to the sense of fiction, considered as a whole, as the epic of the creature, man's vision of his own life as a quest" (p. 15). The reader familiar with Frye's work will recognize such a thesis as being central to the author's traditional concerns.

What follows is a graceful, thoughtful study of the traditions and functions of romance up to the present day. In surveying the conventions of romance, Frye succeeds in using his own categories without seeming to force them on the reader. The proper romance, for Frye, finds its balance between the themes of ascent and descent. His conclusion brings the romance in line with contemporary cultural needs in the following comment on Eliot's "Burnt Norton": "Such a union of past and future in a present vision of a pastoral, paradisal, and radically simplified form of life obviously takes on a new kind of urgency in an age of pollution and energy crisis, and helps to explain why romance seems so contemporary a form of literary experience" (p. 179).

K. K. Ruthven's *Myth* (London: Methuen & Co.) is part of The Critical Idiom series. A short survey, it is intended as a critical introduction to the subject. It gives a capsule history of approaches to myth from the time of Euhemerus to Lévi-Strauss and Northrop Frye. The three chapter titles indicate something of the shape of this short book: "Myths and theorists," "Myths and writers," "Myths and critics." The book is generally effective, although the last chapter is least adequate because Ruthven is not basically sympathetic to myth criticism. He cannot contain a snide condescending tone toward it. William Righter's *Myth and Literature* (see *ALS 1975*, p. 469) is a better introduction to the subject.

William Zinsser's *On Writing Well: An Informal Guide to Writing Nonfiction* (New York: Harper & Row) is a lively, prescriptive, and opinionated book. While it is fun to read, and uses lots of good exemplary quotations, I do not think it would be useful as a textbook. Zinsser is hardheaded and practical, but his book is no replacement for those of Strunk & White, Sheridan Baker, Richard Lehan, or Jacques Barzun.

h. "On the Cutting Edge." I entitle this section "On the Cutting Edge" because it discusses those books which attempt to make a statement that pushes ahead the frontiers of critical thought. This attempt does not necessarily make them the best books of the year, but they are the farthest out on the edge that I consider to represent the major direction of contemporary criticism.

I start with two books by the amazingly prolific Harold Bloom. The first, *Poetry and Repression: Revisionism from Blake to Stevens* (New Haven, Conn.: Yale Univ. Press), completes the major tetralogy that began with *The Anxiety of Influence* and continued with *A Map of Mis-Reading* and *Kabbalah and Criticism*, all previously reviewed in *ALS*. *Poetry & Repression* incorporates the insights of the earlier books and yet shows some evolution and change from *The Anxiety of Influence.*

Poetry and Repression consists of a series of essays on individual poets, including Blake, Wordsworth, Shelley, Keats, Tennyson, Browning, Yeats, Emerson, Whitman, and Stevens, all of them previously subjects of interest to the author. Bloom conducts many close readings of major poems by these poets according to his system of poetic misprision and of strong and weak poets and poems. The application of that system holds the individual chapters together as more than merely essays.

Bloom opposes the canonization of poets and poems, believing instead in "antithetical" readings that show how poems stand against other poems as well as for themselves. In this regard, some of Bloom's interpretations here oppose many of his earlier readings, even ones presented in *The Anxiety of Influence.* Bloom is too "strong" a critic not to subject his own work to "misprision." In many ways, this is Bloom's most convincing book, although I doubt that the reader would find this to be true without reading previously in the tetralogy. As usual, there is something annoyingly self-parodistic in Bloom's mannered, self-conscious tone. And yet it is hard not to believe that although Bloom takes himself quite seriously, it is always with a touch of irony.

A critical statement essential to understanding Bloom's system appears in his chapter on Wallace Stevens: "The function of criticism at the present time, as I conceive it, is to find a middle way between the paths of demystification of meaning, and of recollection or restoration of meaning, or between limitation and representation. But the only aesthetic path between limitation and representation is substitution, and so all that criticism can hope to reach, whether to the common reader or to the poet, is a series of stronger modes of substitution" (p. 270). There can thus be no such thing as a full statement or a genuine interpretation, only a substitution of one statement for another. This is a basic insight in the newest criticism, and it has seldom been better articulated.

It is not the philosophical novelty of Bloom's position that is striking; it is his application of it to literature. He has developed his own sophisticated adaptation of the Oedipal situation as the basic human condition, making Freud viable for the first time for poetry. Still, while Bloom is certainly obsessed with his vision, it is this obsession that leads him to a series of stunning insights. One's reading of poetry can never again be quite the same.

The second of Bloom's 1976 books is *Figures of Capable Imagination* (New York: Seabury Press), 13 essays written during 1970–74, the same years in which the author was writing the four books of his tetralogy. These products of Bloom's furious energy apply in an eminently practical and individual fashion his theory of misprision. For the most part these are well-written, sober applications, with certain concessions made for the Bloomian neophyte. While a newcomer to the "anxiety of influence" could read these essays with pleasure, it would be better to know a little about the theory before attacking this book.

The bulk of the essays is on American subjects, although the book begins with pieces on Coleridge and Pater. There are a number of chapters on A. R. Ammons, to whom *Poetry and Repression* is dedicated. There is also a fine piece on Stevens, reminding one that Bloom has just published a book-length study of that poet that should be as important to Stevens criticism as Bloom's book on Yeats is to the criticism on that poet. Bloom is not always a good close reader. He tends to quote at too great length and he seeks relationships between authors rather than making self-contained analyses. But this tendency is consistent with the tenets of his own theory, with which he seems fully comfortable. It is difficult to predict the lasting viability of Bloom's approach to literature, but even those readers who are most annoyed by his work and his postures owe it to themselves to come to terms with what he is trying to do.

Another product of the newest criticism, heavily influenced by French models, is Leo Bersani, *A Future for Astyanax: Character and Desire in Literature* (Boston: Little, Brown), an excellent book about the relationship between the portrayals of both desire and character in literature since the time of Racine. Bersani believes that the traditional view of character as a unified entity is a literary convention. Through selective in-depth analyses of such writers as Racine, Flaubert, Stendhal, Henry James, Lawrence, Rimbaud, Artaud, and such contemporary theater figures as Joe Chaikin and Robert Wilson, Bersani attempts to show how the development of modern literature has exhibited a growing tendency to "deconstruct" this false unity of character. Students of American literature will find especially interesting Bersani's chapter on Henry James, "The Jamesian Lie."

Although last year saw the publication of a number of first-rate books on Structuralism and Semiotics, this year saw only a few. For the linguistic (as opposed to the anthropological) branch of Structuralism Elmar Holenstein has written a fine survey of *Roman Jakobson's Approach to Language: Phenomenological Structuralism*, trans. Catherine Schelbert and Tarcisius Schelbert (Bloomington: Ind. Univ. Press). Holenstein is himself well prepared to do such a study, being himself a phenomenological linguist, and he makes clear the outlines of Jakobson's thought as well as the contribution of the Moscow and Prague Schools to the movements in language and in structuralist thought throughout this century. Founder of the Moscow School in 1915 and the Prague Linguistic Circle in 1920, Jakobson is at the time of this writing still alive and active professionally. It is amusing to contemplate the fact that Jakobson himself was using the term *Structuralism* as early as 1929. So much for novelty.

Another book on the general subject also published by Indiana University Press is Umberto Eco's *A Theory of Semiotics*, which is part of the Advances in Semiotics series. This book contains a highly technical, full-scale theory of human communication. Eco's orientation is philosophical, but he makes use of insights from a variety of the social sciences as well as from literature. Like most protosciences, Semiotics makes use of a special terminology, which even a glance at the table of contents will reveal. Such words as "code," "signification," "threshold," "sign-function," and "iconism" abound throughout the book, often with quite special uses and meanings. As one reads this book one realizes two things: (1) it demands rereading; (2) we are only now coming to have a rudimentary sense of how people and situations convey information and direction. Eco is one of the current leaders in the movement. The book jacket claims, for instance, that he is the first person appointed in any university for a chair explicitly designated as a professorship of Semiotics.

The third Indiana University Press book that deals with Structuralism and Semiotics is Paul Bouissac's *Circus and Culture: A Semiotic Approach*, another in the Advances in Semiotics series. Originally a collection of essays and talks, the writings here have been welded into a fairly coherent book. The author wishes to develop a "poetics" of the circus using Structuralist-Semiotic premises. He makes heavy use of the ideas of Lévi-Strauss, but I see no mention of Roland Barthes, who tried with reasonable success to do the same kind of analysis of fashion and other elements of popular culture as Bouissac has done with the circus. While Bouissac's attempt is more technical than Barthes's, the unwillingness of the author to deal with the implications of Barthes's achievement strikes me as a serious weakness in an otherwise good book that may well serve as a model for future studies of a similar nature.

Translations of Barthes's works are being published frequently these days, mostly by Hill and Wang. In next year's *ALS* I shall review his delightful autobiography *Roland Barthes by Roland Barthes*, published just recently. In this volume I shall write about *Sade/Fourier/Loyola*, trans. Richard Howard (New York: Hill and Wang), a fascinating followup to *The Pleasure of the Text* (see *ALS 1975*, p. 471). Barthes's technique has become increasingly gnomic over the years, with its attention focused in intense aphoristic bursts.

The three writers chosen for analysis in this book were picked because they are "Logothetes, founders of languages" (p. 3). In his Preface Barthes lays out the four conditions he deems necessary for the founding of a language: "The first is self-isolation. The new language must arise from a material vacuum"; "The second operation is articulation. No languages without distinct signs" (p. 4); "The third operation is ordering; not merely to arrange the elementary signs, but to subject the vast erotic, eudaemonist, or mystical sequence to a higher order, no longer syntactical, but metrical" (p. 5); the fourth is "theatricalization," which Barthes claims "is not designing a setting for representation, but unlimiting the language" (pp. 5–6).

The analyses or reconstructions that follow the Preface are Barthes's attempt to demonstrate the bases for his semiological theory of the interrelatedness of all elements in a communication system. Each author treated in this book develops his language out of certain assumptions and resistances that can only be understood historically and analyzed sociologically. Barthes seems most taken with Sade, least with Loyola. He treats Fourier as a bit of a serious joke. This is a brilliant, gnomic book that should be sipped slowly like a fine brandy.

Another book similar in style and attitude to Barthes's is by the American novelist and critic William Gass, *On Being Blue: A Philosophical Inquiry* (Boston: David R. Godine). The style is gnomic, the attitude philosophic (Gass is also a professional philosopher), and the similarities in its emphasis on the "erotics" of words and ideas reminds one of *The Pleasure of the Text*.

On Being Blue is a meditation of striking literary sensibility on the significance of the color blue in its many connotations. Gass writes of blue moods of depression and of sexually blue thoughts such as those portrayed in jokes, pornographic books, and "blue" movies. He speaks a bit about the theory of colors in painting, in a manner reminiscent of Kandinsky. Gass's use of language is highly sophisticated —poetic, punning, witty, wise, and brilliant. I found this a moving book, impossible to reduce to a brief characteristic description. It is short yet packed, full of autobiographical examples and meditations. Gass seems like a person on whom nothing is lost.

Murray Krieger is clearly an important figure in contemporary American criticism. He has produced a number of its central texts and has recently been involved in founding a School of Criticism at the University of California, Irvine. An entire issue of *Contemporary Literature* (vol. 17, no. 3 [Summer 1976]) was devoted to a special issue edited by Krieger, called "Directions for Criticism: Structuralism and Its Alternatives." The issue was designed as an opening statement by the new School of Criticism on its opening in the summer of 1976, and it contains articles by members of the permanent faculty, Hazard Adams, Ralph Freedman, René Girard, Edward W. Said, and Hayden White.

All the contributors were given the same recent anthologies of critical writings and asked to compose their own overview of the current situation in the field. All the essays were deliberately designed as forms of metacriticism and all are very good, especially the ones by Said, White, and Freedman. Reading the entire issue is a fine way to understand the situation in contemporary literary criticism and theory.

The final book I shall treat is also by Murray Krieger, and it is the most ambitious attempt by an American critic this year to make a comprehensive statement about the literary enterprise: *Theory of Criticism: A Tradition and Its System* (Baltimore: Johns Hopkins Univ. Press).

I have to begin by stating that I disagree with a number of Krieger's fundamental premises, most important of which is his focus on the work of linguistic art as an almost self-contained unity. Krieger believes that one can always find meaning and value inside the work, that in fact the work demands we find all value within its self-contained universe. I find this useful as an attitude but indefensible as a philosophic position. Responding to a work of literature is a form of social behavior, dependent on many varieties of situation, all of which modify to some extent our response to the "self-contained" unity of the work.

With that said, however, I am pleased to recommend the book as an eloquent statement justifying the critical activity. Krieger divides his book into three main sections. The first, "The Problem: The Limits and Capacities of Critical Theory," attempts to define the limits of what criticism can and cannot do. The second, "The Humanistic Theoretical Tradition," is more historical in describing some enterprises in which criticism has been engaged. The third, "A Systematic Extension," tries to define what the critical enterprise is and ought to be at the present time.

Not surprisingly, Krieger comes to conclusions indebted to contemporary French thought about the relationship of the work of literature to the world and the function of the literary work as a model that implies the world without repeating it. The job of the critic is to mediate between the two postulates. As a basic model for criticism, this is a difficult position with which to disagree. But the reader who responds as I did will find many of the details making up Krieger's position to be matters definitely with which to take issue.

At any rate, this is a book worth disagreeing with respectfully. It is sinewy and thoughtful, eminently representative of a school of critical thought that presently dominates American letters.

To sum up, this was a good year for criticism and writings about American literature. While there were fewer outstanding books than in 1975, the general level of quality was high. When one thinks of creative, prolific minds like those of Krieger, Barthes, Bloom, Howe, and Gass, one wonders whether the best literary talents are not turning to critical writing from the more traditional forms of fictional prose and poetry. The relatively small outputs of novelists like Bellow and Styron or of poets like Wilbur and Merwin—when compared to predecessors like Faulkner and Yeats—suggest that it might be easier in this Alexandrian age to be a prolific critic of high quality than anything else. That strikes me as a strange irony.

University of California, Davis

21. Foreign Scholarship

i. French Contributions

Jean Rivière

American literary scholarship produced in France in 1976 can be conveniently divided into the publication of two dissertations and important issues on American literature of five periodicals.

When young scholars are ready to trim their dissertations for publication, they can find a public for their original contributions even in so-called popular collections. That is the case with Pierre Dommergues's *L'aliénation dans le roman américain contemporain* (Paris: Union Générale d'Editions). The book deals with an analysis of alienation in modern American fiction from 1940 to the present. The first half is devoted to a descriptive study of alienation in post–World War II fiction, independent of any reference to a particular novelist. The author tries to assert the novelist's sensitivity to alienation, the level at which he analyzes the phenomenon, the actual impact of his militant stance on alienation, and finally the literary rendering of the problem concerned. Dommergues does not claim to be neutral, but rather to determine how closely the American novelist deals with alienation as it is felt in American society, especially by minorities. The second half of the book is devoted to analyses of the works of five novelists chosen less for their literary value than for their personal or political orientation and the cultural models they build with regard to the problem of alienation. Norman Mailer is considered the most radical in his analysis and the most conservative in his personal behavior. Saul Bellow is depicted as suspended between his refusal of abstraction and theatricality and his acceptance of ordinary life with its extraordinary implications: he stands as the most perfect portrait of the liberal humanist. In spite of her southern and Catholic background, Flannery O'Connor is, according to Dommergues, the writer that undermines most effectively the foundations of Western humanism based on individual competition and on a so-called equality of opportunity through education. LeRoi Jones lays the basis for a new analysis of alienation in the American colonial system through a rewriting of Dante's *Inferno* and the assertion of a new black conscience. Finally, William Burroughs goes as far as any novelist dares to go in his denunciation of the machinery of a police state in its most hypocritical aspects: Burroughs subverts not only the myths most dear to the majority of Americans, but also writing itself. Dommergues's conclusion is that the part played by the novelist in denouncing alienation is similar to that of the journalist, the educator, or the physician: only too often he sets the threshold of tolerance within the limits that the system can bear and thanks to which it can go on working. Although the brilliant analyses of Pierre Dommergues may be questioned, through a masterly use of psychoanalysis, Marxism, and the social sciences, they bring such freshness to the study of modern American fiction that they cannot be ignored by anyone competent in the field of American studies.

With a completely different approach, Georges-Michel Sarotte's *Comme un frère, comme un amant, l'homosexualité masculine dans le roman et le théâtre américains de Herman Melville à James Baldwin* (Paris: Flammarion) is just as fine an achievement in its kind. Sarotte always distinguishes "homoérotisme" (a vague feeling on the part of an individual for a closer contact with a male body) from "homosexualité" (an open and incoercible desire to sleep with a man) and "homogénitalité" (the actual sexual intercourse between two males). The book traces the evolution of the theme through the works of major American writers, particularly Herman Melville, Jack London, Henry James, Ernest Hemingway, Francis Scott Fitzgerald, Norman Mailer, Saul Bellow, James Baldwin, Tennessee Williams, William Inge, Edward Albee, Charles Jackson, Gore Vidal, and Carson McCullers. The author follows the evolution of the American psyche toward the problem of homosexuality in a culture where virility, masculinity, heterosexuality, and brutality were too often confused. In all pre–World War II fiction the homosexual is used as a foil to the beauty, purity, and masculinity of the hero, or his instinct is sublimated into a purer relationship (that of the Indian and the pioneer or the good savage and the sailor in Cooper and Melville), or the homosexual tendencies are depicted between an American and a foreigner (usually a Latin, as in Hemingway). Since 1940 the homosexual hero has been trapped between two attitudes: that of the virile, brutal, and sadistic type (as exemplified in D. H. Lawrence's *The Prussian Officer*) and that of the pure and simple acceptance of female values (with Jean Genet as a prototype). Lately, the American homosexual novel has been deeply influenced by the gay liberation movements that want to force society to consider male homosexuals as normal human beings, not as outcasts or sick people. The predicament of the American homosexual (both in fiction and in real life) is that American culture has always overvalued virility and masculinity and has been less tolerant than European culture of refinement, elegance, and affectivity. In spite of all the recent advances in the condition of the American homosexual, Sarotte thinks that he must still too often find solace in the artificial paradise of drugs or in wishful thinking. Still, American fiction has helped American homosexuals to find their place in the counterculture; the years to come will show if this counterculture rides the wave of the future. Sarotte's major contribution lies in his subtle psychonalytical interpretation of male homosexuality in American literature and his comparisons with the same phenomenon in European culture.

Four periodicals specializing in English studies have published issues on American literature. The old and steady *Etudes Anglaises* (vol. 29, no. 3) pays literary tribute to America's Bicentennial and its contents sound like a roll-call of American literature. Roger Asselineau's statement in the Introduction to the 260-page issue sounds particularly apt: "la littérature américaine est donc la littérature d'une nation encore proche de ses origines qui, faute d'être déjà elle-même, se définit et se constitue d'un même mouvement, tout en allant, se créant ainsi au fur et à mesure et de toutes pièces un caractère propre." Colonial literature, Transcendentalism, Poe, James, Faulkner, Henry Adams, Nathanael West, Jack Kerouac, Anaïs Nin, modern fiction, modern Negro Literature, and modern poetry are highlighted with particular felicitousness by each contributor and always in clear language.

In *Delta*, no. 2, "Flannery O'Connor et le réalisme des lointains," three studies stand out: "Flannery O'Connor ou la vision éclatée" by P. Choffrut emphasizes her split allegiance between the Protestant South and her personal Catholic background in an illuminating study of *The Displaced Person*. "Désir et Destin dans *A Good Man is Hard to Find*" by Claude Richard shows how the short story explores the grandmother's progressive awareness of the universal love God has bestowed on nature. "*The Displaced Person* ou le Christ recrucifié" by D. Lesgoirres is a good study, through the veiled symbolism of the peacock, of Christian redemption as depicted by the author and experienced by the different protagonists. The issue ends with a thorough bibliography of O'Connor, including the French translations of her works.

Delta, issue no. 3, devoted to William Faulkner and mainly the Snopes trilogy, is a chance for the French Faulknerians to show their talents at their best with special emphasis on Faulkner as the novelist of the unconscious; however, the same Faulknerians (André Bleikasten, François Pitavy, Jean Roubérol and Michel Gresset) to gether with Monique Pruvot and Giliane Morell have an even better opportunity in a textual study of *Pylon* in RANAM, no. 9 and articles on Faulkner and history and *The Sound and the Fury*. The same issue contains contributions on southern novelists: an interview with Reynolds Price by Georges Cary, a study of Thomas Wolfe and the South by Jean-Michel Michelet, of Eudora Welty (*Losing Battles* and *The Optimist's Daughter*) by Danièle Pitavy, of Flannery O'Connor by Christiane Beck, of Ernest Gaines by Michel Fabre, and of Marion Montgomery (*The Fugitive*) by Simone Vauthier. In all articles in RANAM or *Delta*, American scholars will find, original approaches to American literature with a heavy (and sometimes obsessional) reliance on what impels a literary artist to write.

The *Revue Française d'Études Américaines* is published and sponsored by the Association française d'études américaines and has as captive subscribers the 300-or-so members of the Association. It should eventually develop as *the* review of American studies in France and the quality of the contributors speaks highly in its favor. The first number (April 1976) opens with an article by Noëlle Batt on "Rupture et déplacement dans l'oeuvre de William Burroughs" (pp. 12–21), in which Batt shows the workings of the cut-up device at a linguistic level and analyzes this method (which consists in breaking and moving the sentences from one paragraph to another within a chapter). Claude Bensimon's article on Stanley Crawford (pp. 23–38) shows how *Log of the S.S. The Mrs Unguentine* (1971) is an important contribution to the analysis of artistic creation since it eliminates the traditional part played by symbolism in the representation of the object and subject. Marc Chénétier's study of Richard Brautigan's *Trout Fishing in America* (pp. 39–53) explains how the novelist's imagery is a commentary on forms that denounce the closedness and circularity of all established discourses. Other articles on Ishmael Reed by Michel Fabre, on John Hawkes by Pierre Gault, on James Purdy by Marie-Claude Profit, and on Flannery O'Connor by Maurice Lévy are each sound contributions on the subject. The last two articles to be considered—"Nabokov's *Pale Fire* or the Purloined Poem" by Maurice Couturier (pp. 56–69) and "Speaking to contemporary American fiction (notes on Robert Coover's fictions)" by Régis Durand (pp. 71–83)—are too involved in Roland Barthes's critical tenets to stand as valuable comments on American literature as such: they are rather reactions of two very sensitive minds to the problems of the relation between the artist and his readers. This is the reason why I think that the new *Revue*, in order to reach beyond its present captive audience, should show determination and above all clarity in its treatment of American literature. New theories of criticism are the salt of literary life, but they must be made accessible to every specialist in the field and not to a coterie only.

Université Paris IX, Dauphine

ii. German Contributions

Hans Galinsky

Without question the bicentennial year caused a distinct increase in Colonial and Revolutionary studies and a rise of comparative studies of the last two centuries. Collections of edited essays on recent literature account for almost half of some 110 items. A new journal, *Gulliver*, adds a new outlet for scholarship.

a. **Literary History—General.** Studies focusing on more than one period are still rare. At least two stages of what is commonly viewed as one period are competently handled by Armin Paul Frank in *Neues Handbuch der Literaturwissenschaft* (Wiesbaden: Athenaion). Volumes 18 and 19 of *Jahrhundertende—Jahrhundertwende (1. Teil)* have been published under the general editorship of Helmut Kreuzer. To volume 18, ed. Klaus von See, Frank contributes "Die amerikanische Erzählliteratur, 1865–1900" (pp. 427–59), while volume 19, ed. Hans Hinterhäuser, includes Frank's "Die amerikanische Literatur 1890–1914/18" (pp. 2–31). The former contribution concentrates on "Mark

Twain: Representative of His Times," "William Dean Howells and American Realism," "Regionalism, Local Color and Hamlin Garland," "Henry James and the International Novel," and "Transition to Naturalism." The latter, after a general sketch of the subperiod, 1890–1914/18, proceeds from "Fiction" via "Emily Dickinson and American Poetry of the Turn of the Century" to "Drama" and "Criticism and Intellectual Development." Frank sticks to traditional historical divisions and their manifestations in the literary genres. Only in his placement of Emily Dickinson does he deviate by preferring the time of the work's public diffusion to the time of its genesis. Whereas the old edition of *Handbuch der Literaturwissenschaft* (Potsdam: Athenaion) put the whole history of American literature (as presented by Walther Fischer in 1929) in one volume with "English literature from the Renaissance through the Enlightenment," the new version is patterned on supranational cultural periods, with each national literature seen as ushering them in, leading them to their climax, lagging behind or developing literary forms of their own. Judging by Frank's treatment of a limited part of American literary history, one has to confine himself to appreciating Frank's balanced presentation of the common international and the individual national features of American letters in the given period. Probably due to limitations of space it emphasizes mainstream literature, neglecting existing or emergent non–Anglo-Saxon writing in the United States.

More than two literary eras are explored in Jürgen Schäfer's *"The American Dream*: Literarische Spiegelungen." It is one of the seven Augsburg University lectures delivered in honor of the Bicentennial and printed in *Weltmacht USA: Sieben Augsburger Universitätsvorträge*, ed. Josef Becker and Rolf Bergmann, Schriften der Philosophischen Fachbereiche der Universität Augsburg (Munich: Vogel), 10:31–48. This subject, particularly dear to foreign audiences, is covered with reference to several less well-known sources and to its onomasiological history.

Even more indispensable to multiperiod literary historians than to one-period specialists, bibliographical tools cutting across period boundaries are represented by *Bibliographie amerikanistischer Veröffentlichungen in der DDR bis 1968*, ed. Michael Hoenisch, Christian Freitag, Dagmar Frost, and Werner Sollors, *Materialien*, 5(Berlin: John F. Kennedy Institute). With this number a group of Berlin's Free University Americanists has added to the Institute's series of useful checklists a bibliography of Americanist publications in the German Democratic Republic through 1968. It comprises research on literary but also linguistic and broadly cultural aspects of American life, past and present.

a–1. **Colonial, Revolutionary and 19th Century.** There is a noticeable decline in 17th-century literary studies, but a happy exception is an exhibition in honor of the Bicentennial focusing on colonial America: "The New World in the Treasures of an Old European Library" (Wolfenbüttel: Duke August Library). The only article in the 17th-century field is Karl Josef Höltgen's "Francis Quarles, John Josselyn and the *Bay Psalm Book*," (*SCN* 34:42–46). Höltgen convincingly argues for John Cotton's rejection of Quarles's Psalm versions which Josselyn had delivered to him. They were not in keeping with Cotton's theological convictions because they were nonliteralist.

The rise of scholarly interest in 18th-century themes is seen by studies in the role of religion in the mounting unrest that preceded the American Revolution, in the ideological position of Thomas Paine, and even in the state of late 18th-century bibliographical research. Characteristically, most of the pertinent publications do not deal with American literature only, but approach it through comparative studies. They will therefore be discussed later in the appropriate section. Of predominantly American literary relevance, however, is Joseph C. Schöpp's "Angloamerikanische Bauernbriefe des 18. Jahrhunderts: Genese und Funktion eines literarischen Genres" (*AmS* 21:187–200). Schöpp describes the growth of an initially subliterary genre from a "predominantly pragmatic function" of "stimulating the pioneering colonists to a life of industry and frugality" to a "propagandistic purpose" of "preaching liberty, independence and happiness" to finally a "fictional purpose" climaxing in Crèvecœur's classic. One wonders whether without the Bicentennial the genesis and development of the genre would have remained unnoticed. Probably due to the same anniversary is K. Dieterich Pfisterer's essay "Religion als ein Ferment der Freiheit in der amerikanischen Revolution" (*AmS* 21:217–38). Although rooted in the history of religious ideas and institutions, this richly documented essay is useful for its frequent references to John Wise and Jonathan Edwards, Ezra Stiles and Benjamin Rush, Thomas Jefferson and James Madison. The student of rhetoric will benefit most.

Ursula Brumm's "A Regicide Judge as 'Champion' of American Independence (*AmS* 21:177–86) furnishes a link between research on Revolutionary and 19th-century literature. Hawthorne's "Gray Champion" receives a succinct interpretation along thematic lines. It is shown to belong with the few works in which America's "creative imagination" in the earlier 19th century transmuted the empiric fact of the revolution. Its main thesis (that "the figure of the Gray Champion is a brilliant achievement of Hawthorne's creative strategy: a character that in its simple and strong outlines projects the basic tensions and contradictions in the Puritan character" and "at the same time illuminates the political situation" has been amply proved.

While no German scholar was attracted to Melville's *Israel Potter*, his creator benefited from the Bicentennial all the same. *Illustrationen zu Melvilles "Moby-Dick"*, ed. Joachim Kruse (Schleswig: Schleswig-Holsteinisches Landesmuseum) was printed on the occasion of a special exposition arranged by the German Federal Republic's most maritime state. Two essays by the editor, "Melvilles Walbilder (pp. 67–81) and "John Hustons 'Moby-Dick'" (pp. 113–17) link the pictorial to the literary art.

Neither American poetry nor drama of the 19th century evoked any scholarly response in 1976. As before, only fiction proved mildly attractive. By way of postscript Hans-Joachim Lang added an essay to Elisabeth Schnack's German translation of George W. Cable's *The Grandissimes* (*Die Grandissimes: Eine Geschichte aus dem tiefen Süden* [Zurich: Manesse] (pp. 511–28). Tracing Cable's creativity to his sense of place, his native New Orleans, and his sense of time, the Reconstruction Era, Lang stresses the 'astonishing consistency' of his work. Aided by Cable's posthumous essay "My Politics," Lang sees this consistency generically in the progress from historiography via the historical short story to the historical novel. As to the consistency of Cable's sociocultural diagnosis, Lang finds it in an early and continuous emphasis on caste and race in southern life. By juxtaposing Irving's attitude toward colonial origins, and Henry Adams's *Democracy* as well as Disraeli's *Tancred* as realizations of the "political novel," Lang illuminates Cable's achievement as "the beginning of the emancipation of literature in the South." For essential information and original comparisons within the narrow space of a postscript this is a remarkable essay.

a–2. 20th-Century Poetry, Drama, and Fiction. In part due to the already mentioned brain drain caused by two large-scale team-work enterprises on post–1945 drama and fiction, publications in what used to be a favorite period of research activity dwindled to one article on poetry and another on drama and fiction combined. Exclusive research on fiction, by producing one monograph and three articles, fared somewhat better. Hans-Joachim Zimmermann contributes a festschrift essay, "Hugh Selwyn Mauberley, Der säkularisierte Odysseus: Zur Metamorphose des Epos bei Ezra Pound," to *Studien zum antiken Epos: Festschrift für Franz Dirlmeier und Viktor Pöschl*, ed. H. Görgemanns and E. A. Schmidt, Beiträge zur Klassischen Philologie, vol. 72 [Meisenheim am Glan: Hain] (pp. 66–84,309–10). The thesis of the transmutation of an ancient epic hero into a 20th-century cultural critic, and, in his turn, a target of authorial criticism is rendered plausible by skillfully applying methods of motif analysis to Pound's Homeric borrowings. Cantos I–III are adduced for comparison and contrast. Franz H. Link's "Das Amerikanische und das Menschliche bei Thornton Wilder," owing to its place of publication, the bicentennial number of *Der Rotarier* (26:283–87), links up with the national jubilee. Here is a drama expert's succinct reasoning on Wilder's thoroughly American trait of rejecting the elitist spirit and on his praise of a universal value, a love that serves.

Exclusive attention to the earlier 20th-century novel is directed at two Californians of two successive generations, Jack London and John Steinbeck. A third contribution is devoted to Virginian novelist Ellen Glasgow. Not a single book-length study on an author or a literary movement, on a regional or social context has appeared. Axel Vielau's "Utopie und Zeitkritik: Jack Londons *The Iron Heel*" (*AmS* 21:39–54) reflects the growth of serious interest among younger German Americanists in the ideological and anticipatory content of what Vielau terms "the first decidedly antifascist novel of the 20th century." London's skill in operating three time levels of narrative perspective is not overlooked. With Horst Groene's "Agrarianism and Technology in Steinbeck's *The Grapes of Wrath*" (*SoR* 9:27–31) interest shifts from the capitalism–socialism dichotomy to the physiocratic vs. industrialist tension in American thought. Groene briefly describes it in its modern garb of agrarianism vs. technology, and evaluates its function in the novel. With "Künstlerischer Archetypus

und Künstlerthematik: Ellen Glasgow und die englische Roman-
tradition" (*AmS* 21:67–73), Renate Noll-Wiemann enters literary
territory rarely traversed by German scholars. Testing Maurice
Beebe's "thesis of the archetypal artist" by applying it to the novelist's
autobiography, *The Woman Within*, and to the characterization of
dramatist Treadwell in her novel *Virginia*, she discovers close affinities between the treatment of the artist in *Virginia* and in the Victorian novel.

a–3. **Fiction since 1945.** For reasons already suggested, this field has
become one of the two cultivated most intensely. Never before has
the short story, and not the novel, been the focus of so much attention.
Die amerikanische Short Story der Gegenwart: Interpretationen, ed.
Peter Freese (Berlin: Erich Schmidt) assembles under its roof 28
scholars—27 German, one American—who explicate one story each
from 32 authors. The editor himself, in addition to a preface and a
selected bibliography, contributes an introductory essay on "themes,
techniques, and tendencies." Ranging from Faulkner's "Was" (1942)
to Brautigan's "The World War I Los Angeles Airplane" (1971), the
collection of interpretations covers nearly 30 years of literary produc-
tivity, with almost 40 separating the oldest storyteller from the youngest. The selection aims to represent "the most important groups and
schools" "by their most significant exponents" and "to document the
traditions from which the contemporary short story has sprung, as
well as the directions in which it is developing." All of these three
aims have been achieved, though in varying degrees. The methods
applied present an instructive panorama of older and more recent
interpretive techniques. Highly experienced scholars like Ursula
Brumm (William Faulkner, "Was"), Horst Oppel (Eudora Welty,
"Livvie"), Rudolph Haas (John Cheever, "The Enormous Radio")
join hands with promising young Americanists adventuring among
the more experimental specimens of the genre. Here Manfred Pütz
(Robert Coover, "The Elevator"; Ronald Sukenick, "The Birds") deserves special mention.

Outside Freese's team-work enterprise, research on modern and
postmodern fiction flourishes much less. Preferences lean toward the
novel and not the short story. Historical and artifact-centered types
of interest can be distinguished in spite of occasional overlappings.
The historical tradition of Romanticism is drawn on by Franz H.

Link in "Nabokov's *Lolita* and Aesthetic Romanticism" (*LWU* 9:37–48) in order to elucidate a work still baffling some critics and readers. Artifact-oriented are two essays on post-1945 Hemingway and John Hawkes. Berthold Schik, in "Rückkehr in die Gesellschaft? Hemingways *The Old Man and the Sea*" (*LWU* 9:100–14), weighs the pros and cons of interpreting the end of Hemingway's parabolic tale as a symbolic return into society. Elisabeth Kraus competently attends to "Psychic Sores in Search of Compassion: Hawkes' *Death, Sleep and the Traveler*" (*Crit* 17:39–52).

a–4. **Drama since 1945.** Missing the shelter of volumes of collected interpretations, investigation of modern and postmodern poetry dropped to zero. Scholarly attention paid to drama, however, kept rising, a phenomenon at least in part attributable to publication prospects in a corresponding collection. They did materialize in *Das amerikanische Drama der Gegenwart*, ed. Herbert Grabes (Kronberg: Athenäum), "Gegenwart" meaning the time span from 1959 through 1970. Neither one of the two preceding German cooperative undertakings in the field of drama, both aiming at historical coverage, had advanced beyond Albee (see *Das amerikanische Drama von den Anfängen bis zur Gegenwart*, ed. Hans Itschert (Darmstadt: Wissenschaftliche Buchgesellschaft, 1972) or beyond Jack Gelber and Charles Gordone (see *Das amerikanische Drama*, ed. Paul Goetsch, noticed in *ALS 1974*, p. 441). Grabes assembles twelve dramatists ranging from Arthur Miller to Ed Bullins, and has their plays interpreted by ten Germans and one American, with himself for twelfth participant. Works selected extend from Lorraine Hansberry's *A Raisin in the Sun* (1959) to Bullins's *Death List* (1970). They are classified as "Calculated Risk on Broadway," "Engagement in Experiments at the 'Other Theatre'—off- and off-off-Broadway" and "Black Drama on Its Way toward a Black Aesthetics." These groupings also furnish the titles for three introductory essays by the editor. His interpretation of LeRoi Jones's (Imamu Amiri Baraka's) *Dutchman* and Helmut Winter's analysis of Lanford Wilson's *The Rimers of Eldritch* stand out as examples of solid explication. Plays of regional and university theatres are excluded on grounds of their largely paralleling off- and off-off-Broadway productions. Another omission, accountable in terms of the common equation of literature with adult literature, concerns the contemporary children's theatre as

represented by the "Paper Bag Players." For information and criticism
the German reader still has to turn to Jens Heilmeyer's "Von *Peter
Pan* zum *creative drama*: Das Kindertheater in den Vereinigten
Staaten." Heilmeyer's essay forms part of the section "The Paper Bag
Players, New York" in *Mannomann! 6 x exemplarisches Kindertheater*,
ed. Melchior Schedler (Köln: DuMont Schauberg, 1973), pp. 151–
83. The entire section needs updating. Another gap, the street theatre
as part of the agit-prop stage, is filled by Dieter Herms's "Agitations
und Strassentheater in den USA" (*Gulliver* 1:237–42). Keeping the
whole modern drama steadily in view, Grabes examines the relationship of art form and ideology, raising the question of the use of allegory and its functions on the contemporary stage. His essay "Allegorie
in modernen amerikanischen Drama? Zum Verhältnis von Kunstform
und Ideologie" (*LWU* 9:9–24) serves as a needed reminder of the
continuity of an old literary technique in the flux of post-1945 experiments in drama.

b. **Literary Criticism and Theory, Comparative Studies, and Didac-
tics.**   Among the almost 30 pertinent contributions there is only one
to American literary criticism. It deals with Lionel Trilling and Ralph
Ellison but extends to cultural and sociopolitical criticism and theory.
For this reason it includes historian Arthur M. Schlesinger, Jr. A
joint undertaking of Klaus Ensslen, Hartmut Keil and Michaela Ulich,
three young Munich Americanists, "Sprache und Ideologie: Konser-
vative Sprachmuster liberaler Intellektueller in den USA um 1950,"
Erzählforschung 1: Theorien, Modelle und Methoden der Narrativik,
ed. Wolfgang Haubrichs (Göttingen: Vandenhoeck), pp. 106–55,
chooses three essays by Trilling, "Manners, Morals and the Novel,"
"*Mansfield Park*," and "*The Princess Casamassima*," "Prologue" and
"Epilogue" of Ellison's *Invisible Man*, his interview "The Art of Fiction," and his address "Brave Words for a Startling Occasion" as well
as two passages from Schlesinger's *The Vital Center: The Politics of
Freedom*. Of these samples those containing literary criticism and
poetics are of direct relevance to literary scholarship. They are subjected to a systematic lexical analysis according to 'semantic field'
principles, and to the more traditional methods of stylistics. Fields
such as the concept of man and society, of culture, of anticommunism,
and of the intellectual as seen by himself are established. The inves-
tigators contend to have detected what they term "political premises"

underlying even the nonpolitical "semantic fields." The premises discovered are labeled 'conservative'. Thus the language of these literary practitioners and critics, whose affinities with the language of a historian like Schlesinger are also worked out, is thought to be a help toward understanding the transformation of former radicals to conformists around 1950. Surely, scrutinizing ideological limitations of literary critics is necessary, but overrating the importance of those limitations is an ever-present temptation.

Literary theory, confined to that of the postmodern novel, is the domain of Joseph C. Schöpp's article " 'It's these interruptions that make it a story' oder von den Unmöglichkeiten fiktionalen Erzählens im Neuen Roman" (*Arcadia* 11:139–49). With a quotation from John Barth's *Lost in the Funhouse* serving as title of his essay, Schöpp illuminates the international phenomenon of the New Novel and its theorists with examples which comprise American postmoderns like Barth and Sukenick, Pynchon and Vonnegut. A difficult topic and its ramifications both philosophical and scientific—religious ones are disregarded—are analysed with clarity. Enlightening, too, is Leo Truchlar's companion essay "Prosatexte zeitgenössischer amerikanischer Autoren. 10 Thesen" (*Sprache im technischen Zeitalter*, no. 59 [July-Sept.]:240–54). Truchlar reduces his observations on these theorists to ten "theses." In addition to the "theses," Barth, Donald Barthelme, Tom Wolfe, Vonnegut, and Richard Brautigan are represented by translated statements of their own on literary theory. Of the two articles Schöpp's usefully marks the point at which German contributions to American literary theory and to comparative studies converge.

The increase of the latter has accelerated in 1976. This is in part due to the Bicentennial because it provided a vantage point from which to survey and assess American-German, American-British, and American-European relations in retrospect. *Americana Germanica 1770–1800: Bibliographie deutscher Amerikaliteratur*, ed. Horst Dippel, *AmS* (monograph series, 42 [Stuttgart: Metzler]) has already proved a reliable bibliographical tool. Günter Moltmann's "200 Jahre USA: Eine Bilanz deutsch-amerikanischer Beziehungen" (*GWU* 27: 393–408) draws up a balance sheet of the German-American relationship since 1776. Aside from politics, economics, and emigration it finds room for the literary exchanges. Equally instructive for literary historians is his essay "Deutscher Anti-Amerikanismus heute und früher," *Vom Sinn der Geschichte*, ed. Otmar Franz (Stuttgart: Seewald), pp. 85–105. It complements a recent American contribution made by Peter Michelsen's "Americanism and Anti-Americanism in German Novels of the XIXth Century" (*Arcadia* 11:272–87). University commemorations of the Bicentennial have resulted in many publications, two of which are especially relevant to American literary scholarship. They are *USA-Universität Tübingen: Die Amerika-Beziehungen der schwäbischen Landesuniversität im Kaleidoskop*, eds. Volker Schäfer and Uwe Jens Wandel, Werkschriften des Universitätsarchivs Tübingen, ser. 2, no. 7, and *The American Colony of Göttingen: Historical and Other Data Collected Between the Years 1855 and 1888*, ed. Paul G. Buchloh and Walter T. Rix, Arbeiten aus der Niedersächsischen Staats und Universitätsbibliothek Göttingen, 15 (Göttingen: Vandenhoeck). Political implications of American-German literary relations are inspected in Hansjörg Gehring's monograph *Amerikanische Literaturpolitik in Deutschland 1945–1953: Ein Aspekt des Re-Education-Programms*, Schriftenreihe der *Vierteljahrsschrift für Zeitgeschichte* (Stuttgart: Deutsche Verlagsanstalt). The role of translation in the German reception of American letters is investigated at two disparate points: Whitman's poetry and McCullers's prose. Monika Schaper's *Walt Whitmans "Leaves of Grass" in deutschen Übersetzungen*, Studien und Texte zur Amerikanistik, 4(Frankfurt: Lang) and Klaus-Jürgen Popp's "Elisabeth Schnack und Carson McCullers: Die Ballade vom traurigen Übersetzen," *Theorie and Praxis des Übersetzens und Dolmetschens*, ed. Horst W. Drescher und Signe Scheffzek (Frankfurt: Lang), pp. 107–23, are among the few critiques of translation techniques. The whole historical panorama of German literary responses to America unfolds in Hans Galinsky's survey, "America's Image in German Literature: A Neglected Field of American-German Literary Relations in Critical Retrospect" (*CLS* 13:165–92).

Another binational (American-British) comparative study exemplifies the entry of linguistics also into comparatistics. Interesting as to method but debatable as to its findings and conclusions, Reinhold Winkler's "Über Deixis und Wirklichkeitsbezug in fiktionalen und nicht-fiktionalen Texten (anhand von Texten Hemingways und des *Daily Express*)" (*Erz* 1:156–74) uses British English newspaper prose and American English literary prose for a comparison of their deictic elements.

The American-European range of literary interrelations is inspected in several Bicentennial-centered publications. Horst Dippel's essays on "Die Wirkung der amerikanischen Revolution auf Deutschland und Frankreich," a contribution to "200 Jahre amerikanische Revolution und moderne Revolutionsforschung," a special number of *Geschichte und Gesellschaft* (2:101–21), and "Amerikanische und europäische Revolutionsideale bei Thomas Paine" (*AmS* 21:203–15) are complementary in that they deal with American-European and European-American directions of influence. Complementary, too, are Hans Läng's and Franz Schmitt-von Mühlenfels's essays. The former's "Der Westen in der europäischen populären Literatur," *Far West: Indianer und Siedler im Amerikanischen Westen*, ed. Jonathan L. Fairbanks, trans. Felix A. Baumann (Essen: Villa Hügel), an insert between pp. 236–37 of a bicentennial exposition catalogue, is the only comparative study undertaken by a German in the image of the American West in Europe's popular literature. The latter's essay "Zur Einwirkung des Kubismus auf die französische und nordamerikanische Literatur" (*Arcadia* 11:238–55) presents the first German attempt to diagnose the impact of Cubism on a European and on American literature along comparative lines. American examples include Wallace Stevens and William Carlos Williams.

The firm place American writing has found in the German educational system, both school and university, is evidenced by a constantly rising number of monographs and articles. Of strictly scholarly value are Jens-Peter Becker's *Das Bild Amerikas im Gedicht, 1606–1966*, Materialien des Kieler Arbeitskreises Didaktik, ed. Hans Hunfeld and Gottfried Schröder (Kiel: Schmidt and Klaunig), and Werner Sollors's "Ethnicity in American Literature," *American Studies in the Teaching of English*, ed. Winfried Fluck (*Materialien*, 9 [Berlin: John F. Kennedy Institute], pp. 77–99. Becker surveys the literary image of America as given shape in the course of 360 years of American poetry, focusing on didactic uses. Sollors offers a rare synthesis of minority literatures on American soil.

c. **Popular Culture.** Hans Läng's above-mentioned essay on the Far West in European popular literature has already supplied a link between comparatistics and popular culture studies. Among noncomparative contributions or such as take only a secondary interest in comparison two stand out. Horst H. Kruse's "Myth in the Making:

The James Boys, the Bank Robbery at Northfield, Minn., and the Dime Novel" (*JPC* 10:315–25) inspects *The James Boys in Minnesota*, a novel by D. W. Stevens (pseud. for the Missouri lawyer, John Roy Musick). Kruse attempts "to assess the function of the dime novel in the myth-making process, and in doing so to arrive at some conclusions about the genre and about the techniques of popular literature." The attempt has been eminently successful. Kruse has explored affinities with the Robin Hood legend and recognized motifs from the Arthurian cycle, especially from *Sir Gawain and the Green Knight*. Paul Goetsch's "Pop Art und die neuere amerikanische Erzählkunst" (Freiburger Universitätsblätter, nos. 53/54[Sept.]:69–83) investigates the appeals and techniques of Pop Art and defines its resemblances to and influences on the art of contemporary fiction.

Johannes Gutenberg Universität, Mainz

iii. Italian Contributions

Rolando Anzilotti

This year has been marked by the appearance of a comparatively large number of books on American literature. Sheer figures show that, in comparison with 1975, almost six times as many books were published in 1976, while exactly the same flow of articles found its way into scholarly reviews, journals, and miscellanies. It has been a good harvest, in many ways representative of the full spectrum of interests of Italian Americanists, of the quality and the methods of their work.

It is perhaps fitting that our survey should start with Biancamaria Tedeschini Lalli's "Gli studi letterari: metodi e prospettive," a report to the convention of the Italian Association for North American Studies in 1974, which is included, together with a summary of the debate that followed, in *Gli studi americani in Italia* (Pisa: Nistri-Lischi). What is America for us now? Which are the best critical methods to apply to American literature? How can we define and make credible nowadays the concept of the literary masterpiece? These were the general questions raised by Tedeschini Lalli's provocative paper. The solutions offered for what the author calls the "crisis of identity" of today's Italian literary Americanists may obviously vary, according to temperament, background, or ideology; however, many aspects call for broader exploration of the potential of interdisciplinary research.

The colonial period received its share of attention. Itala Vivan's "La sfida quacchera alla Nuova Inghilterra" (*SA* 19–20:7–43) is a thoroughly documented, mainly historical, essay on the period of prophetic and missionary zeal of Quakerism in New England. A well-informed discussion of the Non-Conformist experiment in New England from the "Great Migration" to the decline and fall of the Puritan "Third Generation" is conducted by Luigi Sampietro in his article "Gli indipendenti della Chiesa d'Inghilterra tra prescrizione biblica ed esperienza del Nuovo Mondo" (*Spicilegio Moderno* 6:3–29). Franklin's *Autobiography* and Woolman's *Journal* are compared by Lina Unali in her "Proiezione dell'io e concetto di virtù nella letteratura americana del '700: Benjamin Franklin e John Woolman" (*Trimestre* 9:i–ii:17–43). Chiefly using linguistic analysis, Unali intelligently delineates the difference between the two writers as regards both their personalities as projected in their autobiographies and the concept of virtuous living which they upheld, and concludes that they are close to each other in the emphasis they put on man's importance.

Turning to the 19th century, we must notice that until now Francis Parkman had not been the subject of thoughtful study in Italy. To compensate for this neglect, two items appeared this year. An annotated selection from Parkman's works (*Scritti scelti*, Bari: Adriatica) was edited by Luca Codignola, who was also the author of "Francis Parkman: 'wilderness' e progresso" (*SA* 19–20:45–82). In his generally valuable assessment of the historical and literary validity of Parkman's work, Codignola praises the writer for his power of evocation of the wilderness, but resents the historian's ideological bias that aligns him with "progressive" England, against "reactionary" France.

Fiction of the 19th century inspired some interesting and stimulating work. Although its matter is not new (the two essays brought together here had first appeared in 1955 and 1965), Agostino Lombardo's *Un rapporto col mondo: Saggio sui racconti di Nathaniel Hawthorne* (Roma: Bulzoni) deserves more than a fleeting mention. The original texts have been revised and enlarged and the bibliographical notes updated and expanded, so that the volume is easily the most comprehensive study to date on the early Hawthorne: the introductory essay points out the many thematic and stylistic elements in *Fanshawe* that make it a significant anticipation of later works; the second and much longer one is an accurate and perceptive reading of the tales. While he is undoubtedly correct in stressing the great value of Hawthorne's tales both as works that stand comparison with the later, better-known novels and as an achievement highly influential in American and modern literature at large, Lombardo is less convincing where (as in the Preface) he tries to present Hawthorne as a kind of forerunner of contemporary American dissent. "Le finestre di Hawthorne: spazio scenico e tecnica narrativa in *Twice-Told* Tales" by Guido Fink (*Paragone* 316:3–40), a well-written essay whose title does not entirely account for the wealth of the content, can be seen as a complement to and, indeed, an enrichment of Lombardo's book. Just to give an idea of it, suffice it to say that by elaborating with ingenious precision his initial observation that Hawthorne's narrator renounces the privilege of a bird's eye view for the window (a view-point more dangerously involved with the world), Fink convincingly vindicates the literary merits of pieces hitherto ignored (for instance "The Village Uncle"), or dismissed as of minor substance by modern critics ("Sunday at Home"— of which a beautiful close reading is given—and the sketches in general). It must be added that through a dense network of references to the whole canon, most of the crucial points of Hawthorne's work are touched upon and suggestively illuminated with a new light. In "Francesco Caracciolo, Fenimore Cooper and *Billy Budd*" (*SA* 19–20:83–100), Kay S. House, after examining Cooper's *Wing-and-Wing* and the novelist's view of Nelson's role in the Caracciolo execution, points out with much ingenuity attractive similarities and differences between *Billy Budd* and *Wing-and-Wing* to show that Melville's imagination worked on the events of both the *Somers* affair and Nelson's life. Her conclusion is that Vere is based on the character of the British admiral. Nonacademic, but on the whole well-informed from the point of view of scholarship and written in the lively, witty style of a journalist, Beniamino Placido's *Le due schiavitù* (Torino: Einaudi) aims at furnishing a political "analysis of the American imagination" through two literary texts hardly related to each other: *Uncle Tom's Cabin* and "Benito Cereno." An examination of the narrative structure of the former comes to a somewhat startling conclusion: the book has been useful in the process of expansion of American capital. A deeper and less paradoxical investigation of the latter text is conducted by means of a "linguistic model," identified by Placido with what he calls the "hendiadys" (Melville says one thing through two). The "portrait message" delineated by Melville is that of a solipsistic and dull America, incapable, like Delano, of understanding a too complex and variegated reality. The numerous digressions, the oversubtle ingenuity in reasoning, the censorious tone may be found irritating and unscientific; the Marxian interpretation may be debatable or arbitrary—and yet the book merits attention for some insights and intuitions, which are seductive, if not striking. Henry James's late technique is the object of a detailed scrutiny by Giovanna Mochi Gioli. Her " 'The Beast in the Jungle' e l'assenza del referente" (*Paragone* 314:51–76), which focuses on the anomalous use of tenses in the story, is a good structural analysis of the novelist's style. In *Letteratura e società in America 1890–1900: Dialettica di un'integrazione* (Bari: De Donato), Vito Amoruso asserts that in the light of the great changes undergone by American society in the last decades of the 19th century, such writers as Howells, James, Frederic, Crane, Norris, London, and H. Adams show an awareness of the nonrationality of the capitalistic system and react to it not simply by voicing their dissatisfaction with contemporary society but also by attempting to redefine the social role of the American artist under changed historical conditions. Avowedly a hypothesis and not a general reinterpretation of the period, the essay develops the critic's case with cogency, but, while stressing one point of convergence, it overlooks more significant differences among these writers.

Twentieth-century fiction writers exerted their usual appeal. Gertrude Stein stimulated the critical acumen of a group of junior Americanists of the Facoltà di Magistero at the University of Rome under the leadership of Biancamaria Tedeschini Lalli. The excellent results of their research, chiefly encompassing the first period of the writer's maturity, are collected in the volume *Gertrude Stein: L'esperimento dello scrivere*, ed. B. Tedeschini Lalli (Napoli: Liguori). Through a diversity of methods of literary analysis (from semantic to structuralist, from historical-biographical to closely textual) there emerges a well-rounded and comprehensive view of Stein's techniques and style. The eight essays that form the book examine the writer's philosophical background (Emanuela Dal Fabbro) her relations with painters (Paola Bono) and artistic movements (Andrea Mariani, whose very able "Gertrude Stein: Le opere cubiste" must be noted), time and rhythm in "Melanctha" (Maria P. Camboni), the structure of *The Making of Americans* (Caterina Ricciardi's intelligent contribution), Stein's unconventional autobiographies (an enlightening study by Biancamaria Tedeschini Lalli on the narrating voice in *The Autobiography of Alice B. Toklas*; a fine analysis of the evolution of the writer's autobiographical experimentations by Christina Giorcelli). The concluding essay is a general assessment of Stein's last works (Maria Teresa Giuliani). Robert McAlmon is almost forgotten today. Fiorella Ruffini d'Errico thinks that he does not deserve so much neglect and tries to vindicate his memory by drawing a competent profile of the man and his work in "Profilo di Robert McAlmon, scrittore e editore della generazione perduta" (*SA* 19–20:155–200). Marina Gradoli's " 'An Alpine Idyll' di Ernest Hemingway" (*SA* 19–20:309–18) is a perceptive close reading that leads to a reinterpretation of an ironical story.

Two books on Faulkner, written by the same hand and published in the same year, are an uncommon event. Rosella Mamoli Zorzi is the author of *I racconti di Faulkner* (Brescia: Paideia), the first book-length study ever to deal with the entire corpus of Faulkner's short stories and, indeed, a remarkable contribution for its scholarly seriousness. The discussion, always grounded on a thorough knowledge of virtually all the relevant critical bibliography, follows the lines of the chronology and thematic affinity of the stories. Each story is in turn assessed through a painstaking and perceptive analysis of themes, techniques, and style, and at the same time also related to other points in the whole canon, thanks to the author's impressive command of the texts and alertness to the revealing passage or word. Although one may occasionally disagree with the reading of the stories, Mamoli Zorzi's general conclusions are hardly objectionable: Faulkner the story writer is not inferior to Faulkner the novelist (especially when dealing with Yoknapatawpha material); Faulkner's talent as American humorist is best revealed in the stories. In her other book *Invito alla lettura di Faulkner* (Milano: Mursia), Mamoli Zorzi turns to advantage the limitations of format of a series of monographs on contemporary authors and provides an introduction to Faulkner's works which is admirably clear and well-balanced, but also richly informative and critically sound—useful, therefore, to the general reader and student alike. For the same series Giuseppe Picca has written his *Invito alla lettura di Henry Miller* (Milano: Mursia); it is a sound exposition of Miller's ideas as they are exhibited in each work and is more than a profitable discussion of the literary merits of the writer's fiction.

John Barth's "circumlocutions" of thought are hard to discern and to follow. Liana Borghi tries to penetrate the novelist's universe and gives her own ingenious map of it in "Barth e la Chimera: sopravvivenza e/o immortalità (forse)?" (*Antologia Vieusseux* 43–44:62–70). James's "The Madonna of the Future" and Malamud's "A Pimp's Revenge" induce Guido Fink to draw an interesting parallel between them in his "Il colore sul vuoto: James e Malamud a Firenze," a chapter contributed to *America e Europa: La circolazione delle idee*, ed. Tiziano Bonazzi (Bologna: Il Mulino), pp. 11–34. Fink points out some striking similarities in the tales and examines how the two protagonists' negative experience in Florence is "translated" into words, suggesting that in each case the artist's failure to paint his great picture is counterbalanced by the writer's success in giving life to his own all-encompassing picture.

The original vitality of American poets has always attracted the attention of Italian scholars and critics; this year is no exception. Only one article is historical and regards E. A. Poe's fame in America in the years 1845–49. Esther Menascé, in "E. A. Poe e i suoi contemporanei" (*SA* 19–20:101–19), seeks to disprove the widespread French opinion that Poe's poetry was ignored or undervalued in his own country, and furnishes ample evidence of the praise he received in the last five years of his life. Barbara Lanati's "Emily Dickinson: La mia lettera al mondo," appended to her translation of 96 Dickinson poems (*Emily Dickinson: Poesie*, Roma: Savelli) and inspired by the Marxian theories of W. Benjamin, shows remarkable perceptiveness; however, the many stimulating ideas in the essay are often regrettably obscured by psychological and political jargon. An extremely able, mostly structural and semiotic, analysis of a poem by Dickinson is made by Marcello Pagnini in "Emily Dickinson, 'I never told the buried gold.' Un esempio di semiosi pluriisotopica" (*Strumenti Critici* 29:57–86). Pagnini gives an elaborate but plausible interpretation of this cryptic composition, which he sees as adumbrating the Oedipean personality of the poet. Alfredo Rizzardi is the author of the finely written "Walt Whitman, ieri e oggi" (*Spicilegio moderno* 5:94–106), in which he persuasively discriminates between the truly inspired poetry and the histrionic "kitsch" which coexist in *Leaves of Grass*.

As to the poets of this century, we find that Pound still evokes response from scholars and historians. Glauco Cambon contributes a most valuable essay on "Ezra Pound as translator of Italian Poetry" (*SA* 19–20:201–36), giving evidence of Pound's "poignancy of interpretation and expression" as translator of Cavalcanti's poetry. A thorough research into Pound's political and cultural attitude towards Mussolini's fascism is the basis of Niccolò Zapponi's *L'Italia di Ezra Pound* (Roma: Bulzoni). In his clear, well-documented book the author succeeds in showing how Pound was attracted by fascism; what little, almost negligible, impact he had in Italy with his cultural and political action; what his relations were with fascist officials (all lower-rank) and with Italian intellectuals and writers (scanty, and of little import). The author's arguments are founded on unpublished material from archival sources (e.g. Pound's letters to Mussolini) and quotations and extracts from newspapers and reviews now hard to find. More as a historian than a literary critic, Zapponi also writes a chapter on the debate that developed among Italian critics around Pound's work from the thirties up to the present time, describing the poet's influence on Italian culture and especially on the neo-avant-garde poets of the sixties. Barbara Lanati gives a comprehensive and well-grounded assessment of Williams's use of Cubist techniques in *Kora in Hell* and in *Early Poems* in "W. C. Williams e la via americana al cubismo" (*SA* 19–20:237–83). Williams's development, she maintains, is conditioned by the terms on which reality can be recovered by the poet, whether as coherent and all-encompassing, or as a series of unconnected dimensions. Claudia Corradini Ruggiero's "Marianne Moore: A Modern Fabulist" (*SA* 19–20:283–307) concentrates on Moore's animal theme, trying to show that "her interests and subjects are undoubtedly those of the fabulist, but her approach is original and modern." In "Robinson Jeffers: scienza e poesia" (*Approdo* 73:51–61), Franca Bacchiega Minuzzo, as a preface to her translation of some parts of "Cawdor," analyzes Jeffers's tragic narrative and clearly delineates the philosophical ideas that form the basis of his themes. She finds that science and religion are so fused in his verse that one is reminded of Lucretius, whose real subject was the problem of the nature of things. Making use of structural, semiotic, and formal methods, Anthony L. Johnson, in his *Sign and Structure in the Poetry of T. S. Eliot* (Pisa: Editrice Tecnico Scientifica), attempts a definition of the main features in "the paradigmatic structures" of Eliot's poetry and then examines its "formal and anagrammatic components." The ingenious and shrewd work that has gone into making this fat volume is extremely impressive. The theses argued by means of minute and rigorous analysis are certainly original, but debatable and at times perplexing. One of them tends to show that for Eliot the female is the object of disgusted fascination and, at the same time, of terror full of hatred. This constitutes the "sexual dilemma" which the author considers "the main spring in the genesis of the Eliotan poetic."

The impossible but useful art of translation continued to flourish this year, and in addition gave origin to two significant introductory essays. Carlo A. Corsi, the translator of Frank O'Hara's poems (*Poesie*, Parma: Guanda), writes a terse appreciation of the poet's work, tracing its development and pointing out the main themes, foremost among which is an infinite search for identity. Poet Giovanni Giudici, on the strength of the insights gained by admirably translating Sylvia Plath's poems (*Lady Lazarus e altre poesie*, Milano: Mondadori) dwells, with a poet's awareness of what happens in the making of a poem, on those aspects of Plath's style (ironical acceptance of traditional elements like meter and rhyme, precision of diction) which are likely to make her poetical achievement a lasting one.

Interest in the literature of travel, as it concerns Americans in Italy on the one hand and Italians in America on the other, gave occasion to an article and a book, respectively. The image of Italy of an early American traveler, James Sloan, is the theme of Francesco M. Casotti's "Un americano a Trieste negli anni 1816 et 1817" (*Filologia Moderna* [Univ. of Trieste]1:73–102. In his examination of *Rambles in Italy*, Casotti deals particularly with Sloan's long stay in Trieste, noticing that the superficiality of some remarks on the part of the writer is often balanced by sympathetic understanding, genuine concern, and sober judgment. Based on extensive research, Giuseppe Massara's *Viaggiatori italiani in America (1860–1970)* (Roma: Edizioni di Storia e Letteratura) is a partial contribution to the story of Italian images and opinions of America as revealed in books written by Italian travelers from the unification of Italy to 1970. The volume cannot be said to bridge a gap in the scholarship on that subject, since its ideology-burdened method consists in discovering and presenting exclusively the critical attitude taken by Italian travelers towards the United States. The lack of completeness (almost inevitable in works of such a scope) extends also to the entries examined by the author, who unfortunately seems to be unaware of Heinz Reiske's work published in Germany in 1971, which covers the years 1900–1965.

Three articles were written on the reception of American literature in Italy. Giuseppe Gadda Conti's "L'America nel *Corriere* e nella *Stampa*: Mark Twain" (*SA* 19–20:133–53) accurately relates how Twain was often cited as a representative American writer, and his work reviewed, in two influential Italian newspapers between 1900 and 1915. "Una traduzione di Pavese: *The Hamlet* di Faulkner" (*SA* 19–20:319–38) by Maria Stella is an excellent essay that sheds light both on the critical ability and the interpretive skill of Cesare Pavese as a translator of Faulkner's work. Of less import but useful (though incorrect in four items) is Alessandro Gebbia's bibliographical contribution on the fortune of Beat literature in Italy (*SA* 19–20: 389–99).

The only article on drama was Gabriella Ferruggia's "Il teatro di LeRoi Jones" (*SA* 19–20:339–60), a sympathetic but discriminating survey of Jones's theatrical production.

Popular culture is represented by three anthologies that reflect, in part or in whole, the political concerns of the editors. In his second collection of blues lyrics—*Blues, ballate e canti di lavoro afroamericani* (Roma: Newton Compton)—Alessandro Roffeni has included other forms of popular poetry like ballads and work-songs of the Afro-American folk tradition. The transcriptions, facing literal Italian translations, are accurate and benefit from very informative historical and discographical notes. The only limitation of this otherwise valuable book is the diffuseness of Roffeni's introductory essay, in which the black cultural world is schematically divided into two main streams: one reactionary and bourgeois (Booker T. Washington, the gospel songs, soul music), the other politically committed, revolutionary and really creative, with the blues surprisingly belonging only to the line of Malcolm X and the avant-garde jazz musicians. The aim of Alessandro Portelli's *Canzoni e poesie proletarie americane* (Roma: Savelli) is to present an annotated edition of the lyrics, in Italian and English, together with some musical scores, of the

American working classes: black spirituals and blues, songs of miners and farmers, Chicanos and Indians. Religion, love, and other themes are deliberately excluded, since the stress is on the predicament and struggles of the proletariat.

Università di Pisa

iv. Japanese Contributions

Keiko Beppu

A survey of books published on American literature in this country for 1976 shows the diversity of our scholars' interest in American writers. This variety is reflected in Japanese translations not only of creative writings but also of critical works written in English; the amount and kind of translation done in this country is an indicator of our reception of American literature. There has been an even greater output of translation in 1976 than in 1975. The following list of books in translation is by no means complete: *Selected Poems of Sylvia Plath* (Tokyo: Takashobo), *Selected Poems of Ezra Pound* (Tokyo: Kadokawa Shoten); *Short Stories of Sherwood Anderson* (Tokyo: Shinchosha), *Short Stories of Philip Roth, T. Williams, Flannery O'Connor and J. C. Oates* (Tokyo: Taiyosha), Salinger's *Franny and Zooey* (Tokyo: Shinchosha). Translations of 19th-century writers include: *Hawthorne's The Birthmark and Other Stories* (Tokyo: Seibundo), *Melville's Billy Budd,* (Tokyo: Iwanamishoten), *Complete Tales of Mark Twain* in five volumes (Tokyo: Shuppan Kyodosha), two different versions of *A Connecticut Yankee in King Arthur's Court* (Tokyo: Hayakawa Shobo; Tokyo: Sogensha), and Charles Brockden Brown's *Wieland* (Tokyo: Kokusho Kankokai). Translations of *Wieland* and *A Connecticut Yankee* reflect a recent taste of the general public for the gothic and the fantasy world; there are much too many Japanese translations of science-fiction and detective stories. Translations of critical works are: Philip Young's *Ernest Hemingway* (Tokyo: Tohjusha), *Papa Hemingway* (Tokyo: Tokumashoten), Irving Howe's *William Faulkner* (Tokyo: Tohjusha), *Norman Mailer: The Man and His Work*, compiled by Robert F. Lucid (Tokyo: Tohjusha), and Lionel Trilling's *Sincerity and Authenticity* (Tokyo: Chikumashobo). The phenomenon raises a question as to whether translation is an integral part of scholarship dealing with literatures other than one's own, even though thoughtful translation *is* an interpretation of a work of art. One is left with a similar thought after reading Masami Nishikawa's article (in four installments), in *Eigo Seinen* [*The Rising Generation*], "Pioneer Studies on American Literature in Japan" (121:434–39,519–21,570–72; 122:12–15). The article is a succinct survey of Japanese scholarship on American literature, which Nishikawa thinks started with the reading of *Moby-Dick* in the early twenties. Like his critical biography of Ambrose Bierce (1974), Nishikawa's essay is a curious mixture of personal reminiscences and of critical insights into the problem concerning Japanese studies on American writers.

The year 1976 saw the completion of two dictionaries: Shigeru Maeno's *A Melville Dictionary* (Tokyo: Kaibunsha) and Hiroshige Yoshida's *A Sinclair Lewis Lexicon* (Tokyo: The Hoyu Press). Based on Gale's *Plots and Characters in Melville, A Melville Dictionary* is a handbook intended for Japanese readers; naturally it is elementary in its plan and scope and is general in information. Maeno's *Dictionary* includes quite a few self-evident literary and geographical allusions—*The Scarlet Letter*, Wales, the Seine, and Siberia. *A Melville Dictionary* is an important addition to Melville study, however, as Melville is one of the frequent subjects of research in this country. On the other hand, *A Sinclair Lewis Lexicon with a Critical Study of His Style and Method* is a feat of scholarly integrity, exhaustive of sources for colloquial and slangy expressions in Lewis's works and thorough-going in its classification of those Americanisms. Yoshida's critical study of Lewis's style and method in parts 1 and 2 is a useful study in itself, and prepares the way for a lexicon which constitutes part 3. Yoshida discusses Lewis's way of perceiving American life and his literary practice, showing how these are inextricably related to each other. The chart of sources demonstrates an evolution of American as opposed to British English.

To show the diversity of our interest in American literature, two studies on subliterary works deserve attention here: Hiroyuki Takayama's *America no Uta* [*American Folk Songs*] (Tokyo: Kenkyusha) and *America no Taishubunka* [*Popular Culture in America*] (Tokyo: Kenkyusha), ed. Nagayo Homma (an expert on American history) and Shunsuke Kamei (a noted scholar of American literature). The first mentioned is an anthology of American folk songs and ballads to vie with the fad for *Mother Goose* which has been raging some years now in this country. Takayama claims, and rightly, that his book is not so much a study of folk songs per se as an exploration, through the lyrics of songs, of the cultural milieu which has nurtured American literature. An attempt to counterbalance a strong penchant toward the "high" as opposed to "low" literature is made, on a much grander scale, in *Popular Culture in America*, an outcome of the discussions Homma and Kamei had at the 1974 American Literary Symposium. It is a good collection of original essays contributed by our leading artists in different fields (not by literary theorists). The essays are direct reactions to the living America and its people, and cover the whole area of popular culture: pop art, graphics, popular theater, movies, rock and roll, television plays, magazines, detective stories, cartoons, and children's literature. Even pornography receives critical analysis. It is an interesting anthology, but the book leaves an impression that our scholars and artists are too sensitive to literary tastes and trends in the States.

The same thing can be said of women's studies and the subsequent interest in women writers. The only literary criticism published in 1976 on a single literary figure happens to be the books on women writers: Mamoru Ohmori's *Willa Cather no Shosetsu: Hitotsu no Ikikata no Tankyu* [*The Novels of Willa Cather: An Exploration of a Way of Life*] (Tokyo: Kaibunsha) and Miyoko Sasaki's *Senritsu to Risei: Edith Wharton no Sekai* [*The World of Edith Wharton: Its Frisson and Raison*] (Tokyo: Kenkyusha). The books are somewhat overdue recognitions of these major American writers. Cather seems to have fared better in this country than Wharton, who has been overshadowed by Howells and James, who have backgrounds similar to hers. Sasaki's book, then, is the first book-length study done on Edith Wharton in this country, and deserves due recognition. *The World of Edith Wharton* is the Japanese version (translation by the author) of her doctoral dissertation (Yale, 1973); most of the chapters have already appeared as articles in some of the major literary periodicals—*Studies in English Literature* and *Studies in American Literature* published by the English and American Literary Societies of Japan. Sasaki uses Jungian or Freudian psychology to define the nature of fear she finds in Wharton's works. Undoubtedly, the book is a cerebral survey of Wharton's stories—especially ghost stories—and of her novels—*The Age of Innocence, The House of Mirth*, and *Ethan*

Frome. Sasaki's "crowded consciousness" overflows from *The World of Edith Wharton,* which is rich in references to Russian, German, and British writers, and to James. These allusions are generally illuminating, though not always happy. Long quotations from James distract one from the subject, which is Edith Wharton, not Henry James. Considering the fact that *Ethan Frome* is the only novel which has had any impact on Japanese readers, Sasaki's study of Wharton is a significant achievement. Like R. W. B. Lewis's biography of the novelist (1976)—Sasaki acknowledges her indebtedness to Prof. Lewis—*The World of Edith Wharton* has given relief to the "frisson," as the author calls it, the other side of the "grand dame" as well as to the "raison," the familiar façade of the dame's elegant living on both sides of the Atlantic.

Ohmori's aforementioned book on Willa Cather is a conscientious, though pedestrian discussion of Cather's twelve novels taken up one by one in strictly chronological order, because Ohmori sees a steady development in Cather's central theme—the process of living—maturity, fulfillment, degeneration, and finally reconciliation to death. Each chapter begins, consistently and persistently, with a detailed outline of the story; it also has a section discussing the relationship of a particular work to Cather at the time of writing the novel. Ohmori's discussion often overlaps, and reading becomes monotonous at the end, though such is Ohmori's approach, in his present book, to Cather's works. Ohmori is judicious in his judgment of Cather scholarship; also he makes a shrewd observation that Anna in *My Ántonia* is obviously a female counterpart of such American heroes as Rip Van Winkle, Huck Finn, and Natty Bumppo, and that "the strategy of escape," which seems to have characterized these figures, applies to woman characters as well.

Interest in women writers extends to poets: Akio Gotoh's "The World of Sylvia Plath" (*EigoS* 122:584–86), and Ikuko Atsumi's essays on Muriel Rukeyser and Marge Piercy (*EigoS* 122:340–41, 378–79). Atsumi finds Rukeyser and Piercy quite different from Plath in that they are involved with the world outside their immediate concern. She also sees the influence of Zen meditation in their poems, and her discussion becomes a commentary on contemporary American poets in general. Junnosuke Sawazaki's "The Influence of Modernism on Contemporary Poets" (*EigoS* 121:466–69) is another study of a similar topic, though focused on male poets—Ginsberg, James

Wright, Robert Bly, and Lawrence Ferlinghetti. Among the essays on standard subjects (mentioned above), Mihoko Mori's "Natsume Soseki's *Meian* and James's *The Golden Bowl*" (*EigoS* 122:74–76) is an interesting rebuttal to Yasuko Tanimoto's essay on the same subject (*EigoS* 121:392–93). Mori's comparison of the two novelists is convincing, and even though her primary concern is not with James, her observation of James's novel offers some illuminating sug- guestions to James scholars. The subject is worth pursuing, as Soseki studied in London when James was still active there.

Kobe College

v. Scandinavian Contributions

Rolf Lundén

During 1976 the Scandinavian countries showed an increasing en- thusiasm for contemporary American literature. Saul Bellow received the Nobel Prize; Kazin's *Bright Book of Life* and many of the latest American novels have appeared in Scandinavian translations. One publisher even dared introduce such esoteric poets as Gary Snyder in Swedish, a risky undertaking considering the limited market. From a scholarly point of view, however, 1976 was an off-year. No mono- graph or dissertation on American literature was published and only a handful of articles is worth drawing attention to.

As usual Scandinavian scholars devoted themselves primarily to American fiction, while poetry and drama were almost neglected. The focus this year was on traditional authors, most of them belonging to the period before 1930. This was true of Erland Lagerroth's theoret- ical work *Romanen i din hand* [*The Novel in Your Hand*] (Stock- holm: Rabén & Sjögren). This book contains many references to such American novelists as Hawthorne, Melville, Faulkner, and Heming- way, but these are few examples from novels after 1945. For instance, in his discussion of metafiction, Lagerroth gives no sign of being aware of the contemporary American post-Modernists. Lagerroth is skeptical of too much pigeonholing and categorization, of analytical models, of New Criticism and Structuralism. He is rather advocating flexible thought models, which he terms "process" and "world" and which try to catch the unity and the essential theme of a work. The approach may then differ from one text to another. The text should decide the method and not vice versa. The book also clearly shows how dependent European literary theorists have been, and still are, on American (and Canadian) colleagues. Lagerroth disagrees with the ideas of Brooks, Wellek, Warren, and Frye, but confesses to be indebted to those of Robert Scholes and E. D. Hirsch.

Like Lagerroth, John Oakland approaches literature in a theoretical and openminded way in "Romanticism in Melville's *Bartleby* and *Pierre*" (*Moderna Språk* 70:209–19). Romanticism, he says, is generally seen as either "negative, destructively self-obsessed and anti-social" or "positive, revolutionary and striving for possible integration of self and society." Oakland makes it his task to discuss *Bartleby* and *Pierre* from both points of view, and comes to the conclusion that there is some foundation for looking at these works from either angle. However, Oakland prefers to see the protagonists as positive rebels, who do not escape from reality but rather escape *into* it. Øyvind Gulliksen finds the existential probings of the mature Melville also present in his early works. "Into Melville's Intellectual Landscape: A Reading of *Mardi*" (*AmSS* 8:41–53) discusses the various scenes in the novel when the sea is calm. According to Gulliksen, Melville reverses Biblical and Transcendental symbolism by presenting the calm as destructive. At these moments man experiences his ultimate loneliness and the absence of God. Babbalanja, the amateur philosopher, initially professes similar beliefs, which undercut his later Christian conversion. He discovers that nature may "promise immortality to life, but destruction to beings."

Willa Cather also believed that man is doomed to isolation. In "Through the Looking-Glass with Willa Cather" (*SN* 48:90–96), Mona Pers points to the frequency in Cather of window scenes, where a window or a screen stands as a symbolic obstacle between people and what they desire. Giving examples from many short stories and novels, Pers convincingly shows how those outside the window yearn to belong, while those inside long for "freedom," wishes which will not be fulfilled. In another article, "Repetitions in Willa Cather's Early Writings: Clues to the Development of an Artist" (*AmSS* 8:55–66), Mona Pers devotes herself to Cather's early journalism and short stories. It turns out that Cather often repeated long passages almost *verbatim* when turning newspaper articles into short stories. Although the material she presents is rather inconsequential, Pers man-

ages to indicate how the budding artist moves toward increased sim-
plification and a heightened sensitivity to rhythm and word order.

James M. Youngdale treats a subject that was close to Cather's
heart in "The Frontier: Economic Boom and Intellectual Bust" (*AmSS*
8:1–16), but he does not refer to the Nebraska author. He relies instead on examples from Rølvaag and Fitzgerald to show that the
frontier mythology has been a source of tragedy in America. The
ambivalence of such writers as these has taught Americans to chase
the rainbow, which has left them with a "modern sense of sin." Even
today the dream of a lost rural paradise precludes, Youngdale believes, "an imagination for dealing creatively with restructuring and
democratizing the institutions in which our lives are intertwined."
The literary critic should not limit himself to noting this tragic effect
of frontier mythology, Youngdale concludes, but should indicate
practical steps in "the social and political arena for ending the dis-
sonance they sense." In the same issue of *American Studies in Scandinavia*, Per Winther publishes "Joseph Heller on *Something Happened*: An Interview" (pp. 17–31). Heller discusses such aspects of
his narrative technique as transitions, point of view, and the use of
parenthesis. But quite naturally the conversation turns mostly around
the creation of Bob Slocum and what he stands for, his general inability and schizoid personality. Heller confesses that his feelings
for Slocum have changed from contempt to compassion.

When it comes to poetry, the Scandinavian interest is much more
tepid. A book like Paul Borum's *Det Amerikanske* (Copenhagen:
Gyldendal) may warm it a few degrees at least. This collection of
articles is mainly devoted to introducing American poetry. The first
part contains a series of informative studies on Wallace Stevens and
the sublime, Gary Snyder and Zen, Ezra Pound and music (particularly the influence of George Antheil and Arnold Dolmetsch), and
Sylvia Plath's "silence of silence." The last 60 pages constitute a survey of American poetry from Bradstreet to A. R. Ammons. Borum
even manages to include a selection from the poetry of American
Indians. The only scholarly piece on poetry this year was Ronald
Schuchard's " 'Our mad poetics to confute': The Personal Voice in
T. S. Eliot's Early Poetry and Criticism" (*OL* 31:208–23). Schuchard
argues that Eliot's early ideas have been misunderstood. Critics have
focused so much on Eliot's theories of "impersonal" poetry that they
have failed to discover the poet's personal voice underlying the sur-

face pattern. Eliot himself meant, according to Schuchard, that the critic should unearth the temperament of the poet in the impersonal poem. Eliot's Laforgue poems have been dismissed as attempts to master Laforgue's symbolist techniques. Schuchard holds, however, that even in these early pieces Eliot's personal voice is clearly audible. "Nocturne," "Conversation Galante," and the other poems are parodies of Laforgue's lunar symbolism. Eliot's sensibility is here in an artistic and philosophical dialogue with Laforgue's symbolist idealism.

Only one work relating to American drama appeared during 1976. Olav Dalgard published a new expanded edition of his impressive *Teatret i det 20. hundreåret* [*Twentieth-century Theater*] (Oslo: Det Norske Samlaget). The main emphasis of the book is on the Russian, German, and French renewal of the theater, but the development of American drama is also given considerable space. Dalgard presents the growth of the theater from the university theater, the Little Theater movement, the Playwrights' Company, the Theater Union, the Federal Theater, ANTA up to La Mama Experimental Theater Club. He also gives a competent introduction to such American playwrights as O'Neill, Maxwell Anderson, Tennessee Williams, Arthur Miller, and Albee. But the main contribution of the book is that American drama is put into an international context, where influences and parallel developments are easily discernible.

Uppsala University

Author Index

Subject Index